Publisher
China Economic Review Publishing
Editor
Almerindo Portfolio
Editor at Large
Graham Earnshaw
Contributing Editors
James Roy, Nathan Green
Publications Manager
Nicola Crepaldi
Additional Contributors
Ed Gwinn, Lee Perkins, Kenneth Lee
Research Manager
Silvia Zhu
Research Assistants
Magda Qian, Justin Xu
Director of Accounts
Patrick Tam
Deputy Director of Accounts
Patrick Linehan
Advertising Sales Executives
Gavin Murphy, Vivian Au Yeung,
Regan Richardson, Shirley Wang
Sales Adiministrator
Jason Yan
Design Director
Fifi Kao
Design/Layout
Tony Wan, Ricky Deng
Distribution Manager
Rain Ma
Distribution Executive
Rebecca Cao
MIS Manager
Li Guangjie
Technical Support
Cui Qiwei, Bian Lijun

China Economic Review's

CHINA BUSINESS GUIDE

2007

Inquiries
cbg@chinaeconomicreview.com
+86 21 5385 8951
www.chinaeconomicreview.com

ISBN-10: 988-99114-8-5

ISBN-13: 978-988-99114-8-5

© 2006 China Economic Review Publishing

China Economic Review's China Business Guide 2007 is published by
China Economic Review Publishing

Address
Units C&D, 9/F Neich Tower,
128 Gloucester Road, Wanchai, Hong Kong

Foreword

China Economic Review proudly presents China Business Guide 2007, the third edition of our comprehensive guide to doing business in China.

This book is the work of a team of researchers and writers at China Economic Review, as well as several contributors who are experts in their respective fields. It represents not only several months of labor by our team, but also the decade and a half of China business experience and expertise that China Economic Review represents.

For the 2007 edition, we have added several cities to our already vast Destinations section, included a preview of the year to come, and introduced a brand new layout. The pictures spread throughout the book are from our vast photo library and portray an accurate image of today's China.

We wish you success in all your China business dealings!

Almerindo Portfolio
Managing Editor
China Business Guide

CONTENTS

- **Introduction**   11
  - ○ Historical overview   12
  - ○ China's dynasties   24
  - ○ 2007 Preview   25
  - ○ Administrative regions   30
  - ○ China map   31

- **Travel Tips**   33
  - ○ Climate   34
  - ○ Time   37
  - ○ Visas   38
  - ○ Money matters   40
  - ○ Telephones   43
  - ○ Getting online   45
  - ○ Electricity   47
  - ○ Driving   47
  - ○ Air travel   49
  - ○ Hotels   50
  - ○ Shopping   54
  - ○ Dining etiquette   58
  - ○ Drinking and smoking   62
  - ○ Health   65
  - ○ Safety   71
  - ○ Chinese language guide   74

- **Moving to China**   81
  - ○ Registration   82
  - ○ Finding a place to live   83
  - ○ Relocation services   85
  - ○ Getting settled   88
  - ○ Learning Chinese   89
  - ○ Hired help   92
  - ○ Daily necessities   93
  - ○ Schools and education   97

- **Industry overviews**   103
  - ○ Agriculture   104
  - ○ Automobiles   109
  - ○ Aviation   115
  - ○ Banking   119
  - ○ Cement   124
  - ○ Consumer Trends   128
  - ○ Electronics   133
  - ○ Energy   137
  - ○ Environment   141
  - ○ Insurance   146
  - ○ Logistics   150
  - ○ Real Estate   156
  - ○ Retail   160
  - ○ Securities   164
  - ○ Semiconductors   171
  - ○ Steel   175
  - ○ Telecom   179
  - ○ Textiles   184
  - ○ Tourism   188

- **Doing business**   193
  - ○ Company setup   194
  - ○ Registering a company   197
  - ○ Finding staff   198
  - ○ Executive search firms   200
  - ○ Finding an office   202
  - ○ Serviced offices   204
  - ○ Taxation   209
  - ○ Accounting firms   209
  - ○ Lawyers   212

Table of Contents // CHINA Business Guide

○ Law firms	212
○ Business schools	216
○ MBA/EMBA programs	216
○ Logistics	229
○ Logistics providers	229
○ Professional service providers	234
○ Translation firms	234
○ Web design firms	235

• Destinations — 237

○ Anhui	238
Hefei	239
Wuhu	242
Anqing	243
○ Beijing	245
○ Chongqing	276
○ Fujian	283
Fuzhou	285
Xiamen	288
Quanzhou	290
○ Gansu	294
Lanzhou	296
Jiayuguan	299
○ Guangdong	300
Guangzhou	302
Shenzhen	315
Zhuhai	324
Dongguan	328
Zhongshan	333
Shantou	334
Foshan	336
Chaozhou	339
○ Guangxi	340
Nanning	342

Guilin	345
Beihai	348
○ Guizhou	349
Guiyang	351
○ Hainan	354
Haikou	356
Sanya	360
Bo'ao	366
○ Hebei	367
Shijiazhuang	369
Tangshan	371
Baoding	372
○ Heilongjiang	373
Harbin	376
Qiqihar	379
Daqing	380
○ Henan	381
Zhengzhou	382
Luoyang	386
Kaifeng	388
○ Hubei	389
Wuhan	390
Yichang	395
○ Hunan	396
Changsha	397
Xiangtan	401
○ Inner Mongolia	402
Hohhot	404
Baotou	406
○ Jiangsu	407
Nanjing	408
Suzhou	412
Wuxi	416
Nantong	418

CONTENTS

Kunshan 420
Yangzhou 421
Changzhou 422
○ Jiangxi 424
Nanchang 426
Jingdezhen 428
○ Jilin 429
Changchun 431
Jilin City 434
○ Liaoning 436
Shenyang 438
Dalian 441
Anshan 447
○ Ningxia 448
Yinchuan 450
○ Qinghai 451
Xining 452
○ Shaanxi 454
Xi'an 455
Xianyan 460
○ Shandong 461
Ji'nan 462
Qingdao 465
Yantai 470
Weihai 471
○ Shanghai 472
○ Shanxi 497
Taiyuan 498
Datong 501
○ Sichuan 502
Chengdu 504
Mianyang 508
Panzhihua 509
○ Tianjin 510

○ Tibet 518
Lhasa 520
○ Xinjiang 522
Urumqi 524
○ Yunnan 526
Kunming 529
Lijiang 534
○ Zhejiang 535
Hangzhou 537
Ningbo 545
Shaoxing 549
Wenzhou 550
○ Hong Kong 552
○ Macau 560

● **Reference** 563
○ Maps 564
○ China fact file 566
○ PowerPoint fodder 567
○ Economic data 568
○ Chinese leader profiles 574
○ Trade events 2007 582
○ Airlines 587
○ Useful websites 596

● **Index** 599

Introduction

Historical overview	12
China's dynasties	24
2007 Preview	25
Administrative regions	30
China map	31

Historical overview

China is the longest-running show on earth, the only one of the ancient civilizations not to have been submerged by some other upstart culture

The beginnings

The recorded history of the Chinese nation begins some 3,000 years ago, although the first recognizably Chinese societies started to emerge much earlier. Inscriptions have been found on tortoise shells which tell of events during the Shang dynasty, which had its capital near today's Anyang city in the Yellow River valley (the "cradle" of Chinese civilization), and ended sometime around 1122 BC.

The Shang was succeeded by the Zhou dynasty, and in the centuries that followed the Chinese world was often divided into independent states, all sharing a similar culture.

They built long walls to protect themselves from each other and from the "barbarian" tribes to the north. During the Warring States period (476-221 BC), these states fought

amongst each other interminably. Eventually the kingdom of Qin, led by the man known to history as Qin Shi Huang (First Emperor of the Qin Dynasty), conquered the rest of the Chinese world and in 220 BC created the first Chinese empire, at about the time Hannibal was struggling over the Alps with his elephants to attack the Roman Republic.

Qin Shi Huang is largely remembered for three things: he unified the Chinese world; joined together various walls to make the first "Great Wall of China" to keep the barbarians out; and had vast quantities of books burned, saving only technical manuals. But he ruled his new empire for only ten years, and four years after his death the Qin dynasty (probably the origin of the western word "China") fell, to be replaced by the Han dynasty.

The Han dynasty, which lasted 400 years and roughly coincided with the Roman Empire in Europe and the ancient Mediterranean world, saw the first real flowering of Chinese culture. Buddhism was introduced from India, the borders were pushed back north and west into central Asia, and southwards across the Yangtze River. The ideas of Confucius, China's greatest philosopher, became firmly established as the ideological basis for Chinese society. The imperial civil service, which ruled China for more than 2,000 years, was established and the Chinese writing system was formalized, and has remained basically the same ever since.

When the Han dynasty collapsed in the year AD 220, China descended into one of its periodic states of chaos. As before, the country was finally re-unified by a short-lived dynasty which gave way to a powerful, long-lived one: the Tang dynasty (618-907), considered to be classical China's "Golden Age".

Tang dynasty

Tang dynasty China was the world's most powerful state at a time when Western Europe was going through the darkest stretches of the "Dark Ages". Its capital at Chang'an (today's Xi'an) was a cosmopolitan city of over one million people, and the starting and ending point of the Silk Route across central Asia to Europe. The greatest Chinese classical poetry and many of the greatest works of Chinese art were produced during this era.

At the beginning of the tenth century (a century before the Normans conquered England), the Tang dynasty fell, and China entered another time of partition. It was unified once more by the Song dynasty in 960, and enjoyed a renaissance of art, literature and science. Gunpowder, the compass and movable type were invented, putting China well ahead of Europe in science and technology. In 1127, however, northern China was seized by a barbarian tribe from Manchuria, and the Song dynasty retreated to the south of the country.

In the 13th century, the Mongols invaded under the command of Genghis Khan and conquered most of Asia and a large slice of Europe. China was subjugated and Genghis Khan's grandson, Kublai Khan, founded the Yuan dynasty in 1279. The Mongols used foreigners from different parts of their far-flung dominions as officials, and it was in that capacity that the Venetian merchant Marco Polo claimed to have lived in China for many years (although modern scholars tend to believe Marco was never here).

Mongol to Ming

The Mongols were hated by the Chinese, and the incompetent Mongol rulers who succeeded the Great Khan slowly lost their grip on the Chinese empire. Finally, in 1368, a peasant revolt overthrew the Mongol dynasty and the last Mongol emperor fled back to Mongolia.

The peasant leader Zhu Yuanzhang established the Ming dynasty and China underwent another period of confident expansion. Armadas set out under the eunuch Admiral Zheng He to explore the South Seas and to emphasize China's power to vassal states on its southern periphery. They went as far as the Persian Gulf and the coast of East Africa almost a century before Vasco Da Gama made his way round the Cape of Good Hope. But these voyages were just a brief interlude of interest in the outside world. China overall was becoming increasingly isolationist.

The West arrives

Europe began to impinge more and more upon the Chinese consciousness: the Portuguese arrived in 1516 and set up the first foreign settlement on China's coastline at Macau in 1557. Next

came the Dutch, who captured the island of Taiwan, making it a colony. Jesuit priests made their way to Beijing and quietly began work trying to convert the Emperor's courtiers and the empire beyond to Christianity.

In 1644, the Ming Dynasty was overthrown by another peasant rebellion, which itself was crushed almost immediately by the armies of the Manchus, a powerful kingdom far to the northeast of Beijing. Sporadic Chinese resistance to this "barbarian" regime continued for years. Some of the surviving Chinese forces fled to Taiwan, capturing the island from the Dutch and holding it for a few decades before the Manchus regained control.

Opium decline

The Manchus formed their own dynasty, the Qing dynasty. But as with previous foreign invaders, they were quickly "sinified", and under the first Manchu emperors – strong, capable men including the emperors Kang Sheng and Qian Long – the empire and classical Chinese culture prospered once again, a brief reprise ahead of the modern age.

The Manchu court tried to control the foreigners by confining them and their trading activities to the city of Canton (Guangzhou). But by the early 19th century, the traders were getting restless. The British, discovering the high demand that existed for opium, started to ship in tons of the drug from plantations in India. The Chinese tried to halt the imports, sparking the first Opium War in 1839, which the British won easily.

Under the Treaty of Nanking of

1842, China was forced to open up five ports to foreign trade and to cede Hong Kong Island to Britain. The growing foreign influence played a part in the Taiping Rebellion (1850-1864), led by a teacher from Guangxi province, Hong Xiuquan, who believed himself to be the younger brother of Jesus Christ. The Taiping rebels captured much of south China, made their capital in Nanjing and almost took Shanghai, but were finally beaten when Britain and the other western nations intervened on the side of the corrupt but malleable Manchu court.

Meanwhile, China lost the Second Opium War in the late 1850s and was forced to open up more treaty ports to foreign trade and allow foreigners to reside in Beijing. A Chinese force killed 400 British troops arriving to enforce the new agreement, and in

1860 more British forces arrived, razing and looting the old Summer Palace in Beijing in retaliation.

Slicing the pie

The foreign powers, including Russia in the north and Japan in the east, continued to take advantage of China's helplessness throughout the last decades of the 19th century, forcing the Imperial government to agree to new leases and the creation of "spheres of influence". Popular anti-foreign feeling culminated in the Boxer Rebellion of 1900 in which the Legation Quarter in Peking was besieged by Boxer fighters supported by the Imperial government. A foreign force marched on Peking and relieved the legations after a famous 55-day siege.

The strongest personality in China during the last decades of the Empire was the Empress Dowager Ci Xi, who first entered the Imperial palace as a concubine, and rose to power after giving birth to a son for the Emperor. Far more concerned about her own personal power than China's wellbeing, she used any unscrupulous means necessary to keep her control, and almost certainly had the Emperor Guangxu killed one day before her own death in 1908.

The Republic

With the Dowager's demise, the empire could not last long. After several abortive rebellions, an uprising in Wuhan in 1911 sparked a republican revolution, and the empire finally gave way to the Republic of China. Sun Yat-sen was the leader of the republican movement, but when an old, powerful Manchu general named Yuan Shikai threatened trouble, Sun stepped aside and allowed Yuan to become the first president. Yuan decided to make himself emperor, but died in 1916 before ascending the Dragon Throne.

The early republican governments were weak, and most of China was under the control of local warlords. The Chinese Communist Party (CCP

or "the Party") was formed at a secret meeting in Shanghai in 1922, and began collaborating with the larger, stronger Nationalist Party of Sun Yat-sen. In 1925, Sun died, and his successor, Chiang Kai-shek, mounted the Northern Expedition from Canton, re-uniting the country and establishing the capital of the Republic at Nanking (Nanjing).

Chiang then turned on his supposed allies the Communists and tried to exterminate them with successive military campaigns. The 1934 campaign almost succeeded, but the Communist guerrillas in southeast China escaped encirclement and set out on the famous Long March, which ended two years later in Yan'an, northwest China. Yan'an became the base from which the Communist leaders, including Mao Zedong and Zhou Enlai, directed their rise to complete power over China.

Japan invades

Expansionist Japan occupied Manchuria in 1931, and invaded the rest of China in 1937. The Nationalist forces under Generalissimo Chiang Kai-shek led the fight against the Japanese but they often seemed more interested in fighting the Communists than the invaders. The war went badly despite massive aid from the United States and the other Allies, and when the Japanese surrender was announced in August 1945, the Japanese forces in China were still advancing.

With Japan beaten, the Nationalists and Communists could devote themselves whole-heartedly to their own feud. Civil war broke out, and despite an overwhelming superiority in armaments, forces, and supplies, the Nationalists lost, basically because of corruption, bureaucratic inefficiency and their inability to institute meaningful land reforms. In 1949, the remnants of the Nationalist army fled to Taiwan.

The People's Republic

On October 1, 1949, Mao Zedong declared the establishment of the People's Republic of China. The Communists began their rule on a rather sour note, dealing with large numbers of potential and actual opponents. In spite of this harshness, much was achieved. The staggering inflation of the late 1940s was brought under control, industrial production was slowly

INTRODUCTION

increased to pre-war levels, and, most importantly, agricultural land was confiscated from the landlords and handed over to the peasants.

In 1953, the socialization of the economy began. Having just gained control of their land, the peasants were told that it was to be "collectivized". Meanwhile, all major factories, banks and other enterprises were nationalized. Foreign diplomats, missionaries, businessmen and just about all other foreigners were expelled.

The 1950s were viewed by the Party as a "Golden Age", and there certainly was an atmosphere of selflessness and idealism at that time which later dissipated. People worked hard to build the "New China". During its first decade, Communist China was closely allied to the Soviet Union, often officially referred to in those days as "Big Brother", which offered valuable assistance in re-building China's industrial base, shattered after so many years of war.

Great leap "backward"
In 1958, Mao launched the "Great Leap Forward", his first seriously

flawed policy, and Chinese politics became polarized between the radical Maoists and the pragmatists. Mao conceived of the Great Leap as a massive combined effort by China's people to transform the country at one stroke into a developed nation. Instead, it was an economic disaster of the first order, and an example of Mao's ability to pursue idealism in the face of all the evidence of reality.

Mao then announced the establishment of the rural communes, which formalized and completed the collectivization of land that had begun half a decade earlier.

Many in the Party leadership thought the move was premature and would meet with resistance from the conservative peasantry. They were right: many peasants saw the communes as new landlords and huge tracts of land were left fallow that year. At that point, with industry and agriculture in chaos, nature stepped in to deepen the crisis. The harvests failed in 1959, 1960 and 1961, now referred to as the "Three Terrible Years", and many died of starvation.

The early 1960s were years of recovery. The pragmatists were on the ascendant, and Mao himself was pushed into the background. But in 1966, he made his comeback, bypassing the CCP organization in Beijing controlled by his opponents, and appealing directly to the masses and the party structure in Shanghai.

Cultural Revolution
Mao called this new upheaval the Cultural Revolution. During the ten years

in which Maoist radicalism held sway in China, tens of millions suffered from persecution as the country's economy slowly ground towards a halt.

It was a crazy, frightening period, a time of mass psychosis. People disappeared into labor camps, or were declared to be counter-revolutionaries and deprived of their livelihood. Mao was venerated as almost a god and his followers claimed to be able to do almost anything, including heal sickness and reap bumper harvests, using nothing but "Invincible Mao Zedong Thought". During the late 1960s when the Cultural Revolution was at its height, countless old books, paintings and antique treasures were destroyed by Mao's stormtroopers, the Red Guards, whom he ordered to "destroy the Four Olds". Politics was placed "in command". Schools and colleges were shut, and many did not re-open for more than a decade.

The legal system, such as it existed, was terminated; trade dwindled to a handful of deals at the twice-yearly Canton Trade Fair. Basically no novels, plays, movies or anything else of artistic merit were created during those years due to fear of prison or worse.

By the 1980s, China was recovering from this convulsion, but the scars are still visible in myriad ways – in attitudes and in social trends, in manners and in political maneuverings.

An interesting sidelight on the Cultural Revolution was that so many people outside China were taken in by it for so long. At the time, many people in the West really believed that Mao had created the perfect society; John Lennon sported a Mao badge and Maoist groups sprang up all over the world.

But it was much more sordid than the myth of happy workers and peasants suggested. In 1971, the Defense Minister Lin Biao, Mao's official successor, was killed in a plane crash in Mongolia as he was fleeing towards the Soviet Union after a failed attempt to assassinate Mao.

By the early 1970s, Chairman Mao was at the height of his power, but his health was failing. His radical colleagues (including his wife Madame Mao), who had risen to power during the late 1960s, were unpopular with the ordinary people, and needed his support to survive. They attempted to purge their prime opponents, the pragmatists Premier Zhou Enlai and Deng Xiaoping, but in the end, thankfully for China and the world, they eventually lost.

Mao dies

Zhou Enlai died in January 1976, and the radicals had Deng Xiaoping purged in the wake of anti-radical riots in April of that year. But Mao died in September, and less than a month later, Mao's wife and the other leading radicals, immortalized as "The Gang of Four," were seized by the more moderate elements in the leadership, led by Hua Guofeng.

Hua had become Premier in April 1976, a surprise compromise after the pragmatists and the radicals both vetoed each other's candidates. After Mao's death, Hua was also made Party chairman, an unprecedented concentration of power in the hands of one man. He even fashioned for himself a personality cult along the lines of Mao's, but despite some reforms, he was in the end too leftist for the real moderates.

Deng Xiaoping was finally allowed to return to active politics in 1977, and at a crucial party meeting in November 1978 – the 3rd Plenum of the 11th Party Congress – Deng gained support for his revisionist approach of opening and growth. After a long, closely fought battle, Hua finally stepped down in 1981, and Deng consolidated his own hand-picked leadership with protégés Hu Yaobang and Zhao Ziyang as party chief and Premier, respectively.

Both men were dumped by Deng over the next decade partly because they advocated a pace of political re-

form which Deng would not countenance. He appeared to believe firmly that economic growth and prosperity could be achieved within the context of a one-party system.

The opening begins

On January 1, 1979, the United States formally switched its diplomatic recognition from Taipei to Beijing. The US Congress simultaneously passed the Taiwan Relations Act, requiring the US President to provide defensive arms to Taiwan, but the die was cast, and China was back in the world community.

Then, in early 1979, came Democracy Wall, a flowering of free speech through the medium of scrawled posters pasted onto a wall in central Beijing. It lasted for less than a year, and was partly a tool used by Deng to bash his conservative foes. But it was also a safety valve for frustrations, and another important step for China towards normalcy.

Almost immediately afterwards, China had its own Vietnam War. In late January 1979, Chinese forces invaded northern Vietnam in order to take pressure off China's client state, the Cambodian regime led by Pol Pot, and also to "punish" the Vietnamese for forcing hundreds of thousands of people of Chinese ancestry to leave Vietnam, part of the "boat people" tragedy of the late 1970s and early 1980s.

The trial of the Gang of Four, which started in late 1980, was the first opportunity for the country to publicly face the truth of the Cultural Revolution period – the madness, the damage and, most importantly, the blame. The four leftist leaders were convicted, but behind the trial was the shadow of Mao Zedong and the question of the extent to which the Gang were following his instructions or at least acting in the spirit of his wishes. The question was summed up at a meeting later in 1981 at which the Party decided that Mao's contribution was 70-30 – 70% good and 30% bad. Case closed. It was too complicated to pursue any further.

Word plays

Deng then started to make the wonderful word plays on which he built today's China – a series of slogans and phrases so simple that they could not be refuted, which made the policies they represented hard to oppose. "Seek truth from facts" – Maoist dogma was on the run. "Divide production among households" – the agricultural communes collapsed. "One Country Two Systems" – the British surrendered Hong Kong. "First allow a few people to become well-off" – capitalism, consumption, and the middle-class all eventually followed.

Deng knew that foreign money was needed to resuscitate the bankrupt and moribund Chinese economy of 1979. But to allow foreign investors the run of China after decades of propaganda about "self-reliance" and the evils of capitalism was something that had to be introduced with delicacy. So he created the Shenzhen Economic Zone next to Hong Kong, another great piece of Dengist manipulation. He could tell the skeptical conservatives that this capitalist enclave was quarantined and just an experiment, while encouraging Hong Kong capital to plant the seeds of another economy inside the confines of Communist China.

The money flowed in, and the nature of the Chinese communist system changed forever as a consequence. Along with the many positive results came an upsurge in corruption and inflation, which became the triggers for the next major event in China's history – the disturbances of mid-1989.

Despite the obvious negative aspects of that event, there were also numerous positive consequences that followed. The unspoken deal that has emerged out of the ashes of the debacle is: The government lets the people go about the business of getting rich, and the people let the Party keep its hold on power. After watching the Soviet Union collapse into chaos throughout the 1990s, the citizens of China have been willing to accept a gradual shift toward more representa-

tive power.

The onus is now on the Party to meet the steadily rising expectations of the people. As the government allows greater freedom of movement and economic independence, and the outside world beckons the people of China to buy brand name products and surf the Internet, the authoritarian power of the state steadily dwindles (despite active work on the government's part to shore it up). Slowly, the demands of foreign nations and international bodies like the WTO are pushing China inexorably towards market economics, transparency, accountability, shareholder rights, and an impartial and effective legal system.

Change takes hold

Bill Gates could have been talking about China when he famously described technological change as frustratingly slow in the short term, phenomenally fast in hindsight. That was the 1990s. The stock markets of Shenzhen and Shanghai were created in 1990 and 1991. Deng Xiaoping made his southern swing in 1992 and decreed that Shanghai should go for it. He was quoted as saying, "To get rich is glorious." Foreign companies stormed in, and the amount of foreign direct investment continues to soar. China has become the factory of the world, the production point of choice for Fortune 500 companies and beyond.

Hong Kong was returned to Beijing's control in 1997, and Macau in 1999. The holdout is Taiwan, which remains the point of greatest poten-

tial instability in the Chinese world. The economic balance has shifted to the mainland, of course, and while the mainland needs Taiwan investment, Taiwan needs the mainland more. How the Taiwan situation plays out will have a fundamental impact on China. But the likelihood is that it will be an amicable arrangement in the end. There is too much to be lost on both sides, and the pragmatism of the Chinese people is a strong buffer.

What next

Deng certainly helped a "few people to become well-off", and millions have been dragged up with them. China is now turning its attention to completing the job. When Hu Jintao steps down from the country's helm, most probably in 2012, his legacy will be measured against how well his generation has extinguished the last vestiges of poverty.

The "harmonious society" and the "new socialist countryside" are the platforms through which this will be accomplished. The slogans may be red-tinged, but the goal has widespread support, not just from NGOs and China's poor, but also from those who are banking on the transformation of the red-hot but unsustainable growth trajectory of recent decades into an enduring upward march.

The catch-cry of the next half decade will be spend spend spend. Retailers are targeting expansion into second and third tier cities, trading partners are eyeing increased domestic consumption and respite from ever-mounting trade surpluses, and the investment community is counting on China's traditional savers becoming savvy capital market investors.

If Hu can complete Deng's dream, China may well have regained its place as the world's most powerful state. In the meantime, the rest of the world has a choice. Try and contain China's growth, and risk getting left in its wake, or engage with the economic juggernaut and get pulled along for the ride.

INTRODUCTION

China's dynasties

Ancient China	Neolithic	12000-2000 BC	
	Xia	2100-1800 BC	
	Shang	1700-1027 BC	
	Western Zhou	1027-771 BC	
	Eastern Zhou 770-221 BC	Spring & Autumn period 770-476 BC Warring States period 475-221 BC	
Early Imperial China	Qin	221-207 BC	
	Western Han	206 BC-AD 9	
	Hsing (Wang Mang interregnum)	AD 9-25	
	Eastern Han	AD 25-220	
	Three Kingdoms	AD 220-265	
	Western Jin	AD 265-316	
	Eastern Jin	AD 317-420	
	Southern and Northern Dynasties 420-588 AD	Southern Dynasties Song AD 420-478 Qi AD 479-501 Liang AD 502-556 Chen AD 557-588	
		Northern Dynasties Northern Wei AD 386-533 Eastern Wei AD 534-549 Western Wei AD 535-557 Northern Qi AD 550-577 Northern Zhou AD 557-588	
Classical Imperial China	Sui	AD 580-618	
	Tang	AD 618-907	
	Five Dynasties AD 907-960	Later Liang AD 907-923 Later Tang AD 923-936 Later Jin AD 936-946 Later Han AD 947-950 Later Zhou AD 951-960	
	Ten Kingdoms AD 907-979		
	Song AD 960-1279	Northern Song AD 960-1125 Southern Song AD 1127-1279	
	Liao	AD 916-1125	
	Western Xia	AD 1038-1227	
	Jin	AD 1115-1234	
Later Imperial China	Yuan	AD 1279-1368	
	Ming	AD 1368-1644	
	Qing	AD 1644-1911	

2007 Preview

China is a world of extremes. Just as its climate ranges from arctic to tropical and its population from abjectly impoverished to obscenely wealthy, so do the views of those who would call themselves experts of its economy.

Mixed feelings abound. For every newspaper headline extolling the speed and breadth of China's reform, there is another condemning the odor of protectionism emanating from the Middle Kingdom. Less than thirty years ago, the country was in the grips of a strict command economy sealed off from the outside world. The placement of every piece of the economic puzzle was controlled absolutely from the top. But today, not only do those who used to pull all the strings have less and less economic power, but the foreigners that China dreaded for so long are slowly climbing the ladder of domestic involvement.

That China is a vastly different market than it was just a few years ago is well known. In fact, it changes on a near-daily basis. But the restrictions remaining in China's business environment are a source of contention between Beijing and governments around the world, not to mention business people.

The sheer magnitude of everything about China means that what happens here affects the entire world. Should the central bank decide to move its trillion-dollar reserves into euros, or gold, or oil – anything – it would change the nature of the market. When China

buys iron ore or copper, the prices go up, which means Wal-Mart shoppers in Missouri pay more. Inflation is a Chinese export.

With that power comes responsibility. How will China handle it? The best way to move forward with trust is for China to further liberalize its markets. And the serious money is betting that it will.

As China enters its sixth year of membership in the World Trade Organization (WTO), it is due to further open a number of sectors of its economy, most notably banking. And the breakneck speed at which the economy has been growing has brought on concerns of overheating, prompting the government to clamp down on investment. A key question has been: what is the sustainability of annual 10% growth? Surely some cooling is in order for the economy.

Here are several areas to watch in 2007.

Banking

The biggest change for 2007 is a significant further opening of the financial services sector, the most closely watched part of which will be banking. China has committed to allow wholly foreign-owned banks to conduct local currency business, without restrictions by December 11, 2006. Currently foreign banks can only process RMB transactions in certain cities, and only for businesses and foreign customers.

In late 2005 and 2006 China's banking sector made one giant headline after another. First there was the listing of China Construction Bank (CCB) in October 2005, which raised US$8 billion and was vastly oversubscribed as foreigners rushed to get a piece of the first of China's "Big Four" state banks to go public.

Others soon followed. Bank of China (BOC) went public in May 2006, raising over US$11 billion, followed by one of the country's most successful lenders, China Merchants Bank (CMB), which attracted some US$2.5 billion in September 2006. But the giant was Industrial and Commercial Bank of China (ICBC), China's biggest bank, which broke the world record for an IPO with a gargantuan US$19 billion dual listing at home and in Hong Kong.

The banks attracted a healthy dose of foreign investment ahead of their listings: Royal Bank of Scotland, UBS and Temasek of Singapore took stakes in BOC; Goldman Sachs and American Express bought into ICBC; and Bank of America took a piece of CCB.

Foreign money is eager to share the wealth of Chinese banks, despite their large blocs of non-performing loans (NPLs) and other entrenched risks, because of the overwhelming returns possible through controlling a slice of China's financial infrastructure.

There are precious few ways into the market. Building a nationwide network of branches in such a vast country is an expensive undertaking; it's much easier to buy into a big domestic bank that has already done it. Since China's banks are desperate for injections of capital and in dire need of sophisticated corporate governance, so the argument goes, these are perfect matches.

However, some are taking the slow route, hoping to establish brand equity amongst rich Chinese consumers and avoid the potential legacy pitfalls of China's traditionally rotten-to-the-core banking sector. Which is the winning strategy remains to be seen.

Banks are, of course, a strategic part of any country's economy, and it should not be expected that China will allow foreigners to dominate its financial sector. Doubtless there will remain obstacles to setting up shop here. With the sector exposed to unusual amounts of scrutiny, China will almost certainly fulfill its legal obligations. However, it is also likely to shift the burdens on foreigners from the explicit to the implicit; for example, foreign players wishing to introduce new products may see their applications get bogged down in the approval process.

Insurance

The government is due to implement the last of its WTO commitments regarding the insurance sector in 2007, allowing wholly foreign-owned companies to compete in the markets for reinsurance, as well as international marine, aviation, and transport insurance.

Foreign insurers have a lot of ground to make up. They accounted for only 8.78% of the life insurance market in 2005, with US$4.05 billion in premium revenues. But subtracting a one-off US$2.4 billion premium group life transaction undertaken by Generali China Life puts the foreign share of the market at a much more modest 3.75%. In the non-life segment, foreigners only won 1.31% of total revenues, or US$212.2 million.

It is a key growth sector. The number of insured Chinese has been rising over the last decade just as state mechanisms for caring for the population have disintegrated along with the command economy. But still, the numbers are extremely low: total life insurance represents just 2% of GDP; non-life a mere 0.7%. The potential for growth is nearly unlimited. China is forecast to become the fourth-largest life insurance market in the world by premiums in 2008, after the US, Japan and the UK.

How much of this expanding market will come under foreign control is up in the air. Three domestic firms – China Life, Ping An, and China Pacific – control 70% the life insurance market, with China Life the clear leader at over 40% market share. Similar numbers apply to the non-life sector, where PICC controls over half the market. Foreign firms will have their work cut out if they wish to make inroads here.

Still, the foreign competition can take heart from the numbers it has achieved in its limited area of operations. Between 1996 and 2004, for-eign insurers were allowed to sell life insurance through joint ventures in 15 cities. By 2004, these companies had raised their market share to 15%. Now they are specifically targeting newly-opened second- and third-tier cities, which have had less exposure to insurance marketers. When Chinese consumers are given a choice, they often opt for foreign insurance. Look for this trend to increase as the foreign entrants flood the market.

Investment

Over the last few years, analysts and commentators have increasingly worried that China's rampant economic growth was over-reliant on over-investment in many sectors. Growth in fixed-asset investment (FAI) has especially garnered lots of attention; the key macro-economic indicator grew 25.7% in 2005, 27.7% in the first quarter of 2006, and 31.3% (y/y) in the first half of 2006. Each

time FAI figures have been released they have come in well beyond government target, and each time they have been followed by stern proclamations that investment would be scaled back.

By September 2006, tightening measures had dragged FAI growth back to 24%, but many still worried about the government's claim that investment amounted to a total of 45% of GDP – unusually high even considering that China is a developing country.

Real estate has also received special attention from government regulators, with the clear message from Beijing that the frenetic pace of construction – as well as massive amounts of speculative investment, much of it from foreign sources – needs to slow down.

Other areas of concern are steel and cement. China already has too many factories producing both, yet some regions continue to build more and the majority of those in operation do not make a profit. But forcing provincial leaders to close factories is easier said than done: massive layoffs are a cause of social unrest, something the government does not go out of its way to foster.

But sometimes the numbers are misleading. More than anything in China, statistics should be taken with a grain of salt. For starters, the numbers on fixed-asset investment include land purchases, which are only transfers of ownership, not increases in value. And at the same time, the figures released by the government on consumer spending are under-stated because of the poor methods used for tracking services. Adjusting for these discrepancies, a Goldman Sachs economist estimated that investment may only account for 36-40% of GDP (as of October 2006), not outlandish for a country at China's stage of development.

What it all means

China is in a unique period of development;not only economically, but also socially, culturally, and politically. Opportunities that exist now will not exist in five years' time. As its people and leaders adjust to the shifting environment, new rules will be laid down and new methods will emerge for doing business as well as for social interaction. Rules that have been ambiguous and vague will become clear and firm. It is an exciting time to be in this rising nation.

To be sure, there are problems to be worked out. Social stability is a top priority for the leadership as armies of workers continue to be shed by state enterprises wilting in the face of market forces. The environment is in terrible condition, with polluted water and air the dominant trend in cities and towns across the country. The leaders well know the power of mass resistance in China and its history here. They will work hard to keep the people happy, because in the end it is that happiness that will keep them in power.

The world is wise to China. Now that they have got the world's attention, it only remains to be seen what they will do with it.

Administrative regions

INTRODUCTION

China's official name is the People's Republic of China (PRC). Central leadership is concentrated in the capital, Beijing, beneath which the country is divided into 34 administrative areas, provinces, regions and municipalities.

Provinces

There are 22 provinces in the PRC (not including Taiwan which has been under separate rule since the Communist victory in 1949), as follows: Anhui, Fujian, Gansu, Guangdong, Guizhou, Hainan, Hebei, Heilongjiang, Henan, Hubei, Hunan, Jiangsu, Jiangxi, Jilin, Liaoning, Qinghai, Shaanxi, Shandong, Shanxi, Sichuan, Yunnan and Zhejiang.

Regions

There are five "autonomous regions", each named after the minority group that dominates the particular region. They are: Guangxi Zhuang Autonomous Region, Inner Mongolia Autonomous Region, Ningxia Hui Autonomous Region, Tibet Autonomous Region and Xinjiang Uighur Autonomous Region. These regions are governed in effectively the same way as the provinces.

Municipalities

There are four cities designated as centrally administered municipalities as follows: Beijing, Chongqing, Shanghai and Tianjin. Rumors occasionally surface that other bustling metropolises such as Nanjing, Dalian, Shenzhen and Wuhan could be promoted to municipality status. Beijing, Shanghai and Tianjin have operated as separate municipalities since the 1950s while Chongqing became a municipality in 1997, partly to provide more focussed administrative support to the Three Gorges dam project and the huge population and economic changes taking place upstream from the dam along the Yangtze River valley, and also to promote faster growth in the poor and largely neglected western provinces.

Special Administrative Regions

China originally created the concept of the special administrative regions (SARs) to allow for the integration of the former foreign-run colonies of Hong Kong and Macau back into China's administrative structure. The SARs of Hong Kong and Macau are allowed a high degree of administrative independence, although there is a lively debate in Hong Kong over the extent to which the 1997 handover agreement, allowing for "One Country; Two Systems" and fifty years of autonomy, has or has not been observed since. The fact that there is such a debate at all clearly differentiates Hong Kong from the mainland. A long-term goal of the SAR concept is to encourage Taiwan to return to the embrace of the mainland. This issue remains one of the most sensitive on the Chinese political scene.

China

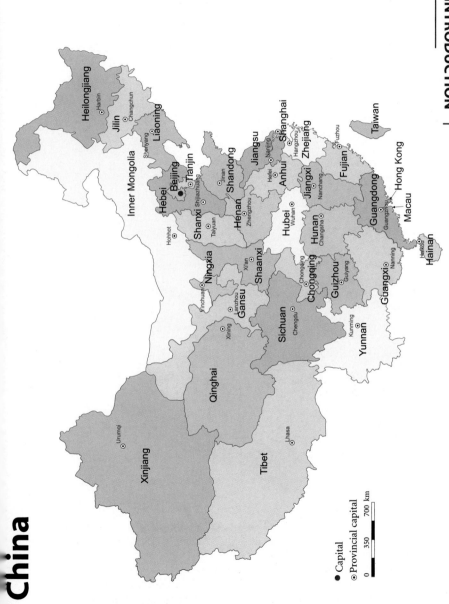

- ● Capital
- ⊙ Provincial capital

0   350   700 km

Travel tips

Climate	34
Time	37
Visas	38
Money matters	40
Telephones	43
Getting online	45
Electricity	47
Driving	47
Air travel	49
Hotels	52
Shopping	54
Dining etiquette	58
Drinking and smoking	62
Health	65
Safety	71
Chinese language guide	74

Climate

In general, northeast regions have short summers and long, cold winters, while northwest regions, which receive little rain, are cold in winter and hot in summer; in central China there are four distinct seasons; and China's southwest corner has vertical seasonal zones, with temperatures varying by altitude.

North and northeast

Northern China experiences extreme temperatures. In winter, temperatures in Beijing can often get as low as -20°C, and areas further north (like Harbin) can get as low as -40°C. In contrast, the summer season is generally hot, with temperatures in Beijing reaching 38°C. Beijing is a dry city, but rain tends to fall in spring and autumn.

Inner Mongolia

Inner Mongolia has short, warm summers, and long, cold winters. The region is snow-covered for 100-150 days of the year and subject to strong winds that create sandstorms as far away as Beijing. Winters may only have 5-6 hours of sunshine a day, compared with up to nine hours in summer. The huge difference in temperatures during the day and night can be the most difficult aspect to adapt to in summer.

Central

Hubei and Jiangsu have high temperatures from April to October. Wuhan and Nanjing are two of China's "furnaces", known for their long, hot and humid summers. During the other seasons, the weather is often wet and mild, with temperatures briefly dipping to 0°C in winter. The coastal

Welcome home to Frasers. When a place makes you feel truly at home, you'll start to think it is home. That's what living at Frasers' serviced residences worldwide is like. From London to Paris, Tokyo to Shanghai, Bangkok to Seoul, Singapore to Sydney. Frasers is best experienced through our personal touch of service and genuine devotion to hospitality. Behind our world-class serviced residences is a closely-knit family, dedicated to taking care of yours. We do everything we can to make you and your loved ones feel completely at home. Frasers. Where you're more than just a guest.

provinces of Shandong and Zhejiang, along with Shanghai, are humid in summer, with temperatures in Shanghai often reaching 35°C, and mild in spring and fall.

South

Monsoons may affect the south from July to September, and temperatures can rise to 38°C. Winters only last from January to March, and temperatures rarely fall below 10°C – in Guangzhou it is warm year-round, though there is frequent rain or drizzle.

Northwest

In the northwest, temperatures can range from over 40°C in the summer to -10°C in the winter. Turpan, a city in Xinjiang 150m below sea level, is called the "hottest place in China" with recorded temperatures of around 47°C. Here it is impor-

tant to bring sunblock and keep bottled water handy. In winter, the northwest gets as cold as the rest of northern China. It is an arid region, with precipitation averaging less than 10mm a year.

Qinghai-Tibet plateau

The capital of Tibet, Lhasa, sits at an elevation of 3,658m and is the highest city in the world. It is nicknamed "Sunlight City" because of the intensity of the sun there. The largest hole in the ozone layer other than at the north and south poles is above Tibet, so take some sunblock with you. The thin air in Tibet can neither block off nor retain heat, so temperatures can reach upper and lower limits within the same day. Temperatures in both Qinghai and Tibet are generally cool in the summer and freezing in the winter.

Average temperatures in China's top cities
Beijing

		YEAR	JAN	FEB	MAR	APR	MAY	JUN	JUL	AUG	SEPT	OCT	NOV	DEC
HIGH	°F	63	33	38	50	67	78	86	87	84	77	66	49	36
	°C	17	1	3	10	19	26	30	30	29	25	19	9	2
LOW	°F	42	13	18	29	43	54	63	69	67	56	43	29	18
	°C	4	-10	-8	-2	-6	12	17	21	20	13	6	-2	-8

Shanghai

		YEAR	JAN	FEB	MAR	APR	MAY	JUN	JUL	AUG	SEPT	OCT	NOV	DEC
HIGH	°F	69	47	48	56	66	76	82	90	90	82	74	63	52
	°C	21	8	9	19	28	24	28	32	30	28	23	17	11
LOW	°F	54	32	34	41	50	60	68	76	76	68	58	47	37
	°C	13	0	1	10	20	15	20	24	24	20	14	9	3

Guangzhou

		YEAR	JAN	FEB	MAR	APR	MAY	JUN	JUL	AUG	SEPT	OCT	NOV	DEC
HIGH	°F	76	67	67	72	79	85	87	90	89	87	83	77	70
	°C	26	19	19	22	26	29	31	32	32	31	29	25	21
LOW	°F	66	51	54	60	67	73	76	77	77	75	69	61	54
	°C	19	11	12	15	19	23	25	25	25	24	21	16	12

Southwest

Chongqing is another of China's "furnaces", as temperatures soar to 40°C here in the summer. Skies here and in Sichuan can stay overcast for weeks on end in the winter, which tends to be damp and cold, though not freezing. Kunming, capital of Yunnan province, is nicknamed the "Spring City" because of its year-round pleasant weather, and southern Yunnan is tropical. Guizhou is the wettest province in the country but temperatures, as in Sichuan, are not extreme.

Time

Beijing time is GMT plus 8 hours. All parts of the country, regardless of longitude, run on "Beijing Time", which was adopted in 1969 as a symbol of a unified nation under Beijing control. This means that in western China in summer, the sun often rises at 9am and sets after midnight. There is no daylight saving time. An attempt to introduce it in 1986 caused com-plete confusion and has never been repeated.

Measurements

China uses the standard metric system for weights, measures and distances. Fruits and vegetables are sold by the jin, approximately 0.5 kilograms or 1.1 pounds. One gongjin equals one kilogram.

Distance is measured in li, one li being around 0.5 kilometers. One gongli equals one kilometer.

Public holidays

The year is divided into three major public holidays, each of which have become 7-10 days long as the government encourages people to spend, travel and generally consume. Avoid business trips during these periods, as most Chinese firms close down, many hotels are fully booked and planes, trains and buses are full to bursting.

The Lunar New Year holiday starts on:

2007 - February 18th
2008 - February 7th
2009 - January 26th
2010 - February 14th

The three major public holidays are:
1. **May Day holiday, starting May 1**
   The traditional Labor Day, also celebrated in other countries.
2. **National Day holiday, starting Oct 1**
   Marks the day on which the People's Republic of China was formally founded in 1949.
3. **Lunar New Year holiday**
   Chinese New Year or Spring Festival. This is the traditional annual holiday, and anyone living away from home will head back to their hometown for this period, with gifts and cash.

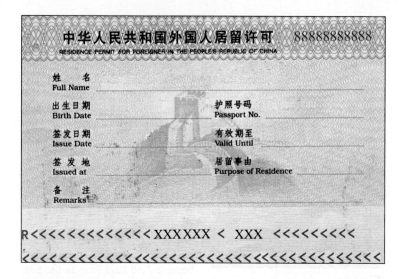

Visas

All foreigners must have a visa to enter China. These are wisely obtained before leaving for China, as those without visas will be detained at the airport with great inconvenience.

Visas can be obtained from China's embassies and consulates in most countries. In Hong Kong, China visas can also be obtained from virtually any travel agency and at the concierge or front desk of most hotels and guesthouses. Visas procured in Hong Kong typically require 1-3 days to process (in other countries, the wait is usually four days). They can be obtained in as little as six hours if you are really in a rush.

Single-entry visas can also be obtained at the border crossings in Shenzhen and Zhuhai in Guangdong province upon arrival from Hong Kong or Macau. Some nationalities may have problems obtaining a visa upon entry from Hong Kong so it's certainly worthwhile making enquiries ahead of time.

Different visas offer different numbers of entries as indicated on the visa itself (see chart). Single-entry visas become invalid as soon as the holder leaves China's borders, regardless of how much time the visa originally permitted the holder to stay in China. Double-entry visas allow the holder to leave China once and then re-enter during the validity of the original visa. Multiple-entry visas enable the holder to cross China's borders at will. Some have a 30-day limit on each stay (be careful), while others have no restrictions during the period of validity of the visa.

Visa applications require a passport valid for at least six months with at least one blank page, one or more passport-sized photos, and an application form. Visas can usually be extended or changed once you are in China without leaving the country.

Fees

Visa fees vary according to a number of factors: the type of visa, the application process, whether the visa is single- or multiple-entry, the turnaround time and the nationality of the applicant. For example, a 30-day single-entry tourist visa obtained by a US citizen from the Chinese embassy in Washington DC costs US$50, however a business visa obtained through a travel agent in Hong Kong may cost between HK$500 and HK$1,500 depending on the factors outlined above.

Visa extensions can only be obtained in-country from the Public Security Bureau via the local Foreign Affairs Branch. The foreign visa office in Shanghai is located at 1500 Minsheng Lu, Pudong, Tel: (021) 6854 1199, while in Beijing is located at 2 Andingmen Dongdajie, Tel: (010) 6404 7799.

Visa Categories

Green Card	The most powerful visa available, it is only available to select applicants, mostly high-profile business-people and spouses of Chinese citizens who have lived in China for five years. As the green card was only introduced in 2004, there are not many holders at this time. It is valid for 10 years.
Z - Employment	A registered company operating in China can assist its employees with the application for this visa, usually valid for one year. Additional supporting documents are needed, including the company's business license, and the holder will be required to undergo a physical examination. This visa also doubles as a residence permit.
F - Business	This visa can be obtained without a sponsoring company, usually with the help of a travel agency. Such visas are usually valid for six months and allow multiple entries and exits. Legally, one is not allowed to accept payment for employment while holding this visa, but is considered a consultant. The visa of choice for young, long-term foreigners operating under the radar as English teachers and freelance writers.
L - Tourist	The easiest visa to obtain, a tourist visa offers the shortest period of stay – usually three months or less. They are a good way to enter China before exploring other options, or if you are only planning a short trip.

Money matters

China's currency is the renminbi (RMB) or "people's currency". The official international abbreviation of renminbi is CNY (for "Chinese yuan"), although the currency is more often shortened to RMB (used throughout this guide). The RMB has been in use for just over half a century, first coming into use shortly before the Communist accession to power in 1949.

The basic unit of the RMB is the yuan. For reasons of consistency, this guide uses the term RMB for cash amounts, but yuan is equally acceptable. Colloquially, the key currency unit is referred to as a *kuai*, both in Chinese and in English, as in: "Have you got 10 *kuai* to pay for the taxi?" One yuan can be divided into 10 jiao (colloquially known as *mao*) or 100 fen (the "cents" of the RMB, which are barely in use anymore).

RMB bills come in denominations of one, five, ten, twenty, fifty and one hundred yuan. There is a one-yuan coin. For change under one yuan, there are one-, two- and five-jiao bills, and one- and five-jiao coins. Most bills feature a prominent portrait of Mao Zedong.

Counterfeiting

With several different bills in circulation it is easy to become confused. A number of features exist to prevent counterfeiting including watermarking. Be sure to check each bill carefully when receiving money from any vendor that frequently caters to tourists. Cashiers and taxi drivers often examine RMB100 or RMB50 notes carefully before accepting them. Counterfeit notes tend to be thinner, smoother and easier to tear than legitimate notes, but the only foolproof way to know is to check them under an ultraviolet light.

The renminbi was effectively pegged to the US dollar at a rate of roughly US$1 to RMB8.28 between 1994 and 2005. The peg was then replaced by a linkage between the RMB and a basket of currencies, and as of November 2006 was trading at about US$1 – RMB7.87. Updated renminbi exchange rates are available at www.xe.com.

Credit cards

Cash is still king, and the most convenient way to pay for things in China, especially as one travels farther inland. Most major international credit cards are now, however, widely accepted in first-tier cities in bars, restaurants and large retail outlets. Major stores, hypermarkets and hotels in secondary cities will also accept them. This is one of the most convenient ways to make purchases, as credit/debit card transactions give you the best exchange rate.

General deposit and savings accounts are easy to open with domestic banks with a minimal deposit, and US dollars or RMB can be used to open the account. A checking account will likely provide an ATM/debit card.

ATMs

ATM cards, or debit cards, come in handy, as many ATMs in large cities accept cards with the Cirrus network logo. You can even use your foreign ATM card to draw RMB from the ATMs, with a fair exchange rate. Be aware, though, that despite the appropriate logo, there are still many ATMs that cannot access your account. The best advice is to go to a Bank of China ATM.

Your bank will usually charge a service fee for each transaction made on a foreign ATM, but most Chinese banks will not levy additional charges, so long as you use an ATM at one of your bank's branches in the city in which your account is locat-

ed. Otherwise, expect a fee between RMB2-5.

It's possible to get cash over the counter at any branch of Bank of China using a credit or debit card provided you take your passport along with you as supporting identification. Be aware that this service is not available at weekends however.

Foreign currency

If you travel to China with foreign currency or travelers' checks, it is easy to exchange for RMB in major banks (Bank of China, CITIC Industrial Bank and HSBC) in the largest and secondary cities and top hotels (although hotels usually don't provide the best exchange rate). Just bring your passport with you. If you are in more remote areas, your best bet is the Bank of China. Be aware that the waiting time in banks can be very long.

It is recommended that you keep the receipts from all exchanges in case customs asks to see them when you leave the country.

Travelers' checks

The Bank of China can cash travelers' checks sold by international commercial banks and travelers' check companies in most foreign countries. The Bank of China also sells travelers' checks for other banking institutions such as American Express, Citibank, Tongjilong Travelers' Check Co., the Sumitomo Bank of Japan and the Swiss Banking Corporation.

Tourists are permitted to take up to RMB6,000 (in cash or travelers' checks) out of the country, but it is advisable to convert all RMB back into foreign currency before you leave, as you will get a better rate. Be sure to keep receipts for all currency transactions so that you may reverse them before you return to your own country.

Telephones

China's mobile phone networks are run largely by the state-owned China Telecom and China Unicom. China Telecom runs a GSM network which is considered to be the most reliable with the best reception. China Unicom offers a CDMA service with slightly cheaper rates and slightly less wide coverage.

China Mobile also offers a GPRS data network that sits on top of the GSM network and allows computers and PDAs with GPRS capability to connect. Speeds vary from very fast to maddeningly slow, but overall the GPRS service is excellent in all major cities.

If you have a mobile phone from your home country, you should find it connects automatically to a local network. Calls you make will be charged to your home account.

China charges for both phoning out and receiving mobile calls.

Buying a mobile phone

It is easy to buy a mobile phone in China – just ask the more than 400 million people who have already done so. There is a huge range of phones available, from the latest internet-enabled devices with digital cameras to the standard no-frills models. Text messaging can be done in English, Mandarin, or other Asian languages, depending on the model.

Prices start at around RMB600. Nokia and Motorola are the most popular names at the moment. Chinese brands such as Panda are well-designed but not yet considered prestigious by the brand-conscious urban Chinese consumer.

There are many places to buy mobile phones in every town and city, including electronics stores, malls, street stalls, and the local China Mobile and China Unicom outlets.

Buying a SIM card

Mobile phones are typically sold separately from the network service, so in addition to your phone you buy a SIM card which gives you a phone number. If you are in China for an extended period, you can set up a mobile phone account and pay the bill on a monthly basis, though you'll need a China-registered company to sponsor your application. More popular are stored-value phone cards (also known as "pay as you go"). You buy a card, charge up your phone, and off you go.

Conveniently, it's also possible to initially buy a SIM card that is charged using stored-value cards and then register at a later date for that same SIM card to be billed monthly, but again you'll need your company to support your application.

SIM cards can be bought for prices starting at around RMB120 and can go up to RMB1,000 depending on the phone number chosen

– phone numbers including several eights and sixes are considered lucky and are sold for a premium, while four is thought to be unlucky, providing a discount opportunity.

SIM cards charged using stored-value cards will usually come with RMB100 worth of credit, and thereafter you will need to recharge manually by buying more charge cards when you need them. These are sold at the China Mobile and China Unicom stores all over the country, and often in supermarkets, post offices, banks and newspaper kiosks in major cities.

Phone charges using a China SIM card are around RMB0.5 for a local call, RMB1 for long distance, and (for example) approximately RMB8 for a one-minute call to the US using an IP service.

Don't forget to bring your mobile phone with you if you're moving to China for any extended period of time since SIM cards bought in

China will work in any standard GSM mobile.

Phone cards

IP cards are the cheapest way to make international calls back home or to head office. These are VOIP (Voice Over Internet Protocol) cards and involve dialing a special five-digit number and the code unique to your card before dialing the number you want – instructions are in English and Mandarin. Call rates to Europe are less than RMB4 per minute, and less than RMB2.5 to the US.

IP cards are sold all over China, just make sure that their use-by date is still valid. The most reliable IP cards are sold by China Telecom, in post offices, major supermarkets and

newspaper kiosks. These cards usually sell for half their face value or less, so be sure you don't get ripped off.

Getting online

With 123 million internet users, China is second only to the US in the size of its online community. Most users congregate in internet cafes, which can range from quiet respites offering tea and snacks to loud, crowded, smoky enclaves full of teenagers playing war games. Fees are usually cheap (RMB2-10 per hour).

Virtually all five-star hotels offer broadband access. An increasing

Wi-Fi hotspots

Beijing	Shanghai
The Bookworm	**KABB**
29 Sanlitun Lu	North Block Xintiandi
Frank's Place	**Sasha's**
Gongti Dong Lu, 200m south of City Hotel	9 Dongping Lu
	St. Regis Shanghai
GL Café Restaurant	889 Dongfang Lu, Pudong
1/F China Trade Center	**Super Brand Mall**
Bar Blu	168 Lujiazui Lu
4/F Tongli Studios, Sanlitun Bei Lu	**Novotel Atlantis**
Be There or Be Square Café	728 Pudong Da Dao, Pudong
BB71 Oriental Plaza	**Pops Plaza**
Beijing Kerry Centre	1/F 1600 Shiji Da Dao, Pudong
1 Guanghua Lu	**Central Plaza**
Gloria Plaza Hotel	38 Huaihai Zhong Lu
2 Jianguomen Nan Dajie	**Xianxia Tennis Center**
Renaissance Beijing Hotel	1885 Hongqiao Lu
36 Xiaoyun Lu	**Manabe Café**
Kunlun Hotel	638 Huashan Lu
2 Xinyuan Nan Lu	1005 Huaihai Zhong Lu
Great Wall Sheraton Beijing	**Va Bene**
10 Dongsanhuan Bei Lu	North Block Xintiandi
Starbucks	**Starbucks**
Various locations around Beijing	Various locations around Shanghai

number of cafes and bars also provide Wi-Fi connection, allowing your laptop computer to connect to the internet through a short-range wireless signal. So long as your laptop is wireless enabled you'll be able to access the internet at the various Wi-Fi hotspots that have sprung up in Beijing, Shanghai and other cities.

Those who live in China can easily hook up broadband access in their homes through the phone company. Fees are about RMB1,500 per year, paid up front in most cases, and allow for unlimited online surfing.

You can also get online via an anonymous dial-up connection. It's possible to either dial one of the many internet service providers (ISPs) that exist in China or use a pre-paid card. Popular ISPs are 163 (China Telecom) and 169 (China Unicom) and this same number is used as the user name and password. The cost of using the internet will then be billed to the phone line that you are using to connect, often at a very low rate.

Electricity

China uses 220-volt electricity, although some five-star hotels are wired for 110-volt electricity. In general, you will need a power converter for 110-volt appliances (most US appliances).

A decent-quality converter will cost anything from US$20 to US$50. It is a good idea to come prepared with one, as most stores and even hypermarkets in China do not carry them. You may also need an adapter plug to use your electrical appliances.

Machines designed for travel, such as laptops, usually don't require a converter, but may need an adapter plug. Be careful with other appliances, such as phones, hairdryers and clocks, which are common travel items but may not be designed to operate at 220 volts. Electrical appliances purchased in continental Europe will usually work fine.

Driving

Getting a driver is a good idea if you are planning to leave the city or visit many locations throughout the day, as taxis can be difficult to find during rush hour or in rainy weather. If you know when and where you would like to be picked up in advance, you can find a driving service when you arrive at the airport, or via the concierge at any large hotel. Most companies require a day's notice.

Drivers have set half- and full-day (about four and eight hours respectively) rates and charge per hour after that. Full-day rental can run anywhere up from RMB500 (US$65) depending on what kind of car and driver (English-speaking or

non-English-speaking) you require. VW Santanas, Buicks and Mercedes are common models and are generally comfortable and clean. A faint cigarette smell is not uncommon, as many drivers smoke, but they will usually ask for your permission before lighting up in the car. Be prepared to pay for tolls yourself, and possibly take your driver out for a meal depending on the arrangements of the company. Tips are not required, although some travelers leave a small gratuity.

Taxis

The alternative to your own driver is the taxi. In every city in China you should be able to find cheap taxis at just about any time of the day or night, although rush hour and weather conditions may make them rarer commodities. All legal taxis have meters. If yours doesn't, find one that does. Do not agree to a fixed price with a taxi driver unless you are sure of the going rate for your trip. The flag fall fare (usually

for the first 3 km) can start as low as RMB5 in smaller or more remote cities and go up to RMB12 in Shenzhen.

It is always a good idea to get the address of your destination written down in Chinese so that you can show the taxi driver. Knowing the nearest crossroads is essential so that the driver can identify your destination. Failing this, use your mobile phone to call the people you are meeting and ask them to give directions directly to the driver – just pass him or her your phone.

Always ask for the receipt, or fapiao, when paying your fare: this can be helpful if you leave something in the taxi, or if you wish to make a complaint.

Airport taxis

Do not take taxi rides from those who offer their services in or near the airport terminal – they will probably overcharge and you will wait just as long or longer. You will also have no recourse if there is a problem or misunderstanding. Better to wait it out in the queue, which usually moves fast anyway.

Renting a car

It is now possible to rent a car without a driver in several cities. If you know your way around and are confident in Chinese traffic, this is obviously a convenient way of traveling, particularly if you are going to out-of-town industrial or development zones.

Air travel

Traveling by air is perhaps the most painless way of traveling in China. Tickets are usually easily obtainable all year, although there may be less choice during the three main national public holidays: May 1-7, October 1-7 and Chinese New Year.

Flights can be bought over the telephone or the internet in major cities and delivered to your office or hotel, and most hotels offer a travel agent service or can recommend one. Failing this, simply turn up at the airport to get a ticket on the day.

Airport procedure

Allow for sufficient time to clear customs and passport control; occasionally there may be a shortage of staff and long queues can form. This is particularly true at Shanghai's Pudong International Airport.

When arriving in China from abroad or when leaving, you must complete an arrival/departure card, and this will be collected when you show your passport.

Flights

The Civil Aviation Administration of China merged most domestic airlines in 2001 into three main companies: Air China, China Southern and China Eastern, but pricing is still largely subject to central control. Standard prices for every route are set but tickets are usually sold at a discount, with full

fare reserved for the holiday seasons. Round trips are generally double the price of a one-way ticket.

In-flight service

Domestic airline service in China, while vastly improved over five years ago, still leaves much to be desired for the average Western traveler. Meals are often unsatisfactory even for Chinese customers – bringing your own snack is advisable. Drink services are fine, and often include complimentary beer and wine. One drastic improvement (for the health-conscious, at least) is that all domestic flights are non-smoking.

Don't forget

There are no direct flights between the Chinese mainland and Taiwan (although there may be in the near future), so you must travel via Macau or Hong Kong, which can make the journey much more expensive. Many Chinese airports claim to be interna-

tional, but this may mean that they offer flights to and from Macau or Hong Kong, so check first.

Sometimes the trains provide a faster and more convenient method of travel. Good examples include the Beijing-Tianjin route (one hour), the Shanghai-Nanjing route (2.5 hours), and the Shanghai-Hangzhou route (two hours). The trains are mostly new and as clean as, if not cleaner than, the trains found in your home country. Express trains are denoted with a letter 'T' before the train number.

Beijing Capital Airport and Shanghai Pudong Airport now stock a reasonable range of gifts and books if you have not had time to go shopping before you return home, or if you need to buy something for your hosts, but the price of goods bought at airports tends to be more expensive than you might expect to pay elsewhere in China.

Air ticket offices

Beijing

Beijing Huaxia Air
26A Baijiazhuang Xi Lu, (010) 6530 3155

Beijing Xingzhongbin
24 Fuwai Dajie, (010) 6858 3801

Shanghai

China Eastern Airline Ticket Office
1720 Huaihai Zhong Lu, (021) 6474 7725

Jinhai Air Service Center
205 Wuning Lu, (021) 6244 3900

Hotels

Hotels in China vary in quality from the extremely plush and high-end, such as the Grand Hyatt in Shanghai or the China World in Beijing, to the damp and neglected. But the overall standard of hotels has risen fast in the past decade, and it is often surprising just how good hotels can be in even out-of-the-way places. Go with low expectations and you may be pleasantly surprised.

The international hotel chains are

now in the China market in force, but almost always only with management contracts. The hotels themselves are typically owned by Chinese companies, often government-owned state enterprises, while the management is done by the international hotel group. The arrangement suits both sides: the foreign hotel chains get to have a China presence with low risk and the Chinese companies get professional management and the advantage of the global booking networks. Domestic hotel chains are beginning to grow on the same principle in provincial cities.

First- and second-tier cities all contain dozens of five- and four-star hotels, and every significant population center across the country has at least one hotel which would be considered acceptable by an international traveler.

The China National Tourism Administration determines a hotel's star rating, with a maximum of five stars available. In cities throughout the country there are invariably hotels that have received rather generous ratings. A small but growing number of foreign-operated hotels in China are declining to apply for ratings and letting their hotels speak for themselves, possibly due to this star inflation.

Most top-end hotels in China add a 15% service charge to all elements of the bill, including food and beverages – something to keep in mind when planning a trip. Unless marked otherwise, all the hotels listed in this guide add a 15% service charge. A deposit is also frequently required when checking in.

When selecting a hotel in China, the best advice is to get a recommendation from someone you trust. Second best is to go with a hotel brand name you have heard of. Third best is to visit the hotel before staying there. If none of these options are possible, you can get a good idea of

the quality of service by calling the hotel and asking some simple questions. If the questions prove difficult for the staff, you may want to consider other options.

It is not advisable to drink the tap water at Chinese hotels, but it is safe to brush your teeth and wash with it. For drinking, use bottled or boiled water. Most of the older hotels offer thermos flasks filled with hot water, while newer ones have electric kettles. In the older establishments in the hinterlands, you may need to obtain the key to your room from the floor attendant.

Male travelers staying alone in Chinese hotels sometimes receive phone calls in the evening from a young woman saying something generally involving the word 'massage'. These women are not masseuses, they are prostitutes. Invite them to your room at your own risk. If you decline and hang up and the woman

calls back, contact the hotel operator and ask them to block the calls.

The most basic requirements for many travelers are hot water, broadband and coffee. Hot water is now no problem anywhere in China, broadband is being introduced very rapidly and is already available probably at most five-star hotels across the country (way ahead of some other countries, including Australia). But coffee can be a problem. In fact, breakfast is often the point at which the past meets the present. Many top hotels in provincial China provide a breakfast buffet which is entirely Chinese, with the exception of fried eggs. Travelers who are particular about their breakfast may want to purchase small portions of necessary foods or condiments in first-tier cities before heading into the hinterland. The top hotels in the distant provinces may be the best places for Western food in the evenings.

Shopping

China is a shopper's heaven. One of the most popular souvenir options – for locals and foreigners alike – is an outdoor market. This is because the merchandise is diverse and prices are low – especially if you know how to play the bargaining game. As you push your way through crowded aisles of purses, shoes, antiques and traditional Chinese and modern clothes, you will be greeted by the chorus of highly motivated vendors vying for your attention.

There are two main approaches to bargaining: starting low and then meeting in the middle or setting one price and sticking to it. Both methods work, as long as you know how much you are willing to pay. The "walk away" is usually a persuasive tool if the vendor is not willing to go any lower, as is indicating that another vendor offered you a better price. Negotiations sometimes happen on a calculator, and the buyer and vendor take turns typing in prices until a number is agreed upon. In general, you should be able to bargain down between a tenth and half of the original asking price.

Here are some suggestions beyond the many available knock-off products, an obvious fancy of most visitors:

Tea and tea sets

China is one of the world's leading producers of tea with more than 1,000 different varieties, and tea is an important part of Chinese culture. Prices for a packet typically range between RMB50-150, but can be much more expensive depending on the quality of the leaves. Many tea shops will let you sample various teas to help you in your decision. China teas divide into two categories: black, or fermented, teas such as Oolong or

Iron Buddha (*tieguanyin*), and green teas such as Dragon's Well (*longjing*). Find out if there are any local teas in the area you are visiting.

Tea in China was traditionally served as part of an elaborate ceremony and shops will usually sell tea sets and teapots. Teapots, especially those from Yixing in Jiangsu province, make particularly beautiful gifts and are usually carefully wrapped in special boxes to avoid breakage. One well-known chain of tea stores is the Tenfu Tea chain, present in most cities in China, which sells a wide range of green, jasmine and Oolong teas in attractive containers, and different style tea sets and accessories.

Silk

You can buy everything from silk tops and pajamas to bedding and rugs made of silk. Most outdoor markets sell a variety of medium-quality silk goods. Pay attention to color consistency and the tightness of the weave. Tailoring of silk garments is often a readily available service. One of the best cities in China to buy silk is Hangzhou and silk embroidery is a famous art form in Suzhou.

Tailored clothing

Tailor-made clothing is one of China's affordable luxuries. As the world's leading producer of textiles, prices are generally far lower in China than anywhere else.

A typical tailor in Beijing or Shanghai may charge between RMB200-RMB600. The quality is usually comparable to a garment costing the same figure in US dollars bought elsewhere. Prices can start as low as RMB70 for a shirt, including fabric. Bring your favorite suit or garment and leave it with the tailor to copy. Fabrics can be picked out in a fabric market and taken to a tailor to be crafted, or alternatively just go

to the tailor and choose there. Shirts and trousers can usually be ready in two days. More complicated articles such as suits and dresses can take up to a week or so but can be ready earlier if you pay extra. If you intend to have clothes made for people at home, be sure to have their measurements ready.

Antiques

Many outdoor markets offer "antiques", most of which are replicas. While they make good novelty gifts for people back home, be aware that customs authorities may charge them as if they are real antiques. If you buy real antiques in proper antique stores, keep all the receipts and documentation. Antiques are not permitted to leave China without the proper "Certificates for the Export of Cultural Relics" from the Chinese authorities, and objects dated pre-1796 are not allowed to leave the country at all.

Art

Scrolls of calligraphy, Chinese landscapes or still life can make good souvenirs, and are usually easy to pack and light to carry. Copies of nature studies and still-life paintings of Qi Baishi, the famous 20th century artist, are delightful and will not date. Scrolls and posters can be bought in major Xinhua bookstores everywhere. Chinese calendars can be a beautiful gift too, and can be found in the main post offices or bookshops. Or go for Chinese modern art. Try some modern art museums and check leisure magazines for the latest happenings in the art scene.

Mao memorabilia

Chairman Mao as an icon of pop culture? Available at most antique and outdoor markets, whether authentic or recent replicas, Mao badges, Little Red Books, or cigarette lighters that play "The East is Red", make fun gifts, as do most Mao memorabilia.

Bookstores

Chinese bookstores stock little of interest to the foreign visitor, aside from perhaps inexpensive reprints of the classics. They might carry "coffee table" books displaying China's landscape, people, and heritage – which can make excellent gifts. Foreign-language bookstores in the major cities are getting better and better and are a good bet for stocking up on English-language reading material.

Dining Etiquette

In some ways, Chinese etiquette is much more relaxed than the Western equivalent. Certain table manners common here would never pass at a Western table. However, there are rules to remember, and a general knowledge of dinner table norms can help first-time visitors avoid embarrassing themselves or insulting their hosts.

There is a pattern to a Chinese banquet which mirrors the courses of Western cuisine – cold dishes first, then meat, then fish, then soup, then something sweet, and finally fruit. But the manner in which food is eaten is patently different. All dishes are ordered by the host (who will almost certainly pay for the meal alone), and shared by the entire table.

Chopsticks

Learning how to eat with chopsticks is not essential to eating in China – restaurants have soup spoons and will give you Western cutlery if required – but it does help make the experience more enjoyable. There are several styles for holding chopsticks, but there is also a standard grip: the top stick is held like a pen and pivots along the thumb and the bottom stick is motionless. The bottom stick should be held in place by the ring finger and wedged in between the thumb and index finger. Novices can

practice with pens before trying in public. As with most things, practice makes perfect.

Once one has learned how to use chopsticks, it is important to keep a few points in mind. Chopsticks should never be stuck vertically into a bowl of rice, as they resemble incense sticks placed before the image of a deceased relative – something that most people don't want to think about while enjoying supper.

It is acceptable for chopsticks to make contact with the mouth, but in general guests should avoid licking or sucking on chopsticks. This is out of respect for the others with whom one is sharing dishes.

Not all food requires chopsticks. Food such as Peking duck, chicken wings and prawns can be eaten directly with your fingers. It is a good idea for hygienic reasons to wash one's hands prior to every meal.

When eating pieces of meat that have been cut on the bone – meat closest to the bone in poultry is con-

sidered the tastiest – or when eating fish, it is acceptable to let the cleaned bone drop gently out of your mouth and on to the side of your plate. It is not good form to remove food from your mouth with your fingers or with your chopsticks.

The banquet

When Chinese take a foreign guest out for dinner, it is typically a lavish affair involving countless cold and hot dishes, snacks, soups, drinks and cigarettes. Chinese are very proud of their country's culinary heritage so they will often order famous dishes in addition to many more obscure dishes that their guests are unlikely to have eaten in their home country. Ordering fish and seafood is a particularly popular way of showing hospitality.

This is a double-edged sword: one dish may be a fantastic new gastronomic discovery, but the next one may make your stomach churn. Some of the Chinese dishes that typically run counter to Western sensibilities include, but are not limited to: dog, brain, pig's lung, snake, chicken feet, sheep penis, camel hoof and bear's paw.

With food that is not appealing, you have two options: eat it or try to get out of eating it. If you opt to eat the item in question, try a small piece with only the minimum chewing necessary to swallow it and perhaps some beverage to wash it down. If it won't go down, the best bet to avoid embarrassment is to inconspicuously spit it into a napkin or excuse yourself to go to the washroom.

When refusing food, it is best to do so in a respectful manner. Refusing something on the grounds that it is disgusting is obviously not the best way to build good relations with a business partner or client. Excuses that are generally acceptable to hosts include stomach discomfort, religious reasons, vegetarianism, or just

"People in my country are not accustomed to eating this". Most hosts in China will not press the issue. Be aware, however, that for many business people in China, your ability to tackle strange new food may be characteristic of your business ability. Your hosts may also simply enjoy testing Westerners.

When eating, one major difference between Chinese customs and those of Western countries concerns finishing dishes. For many westerners, to leave portions of food uneaten in their home countries could be perceived as rudeness. In China, if guests eat everything that is set before them, the Chinese host will think they have failed in their duty by not ordering enough food and will call for more dishes to be prepared. If that food is finished, the cycle will continue. For this reason, it is advisable to always leave some food on every plate and never take the last of any dish unless

you are particularly urged to do so by the host.

When it comes to paying the bill, the Chinese rarely go Dutch. In most instances, the host will pick up the check. Failing that, the person with the highest status or income will pay for the meal. This rule can prove troublesome when such distinctions are not clear, and can occasionally lead to arguments. In most cases it is best to politely offer to pay for the meal and then gratefully accept your host's insistence that he or she pay.

If you are intent on paying, it may be difficult to do so at the table in front of your host. Excusing yourself to go to the washroom and then furtively paying the bill is one of the easiest ways to pay for a meal. Some hosts will find such cleverness impressive, others will find it offensive or feel inadequate. In either of the latter cases, it is likely that your standing will drop in your host's eyes

or your host may insist upon taking you somewhere and getting you drunk. As stated before, it is probably best to just let your host treat you to a meal, no matter how expensive.

Returning the favor

Should you wish to treat your Chinese contacts to a meal, you may want to find a good seafood restaurant, as this tends to be the food of choice for most Chinese. Alternatively, your guests may enjoy being taken to a typically Western restaurant (Italian or French, for example), as this is now considered fashionable, even though they may not enjoy the food. If in doubt, you can always return to a restaurant that your Chinese contacts have taken you to previously.

Make sure that the most senior person you are inviting has a commanding seat, usually facing the door, and that they are served before anybody else.

Other points to remember

In most restaurants, groups will be seated at round tables and the dishes will be placed on a Lazy Susan – a revolving circular tray. This allows all the guests the chance to try all the food without reaching over the table to get at it. It is customary to take a little food from the dishes nearest you, place it on your plate and eat from your plate rather than directly from the dishes presented, and then wait until the tray is turned a few more degrees. It is polite to keep the tray turning in the same direction. If you have a spoon, use this instead of your chopsticks to take servings of smaller, trickier items such as sweet corn or peanuts.

It is best to let your host or the wait staff serve you tea or drinks rather than helping yourself. If service is slack, then pour your host and companions a drink before you help yourself. Traditionally, the spout of the teapot is not supposed to point at anybody, and may be placed facing out with its handle to the centre of the table.

Large official banquets – especially at high levels – can end very abruptly and early, as soon as duty has been seen to be done and toasts have been made. The Chinese prefer to linger in bars, teahouses or karaoke parlors rather than at the remains of a feast, so do not be surprised if at 8pm, say, your hosts leap to their feet and head for the door while the wait staff start removing tables.

Tipping

Tipping is not generally practiced in China, and the service in a large number of restaurants and hotels reflects this. Tipping is widely viewed as a condescending gesture – regardless of how little someone is making at a restaurant, massage parlor or hotel, many people will refuse a tip when offered. But as China continues its rapid change, a 15% to 20% tip is becoming acceptable at five-star hotels and the upper echelon of restaurants in the larger cities. In general, however, there is no situation in China in which tipping is mandatory.

Drinking and smoking

Drinking with Chinese hosts can be an unforgettably good time or can be made awkward by miscommunication or drunkenness. Traditionally, the Chinese thought it "better to make a hole in the stomach than a hole in friendship", meaning that friendship should come before ulcers from alcohol abuse. Men who did not drink were thought not trustworthy, whereas women were not expected to drink at all. These ideas are becoming old-fashioned but may survive to some extent in the backwaters where the Chinese may be less aware of Western habits. In the major cities, many movers and shakers now do business banquets without the need for inebriation at all!

The Chinese enjoy toasting, and will do so by saying *ganbei*, literally "dry glass", meaning bottoms up. Toasts can and often should be done on a group basis or between individuals. **It is considered rude to refuse a toast**. But a "medical condition" is the best possible excuse.

Beer in China is generally inexpensive and of good quality. China's top beer, Tsingtao, was established by industrious Germans during their 16-year stay in east China's Shandong province. Most areas of China produce their own local beers which are typically lagers. But a black beer trend is emerging, led by Tsingtao and Xinjiang Brewery.

When the Chinese order beer, the host will typically pour beer for guests and continue to order until it seems everyone has had more than their fill. Chinese beer is typically low in alcohol content and it is easy to reach your limit from bloating as opposed to drunkenness. If your host seems intent on making you drink

past your limit, make sure to drink plenty of water or tea, and only take small sips of your beer.

Baijiu (literally, **"white liquor"**) **is the most dangerous drink in China**. *Baijiu* comes in many varieties with varying degrees of alcoholic content. It is generally made from rice but can also be made from sorghum, millet or other ingredients. Despite having an alcoholic content similar to western liquors, a fiery shot of *baijiu* packs a punch that seems to go beyond other liquors. Think of it as China's answer to Mezcal. *Baijiu* can be extremely cheap (a few renminbi for a 750ml bottle) or extremely expensive (as much as US$100 for a 750ml bottle). The most famous brands are Maotai and Wuliangye. Typically, it is served in small cups or bowls, the size of small egg cups.

Caution is advised during your first experience with this spirit. Be

aware that once you have drunk one glass of *baijiu*, you may have to continue toasting, often in rounds of threes, as it is not accepted practice to stop at just one small glass.

Grape wine: Chinese are quickly developing a taste for Western wines, and domestically produced wines are improving rapidly. The most widespread Chinese wines are the Dynasty and Great Wall labels, though these would hardly be labeled "fine wines". International brands are available in China in the major cities, but don't be shocked if your host mixes it with Sprite or some other soft drink.

Western liquor is available at many bars and restaurants in China. Whisky, cognac and tequila are frequently the drinks of choice when the Chinese are looking to have a night out at a bar.

Smoking

China is heaven for smokers and hell for non-smokers, as there are few recognized non-smoking areas. Chinese cigarettes are generally stronger than their Western counterparts, with light cigarettes a concept that has yet to gain widespread acceptance.

Many Chinese view smoking as a social activity and offer cigarettes to anyone nearby whenever they reach for one for themselves. They are particularly generous with cigarettes during meals, whenever there is drinking and especially when entertaining foreign guests.

As with food and alcohol, it is a good move to accept offers of cigarettes, and it is not important if a guest finishes or enjoys the cigarette. Often the easiest way to get around smoking is simply to accept the cigarette and light it, holding it and ashing it until it is gone and then declining the second offer.

Visitors who have kicked the nicotine habit may wish to avoid even lighting one cigarette, in which case it may be best to express gratitude for the offer and then explain that they used to be smokers and have since quit. This is generally accepted by most Chinese as a valid excuse. Alternatively, you could accept, but say you will smoke it later.

If you are a smoker, offering cigarettes is one good way to join in, and foreign brands will generally be accepted with alacrity. China produces some good quality cigarettes, the top brands even matching imported brands price-wise. Kunming tobacco is considered the best. Cigar smoking is catching on fast

Cigar Lounges

Beijing
The Country Yard
95 Donghuamen Dajie
Red Moon
1/F Grand Hyatt Hotel
The St. Regis Beijing Cigar Lounge
3/F, 21 Jiangguomenwai Daijie
Centro
1/F Kerry Centre Hotel

Shanghai
Havana Nirvana
1376 Nanjing Lu
Portman Ritz-Carlton Bar
2/F, 1376 Nanjing Xi Lu
Four Seasons Hotel Jazz 37
500 Weihai Lu
House of Blues and Jazz
158 Naoming Nan Lu
Vault Bar at Laris
6/F, 3 On the Bund

too and the top bars in Beijing and Shanghai now have cigar menus or even cigar lounges.

Health

For a trip to the main cities, no special precautions are recommended. Before any extended trips to provincial areas of China, however, a medical and dental checkup is advisable and you would do well to make sure that your immunizations for tetanus, diphtheria and polio are up to date. Depending on how rural your trip will be, typhoid vaccination as well as rabies and hepatitis jabs may be worth considering. Malaria protection is advisable for visits during the wet (summer) season for rural areas in the south of Yunnan and Fujian provinces, and in Guangxi, Guangdong and Hainan.

Should you fall sick in China, there are competent hospitals and clinics available in almost all locations. In Beijing and Shanghai, and in some of the larger cities such as Guangzhou, Shenzhen and Nanjing, there are also a number of excellent foreign clinics and emergency services. Be aware that the prices charged at such foreign clinics are expensive so make sure your insurance covers any treatment.

Hospitals
Beijing
Hong Kong International Medical Clinic 北京香港国际医务诊所
9/F Swiss Hotel, 2 Chaoyangmen Bei

Dajie
(010) 6501 2288 ext. 2346
www.hkclinic.com
Beijing United Family Hospital and Clinics 和睦家医院
2 Jiangtai Lu
(010) 6433 3960
Pinnacle Plaza, 818 Tianzhu Real Estate Dev. Zone
(010) 6433 2345
www.unitedfamilyhospitals.com
Vista Clinic 维世达诊所
B29 Kerry Centre, 1 Guanghua Lu,
(010) 8529 6618
Shanghai
Shanghai United Family Hospital and Clinic 和睦家医院
1388 Xianxia Lu
(021) 5133 1900
www.shanghaiunited.com
World Link 瑞新医疗
203 Shanghai Centre, 1376 Nanjing Xi Lu, (021) 6279 7688
3/F, 170 Danshui Lu,
(021) 6385 9889
Mandarin City, 788 Hongxu Lu,
(021) 6405 5788
www.worldlink-shanghai.com
Shanghai East International Medical Center 上海东方国际医院
12/F, 551 Pudong Nan Lu,
(021) 5879 9999
www.seimc.com.cn
SinoUnited Health
上海戴是凯康复医学门诊部
601 Shanghai Centre, 1376 Nanjing Xi Lu,
(021)6279 8920
www.sinounitedhealth.com

Drugs and pharmacies

If you take any particular medication on a regular basis, bring enough of it with you to last your stay in China. If you need extra medication or have to treat sudden illness, go to a recognized pharmacy, or to a medical clinic that caters to foreigners. Use pharmacies attached to the main hospitals to avoid the risk of buying counterfeit drugs.

For minor ailments, most top-end hotels will be able to provide a doctor to investigate the problem and prescribe the right drugs. Chinese versions of Western medicine are effective for coughs, colds and flu. The most common Western drugs can be obtained in China, although they may appear in a different form or under a different name. Vitamin supplements and aspirin are particularly cheap in China.

Treatment

Unless it is urgent, most business travelers will prefer international clinics to local Chinese hospitals. The service is better although more expensive (consultation fees generally start at around RMB1,000). Also, you are guaranteed to find an English-speaking doctor in an international clinic (although this is not uncommon in good Chinese hospitals in Beijing and Shanghai). Good medical insurance is recommended. Be aware that ambulance services outside major cities are scarce and basic: most ambulances are just white minibuses.

Traditional Chinese Medicine

Traditional Chinese Medicine (TCM) is effective in many instances and has been around for millennia to prove

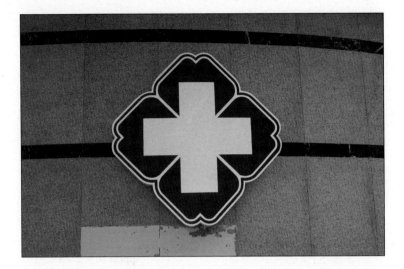

it. TCM uses a holistic approach to healing, and tries to establish a balance in the patient's energy channels – qi (pronounced "chee"). This can involve taking pulse readings and treatment with acupuncture, massage, herbal teas or moxibustion, or a combination of these.

Acupuncture is particularly helpful for easing stress, physical strains and backache, among other ailments, and should be painless. Make sure the practitioner uses new or sterilized needles. Herbal "teas" or decoctions may be prescribed for almost every ailment and can include mineral or animal substances, such as powdered pearl or dried lizards – these can often be made up in advance by the chemist to save time and trouble. China has documented over 5,000 animal and plant substances supposed to have therapeutic properties. Moxibustion involves burning a specially formed stick of dried mugwort and holding this over – but not touching – the patient's skin to stimulate the qi and strengthen the blood.

TCM is traditionally a preventive medicine and ideally should be used in the long term. But it can act swiftly for most ailments if taken correctly.

Basic hygiene

China is not a particularly dirty country, but the bacteria common here may not agree with you or your stomach. For this reason, it is a good idea to wash your hands frequently and keep a small packet of moist tissues or toilet paper handy.

Public bathroom facilities are improving and in the cities they should be clean, if not exactly fragrant. In the less developed areas of the country conditions can be primitive. If you do not mind basic WCs, however, you'll be fine. Just don't forget to bring toilet paper.

Food and drink

General common sense should prevail in matters of hygiene, so do like the Chinese do, and always drink bottled or boiled water, and choose restaurants that are clean-looking and busy – good customer turnover should indicate fresh produce. Avoid salads and raw fruit outside the major cities, or make sure you can peel it yourself. If you are at all unsure about how clean the plates and chopsticks are, ask for freshly boiled water (*kai shui*) to rinse your bowl, cup and chopsticks – this is common practice among the Chinese too.

On the whole, most meat dishes are cooked all the way through in China at high temperatures, and poultry and fish is usually fresh.

Street food, if it looks at all unclean or is lying in the sun, should be avoided, just as anywhere else in the world. But if you want to try typical snacks, such as onion bread (*cong you bing*) or steamed pork buns (*baozi*) then choose a stand that is doing brisk business. Some of China's best food can be found on the streets.

Massage

Chinese massage goes back around 4,000 years and is one of the oldest forms of medicine for which extensive documentation still exists. As an essential part of Traditional Chinese Medicine, it aims to restore balance and harmony both physically and mentally and is used to treat illnesses, since blockages in the flow of *qi* (energy) are considered to be the cause of sickness. It is also more commonly given for relaxation and to promote circulation and a general feeling of well-being.

Massage services can be found in most hotels and hairdressers, as well as on the street, and every Chinese city has a range of massage centers, some operated by specially trained blind masseurs – these usually give the best service. Places with red and purple lights in the windows are not proper establishments, and provide a different service. They should be avoided. Ask the concierge in your hotel for recommendations. Prices can vary but usually start at around RMB40 for 45 minutes in the provinces. For a more medical-type massage, it is best to look for Traditional Chinese Medicine hospitals or clinics.

Chinese massage is usually carried out when you are fully clothed – you just remove your shoes – while you are lying on a special table or sitting on a chair, and in most cases a cotton sheet is placed over you so there is no direct contact with your skin. For maximum benefit, you should wear light cotton clothes, or at least take off your jacket. The massage can range from deep tissue movements to lighter strokes, depending on the practitioner and your requirements. A good massage, as well as helping to ease tension, can be beneficial to those suffering from headaches, neck and shoulder pain, sciatica and back pain, irritable bowel syndrome (IBS), pre-menstrual tension, stress and insomnia.

Foot massage is another popular way to relax after business meetings and is increasingly offered in the major cities. For this, you are usually invited to soak your feet in a warm aromatic footbath for around 10-15 minutes, sometimes while receiving a general shoulder and head massage, before the masseur concentrates on

applying pressure to certain points on your soles or toes to release tension, while you sip tea or listen to soothing music.

Spas

China's booming spa and beauty treatment market reflects the enthusiasm of people in the newly prosperous society to look and feel good. Spas and beauty clinics have sprung up across many cities in China and Hainan Island in south China has also become a popular destination for people to escape to for a few days of spa relaxation.

Spas

Shanghai

Dragonfly 悠庭保健会所
206 Xinle Lu, (021) 5403 9982
20 Donghu Lu, (021) 5405 0008
Villa 5, 3911 Hongmei Lu
(021) 5405 0008
2/F Kerry Centre, 1515 Nanjing Xi Lu, (021) 5405 0008
www.dragonfly.net.cn

Aqua Villa 水泽堂
House 3, 89 Xingguo Lu
(021) 3423 0038

Evian Spa 依云水疗
2/F, Three on the Bund, 3 Zhongshan Dong Yi Lu, (021) 6321 6622
www.threeonthebund.com

Mandara Spa 蔓达梦
6/F JW Marriott Hotel,
399 Nanjing Xi Lu
(021) 5359 4969 ext. 6798, 6799
www.mspa-international.com

CHI Spa CHI 水疗中心
6/FTower 2, Pudong Shangri-La, 33 Fucheng Lu, (021) 6882 8888 ext. 460
www.shangri-la.com/shanghai/

TRAVEL TIPS

*pudongshangri-la/chispa/en/index.
aspx*

Banyan Tree Spa Shanghai 悦榕庄
2/F, 38 Henan Zhong Lu, Westin
Shanghai, (021) 6335 1888 ext. 7272
www.banyantree.com

**David's Camp Men's Spa and Skin
Care** 戴维营专业男子Spa护肤中心
200 Yan'an Xi Lu, by Nanjing Xi Lu
(021) 6247 3602

Hilton Shanghai 希尔顿上海
4/F Hilton Shanghai,
250 Huashan Lu
(021) 6248 0000 ext. 2600
www.hilton.com

Royal Spa Jinmao
1/F Jinmao Tower, 88 Shiji Dadao,
Pudong (021) 5103 6767

Beijing

Pattaya Spa 芭堤雅Spa
Sesson's Club B36 Dongzhimenwai
Dajie, (010) 8453 0399

St. Regis Spa 瑞吉红塔
21 Jiangguomenwai Dajie
(St. Regis Beijing), (010) 6460 6688
www.stregis.com

Club Oasis 绿洲俱乐部

P3/R Grand Hyatt, 1 Dong Chang'an
Dadao, (010) 8518 1234 ext. 3760

Bodhi 菩提
17 Gongti Bei Bei Lu, (010) 6417 9595
www.bodhi.com.cn

Chang An Spa 北京长安水疗中心
10 Dong Chang'an Dadao,
(010) 6522 9988 ext. 6633
www.changanclub.com

Suuma Spa
518-B Xincheng Culture Building,
3 Chongwenmenwai Dajie
(010)6708 9608

Sanya, Hainan

**Pearl River Nantian Resort & Spa
Sanya** 海南三亚市南田温泉
Nantian Dujia Chu Tengqiao Zhen,
(0898) 8881 9888

Crowne Spa Resort Hainan
美体考究SPA馆
1 Qiongshan Dadao, Jiangdong,
(0898) 6596 6888

Bo'ao, Hainan

Sofitel Bo'ao, Hainan
博鳌索菲特大酒店
Dongyu Island, (0898) 6296 6888
www.sofitel.com

Safety

China is far safer than many people traveling here for the first time might imagine. One can walk through just about any part of any city in China at any time of the day or night without worrying about personal safety. Westerners particularly should be relatively safe – on the whole the Chinese people will want you to have a good impression of their country. In practice, the penalties for assaulting or robbing foreigners are more severe than for domestic crime and to some extent this will protect you. That said, be careful, don't carry large amounts of cash on you, and avoid police-related situations wherever possible because of the wasted time and energy they will involve.

Theft

Serious burglary is rare in China but petty theft is widespread, and foreigners can be targets. It is best to carry only as much cash as you need, and keep the rest in travelers' checks. Watch your wallet when you are in crowded areas such as markets, shopping malls and major tourist sights. Cell phones are also frequently stolen so keep them hidden.

If something of yours is stolen, report it immediately to the nearest police station. If they cannot recover your belongings, they can at least provide a loss report for you to claim compensation if you have insurance. The police can be remarkably helpful if you are patient and calm.

If you find yourself involved in a public altercation on the street, keep calm and do not do anything threatening.

Con artists

Here is a common scam: a foreign guy is walking alone along a busy street in a Chinese city is approached by a girl. A conversation ensues, the girl suggests a coffee or a meal. They are ushered into a back room, and at the end of the coffee/meal, the guy calls for the bill and finds it made out for a very large amount. He protests, the girl slides away, two large and potentially violent waiters appear ... the guy does not get out without paying. If he does not have the cash, he may be escorted to a nearby bank machine.

Con artists are a nuisance, but common sense should keep you out of trouble. Beware of overly friendly vendors and sales assistants who may distract you into paying too much for a product or service, substitute fake products or charge you a heavy service fee for their "help". Restaurants, for example, may suggest that you sit in a quieter private room and then give you a more expensive menu, travel agents may try to obtain "VIP" tickets for you and add on a hefty handling fee. Do not be afraid to ask if there is a service fee and how much it is.

One common occurrence is being approached by "art students" who claim that they are holding an exhibition which they want to invite you to, which turns out to be a shop.

Accidents

If you are witness to a street accident,

be careful. By all means give assistance, but be aware that occasionally this can backfire – some would-be good Samaritans have taken people with injuries to hospital only to find themselves accused of causing the accident and being expected to foot the medical bill. Again, it is advisable not to get involved; call a doctor or the police if you wish, and then be on your way.

Violence

Mild street violence occurs in China, though it rarely ever goes beyond loud shouting and pushing. Do not get involved. Laws regarding foreigners and violence are vague but the consequences are likely to be serious.

Traffic

The most dangerous aspect of travel in China is road traffic. The number of private cars on the roads is increasing at a phenomenal rate, but the highway code is still a mere formality. The Chinese driving test does not involve any real road experience, and is usually taken in a special driving center so new drivers generally do not know how to drive in traffic

safely. Add to this the huge migrant population in the cities with little experience of crossing streets safely and you have the makings of a traffic nightmare. The result is some 600 traffic-related deaths in the country per day. If you want to walk around just make sure you keep an eye open for traffic coming in all directions, even from behind: red traffic lights do not have an immediate effect on oncoming vehicles, and one-way streets may not always be.

Politics

Despite the occasional presence of khaki uniforms, China is not a police state and the population is not constantly under surveillance. The exceptions are certain areas that are seen as sensitive by the government, such as Tibet and Xinjiang, which are more heavily policed. Certain dates may also mean more security concerns too, for example during a meeting of the Central Committee of the Communist Party of China, or June 4.

On the whole, if you are not smuggling in illegal literature (works on Falun Gong, Amnesty International human rights reports), arms or drugs, and if you do not talk loudly about Tibetan independence, you should have no problems with the police. The Chinese dislike a fuss, especially involving foreigners, and you will usually find that your hosts will change the subject rapidly if you venture on to dangerous territory.

Prostitution

Prostitution is illegal in China, but is found in all cities, in various guises. Bars in obvious places often feature working girls, and hairdressing salons in many parts of China often provide special services. But the scam warning above applies.

Drugs & alcohol

Drug seizures have increased greatly in China over the past few years. If a foreigner is caught possessing, trafficking, selling or manufacturing drugs, he or she can be subject to the draconian sections of the Criminal Code of the PRC.

There is no legal drinking age in China, but that does not mean that drunken crowds are welcome. In 2004, the southern section of San-litun, the main bar strip in Beijing, was shut down for a time by the government, and Maoming Lu in Shanghai has been closed on a couple of occasions. Disorderly behavior at any bar can get you kicked out.

Police

The Foreign Affairs Branch of the local police, or Public Security Bureau, is responsible for enforcing laws regarding foreigners. If you get into a tangle with hotels, restaurants or cab drivers, this is the body to turn to. If you are lucky, your only interaction with the police will be registering with them if you stay in a residence outside of a hotel for an extended period – the legal requirement is to register within 24 hours of changing your address.

Chinese language guide

Chinese is a tonal language with a writing system that uses ideograms rather than an alphabet. It is the oldest living language, dating back over 3,000 years. The basic grammatical structure of Chinese is similar to that of English (subject-verb-object) but simpler when it comes to dealing with tenses and genders.

A large number of mutually unintelligible dialects are spoken across China. Mandarin, Cantonese and Shanghainese, for example, are as far apart from one another as Italian, Portuguese and Spanish. A wise man once said that the difference between a language and a dialect is that a language has an army and a navy.

The Chinese government has been pushing Mandarin as the national language for the past two decades. Thus, most people that you will run into, if not all, will be able to speak some Mandarin. Accents across the country will differ widely just as English accents vary from Birmingham, England to Birmingham, Alabama.

If you happen to be non-East Asian in appearance, you will have the huge ego-boosting opportunity to be praised for speaking even the most poorly pronounced Chinese. If you are East Asian in appearance, however, you will have the opposite experience.

This language guide is designed for people who will be in China for a short period of time and includes the most common phrases to help you get around and solve problems. We have therefore decided to dispense with phonetics. If you want to get into learning Chinese, it's a whole other book.

Pronouns

I	我	wǒ
You	你	nǐ
He	他	tā
She	她	tā
We	我们	wǒmén
You (plural)	你们	nǐmén
They	他们	tāmén

Numbers

1	一	yī
2	二	èr
3	三	sān
4	四	sì
5	五	wǔ
6	六	liù
7	七	qī
8	八	bā
9	九	jiǔ
10	十	shí
11	十一	shíyī
12	十二	shíèr
13	十三	shísān
20	二十	èrshí
21	二十一	èrshíyī
30	三十	sānshí
100	一百	yībǎi
200	二百	èrbǎi
1,000	一千	yīqiān
3,000	三千	sānqiān
10,000	一万	yīwàn
100,000	十万	shíwàn
One million	一百万	yībǎiwàn
One billion	十亿	shíyì

Greetings and courtesies

Hello	你好	nǐhǎo
Let me introduce myself		

请让我自我介绍
qǐng ràng wǒ zìwǒ jièshào

Good morning
早上好
zǎoshàng hǎo

Good evening
晚上好
wǎnshàng hǎo

Goodbye　　再见　　zàijiàn

See you later 一会儿见
yíhuìr jiàn

Thank you　　谢谢　　xièxie

You're welcome 不客气　búkèqì

No problem　没问题　méi wènti

Sorry　　对不起　duìbùqǐ

Go straight ahead
一直走
yìzhízǒu

Stop here
停在这里
tíng zài zhèlǐ

How long will the trip take?
去那里需要多久?
qù nàlǐ xūyào duōjiǔ?

Please stop here
请停在这里
qǐng tíngzài zhèlǐ

U-turn　　调头　　diàotóu

Is it near?　近吗?　jìnma?

Is it far?　远吗?　yuǎnma?

Introducing yourself

My name is...
我的名字是...
wǒ de míngzì shì...

What's your name?
你叫什么名字?
nǐ jiào shénme míngzi?

Where are you from?
你来自哪里?
nǐ láizì nǎlǐ?

I come from...
我来自...
wǒ láizì...

I am in (profession)
我的职业是...
wǒ de zhíyè shì

Getting around

Excuse me
对不起
duìbùqǐ

I want to go to...
我想去...
wǒ xiǎng qù...

I don't understand
我不明白
wǒ bù míngbai

Turn left　　左转　　zuǒzhuǎn

Turn right　右转　　yòuzhuǎn

Transportation

Taxi　　出租车　chūzūchē

Bus
公共汽车
gōnggòngqìchē

Airplane　飞机　　fēijī

Subway　地铁　　dìtiě

Train　　火车　　huǒchē

Airport　机场　　jīchǎng

Bus stop　车站　　chēzhàn

Train station 火车站　huǒchēzhàn

Subway station 地铁站　dìtiězhàn

One-way ticket
单程票
dānchéng piào

Round-trip ticket
来回票
láihuí piào

First-class
头等舱
tóuděngcāng

Ticket office
售票处
shòupiàochù

Travel agency
旅行社
lǚxíngshè

I'd like to buy a ticket
我想买一张票
wǒ xiǎng mǎi yīzhāngpiào

Where is...?
...在哪里?
...zàinǎlǐ?
What time does it arrive?
什么时候能够抵达?
shénmeshíhòu nénggòu dǐdá?
What time does it depart?
什么时候能够出发?
shénmeshíhòu nénggòu chūfā?

Business

Business	商业	shāngyè
Company	公司	gōngsī
Office	办公室	bàngōngshì

Business Card
名片
míngpiàn

| **Meeting** | 会议 | huìyì |

Deadline
截止日期
jiézhǐrìqī

Boss	老板	lǎobǎn
Client	客户	kèhù
Contract	合同	hétong
Import	进口	jìnkǒu
Export	出口	chūkǒu
Profit	利润	lìrùn
Loss	亏损	kuīsǔn
Revenue	收入	shōurù

Stock market
股票市场
gǔpiào shìchǎng

| **Invest** | 投资 | tóuzī |
| **International** | 国际的 | guójìde |

Money
How much is it?
多少钱?
duōshǎoqián
That's too expensive
太贵了
tàiguìle
Anything cheaper?
有便宜点的吗?
yǒu piányí diǎn de ma?

Can I have a receipt?
可以给我收据么?
kěyǐ gěiwǒ shōujù me

Price	价格	jiàgé
Buy	买	mǎi
Sell	卖	mài

Exchange money
换钱
huànqián

| **Exchange rate** | 汇率 | huìlù |
| **Bank** | 银行 | yínháng |

ATM
自动取款机
zìdòng qǔkuǎnjī

| **Credit card** | 信用卡 | xìnyòngkǎ |

Transfer money
转账　　　zhuǎnzhàng

Dining

| **Restaurant** | 饭店 | fàndiàn |

I want to eat...
我想吃...
wǒxiǎngchī...
Can you recommend anything?
你可以推荐一下么?
nǐ kěyǐ tuījiàn yīxià ma?
I like/don't like
我喜欢/不喜欢
wǒ xǐhuān/bùxǐhuān
Check please 埋单
máidān
Waiter
男服务员
nán fúwùyuán
Waitress
女服务员
nǚ fúwùyuán

Chinese Food	中餐	zhōngcān
Western Food	西餐	xīcān
Beef	牛肉	niúròu
Chicken	鸡肉	jīròu
Pork	猪肉	zhūròu
Lamb	羊肉	yángròu
Seafood	海鲜	hǎixiān
Fish	鱼	yú
Vegetables	蔬菜	shūcài

Soup	汤	tāng
Rice	米饭	mǐfàn
Noodles	面条	miàntiáo
Fruit	水果	shuǐguǒ
Dessert	甜点	tiándiǎn
Beverage	饮料	yǐnliào
Water	水	shuǐ
Soda	汽水	qìshuǐ
Fruit Juice	果汁	guǒzhī
Beer	啤酒	píjiǔ
Wine	葡萄酒	pútaojiǔ
Salty	咸的	xiánde
Spicy	辣的	làde
Sour	酸的	suānde
Bitter	苦的	kǔde
Sweet	甜的	tiánde
Vegetarian	素食的	sùshíde
Oil	油	yóu

Allergy
食物过敏
shíwùguòmǐn

Peanuts	花生	huāshēng
Chopsticks	筷子	kuàizi
Fork	叉子	chāzi
Spoon	汤匙	tāngchí
Knife	刀子	dāozi
Cup	杯子	bēizi
Bottle	瓶子	píngzi

Accommodation

I am staying at…
我住在…
wǒ zhùzài…

Is there a room available?
有空房间吗?
yǒu kōng fángjiān ma?

I would like to stay…days
我要住…天
wǒ yào zhù…tiān

| Hotel | 宾馆 | bīnguǎn |
| Reservation | 预定 | yùdìng |

Single room
单人房
dānrén fáng

Double room
双人房
shuāngrén fáng

| Room Key | 房卡 | fángkǎ |

May I have a hotel name card?
请给我宾馆的名片好吗?
qǐng gěi wǒ bīnguǎn de míngpiàn hǎoma?

Are there any messages for me?
我有没有留言?
wǒ yǒuméiyǒu liúyán?

Health

I have a cold
我感冒了
wǒ gǎnmào le

I have a fever
我发烧了
wǒ fāshāo le

| Hurts | 痛 | tòng |
| Diarrhea | 腹泻 | fùxiè |

Where is the hospital?
请问医院在哪里?
qǐng wèn yīyuàn zài nǎlǐ?

Doctor	医生	yīshēng
Dentist	牙医	yáyī
Medicine	药	yào

Chinese medicine
中药
zhōngyào

| Aspirin | 阿司匹林 | āsīpilín |
| Condoms | 避孕套 | bìyùntào |

Feminine hygiene products
女性用品
nǔxìngyòngpǐn

| Massage | 按摩 | ànmó |
| Acupuncture | 针灸 | zhēnjiǔ |

Visas

| Visa | 签证 | qiānzhèng |
| Passport | 护照 | hùzhào |

Identification
身份证 shēnfènzhèng

I want to extend my visa
我要延长签证有效期
wǒ yào yáncháng qiānzhèng yǒuxiàoqī

TRAVEL TIPS

Public Security Bureau
公安局
gōngānjú

Embassy	大使馆	dàshǐguǎn
Consulate	领事馆	lǐngshìguǎn
Application	申请	shēnqǐng

Mail

Post Office	邮局	yóujú
Address	地址	dìzhǐ

Email/email address
电子邮件
diànzǐyóujiàn

Zip/postal code
邮政编码　yóuzhèngbiānmǎ

Letter	信	xìn
Envelope	信封	xìnfēng

Airmail
航空信
hángkōngxin

Surface mail　平信　píngxìn

Express mail
特快专递
tèkuàizhuāndì

Registered mail
挂号信
guàhàoxìn

Stamps	邮票	yóupiào
Mailbox	邮箱	yóuxiāng

When will it arrive?
什么时候能寄到?
shénme shíhòu néng jìdào?

Telephone

Telephone	电话	diànhuà
Mobile phone	手机	shǒujī

Public telephone
公用电话
gōngyòngdiànhuà

Phone number
电话号码
diànhuàhàomǎ

Fax number
传真号码
chuánzhēnhàomǎ

Area code	区号	qūhào
Extension	分机	fēnjī

International calling card
国际长途电话卡
guójì chángtú diànhuàkǎ

Hello, may I speak with…
你好,请问…在吗?
nǐhǎo,qǐngwèn…zàima?

One moment please
请稍侯
qǐng shāo hòu

I can't get through
电话没有拨通
diànhuà méiyǒu bōtōng

The line is busy
电话忙
diànhuà máng

May I leave a message
我可以留言吗?
wǒ kěyǐ liúyán me

Internet café　网吧　wǎngbā

Time

What time is it?
现在几点了?
xiànzài jǐdiǎn le?

X o'clock
现在x点了
xiànzài x diǎn le

Today	今天	jīntiān
Tomorrow	明天	míngtiān
Yesterday	昨天	zuótiān

The day before yesterday
前天
qiántiān

The day after tomorrow
后天
hòutiān

Monday	星期一	xīngqīyī
Tuesday	星期二	xīngqīèr
Wednesday	星期三	xīngqīsān
Thursday	星期四	xīngqīsì
Friday	星期五	xīngqīwǔ
Saturday	星期六	xīngqīliù
Sunday	星期日	xīngqīrì
January	一月	yīyuè

February	二月	èryuè
March	三月	sānyuè
April	四月	sìyuè
May	五月	wǔyuè
June	六月	liùyuè
July	七月	qīyuè
August	八月	bāyuè
September	九月	jiǔyuè
October	十月	shíyuè
November	十一月	shíyīyuè
December	十二月	shíèryuè
Year	年	nián

2005
二零零五年
èrlínglíngwǔnián

2006
二零零六年
èrlínglíngliùnián

Early	早	zǎo
Late	晚	wǎn
Morning	早上	zǎoshàng
Afternoon	下午	xiàwǔ

Evening
晚上
wǎnshàng

There's not enough time
时间不多了
shíjiān bùduōle

Immediately	马上	mǎshàng
Soon	不久	bùjiǔ
Now	现在	xiànzài
Before	之前	zhīqián
After	之后	zhīhòu
In the future	将来	jiānglái
Jetlag	时差	shíchā

Emergency

Help	救命	jiùmìng
Fire	着火	zháohuǒ
Thief	小偷	xiǎotōu
Police station	警察局	jǐngchájú
Sick	生病	shēngbìng
Injury	受伤	shòushāng
Car accident	车祸	chēhuò
Ambulance	急救车	jíjiùchē
Hospital	医院	yīyuàn

Professions and job titles

Accountant	会计	kuàijì
Architect	建筑师	jiànzhùshī
Assistant	助理	zhùlǐ

Bus. Dev. Manager
市场开发经理
shìchǎng kāifā jīnglǐ

| Consultant | 顾问 | gùwèn |

CEO
首席执行官
shǒuxīzhíxíngguān

Designer	设计师	shèjìshī
Doctor	医生	yīshēng
Editor	编辑	biānji

Engineer
工程师
gōngchéngshī

Factory Manager
厂长
chǎngzhǎng

Financial Advisor
财务顾问
cáiwùgùwèn

General Manager
总经理
zǒngjīnglǐ

HR Manager
人事经理
rénshijīnglǐ

IT Manager
信息部经理
xìnxībùjīnglǐ

| Journalist | 记者 | jìzhě |
| Lawyer | 律师 | lùshī |

Managing Director
总裁
zǒngcái

Marketing Manager
市场经理
shìchǎngjīnglǐ

| Partner | 合伙人 | héhuǒrén |

Operations Manager
运营经理
yùnyíngjīnglǐ

| Photographer | 摄影师 | shèyǐngshī |

Programmer

程序员
chéngxùyuán
PR Manager
公关经理
gōngguānjīnglǐ
Real Estate Agent
房地产经纪人
fángdìchǎnjīngjìrén
Sales Manager
销售经理
xiāoshòujīnglǐ
Stock Broker
股票经纪人
gǔpiàojīngjìrén

| **Teacher** | 教师 | jiàoshī |
| **Translator** | 翻译 | fānyì |

Web Designer
网页设计师
wǎngyèshèjìshī

Countries

Argentina	阿根廷	āgēntíng
Australia	澳大利亚	àodàlìyà
Austria	奥地利	àodìlì
Belarus	白俄罗斯	báiéluósī
Belgium	比利时	bǐlìshí
Brazil	巴西	bāxī
Canada	加拿大	jiānádà
China	中国	zhōngguó
Denmark	丹麦	dānmài
Egypt	埃及	āijí
Finland	芬兰	fēnlán
France	法国	fǎguó
Germany	德国	déguó
Greece	希腊	xīlà
India	印度	yìndù
Indonesia	印度尼西亚	yìndùníxīyà
Iran	伊朗	yīlǎng
Iraq	伊拉克	yīlākè
Ireland	爱尔兰	àiěrlán
Israel	以色列	yǐsèliè
Italy	意大利	yìdàlì
Japan	日本	rìběn
Malaysia	马来西亚	mǎláixīyà
Mexico	墨西哥	mòxīgē
Netherlands	荷兰	hélán

New Zealand	新西兰	xīnxīlán
Norway	挪威	nuówēi
Pakistan	巴基斯坦	bājīsītǎn
Philippines	菲律宾	fēilǜbīn
Poland	波兰	bōlán
Portugal	葡萄牙	pútáoyá
Russia	俄罗斯	éluósī
Singapore	新加坡	xīnjiāpō
South Africa	南非	nánfēi
South Korea	韩国	hánguó
Spain	西班牙	xībānyá
Sweden	瑞典	ruìdiǎn
Switzerland	瑞士	ruìshì
Thailand	泰国	tàiguó
Turkey	土耳其	tǔěrqí

United Kingdom
英国
yīngguó

| **Ukraine** | 乌克兰 | wūkèlán |

United States of America
美国
měiguó

| **Vietnam** | 越南 | yuènán |

Languages

Arabic	阿拉伯语	ālābóyǔ
Chinese	汉语	hànyǔ
Danish	丹麦语	dānmàiyǔ
Dutch	荷兰语	hélányǔ
English	英语	yīngyǔ
Finnish	芬兰语	fēnlányǔ
French	法语	fǎyǔ
German	德语	déyǔ
Greek	希腊语	xīlàyǔ
Hindi	北印度语	běiyìndùyǔ
Irish	爱尔兰语	àiěrlányǔ
Italian	意大利语	yìdàlìyǔ
Japanese	日语	rìyǔ
Korean	朝语	hányǔ
Polish	波兰语	bōlányǔ
Portuguese	葡萄牙语	pútáoyáyǔ
Russian	俄语	éyǔ
Spanish	西班牙语	xībānyáyǔ
Swedish	瑞典语	ruìdiǎnyǔ
Turkish	土耳其语	tǔěrqíyǔ
Vietnamese	越南语	yuènányǔ

Moving to China

Registration 82

Finding a place to live 83

Relocation services 85

Getting settled 88

Learning Chinese 89

Hired help 92

Daily necessities 93

Schools and education 97

MOVING TO CHINA

Moving to China

For some people, the prospect of moving to China can be scary. In reality, most of the common concerns are easily handled and most people find that the shift is much simpler and easier than they imagined.

Relocating your family to China can be an exciting and rewarding experience. Chinese culture stresses hospitality to guests, and since foreign faces are still sparse in many parts of the country, foreigners often find themselves an object of curiosity, which usually translates to special attentiveness and friendliness.

Most foreigners moving to China will be based in one of China's larger and more "cosmopolitan" cities such as Beijing, Shanghai, Shenzhen or Guangzhou. Alternatively, more and more foreigners are moving to the larger provincial cities such

as Tianjin, Nanjing, Chengdu or Qingdao. Given the influx of foreign investment into China in all the above-mentioned cities in recent years, it is not surprising there has also been an increase in the variety of recreational and lifestyle options catering to foreigners. Beijing and Shanghai in particular have evolved in recent years into international metropolises, each providing a full array of commodities and services for foreigners.

Registration

The visa usually issued for long term stay in China is a 'Z' or employment visa. Application for an employment visa will be handled through your employer and will typically be handled before your arrival in China. Many foreigners without such sponsorship (or secure employment for that matter) will typically use an 'F' or business visa, obtained with the help of a visa agent or travel agent in Hong Kong. For more information on visas, see page 38.

In addition to a visa, foreigners are expected to obtain a foreign residency permit within 30 days of arrival in China. A valid passport and visa, health certificate, residence lease, and photos should be submitted with your application to the local office of the PSB (Public Security Bureau – the police). Once again, most of the paperwork will usually be handled by your employer in China.

Finding a place to live

If you are lucky enough to be sent to China on an overseas placement or assignment, it is likely that your employer will either arrange your housing or at the very least provide a generous monthly housing allowance as part of your employment contract. Be sure to check the terms of your employer's offer carefully, making sure it fits your personal requirements. The phrase "fully furnished" lends itself to a variety of interpretations, for instance. Negotiating a good housing package from your employer will probably be worth the effort, especially if you are to be located in a relatively isolated area.

If you are moving to China to look for employment or even start your own business, you will need to find your own housing. There are many options available for all budgets. Foreigners living in Shanghai, for example, can expect to pay anything between RMB2,000 (for a one bedroom apartment) to RMB80,000 or more (for a villa in an expatriate complex) per month. Rental agencies catering to foreigners and with English-

speaking consultants are available in most large Chinese cities (see "Residential property agents" below). Alternatively, a wealth of information and listings are available online.

Serviced apartments catering to foreigners and wealthy Chinese are usually furnished, with utilities, housekeeping, and other services included as part of the package. Most upscale hotels offer serviced apartments designed for long-term stay, as do many independent apartment complexes. Expect monthly rates from around RMB16,000 to as much RMB150,000.

Luxury villas in so-called expatriate complexes have sprouted up on the outskirts of many larger Chinese cities. These developments offer a quieter, more spacious environment than the high-rise apartments that are commonly found in most Chinese cities. Although involving longer commute times, they are often located near development zones, golf courses, and international schools.

Buying a home

Buying a home in China is now a more realistic option than ever, and worth considering for someone who plans to live in China long-term. Regulations restricting foreigners to living in specially designated areas no longer exist in China but it's important to be aware of some of the peculiarities of China's real estate market. The maximum leasehold that can be bought is seventy years.

Real estate prices have been steadily rising in recent years in China's major cities. If you're considering buying a home in China then proceed with caution and secure the help of a reputable agent. Additionally you should consider the property's location and the convenience of public transportation, and all other factors pertaining to valuation. Banks in major cities are happy to provide mortgages to foreigners. For more information, check the overview of the real estate industry on page 156.

Residential property agents
Beijing
CB Richard Ellis
(010) 6539 1288
www.cbre.com.cn
Jones Lang LaSalle
(010) 6505 1300
www.joneslanglasalle.com.cn
Colliers International
(010) 8518 1633
www.colliers.com
Joanna Real Estate
(010) 5108 8028
www.joannarealestate.com.cn
Shanghai
Ark International
(021) 6445 2651
www.ark-shanghai.com
CB Richard Ellis
(021) 6289 1200
www.cbre.com.cn
Jones Lang LaSalle
(021) 6393 3333
www.joneslanglasalle.com.cn
Crispin Property Consultants
(021) 6372 2858
www.cpcproperty.com
Colliers International
(021) 6237 0088
www.colliers.com
Jonna Real Estate
(021) 5109 9888
www.joannarealestate.com.cn
Guangzhou
CB Richard Ellis
(020) 8732 2332
www.cbre.com.cn

Jones Lang LaSalle
(020) 3891 1238
www.joneslanglasalle.com.cn
Colliers International
(020) 8669 5176
www.colliers.com
Chengdu
CB Richard Ellis
(028) 8667 0022
www.cbre.com.cn
Century 21 Real Estate
(028) 8523 7721
www.century21cn.com
Qingdao
Century 21 Real Estate
(0532) 8593 2121
www.century21cn.com
Tianjin
Century 21 Real Estate
(022) 2836 8821
www.century21cn.com
Wuhan
Century 21 Real Estate
(027) 5850 3998
www.century21cn.com
Nanjing
Century 21 Real Estate
(025) 8626 2211
www.century21cn.com

Relocation services

Moving a large amount of personal belongings to China can present many difficulties, not to mention the expense of doing so. Unless your employer provides an allowance for relocating your possessions and furniture, bring along as little as possible – most furniture and appliances can be bought in China for less than the amount required to actually ship similar items from overseas. Bringing a car to China requires reams of paperwork and hefty fees and taxes.

Pets can be brought into China, but airlines have restrictions regarding the transport of animals; inquire ahead of time to ensure your pets can be transported in comfort. China customs rules vary according to animal type, and change frequently. So check for the latest regulations with the authorities both in China and your home country.

Relocation services
Beijing
Asia Pacific Access
(010) 6512 999
www.apachina.com
Asian Tigers
(010) 8580 1471
www.asiantigersgroup.com
Interdean Interconex
(010) 6597 5211
www.interdeaninterconex.biz
Schenker
(010) 6427 6030
www.schenker.com
Allied Pickfords
(010) 8561 8759
www.alliedpickfords.com
Santa Fe Relocation Services
(010) 6947 0688
www.santaferelo.com
DHL Danzas
(010) 8453 4200
www.asia.danzas.com
Links Relocations
(010) 6581 5900
www.linksrelocations.com

UTS Asian Express
(010) 8580 1471
www.aemovers.com.hk
SIRVA Relocation
(010) 5870 0866
www.sirvarelocation.com
Move One Relocations
(010) 6581 4046
www.moveonerelo.com
Shanghai
Asia Pacific Access
(021) 6249 2027
www.apachina.com
Interdean Interconex
(021) 6270 2420
www.interdeaninterconex.biz
Schenker
(021) 5064 3708
www.schenker.com
Allied Pickfords
(021) 6486 0832
www.alliedpickfords.com
Santa Fe Relocation Services
(021) 6233 9700
www.santaferelo.com
DHL Danzas
(021) 6375 9470
www.asia.danzas.com
Links Relocations
(021) 5405 0500
www.linksrelications.com
UTS Asian Express
(021) 6258 2244
www.aemovers.com.hk
Asian Tigers
(021) 6208 3496
www.asiantigersgroup.com
Bridge Worldwide Relocations
(021) 6402 2418
www.bridgerelo.com
SIRVA Relocation
(021) 6332 3322
www.sirvarelocation.com

Move One Relocations
(021) 5212 3989
www.moveonerelo.com
Rhema Mover
(021) 6225 3301
www.rhemamovers.com.sg
Crown Relocations
(021) 6472 0254
www.crownrelo.com
Guangzhou
Asia Pacific Access
(010) 6512 999
www.apachina.com
Schenker
(020) 3879 5308
www.schenker.com
Allied Pickfords
(020) 8730 6001
www.alliedpickfords.com
Santa Fe Relocation Services
(020) 3887 0630
www.santaferelo.com
DHL Danzas
(020) 3887 8801
www.asia.danzas.com
UTS Asian Express
(020) 8659 0616
www.aemovers.com.hk
Asian Tigers
(020) 8666 2655
www.asiantigersgroup.com
Crown Relocations
(020) 8386 3869
www.crownrelo.com
Chengdu
DHL Danzas
(028) 8293 13
www.asia.danzas.com
Qingdao
Santa Fe Relocation Services
(0532) 8386 9455
www.santaferelo.com
Tianjin

Asian Tigers
(022) 2412 4665
www.asiantigersgroup.com
Move One Relocations
(022) 8488 9886
www.moveonerelo.com
Wuhan
DHL Danzas
(027) 8551 0496
www.asia.danzas.com
Nanjing
Asian Tigers
(025) 8454 7861
www.asiantigersgroup.com
DHL Danzas
(025) 3311 123
www.asia.danzas.com
Chongqing
Asian Tigers
(023) 6382 0192
www.asiantigersgroup.com

Getting settled

Settling into your new life in China will be much easier if you get involved with the local foreign community. Not surprisingly, such communities can be very close knit, especially in cities where there are fewer foreigners. There can be no better way to get over some of the peculiarities of living in a foreign country than relating your latest China horror story to a fellow foreigner (or laowai, a Chinese word for foreigner) over a drink, turning a cause of concern into a China learning experience and another great story for friends and family back home.

Even in large cities such as Beijing and Shanghai, with thousands of foreigners, the expatriate community is surprisingly interconnected. Often, a few establishments become unofficial centers for foreigners to congregate. More importantly, if you're looking for a new job such bars can be a great place for networking. Since exchanging business cards is a common practice in China, be sure to have plenty with you at all times. Sports clubs and recreational groups are also common in expatriate communities.

Gyms/sports clubs
Beijing
Softball
Beijing Softball League
www.beijingsoftball.com
Racquet Sports
Kerry Center Tennis and Squash
(010) 6561 8833
Cycling
Mountain Bikers of Beijing
(0) 138 0108 8646
Gyms
Bally Total Fitness
(010) 6518 1666
Clark Hatch Fitness Center
(010) 6770 9900
www.fitnessconcept.com.cn
Kerry Sports Center
(010) 6561 8833
Shanghai
Football
Shanghai International Football

League
www.eteams.com/sifl
(021) 6485 0602
Rugby
Shanghai Rugby Football Club
www.shanghaifootballclub.com
Running
Shanghai Hash House Harriers
www.shanghaihhh.com
Racquet Sports
Shanghai International Tennis Center
(021) 6415 5588 ext. 82
Cycling
Shanghai Bike Club
www.bohdi.com.cn
(021) 3226 0000
Wolf's Bicycle Club
(0) 138 0195 3000
Gyms
Alexander City Club
(021) 5358 1188
Clark Hatch Fitness Center
(021) 6212 9988 ext. 3300
Fitness Concept
(021) 6867 0621

www.fitnessconcept.com.cn
Fitness First Health Club
(021) 6288 0512
Megafit Sports Club
(021) 5030 8118
(021) 5383 6633
www.megafitchina.com
St. Regis Spa and Fitness Center
(021) 5050 4567

Learning Chinese

If you're planning on staying in China for some time then learning some basic Chinese can be not only helpful, but also interesting and fun. While it may take years of intensive study to bring your Chinese to a functional business level, knowledge of even a few polite phrases or sentences about yourself can create a positive impression with your Chinese colleagues and friends. In the meantime, the language guide beginning on page 42 may be of use.

Most cities have private language schools that offer part-time Chinese classes for foreigners. Alternatively, it's easy to find a private tutor so that you can arrange classes to suit your schedule and particular Chinese level. Tutors can be found by contacting the schools below or checking the classified sections of local English-language listings magazines. In addition, there are endless numbers of Chinese people, young and old, eager to learn English and willing to set up a free language exchange arrangement.

There are free English language magazines catering to foreigners in most larger Chinese cities, including Beijing, Shanghai, Guangzhou, Tianjin, Nanjing, Hangzhou, Qingdao, Chengdu and Xi'an, and these can be useful guides to what's going on in the city. Such magazines can normally be picked up in five-star hotels, or bars and restaurants often frequented by foreigners. Perhaps the most popular listing magazine to have sprung up in China in recent years is the That's series, published monthly in Beijing, Shanghai and Guangzhou. Another popular choice is City Weekend, published every two weeks in Beijing and Shanghai.

LifeLine Shanghai: (021) 6279 8990, offers a unique service. Set up early in 2004 and supported by volunteers and contributions, this telephone hotline is open to any 'English speaker needing help', whether that help entails dealing with a serious personal crisis or small daily-life complications. The center welcomes calls from anywhere in China.

A wealth of information is available online on various websites and message boards serving expatriates in China. Most of these websites serve a particular city or locale, and are a good starting point for finding out about life in the city you will be moving to before you actually arrive in China.

Language School
Beijing
Executive Mandarin
3/F Hanwei Mansion,
7 Guanghua Lu
(010) 6561 2486
www.ecbeijing.com
Frontiers Language School
5/Fbuilding 2, 7 Xinhong Jie
Dongzhimenwai Dajie
(010) 6413 1548
www.frontiers.com.cn
Berlitz
801 Sun Joy Mansion, 6 Ritan Lu
(010) 6593 0478
www.berlitz.com.cn
Bridge School
1308, 3/F Guangming Hotel,
Liangmaqiao Lu
(010) 8451 7605
930, 9/F, E-Tower, Guanghua Lu
(010) 6506 4409
www.bridgeschoolchina.com
Beijing Chinese School
805 Building C, Cuojigang,
Dongsanhuan Bei Lu
(010) 8625 2417

www.beijingchineseschool.com
Shanghai
Executive Mandarin
250 Wuyuan Lu, (021) 5403 5500
www.execmandarin.com
East Mandarin
1301 Xinda Mansion, 322 Xianxia Lu
(021) 6209 2529
How Mandarin
2212 Plaza 66, 1266 Nanjing Xi Lu
(021) 6288 2308
www.howmandarin.com
Mandarin House
3/F Far East International Plaza
Tower B, 317 Xianxia Lu
(021) 5257 4040
101 Tower 12, 99 Pucheng Lu
(021) 5054 0033
101 Tower 7, 99 Urumqi Zhong Lu
(021) 5467 0707
Talking China
8E Xinan Building (East Tower), 200
Zhenjing Lu
(021) 6289 4299
www.talkingchina.com
Berlitz
21/F Shui On Plaza,

Huaihai Zhong Lu
(021) 5386 8866
www.berlitz.com.cn
Guangzhou
Berlitz
508 Park View Square,
960 Jiefang Bei Lu
(020) 8666 5444
www.berlitz.com.cn

Hired help

One of the nicest parts about living in China is that hired help is cheap and easy to find. A housekeeper (or *ayi* in Chinese), costs from as little as RMB8 per hour. Some of the services offered by an ayi include cleaning, ironing, cooking, taking clothes to the dry cleaners and the paying of utility bills. If you are living alone it can be great to return home from work to find all your clothes washed and ironed, and your evening dinner waiting in the microwave. Even better, most ayis are wonderful cooks.

It's important to remember that some ayis may not be used to dealing with foreigners and their cultural habits, so be patient with your instructions and expectations. Tipping is not normally expected in China, but if you're satisfied with your ayi's service then a bonus will be more than welcome.

Families can hire a live-in ayi for around RMB1,000 per month. Rates vary by location and dependant upon the ayi's language ability and other skills. Ayis can help with the shopping and babysitting. Many agencies offer ayi referral services, but it is usually best to choose one based upon a recommendation from a friend or colleague.

Other services that are easy to secure in China include drivers (driving your car or theirs) and interpreters. Again, personal referrals are the best.

Daily necessities

It's possible to buy nearly anything in China. As one of the world's leading producers of electronics, textiles and agricultural goods, China can provide the foreign visitor with most of the same goods bought in your home country. Foreign franchises such as Carrefour and Wal-Mart have rapidly opened outlets throughout the country over the past few years, making Western brands of toiletries, clothing and groceries available at reasonable prices. Tending to the huge Chinese consumer pool, these retailers also offer Chinese equivalent goods, which are usually satisfactory in quality and cheaper.

Beyond these familiar outlets lies a diverse range of shopping options. Many modern Chinese cities have everything from old family shops with a range of knick-knacks to opulent malls filled with designer stores. Shopping malls, modeled after those in the West, are fairly straightforward and have signs and directories that are frequently written in English as well as Chinese. Prices in malls tend to be higher and fixed.

Supermarkets

French supermarket chain Carrefour is China's largest foreign retailer, with around 80 hypermarket stores throughout China. It is a great place to buy foreign groceries such as cheese, wine, bread and other foods, but you will also be able to find everything from electronics and clothing to bicycles. Wal-Mart conducts similar business but it has fewer stores throughout the country. N-Mart is another competitor. The prices at these stores are very competitive, and they tend to be very crowded.

Smaller supermarkets carrying imported goods can also be found in Beijing and Shanghai, particularly in areas where lots of foreigners live. Prices at such supermarkets tend to be much more expensive than those at Chinese supermarkets but can be a great place to satisfy your craving for the kinds of snacks and groceries that you might usually buy in your home country.

Delivery

Food delivery services are widely available in China, offered by restaurants specializing in both Chinese and foreign cuisines. Ask your favorite restaurants about their delivery services or use operators that process delivery orders for a network of restaurants like Sherpa's in Shanghai or Goodie's in Beijing. Grocery stores increasingly offer delivery services.

Coca-Cola and Nestle both have drinking water brands, and they along with numerous other local companies are able to deliver purified drinking water to your home or office.

Western supermarkets
Beijing
Friendship Supermarket
Supermarket and grocery delivery service
7 Sanlitun Lu, (010) 6532 1871

Jenny Lou's
Supermarket and grocery delivery service
6 Sanlitun Xiliujie 4 Ritan Bei Lu
(010) 8589 8299

Beijing Goodies
Takeaway food delivery service from some of Beijing's best restaurants
(010) 6416 7676
www.beijinggoodies.com

ASC Fine Wines
Home delivery of fine wines
(021) 6468 1598
www.asc-wines.com

Shanghai
City Supermarket
Supermarket and grocery delivery service
B/F Times Square,
99 Huaihi Zhong Lu

G/F Shanghai Center,
1376 Nanjing Xi Lu
3211 Hongmei Lu, Gubei
(021) 6215 0418
Pines the Market Place
Supermarket and grocery delivery
service
18 Jianhe Lu, (021) 6262 9055
www.pines.com.cn
Sherpas
Takeaway food delivery service from
some of Shanghai's best restaurants
(021) 6209 6209
www.sherpa.com.cn
ASC Fine Wines
Home delivery of fine wines
(021) 6468 1598
www.asc-wines.com
Nanjing
City Supermarket
Grocery delivery service
(025) 6215 0418
Chengdu
Metro Chengdu Store
1 Qingjiang Road Central, Qingyang

(028) 8295 8888
Qingdao
Carrefour Qingdao Store
128 Shandong Rd
(0532) 8508 9156
Tianjin
Carrefour Tianjin Store
168 Bai Di Rd
(022) 2723 2369
302 Nanjing Road
(022) 2721 1585
Wuhan
Carrefour Wuhan Store
1 ZhongBei Road
(027) 8712 4539

News and media
There are two official English-
language newspapers in China
(China Daily and Shanghai Daily)
and several official English language
websites, including several operated
by the official Xinhua News Agency.
Other useful sources of news are
the South China Morning Post

newspaper, published in Hong Kong and available at five-star hotels and foreign language bookstores in China for RMB18, and China Economic Review magazine (www.chinaeconomicreview.com). There is only one official English language television station, CCTV-9.

The best solution to accessing news in China, however, is through the Internet. Though the BBC and CNN websites are not always accessible, there are enough news outlets on the web to ensure that readers will know what's happening in the world.

The foreign language bookstores in the major cities do offer a range of books, but if you're looking for anything obscure your best bet is to order online at Amazon.com. Orders usually arrive to addresses in China in around two weeks.

Convenience stores

24-hour convenience stores are spreading fast in China and are a useful place to buy items such as snacks, beverages, camera film, batteries, stationery, cigarettes, condoms and some toiletries. The 7-Eleven chain, having already conquered other Asian regions like Japan, Taiwan, Hong Kong and Thailand, has so far only opened shops in Guangzhou and Shenzhen. Interestingly, while there seems to be a 24-hour convenience store on every street corner in Shanghai, they have been slower to catch on in Beijing.

Medicines and toiletries

Chinese pharmacies sell prescription and over-the-counter medicines of two varieties: Western drugs and medicines, and traditional Chinese medicines, which are mostly herbal remedies to be boiled and imbibed. Many of the more familiar Western drugs and medicines are now available in China, though it's likely they will be packaged differently from what is available in your home country. If you're trying to locate a particular drug, noting down the medical (or Latin) term for the drug

and showing the pharmacist is a solution that sometimes works.

Watson's, a Hong Kong-based drugstore operator, has outlets in several cities, carrying drugs, medicine, and a large supply of toiletries and personal hygiene products. It can be a great place to buy deodorant, an item that is surprisingly hard to find in China, particularly as you move away from the major cities. Larger supermarkets, hypermarkets and convenience stores (and particularly Carrefour, Metro and Wal-Mart) also include a range of toiletries and medicines.

Schools and education

China's larger cities have international schools for children of expatriate families and the multicultural environment at such schools can have a positive effect on a child's upbringing, providing daily exposure to other children from different cultures. It's worth visiting potential schools before making a final decision, as the curriculum and facilities offered can range widely. Expect teachers to be qualified and experienced. Tuition fees and the overall costs of sending your child to an international school in China can be expensive - as much as US$20,000 per year - though this cost may be covered by your employer as part of your contract.

If you're on a stricter budget, some Chinese schools provide programs for foreign students. All or most of the classes will be delivered in Chinese, but this total immersion approach means your child will quickly become quite fluent in Chinese. Generally, the younger the child, the easier they will find the transition.

Another choice to consider is home-schooling, but make sure your child follows an educational program that will allow for their re-integration into a public school system or one that will be recognized by educational institutions in your home country.

International Schools
Beijing
Kindrgarten and nursery schools
Ivy Academy Beijing
(010) 8451 1380
www.ivyacademy.cn
International Children's House
Montessori Kindergarten
(010) 6505 3869
www.montessoribeijing.com
Primary and secondary schools
Yew Chung International School
Beijing
(010) 8583 3731, *www.ycef.com*
Australian International School
Beijing
(010) 8439 4315
www.aisb.cn
Beijing BISS International School
(010) 6443 3151
www.biss.com.cn

Beijing Concord College of
Sino-Canada
(010) 8959 1234
www.ccsc.com.cn
Beijing Eton International School
(010) 6430 1590
www.etonkids.com
Beijing Zhongguancun
International School
(010) 8213 9966
www.bzis2002.com
Beijing Huijia Private School
(010) 6078 5555
www.huijia2000.com
Beijing World Youth Academy
(010) 6461 7787
www.ibwya.net
British School of Beijing
(010) 8532 3088
www.britishschool.org.cn
Deutsche Botschaftsschule Pekingf
(010) 6532 2535
www.dspeking.net.cn
Fangcaodi Primary School
(010) 6509 4328, *www.fcd.com.cn*
International Academy of Beijing
(IAB)

(010) 6430 1600
www.iabchina.net
International School of Beijing
(010) 8046 2345
www.isb.bj.edu.cn
International Study Group
(010) 6532 2293
www.isg.com.cn
Japanese School of Beijing
(010) 6436 3250
www.jsb.org.cn
Lycee Francais de Pekin
(010) 6532 3498, *www.lfp.com.cn*
New School of Collaborative Learning
(010) 8470 9458
www.nscl-beijing.org
Swedish School
(010) 6456 0826
www.swedishschool.org.cn
Western Academy of Beijing
(010) 8456 4155
www.wab.edu

Shanghai
Kindergarten and nursery schools
Dulwich College Kingergarten (DUCKS)
(021) 5899 3785
www.dulwichcollege.cn
Rainbow Bridge International School
(021) 6268 9773
www.rbik.com
Tiny Tots International Pre-School and Kindergarten
(021) 6431 3788
www.tinytotschina.com
Primary and secondary schools
British International School Shanghai
(021) 5812 7455
www.bisshanghai.com

Concordia International School Shanghai (CISS)
(021) 5899 0380
www.ciss.com.cn
Dulwich College International School
(021) 5899 9910
www.dulwichcollege.cn
German School Shanghai
(021) 6405 9220
www.ds-shanghai.org.cn
Livingston Ameriacan School
(021) 6290 4529
www.laschina.org
Shanghai American School (SAS)
(021) 6221 1445 (Minhang)
(021) 5897 3097 (Pudong)
www.saschina.org
Shanghai Community International Schools
(021) 6252 3688 (Changning)
(021) 5812 9888 (Pudong)
(021) 6261 4338 (Hongqiao)
www.scischina.org
Shanghai Rego International School
(021) 6492 3431
www.srisrego.com
Sino-Canada High School
(021) 5111 3112
www.sinocanada.cn
Yew Chung International School Shanghai
(021) 6242 3243 (Hongqiao)
(021) 6219 5910 (Gubei)
(021) 6856 7202 (Pudong)
www.ycef.com
Yangtze River Delta
Australian International School
Ningbo
Ningbo,Zhejiang
(0574) 8730 6737
www.aussieshool-china.com

MOVING TO CHINA

Community International Schools
Hangzhou, Zhejiang
(0571) 8669 0045
www.scischina.org

Nanjing International School
Nanjing, Jiangsu
(025) 8589 9111
www.najing-school.com

Suzhou Eton House International School
Suzhou, Jiangsu
(0512) 6825 5666
www.etonhouse-sz.com

Sino-Canada High School
Suzhou, Jiangsu
(0512) 6326 1000
www.sinocanada.cn

Suzhou Singapore International School
Suzhou, Jiangsu
(0512) 6761 0082
www.ssis-suzhou.com

Taihu International School
Wuxi, Jiangsu
(0510) 506 3802
www.tis-wuxi.com

Changzhou International School
Changzhou, Jiangsu
(0519) 510 0253
www.czis.com.cn

Pearl River Delta

Concord College of Sino-Canada
Shenzhen, Guangdong
(0755) 2656 8889
www.ccsc.cn

QSI International School of Shekou
Shenzhen, Guangdong
(0755) 2667 6031
www.qsi.org

QSI International School of Zhuhai
Zhuhai, Guangdong
(0756) 815 6134
www.qsi.org

Dongguan Eton House International Pre-School
Dongguan, Guangdong
(0769) 203 8777
www.etonhouse-dg.com

Guangzhou
American International School
(020) 8735 3392
www.aisgz.edu.cn

Clifford School
(020) 8471 1441 (Panyu)
www.clifford-school.org.cn
Guangzhou Nanbu International School
(020) 8706 0862
www.gnischina.com
Utahloy International School
(020) 8704 4299
(020) 8291 3201 (Zeng Cheng)
www.utahloy.com

Other Cities in China
Chengdu International School
Chengdu, Sichuan
(028) 8525 5784
www.iscchengdu.org
QSI International School of Chengdu
Chengdu, Sichuan
(028) 8519 8393
www.qsi.org
Chongqing International School
Chongqing
(023) 6888 7659
www.infls.cn

Yew Chung International School
Chongqing
(023) 6763 8482
www.ycef.com
Dalian Maple Leaf International School
Dalian, Liaoning
(0411) 8790 4790
www.mapleleaf.net.cn
Kunming International Academy
Kunming, Yunnan
(0871) 412 6887
www.kiachina.org
Qingdao MTI International School
Qingdao, Shandong
(0532) 398 5006
www.qmischina.com
QSI International.School of Wuhan
Wuhan, Hubei
(027) 8352 5597
www.qsi.org
TEDA International School Tianjin
Tianjin
(022) 2859 2001
www.tistschool.org

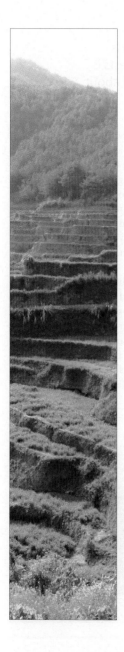

Industry overviews

Agriculture	104
Automobiles	109
Aviation	115
Banking	119
Cement	124
Consumer Trends	128
Electronics	133
Energy	137
Environment	141
Insurance	146
Logistics	150
Real Estate	156
Retail	160
Securities	164
Semiconductors	171
Steel	175
Telecom	179
Textiles	184
Tourism	188

Agriculture

Income levels are rising everywhere, but so is income disparity. The increase in rural protests is evidence that the Party needs to be careful about leaving the peasants behind

U rbanization is taking China by storm. Great swathes of the population are moving out of the fields and into the cities. By the end of 2005, four out of ten Chinese were living in cities – double the number of 20 years ago – and the figure is expected to continue rising. This demographic shift has placed new burdens on the agricultural industry, which faces increased, more varied demands for food from a larger, richer urban population. And since the majority of Chinese still live in rural areas, the government faces some political pressure to see to farmers' wellbeing.

While the lure of higher salaries in the cities reduces the number of available hands to work the land, the land itself is under constant threat from the temptations of developers and their partners in local government. Arable land, already in short supply throughout the country, is often commandeered by officials for the building of factories and apartment blocks.

All too often, these land grabs are illegal. In the first half of 2006, the amount of land seized unlawfully was 20% higher

than the same period in 2005. Protests increasingly crop up around the country as well, as Beijing acknowledged some 87,000 "mass incidents" around the country in 2005, up from 74,000 in 2004 and 58,000 in 2003. Certainly not all of these represent protests against land seizures; but it is safe to say that a large proportion spring from tensions between rich and poor. The fact that the Ministry of Public Security even releases figures like this shows the degree to which the government is worried about social stability.

To alleviate some of its fears, the government is taking steps to relieve the burden on farmers. As part of the 11th National Five-Year Plan, passed in early 2006, the 2,600-year-old agricultural tax was abolished, and subsidies to farmers were raised by 14% to a record-high RMB339.7 billion (US$41.9 billion). This has changed fundamentally the relationship between farmers and the government, for the better.

A brief history

Following the Communist takeover in 1949, land was seized from landowners and given to the peasants, sealing Mao's position as the undisputed leader of "New China". But during the Great Leap Forward of 1958, the land was taken from the peasants again and put in the control of communes. To the farmers facing production quotas and fixed pricing on yields sold directly to the state, government regulation of their livelihood seemed an all-too-familiar return of feudalism. The communes, of course, were a failure.

In late 1978, Deng Xiaoping set a more liberal agricultural market in motion. The communes were dissolved and replaced by the "household responsibility system", whereby land allotments were contracted to farmer families, shifting management responsibility back to households. Essentially this was the introduction of entrepreneurial freedom to millions of Chinese peasants, who could now choose what to grow and sell their produce in the marketplace. This agricultural reform was the first major step in China's greater economic opening.

Now, in the midst of the transition from a planned economy to a free market, prices of agricultural products are still subject to a measure of regulation, grain in particular. But reduced regulation has exposed China's countryside to economic survival of the fittest, where lucky and diligent farmers are seen rising to affluence while others sink further into poverty.

The government introduced national direct subsidies to farmers in 2004. Its intention was twofold: first, the leaders naturally were looking to raise rural incomes; but second, they were also disturbed by the grain harvest of autumn 2003, which was the lowest in 15 years. Over the years, many farmers have given up on rice, opting to grow more lucrative crops like soybeans, fruits and vegetables, or they have switched to farming fish. These choices also reflect changes in the modern Chinese diet, which now includes more meat and dairy products than ever before.

With grain harvests up in 2004, the government said its policies were the cause. But it is just as likely that generally high market prices of early 2004 caused more farmers to plant rice, especially as the government subsidies have been spread so thinly as to mean little to individual farmers. Subsidies in 2004 were valued at RMB11.6 billion, accounting for only 2% of all grain production (as stated earlier, the current level is nearly RMB340 billion)

Modern problems

Irrigation and water pollution are major issues. Generally speaking, northern China tends to be plagued by drought while southern regions are susceptible to flooding. Channeling of water and flood management through construction of dams and canals has already been successful and there are plans for it to be further implemented on a larger scale. In May 2006, construction of the Three Gorges Dam, the largest hydroelectric dam in history, was completed. It required the relocation of over 1 million people.

Changes to the Chinese diet have diversified the types of food now in demand. Consumption of meat, dairy products, and seafood all continue to

Agricultural products trade

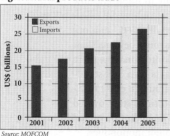

Source: MOFCOM

rise, while demand for rice and wheat is in decline. Despite increases in domestic production, over the last decade China has become the world's third-largest importer of soybeans, for use both in vegetable oils and to feed livestock used for meat. Increases in dairy production have not kept up with more rapid growth in demand.

Additional pressure comes from stipulations relating to China's entry into the WTO, which expose the agricultural industry to greater foreign competition. Utilization of the land area is not nearly as efficient in China as in developed countries, which rely much more heavily on employment of mechanization, chemicals and genetic engineering. However, foreign investment in the sector has been minimal compared to other areas of China's economy, largely due to the lack of ability to own or gain usage of land.

While China has been reforming its barriers to foreign entry in this sector, several non-tariff barriers still remain as obstacles to would-be food importers to China. Tariff quotas and "sanitary and phytosanitary measures" (SPS) are among these. The former refer to tariffs that apply to imports below certain quotas which may be lessened after quotas are filled. SPS are health guidelines published by all WTO-member countries on agricultural imports, which must be consistent with internationally accepted standards. Unfortunately, there have been cases in which China has used its own SPS standards to create restrictions on agricultural trade, in effect turning them into non-tariff barriers. In addition, state-owned enterprises still dominate the agricultural trade in China, and these firms often can restrict imports through monopolies.

Automobiles

Auto production and ownership have exploded since the government announced plans to develop local manufacturers more than a decade ago

by Ed Gwinn

Pronouncements about the future of China's automotive industry are out of date before the ink can dry on the paper. Every forecast that has been made about the industry since the late 1990s has been far short of reality. Actual vehicle production in 2005 reached 5.6 million units. As the most recent news hit the press in late 2006, new changes were underway that could drastically change the shape of the market. What is sure is that the auto industry will continue to grow and China will be a major player in the global market.

Many observers expected China's WTO accession in 2001 to negatively affect its domestic automobile industry. But events played out differently. The automobile market experienced 30% annual growth in 2001 and 2002, and a phenomenal 80% growth in 2003, when a total of 2 million cars were sold in China.

It continued to grow in 2004 and 2005, but at a much reduced rate. Over 3.5 million vehicles were sold in the first half of 2006, up 27% year-on-year. During this same period production was up 29% to 3.6 million units, of which almost 2 mil-

lion units were passenger cars. Total vehicle production capacity in China, including trucks and buses, has reportedly reached 8 million units with another 2 million unit expansion underway.

While the world's major automotive companies are investing more in China, Chinese auto companies are making their way toward the world market. In 2005, China was the third-largest auto producer and the second-largest auto market in the world.

In spite of increasing sales, profit margins continue to drop and are reaching the average levels of the manufacturing industry in general. Many factors are to blame for this change, but chief among them are a rise in steel prices and a significant increase in competition.

Foreign firms dominate

In 2005 there were more than 100 auto manufacturers in China, with the top 15 enterprises accounting for 90% market share. Many of the smaller manufacturers will collapse or be taken over by larger companies. Most of the smaller companies have capacity of fewer than 10,000 vehicles, and some are limited to a capacity of less than 1,000.

The auto industry is among those most sensitive to economies of scale.

Auto trade

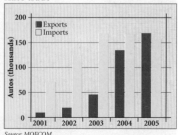

Source: MOFCOM

Less than 10 years ago, China's annual car production did not even match the output of a single large auto company in a developed country, but recent years have seen quite a number of competitive automakers emerge. Yet China still has many vehicle producers, almost as many as the combined number of auto firms in the United States, Japan and Europe.

Volkswagen made its way into China in 1984 when the Chinese government was actively encouraging foreign firms to enter the market through joint ventures. Pairing with Shanghai Automotive Industry Corporation (SAIC) in Shanghai and First Auto Works (FAW) in Changchun, the German automaker was the market leader for 20 years. In 2004, SAIC renewed its joint venture contract with Volkswagen for an additional 20 years. Even with its China sales slipping, Volkswagen is upping production in anticipation of resurgence. Its third factory on the mainland, to be located in Chengdu, Sichuan province, will begin operations in May 2007.

General Motors entered the market much later but saw sales surpass VW's by over 40,000 cars in the first half of 2005 with a total of 308,722 units, and it continued to dominate in 2006. Newer entrants like Honda, Hyundai, and Toyota are growing fast. Toyota is in the process of building several factories in China and could soon be a leading producer.

These partnerships between experienced foreign carmakers and technologically lagging and ill-managed state-owned monoliths have been crucial to the development of China's domestic car manufacturers. Such cooperation allowed com-

panies like SAIC and FAW to streamline management, acquire advanced technologies and increase global exposure.

Other domestic companies like Geely, Chery, Changfeng, Great Wall, Zhongxing and many others have learned quickly. They are expanding production capacity and developing new models. Given the market's increasingly cutthroat nature and China's comparatively low respect for intellectual property rights (IPR), many foreign companies are finding themselves in tough IPR battles. These clashes often involve smaller carmakers which "borrow" everything from design to logos from foreign companies.

In 2005, the government began to work on measures to promote the restructuring of the auto industry, and it is possible that regulators will step up their macro-control over the auto industry and limit the development of new projects. In this case, the strong will become stronger while the weak may have to face the fate of being merged or restructured.

In the coming years, a surge of consolidation will hit China's auto industry in various forms: foreign investors may acquire Chinese companies and large enterprises may buy smaller ones, or vice versa. In the near future, however, China will have a certain number of large auto groups with strong innovative capability, which will finally secure most of the domestic auto market and become players in the global market.

The ins and outs

Car imports are generally limited to luxury vehicles, primarily due to price-inflating tariffs. But current tariffs are not as steep as in years past, due to WTO commitments. Previously as high as 130%, in 2005 they ranged from 38-43%, and dropped to a flat rate of 25% in July 2006. China imported 162,500 motor vehicles in 2005, a year-on-year decrease of 8%. However, the import of luxury cars saw rapid growth during the year.

Official statistics indicate that China exported almost 173,000 vehicles in 2005, up 121% from 2004. The number of sedans exported was more than 31,000, up 233% from a year earlier. It became a net exporter for the first time. In the first four months of 2006 China exported 87,000 vehicles including 23,000 sedans, an increase of 140% and 350% respectively from 2005 levels. Most of the cars were shipped to developing nations and failed to meet standards in Western markets such as the US and Europe.

Volkswagen plans to export its China-made vehicles to 84 countries by 2009. Honda is already exporting to Europe from China. Domestic makers Geely, Chery, Changfeng, Great Wall and Zhongxing could begin shipping vehicles to the US by 2008 or earlier. In June 2006 Shanghai Automotive hired Philip Murtaugh, GM's previous China head, to launch the company's first export to Europe.

In August 2006, China announced plans to establish eight auto export manufacturing bases to help automakers achieve their ambition to expand globally. They include Shanghai, where both GM and VW have joint ventures; the northeastern city of Changchun, headquarters for major automaker FAW Corp; Chongqing, home to Chongqing Chang'an Automobile Co, and Central China's Wuhan, where Dong Feng Group is based. The others are the southeastern city of Xiamen, home to Xiamen Golden Dragon; Wuhu, home to private automaker Chery Automobile Co; Taizhou, production center for Geely Automobile Co, and Tianjin, where Japan's Toyota Motor Corp. has a joint venture with FAW.

Auto parts and related

Seventy percent of the top 100 auto parts suppliers in the world have a presence in China. There are about 1,200 foreign-funded or jointly invested auto spare parts manufacturers in China. These enterprises hold 50% the market. Among them are some world-famous brands, such as Delphi, Bosch, Visteon, Isteon, Valeo, Denso, Marelli and Wanxiang, China's largest maker of auto parts. There are about 5,000 domestic spare parts manufacturers. China has become auto parts supplier to the world and this trade will continue to grow. Other auto-related industries such as auto repair, road transportation, auto insurance, auto finance and auto rental also offer investors great potential in China today.

Aside from the economic benefits of a healthy auto industry, car culture itself is catching on in China. Despite massive investment and campaigns extolling the virtues of public transportation, Chinese people are falling in love with driving. The number of cars in Shanghai reached the 2020 estimate by the beginning of 2005. New highways are saturated with traffic as quickly as they are built. For better or worse, car ownership is fast becoming synonymous with success in China and the automobile is here to stay.

Edward Gwinn, Managing Director
DE Global Limited – Shanghai Guanshu Investment
Consulting Co., Ltd.
1508 Wenjin Building 66 Shanxi Bei Lu
Shanghai, China 200041
Tel: +86 21 5116 0639; 5116 0649 Fax: +86 21 6247 4898
USA Tel: +1 864 248 6291 or 864 335 9607
www.deglobal.net or www.deglobal.com
info@deglobal.net

Aviation

Given the expected trajectory of China's economy, the aviation industry is expected to see rapid growth for the next 20 years

The emergence of a mobile middle class, the growing numbers of Chinese traveling abroad and China's status as factory to the world are spurring market demands for domestic and international travel as well as creating fast-expanding air cargo capacity. In 2005, China surpassed Germany as the world's second-largest air transport market after the US. But fluctuations in world oil prices, together with the intricacies of government intervention, make it difficult to predict the profitability of Chinese airlines.

After the SARS epidemic of 2003 caused a drop in air travel, the total number of air passengers in 2004 was up 38% to 121 million, and 2005 saw traffic jump to 138 million passengers, double the number of five years before. And though the numbers in 2006 look to be leveling off, the government expects traffic to double again by 2011.

Naturally, this is fueling new demand for aircraft. Regulators announced in early 2006 that China's airlines would be buying 100 new planes a year for the next five years, and training 5,000 new pilots during the same period. Boeing and Airbus are in fierce competition to cater to China's voracious demand, with both companies signing big deals with domestic firms in 2005-6.

Between January and May 2006, China imported 135 new planes, altogether worth US$3.73 billion.

Airports across the country are being overhauled in anticipation of rising passenger throughput. As part of Beijing's Olympic facelift, the capital's airport is being converted into the world's biggest, at a projected 420,000 square meters. Guangzhou opened a new US$2 billion facility last year and Shanghai's Pudong debuted a new runway. And both airports are only in the first phases of their expansion plans.

China is the market that most excites those in the aviation business (as in so many businesses) these days. A good sign that the industry's focus is shifting to China is the relocation of Asian Aerospace, the world's third-largest air show, from Singapore to Hong Kong starting in 2007. Airbus has even considered building an assembly plant near Tianjin.

Profit problems

The big three domestic airlines – China Eastern, China Southern and Air China – have had a mixed record in recent years. Of the three, only Air China is expected to be in the black by the end of 2006. China Eastern had a great recovery from SARS when it posted profits of RMB536 million, but the following year saw the margin sink to only RMB60 million. China Southern fared much worse, losing a hefty RMB1.8 billion.

A number of factors are to blame, in-

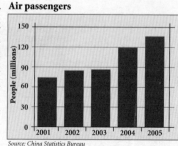

Air passengers

Source: China Statistics Bureau

Aviation // CHINA Business Guide

INDUSTRY OVERVIEWS

cluding all the new investment in expanding fleets (which often involves taking on large new debts), personnel training and excess staff. But by far the largest problem is oil prices. Fuel alone accounts for 40% of total operating costs for Chinese airlines, compared with a global standard around 24%. Fuel is domestically supplied by the scandal-linked state monopoly, China Aviation Oil Supply Corp (CAOSC) at prices fixed by the central government. This arrangement has led to some of the airlines publicly decrying state control, something that never could have happened in the old "New China".

The government has adopted measures such as eliminating ticket surcharges and airport construction fees and allowing domestic ticket prices to float between 55% and 125% of the government-set prices in order help the industry. But the CAOSC continues to readjust fuel prices every three months in line with international rates, while the National Development and Reform Commission sets the cap on fuel surcharges at RMB20-60 per ticket, depending on flight distance. Most firms' profits are getting squeezed between these two figures.

Still, some success

Air China, while of the same relative size as the other two majors in terms of assets and fleets, managed profits of about RMB2.4 billion in both 2004 and 2005. The company has kept competitive with innovative techniques such as hedging jet fuel to lower the impact of high prices. It also operates out of Beijing, a more competitive market than Shanghai (where China Eastern is based) or Guangzhou (China Southern), and it keeps a good balance between domestic and international routes. Air China

has also boosted income through strategic deals with regional powerhouse Cathay Pacific, which owns 20% of the firm.

Global supply chains are increasingly routed through China, with freight traffic increasing by 20% in 2005 to 3 million metric tons. Federal Express is expanding its operations by building its new Asia-Pacific transport hub at Baiyun International Airport in Guangzhou at a cost of about US$200 million.

Besides transporting passengers and cargo, Chinese firms are trying their hand at airplane component assembly. Airbus has been sourcing parts in China for some time, and has committed itself to procurements from local factories worth US$120 million a year by 2010. Guizhou Aviation Industry Group produces the "Mountain Eagle", an internationally competitive trainer model. China also has plans for its own aircraft construction, including the manufacture of turbofan airliners, though the day when they can compete internationally is a long way off.

Foreign airlines are active in China, and the numbers involved will continue to increase. In 2004 China signed its first open skies agreement with Thailand as well as a liberalization agreement with America that will see weekly flights increase from 54 to 249 by 2007 and allow new carriers and routes. Talks with European and other Asian countries on similar agreements are ongoing.

China is forecast to be the key driver for growth in Asia-Pacific air travel; outbound passengers were about 20m in 2004. China is predicted to become the fourth-largest tour destination in the world by 2020 with both the 2008 Olympics and 2010 World Expo. And there are expected to be 100 million outward-bound Chinese tourists a year by 2020. Many of these will be traveling by air. The industry has been cleared for takeoff.

Banking

China's biggest banks made big headlines in 2005 and 2006 as they shaped themselves up to go public. Some of them, anyway

by Ed Gwinn

Bogged down by non-performing loans (NPLs), inefficient structure and ineffective regulations, the banking system remains something of an anachronism in China's otherwise quickly modernizing economy. But much help from the government enabled first China Construction Bank (CCB) and then Bank of China (BOC) to raise large chunks of capital in both the Hong Kong and Shanghai stock exchanges. In October 2006, Industrial and Commercial Bank of China (ICBC) set the all-time record for largest IPO.

Most local banks are performing much better today than they were a few years ago. They have improved operating systems and skills and have a much stronger risk management culture. Some local banks have even become profitable – after the state effectively bought their NPLs, allowing the banks to offload them onto asset management companies. The central bank injected US$22.5 billion into BOC and CCB in 2003. The asset management corporations set up to dispose of these bad loans were able to clear 57% by mid-2005.

INDUSTRY OVERVIEWS

The China Banking Regulatory Commission (CBRC) reported that the ratio of NPLs of China's major commercial banks (state-owned and joint-stock commercial banks) has fallen from 17% in 2003 to 9% in 2005. While this is a welcome improvement, it is still far above the international standard of approximately 1-2%. Domestic banks still extend 65% of their loans to state-owned firms that produce only 25% of the national output.

These problems will be magnified in 2007 when WTO-mandated reforms enable international banks to compete on more equal terms. Against this backdrop Beijing is increasing its efforts to reform the Big Four banks (BOC, CCB, ICBC, and Agricultural Bank of China), as well as 14 national banks, 113 city commercial banks and about 3,500 of the 30,000 official rural credit cooperatives. And what better way to bring about improvements than to enlist the help of those same foreign banks that are causing concern?

China has increased the powers of its banking regulation body. The CBRC has gradually raised the cap on foreign ownership, with foreign investors currently able to acquire up to 25% of the major banks, with no single entity surpassing 20%. It is also clearer on rules and responsibilities and is getting better at enforcement. Fraud cases that used to be hidden are now more public. In mid-2006, the CBRC issued 127 new regulations geared toward bringing international standards of risk management to Chinese banks.

For these banks, foreign investment allows for injections of capital and much-needed management experience. The sales of shares in the major state banks also means that for the first time they will be responsible to their shareholders as well as the government, which should help improve overall transparency and efficiency. Meanwhile, foreign investors gain access to fully established banking networks that stretch throughout China.

As a result, foreign investment reached unprecedented levels in 2005 and shows no signs of slowing. In 2005 foreign investors poured around US$12 billion into the sector, up from only US$111 million for the whole of 2001. By the end of January 2006, CBRC figures showed 18 domestic banks had received a total of about US$18 billion from overseas investors, accounting for 20% of the sector's total capital.

Major transactions

Key deals in 2005 included Temasek of Singapore and Royal Bank of Scotland acquiring 10% of BOC for US$3.1 billion each, while Goldman Sachs, American Express and Allianz AG were major players in the purchase of a US$3 billion stake in Industrial and Commercial Bank of China (ICBC).

A Citigroup-led consortium was given the go-ahead to hold talks for an 85% stake in state-owned Guangdong Development Bank for US$3 billion, which would make it the first

overseas investor to take control of a state-run bank. That bid, however, would put Citigroup over the official foreign ownership quota, and the deal was under serious review by the government in mid-2006, with its future in doubt. The firm already has a large investment in Shanghai Pudong Development Bank.

Newbridge Capital acquired 18% of Shenzhen Development Bank and appointed a foreigner as president. HSBC has made investment in Bank of Communications (BOCOM) and several smaller banks, while Standard Chartered has invested US$123 million in Bohai Bank.

In addition to the financial potential of an economy growing by about 10% a year, the banks are drawn by China's US$2 trillion in household savings and a middle class that could number as many as 200 million. A lack of exposure to consumer banking makes them prime targets for a number of services including wealth management, auto financing and especially credit cards – which now account for less than 3% of consumer loans. The Chinese credit card market has been predicted to be worth US$5 billion by 2013.

Going public

Beijing is encouraging China's biggest banks to list publicly to improve their finances and better compete with international lenders like Citigroup and HSBC Holdings. While the government supports bids to list abroad, they are leaning on the banks to offer shares in the mainland markets as well.

The first of the Big Four to go public was CCB whose US$9 billion IPO in October 2005 was the biggest in the history of the Hong Kong Stock Exchange. Next was BOC in June 2006 raising US$11.4 billion in Hong Kong and an additional US$2.3 billion in Shanghai. ICBC raised a total of US$19.1 billion with simultaneous Hong Kong and Shanghai IPOs in October 2006.

The prospects do not look so rosy for the final member of the Big Four, Agricultural Bank of China (ABC) which is unlikely to meet the listing requirements anytime soon. It has less experienced managers and a mountain of bad debt to deal with.

Going forward

As China opens the financial market further in 2007, it is an excellent opportunity for foreign financial services investment. Entry requirements are still sometimes vague and open to interpretation, but the timing is right for investment. It is estimated that foreign financial groups will own more than 17% of the Chinese banking sector by the end of 2007.

However, in an announcement in September 2006 China said it planned to impose tight restrictions on foreign banks gearing up to compete for local currency deposits despite a pledge to open this sector to overseas lenders starting in December 2006. The proposed rules would require foreign banks to incorporate in China with a minimum of RMB1 billion in capital before they could compete with domestic banks for retail customers.

It is only a matter of time before Chinese banks will become a major force globally. They will learn new risk management skills, implement better corporate governance practices, make managers more accountable, improve their lending guidelines and enforce compliance. There is strong evidence that the changes needed are beginning to happen.

Edward Gwinn, Managing Director
*DE Global Limited – Shanghai Guanshu Investment
Consulting Co., Ltd.
1508 Wenjin Building 66 Shanxi Bei Lu
Shanghai, China 200041
Tel: +86 21 5116 0639; 5116 0649 Fax: +86 21 6247 4898
USA Tel: +1 864 248 6291 or 864 335 9607
www.deglobal.net or www.deglobal.com
info@deglobal.net*

Cement

China's cement factories dominate global production, but greater efficiencies are desperately sought

Despite record growth of 20% in the first half of 2006 and China's solid position as the world's top cement producer, domestic firms still struggle to make a profit in the cement industry. Bottlenecks in production and distribution – as well as overcapacity and waste – are the main reasons that they cannot effectively capitalize on one of the biggest building booms in history. But the government has plans to improve their record.

In January-June 2006, China produced 540 million tons of cement. In each of April, May and June, production exceeded 100 million tons. The reason for the bonanza is simple: China continues to build and expand infrastructure across the country. Fixed-asset investment was up almost 30% during that period, and much of that consisted of new roads and factories.

All of which is good news for the industry. But China's cement production is wasteful. There are nearly 5,000 cement producers in the country, only eight of which produced more than two million tons during the first half of 2006. Another 47 companies produced between one and two million tons. This

disparity is a direct result of the underdeveloped transport infrastructure of the 1970s and 1980s, which encouraged local areas to aim for self-sufficiency in cement production.

The entire industry saw profits of only RMB8 billion (US$1.33 billion) in 2005, down 39% from 2004, and more than one third of producers recorded losses. Clearly, consolidation is now in order.

Streamlining has already begun. In 2005, there were over 6,000 cement enterprises, so the number has already started dwindling. The plan is to reduce the number to 3,500 by the end of the decade. For several years now, the NDRC has been pursuing a policy to shut down underperforming plants. These small operations are typically using outdated technology and contributing more than their share of pollution. But they still employ thousands of people, and therefore create political problems when faced with termination.

Upgrade needed

Shaft kilns and other outdated machinery and processing methods are incapable of producing high-quality cement but are still widely used. Cement production is an energy intensive industry, and using older equipment results in losses from energy waste. This is unacceptable considering China's rising energy needs.

Improved technology is needed not only to raise efficiency and product quality, but also to curtail excessive environmental impact. Dust emissions can be serious, and carbon dioxide released as a byproduct of the calcination process inherent in cement making accounts for about 10% of China's carbon dioxide emissions.

Cement production is concentrated mostly in coastal regions, paralleling economic and urbanization activity. Shandong and Guangdong are the major cement-making provinces, although the government has backed initiatives to develop the industry in western and central regions to support their lagging economic growth. The "Go West" program seeks to bring the level of interior economic development to a level on a par with the coast, which means more roads and bridges, which means more cement.

Foreign investment has helped move production inland. In 2005, Hong Kong property development firm Shui On Construction formed a JV with Lafarge, the world's biggest cement producer, and they jointly bought the parent company of Sichuan Shuangma Cement for $US38 million. By early 2006, Lafarge Shui On owned 14 cement plants and seven grinding stations throughout China, mainly in the southwest.

Germany's Heidelberg Cement, the world's fourth-largest cement producer, has invested in Shaanxi province, purchasing 45% of Jidong Fufeng Cement and a 40% stake of Jidong Jingyang Cement. Meanwhile, another global leader, Holcim, became the first overseas cement investor to control a mainland-listed company when it increased its stake in Hubei province's Huaxin Cement from 26.1% to 50.3%. The Swiss firm, the second-largest cement producer in the world after Lafarge, paid about US$125 million for the stake. The money will help

Huaxin increase capacity to 36 million metric tons a year from 22 million metric tons. Morgan Stanley and the International Finance Corporation, a unit of the World Bank, have taken a 14% stake of the listed unit of China's largest producer, Anhui Conch.

Positive reinforcement

As infrastructure has improved in recent years, increased logistics channels have facilitated consolidation of cement plants, which in turn has improved the efficiency of infrastructure building in a cycle of positive reinforcement. Better roads and bridges have also allowed many cement factories to be moved away from populated centers and closer to raw materials sources, reducing transport and pollution problems. But there is room for further development of bulk cement transport and storage facilities.

Although China exports cement, mostly from the coastal regions and often from stocks produced by foreign-invested firms, domestic demand remains the primary driver of growth. Key importers of Chinese cement include the US, Spain and many Asian countries, most notably South Korea. China has limited need for cement imports, but the industry is looking abroad for related products like new equipment and infrastructure technology.

China's cement exports

Metric tons (millions)

2001	6
2002	5
2003	5
2004	7
2005	11

Source: MOFCOM

Consumer Trends

China's vast second- and third-tier markets are opening up as consumers move from covering needs to satisfying wants

by Kenneth Lee

Fuelled by foreign direct investment and government liberalization, China has achieved strong economic growth over the past 10 years. This growth is allowing more urban and rural Chinese to experiment with foreign brands, broadening their consumer tastes and expectations. These new consumers are part of the burgeoning Chinese middle class that will gradually overtake the affluent consumer segment as a key target for manufacturers.

This new middle class will be relatively young compared to developed markets. Aged 25 to 44, this demographic is a product of unparalleled levels of investment in education by the Chinese government, which previous generations had not enjoyed. Born in a period of economic boom, they have been raised on a steady diet of foreign brands and western notions of consumption which they have adopted rapidly. Their increased consumption will be the backbone of continued growth across China, creating new market opportunities for manufacturers.

Correcting the myths

While startup companies looking for capital may still propagate the myth of 1.3 billion Chinese consumers, the truth is that only 50 to 60 million people in key urban centers have the discretionary income to spend on consumer goods. Though Chinese now aged 15-29 could potentially be the most lucrative target group, they only total around 22% of the population.

Focusing only on urban centers, ACNielsen projects that manufacturers have an untapped market ahead of them worth over RMB844 billion. This is purely based on current key city consumption of RMB1625 per capita; taking into account rising incomes this potential market promises even greater value. Consumption growth in these areas, mirroring that of key cities, supports the projection that these markets will be the true drivers of growth for manufacturers who have already invested heavily in conquering the hearts and wallets of consumers in the main cities.

Nonetheless, companies risk failure if they hope to roll out the same strategy they employed in China's more sophisticated markets. China is a fragmented market defined not just by region but also by culture, language, dialect, tier of city and generation. Consumers in China range from those who were born under the last emperor to a generation, for the first time, throwing off traditional values and paths.

There are however some overriding trends that manufacturers can leverage with confidence. The number of single-person households has increased by 25% over the period 2000-

2005 as Chinese seek work opportunities in the main urban centers. This means that without the support of a family, shopping convenience is becoming more important as single, urban Chinese juggle work and social activities.

These shoppers will increasingly be serviced by the modern retailers which have aggressively expanded their footprint in mainland China. The number of hypermarkets has quadrupled since 2000; supermarkets have grown sixfold and convenience stores have multiplied by a tremendous 23 times over this same period. Less developed regions are catching up fast. With 25% growth in retail outlets from 2004 to 2005, growth of modern trade in areas outside of the main centers is now on par with the key cities and provincial capitals.

Healthy shoppers

Food and non-food categories grew an average of 21% between June 2005 and June 2006. The sales of products offering health or skin benefits achieved greater than average growth over the same period.

Consumers, as well as looking for convenience in shopping, may also be looking for quick fix health solutions to support their busy lifestyles. Sales of added-value health products are soaring. Yogurt drinks and ready-to-drink (RTD) teas have enjoyed sales increases of over 55.7% and 34.8% respectively from June 2005 to June 2006. Such drinks offer benefits such as detoxification and improved digestion.

Increased discretionary income has also seen a greater than

average rise in the demand for personal care. Sales volumes of hair conditioner increased 34.6% between mid-2005 and mid-2006, and sales of facial cleanser and skin moisturizer grew 29.6% and 27% respectively.

Foreign brands stronger, for now

In China, local and foreign brands dominate distinct ends of the market. Multinationals invest heavily in advertising to drive awareness and in turn, build strong brand equity. As a consequence, they enjoy more than double the "spontaneous recall" effect of their local counterparts. Foreign brands also tend to target the premium segment, and through their continuous advertising campaigns, project an image of quality. In comparison, local brands tend to target the lower end of the market, competing for market share via a price proposition, rather than one of image.

Annual disposable personal income

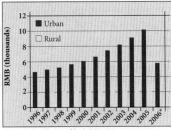

Source: National Bureau of Statistics
*Jan-Jun

The bright side for local brands is that they can learn from their established foreign counterparts. Foreign brands enter a developing market with an advantage because they are often introducing products yet to be developed locally. While this may create a temporary advantage for the foreign brand while local brands catch up, it also means that the foreign brands bear the cost of developing the initial

consumer demand, which usually entails a hefty advertising budget, ultimately benefiting all players in the category.

Foreign brands also tend to focus their market entry strategies on key markets such as Shanghai, Beijing, and Guangzhou, and know less about local brands in 2nd tier markets where local brands, having had the time to learn from their foreign counterparts, have already began building brand loyalty.

Though strapped for time, young urban Chinese are increasingly flush with cash and are behind the growth of China's promising luxury market. Increasing status in the work force is developing young Chinese shoppers' taste for luxury goods. The nature of designer brands makes them highly attractive to young people looking to better project their growing social status.

Despite being a nation of savers, credit cards are making inroads in China. According to ACNielsen Personal Finance Monitor, credit card penetration in 2005 was around 21%, with some 15% of people indicating they were likely to apply for a card in 2006. Most Chinese interviewed indicated that they use plastic in shopping malls, with hyper-and supermarkets being close behind. Banks still have a massive potential consumer credit market in China, but there are more than a few barriers to overcome. The majority of those Chinese without a credit card saw no reason to have one and 12% indicated they still didn't know enough about them.

Kenneth Lee
Executive Director, Customer Research
ACNielson China

Electronics

Televisions, DVD players and mobile phones make up a significant – and growing – part of China's exports

In the past few years, China's manufacturing industry has made a high-tech shift. Those who still think that Chinese factories are concentrated only on toy cars and plastic lighters would be surprised to see the flat screen TVs and PDAs coming off the lines. In 2004, China became the world's largest exporter of information and communications technology (ICT) goods, sending US$180 billion worth of mobile phones, laptop computers, and digital cameras, among other products, out to the technorati of the world.

In 2005, domestic electronics and IT sales together took in US$480 billion, up 28.3% over 2004. And in the first half of 2006, sales were up by an equivalent rate, to US$236.4 billion. Given the growth of the Chinese middle class, steady growth in consumer spending is expected to continue for the next several years. Besides domestic consumption, Chinese electronics manufacturers are also looking to foreign markets to increase their sales.

With cheap labor as the key initial attraction, electronics factories first arrived in the 1980s doing subcontracted assembly

INDUSTRY OVERVIEWS

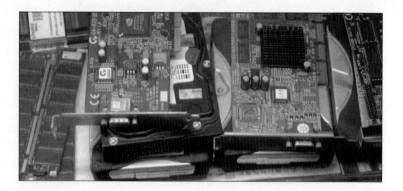

and OEM manufacturing for foreign companies. Labor costs in mainland China are famously low, but rising GDP levels and an increasingly skilled workforce mean that the most menial manufacturing is moving on to places like Vietnam. Other factors, including a stable political scene, good infrastructure, favorable tax conditions and an improving regulatory environment are also attracting manufacturers to China.

The real growth potential lies in selling to China's huge domestic market. Urban China now enjoys all the latest household and personal technology found in the developed world, from refrigerators and microwaves to cell phones and laptops. Even rural residents typically own a television and mobile phone. China has the largest mobile phone market in the world, with over 426 million subscribers in mid-2006. At the same time, China boasted 123 million internet users, second only to the US.

China's electronics sector has expanded into a diverse and comprehensive industry, although foreign brands still make up a significant share of sales. Nokia and Motorola together dominate over 50% of all domestic mobile phone sales. After these giants, a more equitable distribution between foreign and domestic firms emerges. Samsung (South Korea), Bird (China), Lenovo (China), Sony-Ericsson (Sweden) and Xoceco (China) each control between 4% and 10% of the market.

The personal computer market offers an example of China's advancement in electronics. In the early 1990s, half of all electronic production consisted of televisions and radios. The government saw

China's ICT exports

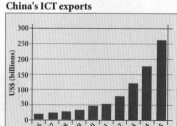

Source: OECD ITS database, MII

computers as an opportunity for growth. Through subsidization of domestic firms and requirements that foreigners share technology in return for market access, PCs and their parts grew to 32% of electronics production by 2000. In 2004, China produced US$81 billion worth of computer hardware, more than any other country. Home-grown superstar Lenovo is the market leader, with 30% of all domestic personal computer sales.

Competing regions

The Pearl River Delta region in Guangdong was the first place to experience an electronics industry boom and remains a focal point of activity today. However, operations in the Yangtze River Delta, encompassing the cities of Shanghai, Suzhou and Hangzhou, are newer and therefore generally have a slight technological advantage over those in Guangdong.

The Yangtze region's high-tech industry experienced a huge influx of operations from Taiwan in the late 1990s, as Taiwanese restrictions on investing in the mainland have loosened, and now it accounts for the majority of China's semi-conductor business. Intel, TSMC and equipment provider Applied Materials have all established operations in Shanghai. Suzhou, now the world's largest laptop-producing city, hosts production centers for Samsung and Fairchild.

But, in line with government efforts, there is some activity inland too. Infineon has a design center in Xi'an in addition to production bases in the Yangtze River Delta. Philips began operating a plant in northeastern Jilin in 2004 while Intel brought a US$375 million facility online in the western city of Chengdu, Sichuan in 2005. The usual investment incentives of cheap land

and tax breaks are attracting these companies, but their decisions are also influenced by a growing pool of low-cost, well-educated technical workers graduating from solid universities in Chengdu, Xi'an and other big western cities.

The northern coast has also emerged as a high-tech leader. Qingdao is home to names such as Haier and Hisense, two of China's best known domestic brands. Dalian has become a center for IT, hosting regional operations of IBM, Hewlett Packard, Microsoft, Dell, Sony, and other IT celebrities.

Low profit margins

Fierce competition in China's domestic market caused protracted deflation during the late 1990s and early 21st century. The prices of electronics appliances here are amongst the lowest in the world. The profit margin of DVD players for sale in Guangdong dropped to about US$1 per machine in 2004. More than 30 suppliers of DVD players closed down in the first few months of that year.

While struggling amid cutthroat domestic competition, Chinese companies have expanded to foreign markets. Electronics comprised 42% of China's total exports in 2005, growing 30% year-on-year to US$322 billion, and achieving similar growth in the first half of 2006.

On the world markets, however, Chinese electronic products are still often known more for low prices than for high quality. China is tightening quality control regulations in the hope of improving this image; for example, new standards were set in 2005 to meet EU quality guidelines for all products exported to that region. China still cannot boast a Sony or a Samsung that is known for quality and reliability the world over. But that may only be a matter of time.

Energy

Explosive growth demands power to keep
the lights on and the machinery humming.
Something must be done to increase efficiency

China's rapidly growing economy is pushing energy consumption to new highs as the increasingly affluent populous plugs in and turns on more appliances than ever, adding to the high-voltage factory hum that has long characterized the country's rapacious modernization efforts.

The chief means of meeting this insatiable demand is China's domestic coal reserve, which accounts for 74% of the total annual power output of 360 gigawatts, dwarfing oil at 13.5%, domestic hydro-power at 8.2%, nuclear energy at 1.1% and natural gas at 0.3%.

But coal presents several problems. Around 70% of the country's coal is transported by rail from the coal-rich north to the energy-hungry coastal regions. While China accounts for 24% of global rail traffic, it only has 6% of the world's rail tracks, resulting in occasional transport network capacity problems followed by regional power shortages. Despite the government committing US$248 billion to rail expansion over the next 15 years, historical underinvestment in railways means there is considerable ground to be made up.

An arguably more serious concern is environmental pollution and the related healthcare and clean-up costs, which are adding ever more weight to the calls for a diversification away from coal. Although China's thirst for fuel means that consumption will still increase in absolute terms, there are plans to reduce coal's contribution to the power supply to around 60% by 2020, with increased output from gas, nuclear and renewable options.

Cleaning up the market

To this end, official muscle has been put behind alternative power sources. China's Renewable Energy Law, which went into effect in January 2006, decreed 20% of total national energy consumption should come from renewable sources by 2020. China is set to spend US$200 billion in the sector over 15 years to achieve this goal. The target has since been reduced to 16%; regardless, this would still make it the world's largest consumer of renewable energy.

In solar power, China already leads the world, with a total of 52 million sq m of solar energy heating panels installed, representing 40% of the global total. Meanwhile, wind power appears to have incredible growth prospects. Installed capacity was just 1.3GW in 2005, but China aims to increase that to 30GW by 2020, more than the 18.4GW currently installed in Germany, the world's wind power capital. China has potential installed capacity of 250GW onshore and 750GW offshore.

Energy consumption

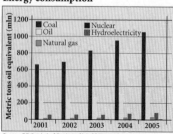

Source: BP Statistical Review of World Energy June 2006

INDUSTRY OVERVIEWS

Electricity usage

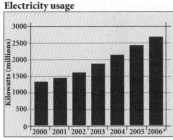

Source: State Statistics Bureau

Nuclear power, and the foreign players queuing up to build the 30 new atomic power stations planned over the next decade and a half, could also win big as China targets a 400% increase in capacity by 2020.

However, alternative energy sources do not produce nearly enough power to replace fossil fuels. Both the OECD's International Energy Agency and the UN's International Atomic Energy Agency reluctantly agree that not only do these sources provide negligible power, the power they do produce is still prohibitively expensive.

Black gold

While renewables may be the Holy Grail for China, it is oil which is increasingly becoming the focus of China's geopolitical strategy. Once a net exporter of oil, China imported 47.3% of its crude in the first half of 2006.

Oil will fall as a proportion of total energy consumption with greater efficiency in coal delivery and the growing emphasis on renewables and nuclear power. But – just like coal – actual oil demand will continue to rise, and imports will be the major source. The US Department of Energy predicts China's crude imports will represent 75% of national oil consumption by 2025, and the major state oil producers are focused on overseas acquisitions to meet this need. Accordingly, Beijing's

diplomatic tentacles have spread to five continents in search of deals, taking in Africa, Asia, Australia, the Middle East and the Americas.

China National Petroleum Corp (CNPC) acquired Petro-Kazakhstan for US$4.2 billion, teamed up with India's Oil and Natural Gas Corp to buy a stake in Syrian oil assets and paid US$600 million for drilling rights in Sudan in a joint bid with China Petrochemical. It has also struck exploration and supply deals in Venezuela and Peru, and acquired a 4% stake in Russian oil giant Rosneft for US$500 million when it went public in July 2006.

China Petrochemical Corp (Sinopec) has also snared a slice of the Russian pie by forming a 25.1% owned joint venture in 2005 with Rosneft to explore the eastern seaboard of Russia for oil and natural gas. Not to be outdone, China National Offshore Oil Corp (CNOOC) paid US$2.7 billion in April for a 45% stake in a Nigerian oil field.

Escalating consumption has hindered conservation efforts in China. Factor in an energy market that is becoming ever more volatile in the current geopolitical landscape and the only certainty for China is that as demand keeps rising, so will the priority attached to securing energy resources.

But such acquisitions will not be used exclusively to serve the home market, unless Beijing seriously makes progress on deregulating energy pricing. Even as global crude prices go through the roof, China's retail prices remain among the lowest in the world, protecting vulnerable sectors from price realities.

Sinopec, the listed arm of China Petrochemical, received a one-off state handout of US$1.17 billion in January 2006 to compensate for losses incurred due to caps on domestic oil-product prices. This was a sweetener to stop the company cutting out the domestic market altogether in order to maximize profits, as they did when they re-exported refined products to Korea and Japan, resulting in 2005's domestic shortages.

Unless there is a substantial rise in domestic prices, companies will continue to siphon off some of their newly acquired foreign oil to use as a source of foreign exchange. For every ton that is traded, swapped or sold abroad, another question mark will be placed against China's energy security.

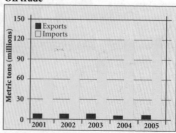

Oil trade

Source: State Statistics Bureau

Environment

As China undergoes the greatest economic transformation ever seen, the stage is set for a green growth revolution. Anything less could be a disaster

According to the World Bank, China contains 16 of the world's 20 most polluted cities. Among the most pressing issues are poor air quality, water pollution and water scarcity, but endemic problems such as land degradation, drought and flooding are increasingly cause for concern, each exacerbated by human activity.

Per capita water scarcity in China is on a par with sub-Saharan Africa, with more than 66% of Chinese cities facing water shortages. Around 75% of the water in the country's seven most important river systems is of a quality unfit for human consumption according to SEPA figures, and only 7.5% of water in inland fresh water lakes and artificial drinking water reservoirs is of an acceptable standard.

Chinese officials have acknowledged that 300 million people drink contaminated water on a daily basis – the World Bank estimates 700 million – and, of these, 190 million drink water that is so contaminated it is making them sick. In August 2006, a government study showed that acid rain fell on one third of China's land mass in the previous year, as China discharged 26 million tons of sulfur dioxide, more than any other country.

INDUSTRY OVERVIEWS

Droughts in the north, northeast and southwest – and flooding in central, eastern and southern regions – are perennial problems. Severe land degradation or desertification already claims around 25% of China's land and is advancing at around 3,000 sq km per year.

The state of China's air is equally dire. Respiratory illness causes premature death of some 400,000 people in China annually, though estimates vary on how many of these can be directly linked to pollution – the World Health Organization (WHO) says 250,000.

China's carbon dioxide emissions increased 33% between 1992 and 2002, according to a recent World Bank survey. Meanwhile European Space Agency tests found that Beijing's skies hold the world's largest amount of nitrogen dioxide, which causes smog. Suspended particle levels were recorded at a dangerous 300 micrograms per cubic meter.

Russia's criticism of the secretive handling of the spill in the Songhua River in northeast China in November 2005, which threatened to contaminate Russian water supplies as well as Chinese ones, shows regional neighbors are growing concerned about China's outsized environmental footprint.

But the global impact of China's economic growth hit home when US researchers traced the surprise reappearance of sulfur and mercury on the

Carbon dioxide emissions by fuel type

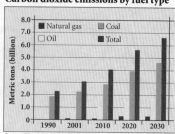

Source: EIA, International Energy Outlook 2004

Washington coast to emissions from coal-fired power plants and factories 3,000 miles away in China. It proved beyond doubt that what is bad for China is bad for everyone, everywhere.

Two steps forward, one back

Of the major economies, only Russia has a worse record on energy efficiency than China, according to Energy Information Administration (EIA) figures. Some estimates have suggested energy efficiency, measured in primary energy consumption per unit of GDP, could be boosted between 30 and 50%.

It is not just the quantity of energy used that is a problem, but also the type of fuel used and the quality of generation. Around 74% of China's electricity comes from coal, often using antiquated power stations with no desulphurization facilities. Factor in the effects of industrial plants with few if any filters, and you have the root cause of much of China's poor air quality.

Central planners want to limit coal generation to 68% of total electricity output by 2010 and 60% by 2020. Central to the government's target is renewable energy, with a target to meet 10% of the country's needs from these sources by 2010 and 16% by 2020.

With US$187 billion expected to be invested in renewable technologies over the coming years, some officials have even touted double the current renewable output by 2010. China is also aiming to increase nuclear capacity 400%, with up to 30 new nuclear power plants expected to come on stream by 2025.

However, experts are skeptical. The consulting firm Capgemnini estimated early in 2006 that China would need to generate an additional 280 gigawatts of energy by 2020 to meet its coal reduction target, on top of the 950 GW already planned, eating into the gains made from alternative fuel sources. The high price of oil is also expected to cause a rethink in China's coal goal, with cheap domestic coal becoming increasingly attractive in the face of uncertainty over the price of oil.

Economic blowback

Overall costs to China's economy from environmental pollution and degradation are estimated to be 8-12% of GDP annually. Economic losses attributed to water shortages were estimated at US$28 billion nationwide in 2003, while acid rain costs agriculture and forestry around US$13 billion every year.

But while business has so far shown an extraordinary ability to plough ahead in the face of escalating environmental degradation, people are not so resilient. This poses a threat to political stability, as social activists organize a population increasingly fed up with contaminated air and water and the poor health that results.

The first national environmental protection law was passed in 1979 and around 375 environmental standards and more than 900 local environmental regulations have been enacted since, to little avail. The challenge is making officials at the local level, where implementation of environmental policy is largely nonexistent, willing to enforce the rules. The balanced growth model outlined in the latest five-year plan is a step in

the right direction, but it remains to be seen whether it will prevail.

A plan for a "green measure" of GDP - whereby the standard figure is adjusted for the impact on the environment - was scrapped in 2006 on the grounds that it is "virtually impossible to calculate accurately". This may just be a reflection of how hard it is for a country in the middle of its own industrial revolution to find a solution to the by-products of rampant growth.

China is integrated so tightly into the world economy that its pollution is not its issue alone, but a challenge for the whole world. Not only does pollution generated in China cross national borders, but foreign-invested companies, which are responsible for around 57% of China's total exports, share some of the blame.

Providing domestic manufacturers with better, cleaner technology can also be a lucrative business for foreign firms. With a significant amount likely to be invested in environmental solutions in coming years, the country will need private know-how and capital from abroad. According to a Deutsche Bank research report, improving the drinking water supply and treating waste water alone will require at least US$200 billion over the next 15-20 years.

Cost of pollution, 2004

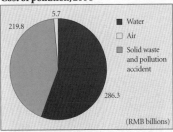

- Water
- Air
- Solid waste and pollution accident

5.7
219.8
286.3

(RMB billions)

Source: State Bureau of Environment Protection

INDUSTRY OVERVIEWS

Insurance

Time is running out for China as it struggles to modernize its traditional cradle-to-grave welfare system in the face of a rapidly aging population

Those Chinese who can are beginning to take their security into their own hands, driving the rapid growth of China's nascent insurance industry and providing a powerful lure for domestic and foreign insurers, banks and financial conglomerates alike.

China Insurance Regulatory Commission (CIRC) figures show insurance premium revenues rocketed to US$61.6 billion in 2005 from just over US$9 billion in 1996. Life insurance accounted for the bulk of the growth, expanding from US$3.76 billion to US$46.25 billion in premium revenues, or 75% of the market. Non-life premiums grew more modestly from US$5.38 billion to US$15.2 billion over the same period.

Low insurance penetration – 2% of GDP in the life sector and just 0.7% in non-life – and a rising middle class are fueling expectations that the good times will continue for insurers. China is forecast to become the fourth-largest life market in the world by premiums in 2008, after the US, Japan and the UK.

According to financial services research and advisory firm Celent LLP, the market is poised to expand to over US$100 billion by 2009. Because the non-life insurance market is under-

served in terms of volume and product mix, Celent LLP estimates that strong growth will see it account for around 40% of all premium revenues by 2009, up from 25% now.

Around 70% of China's 1.3 billion people live in rural areas and have very low incomes. While serious illness can bring devastating financial costs, basic healthcare is more or less affordable. As a result, few people in the countryside choose to buy insurance. While incomes are higher in the cities, so are living expenses, and attitudes toward paying monthly premiums are similarly guarded.

Home advantage

China's insurance sector is still a domestic story, and a limited story at that. Just three domestic players dominated 70% of the life insurance industry, while the top three non-life insurers claimed 72% of their market.

Insurance premium revenues

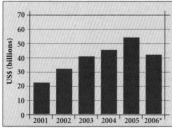

Source: China Insurance Regulatory Commission
* Jan-Aug

Foreign insurers accounted for only 8.78% of the life insurance market in 2005 with US$4.05 billion in premium revenues, up from 2.3% in 2004. But subtracting a one-off US$2.4 billion premium group life transaction undertaken by Generali China Life puts the market share at a much more modest 3.75%. In the non-life segment, foreigners only won 1.31% of total revenues, or US$212.2 million.

Part of the domestic dominance can be

explained by restrictions on geographic expansion of foreign insurers, which until December 2004 were only entitled to operate in 15 major cities. In places that were opened up earlier, such as Shanghai and Guangzhou, the market share of foreign-invested insurance companies had reached 15.3% and 8.2% respectively in 2004.

But these are also the areas where people are most likely to already have insurance, making it harder for new entrants to capture market share. While Shanghai represents just 1.3% of China's population, it accounts for 6.8% of premium revenues. In Guangzhou, 0.8% of China's population accounts for 3.2% of its life revenues, while Beijing-based insurers earn 10% of all life premium revenues from only 1.1% of the national population.

With first-mover advantage gone in the main centers, most foreign insurers are now rapidly surveying China's second- and third-tier cities. But here, consumers are less likely to have the disposable income the insurers are after.

More than one way to grow
Geographical expansion is not the only growth strategy firms can follow, with distribution channels taking on increasing importance. Bancassurance is leading the way, with premiums sold through banks growing 121% in January and February of 2006 alone to US$3.2 billion, or 34% of China's total life insurance premiums for the period.

There is also potential to grow market share through differentiated product offerings. The industry is dominated by simple single-premium, short-term, low-protection products, which do little to develop a strong long-term base for the industry.

Given the shortage of suitable long-term investment vehicles in China with which insurers can offset their liabilities, there

is little appetite for branching out into higher-yielding, higher-protecting and higher-risk products. Official statistics revealed that Chinese insurers had about US$200 billion in gross assets by the end of April 2006, most of it in low-yielding government bonds and bank deposits.

Here the regulator has a key role to play. Since 2004 the CIRC has been working to liberalize investment classes. It is now looking to raise the cap on investment in the domestic stock market, which is currently set at 5% of total assets. Insurers will also be able to invest in asset-backed securities, property, and venture capital projects, and take stakes in strong-performing local banks. Investment will also be permitted in state-level infrastructure projects to 15% of total asset value.

In addition, the CIRC is set to revise rules on overseas investment. In April 2006 it gave the green light for insurers to buy foreign exchange quotas in order to invest in overseas fixed-income and money market instruments, capped at 15% of total assets. This was expected to be expanded to cover other overseas products, including equities and funds.

To offset the increased investment risk, the regulator is also considering moving to a risk-based capital framework in which solvency requirements are matched to asset risks. This is likely to encourage smaller players to raise more capital, opening up opportunities for foreign investors looking for China insurance assets. Domestic listings are also likely.

With domestic players already well in the lead, and progressively given more leash by the CIRC, it remains to be seen what share of new growth foreign players can nab. What is certain is they need to move quickly if they want to insure a slice of the pie.

Logistics

From humble beginnings, the logistics industry in China has blossomed into a pillar industry that has made both global giants and local players excited

by Lee Perkins

INDUSTRY OVERVIEWS

According to the China Logistics Alliance, aggregated turnover of China's logistics industry totalled RMB26.8 trillion (US$3.3 trillion) in the first half of 2006, up 15.3% over the same period the previous year.

However, despite the massive levels of investment there remain areas of concern within the industry. Logistics networks remain fragmented, and outdated hinterland infrastructure slows progress. Logistics accounts for as much as 40% of production costs and 90% of production cycles in China, rates many times higher than developed economies. In general, logistics costs account for around 10% of some developed countries' GDPs, compared with over 21% in China. Taking storage into consideration, the turnover period of Chinese products is 35-45 days compared with less than 10 for many overseas companies.

For the most part, ocean shipping handles the vast bulk of China's import and export volumes. With container throughput at Chinese ports growing by 30% a year there has been an enormous scramble to invest in upgrades. Foreign trade will likely

grow at 15% annually until 2011. In 2005 twenty-foot equivalent unit (TEU) throughput figures for the entire country reached 75.64 million, an increase of 22.8% over 2004. Total ocean cargo handling capacity is expected to reach 5 billion tons by 2010, with container throughput reaching 130 million TEUs.

To meet predicted growth COSCO (China Ocean Shipping Co), China's biggest shipping company, estimates the industry will spend over RMB400 billion (US$49 billion) on ports in 2006-2011. The Ministry of Communications' strategy is to develop five "Port Clusters" – Shanghai, Shenzhen, Tianjin, Xiamen and Haikou – with each cluster consisting of several ports, all of which will be equipped with improved container handling capabilities.

However, with the new Shanghai Yangshan deep-water mega-port now in operation since 2005 and many other major ports (including Ningbo, Tianjin, Qingdao, and Dalian) having aggressively expanded capacity in recent years, Yangshan has already been forced to cut handling rates, prompting fears of potential overcapacity. For many though, the major challenge facing China is linking its port facilities to its less developed hinterland infrastructure.

While rail freight remains China's

Seaport throughput

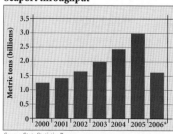

Source: State Statistics Bureau
* Jan-Jun

INDUSTRY OVERVIEWS

dominant transport mode, inland containerized transport remains patchy and most of the network is still best suited to bulk commodities like coal and iron ore. Additionally, damage rates on rail freight are far higher than trucking, and theft so common that manufacturers sometimes employ private security guards to accompany their cargo. Limited availability of containerized road and rail capacity has in the past lead to enormous inefficiencies in hinterland distribution. China's 2002-2007 National Development Plan calls for massive improvements to the rail system with a total of 16 new lines stretching 7,000km planned or under construction.

China's highway network is young but it is already revolutionizing transport options, with trucking becoming a faster and more flexible alternative to rail freight. Trucking is still small compared to rail and water transport, but with the post-WTO opening of China's logistics sector, several major US trucking companies are entering the market gradually leading to an increase in containerized trucking fleets.

Commodities crunch

Another major problem for China has been raw material import-processing capacity. China's ever-growing appetite for natural resources and a dearth of adequate investment in commodity handling infrastructure have strained supply chains across the globe, pushing up both global shipping rates and commodity prices.

Recent logistics crunches in the energy sector have caused brownouts and forced some factories to operate on limited schedules or at night. China's railways handle a quarter of the world's rail traffic on just 6% of the world's track. In the first half of 2006, China's trains carried 1.39 billion tons of freight, a 6.3% rise over the same period in 2005, and coal, oil were major contributors to that rise.

The commodities logjam is the result of inadequate financing, and is representative of the discrepancies between the inefficient state and bustling private sectors. Multinational companies built many of China's modern, efficient container ports to export high-value goods, but China's bulk commodity ports are still largely under-funded municipal government entities. The government estimates China needs to spend US$240 billion expanding the rail system to clear the mountains of imported iron ore and steel that now clog docks in many big ports.

There are no longer obstacles to overseas private capital investing in commodity port projects, but more flexible implementation is required to put policies into practice and most ma-

jor investors remain state-owned enterprises. Rail infrastructure is due under China's WTO commitments to be fully opened to foreign investment by 2008. But foreigners have been slow to express interest, as they are concerned over whether the government will allow freight rates to be determined by the market or continue with the current situation, in which prices are subsidized to prop up failing SOEs.

As a partial solution to backlogs, China plans to utilize its extensive water network. Intensive harbor construction is taking place in the Yangtze River Delta, the Pearl River Delta and the Bohai Bay area with a view to meshing the system with China's inland waterway network. Under the ministry's plan, handling capacity in these major harbor groups will be doubled, reaching 3.5 billion metric tons each before 2010.

Ever watchful of the growing disparity between China's prosperous east and poorer west, the central government's "Go West" policy has become a cornerstone of its 11th Five-Year Plan. The government has invested more than RMB850 billion on 60 key projects to boost development from airports, rail lines, terminals, and pipelines to power stations, and broadband installation.

Into the interior

As the China-ASEAN Free Trade Area (CAFTA) takes shape over the next decade, China's southwest is likely to become a strategically important backdoor to Southeast Asia. Much of the planned infrastructure is designed to integrate Yunnan province into the increasingly important markets of Southeast Asia, bringing cheap Chinese exports to the region and granting China greater access to the region's massive raw material resources.

As part of the overall plan, road links between Kunming and Laos will be completed, forming part of a transnational highway that will eventually link Yunnan with Thailand. Projects such as the Pan-Asian Railway – which will link Kunming to Singapore via Malaysia, Thailand, Cambodia and Vietnam, with a total length of 5,600 km, due for completion by 2010 – are likely to turn Kunming into a major logistics hub.

As the market deregulates and domestic retail volumes rise, the role of third-party logistics (3PL) providers is becoming ever important. 3PL providers currently comprise about 20% of the logistics market. Although many Chinese companies have shown a tendency to shy away from outsourcing such services, large multinationals such as McDonald's have successfully employed 3PL providers, setting an example for others. The 3PL sector in particular is experiencing rapid growth with average annual growth rates around 25% since 2002. Market scope for 3PL providers is vast, with almost every sector of production expanding faster than 3PL capacity.

Now that WTO deregulation has opened the entire logistics sector to fully foreign ownership of logistics service providers, six of the world's top 10 logistics providers have entered the market, and industry analysts predict the China logistics market will continue to grow in excess of 20% per year. Major multinational logistics providers are investing substantially in local partners and distribution centers. Acquisition and consolidation is likely to be a major trend for the foreseeable future.

Lee Perkins is an independent industry consultant and China Correspondent for Cargo Systems, the foremost global container handling and port development publication. Perkins has years of experience analyzing China's logistics and infrastructure development. He is fluent in Mandarin Chinese and has lived in China for seven years.
lee.perkins@meridiangrouphk.com

Real estate

Property in China is booming – so much so that
the government is eager to apply the brakes

China's real estate market has been the big winner from
the disarray of capital markets and controls blocking
offshore investment in recent years. With few alternative
investment vehicles, people have been keener to trade property
than trade stocks.

As a result, not only has China's skyline been transformed at
a remarkable pace, the real estate sector has become a symbol of
the country's rampant growth. It has also become a target for
government efforts to keep a lid on the overheating economy.

This attention is not unwarranted, with the sector showing
many signs of overheating. National Bureau of Statistics figures
showed property developers invested US$35 billion in construc-
tion projects in the first three months of 2006, up 20% from the
same period the previous year. By June 2006, investment was up
22.2% over first-half 2005.

Construction activity came despite a surplus of properties
on the market. At the end of July 2006, 1.3 billion square meters
of real estate – one sq m for every citizen – remained unsold,
up 14% year-on-year. In the residential sector, 66 million sq m

INDUSTRY OVERVIEWS

of housing lay empty, representing about 700,000 unoccupied apartments.

Excess supply had little impact on prices. Overall housing prices in 70 large and medium-sized cities rose 5.8% year-on-year in May 2006, after climbing 5.6% in April and 5.4% in March.

Prices for new properties climbed 6.1% year-on-year in the same period. Several cities, including Dalian, Shenzhen and Inner Mongolia's Hohhot, registered double-digit increases on new properties. Only Shanghai and the northeastern city of Jinzhou experienced declines, by 6.2% and 0.8% respectively.

It is important to bear in mind that despite the pace of contruction and the many empty apartment blocks, there is a strong base of demand that will continue to need more property. Chinese urban masses are starting to demand their own apartments rather than live with their parents after getting married, and foreign investors want a slice of the action, even in China's secondary, interior cities.

Another driver of domestic real estate investment has been the lack of alternative investment channels. According to a 2005 report by Jones Lang LaSalle, some 21.1% of China's newly rich urban citizens – a total of about 15 million individuals – said they preferred to invest in real estate than bank savings or stocks. A wise choice, considering the woeful performance of the mainland bourses until 2006, and the fact that, measured against inflation, bank deposits in China actually lose value over time.

Many of the new Chinese millionaires being targeted by the US$1 mil-

Real estate investment

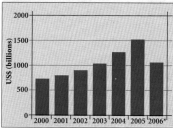

Source: China Statistics Bureau
* Jan-Aug

lion-plus villa complexes sprouting up across the country have themselves made their fortunes in real estate.

Urbanization drive

China's cities are expected to grow by more than 12 million people a year to 2050, taking the urban population rate from just under 40% now to 60% by 2020. More than 600 million people will be added to the urban population by 2050.

According to Macquarie Real Estate Asia, in Shanghai alone, that translates into a need for another 200,000 new units annually for at least the next decade. Added to that, governments at both the central and local level have been looking to increase the amount of living space per person.

But while demand for housing is set to continue, developers have concentrated on luxury housing at the expense of the low-cost accommodation that will be in demand. A 2006 Ministry of Construction survey found the average size of new flats in 16 main cities was more than 120 sq m, much bigger than what an ordinary household can afford.

A Beijing Normal University study found 70% of China's urban residents could not afford to buy a new apartment, based on average housing prices in east China. It is no surprise that the government has been renewing efforts to reel in the sector. Adding to the concerns of civil unrest, dependence on bank credit for 50% of all real estate investment has seen bad loans in the sector soar 16.7% year-on-year to US$13.67 billion at the end of 2005, accounting for 12% of all property loans.

Despite government efforts, the market showed few signs of cooling in 2005, especially in the rapidly developing coastal cit-

ies. Further measures were introduced in May 2006. These included raising down payments on loans for luxury homes from 20% to 30%, taxing proceeds from re-selling homes within five years (instead of two years), and forcing developers to fund at least 35% of project costs with their own capital.

The government also said it would take back land left idle for two years by developers and prosecute those who manipulate market prices and information.

In a controversial step, the government also introduced rules to increase low-cost housing, requiring developers to designate 70% of the units in a property project to apartments of no more than 90 sq m.

Further measures

New regulations restricting speculation in the mainland market by foreign investors were expected at the end of 2006. During the first quarter of that year, foreign investment transactions in the mainland real estate market totaled US$5.4 billion, more than triple the same period last year.

It is still too early to tell whether the moves will be successful – in isolation they are probably not enough. The government raised lending and deposit rates again in August 2006 to try to clamp down on new loans and encourage saving, but the rates were only 27 basis points – hardly a drop in the bucket.

However, as the government continues to develop its capital markets, and opens up offshore opportunities for domestic investors, alternative investment instruments provide a much better hope for cooling real estate flames than any amount of government tinkering.

Retail

An increased foreign presence is raising the competition among the nation's retailers, forcing consolidation and branching out

Multinationals have grasped opportunities for expansion in China's retail sector, particularly since restrictions on operations were eased as part of the country's WTO accession requirements. China is the focus of many global development strategies, but competition in the modern marketplaces of first-tier cities Beijing, Guangzhou and Shanghai is becoming increasingly cutthroat.

Foreign retail enterprises began trickling in as early as 1992, and by 2000, over 350 such enterprises were operating under various local sanctions, but only 40 of them had gained proper approval from the central government. A clampdown followed, requiring foreign investors to conform to a set of trial regulations passed in 1999 which limited investors geographically to provincial capitals and municipalities, and set tough requirements on assets and profitability. But it was a short-lived pullback.

Soon after China's entry to the WTO 2001, the regulations were changed again, liberalized to meet WTO requirements on foreign business access, and also to aid the retail sector's transformation. The rules with regard to geographical limits, joint ventures with domestic enterprises, and limits on the number of

ventures and branch networks were relaxed and have now been dropped completely.

Since then, the big international chains like Carrefour (of France) and Wal-Mart (US), together with domestic competitors like Gome, have saturated top markets like Shanghai and have started to expand to lesser-known cities. And since China has over 100 cities with urban-area populations over 1 million, there is much open land to settle.

The search is taking them beyond the provincial capitals and eastern seaboard hotspots to the untapped cities that fall under the "tier three" category. A prototypical third-tier target is an upwardly mobile prefecture-level city, relatively undeveloped but showing signs of increasing affluence among the population.

In December 2005, Wal-Mart opened its 55th China store in Wuhu, Anhui province, a city with a population of around 2.2 million. Number 56 soon followed in 5 million-strong Yueyang in Hunan province. Both cities are located in the fast-growing Yangtze River Delta region, where clearly Wal-Mart is hoping to ride the consumer wave. By the end of the decade, the company plans to hire 150,000 new employees, quintupling its current Chinese workforce.

Hyper-expansion

Although the number of retail stores in China only increased 2% during 2005, the number of modern trade retail shops – hypermarkets, supermarkets and convenience stores – increased by 25%, with one new outlet opening every minute somewhere in China. Hypermarkets alone increased in store numbers by 37%

in 2005, with an increase in revenue of 26%. Chinese consumers greatly value the attractive shopping environment and consistently high standards provided by these stores. Furthermore, many have established themselves in centrally located areas, greatly increasing convenience. Although prices may be slightly higher than other local stores, consumers are willing to pay more for a more convenient and enjoyable shopping experience.

Both Wal-Mart and Carrefour have large-scale plans to expand throughout China. In mid-2006 Carrefour was already operating 306 stores in China (76 of these were Carrefour outlets, while the other 230 were Dia stores, the company's discount chain). Wal-Mart, at distant second, had 60 stores. Carrefour and Wal-Mart both planned 20 new stores in 2006. The third major foreign retailer, Germany's Metro, has 30 locations with plans to expand to 40 by 2010.

Foreign retailers at this point still occupy a very small share of the traditional department store sector. The Malaysia-based Parkson group has a number of high-end department stores in a few of China's large and medium-sized cities, and Lane Crawford has a flagship store in Shanghai. But huge numbers of outdated state-run department stores still exist, even while they appear headed for extinction.

One of the largest retail trends to watch in the near future is the massive growth of shopping malls. In cities across China, developers are scrambling to build the biggest, glitziest and most imposing malls to win over consumers. Some are or will be among the world's largest shopping complexes. Moreover, with the growth of automobile ownership, malls are springing

up in suburban areas around large cities, particularly Beijing, with massive parking lots to accommodate an army of shoppers all arriving in their own cars. CapitaLand, the Singapore development firm, operated 30 malls inside China in mid-2006, with plans to double its China investments by 2011.

Those Chinese with a bit more money are also indulging in the good life like never before. While the average Chinese still earns only about US$1,700 a year, by 2006 there were over 300,000 Chinese classified as (US-dollar) millionaires. To cater to this market, luxury brands have set their sights on affluent coastal cities. In Shanghai, for example, Prada is investing in an "epistore", a flagship store along the same lines as those in Tokyo and New York. Other than serving as a retail point, luxury mega-stores in China also aim to increase brand awareness for affluent Chinese who often shop while traveling abroad.

As foreign retailers are gaining more and more ground in China, domestic firms are being forced to adapt to the new environment, restructuring and revising their management structure just to stay afloat in the increasingly competitive market. In mid-2006, Gome – China's largest home appliance retailer – bought out China Paradise, the third-biggest in the market, and America's Best Buy was poised to open a Shanghai store by the end of the year. Look for the competition to heat up and spread throughout the country like wildfire.

Retail sales

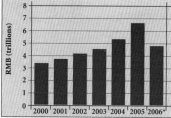

RMB (trillions)

2000 2001 2002 2003 2004 2005 2006*

Source: China Statistics Bureau
* Jan-Aug

Securities

Growing up in the global spotlight, China's
mainland bourses have faced numerous
challenges on their path to maturity

From the first share issue in 1981 to the beginning of formal share trading in 1986, the establishment of stock exchanges in Shanghai and Shenzhen in 1990 and the rapid growth and even faster crash of indices that followed, China's economic success, and the pace at which it has come, has paradoxically been the markets' greatest obstacle.

The markets have paid the price for the investor overconfidence that turned them into a speculators' playpen in the late 1990s and early 2000s, driving the indices to unsustainable levels during an extended bull-run. After a spectacular correction in 2001, investors looking for modest returns in an uneasy world were slow to return.

Worse, as the speculative fervor wore off, those still holding mainland stocks found that what they really owned were the sluggish remains of former state-owned companies, only partially split off from their parents when Beijing began to adopt capitalism's core principles.

These listed arms remained beholden to their state-controlled parents, which generally retained controlling stakes. Further, lax

accounting standards and poor corporate governance enabled the state to reap the majority of any profits. Traditional yardsticks for measuring value, such as dividend yields, barely existed.

Rebirth through reform

When China first experimented with stock offerings, about two-thirds of total stock market capital was held back from general trade, reserved largely in the hands of the state in a bid to prevent state-owned enterprises from falling into the hands of private or foreign parties.

These non-tradable shares have hung menacingly over the market ever since, creating nervousness among investors that the eventual release of these shares onto the market would dilute the value of existing tradable shareholdings. This impact on investor confidence became more pronounced in recent years as the government pursued plans to remove the overhang by forcing state-owned enterprises to list their non-tradable shareholdings. As talk of reform escalated, investor confidence sank to new lows, fearing the resultant equity flood, estimated at more than US$250 billion, would strip whatever value remained in the already suffering markets.

The onus was on the government, through the China Securities Regulatory Commission (CSRC), to manage the reform process gradually, and avoid scaring the horses. But on the couple of occasions the regulator made a move, the market plunged, forcing further delays.

In late April 2005, the CSRC finally announced a pilot

scheme to phase in a reform program involving a number of handpicked state-owned companies. The proposed scheme enabled existing shareholders to negotiate both the selling price and the method by which non-tradable shares would be sold, with a two-thirds majority of all voting stakeholders and voting tradable shareholders required. Owners of non-tradable shares selected for the pilot were bound not to sell their holdings within a year of the float.

The announcement spooked investors once again and the market hit a six-year low in May 2005. To its credit, the CSRC pressed ahead and announced a second round flotation the following month. It also pulled the plug on any new listings, fearing the impact of more equity in the already struggling domestic exchanges. During the hiatus – which lasted 13 months – the regulator also redrafted listings rules to promote a more market-orientated pricing mechanism.

However, although G-shares (the name given to shares of companies that had completed reforms) proved attractive to long-term investors – Qualified Foreign Institutional Investors (QFIIs) invested half of their quotas in G-shares in early 2006 – they still performed poorly as short-term investors sought quick profits. In a controversial aspect of the share reform process, holders of non-tradable shares provided holders of tradable shares a compensation package to make up for any dilution in share price resulting from additional shares entering the market. Speculators seized the opportunity to buy in and out of companies either side of reform to collect the compensation.

宝华大厦

BUSINESS DISTRICT IN SHANG

Despite this hiccup, the overall response of the market was positive, with domestic investors returning to the market in droves. With share reform well underway, the CSRC gave the green light to new listings in May 2006. By the end of the month, more than 100 companies were scrambling to be among the first to offer new shares and a further 60 were aiming to raise new capital with secondary offerings.

Goodbye to the blue chips

While China's past floundered in the domestic markets, China's future, represented by the new breed of lean, innovative and profit-hungry private firms in areas like gaming, software and advertising, were starved of the means for raising capital at home. Instead, they found they could raise more money, and establish a global profile, on foreign exchanges such as the Nasdaq, avoiding the unfashionable and unresponsive local markets altogether.

Hong Kong, in particular, began taking on the role of China's financial hub. The market capitalization of mainland A-shares dropped from almost US$600 billion in 2001 to a low of US$400 billion in 2005, though it had rebounded by mid-2006. At the same time, Hong Kong's doubled from a similar starting point to over US$1 trillion. Mainland companies were responsible for a large portion of this growth: by May 2006, they made up around 39% of Hong Kong's market value, up from only 25% in 2001.

The success of these offshore listings put the spotlight on

the bear market at home, as did China's economic growth of around 10% every year. While foreign investors were capturing a slice of the China growth story on offshore exchanges, domestic investors were staying away.

Many pin the blame for the struggling bourses on a lack of liquidity. But the problem has not been a lack of cash, but rather the absence of a suitable vehicle into which investors could confidently put it. Accumulated personal savings currently deposited in China's banks run in the neighborhood of US$1.9 trillion, earning annual interest of around 2% – barely edging out inflation. In a more developed economy, a large proportion of those savings would be invested in stocks, either through institutional funds or direct investment.

There was something else keeping domestic investors at bay, highlighted by the performance of those mainland stocks like Shenzen Expressway and Yanzhou Coal that were also listed offshore. In 2001, dual-listed companies were trading at an average 380% premium in the H-share market over their price in the A-share market. Although the price gap had narrowed to a much more palatable 30% by 2006, the fact is that the A-share market is still overvalued, adding to the weight of factors undermining investor confidence.

QFII to the rescue

In an effort to find a source of capital more predisposed to investing in stocks, and bring in some much-needed foreign investment expertise, the CSRC introduced the QFII scheme

in 2003. This let foreign institutional investors participate in China's principal A-share stock market for the first time, though they had been able to invest in China's B-share market since 1991.

Initial demand from foreign institutional investors was unenthusiastic. With the markets caught in an extended bear run, and an expectation that Beijing would soon move to revalue the yuan against the greenback, many investors instead diverted quota into fixed-income deposits and RMB-denominated domestic bank accounts. By the end of 2005, approved QFII quotas reached US$3.25 billion, but only about US$2 billion had been invested in the A-share stock market.

Quotas were increased again in 2006 – to US$10 billion – but foreign investors still only have a small impact on domestic markets, at least in dollar terms. The value of yuan-denominated A-shares held by investors outside China equaled 1.6% of the mainland markets' value at the end of 2005, according to China Southern Fund Management, the country's biggest fund management company.

Macroeconomic measures were also introduced to divert domestic money from more attractive investment opportunities like real estate. With reduced lending choices, more bank money became available for equity investments. Although much of this excess cash was diverted into China's bond markets – which climbed 15% in 2005 – rather than its stock markets, it sent a strong signal to investors that the government was serious about improving its capital markets.

Further rule changes introduced in January 2006 allow strategic foreign investors to purchase stakes of more than 10% of a company's A-shares under certain limitations.

Cementing the gains

The CSRC has also introduced measures to improve corporate governance. From early 2006, directors, supervisors, top-level managers and key technology experts have been able to be rewarded with shares if they have contributed to increasing the company's profits. The effect of the rule was immediate, with the Shanghai and Shenzhen indices both rising on the day it was announced.

The government is now looking to improve the depth and quality of the domestic pool by encouraging those that have gone offshore in search of capital to try to replicate their success at home. Air China and Bank of China were early examples of domestic stars to list in Shanghai, to generally good results.

In the long run, the downward trend that has gripped domestic exchanges and forced the regulators into painful but necessary reform could be the market's greatest asset. A-shares are now trading at much more reasonable valuations relative to other markets, companies exposed to good governance practices offshore are looking to return, a range of new instruments have been launched to encourage domestic investment, and foreign investors are requiring, and receiving, a higher caliber of corporate governance.

Semiconductors

Though it now mainly consists of finishing chips produced in other parts of Asia, China's semiconductor industry is ramping up home-grown tech efforts

As a consumer of semiconductors, China has no equal, its appetite driven by booming global demand for Chinese-made electronic goods such as computers, televisions, CD and DVD players, telecommunications equipment and automobiles.

China's semiconductor, or integrated circuit (IC), market grew 32% to US$40.8 billion in 2005, accounting for 21% of global IC consumption. In doing so, it surpassed both the United States and Japan to become the world's biggest, according to IC Insights, a US-based IT consulting firm. As recently as 2000, China only accounted for 6% of global consumption, and was one-fifth the size of the US market.

While demand is hot, domestic production is not. With only US$2.6 billion worth of semiconductors produced domestically in 2005, China's tech exports are largely built using chips im-

ported from elsewhere. In a bid to rectify the imbalance, and capture the lost profits, the government has established preferential regulations to mimic conditions that have seen the semiconductor industry flourish elsewhere in Asia.

Research partners

Chip producers enjoy a five-year zero income tax advantage followed by another five years at half of China's already low tax rates. Officials have promised a continuation of this favorable regulatory environment and reiterated their commitment to the industry's development despite the unpredictable nature of the market.

A research fund has been set up to subsidize the semiconductor industry, something that could well prove more financially beneficial to the industry than the tax breaks. On the R&D front, China is following a typical developing world path by courting global semiconductor giants to form partnerships rather than engaging in the more expensive and time-consuming practice of constructing its own independent research base.

The world's top 10 semiconduc-

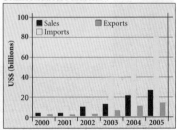

Semiconductor market

Source: MII Electronics Information Center, IC Insights
* Jan-Jun

tor enterprises all have operations of varying scales in China. Getting in early and establishing good relationships with the government is seen as essential to securing a solid share of the burgeoning market. Production centers tend to be found in and around the large eastern cities, especially Shanghai, where Intel, TSMC and equipment provider Applied Materials have all set up shop.

Cities in the surrounding Yangtze River Delta region are also popular, with both Samsung and Fairchild based in Suzhou. Other foreign operators can be found in Beijing and Tianjin in the north and Guangzhou and Shenzhen in the south.

But there is some activity inland too. Infineon has a design center in Xi'an, in addition to production bases in the Yangtze River Delta. Philips began operating a plant in northeastern Jilin in 2004, and Intel opened a US$375 million facility in the western city of Chengdu in 2005.

China's chip industry still has a long way to go, but its efforts are paying off to a certain extent. IC Insights forecasts that domestic chip production will be worth US$12.1 billion by 2010, which equates to annual growth of about 36%. However, given the low base, this will only represent 4% of the expected US$319 billion worldwide production in 2010. Furthermore, it

will only meet about 10% of domestic demand, which is likely to be worth US$124 billion.

The advancement of China's chip industry is hampered by its poor record in intellectual property rights (IPR) protection. Although Beijing issued laws in 2001 addressing IPR in the semiconductor industry, foreign companies are still reluctant to release valuable technologies into the country. This is a major stumbling block with Taiwan, the global home of the semiconductor business, whose government imposes severe limitations on the transfer of semiconductor processing technology to China.

Despite this industry reluctance to share information, China is making progress. The future of its semiconductor industry lies in its high quality design houses, which have been driven by increased investment in research, design, raw materials supply and other support industries. Several of China's major semiconductor enterprises have made impressive advances in their bid to reach international standards.

Global standards

A recent survey by EE Times-China showed that 45% of China's IC design companies – the so called "fab-less" semiconductor companies – chose 0.18 micron for digital IC design in 2005, an increase of about 7% from 2004. Meanwhile, 14% developed chips using the 0.13 micron process, an increase of 8% from the previous year. The move from 0.18 micron to 0.13 micron is expected to speed up with most local houses believing there are no technical barriers to the shift.

In a vote of confidence for the domestic industry, the survey also found local foundries were the top choice for IC design houses, with nearly 60% preferring the mainland for fab processing. The number opting for Taiwan fabs decreased by about 6%, a change attributed to the growth of local manufacturing and the apparent cost advantage.

This preference for home-grown products and services has positioned the industry in a positive feedback cycle that augers well for the future. Many of the newest fabs being constructed on the mainland were originally planned for Taiwan, but have been lured to China not only by lower costs, but also by enhanced local sales potential.

World semiconductor consumption 2004

■	Americas
□	Europe
■	Japan
■	China
■	Rest of world

22.1, 18.3, 18.5, 21.5, 19.6

Source: IC Insights

Steel

Like so much heavy industry in China, the steel sector is vast and inefficient. The government is trying to crack the whip, but obstacles remain

China's steel industry, by far the largest in the world, is hampered by fragmentation and inefficiency. The country represents one-third of global steel production – making 377 million tons in 2005 – but its biggest steelmaker is only the world's sixth-largest. Baosteel had only one-third the output of top producer Mittal in 2005.

China emerged as a viable steel producer and a significant market for iron ore in the 1980s. In 2003, it surpassed Japan as the world's largest importer of iron ore. Now it is a behemoth with three times the imports of second-place Japan, and still growing. In 2005, steel output rose 27%, far higher than the anticipated 10-15%. Analysts predicted 2006 output would go up another 12% despite Beijing's efforts to cool down the economy. Mid-year statistics exceeded these forecasts, as production in January-June 2006 was up 18% over 2005, with no signs of slowing as producers ratcheted up investment in fixed assets.

Similar to its cement industry, much of China's steel comes from small mills that buy a lot of ore but are generally inefficient. According to state media, Beijing plans to shut down a lot of these smaller mills, lower the country's overall steel pro-

duction and cut down demand for iron ore by some 60 million metric tons. Critics, however, have been quick to point out that resistance from local governments – which may depend on these mills for economic growth and employment – may make this task a difficult one.

Still, a more efficient steel industry would be the next natural step for China. By closing down smaller mills located far from the coast, the industry is looking to consolidate into a more flexible and efficient unit. In this way it will be able to respond to the market more quickly, and hopefully play a role in how the market moves.

In 2005, the government made consolidation a priority, focusing on creating large regional steel giants throughout the country. To bolster China's most promising steel enterprises, the government has poured billions of dollars into Baosteel, Shougang in Beijing, Angang of Liaoning province, and Wuhan's Wugang.

A missed opportunity

Given its weighty position in the global steel trade, China sought in 2006 to take a firm stance on iron ore prices. Iron ore is unusual in that prices are negotiated once a year with the world's big three iron ore miners – BHP, Brazil's Cia Vale do Rio Doce (CVRD) and Anglo-Australian group Rio Tinto. After watching 2005 costs shoot up over 70% higher

Steel output

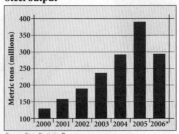

Source: State Statistics Bureau
* Jan-Jun

than 2004, China was determined to drive a hard bargain on behalf of buyers everywhere.

The entire affair was a debacle. China delegated Baosteel to manage the negotiations, and the company stalled for two months without making an offer. Frustrated and out of patience, first German and then Japanese purchasers cut deals with producers, agreeing to a 19% price hike. China attempted to hold out for a better deal, but it was no use. Their hand forced, the embarrassed Chinese agreed to the same price increase soon after.

Still, Baosteel did assert itself and, even if the approach failed to achieve significant results, the message was clear: there is one more big kid on the block and iron ore producers must respect its buying power.

Accessing raw materials

China is now looking to reduce its dependence on the big three producers by investing in new mining efforts. There have been reports of plans to invest up to US$2 billion in projects around the world. To ensure long-term stability, China's steelmakers are not only sourcing from but also buying into overseas mines. China International Trust & Investment Corp (CITIC) purchased two Australian iron ore companies in early 2006 for $415 million. These efforts complement older investments such as Baosteel's joint cooperation with Rio Tinto in Western Australia and with partner CVRD in Brazil.

Shougang Group, China's fourth-largest steelmaker, was in mid-2006 awaiting regulatory approval of its bid for a controlling stake in Australia's Asia Iron Holdings. Shougang also op-

erates Peru's only iron ore mine, a site that has experienced a major strike every year since 2001. The company faced further problems at home, where it was criticized for contributing to Beijing's polluted skies. As a result, the firm plans to relocate its operations with a new plant in Hebei province.

Technological gains in China's steel industry are pushed along by the cycle of death and renewal. Need for better technology has created an opportunity, even necessity, for involvement from abroad. Some of the world's largest steel producers have jumped at the chance. German steel firm ThyssenKrupp owns a 60% stake in a stainless processing operation with Baosteel worth US$1.84 billion. It is also involved in a US$180 million hotdip galvanized steel plate project with Anshan. In a similar project worth US$785 million, the world's number one and two steel producers, Arcelor of France and Nippon Steel of Japan, also teamed up with Baosteel to meet the demands of China's auto industry.

In 2005, however, China put strict limits on control of Chinese steel companies by foreign firms. The government formally declared that no foreign investor could gain a controlling share of any large Chinese steel company. The rules, however, are more flexible when dealing with smaller companies.

Despite the rapid expansion of its steel industry, China is still a net importer of steel, and is likely to remain so for the next few years. But through development and modernization, China has set its sights on becoming a net exporter in the future. Some predictions see China's steel demand peaking in 2010, but with per capita steel consumption still far below the level of developed countries, vast potential for further growth remains.

Telecommunications

With steady growth in what is already the world's largest market in many ways, China's telecoms business is set to become even more competitive

By the end of August 2006, China had over 437 million mobile phone subscribers, more than any other country. But with a national penetration rate of only 32.7%, as against 60% in the US and close to 100% in many European nations, China's mobile market is nowhere near saturation. Analysts have predicted the number of mobile subscribers will climb to almost 600 million by 2009, 200 million of whom will be using 3G services.

Though overtaken by mobile phones as the dominant communication medium in 2003, fixed-line numbers are equally impressive. China had nearly 368 million fixed-line subscribers by the end of August 2006, while around 123 million people had Internet access from home, including 47 million with broadband. The industry is expected to be worth US$100 billion a year by 2009, which is staggering given that it was virtually non-existent well into the 1980s.

China is now regarded as the world's most important telecommunications battleground. As it has rolled out its commu-

nication networks, foreign manufacturers and sellers of network equipment have stolen a march on domestic competitors, with the likes of Siemens, Nokia and Ericsson not only building the networks, but also dominating the mobile phone handset market.

But domestic equipment makers like Huawei and ZTE are fighting back, helped by government loans, credit insurance and other preferential treatment. Faced with intense competition at home, they are also expanding overseas, opening offices in the US and Europe. Huawei's revenues hit US$5.9 billion in 2005, with overseas income surpassing domestic revenue for the first time at 58%.

In April 2006, Huawei announced that it expected to see revenue and orders rise more than 30% to US$7.8 billion for the year. The gains would come as a result of aggressive pricing policies and global expansion. Huawei has struck 3G-equipment deals with Vodafone and BT in Europe, carrier Leap in the US and eMobile in Japan. The company is well on its way to becoming a formidable global competitor for the likes of Motorola and Nokia.

Telecom revenue

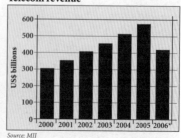

Source: MII
* Jan-Jun

While competition heats up in equipment, services are dominated by a small number of state-owned giants. However, from 2007, this market is also expected to be open to foreign operators in line with World Trade Organization (WTO) accession commitments.

In preparation, China is in the process of reforming the sector. This began in 1994 when China Telecom, the country's only telecom provider, was split, creating a duopoly in basic landline services. There are now four main operators – fixed-line providers China Telecom and China Netcom, and mobile providers China Mobile and China Unicom – and a host of smaller companies. The four main companies are listed on both the New York and Hong Kong stock exchanges.

The 3G revolution

Fixed-line providers, which have been barred from investing in mobile technology, have invested heavily in broadband internet services as per user revenues have declined, in line with global trends. But they have also developed a huge subscriber base for the popular Xiaolingtong ("little smart"), which is a pseudo-mobile service that only works within the subscriber's given region. The inclusion of basic data services, in addition to cheaper voice calling than on a true mobile phone, saw the number of Xiaolingtong users rocket to 78.9 million by mid-2005. The figure is expected to reach 90 million in 2007.

The advent of Xiaolingtong is a clear example of the value fixed-line operators place on offering mobile services. As the government prepares for the next stage of China's telecom revolution, the roll-out of 3G networks, both China Telecom and China Netcom are looking likely to be granted access to the true mobile market, although it may not be on the terms they would wish.

In order to give domestic network equipment and handset providers a boost in the local and global markets, the government has poured enormous capital, both political and real, into developing a domestic 3G standard to compete with global standards WCDMA and CDMA2000. Although the government seems set to release licenses for all three standards in the second half of 2006, it is clear that it will leave no stone unturned in its effort to ensure its own standard has a future.

This means it is certain to entrust the home-grown TD-SCDMA standard to either China Telecom or China Mobile, the dominant fixed-line and mobile providers, respectively. But both have made it clear they would rather provide services on the tested international standards, rather than act as guinea-pigs for TD-SCDMA.

Industry insiders agree that the company awarded the license for the home-grown standard will be at a disadvantage to competitors. A lot of wrangling is still happening behind the scenes, but Beijing is unlikely to let its operators make a purely commercial decision.

Whatever happens, 3G licensing is likely to be combined with a further round of reform and consolidation. The volume of conflicting rumors circulating suggest no one, and possibly not even the leadership in Beijing, yet know how the immediate future of the industry will play out.

Helping hand

But there is good reason to believe that China's telecom giants will retain the lion's share of the market, despite foreign access. The close attention the government has paid to what it considers a strategic sector, despite Chinese companies not being as competitive as they could be, suggests Beijing is loath to allow the market to become any more foreign-dominated than it is right now.

For overseas players, operating in China comes with a number of headaches. As in most industries, there have been ongoing reports of intellectual property violations, and during the WTO accession period there have been complaints that telecom has been a particularly slow industry to meet its obligations.

However, with the current rate of growth, and especially the expected takeoff of 3G technology in the coming years, the benefits to foreign companies of competing in the China market far outweigh the risks.

Textiles

One of the first industries to open up during China's reform period, textiles have been a fundamental driver of the country's economic engine over the last 25 years

Outsourcing production to Chinese textile manufacturers has become increasingly common over the last decade, but it was in 2005 – the deadline for lifting worldwide textile quotas looming – that foreign producers began arriving in droves. Inevitably, when the quotas were removed, textile exports surged more than 40% in 2005 to US$135 billion, despite protectionist measures imposed by US and European nations in the second half of that year.

Chinese-made clothing was initially allowed nearly unfettered access to the markets of Europe and America, with US imports of underwear more than trebling in the first six months of 2005. Cotton shirt imports increased 1,350% and cotton pant imports rose by a factor of 15.

The protectionist backlash, initiated as a result of fierce lobbying by US and European producers who fear for their livelihoods, came in legal form. The rich countries raised the stakes in this long-running textiles war by using a loophole in WTO rules to place new maximums on imports from China. In the EU, these limits were reached by mid-2005, and suddenly thousands of bras and cotton trousers lay in limbo at the ports. Urgent diplomatic talks were held, resulting in a compromise

whereby China agreed to voluntarily limit annual textile increases to 10% until 2008.

Shoes became the focal point of the industry in 2006, when the EU began investigating China for violating anti-dumping regulations. A coalition of shoe-producing European countries led by Italy forced the EU trade commissioner to impose temporary duties of 16.5% on Chinese-made leather shoes. (Tariffs were also levied against Vietnam.) By September 2006, there was a large debate over whether to extend the tariffs. Though China's share of the European leather shoe market had increased fourfold since 2001, it was still only about 9% – hardly dominating.

These disputes show clearly how protectionism remains the only defense for the US and European textile industries against the might of their Chinese competitors. But they have also awakened Beijing to the importance of shifting its focus to quality over quantity if it hopes to remain in top spot. Research and development at major textile companies accounted for only 0.25% of total sales in 2004, meaning products were less profitable and largely focused on the cheaper end of the market.

Textile exports

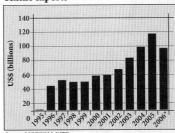

Source: MOFCOM, WTO
* Jan-Aug

As part of an attempt to encourage textile companies to adjust their product mix and turn out more value-added, high-end products, the government raised export tariffs on 74 textile products up to 400% from June 1, 2005. It also plans to help domestic textile firms establish trade cooperation zones overseas, particularly in developing countries, as well as foreign-based R&D, production and sales centers.

The government stepped up its efforts

INDUSTRY OVERVIEWS

at modernization in 2006, announcing textile reforms as part of its new five-year plan. Goals were set to increase production of textile fiber to 3.6 million tons – up 35% – by 2011, while reducing energy and water consumption by 20%. Creating internationally recognized Chinese brands also figured high in the plan.

Fashion hungry

China's textile production tends to be concentrated in the coastal areas. Guangdong has long been a locus of factories (some may be more properly called "sweatshops"), with large textile trade volumes passing in and out of Hong Kong. The Yangtze River Delta region is also a strong textile center; the city of Ningbo alone produces about 1.4 billion pieces of apparel annually, roughly 12% of the country's textiles output.

Opportunities for foreign investment exist throughout the industry, from manufacturing and retail to machinery, design and research. High production capacity together with the ability to meet strict quality control standards makes China's unique, large and inexpensive labor force the world's preferred means of textile manufacturing. Since domestic sourcing cannot meet cotton demand, China has also become the top buyer of US cotton. In 2005, China imported 2.57 billion tons of cotton, and the China Cotton Association forecast that the 2006 number would be close to 4 billion tons.

Chinese consumers – especially in the cities – have shown increasingly broad taste in clothing, as fashion trends have shifted over the past quarter-century from Mao jackets to Moschino knockoffs and on, tentatively, toward the real thing. The huge market for fake brands in the country, both for domestic consumption and export, remains a major irritant in China's trad-

INDUSTRY OVERVIEWS

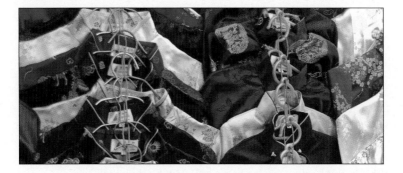

ing relations with the West, although there are signs that the authorities are now serious about cracking down on it.

However, the real impact of fakes on the major brand producers such as Ralph Lauren, Gucci and North Face is hotly debated. Industry advocates naturally say that every sale of a fake Calvin Klein T-shirt represents lost revenue for the company. But it is equally plausible to say that people who buy the fakes wouldn't – or couldn't – pay for the real thing anyway. Furthermore, it can be argued that the spread of fakes actually helps the big labels by providing a free source of advertising. Either way, the warning signs abound for foreign firms looking to manufacture goods in China: IP laws are not up to international standards.

Another worry is that China's domestic market has become saturated with clothing and related goods, resulting in a period of deflation stretching from the late 1990s through to 2005. The government determined that 87% of textile goods were in oversupply and imposed strict limits on the growth of the industry, meaning up to 400,000 textile workers faced salary cuts or possible redundancy. Expansion in capacity is now being actively discouraged in favor of the modernization of existing facilities and quality improvements. Imports of machinery involved in textile production are now in steep decline following several years of steady growth.

As living standards have risen, increasingly affluent Chinese consumers have also started to move upmarket, as evidenced by the myriad boutique shops in Shanghai, Beijing, and other big cities, where the fashion-conscious can search for bargains or splurge a little. The top international brands are now a common sight in the classy malls of all major Chinese cities – those who can afford to shop there are still relatively few in number, but everybody has to buy their clothes somewhere.

Tourism

When a country with a population of 1.3 billion mobilizes for travel, to say it is a massive undertaking is an understatement

With rising amounts of disposable income and more time off from work, Chinese people are clogging the railways, roadways, and airports like never before. This market has been given a boost in the last decade with the introduction of the so-called "Golden Weeks", three week-long national holidays at Chinese New Year, International Labor Day and National Day, first introduced in the wake of the 1997 Asian financial crisis as a means of encouraging consumer spending.

According to official figures, more than 78 million Chinese hit the roads, railways and airlines during the one-week Spring Festival holiday at the end of January 2006. However, every year this mass movement of people sends ticket prices soaring and sees tourist attractions across the country packed to bursting, and therefore has prompted the government to reconsider the future of the mandatory holidays.

"The quality of people's traveling experiences has been negatively influenced during the past six years due to contradictions between consumer demands and service capacity," Wang Zhifa, the vice-director of the China National Tourism Administration

(CNTA), told state media in September 2006, ahead of the National Day weeklong holiday.

But Wang envisions a future in which Chinese will pick and choose when and where they take their holidays, and the demise of mandatory holidays will do little to burst the World Tourism Organization's (the other WTO) forecast that China's domestic travel market will be the world's biggest by the end of the decade.

Outward bound

But people are not just traveling internally. As the concept of leisure travel takes hold, and as incomes continue to rise and travel restrictions ease, more and more Chinese are venturing overseas.

Between 1999 and 2005, the number of Chinese traveling abroad more than tripled from 9.23 million to 31.5 million, according to CNTA figures. By 2020, China is expected to be the world's largest source of departures with 115 million people traveling overseas every year.

Overseas tourism industries have started to realize the impact a flood of Chinese tourists could have on their markets, and cities like Shanghai are festooned with billboards promoting tourism to destinations around the globe. But it's not simply a case of waiting for

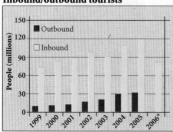

Inbound/outbound tourists

Source: China National Tourism Administration

INDUSTRY OVERVIEWS

the tourists to roll up and spend large, especially in those destinations far from home. According to a survey carried out last November by the International Forum on Chinese Outbound Tourism, 90.4% stick to Asia, with eight of the top 10 outbound destinations located in the home continent.

Chinese tourists spend their money selectively, tending to go for budget to mid-range hotels and eat cheap meals. But they spare no expense when it comes to shopping. According to a study jointly conducted by ACNielsen and Tax Free World Association (TFWA), Chinese travelers spend an average of US$987 shopping each time they take a trip out of China, making them the world's biggest spenders.

Flooding in

China is also becoming a major leisure destination in its own right. Around 120 million tourists visited China in 2005, and numbers grew a further 10.5% in the first four months of 2006, according to the other WTO, or around four times the rate of growth for North America and Europe. Boosted by such events as the Beijing Olympics and the Shanghai World Expo, China is expected to become the most visited country on the planet by 2020, playing host to around 180 million overseas visitors annually.

To accommodate the hordes, gleaming new airports are going up across the country, new rail lines are being laid, and new highways are being paved. China's hotel scene has also seen

furious activity with new hotels under construction in almost all the major cities. In the big economic centers such as Shanghai, Beijing, Guangzhou and Shenzhen, the appetite for hotels shows little sign of abating. Beijing's Olympic Committee, for example, plans to more than double the city's portfolio of 392 star-rated hotels in time for the 2008 Games. Shanghai also plans to double its tally of 342 hotels in time for the opening of the 2010 World Expo.

The rapid rise of China's tourism industry provides foreign tourism operators a great opportunity to take a slice of the domestic market. China is ripe for consolidation from the bookings and travel agency perspective, with 16,846 travel agencies registered across the country at the end of 2005. Of these, 1,590 are capable of planning and booking international vacations.

One of the fastest-growing sectors within the industry is online booking, with companies such as Ctrip and eLong offering a range of services from flights to hotel bookings and car hire over the internet. Such companies are rapidly coming to challenge the traditional travel agent.

Since July 2003, the government has allowed the establishment of wholly foreign-owned travel agencies, four years ahead of China's World Trade Organization obligations. To date, however, few investors other than a small number of Japanese agencies have taken up the opportunity, accounting for only 2% of the total revenues of all of China's agencies on international travel.

For those looking for the next China business goldmine, the time is ripe to try mixing a little business with leisure.

Is giving Corporate Gifts a
Custom or Strategy?

CHINESE - ENGLISH - CHINESE DICTIONARY

Professional bi-lingual high quality leather dictionary with optional languages. Logo can be embossed.

100% LEATHER

Measurements
H:130mm W:85mm

Available colors

SILVER PLATED LETTER OPENER

Elegant high quality "*Sharky Design*" Corporate logo can be laser engraved on both sides of the opener.

Measurements
H:155mm W:30mm

Available colors

SILVER-PLATED BOOK READER

NEW book page separator enabels readers to more comfortably read a book in bed or on a long flight.

100% LEATHER THUMB REST

Available colors

CREDIT CARD SIZE STAINLESS MIRROR

High quality silver-plated stainless Corporate logo can be laser engra Leather holster optional.

Avail

CREDIT CARD SIZE USB MEMORY

One of the worlds flattest USB memory cards. Fits easily into pocket or purse. Capacity 64MB -2GB

SIM CARD RESCUER

Ever lost your mobile? Back up 255 numbers from your SIM card. Corporate logo can be screen printed.

USB + LASER POINTER

Two in one USB storage device with laser pointer. Available in 64MB -2GB. Lanyard included

MAGNETIC LEVITATING PEN

Practical verticaly floating ballpoi in an elegant chrome finish. Corp logo can be screen printed.

LEATHER NAME CARD HOLDER

High quality namecard holder with two slots for easy separation of new and old cards. Logo can be embossed

100% LEATHER

Available colors

RETRACTABLE LEATHER KEY RING

Protective leather keyring holster with retractable key function to avoid pocket wear. Logo can be embossed

100% LEATHER

Available colors

LEATHER NOTEPAD FOR A7 PADS

Pocket size high quality note pad with interchangable standard A7 note pads available in most stationary shops

100% LEATHER

Measurements
H:130mm W:85mm

Available colors

LEATHER MOBILE PHONE H

High quality leather holder availa all size mobile phones, PDA's an Blackberries. Logo can be embossed.

Avai

Doing business

Company setup	194
Registering a company	197
Finding staff	198
Executive search firms	200
Finding an office	202
Serviced offices	204
Taxation	209
Accounting firms	209
Lawyers	212
Law firms	212
Business schools	216
MBA/EMBA programs	216
Logistics	229
Professional service providers	234
Translation firms	234
Web design firms	234

Company setup

Foreign-invested enterprises (FIE) in China are broadly categorized into three models: representative offices, joint ventures, and wholly foreign-owned enterprises. Each approach is accompanied by its own set of advantages and disadvantages, regulatory and otherwise.

The model that is chosen by a particular foreign company will depend on a number of factors, including the specific business area the company operates in and the overall strategic objectives of the company.

The laws and regulations pertaining to the operations of each structure differ, and careful consideration (and perhaps some professional advice) is advisable when determining which form of investment best suits the needs and goals of your business.

Joint ventures

A joint venture (JV) is a partnership between a foreign and one or more Chinese partners. It involves the sharing of capital, expenses, resources, profits, losses and liabilities. There are two different kinds of JVs: equity joint venture (EJV) and contractual joint venture (CJV). In an EJV arrangement, the two partners share the profits and risks according to the percentage of the investment each side holds. In a CJV arrangement, the two partners share the profits and risks according to a ratio agreed to at the beginning of the partnership. Both types of JVs are permitted to repatriate profits after tax dividends in line with the articles of association.

JVs are the most common and, potentially, the most problematic means by which a foreign business can invest in China. Despite the many well-documented stories of Chinese-foreign partnerships that have gone wrong, the JV approach is still encouraged by the Chinese

government because such business partnerships allow the transfer of foreign technology and business practices to Chinese companies.

Choosing the right partner can be the difference between success and failure in a JV relationship. Capable Chinese partners have the benefit of a thorough understanding of local market conditions and the Chinese business environment. They may also have access to established distribution networks and useful *guanxi* (relationships); the latter can be essential to doing business in China, and at times invaluable when dealing with local government bureaucracy.

But it is important to remember that some Chinese partners may carry ambitions widely different from – and at times even competing with – your own company's business interests. Many foreign investors have fallen afoul of China's hazy IPR laws and found that sensitive company information has fallen into the wrong hands. A thorough investigation into your potential business partner's financial history and a consideration of how that company might complement and enhance what your side has to offer is essential.

There is typically a limit on the maximum amount of foreign investment permitted in a JV partnership, depending on the company's area of business operations and its location. Implementation of WTO reforms in most industry sectors has resulted in the lifting of such restrictions on increased foreign participation, with many sectors expected to be further opened to

foreign investment by 2007. As a general rule, strictly regulated industry sectors limit foreign participation to a minority stake of up to 49%, while more open sectors allow the formation of wholly foreign-owned enterprises.

Wholly foreign-owned enterprises

Wholly foreign-owned enterprises (WFOEs) are businesses established entirely with foreign capital, under total foreign control and without any Chinese ownership or participation, and therefore offer a very attractive alternative to the JV. WFOEs are currently the most popular form of FIE in China, but can be troublesome to set up. The capital requirements for WFOEs are set higher than JVs, and there is no Chinese partner to share the expense. WFOEs may also be more limited in their scope of business – some industries are only open to foreign investment by JVs. WFOEs must demonstrate their contribution to China, and are on occasion subjected to export requirements or technology employment standards.

The advantages of setting up a WFOE are that the foreign entity can retain full control of management and sensitive business information, sidestepping the risks inherent in working with a Chinese partner. Without the advantages of market knowledge and distribution offered by a local partner, many choose the WFOE to conduct specialized business targeting a specific client base.

Representative offices

Setting up a representative office

(RO) involves much lower costs than other business structures, but such FIEs are severely limited in their business activities. ROs may only conduct market research and coordination between Chinese customers or suppliers and the foreign parent, and are not allowed to directly engage in any profit-making activities. Furthermore, ROs may not directly hire local employees but must rely on a government authorized employment agency.

An RO can be ideal for foreign companies that operate in a business area where foreign investment is still restricted by the Chinese government; the RO can act as a means to establish business relationships and conduct important market research. The bottom line is that an RO can have expenses but no revenue. This being China, ROs are taxed at a rate which assumes that in fact the company is booking revenue somehow, somewhere – probably offshore.

Holding companies

For investment holding purposes, some foreign investors may establish a holding company in an offshore jurisdiction to "hold" their Chinese-based entity. Hong Kong in particular offers several advantages as a place for establishing a holding company. In establishing such an operation, foreign investors are able to very effectively distance their main overseas business operations from the Chinese entity, therefore diminishing the exposure to potential liabilities. The establishment of a holding company also offers foreign investors increased opportunities for (legal) transfer pricing.

The advantages of Hong Kong over other offshore locations (such as the British Virgin Islands) include the increased transparency of Hong Kong's financial and legal regulations, its geographical proximity to mainland China and the ease and relatively low costs involved in establishing and operating a business there. Also, there is the possible opportunity to take advantage of the CEPA agreement that was signed between Hong Kong and China in June 2003, in which China promised greater access to China markets for Hong Kong-based companies.

Registering a company

All FIE applications are conducted through the Ministry of Commerce (MOFCOM), or its local agents, and the registration process can be long and complicated or quick and easy – it just depends. Overall, the process is getting easier all the time, particularly in Shanghai and Beijing, and can be completed in as little as four weeks. Expect the process to take around 6-7 weeks in other parts of China or away from development zones. Third-party professional service companies are often worth bringing in to facilitate the process.

The authorities will typically scrutinize a WFOE application more closely than they would a JV application to ensure that it fully complies with the relevant regulations. It is important therefore to ensure that the documentation strictly conform to approval requirements so as to avoid further delays in the registration process.

Approval must be obtained before a company can be registered. Documents at this stage may need to include a proposal, feasibility study report and a company's articles of association.

After approval has been granted, it is necessary to apply for a business license. Applicants must show proof of a bank account as registration also needs to be made with the tax bureau, statistics bureau and customs.

To ensure rights to the use of a trademarked name or logo, a company must first register with the Trademark Bureau in Beijing: (010) 68052266. Registration is a fairly simple process requiring a fee of RMB1,000.

Finding staff

Representative offices are required to fill their staffing needs through government affiliated agencies such as FESCO and CIIC (see below for contact details).

These companies are basically happy to sign up any staff that companies propose, or to act as recruitment agencies. FESCO and CIIC are a convenient way of handling staff, in that they handle all staff tax and welfare issues for a company.

Many large corporations send at least a few expatriate personnel to fill high-level management positions, filling out the rest of their needs with local staff. But localization is stretching into ever-higher levels of management, and it is becoming more common for FIEs to promote Chinese staff to the top positions. Some multinationals relocate staff to China on full expatriate terms, which include relocation expenses, housing, education for children and periodic trips home. But it is also increasingly possible to recruit non-Chinese staff within China. These candidates may have the advantages of already being acclimatized to life in China and sometimes fluent in the Chinese language. Jobs for foreigners already living in China are often advertised in local English-language listings and business magazines.

Finding qualified local candidates for upper-level positions often requires more effort and probably requires more effort and probably outside help. Highly qualified talent is in higher demand than supply. Chinese education tends to produce people well grounded in technical and theoretical knowledge but often lacking in practical skills. Many headhunters offer executive search services specifically to find local management talent for foreign firms. Be sure to make thorough background checks, and contact all references. Not only will a background check confirm an applicant's competence, but is essential for countering possible fraud.

Filling lower-level positions in a new company presents the employer with issues of both quality and quantity. The internet has allowed for greater direct access than ever to larger numbers of persons. Newspapers and other print material remain useful options for staff recruitment. But it still may be a good idea to use a local agent. Job applicants in China tend to bend their qualifications to cast themselves in a favorable light more than other countries. After all, there's a lot of competition in the job market. Local HR personnel can be invaluable in interpreting the true abilities of potential staff. Companies can also establish relationships with universities, which can provide good candidates.

Foreign enterprises will often have a competitive edge over local companies in the Chinese market, bringing with them business practices that top the general standard in China. Among these are efficient organization and quality of service. Foreign enterprises benefit from investment in training programs for local staff to retain their advantage.

Employers should be mindful of employee retention in China, especially considering the competitiveness of the market. Money invested in recruiting or training is wasted if workers leave their posts quickly. Employers should continually make themselves aware of salary levels that shift fast in China. If a company expects to deliver service at a level above the common industry standard, it must expect to offer wages accordingly. Labor in China is abundant and usually cheap, but workers are aware of their ability to switch companies.

In China, employers are responsible for paying taxes and social security for staff. These laborious responsibilities can also be outsourced to companies specializing in such services. Foreign businesses should also consider what other benefits are commonly offered to employees in China. Staff at state-owned enterprises often receive full subsidies for housing and medical care. Employers may need to consider offering similar benefits or adjusting wages to compensate for their absence.

Useful job recruitment websites in China include www.51job.com (so called because in Chinese '51' sounds similar to 'I want') and www.zhaopin.com.

DOING BUSINESS

Executive search firms
Beijing
Staff Service
A 1201 Jianguomenwai Dajie, (010) 6527 0988
www.staffservice.com
J.M. Gemini
504 Avic Building, 10B Dongsanhuan Zhong Lu, (010) 6567 0678
www.jmgemini.com
SearchBank
19/F, New York Tower, The General Mall, 6 Xiaozhuang Lu, (010) 6502 3851
www.search-bank.com
St. George's Harvey Nash Ltd
5/F, China Life Tower, 16 Chaowai Jie, (010) 5877 1222
www.stghn.com
Atoz Headhunting
305 Heqiao Mansion , 8A Guanghua Lu, (010) 6581 1468
www.atoz-headhunting.com
Mercer Human Resource Consulting
3501-3506 China World Tower 1, 1 Jianguomenwai Dajie
(010) 6505 9355
www.mercerhr.com
Adecco
2201 CITIC Building, 19 Jianguomenwai Dajie
(010) 8526 1632
www.adecco-asia.com
Boyden Global Executive Search
703 Tower A, Kelun Building, 12A Guanghua Lu, (010) 6581 8456
www.boyden.com
Manpower Business Consulting
605 Building F, Fuhua Mansion, 8 Chaoyangmen Dajie
(010) 6554 5382
www.manpower.com

MRI Worldwide
316 Tower B, Heqiao Mansion, 8A Guanghua Lu, (010) 6505 9180
www.mri-china.com
Spencer Stuart
2709 Tower A, China World Trade Centre 1, 1 Jianguomenwai Dajie, (010) 6505 1031
www.spencerstuart.com
Templar International Consultants
2201 CITIC Building, 19 Jianguomenwai Dajie
(010) 8526 1632
www.templarsearch.com
Shanghai
Staff Service
26/F Kerry Centre, 1515 Nanjing Xi Lu, (021) 5298 6298
www.staffservice.com
J.M Gemini
8E Shanghai Industrial Investment Building, 18 Caoxi Bei Lu
(021) 6428 2460
www.jmdemini.com
SearchBank
2402-3 Times Square, 93 Huaihai Zhong Lu, (021) 6391 0110
www.search-bank.com
The Wright Company
39/F, Plaza 66, 1266 Nanjing Xi Lu, (021) 6288 1855
www.wrightcompany.com
St. George's Harvey Nash Ltd
2010 One Corporate Avenue, 222 Hubin Lu, (021) 6340 6880
Adecco
1208 Tian'an Centre, 338 Nanjing Xi Lu, (021) 6327 2299
www.adecco-asia.com
AdMark International Executive Search
408 Building B, Huanqiu World Building, 1 Wanhangdu Lu

(021) 6249 7809
www.admarkasia.com
Boyden Global Executive Search
6005 Nobel Building, 887 Huaihai
Zhong Lu, (021) 6445 6009
www.boyden.com
EJK Consultants
4108 Hong Kong New World Tower,
300 Huaihai Zhong Lu
(021) 5103 5351
www.kiebaum.com
Hunt and Partners
2008 Huaihai Tower, 885 Renmin
Lu, (021) 6355 0010
Manpower Business Consulting
2008-2811 Shanghai Information
Tower, 211 Shiji Dadao
(021) 5878 2618
26/F Golden Bell Plaza, 98 Huaihai
Zhong Lu, (021) 5385 8006
www.manpower.com
Mercer Human Resource Consulting
3601 Hong Kong New World Tower,
300 Huaihai Zhong Lu, (021) 6335
3358
www.mercerhr.com
Michael Page

1010 Shanghai Kerry Centre, 1515
Nanjing Xi Lu, (021) 3222 4758
www.michaelpage.com
MRI Worldwide
704-705 Hong Kong Plaza South,
283 Huaihai Zhong Lu, (021) 6390
6007
www.mri-china.com
Personnel Decisions International
810 Tomson Financial Building, 710
Dingfang Lu, (021) 5830 9993
www.personneldecisions.com
Russell Reynolds Associates
1513 Central Plaza, 381 Huaihai
Zhong Lu, (021) 6391 5511
www.russellreynolds.com
Spencer Stuart
1107 One Corporate Avenue, 222
Hubing Lu, (021) 6386 1177
www.spencerstuart.com
Templar International Consultants
12/F, Shui On Plaza, 333 Huaihai
Zhong Lu, (021) 5116 0707
The JLJ Group
1806 Shanghai Oriental Centre, 699
Nanjing Xi Lu, (021) 5211 0068
www.jljgroup.com

Finding an office

As in other countries, it helps to use a property agent that is familiar with the city's commercial pulse and can assist in identifying locations that suit the personality of your business. Many foreign property agents in China's larger cities are able to do just that.

It also pays to look into what division and level of government regulates a potential location. Areas named as special economic, industrial or development zones are under special jurisdiction, designated to offer tax breaks or streamlined policies to businesses of a specific industry or trade (more on that below). In the commercial centers of large cities where property is in high demand, authorities are more likely to implement stringent regulations and carry out compliance inspections, whereas in outlying urban areas, local governments are often eager to invite investment, offering a more relaxed and friendly approach.

In larger cities, as most staff use public transport or arrive on foot or bike, consider a location's proximity to the nearest subway station or bus routes. In Shanghai and Beijing, many new subway or light rail lines are under construction around which new high-rise office buildings are being built.

Facilities included in an office lease can vary. A property agent can help to select space that meets your requirements. Most offices will have finished ceilings, inter-tenancy walls and flooring, with installed lighting and adequate electricity, phone, and internet hookups. But sometimes offices – and homes – are provided as concrete shells. Utilities and maintenance costs are sometimes included in the rental quote, but may also be charged in a separate building management fee.

Start-up businesses or those with a limited budget have the option of setting up serviced or virtual offices.

The number of serviced office providers in Beijing and Shanghai in particular has boomed over the past few years and such offices are now available in most important Chinese cities. Serviced offices provide an array of business services, including bilingual secretarial support, handling of mail, fax and telephone calls, courier services, transportation and hotel arrangements. Some also offer translation, telemarketing, employee recruitment, accounting and legal consultancy services.

This one-stop approach to setting up an office allows many companies that are new to China to focus on core business activities by bypassing the technical difficulties of finding an office and hiring staff.

Many smaller foreign companies that have set up in a serviced office in China will stay there for the long-term given that this option can be a particularly effective way of maintaining an office in China with a small number of personnel at a prestigious address.

Virtual offices are an inexpensive option allowing a business to

The Office You Can Call Your Own

serviced office suite | virtual office | meeting facilities | secretarial support

12/F Platinum, 233 Tai Cang Road, Xintiandi, Shanghai 200020, Tel +86.21.5175.7777
5/F Shanghai Times Square Office Tower, 93 Huai Hai Zhong Road, Shanghai 200021, Tel +86.21.5117.9333
info.sh@apbcoffices.com www.apbcoffices.com

circumvent the actual leasing of space. A virtual office can be managed from overseas and leasing a virtual office may start at around US$60 per month. A secretary will answer phone calls using the virtual tenant's company name as well as fielding incoming mail and faxes.

The company can use an address in the building, which will have meeting rooms and office facilities available for use by the hour.

Development zones

Basing your company within a development zone (sometimes also called free trade zones, special economic and technological development zones or high-tech zones depending on their overall focus) can offer several advantages since such zones are able to offer FIEs preferential tax rates and exemptions. Land and rental rates are also generally much cheaper. A complete list of development zones

within China is included within the "Destinations" section of this guide.

Preferential tax rates are sometimes only provided to FIEs engaged in long-term investment and within certain industries. It's therefore worth spending some time looking at the various levels of preferential treatment offered by a number of different national- and state-level development zones to find the zone that most effectively meets the requirements of your company's business operations.

Serviced offices

Beijing

Executive Centre

17/F, Millennium Tower, 38 Xiaoyun Lu, (010) 6410 8588

www.executivecentre.com

The Tower Offices at Oriental Plaza

1 Dong Chang'an Dajie

(010) 8518 4411

Servcorp Beijing

6/F, Tower W2, Oriental Plaza, 1

Grow

With the Executive Centre in CHINA
Choose from 5 Prime Locations in Shanghai & Beijing

TOKYO • SEOUL • BEIJING • SHANGHAI • HONG KONG • TAIPEI • SINGAPORE • JAKARTA • SYDNEY • SOFIA

SHANGHAI:
CITIC SQUARE Telephone: 8621-5252-4618
THE CENTER Telephone: 8621-5116-6888
XINTIANDI Telephone: 8621-6135-7188

BEIJING:
HYUNDAI MOTOR TOWER Telephone: 8610-6410-8588
CHINA RESOURCES BUILDING Telephone: 8610-5811-1888

Asia's leading serviced office provider

THE EXECUTIVE CENTRE

Email: shanghai@executivecentre.com / beijing@executivecentre.com **Website:** www.executivecentre.com

Dong Chang'an Dajie
(010) 8520 0000
www.servcorp.net
Regus: Lufthnansa Centre
C203, Beijing Lufthansa Centre, 1
Dong Chang'an Jie, (010) 8518 4411
C203, Beijing Lufthansa Centre, 50
Liangmaoqiao Lu, (010) 8520 0000
www.regus.com
Regus: Pacific Century Place
14/F, Tower A, IBM Tower, 2A
Gongti Bei Lu, (010) 6539 1020
Regus: NCI Centre
15/F, NIC Tower, 12A
Jianguomeiwai Dajie, (010) 8523
3000
Plaza Business Centre at the Kerry Centre
3/F, North Tower, Beijing Kerry
Centre, 1 Guanghua Lu, (010) 8529
8000
www.kerryprops.com
Plaza Business Centre at China Life
5/F, China Life Tower, No.16
Chaowai Dajie, (010) 5877 1111
www.kerryprops.com

Far Glory
18/F, China Merchants Tower,
No.118 Jianguo Lu, (010) 6567 2299
www.farglory.biz
CEO Suite
10/F, Twin Towers (East), B12
Jianguomeiwai Dajie, (010) 5123
5123
www.ceosuite.com
Shanghai
APBC
26/F, Shanghai Times Square Office
Tower, 93 Huaihai Zhong Lu, (021)
5117 9333
www.asiapacbiz.com
Executive Centre: CITIC Square
3501 CITIC, 1168 Nanjing Xi Lu,
(021) 5252 4618
www.executivecentre.com
The Executive Centre: The Center
989 Changle Lu, (021) 5116 6888
www.executivecentre.com
Asia Biz Center
14/F, Suncome Cimic Tower, 800
Shangcheng Lu, Pudong, (021) 6121
3658

DOING BUSINESS

www.asiabizcenter.com.cn
Regus: One Corporate Avenue
C15/F, One Corporate Avenue, 222
Hubin Lu, (021) 6122 0808
www.regus.com
Regus: Jin Mao Tower
31/F, Jin Mao Tower, 88 Shiji Dadao,
(021) 2809 9888
www.regus.com
CEO Suite
47/F, Hong Kong New World Tower,
300 Huaihai Zhong Lu, (021) 5116
2888, *www.ceosuite.com*
Ortus Premier Serviced Offices
18/F, Bund Center, 222 Yan'an Dong
Lu, (021) 5115 8866
www.ortus.biz
Office General: Plaza 66
39/F, Plaza 66, 1266 Nanjing Xi Lu,
(021) 6288 3288
www.officegeneral.com
Office General: Cross Region Plaza
6/F, Cross Region Plaza, 899 Lingling
Lu, (021) 6468 8833
www.officegeneral.com
Office Lister
14/F, 993 Nanjing Xi Lu

(021) 6272 7899
Omnibiz Centre
250 Caoxi Lu, Zone A 113-115
(021) 5108 9866
Far Glory: Far Eastern International Plaza
3/F, Building A Far Eastern
International Plaza, No.319 Xianxia
Lu, (021) 6270 2222
www.farglory.biz
Far Glory: K. Wah Centre
27/F, K. Wah Centre, 1010 Huaihai
Zhong Lu, (021) 6103 1234
www.farglory.biz
Sercorp Shanghai
21/F, HSBC Building, 101 Yincheng
Dong Lu, (021) 2890 3000
www.servcorp.net
Servcorp Kerry Centre
29/F, Kerry Centre, 1515 Nanjing Xi
Lu, 021) 6103 7000
www.servcorp.net
Guangzhou
Center Plaza
23/F, Center Plaza, 161 Linhe Xi Lu,
(020) 3825 1333
www.centerplaza.com.cn

Taxation

China has two independent tax systems, one for domestic enterprises and one for FIEs. The two systems are distinct from each other and administered independently. There are five taxes most applicable to FIEs in China as follows: corporate income tax, value added tax, business tax, consumption tax and stamp duty. The rates paid by FIEs vary greatly depending on the entity's business area and, most importantly, whether it is based in a development zone (for example FIEs in Shanghai will pay considerably more tax in the Puxi area of the city as opposed to FIEs based in the new Pudong area where the local government is trying to actively encourage greater foreign investment).

China offers foreign investors numerous industry- or geography-based tax incentives for investment purposes and may also offer refunds of tax paid on reinvested profits. One of the most attractive tax concessions usually available to FIEs in China is a one-year tax holiday that usually starts from the first profitable year. If an FIE should terminate operations within ten years after its establishment, however, the company will be required to pay back all of the tax that was exempted as result of the tax holiday.

Individual income tax is imposed on foreign individuals depending upon the individual taxpayer's residence status and source of income.

Accounting firms

Deloitte Touche 德勤华永
www.deloitte.com
Beijing
8/F, Tower W2, Oriental Plaza, 1 Dong Chang'an Dajie, (010) 8520 7788
Shanghai
30/F Bund Centre, 222 Yan'an Dong Lu, (021) 6335 0202
Guangzhou
23/F, Jianlibao Tower, 410 Dongfeng Zhong Lu, (020) 8393 6339
Shenzhen
19/F, Shunhing Square, Diwang Commercial Centre, 5002 Shennan Dong Lu, (0755) 8246 3255
Ernst & Young 安永
www.ey.com
Beijing
16/F, Tower E3, The Towers, Oriental Plaza, 1 Dong Chang'an Jie (010) 6524 6688
Shanghai
23/F, The Centre, 989 Changle Lu, (021) 2405 2000
Guangzhou
36/F, Tower B, Centre Plaza, 161 Linhe Xi Lu, (020) 2881 2888
Shenzhen
26/F, Shenzhen Development Centre, Renmin Nan Lu (0755) 8228 0788
Wuhan
6/F Wuhan Urban Commercial Bank Plaza, 933 Jianshe Dadao (027) 8261 2688
Chengdu
1806 Zongfu Building, 35 Zongfu Lu, (028) 8676 2080
Grant Thronton 中京富
www.grantthronton.com
Beijing

1212 Tower B, Full Link Plaza, 18 Chaoyangmenwai Dajie (010) 6588 6665
Shanghai
1601-1603 Novel Plaza, 128 Nanjing Xi Lu, (021) 6327 2200
HCL Group (Hong Kong) Ltd
www.hclinteriors.com
Beijing
Room 2009, Huayi Building, 42 Dongsanhuan Bei Lu, Chaoyang District, (010) 6581 4044
KPMG 毕马威
www.kpmg.com.cn
Beijing
8/F, Office Tower E2, Oriental Plaza, 1 Dong Chang'an Dajie, (010) 8518 5000
Shanghai
50/F, Plaza 66, 1266 Nanjing Xi Lu, (021) 5359 4666
Guangzhou
2907 Guangzhou International Electronics Tower, 403 Huanshi Dong Lu, (020) 8732 2832
Shenzhen
1007 Shunhing Square, Diwang Commercial Centre, 5002 Shennan Dong Lu, (0755) 8246 3398
LehmanBrown 雷博
www.lehmanbrown.com
Beijing
6/F, Dongwai Diplomatic Building, 23 Dongzhimenwai Dajie (010) 8532 1720
Shanghai
902 Tower A, Shanghai Universal Mansion 172 Yuyuan Lu (021) 6249 0055
Shenzhen
3206 News Building, 2 Shennan Zhong Lu, (0755) 8209 1244
Mazars 马扎尔

www.mazars.com
Beijing
608 Tower E2, Oriental Plaza, 1 Chang'an Dong Jie, (010) 8518 9780
Shanghai
2205 South Tower, Shanghai Stock Exchange Building, 528 Pudong Nan Lu, (021) 6882 5022
PricewaterhouseCoopers 普华永道
www.pwccn.com
Beijing
26/F, Office Tower A, Beijing Fortune Plaza, 23 Dongsanhuan Bei Lu, (010) 6533 8888
Shanghai
11/F, PricewaterhouseCoopers Centre, 202 Hubin Lu, (021) 6123 8888
Guangzhou
25/F, Center Plaza, 161 Linhe Xi Lu, (020) 3819 2000
Shenzhen
37/F, Shunying Square, 5002 Shennan Dong Lu, (0755) 8246 1717
Xi'an
728 Zhongda International Mansion, 30 Nanda Jie, (029) 8720 3336
Tianjin
17/F Tower 1 The Exchange, 189 Nanjing Lu, (022) 2330 6789
Qingdao
4601, Qingdao International Finance Center, 59 Xianggang Zhong Lu, (0532) 8089 1888
Roedl & Partner 罗德
www.roedl.de
Beijing
930 Beijing Sunflower Tower, 37 Maizidian Jie, (010) 8527 5090
Shanghai
28/F POS Plaza, 1600 Shiji Dadao, (021) 5830 0708
Guangzhou
4513-4516 Metro Plaza, 183 Tianhe

Bei Lu, (020) 8755 0930
RSM Salustro 萨理德中瑞
www.rsmi.com
Beijing
601 Tower B, COFCO Plaza,
Jianguomennei Dajie, (010) 6526 3769
Shanghai
2301 Jin Mao Tower, 88 Shiji Dadao,
(021) 5049 2022
**Tianjin Antai Certified Public
Accountants**
天津安泰有限责任会计师事务所
12 Yongyang Dong Lu, Yangcun,
Wuqing, (022) 2934 5162
**Tianjin Xingang Certified Public
Accountants**
天津新港有限责任会计师事务所
35 Xingang Er Hao Lu, Tanggu New
Harbor, (022) 2570 8906
**Tianjin Guocai Certified Public
Accountants**
天津国财有限责任会计师事务所
Tianjin
85 Yongyang Xi Lu, Wuqing, (022)
2937 0001
Tin Wha CPAs 天华
www.tinwhacpas.com
Beijing

17F, Sinochem Tower A, 2
Fuxingmenwai Dajie,(010) 6856 9800
Shanghai
2103 South Tower, Hong Kong
Plaza, 283 Huaihai Zhong Lu
(021) 6390 6501
Guangzhou
Building 3, 398 Guangzhou Bei Lu,
(020) 3886 7839
Shenzhen
1801 Building A, High-Tech Plaza,
Tian'an Cyber Park, (0755) 8343 3600
Nanjing
2305 Jiangsu Telecommunication
Tower, 198 Jiqing Lu, (025) 5230 0356
Qingdao
23/F, Times Square, 52 Xianggang
Zhong Lu, (0532) 5779 588
Shenyang
24 Zegongnanxiang Huigong Jie,
(024) 2272 3980
Xiamen
2/F Zhenxing Tower, 118 Hubin Bei
Lu, (592) 5361 298
Chengdu
803 Building A, World Trade Center,
117 Gulou Nan Jie, (028) 8381 8575
Tianjin

101 Qiongzhou Dao
(022) 8381 8575
Wuhan Tianhai Certified Public Accountants Co., Ltd.
武汉天海会计师事务有限责任公司
Wuhan
3/F Caiyuan Building, 1 Gaoxiong Road, Jiang'an, (027) 8549 4157
Yuehua Certified Public Accountants Co., Ltd.
岳华会计师事务所有限责任公司
www.yhcpa.com
Beijing
B1201 Pengrun Building, 26 Xiaoyun Lu, (010) 8458 4405
Qingdao
709 Section B Yuyuan Building, 75 Xianggang Xi Lu, (0532) 8388 2202
Tianjin
9/F Main Block Kangyue Tower, 35 Xikang Lu, (022) 2304 0215
Chengdu
4/F, 12 Jiuxing Dajie, (028) 8512 7536
Guangzhou
801-802 Yueneng Tower, 45 Tianhe Lu, (020) 6262 4168
Shenzhen
413 Zhuoyue Tower, 98 Fuhuayi Road, Futian, (0755) 8287 7168
Nanjing
12/F Dongpei Tower, 199 Jianye Lu, (025) 5233 6976
Wuhan
A16 Tower A Longyuan International Plaza, 24 Zhongbei Road
(027) 5187 7777
21 ViaNet (China), Inc
www.21vianet.com
Beijing
BOE Science Park, 10 Jiuxianqiao Lu, Chaoyang District, (010) 8456 2121

Lawyers

Naturally, it is a good idea to retain a reputable law firm in China to protect your interests. While the country has attracted record foreign investment in the last decade, the laws are often byzantine in nature and it pays to have a professional keeping track of them so that you can pay attention to your business.

Law firms
Preston Gates Ellis
普盖茨律师事务所
www.prestongates.com
Beijing
1003 Tower E3, Oriental Plaza, 1 Dong Chang'an Dajie, (010) 8518 8528
Allbright Law Offices
锦天城律师事务所
www.allbrightlaw.com.cn
Beijing
1608 Jingcheng Mansion, Xinyuan Nan Lu, (010) 8486 8555
Shanghai
25/F, Jin Mao Tower, 88 Shiji Dadao, (021) 5049 8946
Allen & Overy
安理国际律师事务所
www.allenovery.com
Beijing
522 China World Tower 2, 1 Jianguomenwai Dajie, (010) 6505 8800
Shanghai
601 One Corporate Avenue, 222 Hu Bin Lu, (021) 5386 9988
Baker & McKenzie
贝克麦坚时国际律师事务所
www.bakernet.com

Beijing
3401 China World Tower 2, 1
Jianguomenwai Dajie, (010) 6505 0591
Shanghai
1601 Jin Mao Tower, 88 Shiji Dadao,
(021) 5047 8558
Baker & Daniels LLP
美国贝克·丹尼尔斯律师事务所
www.bakerdaniels.com
Qingdao
4/F Crowne Plaza Office Tower, 76
Xianggang Zhong Lu
(0532) 8575 1051
Beijing
1919 China World Tower 2, 1
Jianguomenwai Da Jie
(010) 6505 7733
Shanghai
1207-1208 Lippo Plaza, 222 Huaihai
Zhong Lu, (021) 5396 5862
Clifford Chance 高伟绅律师事务所
www.cliffordchance.com
Beijing
3326 China World Tower 1, 1
Jianguomenwai Dajie
(010) 6505 9018
Shanghai
40/F, Bund Center, 222 Yan'an Dong

Lu, (021) 6335 0086
Deacons 的近律师行
www.deacons.com.au
Beijing
11, 8/F, Tower W1, The Towers,
Oriental Plaza, 1 Dong Chang'an
Dajie, (010) 8518 2338
Shanghai
2801 Raffles City, 268 Xizang Zhong
Lu, (021) 6340 3588
Fred Kan & Co. 简家骢律师事务所
www.fredkan.com
Tianjin
A1009 International Economic Trade
Center, 59 Machang Lu, 022 2313 9762
Fangda Partners PRC Lawyers
方达律师事务所
www.fangdalaw.com
Beijing
1422-1425 China World Tower 1, 1
Jianguomenwai Dajie, (010) 6505 5557
Shanghai
2202-2207 22/F, Kerry Centre, 1515
Nanjing Xi Lu, (021) 5298 5566
Shenzhen
26/F, Shenzhen Development Bank
Building, 5047 Shennan Dong Lu,
(0755) 8208 0855

Freshfields Bruchhaus Deringer
富而德律师事务所
www.freshfields.com
Beijing
3705 China World Tower 2, 1
Jianguomenwai Dajie, (010) 6505 3448
Shanghai
34/F, Jin Mao Tower, 88 Shiji Dadao,
(021) 5049 1118
Frederick W. Hong
美国康永华律师事务所
www.fwhonglaw.com
Guangzhou
1503 North Tower Guangzhou World
Trade Center, 371-375 Huanshi Dong
Lu, (020) 8760 9933
Beijing
813 Tower W1 Oriental Plaza, 1
Dong Chang'an Jie, Dongcheng,
(010) 8518 2640
Guangsheng & Partners
广盛律师事务所
www.gslaw.com.cn
Qingdao
Room 1406, Hisense Tower No.17
Donghai Xi Lu, (0532) 386 5857
Beijing
Beijing Headquarter 25th Floor,
Zhongfu Tower 99 Jianguo Lu, (010)

6581 3529
Shanghai
Room 806, Changhang Building,
No.800, Zhangyang Lu, Pudong,
(021) 5835 6005
Harbin
Harbin Office Rm, 728-739,
7/F FarEast Business Center, 65
Changjiang Lu, Nangang District,
(0451) 8265 5177
Haarmann Hemmelrath
德国法合联合律师事务所
www.haarmannhemmelrath.com
Beijing
701-703 Tower B COFCO Plaza, 8
Jianguomennei Dajie, (010) 6526
0962
Shanghai
2308 Jin Mao Tower, 88 Shiji Dadao,
Pudong, (021), 5049 8176
Stephenson Harwood & Lo
罗夏信律师事务所
www.shl.com.hk
Guangzhou
1907 Peace World Plaza, 362-366
Huanshi Dong Lu, (020) 8388 0590
Shanghai
8/F HSBC Tower, 101 Yincheng Dong
Lu, Pudong, (021) 6841 0988

Heller Ehrman
国际海陆国际律师事务所
www.hewm.com
Beijing
Unit 01-02 14/F, China World Tower
1, 1 Jianguomenwai Dajie, (010)
5866 9738
INCE & Co. 英士律师事务所
Shanghai
328 The Bund Building 12
12 Zhong Shan Dong Yi Lu
(021) 6329 1212
Jones Day 众达律师事务所
www.jonesday.com
Beijing
3201 China World Tower 1, 1
Jianguomenwai Dajie, (010) 5866 1111
Shanghai
30/F, Kerry Centre, 1515 Nanjing Xi
Lu, (021) 2201 8000
Jun He Law Offices
君合律师事务所
www.junhe.com
Beijing
20/F, China Resources Building, 8
Jianguomenwai Dajie, (010) 8519 1300
Shanghai
32/F, Kerry Centre, 1515 Nanjing Xi
Lu, (021) 5298 5488
King & Wood 金杜律师事务所
www.kingandwood.com
Chengdu
11/F Guancheng Plaza, 308
Shuncheng Da Jie, (028) 8652 7898
Shenzhen
4708-4715 Shunhing Diwang
Commercial Center, 5002 Shennan
Dong Lu, (0755) 8212 5533
Shanghai
21/F Shui On Plaza, 333 Huaihai
Zhong Lu, (021) 6385 2299
Guangzhou
5402B Citic Plaza, 233 Tianhe Bei Lu,

(020) 3891 2080
Beijing
31/F Jianwai SOHO Building A, 39
Dongsanhuan Zhong Lu, (010) 5878
5588
P.C Woo & Co. 胡百全律师事务所
www.pcwoo.com
Chengdu
7K First City Plaza, 308 Shuncheng
Da Jie, (028) 8652 8737
Titan Law Firm 迪泰律师事务所
www.titan-law.com
Chengdu
14B Wangfujin Shopping Centre, 5
Huaxing Zheng Jie, (028) 8678 6200
Linklaters 年利达律师事务所
www.linklaters.com
Beijing
Unit 29 25/F, China World Tower 1,
1 Jianguomenwai Daijie
(010) 6505 8590
Shanghai
16/F, Citigroup Tower 1, 33
Huayuanshiqiao Lu, (021) 2891 1888
Norton Rose 诺顿罗氏律师事务所
www.nortonrose.com
Beijing
C-801 Lufthansa Center, 50
Liangmaqiao Lu
(010) 8448 8881
**Skadden, Arps, Slate, Meagher &
Flom LLP** 世达国际律师事务所
www.skadden.com
Beijing
4/F, East Wing Office, China World
Trade Centre, 1 Jianguomenwai Dajie,
(010) 6505 5511
Sullivan & Cromwell LLP
美国苏利克伦威尔律师事务所
www.sullcrom.com
Beijing
501 China World Trade Centre, 1
Jianguomenwai Dajie, (010) 6505 6120

Business schools

Another great source to tap for talent is China's increasingly sophisticated pool of MBA and EMBA programs. For more news about Chinese business schools, visit www.chinaeconomicreview.com/mba.

MBA/EMBA programs
Beijing
Beijing International MBA at Peking University
101 Beijing International MBA, China Centre for Economic Research, Peking University, Beijing 100871
Tel: (010) 6275 4800/4802/5706
Fax: (010) 6275 7932
admissions@bimba.edu.cn
www.bimba.edu.cn
Guanghua School of Management, Peking University
113 Guanghua Building, Peking University, Beijing 100871
Tel: (010) 6275 7781
Fax: (010) 6275 7754
mbaadmi@gsm.pku.edu.cn
www.mba.pku.edu.cn
Victoria University of Technology-Beijing Jiaotong University
China Australia Business School, Beijing Jiaotong University, Shangyuancun, Xizhimenwai, Beijing 100044
Tel: (010) 5168 8359
cabs@center.njtu.edu.cn
cabs.njtu.edu.cn
Beijing Institute of Technology
1047 Central Teaching Building, Beijing Institute of Technology, 5 Zhongguancun, Nan Dajie, Beijing 100081
Tel: (010) 6894 4997
mbalw@bit.edu.cn
mba.bit.edu.cn
University of Science and Technology Beijing
University of Science and Technology Beijing, Technology Beijing, 30 Xueyuan Lu, Beijing 100083
Tel: (010) 6232 9826
www.ustb.edu.cn
Beijing University of Posts and Telecommunications
Beijing University of Posts and Telecommunications, 10 Xitucheng Lu, Beijing 100876
Tel: (010) 6228 2069
Fax: (010) 6228 3277
mba@bupt.edu.cn
www.sem.bupt.cn/mba/index.asp
Beihang University
School of Economics and Management, Beihang University, 37 Xueyuan Lu, Beijing 100083
Tel: (010) 8233 8230
buaamba@263.net,cn
www.buaamba.net
University of International Business and Economics
University of International Business and Economics, 10 Huixin Dong Jie, Beijing 100029
Tel: (010) 6449 2151
Fax: (010) 6449 5202
mba@uibe.edu.cn
mba.uibe.edu.cn
Renmin University of China
112 Renwen Building, School of Business, Renmin University of China, 59 Zhongguancun Dajie, Beijing 100872

Tel: (010) 6251 1373; 6251 1342
Fax: (010) 6251 6338
mbarbs@ruc.edu.cn
202.112.112.242

China University of Mining & Technology Beijing
School of Management, China University of Mining & Technology Beijing, 11D Xueyuan Lu, Beijing 100083
Tel: (010) 6233 1333
Fax: (010) 6232 8550
sm.cumt.edu.cn/mba/index.asp

Graduate University of Chinese Academy of Sciences
Building 6#, Zhongguancun Campus, School of Management, Graduate University of Chinese Academy Sciences, 80 Zhongguancun Dong Lu, Beijing 100039
Tel: (010) 8268 0833/34
Fax: (010) 8268 0833
zkymba@126.com
www.mscas.ac.cn/mba.htm

Capital University of Economics and Business
Building 1#, East Campus, Capital University of Economics and Business, 2 Jintaili Hongmiao, Beijing 100026
Tel: (010) 8599 6400; 6597 6020
mba.cueb.edu.cn/index.asp

Central University of Finance and Economics
MBA Education Centre, Central University of Finance and Economics, 39 Xueyuan Nan Lu, Beijing 100081
Tel: (010) 6228 8131; 6228 8130
mba@cufe.edu.cn
www.cufe.edu.cn/jgsz/mbal/index.htm

China Agricultural University
210 College of Economic Management, CAU West Campus, 2 Yuanminyun Xi Lu, Beijing 100094
Tel: (010) 6273 1330; 6273 1315
Fax: (010) 6273 1315
office@caumba.com
www.cau.edu.cn/cem/mba/index.htm

North China Electric Power University

North China Electric Power University (Beijing), Zhuxinzhuang Shengdemenwai, Beijing 102206
Tel: (010) 8079 8610
Fax: (010) 8079 8480
hdmba@126.com
www.epmba.com

Shanghai

Boston University-Donghua University
1882 Yan'an Xi Lu, Shanghai 200051
Tel: (021) 6237 9072
Fax: (021) 6219 7600
ico@dhu.edu.cn
www.dhu.edu.cn/englsihnew/index.asp#

Carlton University-Donghua University
1882 Yan'an Xi Lu, Shanghai 200051
Tel: (021) 6237 9072
Fax: (021) 6219 7600
ico@dhu.edu.cn
www.dhu.edu.cn/englishnew/index.asp#

Cheung Kong Graduate School of Management
Building 2#, 2419 Hongqiao Lu, Shanghai 200335
Tel: (021) 6269 6238
Fax: (021) 62696255
ckedp@ckgsb.edu.cn
www.ckgsb.edu.cn

China Europe International Business School (CEIBS)
699 Hongfeng Lu, Pudong, Shanghai 201206
Tel: (021) 2890 5890
Fax: (021) 2890 5678
emba@ceibs.com
www.ceibs.com

City University of London-Shanghai University of Finance and Economics

Shanghai University of Finance and Economics, Shanghai 200233
Tel: (021) 6485 0531 ext. 1113
Fax: (021) 6485 8995
ChinaEmba@city.ac.uk
www.cass.city.ac.uk/china/index/html

Ecole de Management-Shanghai Jiaotong University
535 Fahuazhen Lu, Shanghai 200052
Tel: (021) 6293 2598
Fax: (021) 6293 2591
financeMBA@sjtu.edu.cn
www.financeMBA.net

Ecole Nationale des Ponts et Chausses-Tongji University
501 Yunchou Building,
1239 Siping Lu
Tel: (021) 6598 2011
Fax: (021) 6598 3540
tjsimba@sh163.net
www.simba-tongji.com

Maastricht School of Management-Shanghai Maritime University
1550 Pudong Dadao, Shanghai 200135
Tel: (021) 5885 5200
Fax: (021) 5885 4751
smumba@shmtu.edu.cn
www.msm.nl/programs/omba/intro.htm

Madonna University-Shanghai Institute of International Finance
5 Guiqing Lu, Shanghai 200070
Tel: (021) 6317 5758
Fax: (021) 6317 3080
shiifb@online.sh.cn
www.siif-edu.com

Norwegian School of Management-Fudan University
670 Guoshun Lu, Shanghai 200433
Tel: (021) 6511 0019
Fax: (021) 6564 8069
fdbi@fudan.edu.cn

www.fdms.fudan.edu.cn

Rutgers University-Dalian Technical University

4312 Nanzheng Building, 580 Nanjing Xi Lu, Shanghai 200041
Tel: (021) 6217 6067
Fax: (021) 6218 6823
emba_sh@rutgers.cn
www.rutgers.cn

Sloane School of Management at MIT-Fudan University

208, 670 Guoshun Lu, Shanghai 200433
Tel: (021) 6564 2564
Fax: (021) 6564 4528
imba@fudan.edu.cn
www.fdms.fudan.edu.cn

St. Joseph's University-Donghua University-China Pharmaceutical University

1882 Yan'an Xi Lu, Shanghai 200051
Tel: (021) 6237 9072
Fax: (021) 6219 7600
ico@dhu.edu.cn
www.dhu.edu.cn/englishnew/index. asp#

University of British Columbia-Shanghai Jiaotong University

535 Fahuazhen Lu, Shanghai 200052
Tel: (021) 6293 2604
Fax: (021) 6293 2734
imba@commerce.ubc.ca
www.commerce.ubc.ca/mba/imba

University of Canberra-East China University of Science & Technology

130 Meilong Lu, Shanghai 200237
Tel: (021) 6425 2634
Fax: (021) 6425 2314
mba@ecust.edu.cn
www.ecust.edu.cn/english/Introduction/overview.htm

University of Hamburg-Fudan University

707 Shidai Building 670 Guoshun Lu, Shanghai 200433
Tel: (021) 5566 4801
Fax: (021) 5566 4796
fd-uhh@fudan.edu.cn
www.fdms.fudan.edu.cn

University of Hong Kong-Fudan University

706 Lidasan Building, Shanghai 200433
Tel: (021) 6511 9023
Fax: (021) 6564 6975
shberc@fudan.edu.cn
www.fdms.fudan.edu.cn

University of Maryland Smith School of Business-University of International Business and Economics

550 Shanhai Centre, 1376 Nanjing Xi Lu, Shanghai 200040
Tel: (021) 6279 7657
Fax: (021) 6279 7636
mwang@rhsmith.umd.edu
www.rhsmith.umd.edu/emba

University of Southern California-Shanghai Jiaotong University

535 Fahuazhen Lu, Shanghai 200052
Tel: (021) 6293 2707
Fax: (021) 6293 2713
uscgemba@sjtu.edu.cn
www.asom.sjtu.edu.cn/gemba/index. htm

University of Strthclyde-Shanghai Jiaotong University

535 Fahuazhen Lu, Shanghai 200052
Tel: (021) 6293 2720
Fax: (021) 6282 5427
xwwang@sjtu.edu.cn
www.asom.sjtu.edu.cn

University of Texas at Arlington-Tongji University

216 Yunchou Building, 1239 Siping Lu, Shanghai 200092

Tel: (021) 6598 2396
Fax: (021) 6598 1476
embauta@embauta.com
www.embauta.com
Washington University-Fudan University
3/F, Lidasan Building, Shanghai 200043
Tel: (021) 6564 4263
Fax: (021) 6565 4103
olin-fudan@fudan.edu.com
www.fdms.fudan.edu.cn
Webster University-Shanghai University of Finance and Economics
369 Zhongshanbeiyi Lu, Shanghai 200083
Tel: (021) 6210 6843
Fax: (021) 6210 6843
rick@webster.com
www.websterchina.com
Tianjin
Tianjin University
203 Teaching Building 18, Tianjin University, 92 Weijin Lu, Tianjin 300072
Tel: (022) 2789 1423; 8740 2152
zyxwb@tju.edu.cn
www.tjumba.com
Nankai University
The MBA Centre, Nankai University, 94 Weijin Lu, Tianjin 300071
Tel: (022) 2350 1128; 2350 9396
Fax: (022) 2350 8269
nanhaimba@nankaimba.org
www.nankaimba.org
Tianjin University of Finance & Economics
104 Building B, New Campus MBA Education Centre, Tianjin University of Finance & Economics, 25 Zhujiang Dao, Tianjin 300222
Tel: (022) 2817 1151
Fax: (022) 2817 1151

mba@tjufe.edu.cn
mba.tjufe.edu.cn
Oklahoma City University-Tianjin University of Finance & Economics
104 Building B, New Campus, MBA Education Centre, Tianjin University of Finance & Economics, 25 Zhujiang Dao, Tianjin 300222
Tel: (022) 2817 1151
Fax: (022) 2817 1151
mba@tjufe.edu.cn
mba.tjufe.edu.cn
Hebei University of Technology
MBA Education Centre, 8 Dingziguyihao Lu, Tianjin 300130
Tel: (022) 2656 4102
Fax: (022) 6020 4102
mba@hebut.edu.cn
Chongqing
Chongqing University
Graduate Admission Office, Chongqing University, 174 Shapingbeizheng Jie, Chongqing 400030
Tel: (023) 6510 6914
Fax: (023) 6510 6383
ceba.cqu.edu.cn/jingjixueyuan/MBA/MBAjianjie.asp
Jilin
Jilin University
MBA Education Centre, 212 Management Building, School of Management, Jilin University, 142 Renmin Dajie, Changchun 130012
Tel: (0431) 5095 337; 5094 578
Fax: (0431) 5697 417
jlumba@163.net
gl.jlu.edu.cn/mba
Heilongjiang
Harbin Institute of Technology
MBA Education Centre, School of Management, Harbin Institute of Technology, 92 Xidazhi Jie, Harbin

DOING BUSINESS

150001
Tel: (0451) 8641 2748
mba@hit.edu.cn
som.hit.edu.cn
Harbin Engineering University
MBA Office, Economic and
Management College, Harbin
Engineering University, Nantong
Dajie (3/F Building 21, Harbin
Engineering University), Harbin
150001
Tel: (0451) 8251 9747; 8251 9943
Fax: (0451) 8251 9783
heumba@tom.com
218.7.43.16/sem/mba
Harbin University of Commerce
MBA Education Centre, Harbin
University of Commerce, 1 Xueyuan
Lu, Qianjin Development Zone,
Harbin 210096
Tel: (0451) 8486 5172: 8810 2531
210.46.112.36/mba/MBA.html
Zhejiang
Zhejiang University
MBA Education Centre, 303B
Management Building, Jingang

Campus, Zhejiang University,
Hangzhou 310058
Tel: (0571) 8820 6813: 8820 6812
xdchen@zhu.edu.cn
www.zjumba.org
Zhejiang Gongshang University
525 Administration Building1,
Zhejiang Gongshang University, 149
Jiaogong Lu, Hangzhou 310035
Tel: (0571) 8805 5297: 8807 1024
ext. 8367
mba@mail.hzic.edu.cn
mba.zjgsu.edu.cn
Zhejiang University of Technology
MBA Education Centre, C309
Ziliang Building, Zhejiang University
of Technology, Chaohui 6 Zone,
Hangzhou 310014
Tel: (0571) 8832 0780
MBA@zhut.edu.cn
www.zjut.edu.cn
Hubei
**Huazhong University of Science
and Technology**
MBA Education Centre, 513
Yifu Science and Technology

Building, School of management, Huazhong University of Science and Technology, Wuhan 430074
Tel: (027) 8754 1915: 8754 1806
mba@hust.edu.cn
www.hust.edu.cn/mba/mba.jsp

Wuhan University
MBA Education Centre, Wuhan University, 16 Luojiashan Lu, Wuchang 430072
Tel: (027) 6875 2891
Fax: (027) 6875 4791
mba@whu.edu.cn
www.whmba.com

Wuhan University of Technology
Management School, Mafangshan Dong Campus, Wuhan University of Technology, 205 Luoshi Lu, Wuchang 430070
Tel: (027) 8785 9039
Fax: (027) 8785 9304
202.114.88.130:8080/cm/mba/index.html

Zhongnan University of Economics and Law
MBA Education Centre, Zhongshan University of Economics and Law, 114 Wuluo Lu, Wuchang 430064
Tel: (027) 8804 7866
mba@znufe.edu.cn
mba.znufe.edu.cn

Hunan
Hunan University
MBA Office, Management School Hunan University, Yuelushan Lu, Changsha 410082
Tel: (0731) 8822 216
8822216@sina.com
www.hunu.edu.cn

Central South University
MBA Management Centre, School of Business, Central South University, Lushan Nan Lu, Changsha 410083

Tel: (0731) 8830 317; 8836 711
x-ygzx@csu.edu.cn
bs.csu.edu.cn/mba/index.asp

Guangdong
South China University of Technology
MBA Education Centre, School of Business and Administration, 216 Buiding 12, South China University of Technology, Wushan, Guangzhou 510640
Tel: (020) 8711 4095: 8711 0387
Fax: (020) 8711 4693
bmmba@scut.edu.cn
www.cnsba.com/mba/index.asp

Ji'nan University
MBA Education Admission Office, Literature College Building, Ji'nan University, 601 Huangpu Dadao Xi, Guangzhou 510632
Tel: (020) 8522 0049
omba@jnu.edu.cn
mba.jnu.edu.cn

Guangdong University of Technology
MBA Education Centre, Guangdong University of Technology, 729 Dongfeng Dong Lu, Guangzhou 510090
Tel: (020) 3762 6332
www.gdut.edu.cn

Sun Yat-Sen Unversity
Shansi Hall, School of Business, Sun Yat-Sen University, 135 Xingang Xi Lu, Guangzhou 510275
Tel: (020) 8411 3622; 8411 3623
Fax: (020) 8411 3626
mnmba@zsu.edu.cn
www.mbazd.com/English/lp,html

Guangxi
Guangxi University
MBA Education Office, Business School of Guangxi University, 100 Daxue Lu, Guangxi 530004

DOING BUSINESS

Tel: (0771) 3232 990
Fax: (0771) 3272 602
sxymba@gxu.edu.cn
www.gxumba.com
Fujian
Xiamen University
Jiageng Building 1, School of
Management Siming Nan Lu,
Xiamen 361005
Tel: (0592) 2188 509; 2187 056
sm2.xmu.edu.cn/mba/index.asp
Fuzhou University
324 Liberal Arts Building, School of
Management, 523 Gongye Lu
Tel: (0591) 8376 8207; 8789 3057
glxy.fzu.edu.cn/mba.html
Anhui
University of Science and Technology of China
MBA Centre, University of Science
and Technology of China, 121
Meiling Dadao, Hefei 230052
Tel: (0551) 3492 022
Fax: (0551) 3492 146
mba@ustc.edu.cn
mba.ustc.edu.cn
Hefei University of Technology

School of Management, Hefei
University of Technology, 193 Tunxi
Lu, Hefei 230009
Tel: (0551) 2904 981: 2904 987
Fax: (0551) 2904 985
chenxh216@vip.sina.com
www.hfutmba.com
Shaanxi
Xi'an Jiaotong University
MBA Education Centre, The School
of Management, Xi'an Jiaotong
University, 28 Xianning Xi Lu, Xi'an
710049
Tel: (029) 8266 9604
www.xjtu.edu.cn
Xi'an University of Technology
Graduate Admission Office, Xi'an
University of Technologym, Jinhua
Nan Lu, Shaanxi 710048
Tel: (029) 8323 5148
Fax: (029) 8323 5148
yjsb@xaut.edu.cn
www.xaut.edu.cn
Northwest University
MBA Education Centre School
of Economics and Management,
Northwest University, 1 Taibai Bei

Lu Xi'an 710069
Tel: (029) 8830 2374: 8303 502
Fax: (029) 8302 374
mba@nwu.edu.cn
www.nwu.edu.cn
Northwest Polytechnic University
MBA Centre, 201 School of
Management Building, Northwest
Polytechnic University, 127 Youyi Xi
Lu, Xi'an 710072
Tel: (029) 8849 3557
Fax: (029) 8849 4191
mba@nwpu.edu.cn
mba.nwpu.edu.cn
Sichuan
**University of Electronic Science
and Technology of China**
MBA Office, School of Management,
University of Electronic Science and
Technology of China, 4 Jianshe Bei
Lu Er Duan, Chengdu 610064
Tel: (028) 8320 7285
MBA@uestc.edu.cn
www.mba.uestc.edu.cn
Sichuan University
Business Administration College
Sichuan University, 29 Wangjiang
Lu, Chengdu 610064
Tel: (028) 8541 0216; 8541 1434
mbascu@163.com
www.scumba.org
**Sichuan Finance and Economics
Institute**
MBA Centre, 8/F Guanghua
Building, Guanghua Campus,
Sichuan Finance and Economics
Institute, Chengdu 610074
Tel: (028) 8735 3906
Fax: (028) 8735 2123
mba@swufe.edu.cn
*mba.swufe.edu.cn/2005new/board-
view.asp?type=MBA&board=project*
Southwest Jiaotong University

School of Economic and
Management, Southwest Jiaotong
University, 111Erhuan Lu Beiyiduan,
Chengdu 610031
Tel: (028) 8760 0822
Fax: (028) 8763 4343; 8760 0826
*glxy.swjtu.edu.cn/swjtuintranet/EisWeb-
site/Webinternet/mba/index.aspx*
Jiangxi
**Jiangxi University of Finance and
Economics**
MBA Education Centre, Jiangxi
University of Finance and
Economics, Shuanggang Lu,
Nanchang 330013
Tel: (0791) 3816 962
Fax: (0791) 3816 271
jcmba@jcmba.net
jcmba.jxufe.cn/Index.ASP
**New York Institute of Technology-
Jiangxi University of Finance and
Economics**
Jiaoqiao Campus, Jiangxi University
of Finance and Economics, Changbei
Lushan Zhong Dadao, Nanchang
330013
Tel: (0791) 3816 893: 3816 893
jufe_nyit@yahoo.com.cn
www.jcmba.net
Nanchang University
Graduate Student Institute
Nanchang University, 339 Bejing
Dong Lu, Nanchang 330029
Tel: (0791) 8304 514
Fax: (0791) 8320 289
www.nucmba.com
Gansu
Lanzhou University
School of Management, Lanzhou
University, 222 Tianshui Nan Lu,
Lanzhou 730000
Tel: (0931) 8912 450
ms.lzu.edu.cn/info/index.asp

Shandong
Shandong University
MBA Centre, Economic and
Management Building, East Campus,
Shandong University, 27 Shanda
Nan Lu, Ji'nan 250100
Tel: (0531) 8564 826
219.218.118.131/glxy/outline.
php?sortid=41
Shandong Economic University
Graduate School, Shandong
University, 4 Yanzishan Dong Lu,
Ji'nan 250014
Tel: (0531) 8852 5292; 8859 6201
www.sdie.edu.cn/yjsb/index.asp
Northumbria University-Ocean
University of China
School of International Education,
Yushan Campus, Ocean University
of China, 5 Yushan Lu, Qingdao
266003
Tel: (0532) 590 1060; 864 6617
Fax: (0532) 590 1708
sie@ouc.edu.cn
www.ouc.edu.cn/sie
Heibei
Yanshan university
412 Teaching Building 3, Yanshan
University, 438 Hebei Dajie, Western
Section, Qinhuangdao 066 004
Tel: (0335) 805 7077; 807 4999
Fax: (0335) 805 7077
www.ysu.edu.cn
Shanxi
Shanxi University of Finance &
Economics
Graduate Admission Office
North Campus, Shanxi University
of Finance & Economics, 339
Nanneihuan Jie, Taiyan 030012
Tel: (0351) 766 8044; 766 9924
www.mba.sx.cn
Shanxi University

MBA Education Centre, A 1/F, Dexiu
Gongyu, Shanxi University, 580
Wucheng Lu, Taiyuan 030006
Tel: (0351) 701 9951; 701 9952
Fax: (0351) 701 8644
mba@sxu.edu.cn
www.sxu.edu.cn/mba
Inner Mongolia
Inner Mongolia University-Hohhot
MBA Education Centre, 308 School
of Economics & Management, Inner
Mongolia University, 235 Daxue Xi
Lu, Hohhot 010021
Tel: (0471) 499 0702; 499 3529
imu-mba@imu-mba.org
www.imu-mba.org
Inner Mongolia University-Baotou
MBA Education Centre (Baotou),
211 Innovation Centre, 24 Gangtie
Dajie, Baotou 014030
Tel: (0472) 518 9211; 559 0211
imu-mba@imu-mba.org
www.imu-mba.org
Inner Mongolia polytechnic Uni-
versity
MBA Education Centre, 313 New
Teaching Building, Inner Mongolia
Polytechnic University, 221 Aimin
Jie, Hohhot 01062
Tel: (0471) 657 7191
Fax: (0471) 657 7494
mba@imut.edu.cn
mba.imut.edu.cn
Liaoning
Dongbei University of Fiannce &
Economics
MBA School, Dongbei University of
Finance & Economics, 217 Jianshan
Jie, Dalian 116025
Tel: (0411) 8471 0386
Fax: (0411) 8471 3094
info@mba-edu.net
www.mba-edu.net

Liaoning University
MBA Education Centre, 2/F, Foreign
Language Building, Liaoning
University, 66 Chongshan Zhong Lu,
Shenyang 110036
Tel: (024) 8686 4314
Fax: (024) 8685 6978
www.lnumba.com

Northeastern University
Graduate Admission Office,
Northeastern University, 11 Lane, 3
Wenhua Lu, Shenyang 110004
Tel: (024) 8368 7556: 2390 79820
Fax: (024) 2389 0920
www.neu.edu.cn

Jiangsu
Southeast University
Graduate Admission Office,
Southeast University, 2 Sipailou,
Nanjing 210096
Tel: (025) 8379 5481
www.seu.edu.cn

Nanjing University MBA Program
MBA Education Centre of Business
School, 1909 Yifu Building for
Management Science, Nanjing
University, 22 Hnakou Lu, Nanjing
210093
Tel: (025) 8359 2599
njumba@nju.edu.cn
www.mbanju.com

Nanjing University EMBA Program
EMBA Education Centre of Business
School, 1907 Yifu Building for
Management Science, Nanjing
University, 22 Hankou Lu, Nanjing
210093
Tel: (025) 8368 6117
Fax: (025) 8331 7769
emba@nju.edu.cn
www.embanju.org

University of Missouri-Nanjing
University IMBA Program
MBA Education Centre of Business
School, 1909 Yifu Building for
Management Science, Nanjing
University, 22 Hankou Lu, Nanjing
210093
Tel: (025) 8359 2599; 8359 2461;
8359 3339
njumba@nju.edu.cn
nubs.nju.edu.cn/mba/newnews.htm

DOING BUSINESS

Maastricht School of Management-Nanjing University
Sino-Dutch International Business Centre, 1603 Yifu Building for Management Science, Nanjing University, 22 Hankou Lu, Nanjing 210093
Tel: (025) 8359 2297; 8359 7001
Fax: (025) 8326 0037
sdibc@nju.edu.cn
www.sdibc.org

Cornell University-Nanjing University EMBA Program
1605 Yifu Building for Management Science, Nanjing University, 22 Hankou Lu, Nanjing 210093
Tel: (025) 8359 7244; 8359 7001
www.nimba.cn

China University of Mining & Technology
Graduate School, China University of Mining & Technology, Jiefang Nan Lu, Xuzhou 221008
Tel: (0516) 388 5834
Fax: (0516) 388 5549
Qchzh@cumt.edu.cn
www.cumt.edu.cn

Nanjing University of Science & Technology
MBA Education Centre
Nanjing University of Science & Technology, 200 Xiaolingwei, Nanjing 210094
Tel: (025) 8431 5555; 8431 5726
nustmba@vip.sina.com
www.njust.edu.cn/uni/college/jg/mba

Hohai University
MBA Education Centre, Hohai University, 1 Xikang Lu, Nanjing 210098
Tel: (025) 8378 7509
Fax: (025) 8373 3015
mba@hhu.edu.cn
mba.hhu.edu.cn

Amsterdam School of Business-Hohai University 1+1 MBA Program
MBA Education Centre, Hohai University, 1 Xikang Lu, Nanjing 210098
Tel: (025) 8378 7509; 8378 7820
Fax: (025) 8373 3015
mba@hhu.edu.cn
mba.hhu.edu.cn

Soochow University
Graduate Admission Office, Soochow University
1 Shizi Jie, Suzhou 215006
Tel: (0512) 6511 2816; 6511 2544
Fax: (0512) 6511 2816
www.suda.edu.cn/department/yxsz/mba/default.htm

Jiangsu University
MBA Education Centre
1417 Building 1, Jiangsu University, 301 Xuefu Lu, Zhenjiang 212013
Tel: (0511) 879 1486; 213 0538
Fax: (0511) 878 0186
www.ujs.edu.cn

Hainan

Hainan University
MBA Education Centre
3/F Building 1#, Hainan University, 58 Renmin Dadao, Haikou 570 228
Tel: (0898) 6627 9201
Fax: (0898) 6627 9309
mba@hainu.edu.cn
mba.hainu.edu.cn

Yunnan

Yunnan University
Graduate Admission Office, Yunnan University, 2 Cuihhu Bei Lu, Kunming 650091
Tel: (0871) 503 3837
www.ynmba.com.cn

Kunming University of Science &

Technology

MBA Office, 105 Building of Continuing Education, Kunming University of Science & Technology, 68 Wenchang Lu, Kunming 650093
Tel: (0871) 518 8528
Fax: (0871) 518 8578
glxymba@yahoo.com.cn
www.kmustmba.com.cn

Guizhou

Guizhou University

MBA Education Centre, 2/F, Comprehensive Building, Luohanying Campus, Guizhou University, 14 Luohanying Lu, Guiyang 550003
Tel: (0851) 595 5141
Fax: (0851) 597 3535
www.gzmba.com.cn

Henan

Zhengzhou University

MBA Education Centre, Zhengzhou University, 75 Daxue Bei Lu, Zhengzhou 450052
Tel: (0371) 6776 3101; 6776 3136
Fax: (0371) 6776 7232
www.mbazzu.com

Henan University of Finance &

Economics

MBA Education Centre, 915 Building 10, Henan University of Finance & Economics, 80 Wenhua Lu, Zhengzhou 450002
Tel: (0371) 6351 9153; 6351 9150
cy_mba@sina.com
www3.hnufe.edu.cn/jxky/mba

Xinjiang

Xinjiang Institute of Finance and Economics

The MBA Education Centre, 5313 Teaching Building 3, Xinjiang Institute of Finance and Economics, 15 Beijing Bei Lu, Urumqi 830012
Tel: (0991) 784 2075
Fax: (0991) 784 2071
mba@xjife.edu.cn
www.xjife.edu.cn

Ningxia

Ningxia University

School of Economics and Management, Ningxia University 21 Wencui Lu, Yinchuan 750021
Tel: (0951) 506 3988
Fax: (0951) 506 3008
ndmba@nxu.edu.cn
mba.nxu.edu.cn

Logistics

China's capability of moving things from factory floor to showroom store has improved dramatically over the years. For a detailed view of the industry, see the Logistics piece in the Industry Overviews section of this guide.

Logistics providers

Beijing

Kerry Logistics Network Limited
嘉里物流联网有限公司
1 Dongsihuan Lu, Chaoyang, (010) 8796 6688, *www.kerrylogistics.com*

Schenker 全球货运
5 Tianweisi Jie, Tianzhu Airport Industrial Area, (010) 8048 0049
www.schenker.com

Panalpina 泛亚班拿
3C Guomen Building, 1 Zuojiazhuang, (010) 6461 8866
www.Panalpina.com

DHL 敦豪
2 Jiuxianqiao Lu, (010) 6466 2211
www.dhl.com

ABX Logistics 亨利货运
206 Cencons Plaza Building, 3 Xiaoyun Li, (010) 6467 1551
www.abxlogistics.com

APL Logistics 美集物流
2305-2306 China Resource Building, 8 Jianguomen Dajie, (010) 5870 1095
www.apllogistics.com

Flash Asia
2611 The Spaces International Centre, 8 Dongdamuqiao Lu, (010) 5870 1095
www.flashasia.com

Maersk Logistics 马士基航运
255 BGS Cargo Building, (010) 6459 0773, www.maersk-logistics.com

OOCL 东方海外
1011 Tower W2, The Tower, Oriental Plaza, 1 Dong Chang'an Dajie, (010) 8518 3456, *www.oocl.com*

Senator Lines 胜利航运
2107 B China Resources Building, 8 Jianguomen Bei Dajie, (010) 8519 1596, *www.senatorlines.com*

TNT
9, 8th Avenue, Beijing Shunyi Airport Logistics Base, (010) 6947 7060
www.tnt.com

Shanghai

Kerry Logistics 嘉里物流
1008-1009 Shanghai Kerry Centre, 1515 Nanjing Xi Lu
(021) 6279 3738
www.kerrylogistics.com

Schenker 全球货运
13/F, CITIC Square, 1168 Nanjing Xi Lu, (021) 3222 4877
www.schenker.com

Panalpina 泛亚班拿
3/F, 618 Haitianyi Lu, Pudong, (021) 6105 1500, *www.panalpina.com*

DHL 敦豪
303 Ji'nian Lu, (021) 6536 8888
www.dhl.com

ABX Logistics 亨利货运
10/F, New Hualian Mansion, 775 Huaihai Zhong Lu
(021) 6415 6565
www.abxlogistics.com

APL Logistics 美集物流
5/F, Raffles City, 2668 Xizang Zhong Lu, (021) 2301 2800
www.apllogistics.com

Elee Logistics 铱力物流
7A Hongqiao Business Centre, 2272 Hongqiao Lu, (021) 6237 6247
www.eleechina.com

Maersk Logistics 马士基航运
5/F, Tian'an Centre, 338 Nanjing Xi

Lu, (021) 2306 2666
www.maersk-logistics.con
NYK Logistics 日邮集运服务
20/F, Raffles City, 268 Xizang Zhong
Lu, (021) 6340 4477
www.nyklogistics.com
OOCL 东方海外
21/F, OOCL Plaza, 841 Yan'an Zhong
Lu, (021) 2301 8888, *www.oocl.com*
Senator Lines 胜利航运
24/F, Huadu Mansion, 828
Zhangyang Lu, (021) 5081 8050
www.senatorlines.com
Shanghai Eastern Logistics
上海东方远航物流
66 Jichang Dadao, Pudong
International Airport, (021) 68854385
www.easternlogistics.cn
TNT
45/F, Raffles City, 268 Xizang Zhong
Lu, (021) 5352 4688, *www.tnt.com*
Guangzhou
Schenker 全球货运
20 D Gaosheng Building, 109 Tiyu Xi
Lu, (020) 3879 5989
www.schenker.com
Panalpina 泛亚班拿
2305-2309 Dongshan Plaza, 69
Xianlie Road Central, Dongshan,
(020) 8732 2132
www.panalpina.com
DHL 敦豪
Express Building, Jichang Bei Lu,
(020) 8666 3988, *www.dhl.com*
ABX Logistics 亨利货运
3001 North Tower, World Trade
Centre, 371-375 Huanshi Dong Lu,
(020) 8769 2380
www.abxlogistics.com
Maersk Logistics 马士基航运
2306-2307 Goldlion Digital Network
Centre, 136-138 Tiyu Dong Lu, (020)
3878 0388

Wwwmaersk-logistics.com
NYK Logistics 日邮集运服务
1710-1712 Goldlion Digital Network
Centre, 136-138 Tiyu Dong Lu
(020) 3878 0846
www.nyklogistics.com
OOCL 东方海外
1206 CITIC Plaza, 233 Tianhe Bei Lu,
(020) 8393 6033 , (020) 8393 6033
www.oocl.com
TNT
4/F, Jinquan Shanzhuang, 40
Dajinzhong Lu, (022) 8617 8168
www.tnt.com
Chengdu
APL Logistics 美集物流
1805C Time Plaza, 2 Zongfu Lu
(028) 8672 5090
www.apllogistics.com
P&O Nedlloyd 铁行渣华船务
20-D Sichuan International Building,
206 Shuncheng Dajie, (028) 8652
0532, *www.ponl.com*
**Exel-Sinotrans Freight Forwarding
Co., Ltd.**
金鹰国际货运代理有限公司
715 Bi-Pacific Plaza, 58 Kehua Bei Lu,
(028) 8523 1274, *www.exel.com*
Schenker 全球货运
13A-4 Chuanxin Mansion, 18 Section
2 Renmin Nan Lu, (028) 8619 9299
www.schenker.com
DDAO-DHL Danzas Air & Ocean
丹沙货运
15F First City Plaza, 308 Shuncheng
Dajie, (028) 8652 7328, *www.dhl.com*
Panalpina
泛亚班拿
719 Lidu Plaza, 8 Dakejia Xiang, (028)
8667 3108, www.panalpina.com
Maersk马士基物流
7P First City Plaza, 308 Shuncheng
Dajie, (028) 6770 6700

Kawasaki Kisen Kaisha, Ltd.
川崎汽船株式会社
2907-2908 Sichuan BOC Mansion, 35
Section 2 Renmin Zhong Lu, (028)
8640 2758
www.kline.co.jp
Dimerco Express
中菲行航空货运承揽股份有限公司
7O First City Plaza, 308 Shuncheng
Dajie, (028) 8293 1308
Qingdao
World Shipping Group
世航集团
B526 World Trade Center, 6
Xianggang Zhong Lu
(0532) 8591 0231
www.worldshippinggroup.com
Maersk 马士基航运
26/F Flagship Tower Cyber Port, 40
Xianggang Zhong Lu
(0532) 8388 5500, *www.maersk.com*
M+R Spedag Group 华隆瑞锋货运
1913-1914 Hisense Tower, 17
Donghai Xi Lu, (0532) 8386 2551,
www.mrspedag.com

Air Sea Worldwide Logistics Ltd.
港捷国际货运代理有限公司
B1501-1504 Futai Square, 18
Xianggang Zhong Lu, (0532) 8571
6501, *www.airseaworldwide.com*
Prime Cargo 航运佳国际货运
1116 Hisense Tower, 17 Donghai Xi
Lu, (0532) 8386 6555
www.primecargo.dk
Schenker 全球货运
2913-2914 Shandong International
Trade Mansion, 51 Taiping Lu,
(0532) 8297 1099
www.schenker.com
M+R Spedag Group 华隆瑞锋货运
1913-1914 Hisense Tower, 17
Donghai Xi Lu, (0532) 8386 2551
www.mrspedag.com
THI Group 台骅国际
4/F, Building 2, Pacific Plaza, 35
Donhai Lu, (0532) 8575 7000
www.thi-group.com
BAX Global 伯灵顿全球
716 Post Building, 220 Yan'an San Lu
(0532) 8386 1122

Atlantic Forwarding 瑞士理运
17E Jingguang Tower, Jindu Garden,
18 Donghai Lu, (0532) 8581 0888
www.atlanticforwarding.com

Weiss-Rohlig
伟士德诚运输有限公司
301 Huiquan Dynasty Hotel, 9
Nanhai Lu, (0532) 8287 1157, www.
weiss-rohlig.com

DHL 敦豪
715-717 Times Square, 52 Xianggang
Zhong Lu, (0532) 8571 8081
www.dhl.com

Hapag-Lloyd AG
赫伯罗特
B610 Fullhope Plaza, 12 Xianggang
Zhong Lu, (0532) 8502 6136
www.hlcl.com

Tianjin

M+R Spedag Group
华隆瑞锋货运
2704 Asia Pacific Tower, 35 Nanjing
Lu, (022) 2311 7766
www.mrspedag.com

World Shipping Group 世航集团
C608 Dadi Center, 26 Jieda Lu, Disan
Dajie, Tianjin Eco. & Tech. Dev.
Zone, (022) 6529 2018
www.worldshippinggroup.com

APL Logistics
美集物流
2010 Tianjin International Building,
75 Nanjing Lu, (022) 2330 2040
www.apllogistics.com

BAX Globa
伯灵顿全球
A311 Zhaotong Building, 3 Xiaoyuan
Lu, Diyi Dajie, Eco. & Tech. Dev.
Zone, (022) 2532 4145
www.baxglobal.com

ABX Logistics
亨利货运

906 The Exchange Office Tower, 189
Nanjing Lu, (022) 8319 1437
www.abxlogistics.com

DFDS Transport
得夫得斯国际货运
3809 Golden Emperor Building, 20
Nanjing Lu, (022) 2312 5888
www.dfdstransport.com

Schenker AG
全球货运
2203 Asia Pacific Tower, 35 Nanjing
Lu, (022) 2330 4026
www.schenker.com

Maersk Logistics
马士基物流
37-38/F The Exchange, 189 Nanjing
Lu, (022) 2332 0388
www.maersk.com

Wuhan

THI Group 台骅国际
1303, 69 Yanjiang Lu
(027) 8566 0761
www.thi-group.com

DHL 敦豪
3423 Wuhan World Trade Building,
686 Jiefang Dadao
(027) 5950 2608
www.dhl.com

Hanjin Shipping 韩进海运
502-2 Sinotrans Building, 611 Jianshe
Dadao, (027) 8363 1182
www.hanjin.com

Kerry EAS Logistics Co., Ltd.
嘉里大通物流有限公司
12A Tower A Wuhan International
Tower, Dandong Lu, Jiefang Dadao,
(027) 8542 2537, *www.kerryeas.com*

COSCO Logistics
中国远洋物流有限公司
8-9/F Ocean Building, T1 Hong Kong
Lu, (027) 6882 6888
www.cosco-logistics.com.cn

Maersk 马士基航运

2802 Wuhan China Merchants Bank
Tower, 518 Jianshe Dadao
(027) 8574 3309, *www.maersk.com*

**JHJ International Transportation
Co., Ltd.**
锦海捷亚国际货运有限公司
9A1 Truroll Plaza, Wusheng Lu, (027)
8551 0866, *www.jhj.com.cn*

APC Asia Pacific Cargo
北欧国际货运有限公司
2408 Jinghanmingdu, Sanyang Lu,
(027) 8274 1007, *www.apchk.com.hk*

Nanjing

ABX Logistics 亨利货运
2603 International Business Mansion,
50 Zhonghua Lu, (025) 5226 7802
www.abxlogistics.com

Hellmann Worldwide Logistics
汉宏货运
1002 SOHO Building, 8 Zhongshan
Nan Lu, (025) 8473 2020
www.hellmann.net

M+R Forwarding
华隆瑞锋国际货运
706 Sinotrans Jiangsu Mansion, 129
Zhonghua Lu, (025) 5237 7537
www.mrspedag.com

THI Group 台骅国际
2112, 99 Changjiang Lu
(025) 8479 8007
www.thi-group.com

Maersk Logistics 马士基物流
23/F Huijie Plaza, 268 Zhongshan Lu,
(025) 8479 8171, *www.maersk.com*

United Parcel Service – UPS
联合包裹运送服务有限公司
66 Xiang Ye Shu, Ning Li Lu
(025) 5264 7118
www.ups.com

APL Logistics 美集物流
11E Nanjing Investment Mansion,
414 Zhongshan Nan Lu
(025) 5238 9868
www.apllogistics.com

DOING BUSINESS

Other

Here are some lists of other service providers that can help your business in China succeed.

Professional service providers

Beijing

Staff Service
仕达富新桥人力资源有限公司
A1201 CITIC Building,
19 Jianguomenwai Dajie,
(010) 6527 0988
www.staffservice.com

Foreigner Employee Service
北京市外企服务集团
14 Chaoyangmen Nan Dajie
(010) 8561 8888
www.fesco.com.cn

CIIC 中国国际技术智利合作
25/F, West Wing, Hanwei Plaza, 7
Guanghua Lu, (010) 6561 3920

Beijing Employee Service Centre,
北京市人才服务中心
87 Andingmenwai Dajie
(010) 6440 1188

Shanghai

Staff Service
仕达富新桥人力资源有限公司
2608-09 Kerry Centre, 1515 Nanjing
Xi Lu, (021) 5298 6298
www.staffservice.com

Shanghai Foreign Service
上海市对外服务
28 Jinling Xi Lu
(021) 5456 4999
www.fesco.com

CIIC 中国国际技术智利合作
18/F, Jianhui Building, 922
Hengshan Lu, (021) 6407 2088
www.ciicsh.com

Shanghai Human Resources Service Centre 上海市人才服务中心
620 Zhongshan Xi Lu,
(021) 6233 7211
www.shrc.com.cn

Guangzhou

TUV NORD 汉德技术监督服务
1003 & 1005-2 West Tower Fortune
Plaza, 114 Tiyu Dong Lu
(020) 3891 1187
www.rwtuv.com

SSA Global Technologies, Inc.
系统软件联合全球科技公司
2218 Oriental Plaza, 69 Xianlie
Zhong Lu
(020) 8732 1693
www.ssaglobal.com

Chengdu

Excelpoint Technology Ltd.
世健科技有限公司
27L First City Plaza, 308 Shuncheng
Dajie, (028) 8652 7611
www.excelpoint.com

Qingdao

Aden Services
埃顿酒店服务有限公司
1406 Jinguan Mansion, 56 Hong
Kong Zhong Lu
(0532) 8578 4470
www.adenservices.com

Tianjin

Nalco Company
纳尔科工业服务有限公司
1401 Ocean Tower
(022) 2420 7235
www.nalco.com

Translation firms

Beijing

Global Bridge Translation
环球友联翻译
2182 Sancaitang Building, Tsinghua
Yuan, (010) 8261 2028

www.amtranslation.com

Herald Translation 先驱翻译
2007 Beijing Silver Tower, 2
Dongsanhuan Bei Lu
(010) 6410 7126, *www.herald-ts.com*

WordHouse Localisation
荷兰好字翻译
1002A Gateway Building, 10 Yabao
Lu, (010) 8562 5684
www.wordhouse.nl

Shanghai

SinoMedia Translation Services
中媒翻译服务
12-J, Golden Bell Plaza, 98 Huaihai
Zhong Lu, (021) 5385 8956
www.sinomedia.net

Guangzhou

Langpro Translation 联普翻译
2602-2702, Block A, Hengcheng
Building, 55 Huangpu Lu, (020)
8558 7966, *www.langpro.com.cn*

Web design firms

Base Creative
www.basecreative.com
Shanghai
8 Lane 37, Fuxing Xi Lu
(021) 5117 6318
Hong Kong
2207-2209, Tower 2 Lippo Centre,
Admiralty
(852) 2530 8164

Intermusca
www.Intermusca.com
Shanghai
601, 68 Changping Lu
(021) 6299 4415

Invisible Creative
www.invisible.cn
Shanghai
503 Building 3, Lane 210,
Taikang Lu
(021) 6467 1160

Destinations

Anhui	238
Beijing	245
Chongqing	276
Fujian	283
Gansu	294
Guangdong	300
Guangxi	340
Guizhou	349
Hainan	354
Hebei	367
Heilongjiang	373
Henan	381
Hubei	389
Hunan	396
Inner Mongolia	402
Jiangsu	407
Jiangxi	424
Jilin	429
Liaoning	436
Ningxia	448
Qinghai	451
Shaanxi	454
Shandong	461
Shanghai	472
Shanxi	497
Sichuan	502
Tianjin	510
Tibet	518
Xinjiang	522
Yunnan	526
Zhejiang	535
Hong Kong	552
Macau	560

Anhui

Population: 61.2 million
Area: 139,000 sq km
Capital: Hefei
Airports: Hefei, Wuhu, Anqing, Huangshan, Fuyang, Bengbu
Ports: Wuhu, Tongling

Anhui Province is part of the eastern China region along with Zhejiang, Jiangsu, and Shanghai. But it does not enjoy the coastlines of its neighbors and is considerably poorer. Its population of about 61 million is still largely agrarian, and many of its people serve as migrant labor in construction and other service sectors in neighboring provinces and Shanghai.

The area known today as Anhui province was the first region of southern China to be settled by the Han Chinese. In the third century BC, the original Han settlers left the unpredictable Yellow River floodplain to the north for the equally fertile but equally unpredictable areas along the Huai River and the Yangtze. In the last 1,000 years, Chinese historians estimate that Anhui has experienced more than 8,600 natural disasters such as floods, drought and insect plagues. To try to ameliorate this problem, many public works projects have been built to try to control flood waters and limit damage.

Anhui is primarily an agricultural region. The province is a major producer of rice, corn, wheat, beans, sweet potatoes and sorghum, along with cash crops such as tea, silk, cotton, peanuts, sesame, rapeseed, tobacco and hemp. But recently, Anhui has seen a growth in manufacturing, particularly in household appliances like washing machines and refrigerators, attracting foreign manufacturers such as Bosch-Siemens. Many important

Anhui Economic Data			
	2005	2004	Change%
GDP (RMB bn)	537.5	475.9	12.9
GDP per capita (RMB)	8,675	7,768	11.7
Exports (US$ bn)	5.18	3.94	31.47
Imports (US$ bn)	3.93	3.28	19.82
Cars per 100 households	0.76	0.53	43.39
PCs per 100 households	25.97	19.31	34.49

domestic manufacturers also have production facilities in Anhui including Hefei-based Meiling, the second-largest refrigerator producer in China.

Anhui also has rich mineral resources, particularly copper in and around the city of Tongling. The province's largest employer is Ma'anshan Iron and Steel, located in Ma'anshan city near the border with Jiangsu province. The province has abundant non-metallic minerals including dolomite, calcite and limestone.

Industrial development in Anhui has been strong and steady for the past two decades, with industrial output growth typically averaging around 12%. The majority of businesses to emerge from this development have been small or medium-sized enterprises, leaving much room for consolidation. Provincial officials aim to focus on Anhui's mineral wealth to drive development.

A result of the rapid industrialization, however, has been a marked increase in air and water pollution. To combat this, the local government has taken steps to upgrade water treatment facilities to try to clean up local waterways.

Hefei 合肥

Telephone prefix: 0551
Population: 4.63 million
Bank of China: Changjiang Zhong Lu

Hefei, like a few other provincial capitals, was little more than a small town when the Communist Party took control of China in 1949, a trading center for commodities grown in the surrounding countryside.

Historically, Hefei endured frequent periods of turmoil, particularly from the fourth to 11th centuries AD. Situated at a mountain pass that separated kingdoms in Anhui's northern and southern regions, the city was frequently fought over and changed sides numerous times at great cost to its residents.

Today, Hefei is a key research and development base. Its academic strengths are an asset for the city that has attracted many major brands such as Haier to establish a presence in the city.

Anhui University in Hefei is one of China's eight "key universities" and the city is also home to China Science and Technology University.

DESTINATIONS

Of course, the city's attractions also include some of the lowest wages in eastern China. Retaining talented staff is not easy because of the proximity of Shanghai and the other booming cities of the Yangtze River Delta region.

The city's main economic zone, the Hefei Economic and Technology Development Zone, is situated 8 km north of the city center.

Hefei Economic Data	
GDP 2005 (RMB bn)	85.36
Disposable income 2005 (RMB)	9,684

Hotels

Grand Hotel Overseas Traders Club
★ ★ ★ ★ ★
669 V-1, Changjiang Xi Lu
(0551) 222 9888
Standard room: RMB718
Credit Cards:
Visa, Master Card, JCB, American Express

Holiday Inn Hefei
★ ★ ★ ★ ★
1104 Changjiang Dong Lu

(0551) 220 6666
Standard room:
RMB760 +15% Surcharge
Credit Cards:
Visa, Master Card, JCB, American Express, Domestic Cards

Sofitel Grand Park Hefei
★ ★ ★ ★ ★
Mingzhu Square, Fanhua Jie
(0551) 221 6688
Standard room: RMB546
Credit Cards:
Visa, Master Card, JCB, American Express, Domestic Cards

Anhui Hotel
★ ★ ★ ★
18 Meishan Lu, (0551) 221 8888
Standard room: RMB268
Credit Cards: Visa, Master Card, JCB, American Express, Domestic Cards

Dongyi Hotel
★ ★ ★ ★
169 Funan Lu
(0551) 220 9988
Standard room: RMB358
Credit Cards:
Visa, Master Card, JCB, American Express, Domestic Cards

International Peace Hotel
★★★★
383 Meiling Avenue, (0551) 228 2288
Standard room: RMB660
Credit Cards:
Visa, Master Card, JCB, American
Express, Domestic Cards

Novotel Hefei
★★★★
199 Wuhu Lu, (0551) 228 6688
www.novotel.com/asia
Standard room: RMB429
Credit Cards:
Visa, Master Card, JCB, American
Express, Domestic Cards

Orient Hotel
★★★★
241 Anqing Lu
(0551) 221 1888
www.orienthotel.com.cn
Credit Cards:
Visa, Master Card, JCB, American
Express, Domestic Cards

Swiss-Belhotel Hualun
★★★★
279 Changjiang Zhong Lu
(0551) 228 8688
Standard room: RMB398
Credit Cards:
Visa, Master Card, JCB, American
Express

Angang Hotel
★★★
273 Wuhu Lu
(0551) 228 8999
www.aghotel.com
Standard room: RMB271
Credit Cards: Domestic Cards

Anhui Foreign Economic Hotel
★★★
28 Dongliu Lu, (0551) 349 2588
www.afecc.com
Credit Cards:

Visa, Master Card, Domestic Cards
New Century Hotel
★★★
111 Lujiang Lu, (0551) 228 0114
www.xsjhotel.com
Standard room: RMB200
Credit Cards:
Visa, Master Card, Domestic Cards

Restaurants

Indian
Indian Kitchen 印度小厨
1104 Changjiang Dong Lu
(0551) 220 6666

Barbeque
Brazilian Barbecue 巴西烧烤
Mingzhu Square,
(Sofitel Grand Park Hefei)
(0551) 221 6688

Western
Latin Bistro 必思特烧烤
199 Wuhu Lu (Novotel Hefei)
(0551) 228 6688

Chinese
**Shenji Zhuangyuanlou Restaurant
沈记状元楼大酒店**
168 Funan Lu, (0551) 283 7118

Anhui
Sui Yuan Ju 遂缘居
440 Huaihe Lu, (0551) 262 9286

Hotpot
Tanyutou Hotpot 谭鱼头火锅
127 Tongcheng Lu
(0551) 261 3558

Bars & Clubs

American Pie 美国派
246 Jinzhai Lu, (0551) 281 9911
Madison Bar 廊桥酒吧
456 Meiling Dadao
Moonlight Bar 月光酒吧
2/F, 355 Changjiang Zhong Lu
(0551) 2828 399

DESTINATIONS

Hospitals

Anhui Provincial Hospital
安徽省立医院
17 Lujiang Lu, (0551) 228 3114
Hefei No.105 Hospital
合肥105医院
424 Changjiang Xi Lu
(0551) 514 1123
Hefei Youhao Hospital
合肥友好医院
155 Meilin Dadao, (0551) 466 6688

Industrial parks

Hefei Economic and Technological Development Area
合肥经济技术开发区
(0551) 381 1107
www.hetda.com
Major Industries:
Electronics, equipment manufacturing, chemical engineering and food
Hefei New and High Technology Industrial Development Zone
合肥高新技术产业开发区
(0551) 532 5888
www.hefei-stip.gov.cn
Major Industries:
Bioengineering, information technology, optical-mechanical-electronic integration technology and real estate

Wuhu 芜湖
Telephone prefix: 0553
Population: 2.23 million
Bank of China: 258 Jiahuashan Lu

Wuhu is a port city located on the Yangtze River. Its principle industries include textiles, paper, motor vehicles, and machinery. Certainly not a popular tourist destination, Wuhu is perhaps best known as the location of the Chery Car factory, one of the bright lights of China's domestic auto industry.

Hotels

Conch International Hotel
★ ★ ★ ★
209 Beijing Dong Lu
(0553) 311 8188
Credit Cards:
Visa, Master Card, JCB, American Express
Tieshan Hotel
★ ★ ★ ★
3 Gengxing Lu
(0553) 371 8888
www.ts-hotel.com
Standard room: RMB588
Credit Cards: Visa, American Express

Restaurants

Italian

Jack's Place
杰克地方
3/F, Xinbai Shopping Center,
1 Zhongshan Lu,
(0553) 388 2260

Chinese

Gengfu Xing 耿福兴
10 Fenghuang Meishi Jie
(0553) 384 5577

Siji Chun 四季春
1 Fenghuang Meishi Jie
(0553) 387 9788

American

Carcassonne
卡尔卡松西餐厅
34 Chunan Lu
(0553) 381 1116

Bars & Clubs

Italian

New City
新城俱乐部
3/F, Xinbai Shopping Center,
1 Zhongshan Lu
(0553) 388 2260

Hospitals

Wuhu No.1 People's Hospital
芜湖市第一人民医院
65 Shizishan Lu
(0553) 381 9999

Industrial parks

**Wuhu Economic & Technological
Development Area**
芜湖经济技术开发区
219, Yinhu Beilu
(0553) 584 1876

Major Industries:
Automobiles, auto parts, electronics,
electrical appliances, new construction materials

Anqing 安庆

Telephone prefix: 0556
Population: 6.11 million
Bank of China: 1 Anqing Kaifaqu

Anqing is located on the north bank of the Yangtze River at a point where the river narrows, thus creating an easy crossing point. It is a commercial center for the local tea industry as well as having facilities specializing in oil refining and petroleum processing.

Hotels

Anqing Hotel
★★★★
1 Huxin Bei Lu, (0556) 539 9000
Standard room: RMB270
Credit Cards:
Master Card, JCB, American Express

Quanli Gujing International Hotel
★★★★
Muyanghepan, Tianzhushan Resort
(0556) 814 5666, *www.qlgjhotel.com*
Credit Cards: Domestic Cards

Restaurants

Western

California Sunshine Cafe
加州阳光西餐厅
657 Renmin Lu, (0556) 551 9912

Chinese

Tai Wan Lu Gang Xiao Zhen
台湾陆港小镇
239 Xiaosu Lu, (0556) 556 5777

Hospitals

**Anqing Hospital of Traditional
Chinese Medicine 安庆市中医医院**
26 Longmenkou Jie, (0556) 551 0566

Anqing Municipal Hospital
安庆市立医院
178 Renmin Lu, (0556) 554 2664

Huangshan 黄山
Telephone prefix: 0559
Population: 1.6 million

Yellow Mountain is one of China's four sacred peaks and a major tourist area. An overnight train ride from Shanghai, it is a must-see destination and will provide you with useful conversation material in your business dinners with Chinese clients and partners.

Hotels

Huangshan Pine & Country Club
★★★★★
78 Longjing, Jichang Dajie, Tunxi
(0559) 256 8000
www.chinahsgolf.com
Standard room: RMB780
Credit Cards: Visa, Master Card, JCB, AmericanExpress
Huangshan Guomai Hotel
★★★★
25 Qianyuan Nan Lu
(0559) 235 1188

www.hsgmhotl.com
Standard room: RMB320
Credit Cards: Visa, Master Card, American Express, Domestic Cards
Huangshan Hongta Hotel
★★★★
East Huangkou Bridge, Tunxi
(0559) 232 6666
Standard room: RMB320
Credit Cards:
Visa, Master Card, JCB, American Express
Huangshan International Hotel
★★★★
31 Xiaohuashan Lu, Tunxi
(0559) 256 5678
www.huangshaninterhotel.com
Credit Cards: Visa, Master Card, JCB, American Express, Domestic Cards
Huangshan Xinyuan International Hotel
★★★★
32 Jilingshan Lu, Tunxi
(0559) 257 2588
Credit Cards: Visa, Master Card, JCB, American Express

Beijing

Population: 15.38 million
Area: 139, 000 sq km
Airport: Beijing Capital

Beijing is a municipality with province-level status, under the direct control of the central government. It is China's second-largest city after Shanghai and is a major transportation hub, with dozens of railways, roads and expressways radiating across the country. The city spreads out in bands of concentric ring roads with Tiananmen Square in the center.

For much of its history, the city has been the destination of officials and diplomats from far and wide coming to pay homage to the emperor, and today it still receives a steady stream of state leaders and CEOs from around the globe. While Shanghai is the commercial capital and the place to base business operations, Beijing is where top management must go to be near and possibly influence the real powerbrokers.

The ancient city is also the cultural capital of China, boasting such wonders as the Forbidden City, the Summer Palace, the Temple of Heaven and, not too far away, the Great Wall. While these priceless cultural relics are protected, many culturally and historically significant parts of the city are not and the Olympic-fuelled construction boom of the last few years has demolished huge swathes of the city's ancient architecture, replacing it with shopping malls and highways. Thanks to haphazard urban planning and a booming economy that allows many former cyclists to afford cars, the new roads are clogged with grid-locked traffic at virtually all times of the day.

Beijing Economic Data			
	2005	2004	Change%
GGDP (RMB bn)	688.6	606.0	13.6
GDP per capita (RMB)	45,444	37,058	22.6
Exports (US$ bn)	30.87	20.58	50.00
Imports (US$ bn)	94.64	74.09	27.74
Cars per 100 households	14.06	12.64	11.23
PCs per 100 households	89.16	79.44	12.24

Ancient wonders

Recorded human settlement in the vicinity of today's Beijing goes back more than 5,000 years and the fossil remains of prehistoric Peking Man found in the early 20th century show that humans have been in the area much longer. The city's location on central China's Great Northern Plain was a geographic and political intersection between the farming populations of the Han Chinese to the south and west and the nomadic tribal groups of Mongolia and Manchuria to the north.

The nucleus of the present city was constructed between 1260 and 1290 and was the Mongol emperor Kublai Khan's capital.

The city first assumed the name Beijing, which means 'northern capital', when it was made the capital of the Ming dynasty in 1421. From 1644 it was the capital of the Manchurian Qing dynasty until the revolution in 1911 when the last emperor, the child Puyi, was deposed and the republic formed.

In 1860, during the second Opium war, an Anglo-French force stormed Beijing, burnt down the old Summer Palace on the city's outskirts and forced the Qing government to allow foreigners, including diplomats, to reside in the city. This was seen as a terrible loss of face amongst ordinary Chinese and was one of the factors behind the anti-foreign Boxer Rebellion of 1900. During the uprising, which was actively encouraged by the Qing government, the foreign legation quarter was besieged for seven weeks until relieved by a combined force of European, US and Japanese troops.

After the collapse of the Qing dynasty in 1911, the city fell under the rule of various warlords, and national political power shifted between Beijing, Guangzhou and Hankou. On May 4, 1919, three thousand students gathered in

Tiananmen Square to protest the terms of the Versailles Treaty, which granted former German concessions in China to Japan. What became known as the 'May 4 Movement' had an impact on the growth of the Chinese Communist Party, founded in Shanghai in 1921.

In 1928, Nationalist leader Chiang Kai-shek moved the capital to Nanjing and renamed Beijing as Beiping, or 'northern peace'. Following the Marco Polo Bridge incident in 1937, the Japanese army took control of the city and made it the capital of a puppet state.

At the end of World War II, the city was restored to Chinese rule under the Nationalists. In January 1949, the Communists under Mao Zedong entered the city without a fight and on October 1, 1949, before cheering crowds, Mao mounted the platform above the Tiananmen Gate in the city now renamed Beijing and declared the founding of the People's Republic. Since then, the city has been the undisputed center of power, directing the economy and society across the entire country.

Leading the reform era

In the past half century, Beijing has become an industrial center, containing a vast complex of textile mills, iron and steel works, chemical plants and factories manufacturing heavy machinery, plastics and electronic goods. It also has a sizeable petrochemical industry.

More recently however, heavy industrial development has been in decline and today the economy looks to automobile and parts manufacturing, high tech and IT production, real estate and service industries as the main drivers of growth. With the Olympics just around the corner, the central government has been increasing pressure on highly polluting factories to move out of the city to improve air quality. As heavy industry moves out, global hi-tech firms are moving in to set up research and

BEIJING

BEIJING FACTS 北京实情

- Population: 11 million 人口：1100万
- Age: Created in 1045BC 公元前1045年建立
- Altitude: 43 meters above sea level 海拔43米
- Highest Structure: CCTV Tower (405m) 最高建筑：中央电视塔(405m)
- Most Famous Tourist: Marco Polo (1275) 最著名的旅游家：马可·波罗
- Climate: Dry cold winters, hot wet summers 气候：冬季干冷，夏季湿热
- Oldest Structure: Tianning Temple Pagoda (built 1119) 最古老的建筑：天宁寺
- China Capital: 1272-1368; 1406-1928, 1949-present 中国的首都：1272-1368，1406-1928，1949-今
- Latitude: 40 degrees North (level with Philadelphia & Madrid) 北纬40度（与费城和马德里同一纬度）
- Previous Names: Ji, Yanjing, Zhongdu, Dadu(Khanbaliq), Beiping 曾用名：蓟、燕京、中都、大都(汗八里)、北平

Discover other cities in 3D go to redBANG.com

Order customized city guides in any format and any price range +8610 8580 3165 redBANG.com

redBANG
NEVER EVER LO

development facilities. Multinationals with a high profile in the Beijing area include Siemens, Motorola and Microsoft.

According to official statistics, overall economic growth in Beijing has been steady at an annual rate of about 10% in recent years, but in 2005, the city's GDP increased by an incredible 13.6% (compared with national growth of 10.2%).

Beijing residents are catching up to their Shanghai compatriots, and still earn considerably more than the national average. In 2005, the average annual income in Beijing was about RMB34,191 (US$4,273), up 15.2% from the previous year. While income for all groups has been growing, pay for higher wage jobs has been rising at a faster rate than low level jobs. The result has been an ever widening gap between the richest and poorest in the city.

The population of Beijing in 2005 reached 15.38 million, of which nearly 13 million are considered "urban". Not present in the official tally is the floating population of migrant workers who have come to the city looking for employment but do not have legal residence in Beijing. These people provide the bulk of manual labor fueling the construction boom and often work in substandard conditions for low pay.

An increase in real estate investment coupled with the population explosion and Olympic infrastructure upgrades have transformed the

city into a continuous construction zone. The results, though, are starting to be seen. Large areas of the city are starting to resemble the plans residents have been seeing for the better part of a decade. On the other hand, one area of construction that seems will never be completed is the transportation infrastructure. A high speed rail link between Beijing and Tianjin was started in 2005, and several subway lines are under construction to be completed in time for the Olympics.

The real star (some might say villain) of the transportation network, however, is Beijing's ever-expanding highway system. Concentric ring roads are being built farther and farther away from the city center as fast as Beijingers are buying cars, and six north-south highways linking the ring roads were recently proposed to help deal with the 5 million cars expected on the city's roads by 2020.

To try to cope with its growing problem of sprawl, Beijing is trying to center populations in the outlying areas into satellite cities. The goal is for these cities to be self-sufficient in many aspects, and also serve as mass transit hubs.

Beijing has a lot riding on the Olympic Games. They will serve as a forum both to showcase Beijing as a modern and international city as well as formally introduce the world to a China that is part of the interconnected global community. Most Beijingers are optimistic and confident that the Olympic Games will be a great source of pride for their city and the country as a whole.

Beijing Economic Data	
Disposable income 2005 (RMB)	17,653

Hotels

Hilton Beijing
★★★★★
1 Dongfang Lu, Dongsanhuanbei Lu, Chaoyang
(010) 5865 5000
www.hilton.com
Credit Cards: Visa, Master Card, JCB, American Express

Beijing Asia Hotel
★★★★★
8 Xinzhong Jie West, Gongti Lu North, Chaoyang
(010) 6500 7788
www.bj-asiahotel.com.cn
Standard room:
RMB980 +15% Surcharge
Credit Cards:
Visa, Master Card, JCB, American Express, Domestic Cards

Beijing Canal Family Club & Resort
★★★★★
6 Binhe Lu, Rulin, Tongzhou
(010) 6424 4789
Credit Cards:
Visa, Master Card, JCB, American Express, Domestic Cards

Beijing Hotel
★★★★★
33 Dongchang'an Jie, Dongcheng
(010) 6513 7766
www.chinabeijinghotel.com.cn
Standard room: RMB1,380
Credit Cards:
Visa, Master Card, JCB, American Express, Domestic Cards

Beijing Huandao Boya Hotel
★★★★★
2 Xi Jie, Wanshou Lu, Haidian
(010) 8827 1188
Standard room:
RMB698 +15% Surcharge
Credit Cards:

Visa, Master Card, JCB, American Express, Domestic Cards
Beijing International Hotel
★★★★★
9 Jianguomennei Dajie, Dongcheng
(010) 6512 6688
www.bih.com.cn
Standard room: RMB588
Credit Cards:
Visa, Master Card, JCB, American Express, Domestic Cards

Beijing Marriott Hotel West
★★★★★
98 Xisanhuanbei Lu, Haidian
(010) 6872 6699
Standard room: RMB2,498
Credit Cards:
Visa, Master Card, JCB, American Express, Domestic Cards

Beijing News Plaza Hotel
★★★★★
26 Jianguomennei Dajie, Dongcheng
(010) 6521 1188
www.newsplaza.net
Standard room: RMB1,596
Credit Cards: Visa, Master Card, JCB, American Express

Beijing Shihao International Hotel
★★★★★
25 Gulou Dajie, Miyun County
(010) 6908 6666
www.shihaohotel.com
Standard room: RMB980
Credit Cards:
Visa, Master Card, JCB, American Express, Domestic Cards

Beijing Xinyuan Hotel
★★★★★
6 Shifangyuan, Haidian
(010) 6390 1166
www.telehotels.net.cn
Standard room: RMB618
Credit Cards:

Visa, Master Card, JCB, American Express, Domestic Cards

BTG Fragrant Hill Hotel
★ ★ ★ ★ ★
Fragrant Hill Park, Haidian
(010) 6259 1166
www.xsfd.com
Standard room: RMB800
Credit Cards: Visa, Master Card, JCB, American Express

China World Hotel
★ ★ ★ ★ ★
1 Jianguomenwai Dajie, Chaoyang
(010) 6505 2266
Standard room: RMB3,200
Credit Cards: Visa, Master Card, JCB, American Express

Crowne Plaza Hotel Beijing
★ ★ ★ ★ ★
48 Wangfujing Dajie, Dongcheng
(010) 6513 3388
www.crowneplaza.com
Standard room: RMB3,500
Credit Cards: Visa, Master Card, JCB, American Express

Crowne Plaza Park View Wuzhou Beijing
★ ★ ★ ★ ★

8 Beisihuanzhong Lu, Chaoyang
(010) 8498 2288
www.ichotelsgroup.com
Standard room:
RMB3,200 +15% Surcharge
Credit Cards: Visa, Master Card, JCB, American Express

Days Inn China
★ ★ ★ ★ ★
4/F Days Hotel & Suites Beijing, 27 Huaweili, Chaoyang
(010) 8778 9686
Standard room: RMB2,080
Credit Cards:
Visa, Master Card, JCB, American Express, Diners Club, CUP Card, Domestic Cards

Grand Hotel Beijing
★ ★ ★ ★ ★
35 Dongchang'an Jie, Dongcheng
(010) 6513 7788
Standard room:
RMB2,310 +10% Surcharge
Credit Cards: Visa, Master Card, JCB, American Express

Grand Hyatt Beijing
★ ★ ★ ★ ★

Oriental Plaza, 1 Dongchang'an Jie,
Dongcheng, (010) 8518 1234
www.hyatt.com
Credit Cards:
Visa, Master Card, JCB, American
Express, Domestic Cards
Hotel Kunlun
★★★★★
2 Xinyuan Lu South, Chaoyang
(010) 6590 3388
www.hotelkunlun.com
Standard room: RMB1,620
Credit Cards: Visa, Master Card,
JCB, American Express
**InterContinental Financial Jie
Beijing**
★★★★★
11 Jinrong Jie, Xicheng
(010) 5852 5888
Standard room:
RMB1,095 +15% Surcharge
Credit Cards: Visa, Master Card,
JCB, American Express
Jade Palace Hotel
★★★★★
76 Zhichun Lu, Haidian
(010) 6262 8888
www.jadepalace.com.cn
Standard room: RMB498
Credit Cards:
Visa, Master Card, JCB, American
Express, Domestic Cards
Jing Guang New World Hotel
★★★★★
Hujialou, Chaoyang
(010) 6597 8888
www.jingguangcentre.com
Standard room: RMB650
Credit Cards:
Visa, Master Card, JCB, American
Express, Domestic Cards
Jinqiao Apartment Hotel
★★★★★

55 Guangqumenbeili, Chongwen
(010) 6713 7788
www.jinqiaoapartmenthotel.cn
Standard room: RMB980
Credit Cards: Visa, Master Card,
JCB, American Express
**Kempinski Hotel Beijing
Lufthansa Center**
★★★★★
50 Liangmaqiao Lu, Chaoyang
(010) 6465 3388
Standard room: RMB2,750
Credit Cards: Visa, Master Card,
JCB, American Express
**King Wing Hot Spring Interna-
tional Hotel**
★★★★★
17 Dongsanhuannan Lu, Chaoyang
(010) 6766 8866
www.kingwing.com.cn
Standard room: RMB598
Credit Cards:
Visa, Master Card, JCB, American
Express, Domestic Cards
Loong Palace Hotel & Resort
★★★★★
Longcheng Garden, Huilongguan,
Changping
(010) 8079 9988
www.loongpalacehotel.com
Credit Cards: Visa, Master Card,
JCB, American Express, Domestic
Cards, Diners Club
Luxury Serviced Residence Beijing
★★★★★
17 Jianhua Nan Lu, Chaoyang
(010) 6566 2200
Credit Cards:
Visa, Master Card, JCB, American
Express, Domestic Cards
New Otani Chang Fu Gong Hotel
★★★★★
26 Jianguomenwai Dajie, Chaoyang

(010) 6512 5555
Standard room: RMB3,600-3,890
Novotel Beijing West
★★★★★
36 Haidian Nan Lu, Haidian
(010) 6258 9999
www.novotel.com/asia
Credit Cards:
Visa, Master Card, JCB, American
Express, Domestic Cards
Novotel Oasis Beijing
★★★★★
8 Yanshun Lu, East Yanjiao Eco. &
Tech. Dev. Zone
(010) 6159 2299
Standard room:
RMB1,052 (superior suite)
Credit Cards: Visa, Master Card,
JCB, American Express
Plaza Royal Hotel Beijing
★★★★★
23 Xidawang Lu, Chaoyang
(010) 5879 6666
Standard room: RMB688
Credit Cards: Visa, Master Card,
JCB, American Express

Presidential Plaza Hotel Beijng
★★★★★
A9 Fuchengmenwai Dajie, Xicheng
(010) 5858 5588
www.presidentialplaza.com
Standard room: RMB2,025
Credit Cards:
Visa, Master Card, JCB, American
Express
Prime Hotel
★★★★★
2 Wangfujing Dajie, Dongcheng
(010) 5816 9999
www.primehotel.cn
Standard room: RMB598
Credit Cards: Visa, Master Card, JCB,
American Express, Domestic Cards
Purple Jade Laguna Resort
★★★★★
1 Ziyu Dong Lu, Chaoyang
(010) 6491 7488
www.purplejade.com.cn
Standard room: RMB1,380
Credit Cards:
Visa, Master Card, JCB, American
Express, Domestic Cards

Renaissance Beijing Hotel
★★★★★
36 Xiaoyun Lu, Chaoyang
(010) 6468 9999
Credit Cards:
Visa, Master Card, JCB, American
Express

Shangri-La Hotel, Beijing
★★★★★
29 Zizhuyuan Lu, Haidian
(010) 6841 2211
Standard room:
RMB1,585 +15% Surcharge
Credit Cards: Visa, Master Card,
JCB, American·Express

Somerset Grand Fortune Garden
Beijing
★★★★★
46 Liangmaqiao Lu, Chaoyang
(010) 8451 8888
Credit Cards: Visa, Master Card,
JCB, American Express

Spring Hotel
★★★★★
2 Jichang Lu, Nanxiao Jie, Daxing
(010) 6799 1919
Credit Cards:
Visa, Master Card, JCB, American
Express, Domestic Cards

St. Regis Hotel Beijing
★★★★★
21 Jianguomenwai Dajie, Chaoyang
(010) 6460 6688
Standard room:
RMB3,150 +15% Surcharge
Credit Cards:
Visa, Master Card, JCB, American
Express

Swissotel Beijing Hong Kong Macau
Center
★★★★★
2 Chaoyangmenbei Dajie,
Dongcheng

(010) 6553 2288
Standard room: RMB2,755
Credit Cards: Visa, Master Card,
JCB, American Express

The Ascott Beijing
★★★★★
B108 Jianguo Lu, Chaoyang
(010) 6567 8100
Credit Cards:
Visa, Master Card, JCB, American
Express, Domestic Cards

The Great Wall Sheraton Hotel
Beijing
★★★★★
10 Dongsanhuanbei Lu, Chaoyang
(010) 6590 5566
Standard room:
RMB2,675 +15% Surcharge
Credit Cards:
Visa, Master Card, JCB, American
Express, Domestic Cards

The Kerry Centre Hotel Beijing
★★★★★
1 Guanghua Lu, Chaoyang
(010) 6561 8833
www.shangri-la.com
Standard room:
RMB3,000 +15% Surcharge
Credit Cards: Visa, Master Card,
JCB, American Express

The Peninsula Beijing
★★★★★
8 Goldfish Lane, Wangfujing Dajie,
Dongcheng, (010) 8516 2888
Standard room:
RMB2,800 +15% Surcharge
Credit Cards: Visa, Master Card,
JCB, American Express

Tianlun Dynasty Hotel
★★★★★
50 Wangfujing Dajie, Dongcheng
(010) 6513 8888
Standard room: RMB2,600

Credit Cards: Visa, Master Card, JCB, American Express
Wangfujing Dajie Grand Hotel
★★★★★
57 Wangfujing Dajie, Dongcheng
(010) 6522 1188
Standard room: RMB818
Credit Cards: Visa, Master Card, JCB, American Express
Xiyuan Hotel Beijing
★★★★★
1 Sanlihe Lu, Haidian
(010) 6831 3388
www.xiyuanhotel.com.cn
Standard room: RMB598
Credit Cards: Visa, Master Card, JCB, American Express
Zhaolong Hotel
★★★★★
2 Gongti Bei Lu, Chaoyang
(010) 6597 2299
Standard room: RMB2,158
Credit Cards: Visa, Master Card, JCB, American Express
Baoding Center
★★★★
7 Dongdamochang Jie, Chongwen
(010) 6708 6688

Standard room: RMB688
Credit Cards: Visa, Master Card, American Express, Domestic Cards
Beijing Capital Xindadu Hotel
★★★★
21 Chegongzhuang Dajie, Xicheng
(010) 6831 9988
www.xindadu-hotel.com.cn
Credit Cards:
Visa, Master Card, JCB, American Express, Domestic Cards
Beijing Continental Grand Hotel
★★★★
8 Beichen Dong Lu, Chaoyang
(010) 8498 5588
www.bcghotel.com
Standard room: RMB398
Credit Cards:
Visa, Master Card, JCB, American Express, Domestic Cards
Beijing Dong Jiao Min Xiang Hotel
★★★★
A23 Dongjiaominxiang, Dongcheng
(010) 6524 3311
www.bjdjmx.com
Standard room: RMB680
Credit Cards: Visa, Master Card, JCB, American Express

Beijing Friendship Hotel
★★★★
1 Zhongguancunnan Dajie, Haidian
(010) 6849 8888
www.bjfriendshiphotel.com
Credit Cards:
Visa, Master Card, JCB, American
Express, Domestic Cards

Beijing Guangxi Plaza
★★★★
26 Huaweili, Panjiayuan, Chaoyang
(010) 6779 6688
www.guangxihotel.com
Standard room:
RMB860 +15% Surcharge
Credit Cards:
Visa, Master Card, JCB, American
Express

Beijing HWA (Apartment) Hotel
★★★★
130 Xidan Bei Dajie, Xicheng
(010) 6602 8888
www.huaweihotel.com
Standard room: RMB1,390
Credit Cards: Visa, Master Card,
JCB, American Express

Beijing International Aviation Club
★★★★
200 Jichangfu Lu, Chaoyang
(010) 6459 8822
www.bjaviationclub.com
Standard room: RMB480
Credit Cards:
Visa, Master Card, JCB, American
Express, Domestic Cards

Beijing Landmark Hotel
★★★★
8 Dongsanhuanbei Lu, Chaoyang
(010) 6590 6688
www.beijinglandmark.com
Standard room:
RMB1,600 +15% Surcharge
Credit Cards:
Visa, Master Card, JCB, American
Express, Domestic Cards

Beijing Oriental Culture Hotel
★★★★
101 Jiaodaokoudong Dajie,
Dongcheng
(010) 8403 1188
www.bochotel.com
Standard room: RMB468

DESTINATIONS

Credit Cards:
Visa, Master Card, JCB, American Express, Domestic Cards
Beijing Prince Jun Hotel
★★★★
19 Chaoyanggongyuannan Lu, Chaoyang
(010) 6585 5566
Credit Cards: Visa, Master Card, JCB, American Express, Domestic Cards, Diners Club
Beijing Shanshui Hotel
★★★★
45 Piku Lane, Xidan Bei Dajie, Xicheng
(010) 6606 3388
Standard room: RMB430
Credit Cards:
Visa, Master Card, JCB, American Express, Domestic Cards
Beijing Tibet Hotel
★★★★
118 Beisihuandong Lu, Chaoyang
(010) 6498 1133
www.tibetinfor.com
Standard room: RMB385
Credit Cards:
Visa, Master Card, JCB, American Express, Domestic Cards
Beijing Yanshan Hotel
★★★★
A38 Zhongguancun Dajie, Haidian
(010) 6256 3388
Credit Cards:
Visa, Master Card, JCB, American Express, Domestic Cards
Best Western Premier Beijing
★★★★
15 Dongsanhuannan Lu, Chaoyang
(010) 6762 3993
Standard room: RMB2,490
Credit Cards:
Visa, Master Card, JCB, American

Express, Domestic Cards
BTG Fragrant Hill Hotel
★★★★
Fragrant Hill Park, Haidian
(010) 6259 1166
www.xsfd.com
Standard room: RMB800
Credit Cards:
Visa, Master Card, JCB, American Express
Capital Hotel
★★★★
3 Qianmen Dong Dajie, Chongwen
(010) 6512 9988
www.capitalhotel.com.cn
Standard room: RMB3,042
Credit Cards:
Visa, Master Card, JCB, American Express, Domestic Cards
CCECC Plaza
★★★★
6 Beifengwo, Haidian
(010) 5181 8888
Standard room:
RMB780 +10% Surcharge
Credit Cards: Visa, Master Card, JCB, American Express
Central Garden Hotel
★★★★
18 Gaoliangqiaoxie Jie, Xizhimenwai, Haidian
(010) 5156 8888
www.centralgardenhotel.com
Standard room: RMB475
Credit Cards:
Visa, Master Card, JCB, American Express, Domestic Cards
Chengyuan Plaza
★★★★
19 Jianhua Nan Lu, Jianguomenwai Dajie, Chaoyang
(010) 6567 1305
Standard room: RMB368

Credit Cards:
Visa, Master Card, JCB, American Express, Domestic Cards
China Garment Commercial Hotel
★★★★
26 Dongzhimenwai Dajie, Chaoyang
(010) 6415 3388
www.bjzhongfuhotel.com
Standard room: RMB950
Credit Cards:
Visa, Master Card, JCB, American Express, Domestic Cards
CTS (HK) Grand Metropark Hotel Beijing
★★★★
338 Guang'anmennei Dajie, Xuanwu
(010) 6357 8888
Credit Cards:
Visa, Master Card, JCB, American Express, Domestic Cards
CTS Hotel Beijing
★★★★
2 Beisanhuandong Lu, Chaoyang
(010) 6462 2288
www.ctshotel.com
Credit Cards: Visa, Master Card, JCB, American Express
Dafang Hotel
★★★★
East of South Square, West Station, Fengtai
(010) 6336 2288
Standard room: RMB308
Credit Cards:
Visa, Master Card, JCB, American Express, Domestic Cards
Debao Hotel
★★★★
22 Debaoxinyuan, Xicheng
(010) 6831 8866
www.debaohotel.com
Standard room: RMB1,380
Credit Cards:

Visa, Master Card, JCB, American Express, Domestic Cards
Dragon Spring Hotel
★★★★
Shuizha Lu North, Mentougou
(010) 6984 3366
Credit Cards:
Visa, Master Card, JCB, American Express, Domestic Cards
Foreign Experts Building Beijing
★★★★
8 Huayanbeili, Beisihuanzhong Lu, Chaoyang, (010) 8285 8888
www.feb-hotel.com
Standard room: RMB1,580
Credit Cards:
Visa, Master Card, JCB, American Express, Domestic Cards
Gloria Plaza Hotel Beijing
★★★★
2 Jianguomennan Dajie, Chaoyang
(010) 6515 8855
Standard room: RMB1,370
Credit Cards:
Visa, Master Card, JCB, American Express, Domestic Cards
Golden Harbor Hotel
★★★★
136 Xisihuanbei Lu, Haidian
(010) 8846 1188
www.harborhotel.com.cn
Standard room: RMB660
Credit Cards:
Visa, Master Card, JCB, American Express, Domestic Cards
Golden Palace Silver Street Hotel
★★★★
31 Ganyu Xiang, Wangfujing Dajie, Dongcheng
(010) 8511 0388
Standard room: RMB588
Credit Cards: Visa, Master Card, JCB, American Express

Grand Dynasty Hotel
★★★★
58 Maizidian Jie, Chaoyang
(010) 6506 8888
www.dazonghotel.cn
Standard room: RMB2,688
Credit Cards: Visa, Master Card,
JCB, American Express

Grand View Garden Hotel Beijing
★★★★
88 Nancaiyuan Jie, Xuanwu
(010) 5181 8899
Standard room: RMB1,680
Credit Cards: Visa, Master Card,
JCB, American Express

Guangzhou Hotel Beijing
★★★★
A3 Xidanhengertiao, Xicheng
(010) 5855 9988
www.bjgzds.com.cn
Standard room: RMB2,280
Credit Cards: Visa, Master Card,
JCB, American Express

Holiday Inn Central Plaza Beijing
★★★★
1 Caiyuan Jie, Xuanwu
(010) 8397 0088

Standard room:
RMB780 +15% Surcharge
Credit Cards: Visa, Master Card,
JCB, American Express

Holiday Inn Chang An West Beijing
★★★★
66 Yongding Lu, Haidian
(010) 6813 2299
Standard room:
RMB618 +15% Surcharge
Credit Cards:
Visa, Master Card, JCB, American
Express, Domestic Cards

Holiday Inn Downtown Beijing
★★★★
98 Beilishi Lu, Xicheng
(010) 6833 8822
Standard room: RMB1,929
Credit Cards:
Visa, Master Card, JCB, American
Express, Domestic Cards

Holiday Inn Lido Beijing
★★★★
6 Jichang Lu, Jiangtai Lu, Chaoyang
(010) 6437 6688
Standard room:
RMB1,370 +15% Surcharge

Credit Cards:
Visa, Master Card, JCB, American
Express, Domestic Cards
**Holiday Inn Temple of Heaven
Beijing**
★★★★
1 Ding'andongli, Fengtai
(010) 6762 6688
Standard room:
RMB618-688 (breakfast included)
Credit Cards: Visa, Master Card,
JCB, American Express, Domestic
Cards, Diners Club
**Howard Johnson Paragon Hotel
Beijing**
★★★★
A18 Jianguomennei Dajie,
Dongcheng
(010) 6526 6688
Standard room: RMB628
Credit Cards: Visa, Master Card,
JCB, American Express
Jianguo Garden Hotel
★★★★
17 Jianguomennei Dajie, Chaoyang
(010) 6528 6666

Standard room: RMB558
Credit Cards:
Visa, Master Card, JCB, American
Express, Domestic Cards
Jinglun Hotel
★★★★
3 Jianguomenwai Dajie, Chaoyang
(010) 6500 2266
www.jinglunhotel.com
Standard room:
RMB2,664 +15% Surcharge
Credit Cards:
Visa, Master Card, JCB, American
Express, Domestic Cards
Jiuhua Spa & Resort
★★★★
Xiaotangshan, Changping
(010) 6178 2288
www.jiuhua.com.cn
Credit Cards: Domestic Cards
Minzu Hotel
★★★★
51 Fuxingmennei Dajie, Xicheng
(010) 6601 4466
www.minzuhotel.cn
Standard room: RMB2,407

Credit Cards: Visa, Master Card, JCB, American Express

Moonriver Club & Resort

★ ★ ★ ★

1 Hebin Lu, Tongzhou

(010) 8952 3737

www.moonriver.com.cn

Standard room:
RMB998 +10% Surcharge

Credit Cards:
Visa, Master Card, JCB, American Express, Domestic Cards

New World Courtyard Beijing

★ ★ ★ ★

3-18 Chongwenmenwai Dajie, Chongwen

(010) 6708 1188

Credit Cards:
Visa, Master Card, JCB, American Express, Domestic Cards

Novotel Peace Beijing

★ ★ ★ ★

3 Jinyu Hutong, Wangfujing Dajie

(010) 6512 8833

www.novotel.com/asia

Standard room: RMB1,826

Credit Cards: Visa, Master Card, JCB, American Express, Domestic Cards, Diners Club

Novotel Xinqiao Beijing

★ ★ ★ ★

2 Dongjiaominxiang, Dongcheng

(010) 6513 3366

Standard room: RMB2,075

Credit Cards:
Visa, Master Card, JCB, American Express, Domestic Cards

Oriental Garden Hotel

★ ★ ★ ★

6 Dongzhimennan Dajie, Dongcheng

(010) 6416 8866

www.bjoghotel.com

Standard room: RMB598

Credit Cards:
Visa, Master Card, JCB, American Express, Domestic Cards

Park Plaza Beijing Wangfujing Dajie

★ ★ ★ ★

97 Jinbao Jie, Dongcheng

(010) 8522 1999

www.parkplaza.com

Standard room:
RMB1,784 +15% Surcharge

Credit Cards:
Visa, Master Card, JCB, American Express, Domestic Cards

Plaza Hotel Beijing

★ ★ ★ ★

100 Dongsanhuannan Lu, Chaoyang

(010) 6735 3366

www.plazahotelbj.com

Credit Cards:
Visa, Master Card, JCB, American Express

Poly Plaza

★ ★ ★ ★

14 Dongzhimennan Dajie, Dongcheng, (010) 6500 1188

www.polyhotel.com

Standard room:
RMB1,960 +15% Surcharge

Credit Cards: Visa, Master Card, JCB, American Express

Radisson SAS Hotel Beijing

★ ★ ★ ★

A6 Beisanhuandong Lu, Chaoyang

(010) 5922 3388

Standard room:
RMB2,190 +15% Surcharge

Credit Cards: Visa, Master Card, JCB, American Express, Diners Club, Domestic Cards

River View Hotel

★ ★ ★ ★

2 Dongzhimenwaixiao Jie,

Dongcheng, (010) 8447 8855
Standard room: RMB468
Credit Cards:
Visa, Master Card, JCB, American
Express, Domestic Cards
Rosedale Hotel & Suites Beijing
★ ★ ★ ★
8 Jiangtai Xi Lu, Chaoyang
(010) 6436 2288
Standard room:
RMB1,400 (rack rate)
Credit Cards: Visa, Master Card,
JCB, American Express
Schengen International Hotel
★ ★ ★ ★
5 Laiguangyinxi Lu, Chaoyang
(010) 8490 5555
www.schengenhotel.com
Standard room:
RMB1,494 +15% Surcharge
Credit Cards:
Visa, Master Card, JCB, American
Express, Domestic Cards
SciTech Hotel
★ ★ ★ ★
22 Jianguomenwai Dajie, Chaoyang
(010) 6512 3388
Credit Cards: Visa, Master Card,
JCB, American Express, Domestic
Cards, Diners Club
Shenzhen Hotel
★ ★ ★ ★
1 Guang'anmenwai Dajie, Xuanwu
(010) 6327 1188
www.bjszhotel.com
Credit Cards: Visa, Master Card,
JCB, American Express, Domestic
Cards, Diners Club
Sino-Swiss Hotel Beijing
★ ★ ★ ★
P.O. Box 6913, Xiaotianzhu Lu,
South Capital Airport, Chaoyang
(010) 6456 5588

Standard room: RMB1,300
Credit Cards:
Visa, Master Card, JCB, American
Express, Domestic Cards
The Gorge Hotel
★ ★ ★ ★
Qinglong Tour Holiday Area,
Huairou
(010) 8969 6888
www.gorgehotel.com
Credit Cards: Domestic Cards
The Marco Polo, Beijing
★ ★ ★ ★
6 Xuanwumennei Dajie, Xicheng
(010) 6603 6688
Credit Cards: Visa, Master Card, JCB,
American Express, Domestic Cards
The North Garden Hotel
★ ★ ★ ★
218-1 Wangfujing Dajie, Dongcheng
(010) 6523 8888
www.north-garden.com
Credit Cards:
Visa, Master Card, Domestic Cards
Tianhong Plaza Hotel
★ ★ ★ ★
25 Zhichun Lu, Haidian
(010) 8235 6699
Standard room:
RMB1,280 +15% Surcharge
Credit Cards:
Visa, Master Card, JCB, American
Express, Domestic Cards
Tiantan Hotel Beijing
★ ★ ★ ★
1 Tiyuguan Lu, Chongwen
(010) 6719 0666
www.tiantanhotel.com
Standard room:
RMB598 +15% Surcharge
Credit Cards:
Visa, Master Card, JCB, American
Express, Domestic Cards

Traders Hotel Beijing
★★★★
1 Jianguomenwai Dajie, Chaoyang
(010) 6505 2277
www.shangri-la.com
Standard room:
RMB1,160 +15% Surcharge
Credit Cards: Visa, Master Card,
JCB, American Express
Unisplendour International Center
★★★★
1 Zhongguancundong Lu, Haidian
(010) 6279 1888
www.uniscenter.com
Standard room: RMB906
Credit Cards:
Visa, Master Card, JCB, American
Express, Domestic Cards
**Wancheng Huafu International
Hotel**
★★★★
53 Dong'anmen Dajie, Dongcheng
(010) 5120 9588
www.huafuhotel.com
Standard room:

RMB788
Credit Cards:
Visa, Master Card, JCB, American
Express, Domestic Cards
Winterless Hotel
★★★★
A1 Xidawang Lu, Chaoyang
(010) 6581 2288
www.winterlesshotel.com
Credit Cards:
Visa, Master Card, JCB, American
Express, Domestic Cards
Xinjiang Hotel
★★★★
7 Sanlihe Lu, Haidian
(010) 6833 5599
Standard room: RMB880
Credit Cards:
Visa, Master Card, JCB, American
Express, Domestic Cards
Yongxing Garden Hotel
★★★★
101 Fucheng Lu, Haidian
(010) 8811 1188
www.yongxing-gardenhotel.com

Standard room: RMB980
Credit Cards:
Visa, Master Card, JCB, American Express
York Hotel
★ ★ ★ ★
45 Ciyun Temple, Chaoyang
(010) 6507 8866
Standard room: RMB368
Credit Cards: Domestic Cards
Yu Yang Hotel
★ ★ ★ ★
18 Xinyuanxilizhong Jie, Chaoyang
(010) 6466 9988
www.yuyanghotel.net
Standard room: RMB398
Credit Cards:
Visa, Master Card, JCB, American Express, Domestic Cards
Yu Yang Hotel
★ ★ ★ ★
39 Yuyang Dajie, Pinggu
(010) 6998 9988
www.yuyanghotel.com
Credit Cards: Visa, Domestic Cards

Zhongmin Plaza
★ ★ ★ ★
7 Baiguang Lu, Xuanwu
(010) 6358 9988
Standard room: RMB458
Credit Cards:
Visa, Master Card, JCB, American Express, Domestic Cards
Zhongyu Century Grand Hotel
★ ★ ★ ★
31 Lianhuachi Dong Lu, Haidian
(010) 6398 9999
www.zhongyuhotel.com.cn
Standard room:
RMB747 +15% Surcharge
Credit Cards:
Visa, Master Card, JCB, American Express, Domestic Cards
Anhui Hotel, Beijing
★ ★ ★
1 Huixin Xi Jie
Chaoyang
(010) 6496 5588
www.bjfljg.com
Credit Cards: Domestic Cards

Beijing Grand Hotel
★ ★ ★
2 Yumin Lu, Xicheng
(010) 6201 0033
www.bjyuanshan-hotel.com
Standard room: RMB680
Credit Cards: Visa, Master Card,
JCB, American Express

Beijing Huaxiamingzhu Hotel
★ ★ ★
120-1 Lianhuachidong Lu, Fengtai
(010) 6395 5588
www.bjhxmz.com
Credit Cards:
Visa, Master Card, Domestic Cards

Beijing Konggang Bluesky Hotel
★ ★ ★
Blue Sky Mansion, Area A Tianzhu
Airport Ind. Zone, Shunyi
(010) 8048 9108
www.lantianhotel.com.cn
Credit Cards: Visa, Master Card,
JCB, American Express

Beijing National Jade Hotel
★ ★ ★
19 Huizhongli, Asian Games Village,
Chaoyang
(010) 6496 9988
www.guoyuhotel.com
Standard room: RMB420
Credit Cards:
Visa, Master Card, JCB, American
Express, Domestic Cards

Beijing Rainbow Hotel
★ ★ ★
11 Xijing Lu, Xuanwu
(010) 6302 3575
Credit Cards: Visa, Master Card,
American Express, Domestic Cards

Beijing Resource Yanyuan Hotel
★ ★ ★
1 Yiheyuan Lu, Haidian
(010) 8262 9988

www.zyhotel.com
Credit Cards:
Visa, Master Card, JCB, American
Express, Domestic Cards

Beijing Subway Holiday Resort
★ ★ ★
East Shuiku Lu, Changping
(010) 6071 2288
www.bjdtdjc.com.cn
Credit Cards: Visa, Master Card,
Domestic Cards

Beijing Xiangqing Commercial House
★ ★ ★
5 Landianchangnan Lu, Haidian
(010) 8844 6688
www.xiangqingyuan.com
Credit Cards:
Visa, Master Card, American Express

Bihai Hillside Resort
★ ★ ★
Jinhai Lake, Pinggu, (010) 6999 1201
www.bhsz.com
Credit Cards:
Visa, Master Card, JCB, American
Express, Domestic Cards

Chong Wen Men Hotel
★ ★ ★
2 Chongwenmenxi Dajie, Chongwen
(010) 6512 2211
www.cwmhotel.com
Credit Cards:
Visa, Master Card, American
Express, Domestic Cards

Daxing Hotel
★ ★ ★
118 Section 3 Xingfeng Nan Dajie,
Daxing
(010) 6924 2356
Credit Cards:
Visa, Master Card, JCB, American
Express, Domestic Cards

Guang Yun Hotel
★ ★ ★

A122 Guang'anmenwai Dajie, Xuanwu, (010) 5193 6688
www.guangyunhotel.com
Credit Cards: Visa, Domestic Cards
Guangming Hotel
★★★
Liangmaqiao Lu, Chaoyang
(010) 6467 8822
www.guangming-hotel.com.cn
Credit Cards:
Visa, Master Card, JCB, American Express, Domestic Cards
Guohong Hotel
★★★
A11 Muxidibeili, Xicheng
(010) 6390 8866
www.guohonghotel.com.cn
Credit Cards:
Visa, Master Card, JCB, American Express, Domestic Cards
Hainan Hotel
★★★
188 Andingmenwai Dajie, Dongcheng, (010) 6426 6655
www.hainandasha.com
Standard room: RMB560
Credit Cards: Visa, Master Card, JCB, American Express
Haotian Holiday Hotel Beijing
★★★
1 Gongchen Bei Dajie, Liangxiang, Fangshan, (010) 8935 0800
www.haotianhotel.com
Credit Cards:
Visa, Master Card, Domestic Cards
Huafeng Hotel
★★★
5 Qianmendong Dajie, Dongcheng
(010) 6524 7311
www.hfhotel.cn
Credit Cards:
Visa, Master Card, JCB, American Express, Domestic Cards

Huiqiao Hotel
★★★
19 Huixin Dong Jie, Chaoyang
(010) 6491 8811
www.huiqiaohotel.cn
Credit Cards:
Visa, Master Card, JCB, American Express, Domestic Cards
Jianguo Hotel Qianmen Beijing
★★★
175 Yong'an Lu, Xuanwu
(010) 6301 6688
www.qianmenhotel.com
Standard room: RMB450
Credit Cards:
Visa, Master Card, JCB, American Express, Domestic Cards
Jundu Vacation Resort
★★★
East Shuiku Lu, Changping
(010) 6071 3338
www.jddj.com.cn
Standard room: RMB280
Credit Cards: Visa, Domestic Cards
Loong Garden All-Suite Hotel
★★★
Longcheng Garden, Huilongguan, Changping, (010) 8079 3388
Credit Cards:
Visa, Master Card, JCB, American Express, Domestic Cards
Qinglan Plaza
★★★
24 Dongsishitiao, Dongcheng
(010) 8402 1155
www.qinglanplaza.com
Credit Cards:
Visa, Master Card, JCB, American Express, Domestic Cards
Ritan Hotel
★★★
1 Ritan Lu, Chaoyang
(010) 8563 5588

www.cpits.com.cn
Standard room:
RMB600 +10% Surcharge
Credit Cards: Visa, Master Card,
JCB, American Express
Shengli Hotel Beijing
★★★
3 Beishatan, Deshengmenwai,
Chaoyang, (010) 6487 1155
www.shenglihotel.com
Standard room: RMB280
Credit Cards: Domestic Cards
Suyuan Jinjiang Hotel
★★★
3 Guangwai Dajie, Xuanwu
(010) 6326 7788
www.suyuanjinjianghotel.com
Credit Cards:
Visa, Master Card, JCB, American
Express, Domestic Cards
Taoran Garden Hotel
★★★
19 Taiping Jie, Xuanwu
(010) 6354 3366
www.taorangardenhotel.com
Standard room: RMB580

Credit Cards:
Visa, Master Card, Domestic Cards
Tianzhao Hotel
★★★
18 Gongti Dong Lu, Chaoyang
(010) 6508 0088
Credit Cards: Visa, Master Card,
JCB, American Express, Domestic
Cards, Diners Club
Yong An Hotel
★★★
A5 Nongzhanlanguan Bei Lu,
Chaoyang, (010) 6501 1188
www.yonganhotel.com
Standard room: RMB298
Credit Cards: Visa, Master Card,
JCB, American Express

Restaurants

Beijing
Quan Ju De 全聚德
32 Qianmen Dajie, (010) 65112418
14 Qianmen Xi Dajie
(010) 63018833
9 Shuaifuyuan Hutong,
Wangfujing Dajie, (010) 65253310

1/F Jingxin Dasha, 2A Dongsanhuan
Bei Lu, (010) 6466 0896

Chinese

Xiang Jiang Shui Xiang 香江水乡
A1 Bei Wu Tiao, Tuan Jie Hu
(010) 8597 8069

Wudai 五代
Gongti Nan Lu, (010) 6500 5318

Din Tai Fung 鼎泰丰
Yi Bei Lou, 22 Hujia Yuan
(010) 6462 4502

Red Capital Club 新红资俱乐部
66 Dongsi Jiutiao, (010) 8401 8886

Tian Yu Lou 天雨楼
11 Fangjiayuan Hutong
(010) 6512 7667

Xihe Yaju 羲和雅居
Northeast corner of Ritan Park
(010) 8561 7643

Xiao Wang Fu 北京小王府
4 Gongti Dong Lu
(inside Success club)
(010) 6592 8777
2 Guanghua Lu Dongli
(010) 6591 3255

Cantonese

Chao Fu Cheng 香港潮福城大酒楼
108 Jianguo Lu, (010) 6566 9936

Yunnan

South Silk Road 茶马古道
3/F SOHO New Town, 88 Jianguo Lu
(010) 8580 4286
19A Shichahai Qianhai Xiyan
(010) 6615 5515

Muslim

Afunti 阿凡提
2A Houguaibang Hutong,
Chaoyangmennei Dajie
(010) 6527 2288

International

Zuma 祖玛
1/F Beijing Jingguang Centre Office
Building, Hujialou, (010) 6597 4212

Zone de Comfort 逸生活
4 Gongti Bei Lu, Inner Courtyard
(010) 6500 8070

Thai

Very Siam 非常泰
10A Xinyuan Xili Dong Jie
(010) 8451 0031

Japanese

Sixth Sense 北京和仓六号
6 Jianguomen Dajie
(010) 6559 6606

Jazz-Ya 爵士
18 Sanlitun Lu, (010) 6415 1227

Hatsune 隐泉日本料理
2/F Heqiao Building C,
8A Guanghua Lu, (010) 6581 3939

Matsushin 松伸日本料理
7 Guanghua Lu, (010) 6561 2535

Italian

La Dolce Vita 甜蜜生活
8 Bei Xindong Lu, (010) 6468 2894

Da Giorgio 意餐厅
Oriental Plaza, 1 Dongchangan Jie
(Grand Hyatt Hotel)
(010) 8518 1234

Indian

Tandoor 坦道印度餐厅
1/F Great Dragon Hotel
(010) 6597 2211

The Taj Pavilion 泰姬楼印度餐厅
1/F West Wing, China World Trade
Centre, (010) 6505 288 ext 8

French

Brasserie Flo 福楼
2/F Rainbow Plaza, 16 Dongsanhuan
Lu, (010) 6595 5135

La Cite 紫禁阁
115 Nanchizi Dajie, (010) 6559 6017

First Star 浮士德
18 Xiaoyun Lu, (010) 6464 9970

German

Paulaner Brauhaus
普拉那啤酒坊餐厅
50 Liangmaqiao Lu, Kempinski
Hotel, (010) 6465 3388

Mexican

Mexican Wave 墨西哥酒吧
Dongdaqiao Lu, 200m North of
Guiyou Dasha, (010) 6506 3961

Cafe

Cafe de Niro 霓楼咖啡
1/F Tongli Studios, Sanlitun Bei Jie
(north bar street), (010) 6416 9400

Here 这里
97 Nanluogu Xiang
(010) 8401 4246

Be There or Be Square Cafe
不见不散
2/F, Henderson Shopping Centre, 18
Jianguomennei Dajie
(010) 6518 6515

G7-G9 China Resources Building, 8
Jianguomennei Dajie
(010) 8519 1818

Riverside Cafe Deli 河畔咖啡
10 Sanlitun Beixiaojie
(010) 8454 1031

Seafood

Aria 阿郦雅
2/F, 1 Jianguomen Dajie (China
World Hotel), (010) 6505 3318

Taiwanese

Bellagio 鹿港小镇
35 Xiaoyun Lu, (010) 8451 9988

Malaysian

Cafe Sambal
43 Doufuchi Hutong
(010) 6400 4875

Western

The Courtyard 四合院
95 Donghuamen Dajie
(010) 6526 8883

Hotpot

Ding Ding Xiang
鼎鼎香
1/F, 14 Zhong Dong Jie
(010) 6417 2546

Vegetarian

Lotus in Moonlight
荷塘月色素食
12 Liufang Nanli, (010) 6465 3299

Sichuan
South Beauty 俏江南

DESTINATIONS

3/F, Pacific Century Place,
Gongti Bei Lu, (010) 6539 3502
2/F West Wing, China World Trade
Centre, (010) 6505 0809
Sunshine Plaza, East door
(010) 6495 1201
Across from the International Hotel
(010) 6518 7603
Malls at the Kerry Center, North B1
(010) 8529 9458

American
Steaks and Eggs 喜来中
5 Xiushui Nanjie Jianguomenwai
(010) 6592 8088

Cantonese
Linyipin Fim Restaurant
林一品鱼翅餐厅
38 Maizidian Jie, (010) 6507 7328

Thai
Su Ku Tai Restaurant
粟库泰贵族文化餐厅
6 Zhongguancun Nan Dajie
(010) 6250 1286

Italian
Annie Italian Restaurant
安妮意大利餐厅
1Chaoyanggongyuan Lu
(010) 6591 1931

Hotpot
Little Sheep Hotpot
小肥羊火锅楼
Huangshan Zhong Lu
(010) 8400 1669

Korean
Han Yang Korean Restaurant
汉阳韩国餐厅
40 Liangmaqiao Lu, (010) 6466 3311

Shangdong
Gui Yuan Ju 桂圆居
Zhongguancun Bei Dajie
(010) 6275 6952

Hunan
Xiao Xiang Ju 潇湘居

10 Jiuxianqiao Lu, (010) 6433 8879
Xiang Cai Guan 湘菜馆
69 Banjin Lu, (010) 8846 4046

Brazilian
South America Brazilian BBQ
南美洲巴西烤肉店
Tuanjiehu Lu, (010) 6582 1202

Bars & Clubs

Bar Blu 蓝吧
4/F, Tongli Studios, Sanlitun Beili,
(010) 6416 7567
Bed Tapas & Bar 床
17 Zhangwang Hutong, Jiu Gulou
Dajie (010) 8400 1554
Bubble Cafe 泡点咖啡
2/F, V8-105, Jianwai Soho, 39 Dong-
sanhuan Lu, (010) 5869 2770
Browns
4 Gongti Bei Lu, (010) 6591 2717
Centro 炫酷
First Floor, Kerry Centre Hotel,
1 Guanghua Lu, (010) 6561 8833
Entrance
18 Xingba Lu, Nurenjie
(010) 6465 2284
Frank's Place at Trio
Jiang Tai Xi Lu, West of Rosedale
Hotel, Lido Area, (010) 6437 8399
Houhai Zoo 后海动物园
Building 2, Qianhai, (010) 6403 6690
Vineyard 葡萄院
31 Wudaoying Hutong
(010) 6402 7961
A Che 切
28 Dongzhimen Dajie
(010) 6417 2201
Shooters
Building 40, 5 Sanlitun Beijing
(010) 6416 3726
5:19 Bar & Grill 5:19酒吧
26 Xingba Lu, Nurenjie
(010) 8448 0896

Alfa 阿尔发
5 Xingfu Yicun, (010) 6413 0086
Inner Affair
6 Xiliujie, Sanlitun, (010) 8454 0899
Instituto Cenvantes
A1 Gongti Nan Lu, (010) 5879 9666
John Bull Pub 尊伯英式
44 Guanghua Lu, (010) 6532 5905
Kai 开吧
Sanlitun Beijie (just around the
corner from Poachers)
(010) 6416 6254
Lush
2/F, Building 1, Huaqing Jiayuan,
Chengfu Lu, opposite Wudaokou
train station
(010) 8286 3566
Nanjie 南街
Opposite the Workers' Statium
North Gate, (010) 6413 0963
Nhu
6 Fangyuan Xi Lu, Lido Park South
(010) 6435 6762
Babyface
6 Gongti Xi Lu, (010) 6551 9081
Fusion 派队空间

8A, Gongti Bei Lu, (010) 6551 5138
Mix
Inside the Workers' Stadium North
Gate, (010) 6530 2889

Hospitals

Bayley & Jackson Medical Center
庇利积臣医疗中心
7 Ritan Dong Lu, (010) 8562 9998
**Peking Union Medical College
Hospital** 北京协和医院
1 Shuaifuyuan Hutong
(010) 6529 6114
Beijing University People's Hospital
北京大学人民医院
11 Xizhimen Nan Dajie
(010) 6831 4422
International Medical Center
北京国际医疗中心
C311, 3/F Lufthansa Center, 50
Liangmahe Lu, (010) 6462 2069
Beijing Vista Clinic 维世达诊所
B29 Kerry Center, 1 Guanghua Lu
(010) 8529 6618
Beijing International SOS Clinic
北京国际救援中心

Building C, BITIC Jingyi Building, Sanlitun Xiwu Jie, (010) 6462 9100
Hong Kong International Medical Clinic 北京香港国际医务诊所
9/F Swissotel, 2 Chaoyangmen Bei Dajie, (010) 6501 2288
www.unitedfamilyhospitals.com
Beijing United Family Hospital and Clinics 和睦家医院
Pinnacle Plaza, Unit 818 Tianzhu Real Estate Dev. Zone
(010) 6433 2345
www.unitedfamilyhospitals.com

Bookstores

The Bookworm
Building 4, Nan Sanlitun Lu
(010) 6586 9507
Foreign Language Book Store 外文书店(王府井店)
29 Wangfujing Dajie
(010) 6512 6922
Local English Media
that's Beijing
www.thatsbj.com
City Weekend Beijing
www.cityweekend.com.cn

Embassies

Argentina 阿根廷
11 Dongwu Jie, (010) 6532 1406
Australia 澳大利亚
21 Dongzhimenwai Dajie
(010) 5140 4111
Austria 奥地利
5 Xiushui Nan Jie, (010) 6532 2061
Belarus 白俄罗斯
1Ritan Dongyi Jie, (010) 6532 6427
Belgium 比利时
6 Sanlitun Lu, (010) 6532 1736
Brazil 巴西
27 Guanghua Lu, (010) 6532 2883
Canada 加拿大

19 Dongzhimenwai Dajie
(010) 6532 3536
Czech Republic 捷克共和国
2 Ritan Lu, (010) 6532 6902
Czech Republic 捷克共和国
2 Ritan Lu, (010) 6532 6902
Denmark 丹麦
1 Dongwu Jie, (010) 6532 2431
Finland 芬兰
26/F South Tower, Beijing Kerry Center, 1 Guanghua Lu
(010) 8519 8300
France 法国
3 Dongsan Jie, (010) 6532 1331
Germany 德国
17 Dongzhimenwai Dajie
(010) 8532 9000
Greece 希腊
19 Guanghua Lu, (010) 6532 1588
India 印度
1 Ritan Dong Lu, (010) 6532 1908
Indonesia 印度尼西亚
Diplomatic Office Building B, 14 Liangmaqiao Nan Lu
(010) 6532 5487
Israel 以色列
17 Tianze Lu, (010) 6532 0500
Italy 意大利
2 Donger Jie, Sanlitun
(010) 6532 2131
Korea 韩国
Tayuan Diplomatic Office Building, 14 Liangmahe Nan Lu
(010) 6532 6774
Malaysia 马来西亚
2 Liangmaqiao Bei Jie
(010) 6532 2531
Mexico 墨西哥
5 Dongwu Jie, Sanlitun
(010) 6532 2574
Netherlands 荷兰
4 Liangmahe Nan Lu
(010) 8532 0200

New Zealand 新西兰
1 Ritan Donger Lu
(010) 6532 2731
Norway 挪威
1 Dongyi Jie, Sanlitun
(010) 6532 2261
Pakistan巴基斯坦
1 Dongzhimenwai Dajie
(010) 6532 2504
Philippines 菲律宾
23 Xiushui Bei Jie
(010) 6532 6427
Philippines 菲律宾共和国
23 Xiushui Bei Jie
(010) 6532 6427
Poland 波兰
1 Ritan Lu, (010) 6532 1235
Portugal 葡萄牙
2-15 Tayuan Diplomatic Office
Building, (010) 6532 3497
Russia 俄罗斯
4 Dongzhimenbei Zhong Jie
(010) 6532 2051
Singapore 新加坡
1 Xiushui Bei Jie, (010) 6532 1115
South Africa 南非

5 Dongzhimenwai Dajie
(010) 6532 0171
Spain 西班牙
9 Sanlitun Lu, (010) 6532 3629
Sri Lanka 斯里兰卡
3 Jianhua Lu, (010) 6532 1861
Sweden 瑞典
3 Dongzhimenwai Dajie, Sanlitun
(010) 6532 9790
Switzerland 瑞士
Dongwu Jie, Sanlitun
(010) 6532 2736
Thailand 泰国
40 Guanghua Lu, (010) 6532 1749
Turkey 土耳其
9 Dongwu Jie, Sanlitun
(010) 6532 1715
UK 英国
11 Guanghua Lu, (010) 5192 4000
Ukraine 乌克兰
11 Dongliu Jie, Sanlitun
(010) 6532 6359
US 美国
2 Xiushui Dong Jie, (010) 6532 3431
Vietnam 越南
32 Guanghua Lu, (010) 6532 1155

Airline Offices

Air China 中国国际航空公司
15 Xi Chang,an Jie, (010) 6601 3336
Air France 法国航空公司
5/F Full Link Plaza, 18 Chaoyangmenwai Jie, (010) 6588 1388
Austrian Airlines 奥地利航空公司
S103 Kempinski Hotel, 50 Liangmaqiao Lu, (010) 6462 2161
British Airways 英国航空公司
210 SciTech Tower, 22 Jianguomenwai Dajie, (010) 8511 5599
China Eastern Airlines
中国东方航空公司
1/F, 12 Xinyuan Xili Zhong Jie
(010) 6468 1166
China Southern Airlines
中国南方航空公司
15 Xi Chang'an Jie, (010) 6602 4068
Dragonair 港龙航空有限公司
Rm 1710, Building One, 18 Jianguomennei Dajie, (010) 6518 2533
Finnair 芬兰航空公司
Rm 204, 22 Jianguomenwai Dajie
(010) 6512 7180

KLM 荷兰皇家航空公司
Rm 2432, 1 Jianguomenwai Dajie
(010) 6505 3505
Lufthansa 德国汉莎航空公司
50 Liangmaqiao Lu, (010) 6465 4488
Malaysia Airlines
马来西亚航空公司
Rm 1005, China World Tower 2, 1
Jianguomenwai Dajie
(010) 6505 2681
Northwest Airlines
美国西北航空公司
5/F West Tower, 1 Jianguomenwai
Dajie, (010) 6505 3505
Qantas, 澳大利亚航空公司
S120B Kempinski Hotel Office
Building, (010) 6467 3337
SAS 北欧航空公司
Rm 1830, Sunflower Tower, 37
Maizidian Jie, (010) 8527 6100
Shanghai Airlines 上海航空公司
15 Xi Chang'an Jie, (010) 6601 7755
Singapore Airlines 新加坡航空公司
8/F China World Tower 2, 1 Jian-
guomenwai Dajie, (010) 6505 2233

Industrial parks

Beijing Economic-Technological Development Area
北京经济技术开发区
(010) 6788 1105
www.bda.gov.cn
Major Industries: Electronics, biotechnology and pharmaceuticals.
Zhongguancun Science Park
中关村科技园
(010) 8269 0500
www.zgc.gov.cn
Major Industries:
Information technology, high-tech industry, scientific research
Beijing Economic Technological Development Area
北京经济技术开发区
(010)6788 6732, *www.bda.gov.cn*
Major industries: Electronics, biotechnology, pharmaceuticals
Beijing Shilong Industrial Development Area
北京石龙经济开发区
(010) 6980 3474
www.shilong.com.cn
Major Industries:

Electronic information, CAM manufacturing, environmental protection, biological medicine, new materials industries

Exhibition centers

China World Trade Center
1 Jianguomenwai Dajie, Beijing
(010) 6505 2288, *www.cwtc.com*
Beijing International Convention Center
8 Beisihuan Zhong Lu, Beijing
(010) 8498 5588
www.bicc.com.cn
Beijing Exhibition Center
135 Xizhimenwai Dajie, Beijing
(010) 6831 6677
www.bjexpo.com
China International Science & Technology Convention Center
12 Yumin Lu, Beijing
(010) 8225 2850
www.kezhan.com
National Agriculture Exhibition Hall
16 Dongsanhuan Lu, Beijing
(010) 6509 6688
www.ciae.com.cn

Chongqing
Population: 27.98 million
Area: 82,400 sq km
Airports: Chongqing
Ports: Chongqing

Situated on the upper reaches of the Yangtze River, Chongqing is the commercial, industrial and transportation hub of China's southwest and home to some of China's spiciest cuisine. In 1997, Chongqing City and a large surrounding area of what was then eastern Sichuan Province became the fourth municipality in China, under the direct control of the central government in Beijing. It borders the provinces of Hubei, Hunan, Guizhou, Sichuan and Shaanxi and has been designated as the beachhead for the development of the poorer western regions of the country. The city is the center where resettlement of refugees from

the Three Gorges Dam project was coordinated. It is known as one of the four "furnace cities" in China, with blazing hot, humid summers and cold, foggy winters.

Chongqing means "double celebration" in Chinese and is perhaps better known by its earlier English spelling "Chungking". It was established as a city some 3,000 years ago and given its current name by the Southern Song Emperor Guangzong in 1189, to commemorate his accessions to princely and then imperial rank. It was the capital of a number of early Chinese dynasties and was a stronghold of the Song Empire during the 36 years they spent trying to hold off Mongol invaders in the 13th century. In 1891 the ancient city became the first inland treaty port opened to British and Japanese traders. Following the fall of Nanjing to the Japanese in 1937, Chongqing became the capital of the Republic

Chongqing Economic Data			
	2005	2004	Change%
GDP (RMB bn)	307.0	269.3	14.0
GDP per capita (RMB)	10982	9,608	14.3
Exports (US$ bn)	2.52	2.09	20.57
Imports (US$ bn)	1.77	1.76	0.34
Cars per 100 households	0.67	0.33	103.03
PCs per 100 households	51.33	43.67	17.54

of China, under the Kuomintang leader Chiang Kai-shek, for the duration of WWII. During the war it was inundated with refugees and bombed constantly by the Japanese until very little remained of the original city.

Following its fall to the Communists in 1949, the city was developed as the capital of Sichuan province and the industrial center of southwest China. In 1983, soon after paramount leader Deng Xiaoping's economic reforms began, the local government was granted provincial jurisdiction over the economy and began experimenting with comprehensive economic structural reforms. In 1992, Chongqing was once again designated an open trading port to foreigners and in 1994 was granted the right to operate as an "experimental city at provincial level for the comprehensive reform of the market economic system".

Today the municipality covers a total area of 82,400 sq km and has a population of about 30 million. It is the largest of the country's four municipalities (Beijing, Tianjin and Shanghai are the others), although the actual city is the smallest and makes up less than a quarter of the population and a tiny fraction of the area. The city itself has the distinction of being the only major metropolitan area in China without a significant number of bicycles, which is due to it being very hilly and spread out over the junction of the Jialing and Yangtze Rivers. Because of its hills Chongqing is sometimes known as the "mountain city".

The wild west

As the economic center of the southwest, Chongqing is a thoroughly industrial city, specializing in iron and steel production, construction materials, textiles, motorcycle manufacturing and shipbuilding, as well as chemical and pharmaceutical pro-

duction. It is one of the biggest iron & steel production centers and the major aluminum production base in the country.

Unlike some of the other old industrial bases of the communist command economy era, Chongqing has navigated its transition to a market-oriented exporting economy with reasonable success. The region has done well in growing its offshore export markets by concentrating its exporting efforts on less developed economies around the world, such as Vietnam, Iran and India. Major exports include machinery, chemicals, paper and automobiles, especially motorbikes, with Chongqing rated as one of the major automobile-producing bases in the country.

In addition to heavy industry the region still produces its traditional pre-industrial exports of silk, citrus fruit, tea and grain. The main crop is rice but the area also grows corn, wheat and sweet potatoes, as well as rapeseeds, peanuts, sugar cane, jute and tobacco. Chongqing remains one of China's most important production bases for Chinese medicines. Pigs, goats and rabbits are the main livestock and fish farming is popular all across the rural areas of the municipality with the largest operations based at Changshou Lake and Dahong Lake.

Chongqing is key to the central government's "develop the West" project, which it began in 1999. Since then, large amounts of money and energy have been poured into infrastructure, development and prefer-ential policies designed to encourage foreign and private investment in China's impoverished western regions. As the regional transport and economic hub for the entire southwest of the country, Chongqing has benefited more than almost anywhere else from this policy. Massive public works are currently under way, including overhead and surface commuter rail lines. The city has also benefited financially as the upstream gateway to the controversial Three Gorges Dam project, the largest hydroelectric dam in the world, which is expected to be finished by 2009.

The religious cliff sculptures of Dazu and Baodingshan and the Three Gorges scenic region of the Yangtze River are all nearby, making Chongqing an important center for tourism despite the scarcity of notable sights within the city proper. As is true of most of China, severe air pollution is frequently present, largely as a result of the burning of coal without pollution controls, both for industrial processes and for the production of electric power.

Chongqing is the water, land and air transport hub for the southwest, with rivers, highways and railway lines radiating out across the whole country. The city has flights to all major cities in China as well as routes to Bangkok, Nagoya, Macau and Hong Kong. It is also one of the few airports in China that operates flights to Tibet.

Chongqing Economic Data	
Disposable income 2005 (RMB)	10,244

Hotels

Chongqing Golden Resources Hotel
★★★★★
1 Erzhi Lu, Jianxin Bei Lu
(023) 6795 8888
www.grhotel.com
Credit Cards: Visa, Master Card,
JCB, American Express

Harbour Plaza Chongqing
★★★★★
Wuyi Lu, Yuzhong, (023) 6370 0888
Standard room:
RMB1,300 +15% Surcharge
Credit Cards:
Visa, Master Card, American Express

Hilton Chongqing
★★★★★
139 Zhongshansan Lu, Yuzhong
(023) 8903 9999
Standard room:
RMB1,500 +15% Surcharge
Credit Cards: Visa, Master Card,
JCB, American Express

Hotel InterContinental Chongqing
★★★★★
Pre-Opening Office, 101 Minzu Lu,
Yuzhong, (023) 8906 6888
Credit Cards: Visa, Master Card,
JCB, American Express

JW Marriott Hotel Chongqing
★★★★★
77 Qingnian Lu, Yuzhong
(023) 6388 8888
Credit Cards:
Visa, Master Card, JCB, American
Express, Domestic Cards

**Best Western Garden Hotel
Chongqing**
★★★★
55 Xuetianwanzheng Street, Yuzhong
(023) 6389 2666
Standard room: RMB780
Credit Cards:
Visa, Master Card, JCB, American
Express, Domestic Cards

Chongqing Guest House
★★★★
235 Minsheng Lu, (023) 6384 5888
Standard room: RMB435
Credit Cards: Visa, Master Card,
JCB, American Express

Chongqing Kinglead Hotel
★★★★
9 Pukeyuan'er Lu, Shiqiao
(023) 6851 8888
Standard room:
RMB658 +15% Surcharge
Credit Cards:

Visa, Master Card, JCB, American Express, Domestic Cards

Chongqing Liyuan Hotel
★★★★
15 Tianchen Lu, Shapingba
(023) 6531 6666
www.cqliyuan.com
Standard room: RMB780
Credit Cards: Visa, Master Card, JCB, American Express

Chongqing Xiya Hotel
★★★★
33 Yuzhou Lu, Shiqiaopu
(023) 6860 0999, *www.xiyahotel.com*
Standard room: RMB328
Credit Cards: Visa, Master Card, JCB, American Express

Chuangshiji Hotel
★★★★
1 Xinpaifangyi Lu, Yubei
(023) 8907 8888, *www.csjhotel.com*
Standard room: RMB398
Credit Cards:
Visa, Master Card, JCB, American Express, Domestic Cards

Gloria Plaza Hotel Wanzhou, Chongqing
★★★★
91-97 Taibai Lu, Wanzhou
(023) 5815 8855
Standard room: RMB208
Credit Cards:
Visa, Master Card, JCB, American Express, Domestic Cards

Hoi Tak Hotel Chongqing
★★★★
69 Jiangnan Dajie, Nanping
(023) 6283 8888
Standard room:
RMB680 +10% Surcharge
Credit Cards: Visa, Master Card, JCB, American Express

Holiday Inn North Chongqing
★★★★
66 Wuhong Lu, Yubei
(023) 6786 4888
Standard room:
RMB 410 +15% Surcharge
Credit Cards:
Visa, Master Card, JCB, American Express, Domestic Cards

Holiday Inn Yangtze Chongqing
★★★★
87 Nanpingxin Jie
(023) 6280 3380
Standard room: RMB458
Credit Cards: Visa, Master Card, JCB, American Express

Homehome Inn
★★★★
6 Fenghuangtai, Nanjimen, Yuzhong
(023) 6391 8888
Credit Cards: Domestic Cards

Wanyou Conifer Hotel Chongqing
★★★★
77 Changjiang'er Lu, Yuzhong
(023) 6871 8888
www.wanyouhotel.com
Credit Cards:
Visa, Master Card, JCB, American Express, Domestic Cards

World Traders Hotel
★★★★
118 Zourong Lu, (023) 6378 1111
www.wthotelcq.com
Standard room:
RMB358 +10% Surcharge
Credit Cards: Visa, Master Card, JCB, American Express

Chongqing Grand Hotel
★★★
84 Xiaolongkan Xin Jie, Shapingba, (023) 6533 9888
Standard room: RMB198
Credit Cards: Visa, Master Card, JCB, American Express

Jiangzhou Hotel
★★★
12 Central Section Binjiang Lu
(023) 4752 6888
www.jzhotel.com
Credit Cards:
Visa, Master Card, Domestic Cards
Milky Way Hotel
★★★
49 Datong Lu, Yuzhong
(023) 6380 8585
www.cqyinhe.com
Standard room:
RMB468 +10% Surcharge
Credit Cards: Visa, Master Card,
JCB, American Express
Sunshine Hot-Spring Resort Hotel
★★★
South Hot Spring, (023) 6284 8199
www.wqdjc.com
Standard room: RMB388
Yu Tong Hotel
★★★
18 Hongjin Dajie, Yubei
(023) 6789 0088
www.yutonghotel.com
Standard room: RMB360
Credit Cards: Visa, Master Card,
JCB, Domestic Cards

Restanrants

Western
Dee Dee's Bar 扬子酒吧
86 Nanping Xin Jie, Nan'an
(023) 6613 5941
Mona Lisa Western Restaurant
蒙娜丽莎西餐厅
2/F, 32 Qingnian Lu
(023) 6373 5646
May Flower Coffee House
五月花美福乐西餐厅
2/F, Shaping Opera House, Sanxia
Plaza, (023) 6533 8166
UBC 上岛咖啡
166 Minzu Lu, Jiefang Bei Lu
(023) 8903 3033
Chinese
Wangge Restaurant 旺阁酒楼
2/F Section A, Deyi Shijie Building,
Jiaochangkou, (023) 6860 5356
Waipoqiao Restaurant 外婆桥
7/F Daduhui, 68 Zhourong Lu
(023) 6383 5988
Western
Caesar Western Restaurant
恺撒咖啡西餐厅
84 Xiaolongkanxin Jie (Chongqing
Grand Hotel)
(023) 6533 9888

DESTINATIONS

Sichuan
Ling Yun Chinese Restaurant
凌云楼文化观景餐厅
84 Xiaolongkanxin Jie
(Chongqing Grand Hotel)
(023) 6533 9888
Hotpot
Chongqing Yunyuan Hot Pot Restaurant 韵苑火锅店
123-1 Renmin Lu
(023) 6360 3168
Western & Chinese
Golden Roman 金色罗马西餐茶楼
Zhujiang Garden 5, Zi Gang Dadao
(023) 6843 2966

Bars & Clubs

Dee Dee's Bar 扬子酒吧
86 Nanping Xin Jie, Nan'an
(023) 6613 5941
Notting Hill 诺丁山酒廊
128 Keyuan San Jie
Newcastle Arms
3/F 168 Ba Yi Lu, Jie Fang Bei
Falling Club
Jie Fang Bei
JJ's House Disco
Bayi Lu
Graffiti Bar 涂鸦酒吧
115 Songshi Bei Lu
Windsor Club 温莎夜总会
3/F, 218 Wusi Lu
Normandy Bar 诺曼底酒吧
158 Hubin Lu
MTB Club
Wuyi Lu

Hospitals

Chongqing Shapinba People's Hospital
重庆沙坪坝人民医院
44 Xiaoxin Jie, (023) 6531 1326
Chongqing Red-Cross Hospital

重庆市红十字会医院
1 Honghui Lu, (023) 6763 6835
Chongqing First People's Hospital
重庆市第一人民医院
40 Daomenkou Jie
(023) 6384 1324

Bookstores

Chongqing Xinhua Bookstore
重庆市新华书店
76 Tanzikou, Jiulongpo Qu
(023) 6842 8720

Consulates

Canada 加拿大
Rm 1705, Metropolitan Tower, Wuyi
Lu, (023) 6373 8007
UK 英国
28/F, Metropolitan Tower, Zourong
Lu, (023) 6381 0321

Industrial parks

Chongqing Economic & Technological Development Zone
重庆经济技术开发区
(023) 6746 3079
www.cetz.com
Major Industries:
Information technology, automobiles, scientific research
Chongqing Economic & Technological Development Zone
重庆经济技术开发区
(023) 6298 2932, *www.cetz.com*
Major Industries:
Information technology, automobiles, scientific research

Exhibition centers

Chongqing Exhibition Center
269 4th Lu, Hi-tech Park, Chongqing
(023) 6863 1388
www.super-e.com.cn

Fujian

Population: 35.35 million
Area: 120,000 sq km
Capital: Fuzhou
Airports:
Fuzhou, Quanzhou, Xiamen, Nanping
Ports: Fuzhou, Xiamen, Mawei, Putian,
Zhangzhou

DESTINATIONS

Fujian is a hilly province bordered by Zhejiang to the north, Jiangxi to the west and Guangdong to the south. It is located on China's east coast and faces Taiwan across the 180-km-wide Taiwan Strait. As a result, it has historically had closer ties with the island than any other part of the mainland. Due to its southern location, Fujian enjoys a moist, subtropical climate.

Because of its steep mountains and rugged terrain, the province has always been somewhat isolated from the rest of the country. It traditionally served as a penal colony and a

refuge for deposed dynasties and dissident generals from the north. Successive waves of Han Chinese came to this region over the centuries but geographic isolation kept technology and the economy relatively backward. The region gained economic prominence with its ports, especially Quanzhou, which grew into the largest seaport in the eastern hemisphere under the Mongol Yuan dynasty (1279-1368). A sea trade ban was imposed on Fujian in the mid-Ming dynasty (1368-1644), primarily to stop piracy, which has a long tradition in the area. The ban was eventually lifted in 1550 but by then the region had been surpassed by other ports such as Guangzhou, Hangzhou and Ningbo.

In 1689, the Qing dynasty officially incorporated Taiwan Island into Fujian province. Today an estimated 70% of people in Taiwan are

Fujian Economic Data			
	2005	2004	Change%
GDP (RMB bn)	656.9	576.3	14.0
GDP per capita (RMB)	18,646	17,218	8.3
Exports (US$ bn)	34.84	29.40	18.50
Imports (US$ bn)	19.57	18.15	7.82
Cars per 100 households	1.70	1.42	19.72
PCs per 100 households	54.89	46.56	17.89

descendants of Fujianese emigrants. Many people of Chinese heritage living throughout the world can trace their lineage back to Fujian.

Taiwan and the Fujian coast were ceded to Japan following China's defeat in the first Sino-Japanese war (1894-1895). The region was heavily influenced by the Japanese from then until the end of World War II.

Following the Communist victory and the Nationalist government's retreat to Taiwan in 1949, Fujian had to deal with a US blockade of the Taiwan Strait. The first railway to the province was completed in the mid 1950s, connecting the island city of Xiamen with the rest of the country.

Since the opening up of the late 1970s, Fujian's economy has benefited greatly from its geographic and cultural proximity to Taiwan. Xiamen was one of the first cities in the country to be designated a 'special economic zone' and the region has been at the forefront of the nation's transition to capitalism.

Fujian is one of the country's leading industrial, manufacturing and export processing trade centers. The province's leading industries include electronics, telecommunications, machinery, textiles, food, tea, chemicals, timber products and electric power. The province's main export markets are the US, EU, Japan and Hong Kong, which serves as a transit point to the rest of the world. Imports mainly come from the US, EU, Japan and Malaysia.

Because of its location between the Yangtze and Pearl River deltas as well as its cultural and geographic proximity to Taiwan, Fujian would be the centerpiece in a regional economic zone proposed by the government in 2005. The goal of this zone would be to increase economic integration in the region, including integration with Taiwan. If cross-straight relations are normalized in the near future, Fujian is the province in mainland China that will benefit the most.

Fuzhou 福州

Telephone prefix: 0591
Population: 6.66 million
Bank of China: 27 Gutian Lu

The capital of Fujian province, Fuzhou, is a 2,000-year-old city with a rich cultural heritage. The first city wall was built in 202 BC, and although the name has changed several times, the city has been continuously occupied since then and has never suffered major destruction from war or natural disaster.

At the end of the first Opium War in 1842, Fuzhou became one of the five Chinese ports opened by the Treaty of Nanjing. In 1933 the leaders of the rebel 19th army declared it the capital of the Republic of China, which collapsed after only two months.

The city's economy has flourished since China began its economic opening. Development has been accompanied by a large influx of migrants from the overpopulated regions to the north and west.

As far as the city itself goes, the unsentimental tearing down of ancient buildings in favor of ubiquitous cheaply-made high rises has not yet managed to eliminate all the ancient banyan trees that give Fuzhou its nickname 'the city of banyans'.

Fujian is famous for its high-quality tea production and the mountains surrounding Fuzhou produce many famous varieties. Traditionally renowned for its handicrafts, particularly carving and lacquerware, today Fuzhou's main industries include food processing, chemicals and textiles. It is a center for shipbuilding and steel production and an exit point for many agricultural exports such as rice, sugar, tea and fruit.

Fuzhou attracts more Taiwanese enterprises than almost anywhere else in China and also receives a huge amount of Hong Kong and international investment due to its location and savvy business approach.

Hotels

Fujian Foreign Trade Centre Hotel
★★★★★
73 Wusi Lu, (0591) 8752 3388
Standard room:
RMB550 (discounted)
Credit Cards:
Visa, Master Card, JCB, American Express, Domestic Cards

Fuzhou Lakeside Hotel
★★★★★
158 Hubin Lu, (0591) 8783 9888
www.lakeside-hotel.com.cn
Standard room: RMB470
Credit Cards:
Visa, Master Card, JCB, American Express, Domestic Cards

Golden Resources International Hotel
★★★★★
59 Wenquangongyuan Lu
(0591) 8708 8888
www.g.r.i.hotel.com
Standard room:
RMB800 +15% Surcharge
Credit Cards:
Visa, Master Card, JCB, American Express

Hot Springs Hotel
★★★★★
218 Wusi Lu, (0591) 8785 1818

www.hshfz.com
Standard room: RMB398
Credit Cards:
Visa, Master Card, JCB, American
Express, Domestic Cards
Shangri-La Hotel Fuzhou
★★★★★
9 Xinquan Nan Lu, (0591) 8798 8888
Credit Cards: Visa, Master Card,
JCB, American Express
Banghui Hotel
★★★★
58 Wenquan Lu, (0591) 8755 5555
www.bhhotel.cn
Standard room: RMB600
Credit Cards: Visa, Master Card,
JCB, American Express
Fujian Enjoy Hotel
★★★★
1 Dongda Lu, Gulou
(0591) 8760 2688
Credit Cards: Visa, Master Card
Fujian InterContinental Hotel
★★★★
1/F&20-25/F Dongbai Building,
Dongjiekou, (0591) 8761 5777
Standard room: RMB298
Credit Cards: Visa, Master Card,
JCB, American Express
Ramada Plaza Fuzhou
★★★★
118 Beihuan Xi Lu, (0591) 8788 3999
www.ramada.com
Credit Cards: Visa, Master Card,
JCB, American Express, Domestic
Cards, Diners Club
Sunshine Holiday Hotel
★★★★
26 Gaoqiao Lu, Wuyi Plaza
(0591) 8336 5333
Standard room: RMB268
Credit Cards:
Visa, Master Card, JCB, American

Express, Domestic Cards
Fujian Golden Hotel
★★★
417 Hualin Lu, (0591) 8757 7688
www.aqin.net
Credit Cards:
Visa, Master Card, JCB, American
Express, Domestic Cards
Fuzhou Hotel
★★★
18 Dongda Lu
(0591) 8753 5333
www.fuzhouhotel.net
Standard room: RMB180
Credit Cards:
Visa, Master Card, Domestic Cards
Fuzhou Paul Holiday Hotel
★★★
88 Wuyi Bei Lu
(0591) 8762 7888
www.paulhotel.com
Standard room: RMB255
Credit Cards:
Visa, Master Card, JCB, American
Express, Domestic Cards
Juchunyuan Hotel
★★★
2 Dong Jie
(0591) 8750 2328
www.juchunyuan-hotel.com.cn
Credit Cards:
Visa, Master Card, JCB, American
Express, Domestic Cards
Tang Cheng Hotel
★★★
215 Wuyi Nan Lu, (0591) 8326 9999
Credit Cards:
Visa, Master Card, JCB, American
Express, Domestic Cards

Restaurants

Chinese
Juchunyuan Restaurant

聚春园大酒店
2 Dong Jie, (0591) 8750 2328
Fuzhou Delicacy Restaurant 美食园
101, 817 Bei Lu
(0591) 8755 5816
Fuzhou Antailou Restaurant
安泰楼酒家
39 Jipi Lu
(0591) 8755 0890
International
Fuzhou Hotel 福州大饭店
1 Doudong Lu
(0591) 8333 3333
Sa Ba Yong 萨巴雍
148 Baima Bei Lu, (0591) 8761 9939
Cafe
Gao Shang Dao Cafe
高尚岛西餐咖啡厅
27 Shengfu Lu
(0591) 8760 6941
Western
Chinese Face Music Restaurant
中国脸音乐餐厅
17 Yingji Lu
(0591) 8787 9222
Xin Shi Shanshui Xican Jiulang
新石山水西餐酒廊
Minhui Building, 14 Dong Jie
(0591) 8755-0668
Japanese
Boduo Japanese Restaurant
博多日本料理
2/F, Tianjia Building, 28 Dongda Lu
(0591) 8750 9638
Thai
Singapore Thai Shark's Fin Restaurant 新加坡泰国村鱼翅酒楼
2/F, 58 Yong'an Jie
(0591) 8758 6888
Korean
A Li Lang Korean Restaurant
阿里郎韩国料理
310 Wu Si Bei Lu, (0591) 8771 2678

Hospitals
Fuzhou People's Hospital
福州市人民医院
602 Ba Yi Qi Zhong Lu
(0591) 8325 8135
Xiehe Hospital
协和医院
29 Xinquan Lu
(0591) 8335 7896

Bookstores
Fuzhou Xinhua Bookstore
福州市新华书店
189 Bayiqi Bei Lu,B Antai Center
(0591) 755 3576

Industrial parks
Fuzhou Economic & Technological Development Zone
福州经济技术开发区
(0591) 8368 1407
www.fdz.com.cn
Major Industries: Aquaculture, food, electronic, light industry
Fuzhou Free Trade Zone
福州保税区
(0591) 2832 7751
www.fzftz.gov.cn
Major Industries: Logistics
Fuzhou Mawei High-Tech Industrial Development Zone
福州马尾高科技园
(0591) 8368 7385
www.fdz.com.cn
Major Industries:
Semiconductors, electronics

Exhibition centers
Fuzhou International Conference & Exhibition Center
69 Hot Spring Lu, Fuzhou
(010) 8780 3447
www.ficec.com

DESTINATIONS

Quanzhou 泉州
Telephone prefix: 0595
Population: 7.61 million
Bank of China: 1 Jiuyi Lu

Founded in the Tang dynasty in the early eighth century, the port city of Quanzhou was once the largest seaport in the Eastern hemisphere. Under the Ming dynasty (1368-1644), Quanzhou served as the supply depot for the famous Chinese explorer Zheng He but further development was severely hampered by a sea trade ban introduced later by the emperor.

Quanzhou is visibly less prosperous than better-known Fujian cities Fuzhou and Xiamen. One factor contributing to its slow economic start is that the railroad did not arrive there until 1998. Although the central government was long reluctant to invest in Quanzhou because of the military confrontation with nearby Taiwan, today it is a medium-sized trade center that is developing fast.

A network of industrial parks has been developed and a number of industries involving higher technology are being encouraged including petrochemicals, bioengineering, information technology and electronics. The two main industrial parks are Qingmeng Science and Technology Development Zone and Jiangnan High-tech Industrial Park.

Hotels

Quanzhou Hotel
★★★★★
22 Zhuangfu Xiang, (0595) 2228 9958
www.quanzhouhotel.com
Standard room: RMB1,058
Credit Cards: Visa, Master Card, JCB, American Express
Airlines Quanzhou Hotel
★★★★
339 Fengze Jie
(0595) 2216 4888
www.xiamenair.com.cn
Standard room: RMB799
Credit Cards:
Visa, Master Card, JCB, American Express, Domestic Cards
Humei Hotel
★★★★
Citong Bei Lu, (0595) 2211 8888
www.humeihotel.com

Standard room:
RMB288 +15% Surcharge
Credit Cards:
Visa, Master Card, JCB, American Express, Domestic Cards
Quanzhou Overseas Chinese Hotel
★★★★
Baiyuan Lu, (0595) 2228 2192
www.overseaschinesehotel.com
Standard room:
RMB348 (standard room A), 375 (standard room B)
Credit Cards:
Visa, Master Card, JCB, American Express, Domestic Cards
Licheng Hotel
★★★
Central Section Nanjun Lu, Licheng
(0595) 2227 9888
www.lichenghotel.com
Credit Cards:
Visa, Master Card, Domestic Cards

Restaurants

Chinese
Wen Ling Ting 温陵厅
1/F, Quanzhou Hotel, 22 Zhuangfu Xiang
(0595) 2228 9958
Qingyuan Chun沁园春
2/F, Quanzhou Hotel, 22 Zhuangfu Xiang
(0595) 2228 9958
Western
Paris Town 巴黎城
1/F, Nanxin Lou, Quanzhou Hotel, 22 Zhuangfu Xiang
(0595) 2228 9958
Vegetarian
Bohdi Vegetarian Restaurant
菩提素食馆
1-5 Gongjie Xiang
(0595) 2227 8897

Thai
Yuanfeng Thai Restaurant
远风泰式餐厅
1/F, Quanzhou Hotel, 22 Zhuangfu Xiang, (0595) 2228 9958

Hospitals

Quanzhou Children Hospital
泉州市儿童医院
Fengze Jie
(0595) 2218 3272
Quanzhou No.2 Hospital
泉州市第二医院
Zhongshan Bei Lu
(0595) 2276 8142
Quanzhou No.1 Hospital
泉州市第一医院
134 Dongjie, (0595) 2227 7011

Bookstores

Quanzhou Xinhua Bookstore
泉州市新华书店
2 Wenlin Nan Lu
(0595) 298 4659

Industrial Parks

Qingmeng Science and Technology Development Zone
泉州经济技术开发区
(0595) 2235 3003
www.qingmeng.gov.cn
Major Industries: Bioengineering, information technology, optical-mechanical-electronic integration technology, real estate
Jiangnan High-tech Industrial Park
泉州高新技术产业园区
Nanhuan Lu, Quanzhou
(0595) 2248 3550
www.lcyq.com
Major Industries:
Information technology, biotechnology, pharmaceuticals

Xiamen 厦门

Telephone prefix: 0592
Population: 2.25 million
Bank of China: 40 Hubin Bei Lu

Located directly across the Taiwan Strait from Taiwan, the island city of Xiamen (formerly known to Europeans as Amoy) has a population of over two million and is the hometown of many overseas Chinese. It is one of the cleanest, best-run and most charming cities in China and is notable for its conspicuous lack of pollution, which is maintained by keeping heavy industries out of the city. It has some genuinely lovely beaches, and the ocean is clean and warm – perfect for swimming.

Xiamen was the first trading port to be used by Europeans, beginning in 1541, and in the 19th century it was China's main port for exporting tea. It was one of the five Chinese ports opened by the Treaty of Nanjing in 1842 at the end of the first Opium War between Britain and China.

In 1980 the city was named one of the first four 'special economic zones'

(SEZ) in China and is now one of the country's top ports for international business investment. After 20 years of rapid development, Xiamen boasts the most vibrant economy on China's southeast coast.

Xiamen boasts one of the country's largest container ports and because of its geographical and cultural proximity with Taiwan it is a key trading center between the two and receives much of its investment from there.

The city's economy is based mainly around the high-tech industry, transportation, commerce and trade, banking and insurance, tourism, real estate, information technology and communications. During the Asian economic crisis of the late 1990s, Xiamen did well to attract companies from Europe and the US as the flow of investments from Southeast Asia, on which it had previously relied, disappeared.

Xiamen Economic Data	
GDP 2005 (RMB bn)	102.96
Disposable income 2005 (RMB)	16,403

DESTINATIONS

Hotels

BW Premier Trithorn Hot Spring Resort

★★★★★

5/F, 128 Hetong Lu, Haotou

(0592) 561 9999

Standard room: RMB1,199

Credit Cards:

Visa, Master Card, JCB, American Express, Domestic Cards

Powerlong Hotel, Xiamen

★★★★★

133 Hubin Zhong Lu

(0592) 518 8888

www.powerlonghotel.com

Standard room:

RMB1,250 +4% Government tax

Credit Cards:

Visa, Master Card, JCB, American Express, Domestic Cards

Sofitel Plaza Xiamen

★★★★★

19 Hubin Bei Lu

(0592) 507 8888

Standard room:

RMB698 +15% Surcharge

Credit Cards: Visa, Master Card, JCB, American Express

Xiamen Mandarin Hotel

★★★★★

101 Yuehua Lu, Huli

(0592) 602 3333

Standard room: RMB598

Credit Cards:

Visa, Master Card, JCB, American Express

Riyuegu Hotsprings Resort (Xiamen)

★★★★★

Tang'an Village, Dongfu Town, Haicang, (0592) 631 2222

Standard room: RMB1,160

Credit Cards: Visa, Master Card, JCB, American Express

Best Western Xiamen Central Hotel

★★★★

Changqing Lu, Songbai Xiaoqu

(0592) 512 3333

Standard room: RMB1,120

Credit Cards:

Visa, Master Card, JCB, American Express, Domestic Cards

Crowne Plaza Harbour View Xiamen

★★★★

12-8 Zhenhai Lu, (0592) 202 3333

www.ichotelsgroup.com

Standard room:

RMB1,328 +15% Surcharge

Credit Cards: Visa, Master Card, JCB, American Express

Hongdu Park Hotel

★★★★

201 Bailuzhou Lu, (0592) 222 8888

Standard room: RMB498

Credit Cards:

Visa, Master Card, JCB, American Express, Domestic Cards

Jinyan Hotel

★★★★

99 Hubin Nan Lu, (0592) 221 8888

www.jinyan-hotel.com

Standard room: RMB1,150

Credit Cards:

Visa, Master Card, JCB, American Express, Domestic Cards

Ramada Hotel Xiamen

★★★★

431 Changqing Lu, (0592) 503 1333

Standard room: RMB450

Credit Cards:

Visa, Master Card, JCB, American Express, Domestic Cards

Royal Coast Hotel

★★★★

122 Luling Lu, (0592) 558 1888

Credit Cards:

Visa, Master Card, JCB, American

Express, Domestic Cards
The Marco Polo, Xiamen
★★★★
8 Jianye Lu, Hubinbei
(0592) 509 1888
Credit Cards:
Visa, Master Card, JCB, American
Express, Domestic Cards
Watin Business Hotel
★★★★
8 Honglianzhong'er Lu
(0592) 383 1888, *www.watin.com.cn*
Standard room: RMB880
Credit Cards: Visa, Master Card,
JCB, American Express
Xiamen Gold Coast Hotel
★★★★
40 Hubin Bei Lu, (0592) 530 3333
www.gchtl.com.cn
Standard room: RMB420 +4%
Surcharge (two breakfasts incl)
Credit Cards:
Visa, Master Card, JCB, American
Express, Domestic Cards
Xiamen Huaqiao Hotel
★★★★
70-74 Xinhua Lu, (0592) 266 0888
www.xmhqhotel.com.cn
Standard room: RMB550
Credit Cards:
Visa, Master Card, JCB, American
Express, Domestic Cards
Gulang Villa Hotel
★★★
14 Gusheng Lu, (0592) 888 5578
www.xmgly.com
Credit Cards:
Visa, Master Card, JCB, American
Express, Domestic Cards
Huaxia Hotel
★★★
935 Xiahe Lu, (0592) 588 8888
www.hxhotel.com.cn

Standard room: RMB318
Credit Cards: Visa, Master Card,
JCB, American Express
Xia Men Kingty Hotel
★★★
189 Xianyue Lu, (0592) 511 1888
www.kingty.com
Standard room: RMB638
Credit Cards:
Visa, Master Card, JCB, American
Express, Domestic Cards
Xiamen Jinbao Hotel
★★★
126 Dongdu Lu, (0592) 601 3888
www.jinbaohtl.com
Standard room: RMB760
Credit Cards: Visa, Master Card,
JCB, American Express
Xiamen Longdu Hotel
★★★
878 Xiahe Lu, (0592) 580 6666
www.xmlongdu.com
Standard room: RMB580
Credit Cards: Visa, Master Card,
JCB, American Express
Xiamen Lushan Hotel
★★★
102 Jiahe Lu, (0592) 513 6888
www.xmlushan.com
Credit Cards:
Visa, Master Card, JCB, American
Express, Domestic Cards

Restaurants

Western
Ambert Court 雅博园
158 Changqing Lu Bei, Yuhou Nan
Li, (0592) 512 3333
Cafe Maco 马可咖啡厅
8 Jianye Lu (Marco Polo Hotel)
(0592) 509 1888
Japanese
Shogun 将军日本料理

8 Jianye Lu (Marco Polo Hotel)
(0592) 509 1888

Cafe

Venezzia 维尼西亚
3 Nan Hua Lu, (0592) 219 9503

Pattaya 芭堤雅泰餐厅
37 Lianyue Lu, (0592) 511 2992

French

**Madame Rouge Western Restaurant
红夫人西餐厅**
101 Yuehua Lu (Mandarin Hotel)
(0592) 602 3333

Italian

**Portofino Italian Restaurant
波多菲诺意大利餐厅**
12-8 Zhen Hai Lu
(Crowne Plaza Harborview Hotel)
(0592) 202 3333

Southeast Asian

**Singapore Crab Restaurant
新加坡螃蟹馆**
Jin Xiang Building, 28 Hexiang Dong
Lu, (0592) 580 6448

Vegetarian

**Puzhaolou Vegetarian Restaurant
南普陀寺素菜馆**
515 Siming Nan Lu (Nanpuoto Temple), (0592) 208 7281

Chinese

Rooftop Restaurant 观海花园
56 Lujiang Dao(Lujiang Hotel)
(0592) 202 2922

Sichuan

**Tian Xiang Ge Restaurant
天香阁餐厅**
64 Songbai Lu, (0592) 504 1296

Hunan

**Dongti Lake Hunan Restaurant
洞庭湖湘菜馆**
881 Xiahe Lu, (0592) 580 7278

**Mantanghong Hunan Restaurant
满堂红湘菜**
77 Houbin Lu, (0592) 223 8536

Bars & Clubs

Hollywood Bar 荷里活
Donghui Yuan, 362 Hubin Dong Lu
(0592) 5091 693

Hospitals

**Xiamen No.1 Hospital
福建省厦门市第一医院**
10 Shanggu Jie, Zhenhai Lu
(0592) 2137 327

**Xiamen Zhongshan Hospital
厦门市中山医院**
Hubin Nan Lu, (0592) 2292 201

Bookstores

**Xiamen Xinhua Bookstore
厦门市新华书店**
94 Jiahe Lu, (0592) 8513 7896

Industrial parks

**Xiamen Export Processing Zone
厦门出口加工区**
(0592) 6892 777, *www.amoyepz.com*
Major Industries: Electronics information, biopharmacy, precision machinery, fine chemicals

**Xiamen Torch High-Tech
Industrial Development Zone
厦门火炬高科技产业开发区**
(0592) 603 5175, *www.xmtorch.gov.cn*
Major Industries:
Electronics information

**Xiamen Xiangyu Free Trade Zone
厦门象屿保税区**
(0592) 603 5831, *www.xmftz.xm.fj.cn*
Major Industries:
Logistics, electronics, trading

Industrial parks

**Xiamen International
Conference & Exhibition Center**
198 Huizhan Lu, (0592) 595 9898
www.xicec.com

Gansu

Population: 25.94 million
Area: 454, 000 sq km
Capital: Lanzhou
Airports: Lanzhou, Jiayuguan, Dunhuang, Qingyang
Border crossing: Mazongshan

Gansu is located in the upper reaches of the Yellow River and is considered to be one of the cradles of Chinese culture. Because of its plethora of historical points of interest, most of those visiting Gansu province today do so as tourists. Gansu is home to numerous ethnic groups including Tibetan, Uighur, Mongol, Manchu, Kazakh, Hui and Salar peoples, although Han Chinese still make up the vast majority of the population at about 90%.

Gansu's ethnic diversity is a historical legacy of the Gansu Corridor, a 1,000-km passage at the convergence of the Loess, Qinghai-Tibet and Mongolian Plateaus that was a crucial section of the old Silk Road.

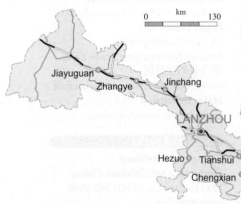

The Gansu Corridor brought peoples and goods from the West and central Asia and facilitated the introduction of Islam to China.

With its proximity to the Qinghai-Tibet Plateau, Gansu also emerged as an important cultural hub for the spread of Buddhism in China. The town of Dunhuang was a center of Buddhist art and scholasticism from the fifth to the 11th centuries, during which many spectacular works of art were produced. Today, Dunhuang's Mogao caves and statues draw both pilgrims and tourists alike. The town of Xiahe in the province's southeast is the second holiest city in Tibetan Buddhism after Lhasa.

Much of Gansu is desert, including stretches of the Gobi Desert, and poorly suited for agriculture and human habitation. Farming is concentrated in the southeastern regions, where the climate is subtropical and humid. The province's northwestern half is temperate and dry. Gansu's main agricultural products are wheat, barley, millet, potatoes, corn, sorghum, rice, soybeans and sugar beet, but the fields are under constant threat by desertification.

Gansu is rich in mineral and energy resources, particularly zinc, nickel, gold, coal, natural gas and oil, and the province's main significance for the rest of the country is related to energy. Gansu sits atop a portion of the Ordos Basin, one of China's largest energy sources, and a gas pipeline connecting Shanghai to energy-rich Xinjiang, part of the massive West-East Gas Pipeline Project, also passes through the province. Gansu has plentiful hydropower resources and its Liujiaxia hydropower station (one of five built in China with Soviet assistance in the 1950s) is one of the country's largest. Recent industrialization of Gansu's economy has chiefly been on the back of development of energy resources.

Both President Hu Jintao and Premier Wen Jiabao began their political careers in Gansu. Hu worked on the construction team of the Liujiaxia Engineering Bureau in the late 1960s and returned in the mid-1970s to serve as Secretary of the Gansu Provincial Construction Committee (GPCC). From 1980 to 1982, Hu served in the GPCC as well as the provincial Communist Youth League. Wen, who studied geology in Beijing, held numerous positions in the Gansu Provincial Geological Bureau from 1968 to 1982.

Gansu is significant to China's rapidly developing space program. The Shenzhou rocket that put Yang Liwei into orbit in 2003 took off from Gansu's Jiuquan base in the Gobi Desert, making China the third nation to successfully launch a manned spacecraft.

Gansu Economic Data			
	2005	2004	Change%
GDP (RMB bn)	193.4	168.8	14.6
GDP per capita (RMB)	7,477	5,970	25.2
Exports (US$ bn)	1.09	1.00	9.44
Imports (US$ bn)	1.88	0.93	100.20
Cars per 100 households	0.46	0.23	100
PCs per 100 households	22.99	20.66	11.28

Lanzhou 兰州

Telephone prefix: 0931
Population: 3.15 million
Bank of China: 589 Tianshui Lu

Very close to the geographic center of today's China, Lanzhou city was founded in the third century BC, during the Qin Dynasty (221 BC-207 BC). Despite being one of China's most interesting cultural crossroads, the city has suffered bad publicity due to its pollution record.

Lanzhou has the reputation of being one of China's - and the world's - most polluted cities. In 1998, the Washington, DC-based World Resources Institute selected Lanzhou as the world's most polluted city. Rampant coal burning and the city's valley location are prime contributors.

The situation has improved to some extent since then, but there is still a pall of dirt hanging over the city on most days, and respiratory diseases are still the city's top cause of death. If you go to Lanzhou in the winter, you may want to consider taking a mask if you have respiratory problems.

Lanzhou is a major transportation hub for north central China, connecting the eastern provinces with Xinjiang, Qinghai and Tibet, and has rail connections to Mongolia and Russia. It also serves as the headquarters of the Lanzhou military region, which encompasses Gansu, Shaanxi, Qinghai, Xinjiang and Tibet.

The city has benefited from the central government's policy of developing the western regions, and a large amount of money has conspicuously been spent on infrastructure, including highways and a large new airport. Meanwhile, there has been considerable foreign investment into the city, with officials saying there are over

1,000 foreign companies with operations in Lanzhou.

The city is laid out along the Yellow River, and divides neatly into two parts – the city center at one end of the valley, and the industrial center at the other. Beyond the city proper, the sparse, grey-brown loess land which is the dominant feature of all of northwest China quickly takes over.

The pollution is far worse in the industrial section. Unfortunately, the Soviet engineers who helped place the factories failed to consider the dominant wind direction, which usually blows the smokestack pall towards the city center.

Across the river from the heart of the city, up on a hill, is a delightful Buddhist temple complex which has been renovated. A little further along is a new calligraphy garden, also overlooking the river and the city beyond, which is filled with stone representations of Chinese characters.

Lanzhou Economic Data	
GDP 2005 (RMB bn)	56.71
Disposable income 2005 (RMB)	8,529

Hotels

Hotel Savoy Muslim
★★★★
788 Xijin Xi Lu, Qilihe
(0931) 293 4888
Standard room: RMB360
Credit Cards:
Visa, Master Card, JCB, American Express, Domestic Cards
JJ Sun Hotel
★★★★

589 Donggang Xi Lu, (0931) 880 5511
www.jjsunhotel.com
Credit Cards:
Visa, Master Card, JCB, American Express, Domestic Cards
Lanzhou Legend Hotel
★★★★
529 Tianshui Nan Lu, (0931) 853 2888
Credit Cards: Visa, Master Card, JCB, American Express, Domestic Cards, Diners Club
Xilan International Hotel
★★★★
39 Dingxi Lu, Chengguan
(0931) 862 8998
www.xilan-hotel.com
Standard room: RMB698
Credit Cards: Visa, Master Card, JCB, American Express
Jincheng Tourism Hotel
★★★
3 Tianshui Zhong Lu
(0931) 841 6638
www.gsjcbg.com
Standard room: RMB248
Credit Cards: Visa, Master Card, JCB, American Express

Restaurants

Chinese
Caesar Delicacy Town
恺撒龙美食城
287 Jingyang Lu, (0931) 848 0969
Chinese Garden Restaurant
中华苑餐厅
486 Donggang Xi Lu (Lanzhou Hotel), (0931) 841 6321
Chaoshan Restaurant
潮汕大酒店
361 Tianshui Lu, Nongmin Xiang
(0931) 888 9484
Zen Chinese Restaurant
天上天中餐厅

529 Tianshui Lu (Lanzhou Legend Hotel), (0931) 853 2888

Muslim

Nation Restaurant 民族饭店餐厅
386 Gannan Zhong Lu (Minzu Hotel)
(0931) 882 4613

Western

Tiffany Restaurant 飞仙
529 Tianshui Lu (Lanzhou Legend Hotel), (0931) 853 2888

Korean

Korean Restaurant 风味阁餐厅
529 Tianshui Lu (Lanzhou Legend Hotel), (0931) 853 2888

Bars & Clubs

Jiuquan Bar 酒泉吧
2/F, 529 Tianshui Lu

Cashbox 西部钱柜
35 Jiuquan Lu, (0931) 8487 000

Hospitals

First People's Hospital

兰州市第一人民医院
1 Wujiayuan Xi Jie, Jianlan Lu
(0931) 233 5411

Bookstores

Lanzhou Xinhua Bookstore
兰州市新华书店
10 Tongwei Lu, (0931) 846 6883

Industrial parks

Lanzhou Economic & Technological Development Zone
兰州经济技术开发区
(0931) 217 5600
www.lzeda.com

Lanzhou National New & High-Tech Industrial Development Zone
兰州高新技术产业开发区
(0931) 855 2467
www.lzhtp.gov.cn

Major Industries:
Science and technology, medical, electronicss chemicals

Jiayuguan 嘉峪关
Telephone prefix: 0937
Population: 0.13 million

Jiayuguan used to be a major stop on the Silk Road and boasts as its tourist draw a fort generally acknowledged as the westernmost point of the Great Wall (though it is technically not). In the old days it represented the divide between the "civilized" east and the "barbaric" and desolate west. The fort itself is located about 6 km outside the city center and is well worth a visit.

Hotels

Jiayuguan Chang Cheng Hotel
★★★★
6 Jianshe Xi Lu
(0937) 622 6306
www.cchotel.com
Credit Cards: Visa, Domestic Cards
Jiayuguan Hotel
★★★★
1 Xinhua Bei Lu
(0937) 620 1588
www.jiayuguanhotel.com
Standard room: RMB568
Credit Cards:
Visa, Master Card, American Express
Guo Tai Hotel ★★★
Xiongguan Square
(0937) 632 6699
www.guotaihotel.com
Standard room: RMB368
Credit Cards: Domestic Cards

Guangdong

Population: 91.94 million
Area: 186,000 sq km
Capital: Guangzhou
Airports: Guangzhou, Shenzhen, Shantou, Zhuhai
Ports: Guangzhou, Chiwan, Shekou, Shantou, Zhuhai

Guangdong province lies in southern China and is bisected by the Tropic of Cancer, giving it warm winters and long, hot summers. Its coastline constitutes more than one fifth of the total coastline in China, thus the ocean has played a vital role in the province's local culture and economy. The Pearl River, the third-longest river in China, winds through the province before meeting the South China Sea at the coast.

The Pearl River Delta (PRD) Economic Zone is the province's economic hub, accounting for 80% of Guangdong's GDP. The PRD Economic Zone covers 14 cities and counties – including Guangzhou (the provincial capital), Shenzhen, Zhuhai, Foshan, Jiangmen, Dongguan, Zhongshan and Huizhou.

Furthermore, Guangdong is the base for the massive Pan-PRD region comprising Guangdong, Sichuan, Fujian, Hunan, Jiangxi, Guangxi, Yunnan, Guizhou and Hainan. A large proportion of import-export traffic involving these provinces flows through Guangdong as does investment capital. The province therefore is a crucial link between Southern China and the rest of the world.

Guangdong has had the highest GDP in China for decades; in 2005 it was roughly US$284 billion, accounting for 12.2% of the national total. Guangdong also has the highest volume of imports and exports in China as well as the highest retail sales figures.

Guangdong's strength lies in the manufacturing of light industry, output of which accounts for over half of the province's total industrial output. Major products include electrical appliances such as television sets, electrical fans and refrigerators, and other consumer products like garments, bicycles, toys, shoes and

electronics. Guangdong is China's top exporter of most of these products.

Guangdong's rapid development is a result of foreign investment, particularly in the PRD economic zones. Guangdong is a major export-processing base for foreign investors mainly from Hong Kong and Taiwan. In recent years the Yangtze River Delta (YRD) comprising Shanghai, Hangzhou, Ningbo, and the surrounding areas, has emerged as a serious rival to the dominance of the PRD. While Guangdong included the first areas in China to liberalize economically, Shanghai is now the fastest-growing region in the country.

But one of the major factors making the PRD more attractive than the Shanghai region is Hong Kong. After the first few years of uncertainty under Chinese rule, Hong Kong has emerged with a new confidence. Hong Kong is becoming much more integrated into Guangdong as a whole. Although some might see the border between Hong Kong and the rest of the province as a logistical barrier, many companies see it as an advantage due to Hong Kong's independent legal and financial systems. Hong Kong dollars are easily exchanged into foreign currency, and the legal environment is much more sophisticated and conducive to foreign enterprises setting up shop. For this reason, it is a popular choice for companies to establish offices in Hong Kong while setting up production facilities just over the border in Guangdong.

Guangdong is aware that it must keep evolving in order to maintain its position of prominence. One of the most innovative infrastructure projects introduced in years was given the green light in 2005 – the Hong Kong-Zhuhai-Macau Bridge. The idea for the bridge was devised as a solution to the logistical difficulties faced when crossing between Guang-

dong, Hong Kong and Macau. It will link the eastern and western banks of the Pearl River, bringing economic advantages to both sides. The bridge will shorten the drive between the two sides to a mere half hour. At a cost of RMB31.5 billion, authorities of the area see it as a worthwhile expenditure to maintain their economic edge.

As home to the first SEZs in China, Guangdong is also known to have some of the most progressive and innovative policies regarding business and investment, thus making it more friendly to international investment than other areas in China. As the rest of China continues to evolve, Guangdong will undoubtedly remain at the forefront of modernization and innovation.

Guangdong Economic Data

	2005	2004	Change%
GDP (RMB bn)	2236.7	1886.5	18.6
GDP per capita (RMB)	24,435	19,707	24.0
Exports (US$ bn)	238.16	191.56	24.33
Imports (US$ bn)	189.81	165.58	14.63
Cars per 100 households	9.69	6.56	47.71
PCs per 100 households	70.34	64.28	9.43 7

Guangzhou 广州
Telephone prefix: 020
Population: 9.48 million
Bank of China: 91 Changdi Lu

Guangzhou, the capital of Guangdong province, is a major deepwater port on the Pearl River Delta with a wealth of history. It has been successively eclipsed by Hong Kong, then by Shenzhen, and lately by Shanghai. But the city, which for a couple of hundred years was the only place foreigners could do business in China, is rising once more in the perceptions and plans of foreign companies.

With a population of about nine million, Guangzhou (formerly known to foreigners as Canton) benefits from its infrastructure, its experience, the flexibility of the local administration, and from the growing depth of manufacturing business right across Guangdong province. Guangzhou is at the heart of the Pearl River Delta, which in the past 25 years has seen tremendous economic growth.

Guangzhou, as the provincial capital, plays a vital role in coordinating this continuing boom, which officials predict will not only continue but also accelerate.

Guangzhou has been an important trading port for more than 2,000 years, and for centuries Arab and Persian traders played a prominent role in the business life of the city. When the Europeans arrived in southern China in the 16th century, the Chinese quarantined them in Macau and also on an island in Guangzhou called Shameen. The island is an oasis of late 19th century European charm with Chinese characteristics, and still has the buildings and some of the feel of those times.

Guangzhou declined in importance when the country was forced open in the 1840s, with foreign trade being dispersed amongst a string of China Treaty Ports along the coast. But after the communist victory in 1949, China's business links with the outside world were once again restricted to Guangzhou. The twice-yearly Canton Trade Fair was for decades a tenuous but crucial link for China with the outside world. It remains an important feature of life in the city even though China is now wide open again. The reason is convenience.

Guangzhou is growing as an air transportation hub for the region and is trying to become a competitor to Hong Kong. The city opened Baiyun airport in 2004 which is serviced by numerous international airlines and is the base for China Southern Airlines, the nation's second-largest passenger carrier. UPS also upgraded its transport links to the city and FedEx declared Baiyun airport would become its regional distribution center in 2005.

Guangzhou Economic Data	
GDP 2005 (RMB bn)	511.58
Disposable income 2005 (RMB)	18,287

Hotels

Bishuiwan Hot Spring Holiday Inn
★★★★★
Hot Spring Holiday Resort, Liuxi, Conghua, (020) 8784 2888
www.bishuiwan.com
Credit Cards:
Visa, Master Card, JCB, American Express, Domestic Cards

China Hotel, A Marriott Hotel
★★★★★
Liuhua Lu, (020) 8666 6888
Standard room: RMB1,300
Credit Cards: Visa, Master Card, JCB, American Express

Grand International Hotel
★★★★★
468 Tianhe Bei Lu, Tianhe
(020) 3880 3333
www.grandinternationalhotel.com
Standard room: RMB900
Credit Cards: Visa, Master Card, JCB, American Express

Holiday Islands Hotel
★★★★★
Shanqian Luyou Dajie, Huadu
(020) 8672 4441
www.holidayislandshotel.com
Standard room: RMB1,080
Credit Cards:
Visa, Master Card, Domestic Cards

Howard Johnson Hawana Resort Guangzhou
★★★★★
1 Xiawanna Dajie, Taiping Town, Conghua, (020) 6170 1188
Credit Cards: Visa, Master Card, JCB, American Express

Nansha Grand Hotel
★★★★★
1 Nan'er Lu, Shangmao Dajie, New Coast City, Nansha, (020) 3930 8888
Standard room: RMB1,160 +15%

Surcharge (deluxe room)
Credit Cards:
Visa, Master Card, JCB, American Express, Domestic Cards

Nanyang King's Gate Hotel
★★★★★
38 Xinghua Lu, Tianhe
(020) 6136 8888
www.nanyanghotel.com
Standard room: RMB468
Credit Cards: Visa, Master Card, JCB, American Express

Novotel Baiyun Airport Guangzhou
★★★★★
North of Domestic Departure, Guangzhou Baiyun International Airport, Huadu, (020) 3606 7899
Standard room:
RMB1,218 +15% Surcharge
Credit Cards:
Visa, Master Card, JCB, American Express, Domestic Cards

Springdale Serviced Residence Guangzhou
★★★★★
Building B1, 105 Tiyu Xi Lu, Tianhe
(020) 3879 2711
Credit Cards:
Visa, Master Card, JCB, American Express, Domestic Cards

The Garden Hotel Guangzhou
★★★★★
368 Huanshi Dong Lu
(020) 8333 8989
www.thegardenhotel.com.cn
Standard room:
RMB1,296 +15% Surcharge
Credit Cards: Visa, Master Card, JCB, American Express

The Phoenix City Hotel Guangzhou
★★★★★
Xintang Section Guangyuan Dong Lu, (020) 8280 8888

www.phoenixcityhotel.com
Credit Cards:
Visa, Master Card, Domestic Cards
Tianlun International Hotel
★★★★★
172 Linhe Zhong Lu, (020) 8393 6388
www.tianlun-hotel.com
Standard room: RMB1,200
Credit Cards:
Visa, Master Card, JCB, American
Express, Domestic Cards
Guangzhou Oriental Resort
★★★★★
1068 Baiyun South Dajie
(020) 8663 2888
www.oriental-resort.com
Standard room: RMB988
Credit Cards:
Visa, Master Card, JCB, American
Express, Domestic Cards
Baihua Resort Hotel
★★★★
Zengcheng, (020) 8261 8888
www.zcbhsz.com
Standard room:
RMB430 +10% Surcharge
Credit Cards: Visa, Master Card,

JCB, American Express
**Best Western Guangzhou Baiyun
Hotel**
★★★★
367 Huanshi Dong Lu
(020) 8333 3998
Credit Cards: Visa, Master Card,
JCB, American Express
Cathay Hotel
★★★★
376 Huanshi Dong Lu
(020) 8386 2888
Standard room: RMB268
Credit Cards: Visa, Master Card,
JCB, American Express
Guangdong Guest Hotel
★★★★
603 Jiefang Bei Lu, (020) 8333 2950
www.ggh.com.cn
Credit Cards: Visa, Master Card,
JCB, Domestic Cards
Guangdong Hotel
★★★★
309 Dongfeng Zhong Lu
(020) 8333 9933
www.guangdong-hotel.com
Standard room: RMB840

Credit Cards:
Visa, Master Card, JCB, American Express, Domestic Cards
Guangdong Victory Hotel
★★★★
53 Shamian Bei Jie, (020) 8121 6688
www.vhotel.com
Standard room: RMB660
Credit Cards: Visa, Master Card, JCB, American Express
Guangzhou International Financial Tower
★★★★
197-199 Dongfeng Xi Lu
(020) 8332 1688
www.financialhotel.com
Credit Cards:
Visa, Master Card, JCB, American Express, Domestic Cards
HNA Hotel Central Guangzhou
★★★★
33 Jichang Lu, (020) 8657 8331
www.hnahotel.com
Standard room:
RMB680 +15% Surcharge
Credit Cards:
Visa, Master Card, JCB, American

Express, Domestic Cards
Holiday Inn City Centre Guangzhou
★★★★
28 Guangming Lu, Huanshidong Overseas Chinese Village
(020) 8776 6999
Standard room:
RMB588 +15% Surcharge
Credit Cards: Visa, Master Card, JCB, American Express
Holiday Inn Shifu Guangzhou
★★★★
188 Dishifu Lu, Liwan
(020) 8138 0088
www.ichotelsgroup.com
Standard room: RMB480
Credit Cards:
Visa, Master Card, JCB, American Express, Domestic Cards
Hotel Canton
★★★★
374 Beijing Lu, (020) 8318 9888
www.hotel-canton.net
Standard room: RMB728
Credit Cards: Visa, Master Card, JCB, American Express, Domestic Cards

Hotel Landmark Canton
★★★★
8 Qiaoguang Lu, Haizhu Plaza
(020) 8335 5988
www.hotel-landmark.com.cn
Standard room:
RMB1,000 +15% Surcharge
Credit Cards:
Visa, Master Card, JCB

Huadu New Century Hotel
★★★★
43 Xiuquan Dajie, Huadu
(020) 8683 2922
Credit Cards:
Visa, Master Card, JCB, American
Express, Domestic Cards

Jin Sui Lou Hotel
★★★★
598 Tianhe Bei Lu, (020) 8529 9277
Credit Cards: Visa, Master Card,
JCB, American Express, Domestic
Cards

Jin Yuan Village Hotel
★★★★
117 Hengfu Lu, (020) 8358 1688
www.gzjy.net
Standard room: RMB680
Credit Cards: Visa, Master Card, JCB,
American Express, Domestic Cards

Ka Ying Hotel
★★★★
418 Huanshi Dong Lu
(020) 8777 1688
Standard room: RMB380
Credit Cards: Visa, Master Card,
JCB, American Express

Liuhua Hotel
★★★★
194 Huanshi Xi Lu, (020) 8666 8800
www.lh.com.cn
Credit Cards:
Visa, Master Card, JCB, American
Express, Domestic Cards

Pearl Garden Hotel
721 Kaifa Dajie, Eco. & Tech. Dev.
Zone, (020) 8222 6688
www.pearlgardenhotel.com
Standard room: RMB998
Credit Cards:
Visa, Master Card, JCB, American
Express

President Hotel Guangzhou
★★★★
586 Tianhe Lu
(020) 8551 2988
www.prehotel.com
Standard room: RMB338
Credit Cards:
Visa, Master Card, JCB, American
Express, Domestic Cards

Ramada Pearl Hotel Guangzhou
★★★★
9 Mingyueyi Lu, Guangzhou Zhong
Dajie, (020) 8737 2988
www.ramada.com
Standard room: RMB1,150 +15%
Surcharge (rack rate)
Credit Cards: Visa, Master Card,
JCB, American Express, Diners Club

Ray Star Hotel
★★★★
95 Chepi Lu, Tianhe
(020) 3860 1999

Riverside Hotel
★★★★
298 Yanjiang Zhong Lu
(020) 8328 8888
www.riverside-hotel.com.cn
Standard room: RMB1,000
Credit Cards:
Visa, Master Card, JCB, American
Express, Domestic Cards

Rong Wei Hotel
★★★★
13 Xindu Dajie, Huadu
(020) 8688 9888

www.rwhotel.cn
Credit Cards:
Visa, Master Card, American Express,
Domestic Cards
Rundu Hotel
★★★★
300 Huangpu Zhong Dajie, Tianhe
(020) 8553 8388
www.runduhotel.com
Credit Cards:
Visa, Master Card, American Express
Silver Bay Bailing Hotel
★★★★
299 Yanjiang Zhong Lu
(020) 6122 2333
www.white-collarhotel.com
Standard room: RMB658
Credit Cards:
Visa, Master Card, JCB, American
Express, Domestic Cards
Warmyes Business Hotel
★★★★
468 Xingang Zhong Lu
(020) 6127 8999
www.warmyes.cn
Standard room:
RMB328 (single), 528 (twin)
Credit Cards: Visa, Master Card,
JCB, American Express
White Palace Hotel
★★★★
111 Yingbin Bei Lu, Dashi Town,
Panyu, (020) 8458 2288
www.whitepalacehotel.com
Standard room:
RMB398 +10% Surcharge
Credit Cards:
Visa, Master Card, JCB, American
Express, Domestic Cards
Zengcheng Hotel
★★★★
Zengcheng Dajie, Licheng
(020) 8261 9888

www.zengchenghotel.com
Standard room: RMB550
Credit Cards:
Visa, Master Card, JCB, American
Express, Domestic Cards
Wei Jing Hotel
★★★★
32 Xingnan Lu, Yingbin Dajie, Panyu
(020) 3482 2888
www.gz-weijing.com
Standard room: RMB570
Credit Cards: Visa, Master Card,
JCB, American Express
Conghua Huguang Holiday Village
★★★
Huangzhulang, Conghua
(020) 8784 3388
www.huguang-holiday.com
Credit Cards: Domestic Cards
Dongyuan Hotel
★★★
8 Dongyuansi Jie, Qingnian Lu, Eco.
& Tech. Dev. Zone, (020) 8221 6668
www.dyhotel.com.cn
Credit Cards:
Visa, Master Card, JCB, American
Express, Domestic Cards
Five Rams City Hotel
★★★
322 Renmin Zhong Lu
(020) 8188 9889
www.wychotel.com
Credit Cards:
Visa, Master Card, American Express,
Domestic Cards, Diners Card
Guangzhou Tian Long Hotel
★★★
118 Guangzhou Zhong Dajie
(020) 3886 9988
www.tianlonghotel.com
Standard room: RMB300
Credit Cards:
Visa, Master Card, Domestic Cards

Guangdong Hotel & Resort
★★★
Lianhua Mountain Tour Zone, Panyu, (020) 8486 2788
www.gdlotus.cn
Credit Cards: Visa, Master Card, JCB, Domestic cards

Guangdong New Xiangjiang Hotel
★★★
183 Huanshi Xi Lu, (020) 8666 3012
www.xxjhotel.com
Standard room:
RMB300 (normal season)
Credit Cards: Visa, Master Card, American Express, Domestic Cards

Guangzhou Baiyun International Airport Hotel
★★★
340 Yunxiao Jie, Jichang Lu
(020) 8663 8838
www.myairporthotel.com
Credit Cards:
Visa, Master Card, JCB, American Express, Domestic Cards

Guangzhou Hotel
★★★
2 Qiyi Lu, (020) 8333 8168

www.gzhotel.com.cn
Standard room: RMB278
Credit Cards:
Visa, Master Card, JCB, American Express, Domestic Cards

Guangzhou New World Hotel
★★★
520 Renmin Bei Lu, (020) 8109 9888
www.new-world-hotel.com
Standard room: RMB270
Credit Cards:
Visa, Master Card, JCB, American Express, Domestic Cards

Guangzhou Sanyu Hotel
★★★
23 Sanyu Lu, (020) 8775 6888
www.sanyuhotel.com
Standard room: RMB488, 328
Credit Cards:
Visa, Master Card, JCB, American Express, Domestic Cards

Guangzhou Shahe Hotel
★★★
318 Xianlie Dong Lu
(020) 3556 6436
www.weare.cn
Standard room: RMB150

DESTINATIONS

Credit Cards: Visa, Master Card, JCB, American Express
Huahai Hotel
★★★
232 Jiangnan Zhong Dajie
(020) 8405 8888
www.huahaihotel.com
Credit Cards: Visa, Master Card, JCB, American Express, Domestic Cards
Huifu Hotel
★★★
38 Huifu Xi Lu, (020) 8130 9888
www.huifuhotel.com
Credit Cards:
Visa, Master Card, JCB, American Express, Domestic Cards
Jiangyue Hotel
★★★
20 Binjiang Xi Lu, (020) 6125 9888
www.gzjyhotel.com
Credit Cards: Visa, Master Card, Domestic Cards
Jin Ying Hotel Guangzhou
★★★

19 Beijiaochang Lu, Yuexiu
(020) 8381 1888
Standard room: RMB398
Credit Cards: Visa, Master Card, JCB, American Express, Domestic Cards
Jing Hua Hotel
★★★
55 Yunshan Dajie, Xinhua Town, Huadu, (020) 3681 0333
www.jinghuahotel.com
Credit Cards: Visa, Master Card, American Express, Domestic Cards
Meiyi Hotel
★★★
151 Jiefang Nan Lu, (020) 8188 8168
www.meiyihotel.com
Standard room: RMB210
Credit Cards: Visa, Master Card, JCB, American Express, Domestic Cards
Overseas Chinese Friendship Hotel
★★★
65 Tianhe Dong Lu, (020) 8551 3298
www.gdhy-hotel.com

Credit Cards: Visa, Master Card, JCB, American Express, Domestic Cards

Overseas Chinese Hotel
★★★
90 Zhanqian Lu, (020) 8666 3488
www.huaqiaoj.com.cn
Standard room: RMB450
Credit Cards: Visa, Master Card, JCB, American Express

Shen Zhou Hotel
★★★
1 Shatai Lu, Tianpingjia
(020) 6136 3888
www.gzszhotel.com
Standard room: RMB328
Credit Cards: Visa, Master Card, JCB, American Express, Domestic Cards

Silver-River Hotel
★★★
268 Shatai Lu, (020) 6108 9688
www.gzsr-hotel.com
Credit Cards: Visa, Master Card, JCB, American Express

Sino Trade Center Hotel
★★★
63 Panfu Lu
(020) 8136 3322
www.sinohotel-gz.com
Standard room: RMB230
Credit Cards: Visa, Master Card, JCB, American Express

Wangxinglou Hotel
★★★
17 Shahe Lu
(020) 6103 5888
Standard room: RMB328
Credit Cards: Domestic Cards

Yuanyang Hotel
★★★
6 Longkou Dong Lu, Tianhe
(020) 6108 2888

www.yyhotelgz.com
Standard room: RMB447
Credit Cards:
Visa, Master Card, JCB, American Express, Domestic Cards

Zhu Hai Special Economic Zone Hotel
★★★
11-15 Haizhu Bei Lu, (020) 6127 6888
www.zh8888.com
Standard room:
RMB338 +13% Surcharge
Credit Cards: Visa, Master Card, JCB, American Express

Restaurants

German
1920 Café
1920咖啡厅
183 Yan Jiang Zhong Lu
(020) 8333 6156

Italian
Anti Pasto
咖啡中途站
1/F Guangyi Plaza, 38 Huale Jie
(020) 8360 1366

Italian Restaurant
小街风情意大利餐厅
3/F East Tower, Pearl River Building,
360 Huan Shi Dong Lu
(020) 8386 3840

Chinese
Datong Restaurant 大同酒家
63 Yuanjiang Xi Lu, (020) 8188 8988

Tangliyuan Restaurant
唐荔园食艺馆
Liwanhu Park, Ruyifang, Huangsha
Dajie, (020) 8181 8002

Chaozhou Restaurant 潮州菜馆
96 Zhanqian Lu, (020) 8667 0276

Seafood
Dongjiang Seafood Restaurant
东江海鲜餐馆

DESTINATIONS

276 Huanshi Zhong Lu
(020) 8322 9188
French
La Seine 塞纳河法国西餐厅
1/F Xing Hai Concert Hall, 33 Qing
Bo Lu, (020) 87352 222
Celebrities Palace 名仕阁
26 Tianhe Dong Lu, (020) 8750 3426
Cantonese
Xin Li Zhi Wan Restaurant
新荔枝湾
7-9 Luhu Lu, (020) 8331 2345
Hunan
Hunan Home 佬湘楼
6/F Times Square, 28 Tianhe Bei Lu
(020) 3882 1850
Western
Gail's Place American Food & Bar
水云轩西餐厅
96 Heng Fu Lu, (020) 8359 2080
American
Samba Restaurant & Bar
森巴西餐厅
2/F, 11 Jian She Liu Ma Lu
(020) 8381 6888
Madison American
麦迪逊美国饮食文化专家
Ocena Harp, Binjiang Dong Lu
(020) 3421 9170
Japanese
Daiwo Story Japanese Restaurant
大和物语日式餐厅
77 Tiyu Xi Lu, (020) 8130 1882
Thai
Welcome Thai Café & Restaurant
沙华地卡泰马星餐厅
1/F, 33 Pan Fu Lu, (020) 8136 3666

Bars & Clubs

B Boss
5/F, Ocean Commercial Plaza, 414
Huanshi Dong Lu
Hill Bar 小山吧

367 Huanshi Dong Lu
Gypsy King 大篷车酒吧
360 Huanshi Dong Lu
Africa Bar 非洲吧
2/F, Zidong Hua Building, 707
Dongfeng Dong Lu
Club Tang 堂会
1 Jianshe Liu
Club Tang 唐会
1 Jianshe Liu
Elephant & Castle 大象堡酒吧
363 Huanshi Dong Lu
Focus 焦点
5/F GITIC Riverside, 298 Yanjiang
Zhong Lu
The Paddy Field
Central Plaza, 38 Huale Lu

Hospitals

**Guangdong Provincial People's
Hospital**
广东省人民医院
102 Zhongshan Er Lu
(020) 8382 7812
Can-Am Int'l Medical Centre
加美国际医疗中心
5/F Garden Tower, 368 Huanshi
Dong Lu, (020) 8386 6988
Global Doctor Clinic
广州市第一人民医院
106 Zhongshan Er Lu (Guangzhou
No.1 People's Hospital)
(020) 8382 7812

Bookstores

Foreign Language Book Store
暨南大学外文书店
Jinan University, 1 Shangye Jie
(020) 8522 1422
Xinhua Bookstore, Guangdong
广东省新华书店
12 Si Malu, Da Shatou
(020) 8227 8655

Local English Media

that's Guangzhou
www.thatsguangzhou.com

Consulates

Australia 澳大利亚
14/F-15/F Guangdong International
Hotel, 339 Huanshi Dong Lu
(020) 8335 0909

Canada 加拿大
801, China Hotel Office Tower,
Liuhua Lu, (020) 8666 0569

Denmark 丹麦
1578 China Hotel Office Tower,
Liuhua Lu, (020) 8666 0795

France 法国
810 Guangdong International Hotel,
339 Huanshi Dong Lu
(020) 2829 2000

Germany 德国
19/F Guangdong International Hotel,
339 Huanshi Dong Lu
(020) 8330 6533

Italy 意大利
5207-5208 CITIC Plaza, 233 Tianhe
Bei Lu, (020) 3877 0556

Japan 日本
368 Huanshi Dong Lu, Garden Hotel
(020) 8334 3090

Korea 韩国
18/F West Tower, Yangcheng International Trade Center
(020) 3887 0555

Malaysia 马来西亚
3/F Ramada Pearl Hotel, 9 Mingyue
Yi Lu, (020) 8739 5660

Netherlands 荷兰
905 Guangdong International Hotel,
339 Huanshi Dong Lu
(020) 8330 2067

Philippines 菲律宾
G/F White Swan Hotel
(020) 8331 1461

Poland 波兰
63 Shamian Dajie, (020) 8121 9993

Sweden 瑞典
1002B-1003, CITIC Plaza, 233 Tianhe Bei Lu, (020) 3891 2383

Thailand 泰国
2/F Garden Hotel, (020) 8380 4277

UK 英国
2/F Guangdong International Hotel,
339 Huangshi Dong Lu
(020) 8335 1354

USA 美国
1 Shamian Nan Jie, (020) 8121 8000

Vietnam 越南
Unit B, 2/F Huaxia Hotel, Qiaoguang
Lu, (020) 8330 5910

Airline Offices

Air China 中国国际航空公司
9/F-10/F 300 Dongfeng Zhong Lu
(020) 8363 7527

Air France 法国航空公司
13/F Gaosheng Building, 109 Tiyu Xi
Lu, (020) 3879 5730

**China Eastern Airlines
中国东方航空公司**
91 Dongfeng Xi Lu, (020) 8135 0075

**China Southern Airlines
中国南方航空公司**
181 Huanshi Xi Lu, (020) 8613 0870

Dragonair 港龙航空有限公司
Garden Hotel, 368 Huanshi Dong Lu
(020) 8388 2498

Shanghai Airlines 上海航空公司
G/F North Tower, Liuhua Hotel, 194
Huanshi Xi Lu, (020) 8668 1149

Singapore Airlines 新加坡航空公司
28/F Dongshan Plaza, 69 Xianlie
Zhong Lu, (020) 8732 0600

Industrial Parks

**Guangzhou Nansha Economic &
Technological Development Zone**

广州南沙经济技术开发区
(020) 8468 8833
www.gzns.gov.cn
Major Industries:
Bonded warehouses, heavy industry, power generation, shipbuilding and mechanical manufacturing, logistics
Guangzhou Economic & Technological Development Zone
广州经济技术开发区
(020) 8221 9000
www.getdd.com.cn
Major Industries:
Plastics, chemistry, electronics, food processing and shipbuilding
Guangzhou Export Processing Zone
广州出口加工区
(020) 8221 9000
Major Industries: Automobile
Guangzhou Free Trade Zone
广州保税区
(020) 8221 9000
www.getdd.com.cn
Guangzhou High-Tech Industrial

Development Zone
广州高新技术产业开发区
(020) 8221 9000
Major Industries: Higher education institutions, scientific research institutions, state-level laboratories

Exhibition centers

Guangzhou International Convention & Exhibition Center
388 Yuejiang Zhong Lu
Guangzhou
(020) 2608 8888
www.cantonfair.org.cn
Guangzhou Jinhan Exhibition Center
119 Liuhua Lu, Guangzhou
(020) 3623 5885
www.jh-gz.com
Chinese Export Commodities Fairground
117 Liuhua Lu, Guangzhou
(020) 2608 8888
www.cftc.org.cn

Shenzhen 深圳

Telephone prefix: 0755
Population: 8.27 million
Bank of China: 2002 Jianshe Lu

Bordering Hong Kong, Shenzhen became China's first Special Economic Zone (SEZ) in 1980, and in less than a quarter century grew from a small village to a metropolis of eight million people. It passed through a wild phase and is now a relatively mature business environment, with good infrastructure and a workforce that comes from all over China to look for work.

Today Shenzhen is one of three lynchpins (together with Hong Kong and Guangzhou) in the powerhouse economy of the Pearl River Delta. From a peasant economy, in less than a generation it has become one of China's richest cities with the country's highest average annual wage. It is home to China's second stock exchange and in 2005 overtook Hong Kong's main Kwai Cheung Port in shipping volume, largely a result of handling costs that are over US$300 less in Shenzhen. The port authorities in Shenzhen have announced that they are going to expand their container handling capacity to cope with the upsurge in demand.

Shenzhen's rise to riches has also made it an important consumer market in its own right. It is one of China's top three markets for private automobiles and a fast growing retail center.

Initially much of the driving force behind Shenzhen's development was its role as a low-cost manufacturing center – an opportunity for thousands of Hong Kong- and Taiwan-based producers to move their production to cheaper plants on the mainland. For much of the 1980s and early 90s therefore, the concentration was overwhelmingly on mass production of textiles, toys, electronics, and, to a lesser extent, chemicals.

Shenzhen displays Chinese freemarket capitalism at its harshest, and those who don't make the grade often have nothing to fall back on. As a result, there are a noticeably high number of beggars in the city. Drugs and street crime, too, have also been a problem – although the city government recently toughened up policing, bringing a noticeable drop in cases. The Luohu area (spelled Lowu on the Hong Kong side) is getting a needed makeover, and the city is investing heavily in a gleaming new CBD further north in the Futian district.

Hotels

Best Western Shenzhen Felicity Hotel
★★★★★
1085 Heping Lu, (0755) 2558 6333
Standard room: RMB1,370
Credit Cards:
Visa, Master Card, JCB, American Express, Domestic Cards
Crowne Plaza Shenzhen
★★★★★
9026 Shennan Dajie, Overseas Chinese Town, (0755) 2693 6888
www.ichotelsgroup.com
Standard room: RMB1,900
Credit Cards:

Visa, Master Card, JCB, American Express, Great Wall, Diners Club
Four Points by Sheraton Shenzhen
★★★★★
5 Guihua Lu, Futian Free Trade Zone
(0755) 8359 9999
Standard room: RMB1,430
Credit Cards: Visa, Master Card, JCB, American Express, Diners Club
Hengfeng Haiyue International Hotel
★★★★★
Xincheng Plaza, 80th Block Baocheng, Bao'an, (0755) 2792 2222
www.hfhotel.com
Standard room:
RMB880 +15% Surcharge
Credit Cards:
Visa, Master Card, JCB, American Express, Domestic Cards
Nan Hai Hotel
★★★★★
1 Gongyeyi Lu, Nanhai Dajie, Shekou, Nanshan, (0755) 2669 2888
www.nanhai-hotel.com
Standard room:
RMB1,560 +15% Surcharge
Credit Cards: Visa, Master Card, JCB, American Express
Shangri-La Hotel Shenzhen
★★★★★
East Side Railway Station, 1002 Jianshe Lu, Luohu, (0755) 8233 0888
Standard room:
RMB1,550 +15% Surcharge
Credit Cards: Visa, Master Card, JCB, American Express
Shenzhen Grand View Hotel
★★★★★
277 Fuhua Lu, Futian
(0755) 8297 6888
www.grand-view-hotel.com
Credit Cards:

Visa, Master Card, JCB, American Express, Domestic Cards
Shenzhen Sunshine Hotel
★★★★★
1 Jiabin Lu, (0755) 8223 3888
Standard room:
RMB1,600 +15% Surcharge
Credit Cards: Visa, Master Card, JCB, American Express
Swiss-Belhotel Suites and Residences Shenzhen
★★★★★
Shennan Xi Dajie, Futian
(0755) 8350 0888
Standard room:
RMB1,400 +15% Surcharge
Credit Cards: Visa, Master Card, JCB, American Express
The Landmark Hotel Shenzhen
★★★★★
3018 Nanhu Lu, (0755) 8217 2288
Credit Cards:
Visa, Master Card, JCB, American Express, Domestic Cards
The Pavilion
★★★★★
4002 Huaqiang Bei Lu, Futian
(0755) 8207 8888
www.pavilionhotel.com
Credit Cards:
Visa, Master Card, American Express
ACK Cyber Hotel
★★★★
Xinzhong Lu, Baishizhou, Nanshan
(0755) 8609 3333
www.ack-cyber.com
Standard room: RMB680
Credit Cards: Visa, Master Card, JCB, American Express
Airland Hotel
★★★★
8 Yanmei Lu, Dameisha, Yantian
(0755) 2506 2299

www.airlandhotel.com
Standard room: RMB880
Credit Cards: Visa, Master Card,
JCB, American Express
Bao Ming Cheng Hotel
★★★★
Jianshe Lu, Gongming Town, Baoan
(0755) 2710 0888
www.bmc-hotel.com
Credit Cards:
Visa, Master Card, JCB, American
Express, Domestic Cards
Bossfield Hotel
★★★★
2 Ziyou Lu, Block 45 Bao'an
(0755) 6115 8888
Standard room:
RMB800 +15% Surcharge
Credit Cards: Visa
Capital Plaza Hotel
★★★★
Baominyi Lu, Baoan
(0755) 2778 3888
www.szcph.com
Standard room:
RMB880 +15% Surcharge

Credit Cards: Visa, Master Card,
JCB, American Express
Century Garden Hotel
★★★★
1 Bagua Lu, Futian, (0755) 6162 1888
www.century-garden-hotel.com.cn
Standard room: RMB348
Credit Cards: Visa, Master Card,
JCB, American Express
Century Plaza Hotel
★★★★
1 Chunfeng Lu, Luohu
(0755) 8232 0888
Standard room: RMB690
Credit Cards:
Visa, Master Card, JCB, American
Express, Domestic Cards
Frontier Hotel Guangdong
★★★★
5 Fujing Lu, Futian
(0755) 8835 8888
www.bianfangjiudian.com
Standard room: RMB268
Credit Cards: Visa, Master Card
Gelan Yuntian Hotel
★★★★

3024 Shennan Zhong Lu
(0755) 8368 9999
www.gslhotel.com
Credit Cards:
Visa, Master Card, JCB, American
Express, Domestic Cards

Golden Lustre Hotel
★★★★
3002 Chunfeng Lu, (0755) 8225 2888
www.sz-jinbi.com
Credit Cards:
Visa, Master Card, JCB

Holiday Inn Donghua Shenzhen
★★★★
Donghua Park, Nanyou Dajie
Nanshan, (0755) 2641 6688
Standard room: RMB1,200 +15%
Credit Cards: Visa, Master Card,
JCB, American Express

Junyuan Hotel
★★★★
Junyuan Tower, 1001 Aiguo Lu,
Luohu
(0755) 2577 1888
www.junyuanhotel.com
Standard room: RMB360
Credit Cards:
Visa, Master Card, Diners Club

La Waterfront Hotel Shenzhen
★★★★
10 Yanmei Lu, Dameisha, Yantian
(0755) 2506 1688
www.szlawaterfront.com
Standard room: RMB898
Credit Cards: Visa, Master Card,
JCB, American Express

Lushan Hotel
★★★★
66 Chunfeng Lu, (0755) 8233 8888
www.lushanhotel.com
Credit Cards: Visa, Master Card,
JCB, American Express, Domestic
Cards, Diners Club

Metropark Hotel Shenzhen
★★★★
2088 Dongmen Zhong Lu, Luohu
(0755) 8231 8388
www.metropolesz.com
Standard room: RMB488
Credit Cards: Visa, Master Card,
JCB, American Express

Ming Wah International Convention Centre
★★★★
8 Guishan Lu, Shekou
Industrial Zone
(0755) 2668 9968
www.mhctr.com
Standard room: RMB595
Credit Cards: Visa, Master Card,
JCB, American Express

Novotel Bauhinia Shenzhen
★★★★
West Gate Yuanbo Garden
Qiaocheng Dong Lu, Futian
(0755) 8282 9966
Standard room: RMB596
Credit Cards:
Visa, Master Card, JCB, American
Express, Domestic Cards

Novotel Watergate Shenzhen
★★★★
1019 Mandalay Tower, Shennan
Zhong Lu
(0755) 8213 7999
Standard room: RMB583
Credit Cards: Visa, Master Card,
JCB, American Express

Seaview Hotel
★★★★
3-5 Guangqiao Jie, Overseas Chinese
Town, Nanshan, (0755) 2660 2222
www.seaviewhotel.com.cn
Standard room:
RMB1,000 +15% Surcharge
Credit Cards: Visa, Master Card,

JCB, American Express
Shenzhen Hotel Oriental Regent
★★★★
Finance Building, Shennan Zhong Lu
(0755) 8224 7838
www.szjingdu.com
Standard room: RMB390
Credit Cards:
Visa, Master Card, JCB, American
Express, Domestic Cards
Shenzhen Jingtian Plaza Hotel
★★★★
Jingtian Lu, Lianhua Lu, Futian
(0755) 8314 0888
www.jingtian-hotel.com
Standard room: RMB340 (luxury
single), 360 (luxury double)
Credit Cards: Visa, Master Card,
JCB, American Express
Shenzhen Xinzhou Hotel
★★★★
9005 Binhe Lu, (0755) 8340 9340
www.xinzhouhotel.com
Credit Cards:
Visa, Master Card, JCB, American
Express, Domestic Cards

South China Harbour View Hotel
★★★★
18 Nanxin Lu, Nanshan
(0755) 2608 8736
Standard room: RMB483
Credit Cards: Visa, Master Card,
JCB, American Express
Sun Island Holiday Hotel
★★★★
34 Dongmen Nan Lu, Luohu
(0755) 8214 3998
Standard room: RMB618
Credit Cards: Visa, Master Card,
JCB, American Express
Sunway Hotel
★★★★
Shenzhen International Airport
(0755) 2730 0888
www.szsunwayhotel.com
Standard room:
RMB340 +13% Surcharge
Credit Cards:
Visa, Master Card, JCB, American
Express, Domestic Cards
Empire Hotel
★★★★

1052 Aiguo Lu, (0755) 2552 3338
www.szempirehotel.com
Standard room: RMB298
Credit Cards:
Visa, Master Card, JCB, American
Express, Domestic Cards
Hongbo Hotel
★★★
10 Qiaocheng Xi Jie, Overseas
Chinese Town
(0755) 2694 9448
www.szspcc.com
Credit Cards:
Visa, Master Card, JCB, American
Express, Domestic Cards
Kindlion Hotel
★★★
89-4 Buji Lu, Buji Town, Longgang
(0755) 2828 9999
www.kindlion.com
Standard room: RMB238
Credit Cards: Visa, Master Card,
JCB, American Express
Minland Hotel
★★★
Zhongnong Building, 68 Gongyeba
Lu, Shekou, (0755) 2681 1888
www.minland-hotel.com
Standard room: RMB298
Credit Cards:
Visa, Master Card, American Express
Petrel Hotel
★★★
6/F Petrel Hotel, Jiabin Lu, Luohu
(0755) 8223 2828
www.petrel-hotel.com
Standard room: RMB333
Credit Cards: Visa, Master Card,
JCB, American Express
Regent Garden Hotel
★★★
473 Shajing Section Guangshen Lu
(0755) 2725 8888

www.shangyuanhotel.com
Standard room: RMB368
Credit Cards:
JCB, American Express
Shenzhen Guest House Hotel
★★★
15 Xinyuan Lu, Luohu
(0755) 8222 2722
www.shenzhenhotel.com.cn
Standard room: RMB495
Credit Cards:
Visa, Master Card, JCB, American
Express
Shenzhen Huizhou Hotel
★★★
2011 Yanhe Nan Lu, Wenjindu
(0755) 8225 2988
Standard room: RMB210
Credit Cards:
Visa, Master Card, JCB, American
Express
Shenzhen Kaili Hotel
★★★
2027 Jiabin Lu, Luohu
(0755) 8237 6188
www.szkailihotel.com
Standard room: RMB438
Credit Cards:
Visa, Master Card, JCB, American
Express, Domestic Cards
Shenzhen Wensha Hotel
★★★
33 Nanxin Lu, Nanshan
(0755) 2666 4860
Standard room: RMB180
Credit Cards: Domestic Cards
Xili Lake Holiday Resort
★★★
Xili Lake Holiday Resort, Nanshan
(0755) 2651 1888
www.xililake.com
Standard room: RMB380
Credit Cards:

Visa, Master Card, Domestic Cards

Restaurants

Western

Gypsys 中澳吉普赛西餐厅
1/F 3 Haibin Business Center, Haishang Shijie, (0755) 2668 2657

Romas Bar & Grill 罗马西餐厅
Back of Taizi Hotel, Taizi Lu
(0755) 2683 8492

Cafe Zentro 西餐厅
9026 Shennan Lu, Overseas Chinese Town (Crowne Plaza Shenzhen)
(0755) 2693 6888

Italian

**Blue Italian Restaurant
意大利海鲜排房**
9026 Shennan Lu, Overseas Chinese Town (Crowne Plaza Shenzhen)
(0755) 2693 6888

**Casablanca Bar and Western
Restaurant 卡萨布兰卡**
1/F Yin Bin Building, Taizi Lu
(0755) 2667 6968

Japanese/Korean

JK 日韩料理
9026 Shennan Lu, Overseas Chinese Town (Crowne Plaza Shenzhen)
(0755) 2693 6888

Cantonese

Marco's 意华轩中餐厅
9026 Shennan Lu, Overseas Chinese Town (Crowne Plaza Shenzhen)
(0755) 2693 6888

Indian

Taj Indian Restaurant 印度宫庭小食
1/F Lianhua Building, Renmin Nan Lu, (0755) 8236 2782

Tandoor Fine Indian Cuisine 檀都
1/F Shenzhen Development Center, Renmin Nan Lu, (0755) 8228 1808

Barbecue

**Garden Grill Brazilian Barbecue
花园巴西烤肉**

1/F, 3 Taizi Lu (Taizi Hotel)
(0755) 2667 6608

Japanese

Enotsuru 江之鹤日本料理
Hairun Plaza, Zhenxing Lu
(0755) 8324 2370

Brazilian

Brazilian Barbecue 入船
Nanhu Lu (outside the Landmark Hotel), (0755) 8217 4568

Bali House 巴里小筑
2023 Honggui Lu, (0755) 2558 2633

Korean

**Cogu Jang Korean Restaurant
巨龟庄韩国料理**
2/F Thai Entertainment City, 218 Hongling Zhong Lu
(0755) 8240 4955

Bars & Clubs

Snake Pit
Taizi Lu

Casablanca 卡萨布兰卡
Taizi Lu
(0755) 2667 6968

True Color 本色酒吧
Shangbunan Lu

Capital Bar 卡碧桃音乐吧
Donghai Garden, Donghai Fang, Xiangxuan Lu

Hospitals

**Shenzhen Nanshan Hospital
深圳南山医院**
89 Taoyuan Lu, (0755) 2655 3111

**Shenzhen Bantian Hospital
深圳坂田医院**
5/F, 18 Bantian Dongpo Lu, Buji Town, (0755) 2702 9846

**Songgang People's Hospital
深圳市宝安区松岗人民医院**
2 Shajiang Lu, Songgang Town
(0755) 2771 8312

Bookstores

Shenzhen Book Mall 深圳书城
Shennan Dong Lu, (0755) 8207 3337
Xinhua Bookstore, Shenzhen
深圳市新华书店
1030 Honggang Lu, (0755) 8226-4582

Industrial parks

Shenzhen Futian Free Trade Zone
深圳福田保税区
(0755) 8359 0305
www.szftz.gov.cn
Major Industries:
Import and export trade, consultancy services, commodities exhibition, high-tech and export-oriented manufacturing, high value-added assembling and compensation trade, bonded warehousing, finance, telecommunications.
Shenzhen High-Tech Industrial
深圳高新技术园区
(0755) 2655 1900
www.ship.gov.cn
Major Industries: Electronics

Shenzhen Shatoujiao Free Trade Zone
深圳沙头角保税区
(0755) 2526 0827
www.szftz.gov.cn
Major Industries:
Import and export, entrepot trade, warehousing and transportation, and real estate.
Shenzhen Yantian Port Free Trade Zone
盐田港保税区
(0755) 2528 0693
www.szftz.gov.cn
Major Industries:
Warehousing, logistics, entrepot trade, bonded commodities exchange, exhibition

Exhibiton centers

China International Hi-tech Fair Exhibition Center
Fuhua Sanlu, Shenzhen
(0755) 8290 7001
www.szcec.com

Zhuhai 珠海

Telephone prefix: 0756
Population: 1.42 million
Bank of China: 1148 Yuehai Dong Lu

Located on the west bank of the Pearl River estuary, just north of Macau, Zhuhai was one of China's first Special Economic Zones. It has a well integrated economy, encompassing hi-tech manufacturing, tourism, logistics and agriculture. Major foreign companies in Zhuhai include BP Chemical, Canon, Mitsumi and Matsushita.

The Zhuhai Southern Software Park is a state-level software production base and universities such as Qinghua University and City University of Hong Kong have set up R&D centers here.

The government plans to develop Zhuhai into a major petrochemical production center, and both British Petroleum (BP) and Taiwan's Eternal have invested in petrochemical plants in Zhuhai.

Hotels

Grand Bay View Hotel Zhuhai
★★★★★
245 Shuiwan Lu, Gongbei
(0756) 887 7998
Standard room: RMB900 +15%
Credit Cards: Visa, Master Card, JCB, American Express, Diners Club

Harbour View Hotel & Resort Zhuhai
★★★★★
47 Qinglu Zhong Lu, Jida
(0756) 332 2888
Standard room: RMB880
Credit Cards: Visa, Master Card, JCB, American Express

International Conference Center Hotel
★★★★★
Qinglu Zhong Lu, Jida
(0756) 332 9988
www.cnicc.com
Standard room: RMB420
Credit Cards: Visa, Master Card, American Express, Domestic Cards

Zhuhai Holiday Resort Hotel
★★★★★
9 Shihua Dong Lu, Jida
(0756) 333 3838
www.zhuhai-holitel.com
Standard room: RMB880
Credit Cards:
Visa, JCB, American Express

Dihao Holiday Hotel
★★★★★
1063 Yingbin Bei Lu
(0756) 262 3333
www.dihaoholidayhotel.com
Standard room:
RMB880 +15% Surcharge
Credit Cards: Visa, Master Card, JCB, American Express

Paradise Hill Hotel Zhuhai
★★★★★
193 Jingshan Lu
(0756) 333 7388
www.paradisehillhotel.com
Standard room: RMB350
Credit Cards: Visa, Master Card, JCB, American Express

Catic Hotel
★★★★
1197 Jiuzhou Dong Dajie
(0756) 388 2222
www.catichotelzh.com
Standard room: RMB380
Credit Cards: Visa, JCB

Greenery Hotel

★★★★
45 Haibin Nan Lu, (0756) 333 3968
www.greenery-hotel.com
Standard room: RMB638
Credit Cards: Visa, Master Card, JCB, Domestic Cards

Guangdong Hotel Zhuhai
★★★★
1145 Yuehai Dong Lu, Gongbei
(0756) 888 8128
www.gdhhotels.com
Credit Cards:
Visa, Master Card, JCB, American Express, Domestic Cards

Holiday Inn Zhuhai
★★★★
188 Jingshan Lu, Jida
(0756) 322 8888
Standard room: RMB1,100
Credit Cards: Visa, Master Card, JCB, American Express

Hotel Jumbo Zhuhai
★★★★
Qiaoguang Xi Lu, Gongbei
(0756) 811 8999
www.hoteljumbo.com
Standard room:
RMB800 +15% Surcharge

Credit Cards: Visa, Master Card, JCB, Domestic Cards

Swan Hotel
★★★★
98 Yinhua Lu, (0756) 265 3333
www.swanhotel.com.cn
Credit Cards: Visa, Master Card, JCB, American Express

Yuwenquan Hotspring Resort
★★★★
Huangyang Dajie, Doumen Town
(0756) 579 7128
www.imperial-hot-spring.com
Credit Cards:
Visa, Master Card, JCB, American Express, Domestic Cards

Zhong Tian Hotel
★★★★
62 Jingshan Lu, Jida, (0756) 336 6888
www.zhongtianhotelzh.com
Standard room: RMB268
Credit Cards: Visa, Master Card, JCB, Domestic Cards

Zhuhai Hotel
★★★★
177 Jingshan Lu, Jida
(0756) 333 3718
www.zh-hotel.com

Standard room: RMB688
Credit Cards: Visa, Master Card, JCB, American Express
Golden Holiday Hotel
★★★★
73 Jinghe Jie, Jida, (0756) 326 3333
www.zhholidayhotel.com
Standard room: RMB238
Credit Cards: Visa, Master Card, JCB, American Express
Chang An Good World Hotel
★★★
327 Lianhua Lu, Gongbei
(0756) 888 0222
www.zhcahotel.com
Standard room: RMB338
Credit Cards: Visa, Master Card, JCB, American Express
Chang An Great Aim Hotel
★★★
1 Qiaoguang Lu, Gongbei
(0756) 889 9668
www.zhcahotel.com
Standard room: RMB308
Credit Cards:
Visa, Master Card, JCB, American Express, Domestic Cards
Chang An Hotel
★★★
196-200 Lianhua Lu, Gongbei
(0756) 811 8828
www.zhcahotel.com
Standard room: RMB220
Credit Cards:
Visa, Master Card, JCB, American Express, Domestic Cards
Hengfu Sunshine Hotel
★★★
143 Jida Lu, (0756) 336 9777
Standard room: RMB200
Credit Cards:
Visa, Master Card, JCB, American Express, Domestic Cards

New Chang An Hotel
★★★
1023 Central Section Jiuzhou Dajie
(0756) 337 7668
www.zhcahotel.com
Standard room: RMB252
Credit Cards:
Visa, Master Card, JCB, American Express, Domestic Cards
Yunhai Hotel
★★★
1263 Jiuzhou Dong Dajie
(0756) 322 6888
www.yunhai-hotel.com
Standard room: RMB368
Credit Cards: Visa, Master Card
Zhu Hai Jin Ye Hotel
★★★
1011 Yingbin Nan Lu, Gongbei
(0756) 813 2668
www.zhjinye.com
Credit Cards:
Visa, Master Card, Domestic Cards
Zhuhai Beijing Hotel
★★★
1 Cuiqian Nan Lu, Qianshan
(0756) 866 5288
www.beijinghotelzh.com
Standard room: RMB338
Credit Cards: Visa, Master Card, JCB, American Express
Zhuhai Bihai Hotel
★★★
1 Bihai Lu, Xiangzhou
(0756) 212 1666
www.bihaihotel.com.cn
Credit Cards: Visa, Master Card, American Express, Domestic Cards

Restaurants

Western
Marco Polo Western Restaurant & Piano Cafe

马可波罗西餐厅
Qiaoguang Xi Lu (Zhuhai Jumbo Hotel), (0756) 8118 999

Indian

Indian
印地安复合式餐厅有限公司
2100 Yingbin Nan Lu
(0756) 815 0615

Cafe

Blue Mountain Cafe 蓝山咖啡厅
3/F Yingbin Building, Yingbin Nan Lu, (0756) 828 3338

Hunan

Xiang Man Lou 湘满楼
3160 Mingzhu Nan Lu
(0756) 850 9860

Seafood

Seafood City 顺风海鲜楼
1/F Haiwan Xinjia, Qinglu Nan Lu
(0756) 818 5668

Cantonese

De Yue Lou得月楼
Middle Section, Jiuzhou Da Dao
(0756) 337 1438

Bars & Clubs

Xiangjiang Football Bar
香江球迷酒吧
5 Haibin Nan Lu
True Love Bar 真爱酒吧
257 Jida Shuiwan Lu
Leopard Bar 豹豪酒吧
Jida Shuiwan Lu
Warriors' Castle 武士堡
Opposite Doumen Stadium

Hospitals

Zhuhai Hospital of Traditional Chinese Medicine 珠海中医院
53 Jingle Lu, (0756) 332 5027
Zhuhai Boai Hospital
珠海博爱医院
Suidao Bei, (0756) 228 9513

Bookstores

Xinhua Bookstore, Zhuhai
珠海市新华书店
36 Jida Jingle Lu, (0756) 335 8950

Industrial parks

Zhuhai Free Trade Zone
珠海保税区
(0756) 868 6619
www.zhfreetradezone.org
Major Industries:
Export-oriented processing, warehousing, international trade, tertiary industries
Zhuhai National High-Tech Industrial Development Zone
珠海国家高新技术产业开发区
(0756) 362 9800
www.zhuhai-hitech.com
Major Industries:
Electronics and communications, PCB industry

Dongguan 东莞
Telephone prefix: 0769
Population: 6.56 million
Bank of China: 72 Guantai Lu

Dongguan is China's third-largest exporting city after Shenzhen and Shanghai. Like other major exporting centers in the Pearl River Delta area, Dongguan was just a village only two decades ago. Its proximity to Hong Kong and the determination of its residents were the key factors behind its development.

Foreign-invested enterprises are the main economic driving force in Dongguan and foreign companies account for two thirds of annual sales of the enterprises in the city. Major international enterprises include General Electric, Duracell, Du Pont, Nestle, Nokia, Thomson, Sony, Canon, NEC and Samsung.

The city government is building a 72 sq km high-tech development zone, Songshan Lake Technology Park, to attract Chinese and foreign enterprises in the areas of optoelectronics, biotech and other high value-added fields.

Hotels

Dongcheng International Hotel
★★★★★
3 Dongcheng Dong Lu, Dongcheng
(0769) 2268 8888
Credit Cards:
Visa, Master Card, JCB, American Express, Domestic Cards

Dongguan Lung Chuen International Hotel
★★★★★
Jinzhou Section Liansheng Lu, Humen Town, (0769) 8518 8688
www.lungchuen.com
Standard room:
RMB830 +15% Surcharge
Credit Cards:
Visa, Master Card, JCB, American Express, Domestic Cards

Gladden Hotel Shilong
★★★★★
Xihu Section Guanlong Lu, Shilong Town, (0769) 8618 8888
www.gladdenhotels.com
Standard room: RMB964
Credit Cards: Visa, Master Card, JCB

Good View Hotel Sangem
★★★★★
Shixin Dajie, Zhangmutou
(0769) 8779 9333
www.htlgvs.com

Credit Cards:
Visa, Master Card, JCB, American Express, Domestic Cards
Grand Noble Hotel
★★★★★
Gangkou Lu, Humen Town
(0769) 8511 7888
Standard room: RMB1,020
Credit Cards: Visa, Master Card, JCB, American Express
Hotel Silverland
★★★★★
48 Guantai Dajie, (0769) 2282 8888
www.hotelsilverland.com
Standard room: RMB980
Credit Cards:
Visa, Master Card, JCB, American Express, Domestic Cards
Jia Hua Grand Hotel
★★★★★
Jiaju Dajie, Houjie Town
(0769) 8592 8888
www.jiahuagrandhotel.com
Standard room: RMB808
Credit Cards: Visa, Master Card, JCB, American Express
Laishing Holiday Resortel
★★★★★
8 Yinxian Resort Dajie, Changping Town, (0769) 8339 8888
www.laishing.com.cn
Credit Cards: Visa, Master Card, JCB, American Express
Metropolitan Yiking Hotel
★★★★★
6 Huanshi Dong Lu, Tangxia
(0769) 8788 3888
Standard room: RMB748
Credit Cards:
Visa, Master Card, JCB, American Express, Domestic Cards
Sheraton Dongguan Hotel
★★★★★

Guantai Section S256 Provincial Highway, Houjie Town
(0769) 8598 8888
Standard room: RMB1,228
Credit Cards: Visa, Master Card, JCB, American Express
Sofitel Royal Lagoon Dongguan
★★★★★
8 Yingbin Lu, Dongcheng
(0769) 2269 8888
Standard room: RMB1,080
Credit Cards: Visa, Master Card, JCB, American Express
The Lotus Villa Hotel
★★★★★
Lianhuashan, Chang'an Town
(0769) 8553 8388
www.lotusvillas.com
Standard room: RMB488
Credit Cards: Visa, Master Card, JCB, American Express
Windsor Park Hotel
★★★★★
Guanzhang Lu, Huangjiang Town
(0769) 8363 6666
www.windsorchina.com
Standard room:
RMB680 +10% Surcharge
Credit Cards: Visa, Master Card, JCB, American Express
Haiyatt Garden Hotel
★★★★★
Houjie Dong Dajie, Houjie Town
(0769) 8588 5888
Standard room:
RMB760 +15% Surcharge
Credit Cards:
Visa, Master Card, JCB, American Express, Domestic Cards
Sofitel Royal Lagoon Executive Resort
★★★★★
Yingbin Lu, Dongcheng

(0769) 2269 9999
Standard room: RMB1,080
Credit Cards: Visa, Master Card,
JCB, American Express
Chang An Hotel
★★★★
Chang'an Town
(0769) 8553 2388
www.changan-hotel.com
Standard room:
RMB680 +13% Surcharge
Credit Cards:
Visa, Master Card, JCB, American
Express, Domestic Cards
Dongguan Hotel
★★★★
11 Dongzheng Lu, (0769) 2222 2222
Credit Cards:
Visa, Master Card, JCB, American
Express, Domestic Cards
Earl Resort Hotel
★★★★
Tangkeng Dev. Zone, Huangjiang
Town, (0769) 8362 1888
Standard room: RMB568
Credit Cards: Visa, Master Card,
JCB, American Express
Gladden Hotel Liaobu
★★★★
1 Jiaoyu Lu, Liaobu Town
(0769) 8332 6328
www.gladdenhotels.com
Standard room: RMB688
Credit Cards: Visa
Golden Lake Guang Dong Hotel
★★★★
99 Tangxia Nan Dajie, Tangxia Town
(0769) 8786 9888
www.gdhhotels.com
Standard room: RMB208
Credit Cards:
Visa, Master Card, JCB, American
Express, Domestic Cards

Hotel Dynasty
★★★★
Guangshen Lu, Shimei, Wanjiang
(0769) 2228 8888
www.hotel-dynasty.com
Credit Cards:
Visa, Master Card, JCB, American
Express, Domestic Cards
Huimei Hotel
★★★★
9 Zhongyuan Jie, Changping Town
(0769) 8391 8888
www.dghuimeihotel.com
Standard room: RMB275
Credit Cards:
Visa, Master Card, JCB, American
Express, Domestic Cards
Jianglong Hotel
★★★★
Guantai Section S256 Provincial
Highway, Houjie Town
(0769) 8583 8888
www.jianglonghotel.com
Standard room: RMB248
Credit Cards:
Visa, Master Card, American Express
Man Wah Hotel
★★★★
Xintang Section Guantai Lu, Houjie
Town, (0769) 8591 1111
www.manwah-hotel.com
Standard room: RMB528
Credit Cards:
Visa, Master Card, JCB, American
Express, Domestic Cards
Resort Lotus Lake Sangem
★★★★
Hubin Lu, Qiaotou Town
(0769) 8334 1868
www.resortlotuslake.com
Credit Cards:
Visa, Master Card, JCB, American
Express, Domestic Cards

Shan Hu Hotel

★★★★

Guantai Section 107 Highway, Hou-jie Town, (0769) 8582 6888

www.shanhu-hotel.com

Standard room:

RMB438 +10% Surcharge

Credit Cards:

Visa, Master Card, JCB, American Express, Domestic Cards

Winnerway Hotel

★★★★

1 Hongyuan Lu, Nancheng

(0769) 2241 8888

www.winnerway-hotel.com

Credit Cards:

Visa, Master Card, JCB, American Express, Domestic Cards

Yinfeng Garden Hotel

★★★★

Yinfeng Lu, Nancheng

(0769) 2280 3888

Credit Cards:

Visa, Master Card, JCB, American Express, Domestic Cards

King Win Hotel

★★★

11 Tiyu Lu, (0769) 2246 3888

www.kingwinhotel.com

Credit Cards:

Visa, Master Card, JCB, American Express, Domestic Cards

Shilong Hotel

★★★

2 Luhua Zhong Lu, Shilong Town

(0769) 8661 3333

www.shilonghotel.com

Credit Cards: Visa, Master Card, JCB, Domestic Cards

Wahtong Cheng Hotel

★★★

Hubin Nan Lu, Qishi Town

(0769) 8673 2288

www.wahtong-hotel.com

Credit Cards:

Visa, Master Card, JCB, American Express, Domestic Cards

Xihu Hotel

★★★

Xihu, Shilong Town

(0769) 8611 2288, *www.ownhotel.com*
Credit Cards:
Visa, Master Card, JCB, American
Express, Domestic Cards

Restaurants

Western
**Star Cafe/ Sky Lounge / Peacock Bar
/ Golden Hall / VIP Room
东莞嘉华大酒店**
Entrance of Furniture Boulevard
(Jiahua Grand Hotel)
(0769) 592 8888

Cafe
UBC 上岛咖啡
Luyin Haoting, East Section of
Jiuzhou Da Dao, (0756) 322 4243
**Mingdian Coffee Language
名典咖啡语茶**
2/F Hong Du Hotel, Yuehai Dong Lu
(0756) 813 5568

Italian
Cappella 卡比拿西餐厅
1/F Yu Hua Yuan, Shuiwantou
(0756) 818 2068
Luigi Italian Restaurant
S256 Provincial Highway, Houjie
Town, (0769) 8958 8888

Cantonese
**Oriental Court Chinese Restaurant
东方宫廷中餐厅**
S256 Provincial Highway, Houjie
Town, (0769) 8598 8888

International
**Botanica Brasserie Restaurant
豫园西餐厅**
S256 Provincial Highway, Houjie
Town, (0769) 8598 8888

Hospitals

**Dongguan Donghua Hospital
东莞东华医院**
1 Dongcheng Dong Lu
(0769) 2233 3333

Bookstores

**Xinhua Bookstore, Dongguan
东莞市新华书店**
32 Xinfen Lu, (0769) 2221 0635

Exhibition centers

**Dongguan International
Conference and Exhibition Centre**
Dongguan Dadao, Dongguan
(0769) 2242 3781
www.dgicec.com

Zhongshan 中山

Telephone prefix: 0760
Population: 2.43 million
Bank of China: 18 Zhongshan San Lu

Zhongshan has witnessed rapid industrial development in recent years, and is fast emerging as one of the Pearl River Delta's main production centers. The area's economy is characterized by a large number of small and medium-sized private enterprises.

It excels at manufacturing household electrical appliances, especially air-conditioners and color TVs.

Many well-known companies, such as domestic giants TCL and Changhong, Taiwan's largest air-conditioner parts manufacturer Shunyi Enterprise, Acer, and Japan's Toshiba have factories in Zhongshan.

Sun Yat-sen, the leader of the 1911 revolution overthrowing the Qing dynasty (China's last), was born in a village here in 1866.

Hotel

Shangri-La Hotel Zhongshan
★★★★★
16 Qiwan Bei Lu, East Area
(0760) 838 6888
Standard room:
RMB980 +15% Surcharge
Zhongshan International Hotel
★★★★★
142 Zhongshanyi Lu
(0760) 863 3388
www.interhotel-zs.com
Standard room: RMB515
Credit Cards:
Visa, Master Card, JCB, American Express, Domestic Cards

Fuhua Hotel
★★★★
1 Fuhua Lu
(0760) 863 8888
www.fuhuahotel.com.cn
Standard room: RMB460
Credit Cards:
Visa, Master Card, JCB, American Express, Domestic Cards
Zhongshan Hot Spring Resort
★★★★
Sanxiang Town, (0760) 668 3888
www.zshs.com
Standard room: RMB350
Credit Cards: Visa, Master Card, JCB, Domestic Cards
China Merchants Club
★★★
Zhaoshang Lu, Yongmo Village, Sanxiang Town, (0760) 668 7888
www.zscmc.com
Credit Cards:
Visa, Master Card, JCB, American Express, Domestic Cards
Fuzhou Hotel, Guangdong
★★★
131 Fuhua Lu, Shiqi
(0760) 861 2888
Credit Cards: Visa, Master Card, JCB, American Express

Restaurants

Western
Fu Shui Yin Coffee
浮水印咖啡西餐厅
36-37, Section A, Hengxin Garden, Tiyu Lu
(0760) 833 8041
Cafe
Discovery Cafe 探索咖啡厅
Huicui Shanzhuang, (0760) 621 0028
Cantonese/Zhongshanese

DESTINATIONS

Shang Palace 香宫
16 Qi Wan Bei Lu, (0760) 838 6888
International
Cafe Plus 尚苑
16 Qi Wan Bei Lu, (0760) 838 6888
Chinese
Yi Garden 江南趣
16 Qi Wan Bei Lu, (0760) 838 6888

Hospitals

Zhongshan Hospital of Traditional Chinese Medicine 中山市中医院
2 Yuelainannan'an Lu
(0760) 880 3661

Industrial parks

Zhongshan Torch High-Tech Industrial Development Zone
中山火炬高技术产业开发区
(0760) 828 3633, www.zstorch.gov.cn
Major Industries:
Packaging and printing, electronics, information technology

Exhibition centers

Zhongshan Torch International Exhibition Center
Kangle Dadao, Zhongshan
(0760) 533 8017, www.zshjexpo.com

Shantou 汕头
Telephone prefix: 0754
Population: 4.94 million
Bank of China: 98 Jiansha Lu

A port city on the Guangdong coast east of Hong Kong, Shantou became a Special Economic Zone in 1980, and now has a fast-growing economy with a mix of light and heavy industries, including shipbuilding and food processing. Shantou is striving to create a national logistics base for plastics and chemicals production.

Major industries are plastic machinery, packaging machinery and printing machinery manufacturing. Chenghai District has become the world's main toy manufacturing and processing base.

Hospitals

Golden Gulf (Jasper) Hotel Shantou
★★★★★
96 Jinsha Dong Lu, (0754) 826 3263
www.goldengulfhotel.com
Standard room: RMB380

Credit Cards: Visa, Master Card, JCB, American Express

Meritus Shantou China

★★★★★

97 Jinsha Dong Lu, (0754) 819 1188

Standard room: RMB1,400

Credit Cards:
Visa, Master Card, JCB, American Express, Domestic Cards

Regency Hotel Shantou

★★★★★

188 Jinsha Dong Lu
(0754) 819 9888

Standard room: RMB428

Credit Cards: Visa, Master Card, JCB, American Express

CITIC Resort Hotel

★★★★

Zhongxin Dajie, Haojiang
(0754) 390 0888
www.citichotel.com

Standard room: RMB480

Credit Cards: Visa, Master Card, JCB, American Express

Garden Hotel Chenghai

★★★★

Wenguan Lu, Chenghai
(0754) 586 8888
www.chgarden.com

Standard room: RMB298

Credit Cards: Visa, Master Card, JCB, American Express

Longhu Hotel

★★★★

2 Dabeishan Lu, (0754) 826 0706
www.stlhhotel.com

Credit Cards:
Visa, Master Card, JCB, American Express, Domestic Cards

Shantou Garden Hotel

★★★★

68 Hengshan Lu, (0754) 886 0666

Standard room: RMB210

Credit Cards:
Visa, Master Card, JCB, American Express, Domestic Cards

Shantou International Hotel

★★★★

52 Jinsha Lu, (0754) 825 1212
www.stih.com

Standard room: RMB598

Credit Cards: Visa, Master Card, JCB, American Express, Domestic Cards, Diners Club

Sun Life Hotel

★★★★

Beishan Bay, Haojiang
(0754) 359 6734
www.sunlifehotel.com

Standard room: RMB243

Credit Cards:
Visa, Master Card, JCB, American Express, Domestic Cards

Gulf Hotel

★★★

Qing'ao Bay, Nan'ao County
(0754) 699 7811
www.nanaogh.com

Credit Cards: Domestic Cards

Jinyuan Hotel

★★★

64 Guangxiang Lu, Chaonan
(0754) 790 2888
www.jydjd.com

Credit Cards:
Visa, Master Card, JCB, American Express, Domestic Cards

Restaurants

Western

Feel Fun Pub 非凡音乐西餐厅

2/F, 99 Changping Lu
(0754) 892 0808

Revolving Restaurant
旋宫

52 Jinsha Zhong Lu (International

Hotel), (0754) 825 1212
Allice Restaurant 亚历士西餐厅
Wenche Lu (Garden Hotel)
(0754) 586 8888
International
**Marco Polo Restaurant
马可波罗餐厅**
Jinsha Dong Lu (Regency Hotel)
(0754) 819 9888

Hospitals

**Shantou Centre Hospital
汕头中心医院**
114 Waima Lu, (0754) 855 045

Bookstores

**Xinhua Bookstore, Shantou
汕头市新华书店**
55 Tianshan Lu, (0754) 873 5083

Industrial parks

**Shantou Free Trade Zone
汕头保税区**
(0754) 359 0278, *www.stftz.gov.cn*
Major Industries: Comprehensive
export processing, transit trade,
bonded warehousing services

Foshan 佛山
Telephone prefix: 0757
Population: 5.80 million
Bank of China: 2 Renmin Xi Lu

Foshan (Buddha Mountain) is a manufacturing center just south-west of Guangzhou. A wide range of foreign companies have set up plants here, including Du Pont from the US, Siemens, Bosch and Hochest from Germany, Panasonic, Toshiba and Sanyo from Japan, and Pohang Steelers from Korea. Consumer electronics predominate. It is also home to one of the four biggest software parks in Guangdong.

Hotels

Butterfiy Valley Resort
Shangri-La Garden, Nanguo Peach
Park
(0757) 8523 3066
www.butterflyvalleyresort.com
Fontainebleau Hotel
★★★★★

Fengdan Lu, Nanguo Peach Garden
(0757) 8523 2288
www.ftbl-hotel.com.cn
Standard room: RMB698
Credit Cards:
Visa, Master Card, JCB, American
Express, Domestic Cards
Foshan Hotel
★★★★★
75 Fenjiang Nan Lu
(0757) 8298 6881
www.foshanhotel.com
Credit Cards: Visa, Master Card,
JCB, American Express, Domestic
Cards, Diners Club
Chancheng Hotel
★★★★
103 Fenjiang Zhong Lu
(0757) 8296 6888, *www.fscchotel.com*
Standard room:
RMB498 +10% Surcharge
Credit Cards: Visa, Master Card,
JCB, American Express
Country Garden Holiday Resorts
★★★★
Bijiang Bridge, Beijiao Town
(0757) 2633 2228, *www.bgy.com.cn*
Standard room: RMB690
Credit Cards:
Visa, Master Card, American Express
Ever Profit Hotel
★★★★
42 Guanghai Zhong Dajie
(0757) 8773 3888
www.ever-profit-hotel.com
Credit Cards:
Visa, Master Card, JCB, American
Express, Domestic Cards
Foshan Carrianna Hotel
★★★★
Huaqiao Building, 14 Zumiao Lu,
Chancheng, (0757) 8222 3828
Credit Cards: Visa, Master Card,

JCB, American Express
Golden City Hotel
★★★★
48 Fenjiang Nan Lu, (0757) 8328 8888
www.fs-goldencityhotel.com.cn
Credit Cards: Visa, Master Card,
JCB, American Express
Jin Du Hotel
★★★★
Foshan Jichang Lu, Nanhai
(0757) 8555 8328
www.jindu-hotel.com.cn
Standard room: RMB598
Credit Cards: Visa, Master Card,
JCB, American Express
New World Courtyard Shunde
★★★★
150 Qinghui Lu, Daliang, Shunde
(0757) 2221 8333
Standard room:
RMB600 +15% Surcharge
Credit Cards:
Visa, Master Card, JCB, American
Express, Domestic Cards
Peach Garden Hotel
★★★★
Nanguo Peach Garden Resort, Song-
gang Town, (0757) 8523 3668
www.peach-garden-hotel.com
Standard room: RMB380
Credit Cards:
Visa, Master Card, JCB, American
Express, Domestic Cards
Silversea Hotel
★★★★
483 Yanjiang Lu, (0757) 8882 1128
www.silveroceanhotel.com
Credit Cards:
Visa, Master Card, JCB, American
Express, Domestic Cards
Yun Ying Qiong Lou Hotel
★★★★
Baiyundong Resort, Xiqiaoshan,

Nanhai, (0757) 8688 6799
www.nanhai-cts.com
Standard room: RMB498
Credit Cards: Visa, Master Card
Golden Sun Hotel
★★★
2 Guanghai Dong Dajie, Xinan
Town, Sanshui
(0757) 8776 1888
www.jty.cc
Credit Cards:
Visa, Master Card, Domestic Cards
Nanguo Hotel
★★★
67 Fenjiang Nan Lu
(0757) 8298 3888
www.nanguohotel.com
Credit Cards: Visa, Master Card
Shi Wan Hotel
★★★
15 Fenjiang Xi Lu
(0757) 8332 8813
www.shiwanhotel.com
Credit Cards: Visa, Master Card,
American Express, Domestic Cards
Xiqiao Mountain Hotel
★★★
Baiyun Cave Scenic Spot, Xiqiao
Mountain, Nanhai, (0757) 8688 6799
www.nanhai-cts.com
Standard room:
RMB268 (double room)
Credit Cards: Visa, Master Card,
JCB, American Express

Restaurants

Western
Leaflet Western Restaurant 枫菲厅
Fengdan Lu, Nanguo Taoyuan
(Fontainebleau Hotel)
(0757) 8523 2288
French
Heidelberg 海德堡

75 Fenjiang Nan Lu (Foshan Hotel)
(0757) 8298 6881
Cafe
Coffee Shop 中庭咖啡厅
75 Fenjiang Nan Lu (Foshan Hotel)
(0757) 8298 6881
Japanese
Japanese Restaurant
海悦寅福门日本料理店
75 Fenjiang Nan Lu
(0757) 8298 6881
Western
Personable Restaurant
柏逊堡西餐厅
75 Fenjiang Nan Lu, (0757) 8298 6881

Hospitals

First People's Hospital of Foshan
佛山第一人民医院
3 Dafu Nan Lu, (0757) 8383 3633

Bookstores

Xinhua Bookstore, Foshan
佛山市新华书店
23 Tangyuan Dong San Jie
(0757) 8333 0514

Industrial parks

Foshan High-Tech Industries
Development Zone
佛山国家高新技术产业开发区
(0757) 8221 2609
www.fs-hitech.gov.cn
Major Industries:
Electronics, textiles, chinaware, plastic, building materials, food

Exhibition centers

Foshan International Convention &
Exhibition Center
Huaxia Ceramic Exposition City,
Foshan, (0757) 8532 0083
www.foshanfair.com

Chaozhou 潮州

Telephone prefix: 0768
Population: 4.13 million
Bank of China: Heng Tong Building, Chaofeng Lu

Situated 40 km north of Shantou, Chaozhou is one of Guangdong's most historic towns, and a major source of emigrants and entrepreneurs. Its economy is based upon textiles, machinery, porcelain, and sugar-refining.

Li Ka-Shing, Chairman of Cheung Kong (Holdings) Limited and Hutchison Whampoa Limited – and one of the richest men in East Asia – was born in Chaozhou.

Hotels

Chaozhou Hotel
★★★★
Chaofeng Lu, Yonghu Lu
(0768) 233 3333
www.chaozhouhotel.com
Credit Cards:
Visa, Master Card, JCB, American Express, Domestic Cards
Chaozhou Guest Hotel
★★★★
Central Section Chaofeng Road
(0768) 239 9888, *www.czybg.com*
Standard room: RMB388
Credit Cards:
Visa, Master Card, JCB, American Express, Domestic Cards

Restaurants

Cafe
UBC 上岛咖啡
26 Chaofeng Lu, (0768) 228 2747
Yinhe Zhi Xing 银河之星
2-3 Lurong Lu (next to Yiyuan)
(0768) 220 4410
Chinese
Mudan Yuan Restaurant
牡丹苑大酒店
At the cross of middle section of Chaofeng Lu and Chaozhou Da Dao
(0768) 280 0777

Hospitals

Chaozhou Central Hospital
潮州中心医院
84 Huancheng Xi Lu, (0768) 222 4092

Guangxi

Population: 46.6 million
Area: 236,300 sq km
Capital: Nanning
Airports:
Nanning, Guilin, Beihai, Liuzhou,
Wuzhou
Border crossings: Pingxiang, Dongxing,
Longzhou, Fangcheng

Long considered one of the most beautiful areas in the country by artists and tourists alike, Guangxi is located on China's southern coast. It is bordered by the provinces of Yunnan to the west, Guizhou to the north, Hunan to the northeast, Guangdong to the southeast and by Vietnam and the Beibu Bay (Gulf of Tonkin) to the southwest.

A subtropical, monsoon climate makes Guangxi one of China's wettest areas, with short winters and long humid summers. The area officially became part of China in 214 BC,

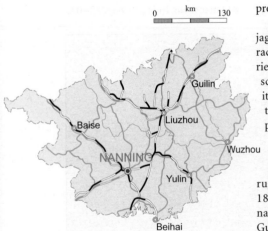

when the army of the Qin dynasty claimed most of the southern provinces. Guangxi has a long revolutionary history and was the base from which the quasi-Christian Taiping Rebellion spread in the 1850s and 1860s. They were exterminated with the help of foreign troops in 1864.

The region was opened to direct foreign trade following the 1889 Sino-French treaties which established Longzhou as a port. The interior of Guangxi was made much more accessible to foreign trade when the French established a rudimentary railway network in Vietnam which easily and cheaply brought foreign products up to the border.

The region's dramatic scenery of jagged karst peaks and steeply terraced hillsides has provided centuries of inspiration to Chinese landscape painters. Characterized by its wide variety of flora and fauna, the region is also populated by a plethora of ethnic minority peoples whose cultures have remained relatively intact due to the isolation provided by Guangxi's rugged terrain. Almost all of the 18 million-strong Zhuang, China's largest minority group, live in Guangxi, hence the region's official title "Guangxi Zhuang Autonomous Region". Despite their separate language and customs the Zhuang are actually quite similar to China's dominant Han and are well assimilated into the wider population.

Because of its diversity, Guangxi is a favorite tourist destination. As the only one of the poorer western provinces with a coastline, Guangxi also plays an important role in the central government's western development campaign. Begun in 1999, this initiative has seen huge amounts of investment directed at leveling out the imbalance between China's coastal regions and the poorer western hinterland.

With its ports and proximity to Vietnam and Southeast Asia, Guangxi is well placed to take advantage of what is being touted as the world's largest free-trade zone, incorporating southwest China and the Association of South East Asian Nations (ASEAN). This agreement is set to come into effect in 2010 and will include 1.7 billion consumers with a combined GDP of US$2 trillion.

Apart from its potential as a logistics center, local and international business in Guangxi is increasingly driven by vast mineral resources. Offshore oil and natural gas resources have been identified and the region has emerged as a major nonferrous metal production base boasting the largest deposits of tin, manganese and indium in the country.

A large proportion of the population continues to make a living from agriculture. In addition to growing staple crops such as rice, wheat, corn, peanuts and tea, Guangxi is the largest sugarcane production base in China and a major producer of ingredients for Chinese traditional medicine.

The province also has a significant machinery and equipment industry, based primarily around its five industrial cities, producing automobile parts, heavy machinery, electronic equipment and instruments.

Somewhat controversially, energy production in Guangxi has been dramatically increased in recent years. The Hongshui River will host the Longtan hydropower station, which will be second in size only to the Three Gorges Dam on completion in 2009.

Guangxi Economic Data			
	2005	2004	Change%
GDP (RMB bn)	407.6	343.4	18.7
GDP per capita (RMB)	8,788	7,196	22.1
Exports (US$ bn)	2.88	2.39	20.50
Imports (US$ bn)	2.30	1.89	21.69
Cars per 100 households	1.88	0.48	291.67
PCs per 100 households	46.67	32.64	42.98

Nanning 南宁
Telephone prefix: 0771
Population: 6.46 million
Bank of China: 39 Gucheng Lu

Guangxi's provincial capital, Nanning, was a relatively small market town at the beginning of the 20th century but it grew rapidly in the post-1949 period and is now a prosperous industrial city. It is situated along the Yong River, a tributary of the Pearl River that forms a fertile valley north of the mountains that lie on the Sino-Vietnamese border.

Nanning served in the past as a staging point for several historic conflicts with the Vietnamese, the most recent of which was fought in 1979. But today, China's friendly relations with its neighbor allow for convenient border crossings and lots of trade. With the proposed free trade zone between ASEAN and China, Nanning's proximity to Vietnam will make it a key transport hub into the rapidly expanding market of Southeast Asian nations. Because of this, the city has been made the permanent host of the annual China-ASEAN Expo. Guangxi's provincial government in Nanning is making a concerted effort to industrialize the area's energy and mineral resources.

The city is popular with visitors for its easy accessibility and modern amenities, including five-star hotels near the train station as well as centrally located banks and post offices. As a tourist destination, Nanning is particularly famous for its Medicinal Herb Garden, considered the best in China. Manufacturing activities include iron and steel, aluminum, food processing, fertilizers, and machinery.

Trains and buses link Nanning with Hanoi, with travel time of between 10 and 15 hours.

Nanning Economic Data	
GDP 2005 (RMB bn)	72.27
Disposable income 2005 (RMB)	9,203

Hotels

Mingyuan Xindu Hotel
★★★★★
38 Xinmin Lu, (0771) 211 8668
www.nn-myxd.com
Standard room:
RMB858 +10% Surcharge
Credit Cards: Domestic Cards

Nanning Hotel
★★★★★
38 Minsheng Lu, (0771) 210 3888
www.nnhotel.cn
Standard room: RMB488
Credit Cards: Visa

Yong Jiang Hotel
★★★★★
1 Linjiang Lu, (0771) 218 0888
www.yongjianghotel.com
Credit Cards:
Visa, Master Card, JCB, American
Express, Domestic Cards

Jindu Hotel
★★★★
17 Zhonghua Lu, (0771) 210 8188
www.nnjd.cn
Standard room: RMB268
Credit Cards:
Visa, Master Card, JCB, American
Express, Domestic Cards

Jinhua Hotel
★★★★
1 Dongge Lu, (0771) 208 8888
Credit Cards: Visa, Master Card,
JCB, American Express, Domestic
Cards, Diners Club

Nanning Phoenix Hotel
★★★★
63 Chaoyang Lu, (0771) 211 9888
www.phoenixhotel.cn

Nanning Taoyuan Hotel
★★★★
74 Taoyuan Lu, (0771) 209 6868
Credit Cards:

Visa, Master Card, JCB, American
Express, Domestic Cards

Camellia Hotel
★★★
48 Zhonghua Lu, (0771) 208 8090
Credit Cards: Domestic Cards

Guangxi Xinhua Hotel
★★★
69 Minzu Dajie, (0771) 208 5888
Standard room: RMB318
Credit Cards: Domestic Cards

Nanning Tianhu Hotel
★★★
3 Hangzhou Lu, (0771) 219 5588
www.tianhu-hotel.com
Credit Cards: Visa, Master Card,
JCB, Domestic Cards

Nanning Wanxing Hotel
★★★
42-1 Beining Jie, (0771) 210 2888
www.nnwxhotel.com
Standard room: RMB218
Credit Cards:
Visa, Master Card, JCB, American
Express, Domestic Cards

Xiangyun Hotel
★★★
59 Xinmin Lu, (0771) 210 1999
www.nnxyhotel.com
Standard room: RMB380
Credit Cards:
Visa, Master Card, JCB

Yinhe Hotel
★★★
84 Chaoyang Lu, (0771) 211 6688
www.yhhotel.com
Standard room: RMB380
Credit Cards: Visa, Master Card,
JCB, American Express

Restaurants

Western
Red Star 3 红星3号

19-1 Jiaoyu Lu, (0771) 532 6660
Louis XIII 路易十三
5 Dongge Lu, (0711) 281 7888
Cafe
Yesterday Once More Cafe
昨日重现咖啡厅
6 Xinzhu Lu, (0771) 589 0939
International
Tropical Island 热带岛
6 Guangyuan Lu, (0771) 570 6060
Chinese
Shenzhou Shifu 神州食府
88 Minzu Dong Dajie, Wharton
International Hotel
(0771) 211 1999
Chinese Restaurant 中餐厅
88 Minzu Dong Dajie, Wharton
International Hotel
(0771) 211 1999

Bar & Clubs

Mingdu Club 明都娱乐城
38 Xinmin Lu, Mingyuan Xindu
Hotel, (0771) 280 7846
Hailan Yuntian Club
海蓝云天夜总会
4/F, 81 Minzu Da Dao
(0771) 588 0000

Hospitals

First Affiliated Hospital of Guangxi
Medical University
广西医科大学第一附属医院
6 Shuangyong Lu, (0771) 5359 339
First People's Hospital of Nanning
南宁市第一人民医院
99 Qixing Lu, (0771) 263 6235

Bookstores

Xinhua Bookstore, Nanning
南宁市新华书店
69 Minzu Dadao, (0771) 585 1848

Industrial parks

Nanning Economic & Technological
Development Zone
南宁经济技术开发区
(0771) 451 8881
www.nnda.gov.cn
Major Industries:
Chemical engineering, automobiles,
electronics, biotechnology
Pingxiang Border Economic Zone
凭祥市边境经济合作区
(0771) 855 0500, *www.gxpxhzq.com.cn*
Major Industries:
Electronics, new materials
Nanning National Hi-Tech Indus-
trial Development Zone
南宁国家高新技术产业开发区
(0771) 581 6999
www.nnhitech.gov.cn
Major Industries:
Electronics, pharmaceuticals, environmental protection

Exhibition centers

Nanning International Convention
& Exhibition Center
106 Minzu Dadao, Nanning
(0771) 209 2223
www.nicec.cn

Guilin 桂林

Telephone prefix: 0773
Population: 4.79 million
Bank of China: 5 Shanhu Bei Lu

Ask anyone in China what the most beautiful place in the country is and they will likely tell you Guilin. Easily accessible from the capital Nanning, Guilin's location on the Li river has made it a booming tourist town. The city itself maintains a pleasant but bustling environment, with the majority of its population engaging in tourism and hospitality-related work.

Several prominent natural attractions are located around Guilin, including karst mountains – the dragon's teeth towers of rock depicted in traditional Chinese paintings caves and the river, which hosts the boating tours that have become a required adventure for China's burgeoning tourist population. Just north of Guilin is the town of Yangshuo which is less well known and therefore cheap-

er and a haven for backpackers. The Guilin Liangjiang International Airport offers direct flights to a number of major cities in China as well as Fukuoka, Seoul, Bangkok, Macau, and Hong Kong.

Hotels

Guilin Merryland Resort Hotel
★★★★★
Zhiling Lu, Xing'an County
(0773) 622 9898
Credit Cards: Visa
Guilin Royal Garden Hotel
★★★★★
186 -1 Linjiang Lu, (0773) 568 8888
www.gldy.com.cn
Credit Cards: Visa, Master Card, JCB, American Express
Lijiang Waterfall Hotel
★★★★★
1 Shanhu Bci Lu, (0773) 282 2881
www.waterfallguilin.com
Credit Cards: Visa, Master Card, JCB, American Express
Sheraton Guilin Hotel
★★★★★
15 Binjiang Lu, (0773) 282 5588

DESTINATIONS

Standard room: RMB550
Credit Cards: Visa, Master Card,
JCB, American Express
Guilin Bravo Hotel
★★★★
14 Ronghu Nan Lu, (0773) 289 8888
www.glbravohotel.com
Standard room: RMB646
Credit Cards: Visa, Master Card,
JCB, American Express, Domestic
Cards, Diners Club
Guilin Park Hotel
★★★★
1 Luoshishan, (0773) 255 8899
Standard room: RMB830
Credit Cards: Visa, Master Card,
JCB, American Express
Guishan (Jasper) Hotel
★★★★
Chuanshan Lu, (0773) 581 3388
www.guishanhotel.com
Credit Cards: Visa, Master Card,
JCB, American Express
Jun Hao Hotel
★★★★
28 Guanlian Lu, Yangshuo
(0773) 691 0168
Standard room: RMB258

Credit Cards:
Visa, Master Card, JCB, American
Express, Domestic Cards
New West Street Hotel
★★★★
68 Pantao Lu, (0773) 881 8888
www.nwshotel.com
Standard room: RMB688
Credit Cards:
Visa, Master Card, JCB, American
Express, Domestic Cards
Paradesa Yangshuo Resort
★★★★
116 Yangshuo Xi Jie, (0773) 882 2109
Standard room: RMB784
Credit Cards: Visa, Master Card,
JCB, American Express
Yangshuo New Century Hotel
★★★★
Yangshuo Park, Pantao Lu
(0773) 882 9819, *www.ysxsj.com*
Credit Cards:
Visa, Master Card, JCB, American
Express, Domestic Cards
Guilin Fubo Hotel
★★★
27 Binjiang Lu, (0773) 256 9898
www.fubohotel.com

Standard room:
RMB666 +10% Surcharge
Credit Cards: Visa, Master Card,
JCB, American Express
Guilin Osmanthus Hotel
★★★
77 Zhongshan Nan Lu
(0773) 383 4300, *www.glosm.com*
Credit Cards:
Visa, Master Card, JCB, American
Express, Domestic Cards
Jing Xiu Grand Hotel
★★★
8 Lingui Lu, (0773) 286 9818
www.jingxiuhotel.com
Credit Cards:
Visa, Master Card, JCB, American
Express, Domestic Cards
Shanshui Hotel
★★★
48 Qixing Lu, (0773) 581 5151
www.glshanshui.com
Credit Cards: Domestic Cards

Restaurants

Japanese
Ronghu Fuji 榕湖富士总店
17 Ronghu Bei Lu, (0773) 281 8606
Korean
Korean Restaurant 韩国餐厅
36 Binjiang Lu (Golden Elephant
Hotel), (0773) 280 8888
Cantonese
Tai Lian Hotel
102 Zhongshan Zhong Lu
(0773) 282 2888
Chinese
Weixiangguan Restaurant 味香馆
240 Zhongshan Zhong Lu
(0773) 282 2559
Lijiang Restaurant 漓江厅
14 Ronghu Nan Lu, Guilin Bravo
Hotel, (0773) 282 3950

Western
Qinyuan Cafe 沁园咖啡厅
14 Ronghu Nan Lu, (0773) 282 3950

Bars & Clubs

Jiulong Night Club 九龙夜总会
1 Nanmenqiao
Taibai Bar 太白吧
Windsor Guishan Hotel
Under Moon 月亮下
Xi Jie (in Yangshuo)
Animal House 原始人酒吧
Xi Jie (in Yangshuo)
Meiyou Restauarant 没有饭店
Yangshuo Xi Jie, (0773) 881 9355

Hospitals

Guilin People's Hospital
桂林市人民医院
12 Wenming Lu, (0773) 282 7626
Nanxishan Hospital 南溪山医院
96 Chongxin Lu, (0773) 383 2001

Bookstores

Guilin Xinhua Bookstore
桂林新华书店
28 Zhongshan Zhong Lu
(0773) 288 0519

Industrial parks

**Guilin National New & Hi-Tech
Industrial Development Zone**
桂林国家高新技术产业开发区
(0773) 581 1341, *www.eguilin.org*
Major Industries:
Electronics, biotechnologies, pharmaceuticals, environment protection

Exhibition centers

**Guilin International Convention &
Exhibition Center**
22 Lijiang Lu, (0773) 5869 856
www.glcec.com

Beihai 北海
Telephone prefix: 0779
Population: 1.4 million

Located on the southern coast of China, on the Beibu Gulf, Beihai is home to Silver Beach, one of the finest in China. Naturally seafood is a local delicacy. The city was opened to international commerce in 1984 and has helped increase trade between China and Southeast Asia with its sea ports.

Hotels

Shangri-La Hotel Beihai
★★★★★
33 Chating Lu
(0779) 206 2288
Standard room:
RMB700 +15% Surcharge
Credit Cards:
Visa, Master Card, JCB, American Express, Domestic Cards
Beihai International Hotel Jiatianxia
★★★★
8 West Section Beihai Dajie

(0779) 306 5666
www.jtxhotel.com
Credit Cards:
Visa, Master Card, JCB, American Express, Domestic Cards
Haitan Hotel
★★★★
Yintan Dajie, (0779) 388 8888
Li Yuan International Hotel
★★★
Beijing Lu, (0779) 322 0688
www.lyhotel.cn
Credit Cards:
Visa, Master Card, JCB, American Express, Domestic Cards
Stone Forest Hotel
★★★
35 Beibuwan Xi Lu, (0779) 390 8088
www.bhslhotel.com
Standard room: RMB200
Credit Cards: Visa, Master Card, JCB, American Express

Restaurants

Danjia
Beibuwan Dong Lu
(0779) 205 4734
Dexing
Beibubei Square, (0779) 303 3616

Guizhou

Population: 37.3 million
Area: 174, 000 sq km
Capital: Guiyang
Airport: Guiyang, Tongren

Guizhou, located in central southwest China, is one of the country's poorest provinces. Its hilly terrain is home to 38.7 million inhabitants many of whom are ethnic minorities. Guizhou is relatively rich in natural mineral resources, and also stands to become an important source of hydroelectric power for China.

Guizhou occupies the eastern part of the Yunnan-Guizhou Plateau and averages an altitude around 1,000 meters above sea level. The province is almost entirely composed of mountains and valleys, its numerous rivers and tributaries fed by the highest annual precipitation of all China's provinces. Less polluted than most

eastern provinces, Guizhou has an average annual temperature of 14 to 16 degrees Celsius.

Guizhou has one of China's largest non-Han Chinese populations with ethnic minorities such as the Miao, Yao, Yi, Qiang, Dong, Zhuang, Bai, Buyi and Tujia comprising 37% of its people. The Miao were the dominant ethnic group in the Guizhou region until the area began to be settled by Han Chinese during the Ming Dynasty (1368-1644).

Due to its non-Han roots, remoteness and difficult terrain, Guizhou has often been on the fringes of control by Beijing and colonial powers alike. In the early 20th century, Guizhou provoked the ire of foreign opium traders when it emerged as a major poppy producer, undercutting opium imports to the Chinese market. In 1916, after president Yuan Shikai attempted to promote himself to emperor, Guizhou declared independence, a situation that remained more or less in place through the upheavals of the early 20th century, until the province was captured by Communist forces in 1949.

Guizhou's economy is largely built on mining and agriculture, but its value as a power source to

Guangdong's Pearl River Delta cities has grown steadily in recent years. The province's rivers, particularly the Wu River, are a rich source of hydroelectric power. Several hydro-power projects have been launched in recent years as part of a drive to harness the energy resources of the country's west to satisfy the needs of the booming coastal provinces.

Guizhou's mining sector has proven to be the most attractive economic area for foreign investors, with numerous small exploration deals between foreign mining com-panies and the provincial geological bureau. The province holds large reserves of gold, copper, zinc, baux-ite and mercury. It is also one of China's largest producers of phos-phate fertilizers.

Guizhou's coal and coal bed gas reserves are some of the largest in southwest China. Much of the prov-ince remains unexplored and there are major discoveries occurring every year. Guizhou's mines, not unlike others nationwide, are plagued by accidents and have yet to resolve fun-damental safety issues.

Agriculturally, Guizhou produces small quantities of grains and sta-ple foods, with tobacco, tea, banan-as, chilies, garlic, bamboo shoots and edible fungus constituting the bulk of agricultural production. Guizhou's tobacco production is second in China only to neighbor-ing Yunnan, but its production lacks the organization and regulation of its wester neighbor. Textiles have a long tradition in Guizhou, with locally made batiks gaining increas-ing international attention.

Alcohol from Guizhou is famous, with *maotai*, named after the town where it is produced, being the most famous local spirit. Prices of the best *maotai* can reach RMB3,000 per bot-tle, so it is not cheap, but it is drunk like water by those who can afford it – officials and rich business people – and local restaurants wisely offer yogurt to drink with it to prevent the lining of your stomach from being eaten away.

Guizhou Economic Data			
	2005	2004	Change%
GDP (RMB bn)	197.9	167.8	17.9
GDP per capita (RMB)	5,052	4,215	19.9
Exports (US$ bn)	0.86	0.87	-1.15
Imports (US$ bn)	0.54	0.65	-16.92
Cars per 100 households	1.81	0.38	376.32
PCs per 100 households	23.99	21.02	14.13

Guiyang 贵阳

Telephone prefix: 0851
Population: 3.88 million
Bank of China: 30 Dusi Lu

Guiyang's reputation as being underdeveloped and poor is not borne out by reality – it has the same highways, shopping plazas, KFC and Giordano outlets, luxury goods and nightclubs as every other provincial capital, but prices are significantly lower than most, providing some investment opportunities.

Infrastructure in Guiyang is good, the electricity supply (largely from hydroelectric dams) is plentiful and there are many state-owned factories that are eager to do business with private investors.

Guiyang is rich in minerals and pharmaceutical materials and prospects for the city becoming a key hub for southwest China are good. The central government's 'Go West' initiative to encourage investment in China's remote western regions also means tax breaks for foreign investors.

Although not as obvious as in the coastal cities, the private enterprise element of the city's economy is growing. State enterprise is well entrenched in Guiyang and is retreating only slowly, but already half of the taxis are privately owned, compared to less than 1% in either Beijing or Shanghai.

The foreign investment that continues to flood into China heads almost always for the coastal strip from Dalian to Shenzhen. But there is an argument for avoiding these well-developed regions in favor of inland China with its lower costs and less competitive environment. Guiyang is part of the proof. Growing numbers of foreign investors are looking at such places to build businesses on the big fish-small pond principle.

There are obviously significant business opportunities. Guizhou has very low labor costs, good air transport links, a tradition of manufacturing (thanks to Chairman Mao's policy of diversification in the 1950s and 1960s to prepare for a possible attack by either the Soviet Union or the US), and one of the most pleasant climates of any part of China.

Low levels of education and training amongst local staff can be a problem. Another is a local government structure which could be more responsive and efficient.

Tourism is an obvious opportunity and the right pitch would seem to be "The Last Frontier". Guizhou has natural scenery on a par with Guilin and Sichuan, but it is much less developed. There will be foreign tourists who want to see the natural beauty of Guizhou, without the rafting, trekking and other activities available elsewhere. But the main market will surely be the urban middle class Chinese from the coastal cities who want to see China as it was, before it disappears.

Guiyang Economic Data	
GDP 2005 (RMB bn)	52.56
Disposable income 2005 (RMB)	9,928

Hotels

Guizhou Park Hotel
★★★★
66 Beijing Lu, (0851) 682 3888
www.gz-hotel.com.cn
Credit Cards:
Visa, Master Card, JCB, American Express, Domestic Cards
Guilong Hotel
★★★★
52 Shenqi Lu, (0851) 559 2888
Credit Cards: Visa, Master Card, JCB, American Express, Domestic

Cards, Diners Club
Howard Johnson Plaza Hotel Guizhou
★★★★
29 Zaoshan Lu, (0851) 651 8888
Standard room: RMB500
Credit Cards: Visa, Master Card, JCB, American Express
Jinjiang Flower Hotel
★★★★
1 Zhonghua Nan Lu, (0851) 586 7888
www.jjxhhotel.com
Standard room: RMB468
Credit Cards:
Visa, Master Card, JCB
Miracle Hotel Guiyang
★★★★
1 Beijing Lu, (0851) 677 1888
www.miraclehotels.com
Credit Cards:
Visa, Master Card, JCB, American Express, Domestic Cards
Miracle Plaza Hotel Guiyang
★★★★
219 Baoshan Bei Lu, (0851) 682 5888
Standard room:
RMB660 (published rate)
Credit Cards: Visa, Master Card, JCB, American Express
Regal Hotel Guizhou
★★★★
115 Ruijin Bei Lu, (0851) 652 1888
www.gzregal.com.cn
Standard room: RMB880
Credit Cards:
Visa, Master Card, JCB, American Express, Domestic Cards
Trade-Point Hotel
★★★★
18 Yan'an Dong Lu, (0851) 582 7888
www.trade-pointhotel.com
Credit Cards:
Visa, Master Card, JCB, American

Express, Domestic Cards
Hualian Hotel
★★★
137 Zhonghua Zhong Lu
(0851) 581 0999
Standard room:
RMB328 +10% Surcharge
Credit Cards:
Visa, Master Card, JCB, American
Express, Domestic Cards

Restaurants

Cantonese
Tianwaitian Restaurant 天外天渔城
1/F- 6/F, 36 Ruijin Nan Lu
(0851) 581 5555
Chinese Vegetarian
Jueyuan 觉园餐厅
11 Fushi Bei Lu, (0851) 552 0999
Chinese
Mingjianwagang 民间瓦缸
118 Ruijin Nan Lu, (0851) 583 3777

Bars & Clubs

The Little Beer House 小小啤酒屋
64 Beijing Lu, (0851) 683 6301

Hospitals

Affiliated Hospital of Guiyang Medical College 贵阳医学院附属医院
28 Guiyi Jie, (0851) 683 2942
**First People's Hospital of Guiyang
贵阳第一人民医院**
97 Bo'ai Lu, (0851) 583 3214

Bookstores

**Xinhua Bookstore, Guiyang
贵阳市新华书店**
1 Ruijin Bei Lu
(0851) 657 1890

Industrial parks

**Guiyang Economic & Technological Development Zone
贵阳经济技术开发区**
(0851) 380 6943
www.geta.gov.cn
Major Industries:
Engineering, electronics, machinery,
automotive and aviation parts
**Guiyang High-Tech Industrial Zone
贵阳高新技术产业开发区**
(0851) 470 1272
www.gyhtz.gov.cn
Major Industries: Biotechnology,
pharmaceuticals, electronics.

Hainan

Population: 8.28 million
Area: 34, 000 sq km
Capital: Haikou
Airports: Haikou, Sanya
Ports: Haikou, Sanya, Yangpu

For centuries, Hainan was known to the Chinese as "the end of the world"; a place where those who fell out of favor with the emperor were sent to live out their lives in obscurity. Now a Special Economic Zone, Hainan is using its remote southern location to transform itself into a tourist haven, particularly for the Chinese who live in chilly northern climes.

Hainan is China's southernmost province, separated from the southwestern tip of Guangdong province (only 18 km away) by the Qiongzhou Straits, a divide that has now been bridged by a rail line. Hainan's two main cities, Haikou and Sanya, are located at the island's northeast and southwest, respectively, and the island

is flanked by the Gulf of Tonkin to the west and the South China Sea to the east. About 85% of its 8.2 million inhabitants are Han Chinese, with the next largest ethnic group, the Li people, totaling approximately 1 million. The island is also home to Miao (Hmong) and Hui minorities.

For hundreds of years, Hainan was one of China's poorest and most backward regions, despite being a treasure trove of natural resources such as iron, salt, minerals, petroleum (under the South China Sea) and a range of aquatic products.

Toward the end of the Qing Dynasty (1644-1911), Hainan began to see some interaction with the West. Haikou was one of the second wave of "treaty ports", opened to trade with the West in 1858. At the end of the 19th Century, France claimed "special rights" over Hainan, as well as Guangdong, Guangxi and Yunnan.

China's largest island after Taiwan, Hainan has struggled in the past few decades to find its place in China's development. The island was a special administrative region of Guangdong province until 1988, when it was promoted to provincial status and declared a Special Economic Zone (SEZ).

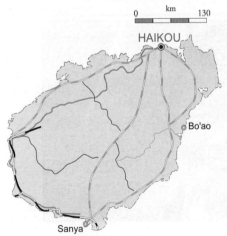

Far from Beijing, Hainan has not always been easy for the central government to control. Official corruption has led to several embarrassing scandals. In the most egregious case, freewheeling officials in the mid-1980s imported 90,000 Japanese cars and trucks duty free before shipping them to the mainland, assisted by local naval units, at a 150% profit.

Hainan's tropical appeal and SEZ status led to a major influx of foreign capital in the early 1990s, during which a number of large projects were initiated in anticipation of a bright economic future for the island. A property market boom resulted, which ended in a crash when Beijing implemented measures to cool down the country's overheating economy. Shortly afterwards, in 1997, the Asian financial crisis returned Hainan to investment backwater status, from which it is only starting to emerge. The provincial capital of Haikou still features numerous skeletons of large buildings whose capital ran out before they could be completed.

With inland and offshore reserves estimated at 5.8 trillion cubic meters of gas and 29.1 billion tons of oil, Hainan is endowed with some of the largest oil and gas reserves of any Chinese province. The island supplies 2.9 billion cubic meters of gas to Hong Kong every year via a 770-km pipeline.

In recent years, the island's industrial development plan has focused on technology-intensive, low-pollution manufacturing, particularly in the electronics, petrochemical and pharmaceutical sectors. The island has made progress on consolidating and regionalizing industries – moving integrated industry to the island's north, light industry to the east and heavy industry to the west. The south has essentially been reserved for tourism.

Hainan's tropical climate has helped make it China's largest producer of raw rubber, and it is also a major producer of finished rubber products such as latex gloves, tires and conveyor belts.

Hainan's year-round warm weather also makes it one of China's top fruit-producing regions, producing about one million tons of banana

products annually. Other produce includes coconuts, pepper, coffee and aquatic products, especially shrimp and shellfish. The warm weather also brings many tourists to Hainan's beautiful beaches.

The overall development of industry on Hainan has been made difficult by its isolation from the mainland. It does not have major transport facilities that would spur development, and most industries are reluctant to invest in regions where suitable facilities do not already exist. For this reason, in 2005 the island's governor set aside US$2.4 million to study the feasibility of building a bridge from the island to Guangdong province.

Tourism has for some time been Hainan's most promising sector, yet this potential remains unrealized and the island has failed to compete with regional rivals Thailand and the Philippines. Of 12 million visitors to Hainan in 2002, only 3% were from overseas. This is changing however, as more and more vacation home communities and golf courses are springing up around the island. Sanya is set to become the island's hub of tourism, with multinational hotel chains like Mariott and Sheraton building resorts nearby. China's goal is to transform Hainan into the "Hawaii of China".

Hainan Economic Data			
	2005	2004	Change%
GDP (RMB bn)	89.5	79.9	12.0
GDP per capita (RMB)	1,087	9,450	-88.5
Exports (US$ bn)	1.02	1.09	-6.42
Imports (US$ bn)	1.52	2.31	-34.20
Cars per 100 households	3.52	2.25	56.44
PCs per 100 households	36.21	18.96	90.98

Haikou 海口

Telephone prefix: 0898
Population: 1.73 million
Bank of China: 38 Datong Lu

Hainan's provincial capital Haikou is situated at the island's northeast corner, on the Qiongzhou Straits. Due to its position facing the mainland, the city has traditionally been the island's commercial center and has had port operations for around 1,000 years.

Haikou first came under Chinese influence during the Han Dynasty around 100 BC. Haikou was opened to trade with the West in 1858 by the Treaty of Tianjin, after the second Opium War.

Haikou is a pleasant and clean city with a warm climate, but it is primarily seen by tourists as a gateway to the more popular Sanya. Beyond tourism, Haikou's economy is built upon agriculture, light industry, food processing and textiles. Coconut milk and rubber products are key exports.

Mazda Motors has a plant in the city and Korean electronics giant Samsung completed a new fiber optic cable in Haikou in late 2004. The city also has ambitions to become a regional chemical and pharmaceutical hub. Haikou itself is composed of two sections, the port area in the city's west and the colonial district in the north. The colonial district is good for a relaxing walking tour.

Haikou Economic Data	
GDP 2005 (RMB bn)	30.13
Disposable income 2005 (RMB)	9,740

Hotels

Crowne Spa Resort Hainan
★★★★★
1 Qiongshan Dajie, Jiangdong
(0898) 6596 6888
www.ichotelsgroup.com
Standard room: RMB1,400
Credit Cards:
Visa, Master Card, JCB, American
Express, Domestic Cards

Golden Coast Lawton Hotel
★★★★★
68 Renmin Dajie, (0898) 6625 9888
www.golden.com.cn
Standard room: RMB1,100
Credit Cards: Visa, Master Card,
JCB, American Express

Huandao Tide Hotel
★★★★★
18 Heping Dajie
(0898) 6626 8888
Standard room:
RMB1,176 +15% Surcharge
Credit Cards:
Visa, Master Card, JCB, American
Express, Domestic Cards

Huayun Gloria Grand Hotel Haikou
★★★★★
239 Binhai Dajie, Xiuying
(0898) 3168 8855
Standard room:
RMB368 (one buffet breakfast)
Credit Cards: Visa, Master Card,
JCB, American Express

Kangle Garden HNA Resort
★★★★★
Kangle Garden, Wanning
(0898) 6256 8888
www.kangleresort.com
Standard room:
RMB1,550 +15% Surcharge
Credit Cards: Visa, Master Card,
JCB, American Express

Meritus Mandarin Haikou
★★★★★
18 Wenhua Lu, (0898) 6854 8888
Standard room: RMB1,200
Credit Cards:
Visa, Master Card, JCB, American
Express, Domestic Cards

Sheraton Haikou Resort
★★★★★
199 Binhai Dajie, (0898) 6870 8888
www.sheraton.com
Standard room: RMB1,000
Credit Cards: Visa, Master Card,
JCB, American Express

Sofitel Fizi Hainan
★★★★★
Yingbin Peninsula, Old City Dev.
Zone, Chengmai County
(0898) 6749 8888
www.sofitel.com/asia
Credit Cards:
Visa, Master Card, JCB, American
Express, Domestic Cards

Golden Sea View Hotel
★★★★
67 Binhai Dajie, (0898) 6853 7718
www.goldenhotel.com.cn

**Haikou International Financial
(Jasper) Hotel**
★★★★
29 Datong Lu, (0898) 6677 3088
www.hkjr-jasper.com.cn
Credit Cards:
Visa, Master Card, JCB, American
Express, Domestic Cards

Haikou Tower Hotel
★★★★
2 Taihua Lu, Binhai Dajie
(0898) 6677 2990
www.towerhotel.cn
Standard room: RMB888
Credit Cards:
Visa, Master Card, JCB, American

Express, Domestic Cards
Hainan Airline Hotel
★★★★
38 Datong Lu, (0898) 6679 6999
Credit Cards:
Visa, Master Card, JCB, American
Express, Domestic Cards
Hainan Huatian Hotel
★★★★
9-1 Longkun Bei Lu
(0898) 6679 9988
Standard room:
RMB788 (deluxe room)
Credit Cards: Visa, Master Card,
JCB, American Express
Hainan New Hot Spring Hotel
★★★★
50 Longkun Bei Lu, (0898) 6671 1111
www.newhotspringhtl.com.cn
Standard room: RMB200-230
Credit Cards: Visa, Master Card,
JCB, American Express
Hainan Xinyuan Hot Spring Hotel
★★★★
18-8 Haixiu Lu, (0898) 6673 5111
www.xinyuanhotel.com
Standard room: RMB338
Credit Cards:
Visa, Master Card, JCB, American
Express, Domestic Cards
Hainan Yantai Int'l Hotel
★★★★
18 Wudong Lu, Haidian
(0898) 6625 0888
www.hnyantaihotel.com
Treasure Island Hotel
★★★★
16 Lantian Lu, (0898) 6676 3388
www.treasureisland-hotel.com
Credit Cards:
Visa, Master Card, JCB
Hainan Asgard Hotel
★★★★

55 Renmin Dajie, (0898) 6619 5888
Standard room: RMB788
Credit Cards: Visa, Domestic Cards
Seaview International Hotel
★★★★
6 Haixiu Dong Lu, (0898) 6677 3392
www.wh-hotel.com
Sun City Hotel
★★★★
A16 Longhua Lu, (0898) 6624 3333
www.suncityhotel.com.cn
Ye Hai Hotel
★★★★
46 Yusha Lu, (0898) 6859 8888
www.yehaihotel.com
Hai Wai Hotel
★★★
11 Wuzhishan Lu, (0898) 6523 5999
Credit Cards:
Visa, Master Card, JCB, American
Express, Domestic Cards
Haikou Hotel
★★★
4 Haifu Dajie, (0898) 6535 1234
www.haikouhotel.com
Standard room: RMB688
Credit Cards:
Visa, Master Card, JCB, American
Express, Domestic Cards
Haikou Huitong Hotel
★★★
26 Guomao Lu, (0898) 6853 1881
www.huitong-hotel.com
Standard room: RMB575
Credit Cards: Visa, Master Card,
JCB, American Express

Restaurants

Cafe
Fengge Cafe 风格咖啡店
2/F, 4 Datong Lu, (0898) 6623 8890
Hotpot
Henry Beef Restaurant

亨利肥牛酒店
10-20 Jinlong Lu, (0898) 6855 0800

Russian

**Yawen Russian Restaurant
亚雯俄罗斯斯西餐厅**
23 Nanhang Dong Lu
(0898) 6677 9818

Korean

**Jingfu Palace Korean Restaurant
名人泰国鱼翅餐厅**
6 Jichang Xi Lu, (0898) 6676 7819

Italian

**Bologna Italian Restaurant
波洛尼亚意大利餐厅**
18 Wenhua Lu (Hainan Mansion)
(0898) 6854 8888

Seafood

**New Longquan Seafood Restaurant
新龙泉海鲜酒家**
9 Longkun Nan Lu, (0898) 6672 3944

Bars & Clubs

Hot Bar 热点酒吧
1 Haidian Sandong Lu, Heping Da
Dao

Football Bar 快乐足球酒吧
G/F Art Gallery, Haidian Xi Lu

Village Bar 乡村吧
Crowne Plaza

Along Story 阿龙故事
49 Guomao Dadao, (0898) 6851 2128

Hospitals

**Xiuying Yifu Hospital
秀英逸夫医院**
19 Xiuhua Lu, (0898) 6864 2654

Affiliated Hospital of Hainan Medical College 海南医学院附属医院
31 Longhua Lu, (0898) 6677 2248

Bookstores

**Xinhua Bookstore, Haikou
海口市新华书店**
27 Nansha Lu, (0898) 6650 3004

Industrial parks

**Haikou Free Trade Zone
海口保税区**
(0898) 6680 1295
www.hkftz.gov.cn

Major Industries:
Export processing industries, free trade storage, international trade, finance, insurance, information, consulting

Sanya 三亚

Telephone prefix: 0899
Population: 0.52 million
Bank of China: 35 Jefang Si Lu

Haikou is Hainan's provincial capital, but the resort city of Sanya on the island's south coast was placed squarely in the international limelight when it hosted the Miss World contest in December 2003. It was such a success that it was held there again in 2004 and 2005. Sanya is Hainan's leading tourist destination. Most of the factories previously located in the city have been moved elsewhere, making the city's tourism market more attractive, but also crucial to its economic health.

There are two main areas in Sanya: Dadonghai, which is closer to downtown Sanya, and Yalong Bay, which is about a RMB40-taxi from the downtown area and has attracted more of the city's upscale hotel chains such as the Sheraton. Both areas have long, wide beaches with white sand and clear blue water, and there is a thriving beach culture (unlike, for example, Xiamen beaches) with rubber boats, jet ski rides, and even paras-

ailing available. Seafood barbeque is ubiquitous and delicious.

The government is determined to turn Hainan into a successful international tourist destination. Chinese guests currently constitute 90% of the current occupancy in Sanya. Foreign businesspeople living in China are also still very much the minority in Sanya, perhaps because it is often cheaper to fly from Shanghai to Bangkok than to Sanya.

Sanya's government invested heavily to ensure selection as the venue for the Miss World 2003 contest, and the beauty pageant proved to be an effective marketing tool, raising the global awareness of Sanya in particular and Hainan in general. For meetings, incentives, conferences and exhibitions, known in the trade as MICE, Sanya is becoming a China favorite.

Sanya sees a lot of Korean honeymooners and Japanese golfers, as flight times are significantly shorter than to Southeast Asia. Many in the local hotel industry see an opportunity for high-end boutique hotels. At present, most operators compete head-to-head with large mid- to high-end chain hotels.

Hotels

Crowne Plaza Sanya
★★★★★
Yalong Bay National Resort
(0898) 8855 5888
www.ichotelsgroup.com
Standard room: RMB888
Credit Cards:
Visa, Master Card, JCB, American
Express, Domestic Cards

Gloria Resort Sanya
★★★★★
Yalong Bay National Resort
(0898) 8856 8855
Standard room: RMB1,488
Credit Cards: Visa, Master Card,
Diners Club

Guest House International Hotel Sanya
★★★★★
33 Yuya Lu
(0898) 8828 6688
www.gh898.com
Standard room: RMB1,080
Credit Cards: Visa, Master Card,
American Express, Domestic Cards

Hilton Sanya Resort & Spa
★★★★★
Yalong Bay National Resort
(0898) 8858 8888
www.hilton.com
Standard room: RMB1,580
Credit Cards:
Visa, Master Card, JCB, American
Express, Domestic Cards

Holiday Inn Resort Yalong Bay Sanya
★★★★★
Yalong Bay National Resort
(0898) 8856 5666
Standard room: RMB1,438
Credit Cards:
Visa, Master Card, JCB, American
Express, Domestic Cards

Holiday Inn Sanya Bay Resort
★★★★★
Sanya Bay Haipo Tourism Resort
Zone, (0898) 8833 9988
Standard room:
RMB565 +15% Surcharge
Credit Cards: Visa, Master Card,
JCB, American Express, Domestic
Cards, Diners Club

Horizon Resort & Spa
★★★★★
Yalong Bay National Resort
(0898) 8856 7888
www.horizon.com.cn
Standard room: RMB1,458
Credit Cards:
Visa, Master Card, JCB, American
Express, Domestic Cards

International Asia Pacific Convention Center & HNA Resort Sanya
★★★★★
Sanya Bay Resort, (0898) 8833 2666
www.iapccsanya.com
Standard room: RMB1,288
Credit Cards: Visa, Master Card,
JCB, Domestic Cards

Nanshan Hotel
★★★★★
Nanshan Resort
(0898) 8883 8088
www.nsybg.com
Standard room: RMB668
Credit Cards: Visa, Master Card

Resort Intime Sanya
★★★★★
Dadonghai Resort, (0898) 8821 0888
www.resortintime.com
Standard room: RMB1,288 (standard), 1,488 (superior ocean view)
Credit Cards:
Visa, Master Card, JCB, American
Express, Domestic Cards

Sanya Marriott Resort & Spa
★★★★★
Yalong Bay National Resort
(0898) 8856 8888
Standard room: RMB2,323
Credit Cards: Visa, Master Card,
JCB, American Express

Sanya Shanhaitian Hotel
★★★★★
88 Haiyun Lu, (0898) 8821 1688
www.shthotel.com
Standard room: RMB400
Credit Cards: Visa, Master Card,
JCB

Sanya Tian Fu Yuan Resort
★★★★★
208 Sanyawan Lu, (0898) 8833 3888
www.tianfuyuan.com
Standard room: RMB350
Credit Cards: Visa, Master Card,
JCB, American Express

Sanya Tianhong Resort Hotel
★★★★★
Yalong Bay National Resort
(0898) 8855 0088
www.tianhongresort.com
Standard room: RMB1,388
Credit Cards: Visa, Master Card,
JCB, DLC, GWC

Sheraton Sanya Resort
★★★★★
Yalong Bay National Resort
(0898) 8855 8855
Standard room: RMB1,550
Credit Cards: Visa, Master Card,
JCB, American Express

Universal Resort
★★★★★
Yalong Bay National Resort
(0898) 8856 6666
www.universalresort.com
Standard room: RMB1,380
Credit Cards: Visa, Master Card,

JCB, American Express, Domestic
Cards

Yalong Bay Mangrove Tree Resort
★★★★★
Yalong Bay National Resort
(0898) 8855 8888
www.mangrovetreeresort.com
Credit Cards: Visa, Master Card,
JCB, American Express

Cactus Resort Sanya
★★★★
Yalong Bay National Resort
(0898) 8856 8866
Standard room: RMB508
Credit Cards:
Visa, Master Card, JCB, American
Express, Domestic Cards

Golden Phoenix Sea View Hotel
★★★★
Haiyue Square, Binhai Dajie
(0898) 8866 1888
www.sygphotel.com
Credit Cards: Domestic Cards

Golden Sea Hotel
★★★★
Hai Po Resort, (0898) 8833 1288

Guoxi Hotel
★★★★
Jie Fang Si Lu, (0898) 8825 4888
www.guoxihotel.com

Harvest Qilin Hotel Sanya
★★★★
26 Hedongyi Lu, (0898) 8898 8999
www.harvestqilin.com
Standard room: RMB888
Credit Cards: Visa, Master Card,
JCB, American Express, Domestic
Cards

Huandao Beach Hotel
★★★★
Yalong Bay Resort
(0898) 8856 5588
www.underwatersightseeing.com

Standard room: RMB858
Credit Cards: Visa, Master Card, JCB, American Express
Jinling Holiday Resort
★★★★
Dadonghai Resort, (0898) 8822 8088
www.syjinling.net
Credit Cards:
Visa, Master Card, JCB, American Express, Domestic Cards
Kempinski Resort & Spa Sanya
★★★★
Sanya Bay
(0898) 8895 8686
Landscape Beach Hotel Sanya
★★★★
Dadonghai Resort
(0898) 8822 8666
www.sanyaliking.com
Credit Cards: Visa, Master Card, JCB, American Express, Domestic Cards
Linda Sea View hotel
★★★★
Dadonghai District
(0898) 3180 8888
www.hnlinda.com
Resort Golden Palm
★★★★
Yalong Bay National Resort

(0898) 8856 9988
www.resortgp.com.cn
Romantic Sea View Hotel
★★★★
Dadonghai Resort
(0898) 8821 6888
www.romantichel.com
Credit Cards: Visa, JCB, American Express, Domestic Cards
Sanya Bay Asgard Hotel
★★★★
Central Section Binhai Dajie, Sanya Bay
(0898) 8827 9888
www.syasgard.com
Standard room: RMB988
Credit Cards: Visa, Master Card, JCB, American Express
Sanya Haitian Grand Hotel
★★★★
Yuya Dajie
(0898) 8821 1666
www.hyton.com
Standard room: RMB278
Credit Cards: Visa, Master Card, JCB, American Express, Domestic Cards
Sanya Holiday Resort
★★★★
168 Sanyawan Lu
(0898) 8833 1328

www.syresort.com
Standard room: RMB268
Credit Cards: Visa, Master Card,
JCB, American Express, Domestic
Cards
Sanya Huayuan Resort
★★★★
Sanya Bay Tourist Spot
(0898) 8833 3999
www.hyholiday.com
Standard room: RMB1,088
Credit Cards: Visa, Master Card,
American Express, Domestic Cards
Sanya Maintint Hotel
★★★★
Linchunqiao, Xinfeng Lu
(0898) 8823 6888
www.maintint.com
Standard room: RMB688
Credit Cards:
Visa, Master Card, JCB, American
Express, Domestic Cards
Sanya Orient Bay View Hotel
★★★★
176 Jiefangsi Lu
(0898) 8829 8080
Standard room: RMB780
Credit Cards: Visa, Master Card,
American Express
Sanya Pearl River Garden Hotel
★★★★
Dadonghai Resort
(0898) 8821 1888
www.prgardenhotel.com.cn
Standard room: RMB980
Credit Cards: Visa, Master Card,
JCB, American Express
Sanya Pearl Seaview Hotel
★★★★
Dadonghai Resort, (0898) 8821 3838
www.pearlresort.com
Standard room: RMB1,188
Credit Cards: Visa, Master Card,

JCB, Domestic Cards
Sanya Royal Garden Resort
★★★★
Luling Lu, Dadonghai
(0898) 8822 8888
www.sanyaroyalgarden.com
Credit Cards:
Visa, Master Card, JCB, American
Express, Domestic Cards
Sanya Treasure Island Hotel
★★★★
1 Xinglong Wenquan Jie
(0898) 6255 5888
www.treasureisland.com.cn
South China Hotel
★★★★
Dadonghai Resort Area
(0898) 8821 9888
www.southchinahotel.com
Standard room: RMB980
Credit Cards: Visa, Master Card,
JCB, Domestic Cards
Viable Hot-Spring Sea View Village
★★★★
Binhai Dajie, Sanya Bay
(0898) 3889 9888
www.sanyawanbo.com
Standard room: RMB580
Credit Cards: Domestic Cards
Xinglong Treasure Island Hotel
★★★★
1 Wenquan Dajie, Xinglong
(0898) 6255 5888
www.treasureisland.com
Standard room: RMB500
Credit Cards:
Visa, Master Card, JCB, American
Express, Domestic Cards
Jing Wei Hotel
★★★
Haiyue Square, Sanyawan Lu
(0898) 8866 1323
www.syjingweihotel.com

Credit Cards: Visa, Master Card, JCB, American Express, Domestic Cards

Wenchang Jingwei Garden Hotel

★★★

Luyou Dajie, Qinglan Eco. Dev. Zone, Wenchang

(0898) 6332 2760

Restaurants

International

Coffee Time 咖啡时间西餐厅

Lanhai Garden, Binhai Lu

(0898) 8829 8848

BBQ & Seafood

Window Pavilion 云天阁

Yalong Bay (Resort Golden Palm Hotel)

(0898) 8856 9988

Seafood

**Chinese Restaurant
三亚珠江花园酒店**

Sea Sanya City (Pearl River Hotel)

(0899) 8821 1888

Western

**Coconut Grove Plaza
三亚东方海景大酒店**

176 Jiefang Lu (Oriental Hotel)

(0899) 8829 8080

Chinese

Dangui Lou 丹桂楼

Yalong Bay (Resort Golden Palm Hotel)

(0898) 8856 9988

Bars & Clubs

Sand Beach Bar 沙滩吧

Dadonghai Square

Hello Bar

Dadonghai Square

Samba Club 桑巴夜总会

Sheraton Hotel

Hospitals

**Sanya People's Hospital
三亚市人民医院**

32 Jiefang San Lu

(0899) 827 3806

**Sanya Chinese Medical Hospital
三亚市中医院**

Xinfeng Lu

(0899) 827 5345

Bookstores

**Xinhua Bookstore, Sanya
三亚市新华书店**

3 Jiefang Er Lu

(0899) 8827 3520

Bo'ao 博鳌
Telephone prefix: 0898
Population: 30,000
Bank of China: 119 Renmin Lu, Qionghai

Bo'ao is a fishing village that is receiving increasing international attention for its role as the host of the Bo'ao Forum for Asia (BFA), the first international cooperation organization based in China. In theory, BFA is intended to serve as the Asian answer to the World Economic Forum in Davos, Switzerland.

The main goals of the forum are to promote dialogue on regional, economic and social matters and concerns facing the member nations as well as discuss the important issues facing the region with respect to its place in the global community. Highlights from the 2006 conference included discussions on the banking, real estate, and automotive sectors, as well as how to meet energy needs and reform China's state-owned enterprises.

Hotels

Bo'ao Golden Coast Hot Spring Hotel
★★★★★
8 Jinhai'an Dajie
(0898) 6277 8888
www.boao-golden.com.cn
Standard room: RMB1,680
Credit Cards:
Visa, Master Card, JCB, American Express, Domestic Cards
Sofitel Bo'ao
★★★★★
Dongyu Island, (0898) 6296 6888
Standard room:

RMB1,992 +15% Surcharge
Credit Cards: Visa, Master Card, JCB, American Express
Gold Hibiscus Holiday Village
★★★★
Resort Dev. Zone, (0898) 6277 7888
www.jinfurong.net
Standard room: RMB680
Credit Cards: Visa, Master Card, JCB, American Express, Domestic Cards, Diners Club
Jinjiang Hot Spring Hotel
★★★★
1 Jinhai'an Dajie, (0898) 6277 8588
Standard room: RMB880
Credit Cards:
Visa, Master Card, JCB, American Express, Domestic Cards

Restaurants

Seafood
Aozhuang Seafood Restaurant
鳌庄海味馆
Bo'ao, Qionghai
(0898) 6277 7099
Western
Lagoon Cafe 乐泉咖啡厅
8 Jinhai'an Dadao, Golden Coast Hot Spring Hotel, (0898) 6277 8888
Riverside Cafe 玉带滩咖啡厅
8 Jinhai'an Dadao, Golden Coast Hot Spring Hotel
(0898) 6277 8888
Chinese
Royal Court Restaurant
御园中餐厅
8 Jinhai'an Dadao, Golden Coast Hot Spring Hotel, (0898) 6277 8888

Bars & Clubs

Fairyland Bar鳌仙吧
8 Jinhai'an Dadao, Golden Coast Hot Spring Hotel, (0898) 6277 8888

Hebei

Population: 68.51 million
Area: 18, 740 sq km
Capital: Shijiazhuang
Airports: Shijiazhuang, Qinhuangdao
Ports: Qinhuangdao, Jingtang, Huanghua

The name Hebei means "north of the (Yellow) River", even though the province's modern border does not touch the Yellow River at any point. Hebei is one of the most densely populated regions in China, with a population that has more than doubled since the 1950s to surpass 68 million. The province surrounds Beijing and Tianjin municipalities and because of this has managed to hitch a ride on the economic boom of the capital.

It is the gateway to China's old industrial base in the northeast and shares a border with Liaoning and Inner Mongolia to the north, Shanxi to the west, Henan to the south and Shandong to the southeast. To the east are Bohai Bay and the Yellow Sea. Hebei has four distinct seasons with cold winters and hot summers. Sand and dust storms are common in spring and it often rains heavily in summer.

The plains of Hebei were once the home of the prehistoric 'Peking Man' and have been an important region for Chinese rulers and foreign invaders since history began. The Great Wall, China's most iconic construction, runs across the north of the province and provides a striking reminder that this region has always been a frontier and a battleground for competing dynasties.

The area was formally designated "Hebei" for the first time during the Tang dynasty (618-907), but under the Ming (1368-1644) and subsequent Qing (1644-1911) dynasties came to be known as "Zhili", which means "directly ruled", because it was directly under the control of the imperial court.

After the Republic of China was founded in 1911, warlords took over much of the country and a group called the Zhili Clique ruled the region.

In 1976, the city of Tangshan was struck by a powerful earthquake which killed over 250,000 people, making it the deadliest of the 20th century.

Hebei's geographical location is the most important feature of its economy. As the province that surrounds Beijing and Tianjin, Hebei maintains long-standing ties with the two metropolises. It links the cities with the rest of China and bridges inland regions with the seaports along its Bohai Sea coastline. To accommodate increasing traffic, Hebei has built the largest number of highways and railway lines in the country. The Beijing-Tianjin-Hebei Economic Zone has been formed to allow the province's economy to benefit from integration with Beijing and Tianjin.

Furthermore, Hebei's population, rural and impoverished when compared with that of its neighboring metropolises, serves as a constant stream of manual labor, primarily in construction. Unfortunately for residents, as people have gravitated to the cities, heavily polluting industries have been moving out of Beijing and Tianjin, often relocating to Hebei. The environmental deterioration and land confiscation associated with this has resulted in increased protests and peasant revolts in recent years.

With its large area of cultivated land, Hebei is chiefly an agricultural province and one of the country's major producers of cereals, cotton, vegetables and vegetable oils. The province's output of fruit and milk rank second in China and tobacco is also a major industrial crop.

The province is rich in mineral resources and a large industrial base for coal and steel. The Tangshan Iron and Steel Group is one of the ten largest iron and steel enterprises in China, while the Kailuan Coal Mine, not far from the port of Tianjin adjoining northeast Hebei, is one of the largest coal producers in China. Oil deposits have been found in the province and are tapped on a sizeable scale in the Renqiu Area in the southeast.

The leading industrial sectors in Hebei include metallurgy, textiles, machine-making, construction materials, power generation and chemicals. Great Wall Automobile produces the largest number of pickup trucks in China at their factories in the province and Shijiazhuang Aircraft Industry produces the 'Little Hawk 500' light aircraft. The production of more high-tech products such as computers, telecom equipment and software is being actively encouraged.

Hebei has a host of tourist destinations besides the Great Wall, which runs through the north of the province and meets the sea at Shanhaiguan. World heritage sites include the imperial summer resorts and temples around Chengde city.

Hebei Economic Data			
	2005	2004	Change%
GDP (RMB bn)	1,009.6	847.8	19.1
GDP per capita (RMB)	14,782	12,918	14.4
Exports (US$ bn)	10.92	9.34	16.92
Imports (US$ bn)	5.15	4.19	22.91
Cars per 100 households	3.94	2.23	76.68
PCs per 100 households	37.63	23.82	57.98

Shijiazhuang 石家庄

Telephone prefix: 0311
Population: 9.27 million
Bank of China: 80 Xinhua Lu

The provincial capital Shijiazhuang is located in the center of the province, 280 km southwest of Beijing. It is a major hub for China's rail network and home to the biggest People's Liberation Army School and the biggest pharmaceutical factory in China. It is also a center for the study of traditional Chinese medicine.

Shijiazhuang was little more than a village until the beginning of the 20th century, when it became a transit point on the railway from Beijing to Wuhan. Construction of a second rail line between nearby Zhengding and the northern city of Taiyuan in 1907 led to further expansion of the city. Since the founding of the People's Republic in 1949, Shijiazhuang has become the political and economic center of Hebei Province.

The main industries in the city are textiles, chemicals, food processing, fertilizer, machinery, and agricultural equipment. Coal is mined nearby. Shijiazhuang New and High-tech Development Zone is a state-level development zone aimed at developing industries like telecommunications, electronic information and biochemicals.

The most famous tourist site in Shijiazhuang is the Zhaozhou Bridge, the oldest bridge in China and an impressive example of ancient engineering.

Shijiazhuang Economic Data	
GDP 2005 (RMB bn)	185.2
Disposable income 2005 (RMB)	10,040

Hotels

Hebei Century Hotel, Shijiazhuang
★★★★★
145 Zhongshan Xi Lu
(0311) 8703 6699
www.hebei-centuryhotel.com
Standard room: RMB338
Credit Cards:
Visa, Master Card, JCB, American Express, Domestic Cards

World Trade Plaza Hotel
★★★★★
303 Zhongshan Dong Lu
(0311) 8667 8888
www.wtphotels.com
Standard room: RMB590
Credit Cards:
Visa, Master Card, JCB, American Express, Domestic Cards

Hebei Grand Hotel
★★★★
168 Yucai Jie, (0311) 8526 6666
www.hb-hg.com
Standard room: RMB278
Credit Cards:
Visa, Master Card, JCB, American Express, Domestic Cards

Hebei Sunshine Hotel
★★★★
33 Ping'an Nan Dajie
(0311) 8862 5566
www.hbsunshine.com
Standard room: RMB316
Credit Cards:
Visa, Master Card, JCB, American Express, Domestic Cards

Jinyuan Grand Hotel
★★★★
3 Zhonghua Bei Dajie
(0311) 8861 4888
www.jinyuanhotel.com.cn
Credit Cards: JCB, Domestic Cards

Kingshine Hotel

DESTINATIONS

1 Dong Dajie, (0311) 8526 8888
www.kingshinehotel.com
Credit Cards:
Visa, Master Card, JCB, American
Express, Domestic Cards
NCPC Building
★★★★
56 Tiyu Bei Dajie, (0311) 8691 5888
www.hbhotel.com.cn
Standard room: RMB480
Credit Cards:
Visa, JCB, Domestic Cards
Shijiazhuang International Hotel
★★★★
301 Zhongshan Dong Lu
(0311) 8591 9999
www.guoda-hotel.com
Standard room: RMB285
Credit Cards: Visa, Master Card, JCB,
American Express, Domestic Cards
Ximei Business Hotel
★★★★
6 Jianshe Nan Dajie, (0311) 8691 8888
www.ximeihotel.com
Credit Cards: Visa, Master Card,
JCB, American Express
Youngsun Hotel
★★★★
158 Yuhua Xi Lu, (0311) 8701 2233
www.yshotel.com.cn
Standard room: RMB355
Credit Cards: Visa, Master Card, JCB,
American Express, Domestic Cards
Guobin Hotel Hebei
★★★
99 Zhongshan Dong Lu
(0311) 8691 1666, *www.gb-hotel.com*
Credit Cards: Visa, Master Card, JCB,
American Express, Domestic Cards
Hui Yuan Grand Hotel
★★★
46 Zhonghua Nan Dajie

(0311) 8701 1001
www.huiyuanhotel.cn
Credit Cards: Visa, Master Card, JCB,
American Express, Domestic Cards

Restaurants

Chinese
Yanchun Restaurant
燕春花园酒店
195 Zhongshan Dong Lu
(0311) 8667 1188
Cafe
Bu Jian Bu San不见不散西餐厅
15 Jianshe Nan Dajie
(0311) 667 4673
Manabe 真锅
B1/F-2/F, 47 Jianshe Bei Dajie
(0311) 606 5999
Barbeque
Seventh Day 第七日休闲餐吧
33 Pingan Nan Dajie
(0311) 862 5183

Hospitals

**Affiliated No.2 Hospital of Hebei
Medical Hospital**
河北医科大学第二附属医院
Heping Xi Lu, (0311) 8668 4343

Bookstores

Xinhua Bookstore, Shijiazhuang
石家庄市新华书店
1 Jianshe Bei Dajie, (0311) 605 1640

Industrial parks

**Shi Jiazhuang Hi-Tech Industrial
Development Zone** 石家庄高新区
(0311) 8509 5113
www.shidz.com
Major Industries: Electromechanical
integration, biological engineering,
new materials, new energy sources,
information industry

Tangshan 唐山

Telephone prefix: 0315
Population: 7.15 million
Bank of China: 67 Xinhua Xi Lu

Tangshan was a small village until coal deposits began to be exploited in the 1880s. The mines were modernized after 1953 and the city grew rapidly.

Tangshan was completely destroyed by a massive earthquake on July 28, 1976, in which the government estimated over 250,000 people were killed. It has since been rebuilt and is today a major industrial city situated in the Kailuan coalfield about 135km east of Beijing. The coal is used to generate electricity to support a number of heavy industries including steel, machinery, motor vehicles, chemicals, textiles, glass, petrochemicals, and cement. Tangshan is sometimes called 'the porcelain capital' of north China. The Eastern Tombs of the Qing dynasty are located nearby.

Hotels

Tangshan Jinjiang Grand Hotel
★★★★
46 Jianshe Nan Lu, (0315) 282 1611
www.ts-hotelgroup.com.cn
Standard room: RMB453
Credit Cards: Visa, Master Card, JCB, American Express
Bluesky Hotel
★★★
131 Xishan Lu, (0315) 234 2501
www.lt-hotel.com
Credit Cards: Domestic Cards

Restaurants

International
Tangshan Hotel 唐山宾馆
25 Jianshe Bei Lu, (0315) 282 2210
Chinese
Jiang Nan Cun 江南村
2/F, 46 Jianshe Nan Lu (Tangshan Jinjiang Grand Hotel), (0315) 282 1611
Jinjiang Fu 锦江府
46 Jianshe Nan Lu (Tangshan Jinjiang Grand Hotel), (0315) 282 1611
Cantonese
Changcheng Restaurant
长城大酒店
168 Changning Dao, (0315) 201 6868

Hospitals

Tangshan Gongren Hospital
唐山工人医院
27 Wenhua Lu, (0315) 284 6904
Tangshan People's Hospital
唐山市人民医院
65 Shengli Lu, (0315) 287 3943

Bookstores

Xinhua Bookstore, Tangshan
唐山市新华书店
12 Xinhua Dongdao
(0315) 282 1771

Baoding 保定

Telephone prefix: 0312
Population: 7.15 million
Bank of China: 2 Yuhua Xi Lu

Baoding is a medium-sized city that lies in the middle of a vast fertile plain on the main road and rail connection between Beijing and Shijiazhuang. Beijing is a short train ride north. Baoding has been considered a strategic southern gateway and protectorate for the capital through the centuries. During the early 1940s it served as a headquarters for the Japanese occupying armies.

Hotels

Hengtong Fortune Centre
★★★★
218 Chaoyang Bei Dajie, Gaokai
(0312) 332 1666
www.ht-center.com.cn
Standard room: RMB378
Credit Cards:
Visa, Master Card, JCB, American Express, Domestic Cards
Zhongyin Hotel

★★★★
16 Chaoyang Nan Dajie
(0312) 309 8888
Standard room: RMB405
Credit Cards:
Visa, Master Card, JCB, American Express, Domestic Cards

Restaurants

Sichuan
Tangren Meishishan Restaurant
唐人美食山
106 Jindi Lu
(0312) 311 8888
Hotpot
Laochenggen Hotpot Restaurant
老城根涮肉店
253 Huancheng Nan Lu
(0312) 201 3377

Hospitals

Sixth People's Hospital of Hebei
河北省第六人民医院
64 Weisheng Lu, (0312) 507 9256

Bookstores

Xinhua Bookstore, Baoding
保定市新华书店
Chaoyang Lu, (0312) 331 1612

Heilongjiang

Population: 38.2 million
Area: 469, 000 sq km
Capital: Harbin
Airports: Harbin, Qiqihar, Jiamusi, Mudanjiang
Border crossings: Yichun, Heihe, Dongning, Tongjiang, Fuyuan, Mohe

Named after the river that separates it from Russia, Heilongjiang, or "Black Dragon River" province is known for being the coldest part of China as it experiences brutally long winters with temperatures frequently plunging to -30 degrees Celsius and the ground is covered with snow for months at a time.

Heilongjiang is the northernmost of the three provinces that make up the area formerly known as Manchuria (*Dongbei* in Chinese) and borders Jilin province to the south and Inner Mongolia to the east. The area was originally inhabited by nomadic tribal people and came under the sway of various warring kingdoms and empires. Under the Manchu Qing dynasty, Chinese power extended well into present day Russia and was closed to ordinary Han Chinese. After 1860, when the Qing government was forced to cede large tracts of land and withdraw the northeastern borders to where they lie today, the area was opened to Han migration in order to ensure that it stayed in Chinese hands. Today the majority of Heilongjiang's population is Han Chinese, while ethnic minorities in the area include Manchu, Mongolians, Hui, Koreans, Daur, Oroqin and Hezhen.

In 1932 the area was incorporated into the Japanese puppet state of Manchukuo and suffered more than almost anywhere else in the country under Japan's repressive military rule. Heilongjiang was the site where Japanese troops, including the infamous Unit 731, developed and tested chemical and biological weapons on entire villages of unsuspecting Chinese civilians.

After Japan's unconditional surrender in 1945, Soviet forces entered

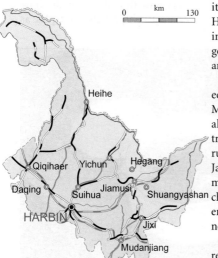

0   km   130

Manchuria and handed the Chinese Communists control over most of the area. Heilongjiang became the first complete province to be controlled by the Communists, and Harbin the first major city. From here they launched their campaign against the Nationalists, whom they eventually defeated in 1949.

Along with the rest of the northeast, Heilongjiang was developed as the industrial base for China's planned economy. Industry here has traditionally focused on coal, petroleum, lumber, machinery and food. While heavy industry and mining still contribute a large percentage to the economy, today electronics, automotives and animal feed production, which all depend on imported capital and advanced technology, are being promoted as the province's pillar industries. It is an important gateway for trade with Russia and major exports include garments, textiles, mechanical and electrical products, footwear and cereals.

The agriculture of the province, heavily defined by its cold climate, is based on crops such as soybeans, maize, and wheat. Commercial crops grown include beets, flax, and sunflowers. The principal livestock are horses and cattle; the province has the largest number of milk cows and the highest production of milk in the country. Heilongjiang is also an important source of lumber for China, especially pine and larch.

The province's deposits of gold are among the largest in China and other significant mineral and metal deposits include silver, copper, graphite, lead, aluminum, zinc, crude oil and coal. Heilongjiang ranks first in the country in the production of petroleum, which is mainly found in the Daqing oil fields, China's oldest and largest. The production from Daqing has been in steady decline for several years now though, so in the long term oil will probably not play as

important a role in the region as in the past. The area also has great potential for wind power.

Compared to provinces in the coastal regions, Heilongjiang is relatively less reliant on foreign-invested enterprises. Foreign investment is mainly concentrated in real estate, manufacturing, retail and catering. Hong Kong is the largest foreign investor in the province but large US companies like Wal-Mart and Coca-Cola, and Japanese corporations like Mitsubishi and Kirin Brewery, also have a strong presence.

Since economic reforms began in the late 1970s Heilongjiang has fared badly, along with the rest of China's northeast. The move from a planned economy built around heavy industry to a market-oriented one has left the old industrial base behind. In 2003 the central government introduced its "revitalize the Northeast" plan, intended to boost foreign and domestic investment in the region and transform it into a vibrant exporting base. In response to the initiative Heilongjiang is in the process of restructuring its traditional key industries, including petrochemicals and food processing.

Because of historical and geographic factors, Heilongjiang is also seen as a major gateway to Russia. Numerous trade agreements have been signed at provincial levels on both sides of the border, and infrastructure projects are currently linking the region more closely to allow both countries to benefit from increased trade.

Heilongjiang Economic Data			
	2005	2004	Change%
GDP (RMB bn)	551.2	475.1	16.0
GDP per capita (RMB)	14,434	13,897	3.9
Exports (US$ bn)	6.07	3.68	64.95
Imports (US$ bn)	3.50	3.11	12.54
Cars per 100 households	1.51	0.95	58.95
PCs per 100 households	25.94	17.29	50.03

Harbin 哈尔滨

Telephone prefix: 0451
Population: 9.75 million
Bank of China: 19 Hongjun Jie

Harbin is known variously as the "oriental Moscow", the "ice city" and "the pearl on the swan's neck". This last title derives from the shape of Heilongjiang province and its vague resemblance to a swan. The thriving industrial city lies on the south bank of the Songhua River and is the gateway to trade with Russia and the economic, cultural and political center of the far northeast. Its central shopping district contains stunning examples of colonial, particularly Russian, architecture.

The modern city of Harbin originated in 1898 with the construction of the Chinese Eastern Railway by Russia. Russian White Guards took the city with Chinese assistance in December 1918, during the Russian Civil War. It subsequently became the new home of a large White Russian and Jewish community who added to the already large foreign population. At the time, sixteen countries had established consulates in Harbin and several thousand foreign-owned industrial, commercial and banking companies flourished in the city. The Chinese also established businesses in brewing, foodstuffs and textiles.

Japanese troops occupied Harbin from 1932 until their defeat in 1945, when the Soviet army took the city. During the Second World War the notorious Japanese Unit 731, a germ warfare experimental base, was located here and carried out widespread biological and chemical weapons tests on the local population. After a brief period under the Nationalists, Harbin was the first city to be controlled by the communist People's Liberation Army.

After the founding of the People's Republic in 1949, Harbin quickly recovered from the war and, with the help of Soviet aid projects, was established as a heavy industrial base and one of the few major economic cities in China. It also provided a strong backup to the Chinese army fighting the Americans in North Korea in the early 1950s.

Since the opening up and reform of China in the late 1970s, Harbin has experienced rapid economic and urban development. The city has grown into a major river port and hosted eight international trade fairs and the third Asian Winter Games. Since 1985, it has held the annual month-long Harbin International Ice and Snow Festival in January, a world-renowned extravaganza of ice sculpture and related events. Furthermore, Harbin is starting to capitalize on the growing affluence and free time of China's expanding middle class by constructing winter sports facilities including ski slopes in the nearby mountains.

Harbin Economic Data	
GDP 2005 (RMB bn)	183.04
Disposable income 2005 (RMB)	10,065

Hotels

Fortune Days Hotel
★★★★★
20-22 Ganshui Lu, Xiangfang
(0451) 8236 8888
www.fortunedayshotel.com
Credit Cards:
Visa, Master Card, JCB, American
Express, Domestic Cards
Shangri-La Hotel Harbin
★★★★★
555 Youyi Lu, Daoli, (0451) 8485 8888
Standard room:
RMB1,228 +15% Surcharge
Credit Cards: Visa, Master Card,
JCB, American Express
Singapore Hotel
★★★★★
68 Ganshui Lu, Xiangfang
(0451) 8233 6888
Credit Cards:
Visa, Master Card, JCB, American
Express, Domestic Card
Baoye Hotel
★★★★
399 Youyi Lu, Daoli, (0451) 8489 0888
www.haerbindaily.com
Credit Cards:
Visa, Master Card, JCB, American
Express, Domestic Cards
Holiday Inn City Centre Harbin
★★★★
90 Jingwei Lu, Daoli
(0451) 8422 6666
Standard room: RMB880
Credit Cards:
Visa, Master Card, JCB, American
Express, Domestic Cards
Jin Gu Hotel
★★★★
185 Zhongyang Dajie
(0451) 8469 8700
www.jinguhotel.com.cn

Credit Cards:
Visa, Master Card, JCB, American
Express, Domestic Cards
Join Us Plaza
★★★★
15 Songhuajiang Jie, Nangang
(0451) 5367 9898
www.huayi-hotel.com
Standard room: RMB405
Credit Cards:
Visa, Master Card, JCB, American
Express, Domestic Cards
Kunlun Hotel
★★★★
8 Tielu Jie, (0451) 5361 6688
www.hljkunlun.com
Credit Cards:
Visa, Master Card, JCB, American
Express, Domestic Cards
Power Hotel
★★★★
79 Youzheng Jie
(0451) 5390 8555
www.power-tourism.com
Standard room: RMB358
Credit Cards: Visa, Master Card,
JCB, American Express
**Songhuajiang Gloria Plaza Hotel
Harbin**
★★★★
259 Zhongyang Dajie, Daoli
(0451) 8677 0000
Standard room: RMB638
Credit Cards: Visa, Master Card,
JCB, American Express
Harbin Flamingo Confier Hotel
★★★
118 Minsheng Lu, Dongli
(0451) 8679 8888
www.hrbflamingohotel.com
Standard room: RMB580
Credit Cards: Visa, Master Card,
JCB, American Express

Lung Men Hotel
★★★
85 Hongjun Jie, Nangang
(0451) 8679 1888
www.hotellm.com
Standard room: RMB480
Credit Cards:
Visa, Master Card, JCB, American
Express, Domestic Cards

Restaurants

Western
Portman Bar 波特曼西餐厅
63 Xiqi Dao Dajie, (0451) 8468 6888
Cafe
Russia 1914 露西亚咖啡西餐厅
57 Xi Toudao Dajie, Zhong Yang
Dajie, (0451) 8456 3207
Chinese
Liyuan Restaurant 利园餐厅
87 Xiaojianhe Jie, (0451) 8460 8661
Laodu Yichu Dumpling Restaurant
老都一处
58 Xi Shi'er Dajie, (0451) 8461 5895
International
Tongshang 通商
36 Andao Jie, (0451) 8421 0321
Jiaozi
Dongfang Jiaozi Wang 东方饺子王

39 Zhongyang Dajie
(0451) 8465 3920

Hospitals

**Harbin Medical College First Affili-
ated Hospital**
哈尔滨医科大学第一附属医院
23 Youzheng Jie, (0451) 5364 3849

Bookstores

Xinhua Bookstore
哈尔滨市新华书店
64 Yimian Jie, (0451) 8468 0554

Industrial parks

**Harbin Economic and Technology
Development Zone**
哈尔滨经济技术开发区
(0451) 8229 4322, *www.kaifaqu.com.cn*
Major Industries: Textiles, petrochemicals, machinery, electronics,
medical equipment, automobiles,
construction materials
**Harbin High-Tech Industrial
Development Zone**
哈尔滨高新技术产业开发区
(0451) 8229 4322, *www.kaifaqu.com.cn*
Major Industries: Telecommunications, electronics, machinery

Qiqihar 齐齐哈尔

Telephone prefix: 0452
Population: 5.57 million
Bank of China: 2 Gonghui Hutong

Qiqihar, located in the south of Heilongjiang province, is a port city on the Nen river. It is connected by rail with Harbin, Shenyang, and Dalian. Founded in 1691 as a Chinese fortress, it was formerly the capital of Heilongjiang. From 1932 to 1945 it was an important military center for Japanese-controlled Manchuria.

The city is an important heavy industrial base boasting more than 15,000 industrial enterprises including the No.1 Heavy Machinery Group – the biggest heavy machinery producing enterprise in Asia. Major manufacturing includes steel, chemicals, engines, machine tools, wood and paper products. The city is also a processing center for soybeans, grain, and sugar beet.

Hotels

Guomai Hotel 国脉大厦
★★★★★
1 Junxiao Jie Longhua Lu

(0452) 241 0000
Standard Room: RMB 320
H.C. Aviation Hotel 民航大厦
★★★★
4 Pukui Dajie, (0452) 238 8888
Standard Room: RMB 140

Restaurants

Barbecue
Baokun Barbecue Restaurant 宝坤烧烤
2 Yongan Dajie, (0452) 240 1125
Seafood
Guangzhou Seafood Restaurant 广州海鲜大排档
Building 4, Yongan Dajie
(0452) 244 1199
Chinese
Qing Yang Lou 清羊楼
Zhanqian Dajie

Hospitals

First Hospital of Qiqihar
齐齐哈尔市第一医院
20 Gongyuan Lu, (0452) 2459 615

Bookstores

Xinhua Bookstore
齐齐哈尔市新华书店
90 Pukui Dajie
(0452) 268 8265

DESTINATIONS

Daqing 大庆

Telephone prefix: 0459
Population: 2.64 million
Bank of China: 168 Jingliu Jie

Established only in 1979, Daqing's existence is owed to the nearby oil fields of the same name. Not surprisingly, Daqing's economy is heavily reliant on the oil and petrochemical industries.

Restaurants

Western & Chinese

Pujing Western Restaurant
谱京酒店
8 Kaerjiali Lu
(0459) 631 1999

Bars & Clubs

Daqing Hotel Bar
大庆宾馆酒吧
1 Dongfeng Lu
Daqing Hotel
(0459) 610 3121

Hospitals

Daqing Hospital of Traditonal Chinese Medicine
大庆市中医医院
35 Youyi Dajie
(0459) 631 3405

Bookstores

Xinhua Bookstore
大庆市新华书店
27 Huizhan Dajie, Sa Qu
(0459) 632 2658

Henan

Population: 93.8 million
Area: 167, 000 sq km
Capital: Zhengzhou
Airports: Zhengzhou, Luoyang, Nanyang

Located south of the Yellow river, Henan's name roughly translates to "south of the river". As one of the most important centers for development in ancient Chinese culture, the Yellow River Valley in Henan has been inhabited for thousands of years and is considered to be one of the cradles of Chinese civilization.

Located in the center of eastern China, Henan shares borders with six provinces: Hebei to the north, Shandong to the northeast, Anhui to the east, Hubei to the south, Shaanxi to the west and Shanxi to the northwest.

The area is also right in the middle of China's weather extremes. Under the central planning system, anywhere north of the Yellow River is entitled to government-provided central heating while anywhere south of the river is not. Despite its cold winters, most of Henan is not eligible.

The region's history dates back at least as far as the 6,000-year-old remains of the Yangshao people and was the center of power for many succeeding civilizations. This rich heritage has endowed Henan with many historic treasures and destinations for tourists. The most popular of these are the Longmen Caves, with their ornate Buddhist carvings and giant replicas of the Buddha, and the Shaolin Temple, the home of Chinese kung fu.

The region is politically important in China's modern history as the place where Chairman Mao's disastrous Great Leap Forward was launched in 1958. This campaign was aimed at pushing China instantly through to indus-

trialization by mobilizing the entire population to produce steel. It failed miserably. Agriculture was neglected, and when a rash of natural disasters hit the country millions died in the ensuing famine.

In another unfortunate incident, blood banks the late 1990s increased their drive to collect blood in the rural areas of Henan with promises of upfront cash payments. Whole villages of peasant farmers lined up to give blood. Unsanitary practices and contaminated blood spread HIV to many people across the province.

Henan's large population of more than 93 million people is predominantly based in the rural areas and agriculture is the mainstay of the region's economy. It is China's biggest grain producer and is top in yields of corn, wheat and sesame. It ranks second in China in the production of cotton, oil plants and tobacco. Fruit and traditional Chinese medicine are also important products.

Aluminum, bauxite, gold and silver are the four major mineral products of the province. Besides agriculture, pillar industries include electronics, machinery, chemicals, food processing, textiles and building materials.

Henan Economic Data

	2005	2004	Change%
GDP (RMB bn)	1058.7	855.4	23.8
GDP per capita (RMB)	11,346	9,470	19.8
Exports (US$ bn)	5.08	4.18	21.53
Imports (US$ bn)	2.64	2.45	7.76
Cars per 100 households	1.58	0.76	107.89
PCs per 100 households	31.82	22.09	44.05

Zhengzhou 郑州

Telephone prefix: 0371
Population: 7.16 million
Bank of China: 40 Huayuan Lu

Zhengzhou is the capital city of Henan province and an important railway junction on the Beijing-Guangzhou and Xi'an-Shanghai rail lines. Situated south of the Yellow River and east of the Songshan River, it is one of China's earliest cities and is thought to have been the walled capital of the Shang dynasty some 3,500 years ago. China's early bronze industry developed here and the city later became a transport and economic center during the Sui and Tang periods (late sixth to early 10th century), when Zhengzhou's grain markets were connected by canal to the Yellow River. With the building of railway lines in the early 20th century, the city saw a revival of its traditional economic role and today it is one of Asia's most important freight transfer hubs.

Zhengzhou is home to the Zhengzhou Commodity Exchange, the national grain wholesale market and the country's first grain futures market. It is also known as the textile center of Henan province. Other industrial products include tractors, cigarettes, fertilizer, agricultural machinery and electrical equipment.

Foreign investment in Henan is mainly concentrated in Zhengzhou in the fields of agriculture, electronics, petrochemicals, machinery and infrastructure. A number of well-known multinational enterprises such as Mitsui, Sumitomo and C Itoh & Co from Japan, General Electric and International Telephone & Telegraph (ITT) from the US and Renault from France have set up joint ventures here.

Zhengzhou's Zhengdong New District, intended as a new CBD similar to Shanghai's Pudong area, is scheduled to open in 2015. Depending on your point of view this high-tech city is either a vision of the future or the height of folly. In 2004 Beijing actively discouraged such local government "prestige projects" that replaced large areas of arable land. The new district is to be built over an area of 15,000 hectares east of the city and will be constructed under a Japanese team's supervision. The district is being touted as East Asia's first hybrid transportation city combining water and road transport and is intended to function as a commercial and business center in Henan.

Zhengzhou Economic Data	
GDP 2005 (RMB bn)	165
Disposable income 2005 (RMB)	10,640

Restaurants

Crowne Plaza Holiday Inn Zhengzhou
★★★★★
115 Jinshui Lu, (0371) 6595 0055
www.ichotelsgroup.com
Standard room: RMB698
Credit Cards: Visa, Master Card, JCB, American Express

Sofitel Zhengzhou
★★★★★
289 Chengdong Lu, (0371) 6595 0088
Standard room: RMB1,284
Credit Cards: Visa, Master Card, JCB, American Express

Yuda Palace Hotel
★★★★★
220 Zhongyuan Zhong Lu
(0371) 6743 8888
www.yudapalacehotel.com.cn
Standard room:
RMB668 +15% Surcharge
Credit Cards: Visa, Master Card, JCB, American Express, Diners Club

Deyi Hotel
★★★★
9 Jichang Lu, (0371) 6597 9999

Credit Cards: Visa, Master Card, JCB, American Express

Fengleyuan Hotel
★★★★
North Section Nanyang Lu
(0371) 6677 1188
www.fengleyuan.net
Standard room: RMB960
Credit Cards: Visa, Master Card

Holiday Inn Zhengzhou
★★★★
115 Jinshui Lu
(0371) 6595 0055
www.holiday-inn.com
Standard room: RMB598
Credit Cards: Visa, Master Card, JCB, American Express

Kai Lai Hotel
★★★★
111 Fengchan Lu, (0371) 6676 7777
Credit Cards: Visa, Master Card, JCB, Domestic Cards

Red Coral Hotel
★★★★
20 Erma Lu
(0371) 6698 6688
www.redcoralhotel.com
Standard room: RMB388
Credit Cards: Visa, Master Card, JCB, Domestic Cards

Weilai Conifer Hotel
★★★★
69 Weilai Dajie
(0371) 6561 2288
www.weilaiconifer.com
Credit Cards:
Visa, Master Card, JCB, American Express, Domestic Cards

Angang Hotel Zhengzhou
★★★
68 Jichang Lu, (0371) 6596 8899
Credit Cards: Domestic Cards

Express by Holiday Inn Zhengzhou

★★★
114 Jinshui Lu, (0371) 6595 6600
www.hiexpress.com
Standard room: RMB448
Credit Cards: Visa, Master Card, JCB, American Express

Golden Sunshine Hotel
★★★
86 Erma Lu
(0371) 6696 9999
www.goldensunshinehotel.com
Credit Cards: Domestic Cards

Henan New Century Hotel
★★★
50 Huayuan Lu
(0371) 6570 0588
www.hnnchotel.com
Credit Cards:
Visa, Master Card, Domestic Cards

Huanghe Hotel
★★★
106 Zhongyuan Lu
(0371) 6780 9999
www.huanghehotel.net
Credit Cards: Visa, Master Card, JCB, Domestic Cards

Samost Hotel
★★★
18 Xinghua Bei Jie
(0371) 6677 6168
www.samosthotel.com
Credit Cards: Visa, Domestic Cards

Tianquan Hotel
★★★
1 Xidatong Lu
(0371) 6698 6888
www.tqhotel.com
Standard room: RMB278
Credit Cards: Domestic Cards

Restaurants

Chinese
Li's Mutton 李记红焖羊肉

146 Dongming Lu
(0371) 6599 3133

Western

Origus 好伦哥餐厅
52-6 Dongtaikang Lu
(0371) 6620 0733

Dome Bressa 圆顶阁西餐厅
289 Chengdong Lu (Hotel Sofitel
Zhengzhou), (0371) 6595 0088

Italian

Peppino 皮皮鲁比萨西餐
Yousheng Nan Lu, Zhong Duan
(0371) 6391 4920

Chinese

Henan Restaurant 河南食府
25 Renmin Lu, (0371) 6621 3336

**Yushunlou Restaurant
豫顺楼饭庄**
53 Jinshui Lu, (0371) 6793 3777

Hospitals

**Seventh People's Hospital of
Zhengzhou 郑州第七人民医院**
12 Ruhe Lu, (0371) 6887 7120

Second People's Hospital of

Zhengzhou 郑州第二人民医院
81 Jiefang Xi Lu, (0371) 6626 0137

Bookstores

**Xinhua Bookstore
郑州市新华书店**
19 Xi Taikang Lu
(0371) 6621 0640

Industrial parks

**Zhengzhou New & Hi-Tech Industries Development Zone
郑州高新技术产业开发区**
(0371) 6799 1110, *www.zzgx.gov.cn*

Major Industries:
New materials, biopharmaceutical,
photo machinery, software

**Zhengzhou Economic and Technological Development Zone
国家郑州经济技术开发区**
(0371) 6678 1251
www.zz-economy.gov.cn

Major Industries:
New materials, telecommunications,
food processing, auto mobile parts

Luoyang 洛阳

Telephone prefix: 0397
Population: 6.42 million
Bank of China: 439 Zhengzhou Zhong Lu

Luoyang lies in northwest Henan. It is an important base for China's machinery industry and a famous historical city that in ancient times served as the capital for the East Zhou dynasty, East Han dynasty, Cao dynasty, Wei dynasty and another nine dynasties.

Luoyang today is an industrial center of more than half a million – a small city by China's standards. The surrounding area produces an abundance of wheat, cotton, corn, oil and tobacco and there are significant reserves of molybdenum, aluminum, sulfuric iron ore, clay, and cement rock.

The main industries in Luoyang are machine making, metallurgy, textiles, building materials and petrochemical processing.

Near Luoyang are the Longmen caves, featuring ornate Buddhist carvings and giant replicas of the Buddha. The White Horse Temple (Bai Ma Si) in Luoyang is thought to be the oldest temple in China.

Hotels

Jing'an Peony Plaza
★★★★
2 Nanchang Lu, (0379) 6468 1111
www.jingan-peonyplaza.com
Credit Cards: Visa, Master Card, American Express, Domestic Cards

Jun Shan Hotel
★★★★
3 Junshan Dong Lu, Luanchuan
(0379) 6681 0988
www.junshanhotel.com.cn
Standard room: RMB480
Credit Cards: Visa, Master Card

Luo Yang Penoy Hotel
★★★★
15 Zhongzhou Xi Lu
(0379) 6468 0000
Standard room: RMB550
Credit Cards:
Visa, Master Card, JCB, American Express, Domestic Cards

Luoyang Grand Hotel
★★★★

South Section Nanchang Lu
(0379) 6432 7408
www.ly-grandhotel.com
Standard room: RMB500
Credit Cards:
Visa, Master Card, JCB, American
Express, Domestic Cards
Luoyang International Financial Hotel
★★★
439 Zhongzhou Zhong Lu
(0379) 6390 3888
www.lyhotel.com.cn
Credit Cards:
Visa, Master Card, Domestic Cards
New Jianlong Hotel
★★★
3 Kaixuan Dong Lu
(0379) 6325 1111
www.newjianlong.com
Standard room: RMB468
Credit Cards: Visa, JCB
New Juhe Hotel
★★★
19 Jiefang Lu, (0379) 6256 8666
www.newjuhe.com
Standard room: RMB468
Credit Cards: Visa, Domestic Cards
Xiao Lang Di Mansion
★★★
South Section Nanchang Lu
(0379) 6494 6688
www.xldmansion.com.cn
Standard room: RMB380
Credit Cards:
Visa, Master Card, JCB, American
Express, Domestic Cards
Xiaolangdi Hotel
★★★
Xiaolangdi Scenic Area
(0379) 6390 5555
Standard room: RMB368
Zhuogengyuan Hotel

★★★
71 Longmen Dajie, (0379) 6552 5666
www.zhuogy-hotel.com
Credit Cards: Visa, Master Card,
JCB, Domestic Cards

Restaurants

Chinese
Luoyang New Friend Hotel
洛阳新聚合大酒店
19 Jiefang Lu
(0379) 6256 8666
Zhen Butong Restaurant
洛阳真不同
359 Zhongzhou Dong Lu
(0379) 6399 5080
Cafe
Roman Holiday Cafe
罗马假日咖啡吧
Guanzhou Shichang
(0379) 6493 5263

Hospitals

Central Hospital of Luoyang
洛阳市中心医院
288 Zhongzhou Zhong Lu
(0379) 6389 2222

Bookstores

Xinhua Bookstore
洛阳市新华书店
283 Zhongzhou Zhong Lu
(0379) 6325 1588

Industrial parks

**Luoyang Hi-Tech Development
Zone** 洛阳高新技术产业开发区
(0379) 6490 2654
www.lhdz.gov.cn
Major Industries:
New materials, photoelectricity, elec-
tromechanics, electronic information, bioengineering

Kaifeng 开封

Telephone prefix: 0378
Population: 4.76 million
Bank of China: Zhongshan Nan Lu

Known as "the capital of seven dynasties", Kaifeng is a famous historic and cultural city in China with a history of more than 2,700 years. During the Northern Song dynasty (960-1137) the city was the political, economic and cultural center of the whole country, with bustling commerce and well-developed handicrafts and communications.

Located in the central plain of Henan province on the south bank of the Yellow River, Kaifeng is today best known as a center for refined chemical production. The city is a production base for the region's cereals, cotton and oil crops and has developed a livestock breeding industry.

The main industries in Kaifeng are food processing, chemicals, and machinery. Textiles, cigarettes, electronics and construction materials are also produced here.

Kaifeng Economic & Technological Development Zone, authorized by Henan provincial government in 1992, is a 54-sq-km industrial park.

A source of curiosity is the Kaifeng Jewish community, whose ancestors were said to have arrived in China from Persia and India during the Tang dynasty (618-907). For centuries the Jews of Kaifeng recited the prescribed daily and Sabbath prayers, followed strict diets and observed their religious holidays.

Kaifeng was also the city where Liu Shaoqi, a prominent communist leader, was imprisoned and died in 1969 after falling out of favor with Mao.

Hotels

Kaifeng Guest House
★★★
66 Central Section Ziyou Lu
(0378) 595 5589
www.kaifengbinguan.com
Standard room: RMB260-468
Yi Yuan Hotel
★★★
88 Dingjiao Jie, Gulou
(0378) 397 2211
Standard room: RMB268
Credit Cards: Domestic Cards

Restaurants

Cafe
Serne Spring Cafe
塞纳春天咖啡西餐厅
1 Jinming Dong Jie, (0378) 256 2777
Chinese
Dongjing Hotel 东京大饭店
99 Yingbin Lu, (0378) 398 9388

Bars & Clubs

Mingdian Coffee Language
名典咖啡语言
56 Gulou Jie, (0378) 597 7606

Hospitals

First People's Hospital of Kaifeng
开封市第一人民医院
85 Hedao Jie, (0378) 567 1288

Bookstores

Xinhua Bookstore
开封新华书店批销中心
Xinhua Tower, Daliang Lu, Kaifeng
Eco & Dev District, (0378) 387 9999

Hubei

Population: 57.1 million
Area: 185,900 sq km
Capital: Wuhan
Airports:
Wuhan, Yichang, Xiangfan, Shanshi, Enshi
Ports: Wuhan, Yichang, Huangshi, Shashi

Hubei province is in the heart of China, in the center of the Yangtze River valley. Most of the province is rich agricultural land interspersed with lakes and rivers. It is a major producer of rice, wheat, rapeseed and freshwater seafood products, and is known as "the homeland of rice and fish."

The Three Gorges Dam, the world's biggest hydroelectric project, is just within the provincial border, although the reservoir to the west, behind the dam, is mostly in Chongqing municipality. There are significant mineral deposits in the province, including iron, copper and phosphate.

The river towns along the Yangtze have always been important trading centers, particularly in the latter half of the 19th century when the Western powers were eager to open up inland China to their goods. Wuhan was one of the first places in China to be industrialized, and the city was the site of the revolution in 1911 which toppled the last emperor and established a Chinese republic.

The construction of the Three Gorges Dam near Yichang has changed the region fundamentally, leading to the relocation of over one million people and big infusions of infrastructure funds. Construction was completed ahead of schedule in May 2006 but the project will not reach its full power-producing potential until 2009, when it will be able to pump out some 18 million kilowatts.

In northwest Hubei is an inaccessible mountain area called Shennongjia in which it is said lives a tribe of apelike semi-human known as Wild Men, cousins of the Himalayan Yeti and of Big Foot in North America. There have been many reported sightings but the Wild Men always seem to avoid detection, hopefully because they are clever and lucky, not because they are a figment of China's collective imagination.

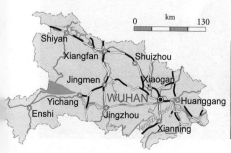

Hubei Economic Data			
	2005	2004	Change%
GDP (RMB bn)	652.0	563.3	15.7
GDP per capita (RMB)	11,431	10,500	8.9
Exports (US$ bn)	4.43	3.38	31.07
Imports (US$ bn)	4.63	3.39	36.58
Cars per 100 households	0.92	0.31	196.77
PCs per 100 households	42.42	32.40	30.03

Wuhan 武汉

Telephone prefix: 027
Population: 8.58 million
Bank of China: 233 Jiuhuasan Lu

Wuhan is easily the most important city in the middle stretches of the Yangtze River, standing at the confluence of the Yangtze and the Han Rivers. It is composed of three separate cities – Wuchang, Hanyang and Hankou. The name Wuhan is an amalgam of their names.

The city is the fifth-largest in China and a major heavy industrial center noted for the production of steel and vehicles. Chairman Mao Zedong was a regular visitor to Wuhan, and in 1966 staged a famous swim on the Yangtze here which became a part of his mythology.

Wuhan has always lived with and against the mighty Yangtze, depending on it for commerce and irrigation but also fearing its summer floods. The flood crest in 2004 passed Wuhan about one meter lower than

2003, and experts attribute this to the impact of the new Three Gorges dam, which is now controlling the flow of the Yangtze.

The Wuhan municipal government has invested huge sums in upgrading the infrastructure of the city to attract foreign investment. Roads are being widened, new apartment blocks being built, polluting industries are being relocated, and a subway network is under construction. The first bridge across the Yangtze River at Wuhan was opened in 1957, allowing north and south China to be connected by rail for the first time. Now, there are a total of 13 major bridges near Wuhan.

The city attracts companies largely on the basis of cheaper costs – both of property and labor – and its central location. The Shui On Group, the property development firm from Hong Kong, gained the rights to develop a parcel of land in the city center in 2005 on which it plans to build luxury hotels, office buildings, residential apartments, and retail space. Wuhan has the

biggest concentration of universities and research institutes in China after Beijing and Shanghai. But it is heavy industry which built the city, and heavy industry which is leading its revival. Peugeot-Citroen and Honda both have JVs with Wuhan's Dongfeng Auto. Wuhan Steel is the third-biggest producer of iron and steel in China, and has been upgrading and expanding production with assistance from firms including Alstom and Siemens.

Wuhan Economic Data	
GDP 2005 (RMB bn)	223.8
Disposable income 2005 (RMB)	10,849.72

Hotels

Best Western C-bank Hotel Wuhan
★★★★★
933 Jianshe Lu, Hankou
(027) 8265 6688
Standard room:
RMB980 +15% Surcharge
Credit Cards: Visa, Master Card, JCB, Domestic Cards

Best Western Premier Mayflowers Hotel Wuhan
★★★★★
385 Wuluo Lu, Wuchang
(027) 6887 1588
Standard room:
RMB488 +15% Surcharge
Credit Cards:
Visa, Master Card, JCB, American Express, Domestic Cards

East Lake Hotel
★★★★★
231 Yaojialing, Wuchang
(027) 6781 3999
www.eastlakehotel.com
Standard room: RMB880

Credit Cards: Visa, Master Card, JCB, American Express

HK & Macau Center Business Hotel
★★★★★
118 Jianghan Jie, Hankou
(027) 6882 9999
www.999jiuhui-hotels.com
Standard room: RMB298
Credit Cards: Visa, Master Card, JCB, American Express

Howard Johnson Pearl Plaza Wuhan
★★★★★
182 YanJiang Dajie, Hankou
(027) 8277 6666
Standard room:
RMB1,207 +15% Surcharge
Credit Cards: Visa, Master Card, JCB, American Express

Novotel Xinhua Wuhan
★★★★★
558 Jianshe Dajie, Hankou
(027) 8555 1188
Standard room: RMB658
Credit Cards:
Visa, Master Card, JCB, American Express, Domestic Cards

Ramada Plaza Tian Lu Hotel Wuhan
★★★★★
5 Qingnian Lu, Hankou
(027) 8363 0888
www.ramada.com
Credit Cards: Visa, Master Card, JCB, American Express

Shangri-La Hotel Wuhan
★★★★★
700 Jianshe Dajie, Hankou
(027) 8580 6868
Credit Cards:
Visa, Master Card, JCB, American Express, Domestic Cards

Barony Resort at Longquan
★★★★
Longquan Sancha Harbor

(027) 8790 1111
Standard room: RMB680
Credit Cards: Visa
Chu Yuan Hotel
★★★★
Zhuodaoquan Bei Lu, Wuchang
(027) 6788 6888
www.whcyhotel.com
Standard room: RMB238
Credit Cards: Domestic Cards
Crown Hotel
★★★★
281 Ziyang Lu, Wuchang
(027) 8830 8888
Standard room: RMB830
Credit Cards: Visa, Master Card,
JCB, American Express
Holiday Inn Riverside Wuhan
★★★★
88 Ximachang Jie, Hanyang
(027) 8471 6688
Standard room: RMB930
Credit Cards:
Visa, Master Card, JCB, American
Express, Domestic Cards
Holiday Inn Tian An Wuhan City
Center
★★★★
868 Jiefang Dajie, Hankou
(027) 8586 7888
Standard room: RMB1,315
Credit Cards:
Visa, Master Card, JCB, American
Express, Domestic Cards
Hong Yi Hotel
★★★★
136 Donghu Lu, Wuchang
(027) 6781 9888
www.wdhy-hotel.com
Standard room: RMB568
Credit Cards: Visa, Master Card,
JCB, American Express
Hubei Taihua Hotel

★★★★
101 Donghu Lu, (027) 8732 8686
www.taihua-hotel.com
Standard room: RMB568
Credit Cards: Visa, Master Card,
JCB, American Express
Lake View Garden Hotel
★★★★
115 Luoyu Lu, (027) 8778 2888
Standard room: RMB717
Credit Cards: Visa, Master Card,
JCB, American Express
Marshal Palace Hotel
★★★★
98 Bayi Lu, Wuchang
(027) 8716 8888
www.sfhotel.com.cn
Standard room: RMB300
Credit Cards: Visa, Master Card, JCB,
American Express, Domestic Cards
Swiss-Belhotel on the Park
★★★★
9 Taibeiyi Lu, Hankou
(027) 6885 1888
Credit Cards: Visa, Master Card, JCB,
American Express, Domestic Cards
White Rose Hotel, Wuhan
★★★★
788 Minzhu Lu, (027) 6887 6888
Standard room: RMB468
Wu Gang Hotel
★★★★
943 Heping Dajie, (027) 6886 4899
www.wghotel.com
Credit Cards:
Visa, Master Card, JCB, American
Express, Domestic Cards
Wuhan Asia Hotel
★★★★
616 Jiefang Dajie, (027) 8380 7777
www.whasiahotel.com
Standard room:
RMB966 +15% Surcharge

Credit Cards:
Visa, Master Card, JCB, American Express, Domestic Cards
Changhai Hotel
★★★
111 Yanjiang Dajie, Hankou
(027) 8281 8980
Credit Cards:
Visa, Master Card, JCB, American Express, Domestic Cards
Gaoxiong Hotel
★★★
907 Jianshe Dajie, Hankou
(027) 8549 2288
www.whgxhotel.com
Credit Cards: Visa, Master Card, JCB, American Express
Hongshan Hotel
★★★
1 Zhongbei Lu, (027) 8782 4112
www.hshotel.com
Credit Cards:
Visa, Master Card, Domestic Cards
Hubei Lijiang Hotel
★★★
5 Tiyuguan Lu, Wuchang
(027) 8713 6666
www.lijianghotel.com
Credit Cards:
Visa, Master Card, JCB, American Express, Domestic Cards
Jiangcheng Hotel
★★★
North Hankou Railway Station
(027) 8587 6508
Standard room: RMB438
Credit Cards: Visa, Master Card, JCB, American Express
Jinhai Hotel of Hubei Civil Aviation
★★★
97 Jianghan Bei Lu, (027) 6885 2000
www.hb-phoenixhotel.com
Standard room: RMB368

Credit Cards: Visa
Jiuye Hotel
★★★
38 Dongyi Lu, (027) 8723 7766
Credit Cards: Domestic Cards
Li Yuan Hotel
★★★
343 Xudong Dajie, Wuchang
(027) 8677 2029
www.lyhotel.com
Standard room: RMB460
Credit Cards: Visa, Master Card, JCB, American Express
New Land Hotel
★★★
330 Wuluo Lu, Wuchang
(027) 8781 2788
Credit Cards:
Visa, Master Card, JCB, American Express, Domestic Cards
Wuhan Changhang Hotel
★★★
15 Huiji Lu, (027) 6882 5188
www.chdjd.com
Credit Cards:
Visa, Master Card, JCB, American Express, Domestic Cards
Wuhan Wesun Hotel
★★★
234 Yanjiang Dajie, Hankou
(027) 6882 6666
Standard room: RMB550
Credit Cards: Visa, Master Card, JCB, American Express
Wuhan Xuangong Hotel
★★★
57 Jianghanyi Lu, (027) 6882 2588
www.xuangonghotel.com
Standard room: RMB638
Credit Cards:
Visa, Master Card, Domestic Cards
Xin Dong Fang Hotel
★★★

563 Minzhu Lu, Wuchang
(027) 8781 6688, *www.whxdf.com*
Standard room: RMB218
Credit Cards: Domestic Cards

Restaurants

American
Kanglong Taizi Wineshop
武汉亢龙太子酒轩
226 Shengli Jie, (027) 8271 2228
Chinese
Kanglong Taizi Wineshop
武汉亢龙太子酒轩
735 Jianshe Da Dao, (027) 8579 8288
Mr. Xie Restaurant 谢先生餐厅
910 Jiefang Da Dao, (027) 8581 3580
Cafe
Blue Sky 蓝色天空
735 Jianshe Da Dao, (027) 8580 7466
Western/Cafe
Bitter Rain Cafe 苦雨咖啡
18 Wansongyuan Lu, (027) 8556 0505
Wuhan Oriental Hotel
武汉东方大酒店
185 Fazhan Da Dao, (027) 8588 8558
Best World Restaurant
好世纪大酒店
705 Jianshe Da Dao, (027) 8573 3333
Indian
Imperial Indian Kitchen
帝皇印度小厨
868 Jiefang Dadao, (027) 8586 7888
Western
Toscana 托斯卡娜意大利经典餐厅
328 Qingnian Lu, (027) 8575 8688
Buffet
Yajing Yuan Revolving Restaurant
雅景园旋转餐厅
5 Qingnian Lu, (027) 8363 0888

Hospitals

Tongji Hospital
华中科技大学同济医学院附属同

济医院
(027) 8366 2688
Union Hospital
华中科技大学同济医学院附属协
和医院
1277 Jiefang Dadao, (027) 8572 6114

Bookstores

Xinhua Bookstore 武汉市新华书店
93 Wusheng Lu
(027) 800 880 9588

Consulates

France 法国
809, International Trade Center, 566
Jianshe Da Dao
(027) 8577 8423

Industrial parks

Wuhan East Lake High-Tech Industrial Development Zone
武汉东湖高新科技工业园
(027) 8717 2020
www.elht.com
Major Industries: Telecommunications, bioengineering, new materials, software, laser technology
Wuhan Economic & Technological Development Zone
武汉经济技术开发区
(027) 8489 1443
www.wedz.com.cn
Major Industries:
Auto industry and hi-tech industry, machinery, electronics, food and beverage processing, building material processing, pharmaceutical, biological engineering

Exhibition centers

Wuhan International Convention Exhibition Center
372-374 Jiefang Dadao
(027) 8581 6012, *www.whicec.com*

Yichang 宜昌
Telephone prefix: 0717
Population: 4.05 million
Bank of China: 10 Shengli Si Lu

Yichang is the closest city to the massive Three Gorges Dam. Before the construction of the dam, the city was largely known to foreigners as the place to board or disembark from a Three Gorges boat tour. With the dam completed, the city is gaining tourists who see the massive infrastructure project as an attraction. Furthermore, a museum in the city houses ancient relics recovered from the river valley that would have been buried by the rising waters had they not been removed.

Hotels

Guobin Garden Hotel
★★★★★
40 Chengdong Dajie
(0717) 633 1111
www.gbhyhotel.com
Standard room: RMB558
Credit Cards: Visa, Master Card, JCB, American Express, Domestic Cards
Ge Zhou Ba Hotel
★★★★
3 Yiling Lu, (0717) 886 6666
www.gzbhotel.com
Standard room: RMB426
Credit Cards: Visa, Master Card, JCB, American Express, Domestic Cards
Innca Hotel
★★★★
12 Zhenzhu Lu
(0717) 673 6666
www.innca.cn
Standard room: RMB559
Credit Cards: Visa, Master Card, JCB, American Express, Domestic Cards
Peninsula Hotel
★★★★
25 Shenzhen Lu
(0717) 634 5666
www.peninsulahotel.cn
Standard room: RMB588
Credit Cards: Visa, Master Card, JCB, American Express, Domestic Cards
Three Gorges Project Hotel
★★★★
Bahekou, Sanxia
(0717) 661 3666
www.sxdaba.com
Standard room: RMB468
Credit Cards: Visa, Master Card, JCB, American Express, Domestic Cards
Yichang International Hotel
★★★★
127 Yanjiang Dajie
(0717) 622 2888
www.ycinthotel.com
Standard room: RMB424
Credit Cards: Visa, Master Card, JCB, American Express, Domestic Cards

Restaurants

Chinese
Peach Blossom Restaurant
桃花岭饭店
29 Yunji Lu (Taohualing Hotel)
(0717) 623 6666

Hospitals

First People's Hospital of Yichang
宜昌市第一人民医院
4 Huti Jie, (0717) 624 3951

Bookstores

Xinhua Bookstore
宜昌市新华书店
5 Xinlin Yi Lu, (0717) 644 6577

Hunan

Population: 63.26 million
Area: 210, 000 sq km
Capital: Changsha
Airports: Changsha, Changde, Zhangjiajie
Port: Chenglingji

In the center of the central China plain is the province of Hunan, whose name means "south of the lake", derived from its location south of China's second-largest freshwater lake, Dongting Lake. This is rich agricultural country; Hunan produces more than 10% of all the rice consumed in China. The region is also a major producer of freshwater fish, tea, tobacco and meat. It is a watery land filled with lakes, and rivers, including the Yangtze River, and flooding is a problem most years.

Hunan is known for its hot spicy food and the fact that it was the birthplace of Mao Zedong, the man who led the Chinese Communists to victory. His home village of Shaoshan was once a place of pilgrimage, but has morphed over the decades into a tourist attraction. If you want a Mao souvenir of some sort, this is the best place to get it.

The province is rich in minerals with generous deposits of copper, lead and zinc. Much of the province's industrial output relates to processing of these minerals, but production of consumer goods, including electrical appliances and textiles is also important. Hong Kong is by far the largest external investor in the province, which usually means mainland funds diverted through Hong Kong and back home to benefit from foreign investment tax breaks.

Overall, the province is undeveloped compared to the coastal regions, but that is something of an advantage in terms of what will probably be one of the biggest money makers in coming decades – domestic tourism. Key tourist destinations, apart from the politically profound Shaoshan, include

Zhangjiajie, a nature reserve in the northwest of the province which is a world heritage site.

Furthermore, the province serves as a bridge between the two most important regions in China – the Yangtze River Valley and Guangdong province. To take advantage of this location, the province is building an industrial corridor along the Beijing-Guangzhou railway that connects the two regions.

Changsha 长沙
Telephone prefix: 0731
Population: 6.39 million
Bank of China: 127 Furong Zhong Lu

Changsha, founded in the third century, is a city historically noted as a center of learning and cultured mandarins. But it is as a trading center that it earned its keep. It was one of the first cities in central China to be opened up officially to foreign trade, being given the status of Treaty Port in the early 1900s. Mao Zedong spent several years here at school, a stop on his way from village youth to supreme leader.

The city was one of the many inland cities that benefited, if that is

Hunan Economic Data			
	2005	2004	Change (%)
GDP (RMB bn)	651.1	564.2	15.4
GDP per capita (RMB)	10,426	9,117	14.4
Exports (US$ bn)	3.75	3.10	20.97
Imports (US$ bn)	2.25	2.34	-3.85
Cars per 100 households	1.10	0.56	96.43
PCs per 100 households	34.94	27.67	26.27

the word, from the decision in the 1950s and 1960s to shift factories and manufacturing capacity into the interior to make them less vulnerable to attack from the US or the Soviet Union. As a result, Changsha now has machinery and transportation equipment factories.

Changsha has established several economic zones to help attract investment, of which the largest is the Changsha National Economic Technical Development Zone (CNETDZ), established in the early 1990s. More than 40 foreign companies have operations in the zone.

In 2005 Microsoft, in conjunction with its regional partner Powerwise, invested in a software technology development center in the city. The goal for the center will be software development as well as sales and marketing.

Changsha is located on the main north-south rail line through China, from Beijing to Guangzhou, and its airport has flights to 45 cities in China as well as international flights to Hong Kong, Bangkok and Seoul.

Changsha Economic Data	
GDP 2005 (RMB bn)	151.99
Disposable income 2005 (RMB)	12,434

Hotels

Dolton Hotel Changsha
★★★★★
159 Shaoshan Bei Lu
(0731) 416 8888
Standard room: RMB596
Credit Cards: Visa, Master Card, American Express
Gaoyuanhong Hotel
★★★★★
407 Bayi Zhong Lu
(0731) 276 6666
www.gyh-hotel.com
Standard room: RMB358
Credit Cards:
Visa, Master Card, American Express
Grand Sun City Hotel
★★★★★
269 Section 3 Furong Zhong Lu
(0731) 521 8888
www.grandsuncityhotel.net
Standard room: RMB468
Credit Cards:
Visa, Master Card, JCB, American Express, Domestic Cards
Huatian Hotel
★★★★★
300 Jiefang Dong Lu
(0731) 444 2888
www.huatian-hotel.com
Standard room: RMB510
Credit Cards:
Visa, Master Card, JCB, American Express, Domestic Cards
Hunan International Convention & Exhibition Hotel
★★★★★
Jinying Movie & TV Culture City, Liuyang River Bridge East
(0731) 425 2333
www.icec-hotel.com
Credit Cards: Visa, Master Card, JCB, American Express, Domestic Cards, Diners Club
HN Furama Hotel
★★★★
88 Bayi Lu, (0731) 229 8888
www.furama.com
Standard room: RMB698
Credit Cards:
Visa, Master Card, American Express
Hunan Jinhui Jinjiang Hotel

★★★★
332 Sanyi Dajie
(0731) 452 8888
www.jhjj-hotel.com
Standard room: RMB328
Credit Cards:
Visa, Master Card, JCB, American
Express, Domestic Cards
Junyi Conifer Hotel
★★★★
508-3 Furong Zhong Lu
(0731) 233 3333
www.junyiconiferhotels.com
Standard room: RMB388
Credit Cards: Visa, Master Card,
JCB, American Express
Lotus Huatian Hotel
★★★★
176 Wuyi Dajie
(0731) 440 1888
www.chhtg.com
Standard room: RMB518
Credit Cards: Visa, Master Card,
JCB, American Express

New Oriental Hotel
★★★★
87 Shaoshan Zhong Lu
(0731) 554 8888
Credit Cards: Visa, Domestic Cards
Royal Seal Hotel
★★★★
518 Furong Zhong Lu
(0731) 516 9999
www.rshotel.com.cn
Standard room: RMB400
Credit Cards:
Visa, Master Card, JCB
Xinshikong Conifer Hotel
★★★★
398 Section 3 Furong Zhong Lu
(0731) 501 2222
Standard room: RMB368
Credit Cards: Visa, Master Card,
JCB, American Express
King Year Hotel
★★★
248 Shuguang Zhong Lu
(0731) 548 1188

www.kingyear.com
Standard room: RMB198
Credit Cards: Domestic Cards
Yinhua Hotel
★★★
618 Wuyi Dajie, (0731) 430 8188
www.yinhua-hotel.com
Credit Cards: Domestic Cards

Restaurants

International
Wing 咖啡之翼
603 Furong Zhong Lu
(0731) 441 8059
Western
Shuiguo Lao
水果捞主题餐厅
2/F Wangfujing Department Store,
Huangxing Zhong Lu
(0731) 442 5477
Western/Cafe
Luyin Ge 绿茵阁
312 Jiefang Dong Lu

(0731) 416 9555
379 Laodong Xi Lu, (0731) 550 0562
198 Huangxing Nan Lu
(0731) 513 8957
Seafood
Xin Changfu
新长福酒楼
228 Furong Zhong Lu
(0731) 441 5222
Hunan
Fire Palace
火宫殿
Dong Tang Plaza
(0731) 556 8303
107 Wuyi Dong Lu
(0731) 412 0580
Yu Lou Dong 玉楼东
115 Wanjiali Lu, Fujiawan
(0731) 468 3818

Hospitals

Second Xiangya Hospital
中南大学湘雅二医院

156 Renmin Lu
(0731) 529 5999
**Hunan Provincial
People's Hospital**
湖南省人民医院
253 Jiefang Zhong Lu
(0731) 227 8287

Bookstores

Xinhua Bookstore
长沙市新华书店
285 Wuyi Dadao
0731) 412 2407

Industrial Parks

Changsha Economic & Technological Development Zone
长沙经济技术开发区
(0731) 402 0088
www.cetz.gov.cn
Major Industries:
Micro-electronics, new materials,
bioengineering, information
technology
Changsha High-Tech Industrial
长沙高新技术产业开发区
(0731) 899 5638
www.cshtz.gov.cn
Major Industries:
Telecommunications, biopharmaceuticals, new materials

Exhibition Centers

Hunan International Exhibition & Convention Center
Liuyang River Bridge East
(0731) 483 8114
www.hnicec.com
Hunan Hongxing International Exhibition Center
Sourth Shaoshan Lu
(0731) 264 6798
www.hnhxsy.com

Xiangtan 湘潭
Telephone prefix: 0731
Population: 6.39 million
Bank of China: 127 Furong Zhong Lu

Located in central Hunan, Xiang-
tan lies on the banks of the Xiang
River and is the urban center of
which Shaoshan village, Mao's birthplace, is a suburb. Once dependent
solely on agriculture, the city is now
supported by the textile, iron, steel,
manganese ore, and cement industries.

Hotels

Paragon Hotel
★★★★★
1 Hongqi Dajie, Hedong
(0732) 251 8888
www.paragon-hotel.com
Standard room:
RMB698 +15% Surcharge
Credit Cards: Visa, Master Card,
JCB, American Express
Desheng Hotel
★★★
1 Chezhan Lu, (0732) 568 0088
www.china-shaoshan.net
Standard room: RMB368
Credit Cards: Visa, Master Card

Inner Mongolia

Population: 23.86 million
Area: 1,183,000 sq km
Capital: Hohhot
Airports: Hohhot, Baotou, Hailaer, Xilinhaote, Chifeng, Tongliao, Wulanhaote
Ports: Erlianhaote, Zhuengedabuqi, Aershan

Located in extreme northern China and sharing a border with both Russia and Mongolia, Inner Mongolia is one of the poorest regions in the country. Although a majority of its 24 million residents are Han Chinese, there are also a large number of minorities, most notably Mongolians at 16%. Inner Mongolia has a relatively dry climate with long, cold winters and short, hot summers.

Throughout its history, this area was controlled in turn by Chinese agriculturalists from the south and nomadic tribes from the north. Outer Mongolia, with the help of Russia, passed out of Chinese control during the Republic of China period. Eastern Inner Mongolia came under control of the Japanese puppet state of Manchukuo in 1931, while the remainder of the province simultaneously declared independence from China and also became a puppet of the Japanese Empire.

The region remained under Japanese control until the end of the war in 1945 when the Soviet-backed Communists took the area and established the Inner Mongolia Autonomous Region, incorporating most of the areas in China's north with sizeable Mongol populations. Inner Mongolia constitutes 12% of China's land area and is the third-largest administrative region after Xinjiang and Tibet.

Inner Mongolia has two major economic resources – its livestock industry and the production of its mineral reserves. It is rich in natural resources like forestry, grains and mineral deposits but currently faces an ecological disaster of immense proportions. Desertification caused by overgrazing and global warming presently claims 670,000 hectares of grass and farmland (out of a total area of 112 million hectares) a year. At present, 60% of the province's land is sterile desert.

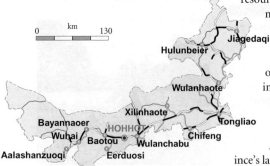

Some of the primary contributors to this massive problem are the industries of animal husbandry and dairy farming, which make up a significant proportion of the province's economy. The province has the largest number of horses, cattle, fine-wool sheep, white goats and camels in China and produces 35% of the world's cashmere.

Milk consumption in China is slowly increasing and Inner Mongolia is carrying out ambitious plans to boost its dairy industry. The Yili Company is one of China's largest dairy products companies and the top producer of ice cream in the country.

The region is a national production base for grain, oil and sugar and principal crops produced include wheat, corn, rice, linseed, millet, soybeans, sugar beet, oats, potatoes, flax and rapeseed.

It is also an important steel and coal producing base, with the second-largest reserves of coal in the country and the largest niobium, selenium, platinum, rare earth and agate reserves in the world. It boasts large reserves of other minerals including abundant oil, gas, salt and calcium deposits and is the site of four of China's six biggest gold mines. Mineral deposits remain only partially exploited.

Inner Mongolia is an important iron and steel producing region and the city of Baotou is home to one of the country's largest steel producers – the Baotou Iron and Steel Company. The largest military products plants in the country are also located here. Other industries of note include forestry, farm produce processing, machine manufacturing, chemicals, electronics, textiles, papermaking, light industry and power production. It is an important supplier of power to Beijing: the Inner Mongolia Power Group, the region's largest power supplier, is in the process of rapidly expanding its capacity.

The province's trade with Russia and Mongolia thrives through its 18 land-locked ports, two of which, Manzhouli and Erenhot, are gateways for trade with eastern and western Europe through Russia. A railway built in 1958, linking Russia (through Mongolia) with Lanzhou in Gansu province, passes through Hohhot and Baotou. The Beijing-Ulan Bator road traverses the region.

Inner Mongolia is included as one of the targets of the western development campaign, with an emphasis on tackling its daunting environmental problems. Investment is starting to pay off as its GDP expanded 28.1% in 2005, more than any other province in China.

Also notable is the cultural impact that Inner Mongolia is having on Mongolia. Some of the most popular television broadcasts in Ulan Bator are programs produced over the border in Inner Mongolia.

Inner Mongolia Economic Data			
	2005	2004	Change (%)
GDP (RMB bn)	389.6	304.1	28.1
GDP per capita (RMB)	16,331	11,305	44.5
Exports (US$ bn)	1.77	1.36	30.15
Imports (US$ bn)	3.10	2.37	30.80
Cars per 100 households	3.64	3.47	4.89
PCs per 100 households	23.17	19.02	21.82

Hohhot 呼和浩特

Telephone prefix: 0471
Population: 2.48 million
Bank of China: 88 Xincheng Dong Jie

The provincial capital of Hohhot lies at the center of Inner Mongolia on the Tumochuan Plain, about 670 km from Beijing. The city's name means 'green city' in Mongolian and with a population of 2.5 million people, it is the cultural, financial and economic hub for the province. It is China's leading center for woolen textiles and has also developed industries in leather, sugar, machine making, steel and animal product processing.

The city was founded during the Ming Dynasty around 1580 by Altan Khan, a leader who had sacked Beijing some 30 years earlier, greatly increasing the trading rights, and thus the prosperity, of his people.

Apart from the harsh climate the city is relatively pleasant, with a mixture of modern and traditional architecture surrounded by grasslands. There are several tourist attractions of note in the city, including the Tomb of Zhao Wujun and the Temple of the Five Pagodas.

Hohhot is also an important provincial transportation center linking Inner Mongolia with the rest of China by both rail and air.

Hohhot Economic Data	
GDP 2005 (RMB bn)	80
Disposable income 2005 (RMB)	12,500

Hotels

Inner Mongolia Hotel
★★★★★
31 Wulanchabuxi Lu, (0471) 693 8888
www.nmghotel.com
Credit Cards:
Visa, Master Card, JCB, American Express, Domestic Cards

Xincheng Hotel
★★★★★
40 Hulun Nan Lu, (0471) 629 2288
www.xincheng-hotel.com.cn
Credit Cards:
Visa, Master Card, JCB, American Express, Domestic Cards

Holiday Inn Hohhot
★★★★
185 Zhongshan Xi Lu
(0471) 635 1888
Standard room: RMB900
Credit Cards: Visa, Master Card, JCB, American Express

Inner Mongolia Bin Yue Hotel
★★★★
Zhaowuda Lu, Saihan
(0471) 660 5588
Standard room: RMB760
Credit Cards: Visa, Master Card, American Express, Domestic Cards

Jin Sui Hotel
★★★★
60 Xing'an Nan Lu, (0471) 660 6688
www.jinsui-hotel.com.cn
Standard room: RMB600
Credit Cards: Visa, Master Card, JCB, American Express

Phoenix Hotel Inner Mongolia
★★★★
Xincheng Bei Jie, (0471) 660 8888
www.ni-phoenix.com.cn
Credit Cards:
Visa, Master Card, JCB, American Express, Domestic Cards

Yitai Hotel
★★★★
1 Dongying Nan Lu, (0471) 223 3388

www.yt-hotel.com
Credit Cards:
Visa, Master Card, JCB, American
Express, Domestic Cards
Jinhui Hotel
★★★
105 Xilin Bei Lu, (0471) 694 0099
www.jh-hotel.com.cn
Standard room: RMB500
Credit Cards: Visa, Master Card,
JCB, American Express
Zhaojun Hotel
★★★
69 Xinhua Dajie, (0471) 666 8888
www.zhaojunhotel.com.cn
Standard room: RMB360
Credit Cards: Visa, Master Card,
JCB, American Express
Pearl Inner Mongolia Hotel
★★
108 Zhelimu Lu, (0471) 339 9888
www.pearl-hotel.com
Standard room: RMB580
Credit Cards: Visa, Master Card,
JCB, American Express

Restaurants

Inner Mongolia Hotel 内蒙古饭店
31 Wulanchabu Xi Lu
(0471) 693 8888
Cafe
Victoria Cafe 维多利亚咖啡厅

69 Dongying Nan Jie (Yi Tai Hotel)
(0471) 223 3308
International
Caoyuan Mingzhu Restaurant
草原明珠大酒店
2 Xincheng Bei Jie, (0471) 628 0088

Hospitals

Inner Mongolia People's Hospital
内蒙古人民医院
20 Zhaowuda Lu, (0471) 662 0000
Inner Mongolia Medical College
Affiliated Hospital
内蒙古医学院附属医院
1 Tong Dao Bei Jie, (0471) 663 6630

Industrial parks

Hohhot Economic and Technologi-
cal Development Zone
呼和浩特经济技术开发区
(0471) 461 2615
www.hetdz.gov.cn
Major Industries:
Bio-engineering, electronic information, fine textiles, new materials
Huhhot Export Processing Zone
呼和浩特出口加工区
(0471) 460 6491
www.hetdz.gov.cn/tzzn/export_zone.
asp
Major Industries: Ware-housing,
logistics, export processing

Baotou 包头

Telephone prefix: 0472
Population: 2.43 million
Bank of China: Xingyuan Hotel Gangtie Dajie

Baotou is the largest industrial city and the second-largest city in Inner Mo ngolia. With a population of around 2 million, it is the regional center for the province's main industries and the home of a large number of iron and steel mills. It also has numerous plants producing fertilizer, cement, textiles and machinery.

Following the founding of the People's Republic of China in 1949, Baotou was recognized as one of the "newly-built iron and steel centers in North China" and the eponymous Baotou Iron and Steel Company is based here.

The city is located close to the rich mineral resources found in the Yinshan – Tianshan Mountain Zone. There are hundreds of mines in the area extracting various metals and non-metals, including coal. Baotou and its surrounding area boast 25% of the nation's total coal reserves and 73% of the world's proven rare earth deposits.

Founded in 1992, the Baotou Rare-Earth High-Tech Development Zone is the only high-tech zone in the country devoted to the development of rare earth related production.

Considerable road and rail improvements have been made with the vigorous industrialization of Baotou.

Hotels

Shenhua International Hotel
★★★★★
1 A'erding Jie, Kundulun

(0472) 536 8888
www.shenhuahotel.com
Bao Tou Hotel
★★★
33 Gangtie Dajie, Kundulun
(0472) 515 6655
www.baotouhotel.com.cn

Restaurants

Cafe
UBC 上岛咖啡
Minzu Dong Lu (0472) 591 0797
Chinese
Jian Pu Zhai 简朴寨
512-15 Xihua Shangye Jie, Shifu Dong Lu, (0472) 591 0077
Western
Western Restaurant 西部之光
22/F, 1 A'erding Dajie (Shenhua International Hotel), (0472) 536 8888
Japanese
Fuji Japanese Restaurant 富士铁板烧
1 A'erding Dajie (Shenhua International Hotel), (0472) 536 8888

Hospitals

Baotou Central Hospital 包头市中心医院
1 Huan Cheng Xi Lu, (0472) 414 1084

Bookstores

Xinhua Bookstore 包头新华书店
14 Wenmin Lu, Shahe Town
(0472) 715 5795

Industrial parks

Baotou Rare-Earth High-Tech Industrial Development Zone
包头稀土高新技术产业开发区
(0472) 515 6625, *www.rev.cn*
Major Industries: Raire-earth processing and products

Jiangsu

Population: 74.75 million
Area: 102,600 sq km
Capital: Nanjing
Airports: Nanjing, Suzhou, Wuxi, Changzhou, Nantong, Lianyungang, Xuzhou
Ports: Liangyungang, Zhenjiang, Nantong

Jiangsu province is located on the Yangtze River Delta just north and west of Shanghai. It has some of the best road and rail transport links in the country, including the heavily traveled Shanghai-Nanjing line. Although it is deficient in natural resources like timber and minerals, Jiangsu has developed a sophisticated manufacturing sector, making it one of the wealthiest provinces in China.

Technology- and capital-intensive industries have seen rapid development in Jiangsu, especially electronics and telecommunications. Other primary industries include metal smelting and pressing, machine production, medical and pharmaceutical production and tobacco processing.

In recent years, Jiangsu has moved towards the development of high technology products. Many Taiwanese and international IT manufacturers have invested in Suzhou and Kunshan which are close to Shanghai but have more attractive land and labor costs.

In addition to its industrial sectors, Jiangsu's service sector has also attracted much foreign investment. Many multinational retail enterprises like Wal-mart from the US, Metro and OBI from Germany, Carrefour from France and B&Q from the UK have also targeted Jiangsu.

Jiangsu's economy owes a large part of its prosperity to its proximity to Shanghai. It has one of the most developed infrastructures in the country linking it with its neighbor to the east, facilitating logistics and the flow of investment into the province.

Jiangsu Economic Data			
	2005	2004	Change (%)
GDP (RMB bn)	1830.6	1500.4	22.0
GDP per capita (RMB)	24,560	20,705	18.6
Exports (US$ bn)	122.97	87.50	40.54
Imports (US$ bn)	104.96	83.36	25.91
Cars per 100 households	4.29	1.83	134.43
PCs per 100 households	46.35	31.68	46.31

Nanjing 南京

Telephone prefix: 025
Population: 6.86 million
Bank of China: 148 Zhongshan Nan Lu

Just over three hours from Shanghai by train, Nanjing, literally "Southern Capital", has long been celebrated as a literary and political center. It served as capital during the early years of the Ming dynasty, again during the short-lived Taiping Rebellion in 1853, and once more during the Republic of China under Chiang Kai-Shek. The Treaty of Nanjing, signed in 1842 at the conclusion of the First Opium War, opened China to foreign trade. In late 1937, the Japanese entered the city, and embarked on a campaign of widespread slaughter, which became known as the "Rape of Nanjing". Chinese forces reoccupied the city in 1945, which fell to the Communists in April 1949, becoming the provincial capital of Jiangsu.

The city's long and turbulent history provides visitors with a generous crop of historical sights, including the tomb of Sun Yat-sen, the Confucius Temple (Fuzimiao) and the Taiping Heavenly Kingdom History Museum. Nanjing is also famous for its educational institutions, which include Nanjing University and Nanjing Institute of Technology.

Nanjing today is a prosperous city, with an integrated iron-steel complex, an oil refinery, food-processing establishments and hundreds of plants producing a variety of items including chemicals, textiles, cement, fertilizers, machinery, weapons, electronic equipment, optical instruments, photographic equipment, and trucks. Nanjing also aims to become an international leader in the manufacturing sector. Urban infrastructure projects include two major bridges across the Yangtze.

Nanjing offers excellent conditions for investment in the petrochemical industry. A US$2.9 billion joint venture between Germany's BASF and Yangtze Petrochemical (a subsidiary of Sinopec), is expected to transform Nanjing into China's leading chemical production center.

Nanjing boasts many museums and other places of tourist interest, such as the Taiping Kingdom History Museum, the Nanjing Massacre Memorial, the Sun Yat-sen Mausoleum, and large sections of the old city wall.

Nanjing Economic Data	
GDP 2005 (RMB bn)	241.3
Disposable income 2005 (RMB)	14,997

Hotels

Celebrity City Hotel Nanjing
★★★★★
30 Zhongshan Bei Lu
(025) 8312 3333
Standard room: RMB1,080
Credit Cards:
Visa, Master Card, JCB, American Express, Domestic Cards

Crowne Plaza Nanjing
★★★★★
89 Hanzhong Lu, (025) 8471 8888
www.ichotelsgroup.com
Standard room: RMB1,494
Credit Cards:
Visa, Master Card, JCB, American Express, Domestic Cards

Grand Metropark Hotel Nanjing
★★★★★
319 Zhongshan Bei Lu
(025) 8480 8888
www.metroparkhotels.com
Credit Cards: Visa, Master Card, JCB, American Express

Jinling Hotel
★★★★★
1 Hanzhong Lu, (025) 8471 1888
www.jinlinghotel.com
Standard room: RMB598
Credit Cards:
Visa, Master Card, JCB, American Express, Domestic Cards

Jinling Resort
★★★★★
1 Jinling Hotel Lu, Jiangning
(025) 5210 7666
www.jinlinghotel.com
Credit Cards: Visa, Master Card, JCB, American Express

Mandarin Garden Hotel Nanjing
★★★★★
9 Zhuangyuanjing, Fuzimiao
(025) 5220 2555
Standard room:
RMB990 +15% Surcharge
Credit Cards: Visa, Master Card, JCB, American Express

Nanjing Grand Hotel
★★★★★
208 Guangzhou Lu, (025) 8331 1999
www.njgrandhotel.com
Credit Cards: Visa, Master Card, JCB, American Express

Nanjing Lakeview Xuanwu Hotel
★★★★★
193 Zhongyang Lu, (025) 8335 8888
Standard room: RMB1,000
Credit Cards: Visa, Master Card, JCB, American Express

Sheraton Nanjing Kingsley Hotel & Towers
★★★★★
169 Hanzhong Lu, (025) 8666 8888
Credit Cards: Visa, Master Card, JCB, American Express

Sofitel Galaxy Nanjing
★★★★★
9 Shanxi Lu, (025) 8371 8888
www.sofitel.com/asia
Credit Cards:
Visa, Master Card, JCB, American Express, Domestic Cards

Sofitel Zhongshan Golf Resort Nanjing
★★★★★

9 Huanling Lu, (025) 8540 8888
www.sofitel.com/asia
Standard room: RMB668
Credit Cards: Visa, Master Card,
JCB, American Express
Suning Universal Hotel
★★★★★
188 Guangzhou Lu, (025) 8323 2888
www.suningsuitehotel.com
Standard room: RMB1,300
Credit Cards: Visa, Master Card,
JCB, American Express
Central Hotel
★★★★
75 Zhongshan Lu, (025) 8473 3888
Standard room: RMB1,280
Credit Cards:
Visa, Master Card, American Express
Guoxin Hotel
★★★★
88 Changjiang Lu, (025) 8470 0688
www.jsgx.net
Credit Cards:
Visa, Master Card, JCB, American
Express, Domestic Cards
Jinling Star Hotel
★★★★
169 Longpan Lu, (025) 8509 7888
www.jlzxhotel.com

Credit Cards:
Visa, Master Card, JCB, American
Express, Domestic Cards
**Nanjing International Conference
Hotel**
★★★★
2 Sifang City, Zhongshanling
(025) 8443 0888
www.nic-hotel.com
Credit Cards:
Visa, Master Card, JCB, American
Express, Domestic Cards
Nanjing Shanshui Grand Hotel
★★★★
118 Longpan Zhong Lu
(025) 8481 1888
Standard room: RMB378
Credit Cards:
Visa, Master Card, JCB, American
Express, Domestic Cards
Nanjing Zhongshan Plaza
★★★★
200 Zhongshan Lu, (025) 8336 1888
www.zhongshan-hotel.com
Standard room:
RMB668 +15% Surcharge
Credit Cards: Visa, Domestic Cards
New Century Hotel
★★★★

278-2 Longpan Lu, (025) 8688 8888
www.jsnch.com
Standard room: RMB360
Credit Cards: Visa, Master Card, JCB, American Express, Domestic Cards
New Era Hotel
★★★★
251-1 Zhongshan Lu, (025) 8681 2222
www.newerahotel.com
Standard room: RMB680
Credit Cards: Visa, Master Card, JCB, American Express
Phoenix Palace Hotel
★★★★
47 Hunan Lu, (025) 8683 8888
www.pphotel.com.cn
Credit Cards: Visa, Master Card, JCB, American Express, Domestic Cards
Ramada Plaza Nanjing
★★★★
45 Zhongshan Bei Lu
(025) 8330 8888
www.ramada.com
Standard room: RMB498 +15% Surcharge (including breakfast)
Credit Cards: Visa, Master Card, JCB, American Express
Shuixiu Garden Hotel
★★★★
9 Jiahu Xi Lu, Baijiahu
(025) 5210 5588
www.shuixiuyuan.com
Standard room: RMB398
Credit Cards: Visa, Master Card, JCB, American Express
Egret Hotel
★★★
68 Dashiba Jie, Fuzimiao
(025) 8687 9999
www.egrethotel.com
Credit Cards:
Visa, Master Card, Domestic Cards

Restaurants

Italian
Jack's Place 杰克地方西餐厅
160 Shanghai Lu, (025) 8332 3616
2 Shizi Qiao, (025) 8326 0148
35 Wangfu Dajie, (025) 8420 6485
Western
Henry's Home 亨利之家
33 Huaqiao Lu, Xinjiekou
(025) 8470 1292
3 Lanjia Zhuang, Beijing Dong Lu
(025) 5771 6816
2 Shizi Qiao (near Hubei Lu)
(025) 8320 5677
Brazilian
Carioca 里约人拉丁餐厅
103 Zhongshan Bei Lu (Inside the Soldier's Club), (025) 8323 2163
3/F, 169 Hanzhong Lu (Sheraton Hotel), (025) 8679 5777
Mexican
Tacos 塔可
228-3 Guangzhou Lu, (025) 8323 1981
International
La Seine 塞纳河西餐厅
27/F, 188 Guangzhou Lu (Suning Universal Hotel), (025) 8323 2888
Tiramisu House 威雀提拉米苏餐厅
19 Jinyin Jie, (025) 8323 1353
Chinese
Tianyige Restaurant 天一阁大酒店
Zhongshan Dong Lu, Yixian Bridge
(025) 8445 3737
**Zhenbaofang Restaurant
珍宝舫大排档平江府店**
135 Pingjiangfu Lu, (025) 5230 0999
Thai
**Golden Harvest Thai Opera Cafe
金禾泰大餐厅**
2 Shiziqiao, Hunan Lu
(025) 8324 1823
Cantonese
Nihero Cantonese Cuisine 粤鸿和

11/F Suning Shopping Center, 18
Hunan Lu, (025) 5792 3518
Shanghainese
Shanghai Mansion 上海公馆菜
28 Wangfu Dajie, (025) 8420 5197

Hospitals

**People's Hospital of Jiangsu
江苏省人民医院**
300 Guangzhou Lu, (025) 8371 4511

Bookstores

Xinhua Bookstore 南京市新华书店
6 Zhongshan Dong Lu
(025) 8664 5151

Industrial parks

**Nanjing High-Tech Industrial
Development Zone
南京高新技术开发区**
(025) 5864 1118, www.njnhz.com.cn
Major Industries: Electronics, bioengineering, pharmaceuticals
**Nanjing Economic & Technological
Development Zone
南京经济技术开发区**
(025) 8580 0800
www.njxg.com
Major Industries:
Electronics, household appliances,
biopharmaceuticals, new materials,
export-oriented processing
**Nanjing Export Processing Zone
南京出口加工区**
(025) 5272 4998, www.njepz.gov.cn
Major Industries: Information technology, auto manufacturing

Exhibition centers

**Nanjing International Exhibition
Center**
88 Longpan Lu, (025) 8689 1058
www.njiec.com

Suzhou 苏州
Telephone prefix: 0512
Population: 7.53 million
Bank of China: 188 Ganjiang Lu

Famous throughout history for its
silk production, Suzhou is now a
major international hi-tech production hub as well as a manufacturing
base for other products including
steel, chemicals, paper, machine tools
and motor vehicles.

Suzhou has experienced an
impressive average annual growth
rate of about 17% in recent years,
and has become a major target of
foreign direct investment. Suzhou
Industrial Park, Suzhou Hi-tech
Development Zone and the Zhangjia-
gang Bonded Zone have all attracted
large amounts of foreign investment.
Between Suzhou Industrial Park and
Shanghai, leading IT producers such
as TSMC, UMC, GSMC, Samsung,
Hitachi and Phillips have created
what is known as the "silicon corridor".

Conveniently located about an
hour from Shanghai, Suzhou is worth
a leisure visit for its beautiful gardens
and pagodas. It is said in China that
"Above they have the heavens; below
we have Hangzhou and Suzhou".

Hotels

Crowne Plaza Suzhou
★★★★★
168 Xinggang Jie, Ind. Park
(0512) 6761 6688
www.crowneplaza.com
Standard room: RMB898
Credit Cards:

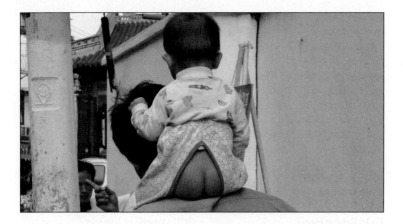

Visa, Master Card, JCB, American Express, Domestic Cards
Sheraton Suzhou Hotel & Towers
★★★★★
259 Xinshi Lu, (0512) 6510 3388
Standard room: RMB1,660
Credit Cards:
Visa, Master Card, American Express
Sofitel Suzhou
★★★★★
818 Ganjiang Dong Lu
(0512) 6801 9699, *www.sofitel.com*
Standard room: RMB1,700
Credit Cards:
Visa, Master Card, JCB, American Express, Domestic Cards
Renaissance Hotel Suzhou
★★★★★
229 Suhua Lu, Suzhou Ind. Park
(0512) 6761 8888
Credit Cards:
Visa, Master Card, JCB, American Express, Domestic Cards
Aster Hotel
★★★★
488 Sanxiang Lu, (0512) 6829 1888
Standard room:
RMB830 +15% Surcharge

Credit Cards: Visa, Master Card, JCB, American Express
Bamboo Grove Hotel
★★★★
168 Zhuhui Lu, (0512) 6520 5601
Standard room: RMB998
Castle Hotel
★★★★
120 Sanxiang Lu, (0512) 6828 6688
www.castlehotel.com.cn
Credit Cards: Visa, Master Card, JCB, American Express, Domestic Cards, Diners Club
China Garden Hotel
★★★★
198 Jinshan Lu, Mudu
(0512) 6625 6666
www.chinagardenhotel.com
Standard room: RMB520
Credit Cards: Visa, Master Card, JCB, American Express
Delight Mansion Hotel
★★★★
201 Shiquan Jie, (0512) 6801 7788
www.baiyuehotel.com
Standard room: RMB348
Credit Cards: Visa, Master Card, JCB, American Express

Glamor Hotel
★★★★
538 Tongjing Bei Lu
(0512) 6801 6088
www.glamorhotel.com
Standard room: RMB388
Credit Cards: Visa, Master Card,
JCB, American Express

Gloria Plaza Hotel Suzhou
★★★★
535 Ganjiang Dong Lu
(0512) 6521 8855
Credit Cards: Visa, Master Card,
JCB, American Express

Gold Bridge Hotel
★★★★
437 Jingde Lu, (0512) 8210 6008
www.szgbhi.com
Credit Cards:
Visa, Master Card, Domestic Cards

**Jin Cheng Jin Jiang International
Hotel**
★★★★
260 Xingtai Lu, Taiping Town,
Xiangcheng, (0512) 6543 1888
Standard room: RMB780
Credit Cards: Visa, Master Card,
JCB, American Express

Lexiang Hotel
★★★★
18 Dajing Lane, Guanqian Jie
(0512) 6522 8888
Standard room: RMB399
Credit Cards:
Visa, Master Card, JCB, American
Express, Domestic Cards

Lidu (Jasper) Hotel
★★★★
168 Ganjiang Xi Lu, (0512) 6511 9358
www.lidu-h.com
Credit Cards:
Visa, Master Card, JCB, American
Express, Domestic Cards

New City Garden Hotel
★★★★
1 Shishan Lu, (0512) 6825 0228
www.ncghotel.com.cn
Credit Cards:
Visa, Master Card, JCB, American
Express, Domestic Cards

Suzhou Hostun Hotel
★★★★
41 Dongwu Bei Lu, Wuzhong
(0512) 6565 6666
www.hostunhotel.com
Standard room: RMB248
Credit Cards: Visa, Master Card,
JCB, American Express

Suzhou Hotel
★★★★
345 Shiquan Jie, (0512) 6520 4646
www.suzhou-hotel.com
Standard room: RMB295
Credit Cards: Visa, Master Card,
JCB, American Express

Suzhou Plaza Hotel
★★★★
1168 Renmin Lu, (0512) 6523 3333
www.suzhouplazahotel.com
Standard room: RMB598

Suzhou Xishan Hotel
★★★★
Shigongshan Resort, (0512) 6627 8888
www.szxishanhotel.com
Standard room: RMB580
Credit Cards: Visa, Master Card,
JCB, American Express

Tian Ping Hotel
★★★★
168 Jinshan Lu, Mudu
(0512) 6626 8888
www.sz-tianpinghotel.com
Standard room: RMB650
Credit Cards:
Visa, Master Card, JCB, American
Express, Domestic Cards

Restaurants

Western

Sicily Pub & Restaurant
西西里西餐厅
1 Shaomozhen Xiang
(0512) 6523 2393
Tasty 西堤牛排
35 Shishan Lu, (0512) 6878 1971

Chinese

Deyuelou Restaurant 得月楼
43 Taijian Nong, Guanqian Jie
(0512) 6523 8940
Lao Dongwu Restaurant
老东吴食府
611 Changxu Lu, (0512) 6533 2093
Nakai Restaurant 南开大酒店
123 Dongwu Bei Lu, (0512) 6563 1749

Cantonese

Jiangnan Shouxi 江南首席
40-41/F International Jinhe Tower,
35 Shishan Lu, (0512) 6808 0000

Hospitals

Third People's Hospital of Suzhou
苏州第三人民医院
242 Guangji Lu, (0512) 6533 1688

Bookstores

Xinhua Bookstore 苏州市新华书店

166 Guanqian Jie
(0512) 6727 0241

Industrial parks

**Suzhou High-Tech Industrial
Development Zone**
苏州高新技术产业开发区
(0512) 6825 1888, *www.snd.gov.cn*
Major Industries: Information
technology, pharmaceutical, textiles,
paper, packaging, machinery
Suzhou Industrial Park
苏州工业园
(0512) 6668 0114
www.sipac.gov.cn
Major Industries: Electronics, pharmaceuticals, automobile parts
**Suzhou Industrial Park Export
Processing Zone**
苏州工业园出口加工区
(0512) 6258 1926, *www.sipepz.gov.cn*
Major Industries: Electronics, pharmaceuticals, automobile parts

Exhibition centers

Suzhou International Expo Center
Expo Plaza, Xiandai Dadao
(0512) 6258 0111
www.suzhouexpo.com

Wuxi 无锡

Telephone prefix: 0510
Population: 5.57 million
Bank of China: 258 Zhongshan Lu

A silk producing town, Wuxi sits on the north bank of Tai Lake, northwest of Shanghai. Wuxi processes grain and produces machine tools, paper products, fertilizer, and motor vehicles. The city's name literally means "without tin", referring to the tin mines in the area that were exhausted during the Han dynasty.

Wuxi lies on the main railroad line west from Shanghai. To exploit its advantageous location, eight zones including the Wuxi State Hi-Tech Industrial Development Zone were established. The city has become a major target for international investment and several internationally-recognized names, including Seagate and Sharp, have a presence in the city.

Hotels

Hubin Hotel
★★★★★
Liyuan Garden, Huanhu Lu
(0510) 8510 1888
www.hubinhotel.com
Credit Cards:
Visa, Master Card, JCB, American Express, Domestic Cards
Sheraton Wuxi Hotel & Towers
★★★★★
403 Zhongshan Lu, (0510) 8868 8688
Standard room: RMB1,380
Credit Cards: Visa, Master Card, JCB, American Express
Taihu Hotel
★★★★★
Huanhu Lu, Meiyuan
(0510) 8551 7888
www.taihuhotel.com
Standard room:
RMB860 +15% Surcharge
Credit Cards: Visa, Master Card, JCB, American Express
Courtyard by Marriott Hotel
★★★★
335 Zhongshan Lu, (0510) 8276 2888
Credit Cards:
Visa, Master Card, JCB, American Express, Domestic Cards
Gold Coast Hotel
★★★★
1 Caishu Lane, Bei Dajie
(0510) 8261 6888
www.goldcoasthotel-cn.com
Standard room: RMB880
Credit Cards: Visa, Master Card, JCB, American Express
Jinlun Hotel
★★★★
58 Wuai Bei Lu, (0510) 8271 5858
www.jinlun-hotel.com
Standard room: RMB458
Credit Cards:
Visa, Master Card, American Express
Lakeview Park Resort
★★★★
8 Shanshui Dong Lu
(0510) 8555 5888
Standard room: RMB700
Credit Cards: Visa, Master Card, JCB, American Express
Sainty Lakeside Resort
★★★★
9 Bibozhi Lu, (0510) 8599 6666
www.saintylakeside.com
Credit Cards: Visa, Master Card, JCB, American Express, Domestic Cards, Diners Club
Shan Ming Shui Xiu Hotel

DESTINATIONS

★★★★
369 Hubin Lu, (0510) 8511 1888
Credit Cards:
Visa, Master Card, JCB, American
Express, Domestic Cards
Taihu Pearl International Hotel
★★★★
Shilimingzhudi, Taihu National
Tourist Resort, Mashan
(0510) 8599 8888
Standard room: RMB398
Credit Cards: Visa, Master Card,
JCB, American Express
Wuxi Grand Hotel
★★★★
1 Liangqing Lu, (0510) 8580 6789
Standard room: RMB1,170
Credit Cards: Visa, Master Card,
JCB, American Express
Wuxi International Hotel
★★★★
118 Xianqian Dong Jie
(0510) 8231 8888
www.wuxiinternational.cn
Standard room: RMB380
Credit Cards:

Visa, Master Card, JCB, American
Express, Domestic Cards
Wuxi Jin Jiang Grand Hotel
★★★★
218 Zhongshan Lu, (0510) 8275 1688
Standard room: RMB468
Credit Cards:
Visa, Master Card, JCB, American
Express, Domestic Cards
Xihai Garden Hotel
★★★★
207 Suxi Lu, Zhongqiao
(0510) 8540 1888, *www.xihaihotel.com*
Credit Cards:
Visa, Master Card, JCB, American
Express, Domestic Cards
Arcadia Resorts
★★★
2 Taowudongniu, Mashan, Binhu
(0510) 8568 0111
www.wxtysz.com
Credit Cards: Domestic Cards

Restaurants

French
Provence Western Restaurant

普罗旺斯西餐厅
2 Yongding Xiang, Xianqian Xi Jie
(0510) 8276 9177
International

Jinxi Yuan Revolving Restaurant
锦锡园旋转餐厅
218 Zhongshan Lu, (0510) 8275 1688
Coffee House 咖啡屋
335 Zhongshan Lu (Marriott Hotel)
(0510) 8276 2888
Coffee Language 尚典咖啡
427 Qingshi Lu, (0510) 8260 7578
Chinese
Huamei Xuan 华美轩
335 Zhongshan Lu (7/F Marriott
Hotel), (0510) 8276 2888
Jufengyuan 聚丰园大酒店
555 Zhongshan Lu, (0510) 8275 7888

Hospitals

First People's Hospital of Wuxi
无锡第一人民医院
111 Renmin Lu, (0510) 8270 0778
Fourth People's Hospital of Wuxi
无锡第四人民医院
200 Huihe Lu, (0510) 868 2999

Bookstores

Xinhua Bookstore 无锡市新华书店
145 Zhongshan Lu, (0510) 8272 2127

Industrial parks

Wuxi New District 无锡新区
(0510) 8521 0633, www.wnd.gov.cn
Major Industries: Microelectronics,
machinery, biological engineering,
fine chemicals, new materials

Exhibition centers

**Wuxi Stadium and Convention
Center**
1500 West Taihu Dadao, Wuxi
(0510) 8512 8576

Nantong 南通
Telephone prefix: 0513
Population: 6.41 million
Bank of China: 8 Yaogang Lu

Nantong is a port city strategi-cally located at the mouth of the Yangtze River which became a textile center about a century ago. This industrial base later expanded to embrace light industry, machine-building, electronics, chemicals, pharmaceuticals, building materials, power production, ship-building and metallurgical sectors.

Nantong Port is an important transshipment point for exports and imports, particularly for goods enter-ing and leaving the Yangtze River valley, all the way west to Sichuan. The Nantong Economic & Techno-logical Development Area, one of the largest in China, occupies 147 square km and faces Shanghai across the Yangtze River. Companies from countries including Taiwan, Hong Kong, Japan, and Singapore have set up plants in Nantong, encouraged by preferential government policies designed to attract foreign invest-ment.

Nantong will no doubt benefit from recent infrastructure expansion projects in the region that include two bridges crossing the Yangtze River, linking it to Shanghai.

Hotels

Nantong Hotel
★★★★
81 Qingnian Dong Lu
(0513) 8501 8989

www.nthotel.com
Standard room: RMB572
Credit Cards:
Visa, Master Card, JCB, American Express
Qi Dong Hotel
★★★★
490 Minle Zhong Lu, Qidong
(0513) 8331 6621
www.qidonghotel.com
Standard room: RMB538
Credit Cards:
Visa, Master Card, American Express
Qidong Grand Hotel
★★★★
578 Gongyuan Zhong Lu, Qidong
(0513) 8332 9666
Standard room: RMB380
Credit Cards: Visa, Master Card, JCB, American Express
San Teh Hotel
★★★★
1 Duanjiaba Lu
(0513) 8512 3888
Standard room: RMB700
Credit Cards: Visa, Master Card, JCB, American Express

Restaurants

Chinese
Riyuetan Restaurant
日月谈大酒楼
195 Gongnong Lu
(0513) 8522 7777
Xiyangyang Restaurant
喜洋洋大酒店
8 Qingnian Zhong Lu
(0513) 8515 1511
Western
Nantong Captain'es Bar
南通船长酒吧
9 Qingnian Zhong Lu
(0513) 8559 8856

Chef Richard Cafe
20 Haonan Lu
(0513) 8551 9996
International
Wen Feng Hotel 文峰饭店
1 Qingnian Dong Lu
(0513) 8501 1551
Nantong Hotel 南通大饭店
81 Qingnian Dong Lu
(0513) 8501 8989

Hospitals

First People's Hospital of Nantong
南通市第一人民医院
6 Hai'erxiang Bei Lu
(0513) 512 9000
Affiliated Hospital of Nantong Medical College
南通医学院附属医院
20 Xisi Lu, (0513) 8505 2222

Bookstores

Xinhua Bookstore 南通市新华书店
80 Renmin Zhong Lu
(0513) 8506 2591

Industrial parks

Nantong Economic & Technological Development Area
南通经济技术开发区
(0513) 8592 2110
www.netda.com
Major Industries:
Chemicals, materials, electronics, textiles, food and oil processing, warehousing and storage
Nantong Export Processing Zone
南通出口加工区
(0513) 8598 0289
www.ntepz.com
Major Industries:
Electronic information, biomedicine, precision machinery, textiles, hi-tech

DESTINATIONS

Kunshan 昆山
Telephone prefix: 0512
Population: 1.34 million
Bank of China: 162 Qianjin Zhong Lu

Kunshan city – the birthplace of Kun Opera, a traditional favorite in east China - is located less than an hour west of Shanghai. Only a tiny and undeveloped town until Taiwanese businesses moved in and expanded the domestic market in the 1980s, it is experiencing rapid economic development. More than 1,200 Taiwanese companies are based in Kunshan and other leading foreign investors include companies from Hong Kong, the US and Japan.

Hotels

Kunshan KG Landmark Hotel
★★★★★
198 Qingyang Zhong Lu
(0512) 5770 3999
www.chinatrust-hotel.com
Standard room: RMB500
Credit Cards:
Visa, Master Card, JCB, American Express, Domestic Cards
Ramada Lakeside Villas Kunshan
★★★★★
18 Hubin Nan Lu, Bacheng Town
(0512) 5789 0088
www.ramada.com
Standard room: RMB980
Credit Cards: Visa, Master Card
Sovereign Hotel Kunshan
★★★★★
33 Qianjin Zhong Lu
(0512) 5716 8888
www.huaminsovereign.com
Standard room: RMB980

Credit Cards: Visa, Master Card, JCB, American Express
Traders Hotel Kunshan
★★★★★
387 Qianjin Zhong Lu
(0512) 5788 5788
www.shangri-la.com
Credit Cards:
Visa, Master Card, JCB, American Express, Domestic Cards
Garden Holiday Hotel
★★★★
18 Ma'anshan Dong Lu
(0512) 5755 8888
www.gardenholidayhotel.com
Credit Cards:
Visa, Master Card, JCB, American Express, Domestic Cards
Wealth Grand Hotel
★★★★
459 Chaoyang Zhong Lu
(0512) 5716 6888
Credit Cards: Visa, Master Card, JCB, American Express, Diners Club, Domestic Cards
Xingda Hotel
★★★
Diannan Lu, Zhouzhuang Scenery Area, (0512) 5721 6779
www.xingdahotel.com

Restaurants

French
Le Moulin de Qin Qin
乐磨坊法国餐厅
17 Zhongyin Square
(0512) 5736 4121
Chinese
Grandma's 外婆家
278 Zhujiang Bei Lu
(0512) 5739 2828
Local traditional
Aozao Mianguan 奥灶面馆

49 Tongjing Lu, Lujia Town
(0512) 5089 2195
Japanese
Yi Japanese翼日本料理
88 Heiliongjiang Bei Lu
(0512) 5755 0907

Hospitals

Kunshan Hospital of Traditional Chinese Medicine
昆山中医医院
189 Chaoyang Lu
(0512) 5731 0000

Bookstores

Xinhua Bookstore
昆山市新华书店
68 Renmin Lu
(0512) 5753 8864

Industrial parks

Kunshang Export Processing Zone
昆山出口加工区
(0512) 5735 2662
www.jseport.gov.cn
Major Industries:
Electronic information, optic electronics and precision machinery
Kunshan Economic and Technological Development Zone
昆山经济技术开发区
(0512) 5731 3838
www.ketd.gov.cn
Major Industries:
Information technology, precision machinery

Exhibition centers

Kunshan Science & Culture Exhibition Center
109, Qianjin Zhong Lu, Kunshan
(0512) 5736 7396
www.ks-bl.com

Yangzhou 扬州
Telephone prefix: 0541
Population: 4.51 million
Bank of China: 279 Wenchang Zhong Lu

Located near the juncture of the Grand Canal and the Yangtze River, Yangzhou was an ancient center of commerce in the Sui and Tang Dynasties. Today it is mainly a tourist town, known for canals, bridges, and gardens.

Hotels

Garden International Hotel
★★★★
236 Jiangyang Zhong Lu
(0514) 780 3333, *www.yzhyhotel.com*
Credit Cards: Visa, Master Card, JCB, American Express, Domestic Cards
Metropark Hotel Yangzhou
★★★★
559 Wenchang Zhong Lu
(0514) 732 2888
Standard room: RMB700
Credit Cards: Visa, Master Card, JCB, American Express
Hotel Shita
★★★
590 Wenchang Zhong Lu
(0514) 780 1188, *www.yzstbg.com*
Credit Cards: Visa, Master Card, JCB, Domestic Cards
Liming Hotel
★★★
121 Zhenzhou Xi Lu, (0514) 340 0088
www.liminghotel.com
Credit Cards: Visa, Master Card, JCB, American Express, Domestic Cards

Restaurants

Yangzhou

DESTINATIONS

Houcaller豪客来
37 Wenhe Bei Lu, (0514) 734 2769
Barbeque
Boca Latin Restaurant & Club
博卡阿根廷烤肉餐厅
46 Siwangting Lu
(0514) 793 6177
Pizza
Champion Pizza 千尊比萨
12 Wenhe Bei Lu, (0514) 732 4508
Japanese
Japanese Restaurant 日本料理
26-3 Dahongqiao Lu, (0514) 733 0699
Seafood
Dock Restaurant 公爵渔港
51 Wenchang Xi Lu, (0514) 787 1888
Cantonese
Zijing Goose 扬州紫京烧鹅仔
197 Weiyang Lu, (0514) 776 0717
Chinese
Fuchun 富春茶社
35 Deshengqiao, 299 Yangzijiang Bei
Lu, (0514) 723 3326
Fumanlou Restaurant
福满楼大酒店
2 Meishi Jie, near Siwang Ting
(0514) 734 4777
Fumanlou Restaurant
福满楼大酒店
202 Wenchang Xi Lu, (0514) 786 2777
Chouxiaoya Restaurant 丑小鸭酒楼
108 Wenhui Dong Lu
(0514) 731 8528

Hospitals

Third People's Hospital of
Yangzhou 扬州第三人民医院
13 Youyi Lu, (0514) 762 5350

Bookstores

Xinhua Bookstore
扬州市新华书店
65 Wenhe Nan Lu, (0514) 734 4427

Changzhou 常州
Telephone prefix: 0519
Population: 2.52 million
Bank of China: 150 Heping Nan Lu

An ancient town on the Grand Canal, Changzhou was originally founded over 3,000 years ago. During the first half of the twentieth century, cotton production was its principle industry. Today, it has factories mainly specializing in textiles, food production, engineering, and some high technology.

Hotels

Changzhou Grand Hotel
★★★★★
65 Yanling Xi Lu, (0519) 810 9988
www.czghotel.com
Standard room: RMB730
Credit Cards: Visa, Master Card, JCB, American Express
Traders Fudu Hotel Changzhou
★★★★★
398 Tongjiang Dajie, (0519) 516 8888
www.shangri-la.com
Standard room:
RMB998 +15% surcharge
Credit Cards:
Visa, Master Card, JCB, American Express, Domestic Cards
Jinling Mingdu Hotel
★★★★
39 Heping Bei Lu, (0519) 811 8888
www.hotelworld.com.cn
Standard room: RMB550-880
Credit Cards:
Visa, Master Card, Domestic Cards
Jintan Sakura Hotel
★★★★
88 Ximen Dajie, (0519) 239 6666

www.sakura-hotel.com
Credit Cards: Visa, Master Card, JCB, American Express, Domestic Cards

Legend Holiday Hotel
★★★★
151 Heping Nan Lu, (0519) 816 3388
www.hotelren.cn
Standard room: RMB528
Credit Cards: Visa, Master Card, JCB, American Express

Zhongyou International Hotel Changzhou
★★★★
45 Huaide Zhong Lu, (0519) 660 6888
www.zyint.cn
Standard room: RMB458
Credit Cards: Visa, Master Card, JCB, American Express

Changzhou Zhangshengji Hotel
★★★
317 Jinling Zhong Lu
(0519) 812 9688
www.zsj-hotel.com
Credit Cards:
Visa, Master Card, Domestic Cards

Guorui Hotel
★★★
Hengshanqiao Town, Wujin
(0519) 860 3888
www.czgr.com
Standard room: RMB380
Credit Cards: Domestic Cards

Restaurants

French
Spring Cafe春天咖啡西餐厅
65 Yanlin Xi Lu, (0519) 816 9988

Chinese
Changzhou Grand Hotel
常州大酒店
65 Yanlin Xi Lu, (0519) 810 9988

Sanpinyuan Restaurant

三品苑大酒店
338 Jinlin Zhong Lu, (0519) 660 0778
Jiangnanchun Hotel
江南春宾馆
39 Yingbin Lu, (0519) 664 3663

Barbecue
Oscar Restaurant
奥斯卡电影主题餐厅
21 Huaide Zhong Lu
(0519) 680 6666

Hospitals

First People's Hospital of Changzhou常州市第一人民医院
185 Juqian Jie, (0519) 618 0000

Bookstores

Xinhua Bookstore常州市新华书店
3/F Nan Dajie, Buxing Jie
(0519) 668 2720

Industrial parks

Changzhou New & High-Tech Industrial Development Zone
常州国家高新技术产业开发区
(0519) 510 7129
www.cznd.com
Major Industries: Electronics, precision machinery, bio-engineering, new materials, new energy, fine chemicals, environment protection

DESTINATIONS

Jiangxi
Population: 43.11 million
Area: 166,600 sq km
Capital: Nanchang
Airports: Nanchang, Jingdezhen, Jiu-jiang, Ji'an, Ganzhou, Lushan
Ports: Jiujiang

Jiangxi province is just west of Zhejiang and Fujian provinces and north of Guangdong, but does not share the in the wealth of its coastal neighbors. Aside from its natural resources, Jiangxi is known chiefly for its ceramics industry and its rich communist history.

Jiangxi has a subtropical climate and is primarily mountainous and hilly, with slopes that trend downward towards the Yangtze River. Northern Jiangxi is home to the Poyang Lake, China's largest freshwater lake and a major source of fish.

The region has been famed for its ceramics since the Han dynasty (206 BC-220 AD), particularly porcelain. The eastern town of Jingdezhen, with its proximity to kaolin and feldspar deposits, became the center of China's ceramics industry and was one of the world's first industrial cities a thousand years ago. The kilns were destroyed during the Taiping Rebellion (1851-64 AD) but the porcelain industry rose from the ashes and returned to production in the 1950s.

In Jiangxi during the late 1920s and early 1930s, Mao Zedong experienced some of his most significant development as a leader and it was here that he decided that the peasants in the countryside should be the engine of the Chinese revolution, not industrial workers as in Europe.

Today, Jiangxi province is struggling to keep up with its neighbors and road links are still primitive. Jiangxi has succumbed to a North-South divide, with Poyang Lake acting as the divider. The South remains largely agricultural, with only Jinggangshan as a tourist draw for diehard Communist pilgrims. The northern part of the province has a large port on the Yangtze in Jiujiang (which now has Jiangxi's first container service), the city of Jingdezhen, now as well-known for pollution as for porcelain, and Jiangling Motors Corp in Nanchang.

Jiangxi's economy is dependant upon agriculture, with top crops of rice and tea, among others. Because of its subtropical climate, citrus fruits are also grown here.

Mineral resources are Jiangxi's top non-agricultural asset, with copper and coal leading the list. The Dexing mine has China's largest copper reserves. Jiangxi is also a major producer of rare earth – tantalum and niobium in particular – and kaolin, essential for the province's most famous export, porcelain china. Additionally, Jiangxi is one of the top ten copper producers in the world.

Jiangxi's western area, near its border with Hunan, is one of the country's oldest and most important coal mining regions. With innumerable mines both large and small, legal and illegal, Jiangxi is plagued by mining accidents.

Heavy industry is also a major contributor to Jiangxi's economy, although it has yet to attract much in the way of foreign investment. Major industrial products include automobiles, steel, machinery, petrochemicals, electronics and textiles.

The mountain resort of Lushan in northern Jiangxi makes for an interesting trip both for natural beauty and the colonial architecture left behind by its former Western residents. Longhushan, not far from the Fujian border in the east, is being touted as a new Guilin-style holiday resort.

Jiangxi Economic Data			
	2005	2004	Change (%)
GDP (RMB bn)	405.7	345.7	17.4
GDP per capita (RMB)	9,440	8,189	15.3
Exports (US$ bn)	2.43	2.00	21.80
Imports (US$ bn)	1.63	1.53	6.54
Cars per 100 households	0.73	0.36	102.78
PCs per 100 households	32.03	19.98	60.31

DESTINATIONS

Nanchang 南昌

Telephone prefix: 0791
Population: 4.51 million
Bank of China: 1 Zhanqian Xi Lu

Like much of Jiangxi, Nanchang is full of significant moments in China's Communist history. The Nanchang Uprising, which took place on August 1, 1927, was one of the first major clashes between Communist forces and Chiang Kai-shek's Nationalist troops. August 1 is celebrated today as the anniversary of the founding of the People's Liberation Army (PLA).

Nanchang has three investment zones, but its inland location and the fact that it is surrounded by more appealing investment destinations and regional markets has relegated the city to investment hinterland status.

The city suffers from scorching summers and freezing winters made even less pleasant by the area's high humidity.

Nanchang Economic Data	
GDP 2005 (RMB bn)	100.77
Disposable Income 2005 (RMB)	10,301

Hotels

Gloria Plaza Hotel Nanchang
★★★★★
88 Yanjiang Bei Lu
(0791) 673 8855
Standard room: RMB980
Credit Cards:
Visa, Master Card, JCB, American Express, Domestic Cards
Jiangxi Hotel
★★★★★
368 Bayi Dajie, (0791) 620 6666

www.jxh.com.cn
Credit Cards:
Visa, Master Card, JCB, American Express, Domestic Cards
Civil Aviation Hotel
★★★★
587 Hongcheng Lu, (0791) 889 8888
www.jxmhotel.com
Standard room: RMB368
Credit Cards: Visa, Master Card, JCB, Domestic Cards
Jin Feng Hotel
★★★★
281 Zhanqian Xi Lu, (0791) 886 7777
www.jinfenghotel.com.cn
Standard room: RMB568
Credit Cards: Visa, Master Card, JCB, American Express, Domestic Cards
Jinjiang Crown Hotel
★★★★
99 Hongcheng Lu, (0791) 642 9999
www.jjhghotel.com
Standard room: RMB360
Credit Cards: Visa, Master Card, JCB, American Express
Regal Hotel
★★★★
160 Hongcheng Lu, (0791) 640 8888
www.regalhotel.cn
Standard room: RMB480
Credit Cards: Visa, Master Card, JCB, American Express, Domestic Cards
Ruidu Hotel
★★★★
399 Guangchang Nan Lu
(0791) 620 1888
Credit Cards: Visa, JCB, American Express, Domestic Cards, Diners Club
The Lake View Hotel Nanchang
★★★★
99 Hubin Nan Lu, (0791) 852 1888
www.lakeviewhotel.com.cn
Standard room:

RMB780 +10% Surcharge
Credit Cards: Visa, Master Card, JCB, American Express

Restaurants

International
Jin Mei Yuan 尽美苑
368 Bayi Da Dao (Jiangxi Hotel)
(0791) 620 6666
Cafe
Star Coffee Lounge 星运咖啡廊
368 Bayi Da Dao (Jiangxi Hotel)
(0791) 620 6666
Greenery Cafe 绿茵阁西餐厅
191 Ruzi Lu, (0791) 622 9788
Chinese
Nanchang Ren Jia Hotel 南昌人家
148 Ruzi Lu, (0791) 629 2777

Hospitals

Jiangxi Provincial People's Hospital
江西省人民医院
92 Aiguo Lu, (0791) 689 5510
First Affiliated Hospital of Jiangxi
Medical College
江西医学院第一附属医院
17 Yongwai Zheng Jie
(0791) 869 2711

Bookstores

Xinhua Bookstore 南昌市新华书店
272 Bayi Dadao, (0791) 626 2026

Industrial parks

Nanchang Economic & Technological Development Zone
南昌经济技术开发区
(0791) 380 5600
www.china-taiwan.com/TZZS/nanchang
Major Industries: Textiles, automotive components, electronics
Nanchang High-Tech Industrial
南昌高科技产业开发区
(0791) 816 1090
www.nchdz.net
Major Industries: Information technology, bioengineering, textiles

Jingdezhen 景德镇

Telephone prefix: 0798
Population: 1.54 million
Bank of China: 1 Taoyang Lu

Jingdezhen is chiefly known for porcelain production. In the 11th century, emperor Jingde decreed that all imperial porcelain was to come from this small town. The town was subsequently renamed after the emperor, its name meaning simply 'Jingde town', and has been well known for fine porcelain products ever since.

Hotels

Kai Men Zi Grand Hotel
★★★★
1055 Cidu Dajie, (0798) 857 7777
www.kmz.cn
Standard room: RMB488
Credit Cards:
Visa, Master Card, JCB, American Express, Domestic Cards
Jinye Hotel
★★★
1168 Cidu Dajie, (0798) 858 8888
www.jdzjinye.com.cn
Standard room: RMB358

Credit Cards: Visa, Master Card, JCB, American Express, Domestic Cards

Restaurants

Chinese
Xiaomaque Restaurant 小麻雀
58 Lianshe Bei Lu, (0798) 823 6777
China Town Restaurant
唐人街酒店
Xilukou, near Tiyu Gong
(0798) 822 5777
Xilaideng Restaurant 喜来登酒楼
6 Xincun Nan Lu, (0798) 821 5777
Kaimenzi Grand Hotel
开门子大酒店
1 Xinfeng Lu, (0798) 857 7777

Hospitals

First Hospital of Jingdezhen
景德镇市第一医院
37 Zhonghua Bei Lu
(0798) 852 3661
Third People's Hospital of Jingdezhen 景德镇市第三人民医院
Linyin Lu, Changjiang Square
(0798) 841 7496

Bookstores

Xinhua Bookstore
景德镇市新华书店
Xinde Yuan, (0798) 822 8154

Jilin

Population: : 27.16 million
Area: 187, 400 sq km
Capital: Changchun
Airports: Changchun, Jilin, Yanji, Liuhe
Ports: Jilin, Da'an, Fuyu
Border crossings: Tumen

Located in the center of China's northeast region (Dongbei), Jilin is surrounded by Liaoning to the south, Inner Mongolia to the west, Heilongjiang to the north, and Russia and North Korea to the east. After the communist revolution, Jilin became one of the main industrial and agricultural centers of China. Since economic reform began in the 1970s the local economy has suffered, while regions to the south have grown and prospered. Still a large producer of grain, Jilin has not been hurt as much by the recent economic shifts as its neighbors. The province is home to over 40 ethnic minorities including Korean, Manchu, Mongolian, Hui, and Sibo.

Positioned at a crossroads between the distinct ethnic regions of Russia, Japan, Korea and China, Jilin has a turbulent history. The area has been constantly fought over and invaded since records began, most recently by the Japanese. During the Qing Dynasty (1644-1911), the area was under the control of the General of Jilin, whose influence extended to the Sea of Japan to encompass much of what is Russian territory today. This area was ceded to Russia in 1860 as the regime weakened under the foreign onslaught of the Opium wars.

In 1932, the area was incorporated into the Japanese puppet state of Manchukuo and Changchun was made the capital. The Japanese ran a brutal regime with the deposed last emperor Puyi as their puppet ruler. After the defeat of Japan in 1945 the region, together with the rest of Manchuria, was handed to the communists by the Soviet Union and became the base from which the communists defeated the Nationalists in the civil war. It soon became the staging ground for Chinese assistance to North Korea in the Korean War.

During the Cultural Revolution of 1966-1976 the cities of Jilin and Changchun were the scene of the heaviest fighting in the country as rival Red Guard factions, armed with heavy artillery, did battle with each other and the army. When relations with the Soviet Union turned sour in the late 1960s, the region prepared itself for invasion. Today the larger cities in Jilin have converted the old bomb shelters built then into underground shopping malls.

With a sown area of over 3,500 million hectares, the province's fertile soil is suitable for growing grains, beans, oil crops, tobacco, potato, ginseng, traditional Chinese medicinal herbs, and fruits. Ginseng, sable and deer antlers are produced in abundance here and are known in China as the "three northeastern treasures". Jilin is also relatively rich in natural and mineral resources. It has reserves of oil, gas, coal, iron ore, nickel, gold and silver and ranks as the sixth-largest timber-producing province in China.

Jilin is also an important petrochemical production base in China producing a wide variety of chemical materials for foodstuffs, medicine, textiles and other light industries. The region's petrochemical industry was all over the news in November 2005 when a factory of the China National Petroluem Company leaked benzene into the Songhua River, sending a toxic slick through Harbin and all the way to Russia. Sadly, the incident was not an isolated occurrence. Pollution from industry plagues the region.

In 2003, the central government launched an initiative similar to its earlier drive to "develop the West" when it called for all patriots to "revive the Northeast". More than just political sloganeering, the program involves tax breaks and other preferential policies for locals and foreign businesses wanting to set up in the northeast. It also means increased infrastructure investment and throwing the full weight of the central government behind new projects and ventures, especially those involved in exporting overseas.

The climate in Jilin is harsh, with long, cold winters and short, hot summers. Severe droughts have exacerbated a shortage of clean water caused by industrial pollution and overuse.

In the last few years, as conditions in North Korea have steadily worsened, a clandestine flow of North Korean refugees have illegally crossed the border into China, mostly into Jilin. But after the DPRK successfully tested a nuclear bomb in October 2006, China redoubled efforts to strengthen the border. It was unclear whether the new barriers would also prevent videos of South Korean television dramas and other contraband that have been smuggled from China into North Korea.

Jilin Economic Data			
	2005	2004	Change (%)
GDP (RMB bn)	362.0	312.2	16.0
GDP per capita (RMB)	13,348	10,932	22.1
Exports (US$ bn)	2.47	1.72	43.60
Imports (US$ bn)	4.06	5.08	-20.08
Cars per 100 households	1.41	1.16	21.55
PCs per 100 households	30.06	20.85	44.17

Changchun 长春

Telephone prefix: 0431
Population: 7.33 million
Bank of China: 11 Xi'an Da Lu

Changchun is affectionately referred to as 'Car City', the name of one of its suburbs, due to its hosting of China's first and largest car factory, Changchun First Auto Works (FAW). It was the capital of the Japanese puppet state of Manchukuo and today it is still possible to visit the palace where the last emperor, Puyi, lived for 14 years before the communists made him a gardener.

As the industrial center of Jilin, Changchun is home to a large array of heavy industrial corporations. First, of course, are FAW and its enormous joint venture with Volkswagen. It was set up originally by the Russians and specialized in "Liberation" trucks, "Red Flag" lim-

ousines and later the ubiquitous VW Santanas. Toyota has also signed a deal with FAW to make engines, and General Motors is producing trucks in the city.

Changchun New and High-Tech Industries Development Zone is touted as one of the best development zones in the country, with more than 700 high-tech enterprises, over 200 of which are foreign-funded. Changchun Economic and Technological Development Zone is a state-level development zone with 1,038 domestic and foreign enterprises.

The city is the rail and road hub of the northeast and flights from Changchun Airport leave for most major cities in China. There are also direct flights to Sendai, Scoul and Hong Kong.

Changchun Economic Data	
GDP 2005 (RMB bn)	167.54
Disposable income 2005 (RMB)	9,830

Hotels

Changchun Noble Hotel
★★★★★
4501 Renmin Dajie, (0431) 562 2888
www.noblehotel.com
Standard room: RMB1,050
Credit Cards:
Visa, Master Card, JCB, American
Express, Domestic Cards

Redbuds Hotel
★★★★★
5688 Renmin Dajie, (0431) 568 7888
www.redbudshotel.com
Standard room: RMB468
Credit Cards:
Visa, Master Card, JCB, American
Express, Domestic Cards

Shangri-La Hotel Changchun
★★★★★
569 Xi'an Dajie, (0431) 898 1818
Standard room:
RMB1,320 +15% Surcharge
Credit Cards: Visa, Master Card,
JCB, American Express, Diners Club,
Domestic Cards

Changbaishan Hotel
★★★★

1448 Xinmin Dajie, (0431) 558 8888
www.cbshotel.0431-114.com
Credit Cards:
Visa, Master Card, JCB, American
Express, Domestic Cards

Changchun International Conference Center
★★★★
4288 Ziyou Dajie
(0431) 461 8888
Standard room: RMB488
Credit Cards: Visa, Master Card,
JCB, American Express, Domestic
Cards, Diners Club

Changchun Yanminghu Spa Hotel
★★★★
8777 Beihuancheng Lu
(0431) 587 9999
Standard room: RMB328
Credit Cards: Visa, Master Card,
American Express, Domestic Cards

Jixiang Hotel
★★★★
2228 Jiefang Dajie
(0431) 558 9888
Credit Cards: Visa, Master Card,
JCB, Domestic Cards

Maxcourt Hotel
★★★★
823 Xi'an Dajie, (0431) 896 2688
Credit Cards: Master Card, JCB,
American Express, Domestic Cards
Paradise Hotel
★★★★
1078 Renmin Dajie, (0431) 209 0999
Standard room: RMB448
Credit Cards:
Visa, Master Card, JCB, American
Express, Domestic Cards
Songyuan Hotel
★★★★
1169 Xinfa Lu, (0431) 272 7001
Credit Cards: Domestic Cards
Swiss-Belhotel Changchun
★★★★
1447 Chuangye Dajie, Lvyuan
(0431) 598 8888
Standard room: RMB720
Credit Cards: Visa, Master Card,
JCB, American Express

Restaurants

Chinese
Shang Gong 香宫
569 Xianda Lu, (0431) 898 1818
French
French Bakery 红磨坊
745 Guilin Lu, Tongzhi Jie
(0431) 562 3994
Western
Cafe 咖啡厅
569 Xianda Lu, (0431) 898 1818
Japanese
Zhudi Japanese Restaurant
筑地日本料理
569 Xianda Lu, (0431) 898 1818

Bars & Clubs

Xanadu 仙乐都
Shangri-La Hotel

Ferry Port Bar 渡口酒吧
17 Guilin Lu

Hospitals

**Jilin University China-Japan Union
Hospital**
吉林大学中日联谊医院
126 Xiantai Dajie, (0431) 499 5114

Bookstores

Xinhua Bookstore 长春市新华书店
40 Chongqing Lu, (0431) 895 8836

Industrial parks

**Changchun Economic & Techno-
logical Development Zone**
长春经济技术开发区
(0431) 463 0011, www.cetdz.com.cn
Major Industries: Automotive components, corn processing, photoelectronics and electronics, biopharmaceutical, new materials
**Changchun High-Tech Industrial
Development Zone**
长春高科技产业开发区
(0431) 553 0623
www.chida.gov.cn
Major Industries:
Automotive, biopharmaceutical,
photoelectronics, new materials
Huichun Export Processing Zone
珲春出口加工区
(0440) 761 2219
www.hcexport.com
Major Industries:
Foodstuffs, new materials

Exhibition centers

**Changchun International Conven-
tion & Exhibition Center**
100 Huizhan Dajie, Changchun
(0431) 460 6101
www.ccicec.com

Jilin City 吉林市

Telephone prefix: 0432
Population: 4.51 million
Bank of China: 1 Shenzhen Da Dao

Located about 700 kilometers northeast of Beijing, Jilin translates to "lucky forest". As with Changchun, which means "long spring", the name is almost certainly meant to be loaded with irony.

The largest enterprise in Jilin is the state-owned Jilin Paper Company, which engages in electric power generation along with papermaking. Three power stations close to Jilin City along the Songhua River provide 83.3% of the total hydroelectric power in the northeast, and also provide power to North Korea.

The Jilin Ferroalloy Factory is China's oldest and largest metallurgy plant and the Jilin Carbon Factory is the country's largest, exporting carbon and graphite products to 26 countries. The city has its own New and High-tech Industries Development Zone and the government has laid out a series of regulations and preferential policies to encourage foreign investment.

One of Jilin's foremost claims to fame is its Meteor Shower Museum, which houses the largest piece of a meteorite ever found anywhere in the world.

Hotels

Century Hotel Jilin
★★★★★
77 Jilin Dajie, (0432) 216 8888
www.centuryhotel.com.cn
Standard room: RMB484
Credit Cards:
Visa, Master Card, JCB, American Express, Domestic Cards
Empire Garden Hotel
★★★★★
10 Liaoning Lu, North Section Jiefang Dajie, (0432) 216 9999
www.eghotel.com

Standard room: RMB328
Credit Cards:
Visa, Master Card, JCB, American Express, Domestic Cards
Jilin Crystal Hotel
★★★★
29 Longtan Dajie, (0432) 398 6200
www.crystal-hotel.com.cn
Credit Cards:
Visa, Master Card, JCB, American Express, Domestic Cards
Shen Zhou Hotel
★★★
1 Songjiang Dong Lu
(0432) 216 1000
www.jlszhotel.com
Standard room: RMB266
Credit Cards:
Visa, Master Card, JCB, American Express, Domestic Cards

Restaurants

Cafe
Rhine Cafe 莱茵河咖啡厅
Yinlong Building, 8 Jiefang Da Lu
(0432) 209 3555
Jingfu Palace 竞福宫
Jiefang Da Lu, (0432) 202 9999
Chinese
Zhuangjiayuan 庄稼院饭店
48 Jilin Dajie, (0432) 467 8315
Papa's 啪啪斯
Beiqi Building, 8-18 Jiefang Da Lu
(0432) 245 8884

Hospitals

Jilin Municipal Hospital
吉林市医院
57 Shanghai Lu, (0432) 256 9654

Bookstores

Xinhua Bookstore 吉林市新华书店
512 Chongqing Lu
(0431) 249 9881

Industrial parks

Jilin High-Tech Industrial Development Zone
吉林高新技术产业开发区
(0432) 479 8019
www.jlhitech.com
Major Industries:
Machinery, electronics, biopharmaceutical, new materials

Liaoning

Population: 42.21 million
Area: 145,700 sq km
Capital: Shenyang
Airports: Dalian, Shenyang, Jinzhou, Dandong, Zhaoyang, Changhai
Ports: Dalian, Yinkou, Dandong
Border crossings: Dandong, Taipingwan

Jutting out between the Bohai Sea and the Yellow Sea, Liaoning is located on the coast of China's northeast region. Bordering North Korea to the east, Jilin and Inner Mongolia to the North, and Hebei to the west, Liaoning experiences a more balanced climate than its inland neighbors due to its maritime location, although it is still quite cold in the winter.

The main ethnic group is Han Chinese, but the province also includes Manchu, Mongolian, Hui,

Korean, Sibo and many official ethnicities amongst its population. The Manchurian Qing Dynasty (1644-1911) originated here, and after conquering the rest of China they sealed off the area to all non-Manchus until the mid-19th century when the declining power of the central administration made it impossible to stop the flow of Han Chinese into Manchuria.

The region came under the sway of Russia and Japan in the late nineteenth century, but Russia's defeat in the war of 1904-5 gave Japan the upper hand. From then until the end of World War II, Japan ruled the territory, investing massively in industrial infrastructure. Liaoning was incorporated into the Japan's Manchukuo state in 1932 and was the site of a decisive battle between the Communists and Nationalists in 1948.

After their victory in 1949, the communists built on the existing heavy industry infrastructure, and Liaoning became China's number one producer of steel, cement and crude oil. The province is rich in mineral resources, especially iron ore and coal, with the largest iron ore mines in the country located at Anshan and Benxi.

Besides iron and coal, Liaoning also has the country's largest reserves of boron, magnetite, diamonds and jade. It is also an important source of petroleum and natural gas. In terms of agriculture, the main products include maize, Chinese sorghum, soybeans and cotton. As probably China's most important industrial base, the leading industries in the province include petrochemicals, iron and steel, coal, metallurgy, construction materials, machinery, electronics and textiles.

Liaoning has probably fared the worst of all China's provinces in the reform process of the past two decades as its heavy industry has been gradually dismantled. The area has seen widespread social unrest triggered by massive layoffs in inefficient state-owned industrial enterprises.

The situation led to a central government initiative begun in 2003 and known as the "revitalize the northeast" campaign, offering tax breaks and infrastructure investment to encourage foreign and domestic investment. As a result, actual foreign direct investment in Liaoning jumped 91% in 2004, to reach US$654 million, with Japanese investors leading the way. Recent major investors include Pepsi and Mitsubishi Heavy Industries.

In 2005 the government announced it planned to spend US$8.7 billion on port facilities in the province, aiming to upgrade its capacity to 579 billion tons by 2010.

Liaoning Economic Data			
	2005	2004	Change (%)
GGDP (RMB bn)	800.9	667.2	20.0
GDP per capita (RMB)	18,983	16,297	16.5
Exports (US$ bn)	23.44	18.92	23.89
Imports (US$ bn)	17.57	15.52	13.21
Cars per 100 households	1.16	0.42	176.19
PCs per 100 households	32.88	27.87	17.98

Shenyang 沈阳

Telephone prefix: 024
Population: 7.40 million
Bank of China: 9 Yan'an Lu

The provincial capital city of Shenyang is an hour's flight or a nine-hour train ride from Beijing. This large industrial city serves as a railway junction and a banking center for the region. Established as early as the 11th century as a trading center for nomads, the city was the original capital of the Manchus, who went on to conquer all of China and establish the Qing dynasty in 1644. The city was known as Mukden and was a center of the ginseng trade. You can still visit the original Manchu palace, which served as the model for the Forbidden City in Beijing.

The city was occupied by the Russians around the turn of the century while they were building the South Manchurian railway and was a key battleground during the Sino-Japanese (1894-95) and Russo-Japanese (1904-05) Wars. Since the communist victory in 1949 the city's population has increased tenfold.

The major pillars of Shenyang's economy are heavy industry, automobiles, and manufacturing. Shenyang Aircraft Corporation, with 30,000 employees, has emerged as China's largest fighter aircraft producer since its establishment in 1953.

Following the lead of many other Chinese cities, Shenyang will soon introduce the first of what will eventually be a multiple-line subway.

Shenyang Taoxian International Airport has flights to all major domestic cities as well as several regional international destinations.

Shenyang Economic Data

GDP 2005 (RMB bn)	208.41
Disposable income 2005 (RMB)	10,098

Hotels

InterContinental Shenyang
★★★★★
208 Nanjing Bei Jie, Heping
(024) 2334 1999
Standard room: RMB1,500
Credit Cards: Visa, Master Card, American Express, Domestic Cards

Kempinski Hotel Shenyang
★★★★★
109 Qingnian Dajie, (024) 2298 8988
Standard room: RMB1,552
Credit Cards: Visa, Master Card, JCB, American Express, Domestic Cards

Shenyang Green Island Forest Park Hotel
★★★★★
Taoxian Airport Exit, Shenyang Benxi Expressway
(024) 8957 9797
Credit Cards: Domestic Cards

Shenyang Marriott Hotel
★★★★★
388 Qingnian Dajie, Heping
(024) 2388 3456
Standard room: RMB868
Credit Cards: Visa, Master Card, JCB, American Express

Sheraton Shenyang Lido Hotel
★★★★★
386 Qingnian Dajie, Heping
(024) 2318 8888
Standard room:
RMB766 +15% Surcharge
Credit Cards: Visa, Master Card,

JCB, American Express
Sunrise International Hotel
★★★★★
10 Chang'an Lu, Dadong
(024) 2435 9999
Standard room: RMB515
Credit Cards:
Visa, Master Card, JCB, American
Express, Domestic Cards
Gloria Plaza Hotel Shenyang
★★★★
32 Yingbin Jie, Beizhan, Shenhe
(024) 2252 8855
Standard room: RMB458
Credit Cards:
Visa, Master Card, JCB, American
Express, Domestic Cards
Golden Hotel Shenyang
★★★★
52 Qingnian Dajie, Shenhe
(024) 2281 8888, *www.goldensy.com.cn*
Standard room:
RMB747 +15% Surcharge
Credit Cards: Visa, Master Card,
JCB, American Express
Green Hotel
★★★★
72 Beizhan Lu, Shenhe
(024) 2257 6688
www.greenhotel.com.cn
Standard room: RMB358
Credit Cards:
Visa, Master Card, JCB, American
Express, Domestic Cards
Holiday Inn City Centre Shenyang
★★★★
204 Nanjing Bei Jie, Heping
(024) 2334 1888
Standard room: RMB1,200
Credit Cards: Visa, Master Card,
American Express, Domestic Cards
Hotel Eletel
★★★★

235 Zhongjie Lu, (024) 3130 7777
Standard room: RMB638
Credit Cards: Visa, Master Card,
JCB, American Express
New World Hotel Shenyang
★★★★
2 Nanjing Nan Jie, Heping
(024) 2386 9888
Credit Cards: Visa, Master Card, JCB,
American Express, Domestic Cards
Shenyang Kingdom Hotel
★★★★
189 Taiyuan Nan Jie, Heping
(024) 2351 0888
www.kingdomhotel.cn
Standard room: RMB368
Credit Cards: Visa, Master Card,
JCB, American Express
Times Plaza Hotel Shenyang
★★★★
99 Beizhan Lu, (024) 2253 2828
Credit Cards: Visa, Master Card, JCB,
American Express, Domestic Cards
Traders Hotel Shenyang
★★★★
68 Zhonghua Lu, Heping
(024) 2341 2288, *www.shangri-la.com*
Standard room:
RMB530 +15% Surcharge
Credit Cards:
Visa, Master Card, JCB, American
Express, Domestic Cards
Gloria Inn Shenyang
★★★
8 Wenhua Dong Lu, Dongling
(024) 2456 8866
Standard room: RMB258
Credit Cards:
Visa, Master Card, JCB, American
Express, Domestic Cards
Liaoning Trade Union Mansion
★★★
40 Chongshan Dong Lu, Huanggu

(024) 6223 5999, *www.lnghds.com*
Standard room: RMB398
Credit Cards: Visa, Master Card,
JCB, Domestic Cards

Restaurants

Pizza
Summer Christmas 夏日圣诞
99 Xita Jie, (024) 2347 4704
American
Traders Cafe 商贸咖啡厅
68 Zhong Hua Lu (024) 2341 2288
Chinese
Shang Palace 香宫
68 Zhong Hua Lu, (024) 2341 2288
Seafood
Sampan Seafood Restaurant 中餐厅
32 Yinbin Jie (Gloria Plaza Hotel)
(024) 2252 8855
Western
Marriott Cafe 万豪咖啡厅
388 Qingnian Dajie (Marriott Hotel),
(024) 2388 3456
Japanese
Mikado 御门铁板烧
388 Qingnian Dajie (Marriott Hotel),
(024) 2388 3456

Bars & Clubs

Mazza 回廊吧
Sheraton Hotel
San Marco 圣马可
21 Shisiwei Lu (opposite the American Consulate)

Hospitals

China Medical University First Affiliated Hospital
中国医科大学附属第一医院
155 Nanjing Bei Jie, (024) 2326 9368
China Medical University Second Affiliated Hospital
中国医科大学附属第二医院

36 Sanhao Jie, (024) 8395 6220
Liaoning People's Hospital
辽宁省人民医院
33 Wenyi Lu, (024) 2414 7900

Bookstores

Xinhua Bookstore 沈阳新华书店
81 Guangzhou Jie, (024) 2285 1681

Consulates

Japan 日本
50 Shisiwei Lu, (024) 2322 7492
Korea 韩国
13/F-14/F Mingzhe Building
(024) 2385 7820
USA 美国
31 Shisanwai Nan Lu
(024) 2322 3927

Industrial parks

Shenyang High-Tech Industrial
沈阳高新技术产业开发区
(024) 2378 7666, *www.hunnan.gov.cn*
Major Industries:
Electronics, information technology
Dandong Border Economic Area
丹东边境经济合作区
(0415) 312 7399, *www.dbecz.ddptt.ln.cn*
Major Industries: Food supplies, trade
Shenyang Economic & Technological Development Zone
沈阳经济技术开发区
(024) 2581 1100, *www.sydz.gov.cn*
Major Industries: Automotive parts,
chemicals, foodstuffs and medicine
Shenyang Exporting Processing Zone
沈阳出口加工区
(024) 2469 9098
www.syepz.gov.cn

Exhibition centers

Liaoning Industry Exhibition Hall
Caita Jie, (024) 2389 2990

Dalian 大连

Telephone prefix: 0411
Population: 6.13 million
Bank of China: 9 Yan'an Lu

Dalian is one of the most pleasant and prosperous cities in China. With only 100 years or so of history, it spent more than half a century under colonial rule, first under the Russians and then under the Japanese, who ruled the city for 40 years. Today's Dalian, surrounded on three sides by the Yellow Sea, incorporates the major seaport town at the southwestern tip of the Liaodong peninsula (previously known as Port Arthur) and Dalian port on Korea Bay. The city is free of ice all year round and features an important naval base, which guards the entrance to the gulf of Bohai, and the main commercial port for industrialized northeast China.

Dalian is connected by pipeline to the Daqing oil field and since the 1970s has traditionally served as the leading petroleum-exporting point in the country. It can accommodate supertankers and also boasts the largest shipbuilding yards in the country.

Built up in the 1950s and 1960s as a center for heavy industry, Dalian's main manufactured goods include refined petroleum, chemicals, fertilizer, machinery, iron and steel, and transportation equipment. The State Council opened the city to foreign investment and economic reform in 1984, long before such reforms had begun in many other parts of the country, and the city has flourished ever since.

The beautiful Japanese and Russian colonial architecture, relatively mild climate and thriving economy make Dalian the closest thing to a popular coastal resort town in China. These attributes make the city a popular destination for foreign and domestic investors alike. The city boasts an abundance of great hotels and entertainment spots.

DESTINATIONS

Hotels

Best Western Premier Dalian Harbour View Hotel
★★★★★
2 Gangwan Jie, Zhongshan
(0411) 8272 8888
Standard room: RMB728
Credit Cards:
Visa, Master Card, JCB

Furama Hotel Dalian
★★★★★
60 Renmin Lu, (0411) 8263 0888
www.furama.com
Credit Cards:
Visa, Master Card, JCB, American Express, Domestic Cards

Furama Nanshan Garden Hotel
★★★★★
56 Fenglin Jie, (0411) 8271 5555
www.nanshangardenhotel.com
Standard room:
RMB458 +15% Surcharge
Credit Cards: Visa, Master Card, JCB

Hotel Nikko Dalian
★★★★★
123 Changjiang Lu, Zhongshan
(0411) 8252 9999
www.orientalpalace.com.cn
Standard room: RMB935
Credit Cards: Visa, Master Card, JCB, American Express

Kempinski Hotel Dalian
★★★★★
92 Jiefang Lu, Zhongshan
(0411) 8259 8888
www.kempinski.com
Standard room: RMB676
Credit Cards:
Visa, Master Card, JCB, American Express, Domestic Cards

Shangri-La Hotel Dalian
★★★★★
66 Renmin Lu, (0411) 8252 5000

Credit Cards: Visa, Master Card, JCB, American Express

Somerset Harbour Court Dalian
★★★★★
55 Renmin Lu, Zhongshan
(0411) 8899 1888
Credit Cards:
Visa, Master Card, JCB, American Express, Domestic Cards

Swissotel Dalian
★★★★★
21 Wuhui Lu, Zhongshan
(0411) 8230 3388
Standard room: RMB1,453
Credit Cards: Visa, Master Card, JCB, American Express

Air China Hotel Dalian
★★★★
578 Zhongshan Lu, Shahekou
(0411) 8480 1188
Credit Cards:
Visa, Master Card, JCB, American Express, Domestic Cards

Baoyue Hotel
★★★★
2 Gangwan Jie, Zhongshan
(0411) 8273 6666
www.baoyuehotel.cn
Standard room: RMB258
Credit Cards:
Visa, Master Card, JCB, American Express, Domestic Cards

Central Plaza Hotel Dalian
★★★★
145 Zhongshan Lu, Xigang
(0411) 8369 9988
www.xiangzhouhotel.com
Standard room: RMB398
Credit Cards:
Visa, Master Card, JCB, American Express, Domestic Cards

Dalian Bohai Pearl Hotel
★★★★

8 Shengli Square, Zhongshan
(0411) 8882 8333
Credit Cards:
Visa, Master Card, American
Express, Domestic Cards
Dalian East Hotel
★★★★
67 Liaohe Xi Lu, Eco. & Tech. Dev.
Zone, (0411) 8761 2988
Standard room: RMB690
Credit Cards: Visa, Master Card, JCB
Dalian Regent (Jasper) Hotel
★★★★
12 Hutan Jie, Zhongshan
(0411) 8289 2811
www.jasperhotels.com.cn
Standard room: RMB680
Credit Cards: Visa, Master Card,
JCB, American Express
Dalian Sea Horizon Hotel
★★★★
81 Binhai Xi Lu, Xigang
(0411) 8240 3399

Standard room: RMB268
Credit Cards:
Visa, Master Card, JCB, American
Express, Domestic Cards
Dalian Yushengyuan International
Hotel
★★★★
6 Taiyuan Jie, Shahekou
(0411) 8882 8888
www.ysyhotel.com
Credit Cards: Visa, Master Card, JCB
Dalian Zhongxia Hotel
★★★★
222 Bayi Lu, Xigang, (0411) 8249 2222
www.zhongxiahotel.com
Standard room: RMB580
Credit Cards: Visa, Master Card,
JCB, American Express
Delight Hotel Dalian
★★★★
81 Renmin Lu, (0411) 8280 9000
Standard room: RMB898
Credit Cards: Visa, Master Card,

JCB, American Express

Gloria Plaza Hotel Dalian

★★★★

5 Yide Jie, Zhongshan

(0411) 8280 8855

Standard room: RMB398

Credit Cards: Visa, Master Card,

JCB, American Express

Inn Fine Hotel

★★★★

135 Jinma Lu, (0411) 8896 8888

Credit Cards:

Visa, Master Card, JCB, American

Express, Domestic Cards

Lee Wan Hotel

★★★★

8 Minzhu Square, Zhongshan

(0411) 8212 3651

www.dlleewan.com

Credit Cards:

Visa, Master Card, JCB, American

Express, Domestic Cards

Merro Hotel Dalian

★★★★

112 Zhongshan Lu, Zhongshan

(0411) 8363 1991

Standard room: RMB268

Credit Cards:

Visa, Master Card, JCB, American

Express, Domestic Cards

Ramada Hotel Dalian

★★★★

18 Victory Plaza, Zhongshan

(0411) 8280 8888

www.ramada.com

Credit Cards:

Visa, Master Card, JCB, American

Express, Domestic Cards

The Golden Shine International

Hotel

★★★★

53 Wuwu Lu, Zhongshan

(0411) 8272 7999

www.jiaxinhotel.com

Standard room: RMB258, 368

Credit Cards: Visa, Master Card,

JCB, American Express

Wanda International Hotel Dalian

★★★★

539 Changjiang Lu, Xigang

(0411) 8362 8888

Standard room: RMB408

Credit Cards:

Visa, Master Card, JCB, American

Express, Domestic Cards

Xinhaitian International Hotel

★★★★

136 Huanghai Xi Lu, Eco. & Tech.

Dev. Zone, (0411) 8762 9999

Credit Cards:

Visa, Master Card, JCB, American

Express, Domestic Cards

Zhongshan Parkwin Hotel Dalian

★★★★

3-5 Jiefang Lu, Zhongshan

(0411) 8281 2888

www.zs-hotel.com

Standard room: RMB460

Credit Cards:

Visa, Master Card, JCB, American

Express, Domestic Cards

Da Lian Hotel

★★★

4 Zhongshan Square

(0411) 8263 3111

www.dl-hotel.com

Standard room: RMB350

Credit Cards:

Visa, Master Card, JCB, American

Express, Domestic Cards

Dalian Everbright Hotel

★★★

99 Liaohe Xi Lu, (0411) 8733 8888

www.everbright-hotel.com

Credit Cards:

Visa, Master Card, JCB, American

Express, Domestic Cards
Dalian Norinco Hotel
★★★
19 Renmin Lu, Zhongshan
(0411) 8281 8388
www.norinco-hotel.com
Standard room: RMB338
Credit Cards: Visa, Master Card,
JCB, American Express

Restaurants

Pizza
Pizza King Italian Restaurant
比萨王意式餐厅
122 Youhao Lu
(0411) 8280 6888
Pizza King Italian Restaurant
比萨王意式餐厅
122 Youhao Lu, (0411) 8280 6888
Japanese
Tairyo Jroup 大渔日本料理
2 Luxun Lu, Zhongshan Square
(0411) 8210 9060
Jujiuwu Wuzang
居酒屋武藏日本料理店

36 Changjiang Lu, (0411) 8263 2825
Korean
Qiying 奇莹
18 Minyi Jie, (0411) 8282 0055
Thai
Baishiwei Restaurant
百世威鱼翅酒楼
78 Luxun Lu, (0411) 8272 7661
Seafood
Tian Tian Yu Gang 天天渔港酒楼
45 Tongtai Dajie
(0411) 8450 9000
26 Huachang Jie
(0411) 8450 9111
Chinese
Shuangshengyuan 双盛园
1 Anle Jie, (0411) 8264 7800
International
Harbour View Restaurant
大连海景酒店
2 Gangwan Jie, Zhongshan district
(0411) 8272 8888
New Orient Delicacies City
新东方美食城
3 Gangwan Square, (0411) 8270 6999

DESTINATIONS

Western/buffet
West Bank Restaurant 左岸西餐厅
45/E Xinghai Square
(0411) 8480 3188

Bars & Clubs
ZZ TOP 最最音乐酒吧
1/F, 108 Nanshan Lu
Fashion Bar 时尚酒吧
8/F, 21 Wuhui Lu
Hans Bar 汉斯啤酒屋
268 Jiefang Lu
F.A.T.S 肥吧
Shangri-La Hotel
Hollywood Café & Pub 好莱坞影城
1/F Royal Gourmet Court, Victory
Plaza

Hospitals
Dalian Railway Hospital
大连铁路医院
6 Jiefang Jie, (0411) 6289 3015
First Affiliated Hospital of Dalian
Medical College
大连医科大学附属第一医院
222 Zhongshan Lu, (0411) 8363 5963
Dalian Friendship Hospital
大连市友谊医院
8 Sanba Square, (0411) 8271 8822

Bookstores
Xinhua Bookstore 大连市新华书店
69 Tongxing Jie, (0411) 8265 4448

Consulates
Japan 日本
3/F, 147 Zhongshan Lu
(0411) 8370 4077

Industrial parks
Dalian Economic & Technological
Development Zone
大连经济技术开发区
(0411) 8762 2666, *www.ddz.gov.cn*
Major Industries:
Telecommunications, construction
materials, heavy industry
Dalian Export Processing Zone
大连出口加工区
(0411) 8762 2666, *www.dlftz.gov.cn*
Major Industries:
Electronics, plastics, machinery
Dalian Free Trade Zone
大连保税区
(0411) 8730 2951
www.dlftz.gov.cni
Major Industries:
International trade, export process-
ing, bonded warehousing
Dalian High-Tech. Industrial
Development Zone
大连高新技术产业开发区
(0411) 8479 3643
www.dlhitech.gov.cn
Major Industries:
Telecommunications, construction
materials, heavy industry

Exhibition centers
Xinghai Exhibition Center
18 Huizhan Lu, Dalian
(0411) 8480 9777
www.exhibition.com.cn

Anshan 鞍山

Telephone prefix: 0412
Population: 3.61 million
Bank of China: 4 Eryaojiu Lu

With a population of 3.6 million, Anshan is located southwest of Shenyang. Known primarily for steel and iron production, Anshan was once called the steel capital of China. It has a troubled history. Anshan was destroyed during the Boxer Rebellion, and again in the Russo-Japanese War; it was bombed by the Americans and looted by the Soviets in World War II before being taken by the Communists under Mao in 1948.

The city is well known for its many natural hot springs, as well as the Anshan Jade Buddha, a statue of Buddha – nearly eight meters tall – made entirely of jade.

Hotels

Anshan World Hotel
★★★★
1 Minfeng Lane, Tiedong
(0412) 298 8888
Credit Cards:
Visa, Master Card, JCB, American Express, Domestic Cards
Haicheng Hotel
★★★★
18 Beishuncheng Lu, Beiguan Jie
(0412) 322 0888
www.hchotel.com
Credit Cards:
Visa, Master Card, JCB, American Express, Domestic Cards

Restaurants

International

Anshan International Hotel
鞍山国际大酒店
219 Yuanlin Lu
(0412) 555 5888
Cantonese
Shitongtian Restaurant
食通天大酒店
37 Zhanqian Jie
(0412) 224 9028
Jiaozi
Laobian Dumpling Restaurant
老边饺子馆
919 Wuyi Lu
(0412) 553 3008
Barbeque
Sanbao Barbecue 三宝烧烤
36-12 Bagua Jie, near Xin Yijia
Supermarket, (0412) 292 8688

Hospitals

Anshan Angang Tiedong Hospital
鞍山鞍刚铁东医院
3 Jiankang Jie
(0412) 631 3773
Anshan Angang Tiexi Hospital
鞍山鞍刚铁西医院
166 Renmin Lu, (0412) 881 3788

Bookstores

Xinhua Bookstore
鞍山市新华书店
Wenhua Jie, Tiedong District
(0412) 222 6274

Industrial parks

Anshan High-Tech Industrial Development Zone
鞍山高新技术产业开发区
(0412) 521 2000
www.asht-zone.gov.cn
Major Industries:
New materials, telecommunications, biopharmaceutical

Ningxia

Population: 5.96 million
Area: 66,400 sq km
Capital: Yinchuan
Airports: Yinchuan

One of the country's smallest administrative units, comprising 66,400 sq km of mostly desert or semi-desert and a thin strip of arable land following the Yellow River, Ningxia is rich in mineral resources. But economic development has been hindered by its remote location and underdeveloped transport and communications infrastructure.

Ningxia, now known officially

as the Ningxia Hui Autonomous Region, was once part of the Silk Road connecting China with Central Asia and Europe, and its people to some extent reflect that legacy. Roughly one-third of the population is Hui minority, descendants of Persian traders who came to China in the Tang dynasty nearly 2,000 years ago. The Hui people are almost indistinguishable from Han Chinese in appearance, but they are usually devout Muslims.

This is an isolated and mostly desolate region. Yinchuan, the capital and largest city in Ningxia, has less than a million people, making it China's smallest provincial capital after Lhasa. It is 500 km from the nearest major city. The primary environmental challenge is severe water shortage, and the already harsh environment is becoming less hospitable due to increasing erosion and desertification, largely due to overgrazing by nomadic herders. A ban on nomadic herding was passed in 2003 in an attempt to improve the situation.

Ningxia has sizable deposits of natural gas, coal, quartz and tantalum, an important material in the manufacturing of silicon chips.

More than 80% of China's domestic tantalum production occurs in Ningxia. The region covers part of the Erdos Basin, a loess depression that China National Petroleum Corp has estimated to contain 2.85 billion tons of oil and gas resources.

However, the exploitation of these resources is limited by Ningxia's poor transportation links: the Yellow River is too shallow here for large vessels, and the highway network is still under construction. There is a one-line train track linking Yinchuan with Xi'an in one direction and Lanzhou in the other. Yinchuan airport is large and new, and has flights to Beijing and Shanghai.

Foreign JVs are as yet a rarity, but some investment is taking place. In July 2006, International Finance Corporation agreed to invest US$19.5 million in Ningxia Darong Chemicals and Metallurgy to expand a calcium cyanamide and dicyandiamide production facility, and Royal Dutch Shell was exploring the possibility of a large coal-to-liquid fuel plant in western Ningxia, expected to cost some US$5 billion – US$6 billion.

Ningxia Economic Data			
	2005	2004	Change (%)
GDP (RMB bn)	60.6	53.7	12.8
GDP per capita (RMB)	10,239	7,880	29.9
Exports (US$ bn)	0.69	0.65	6.15
Imports (US$ bn)	0.28	0.26	7.69
Cars per 100 households	1.27	0.36	252.78
PCs per 100 households	23.15	15.04	53.92

Yinchuan 银川
Telephone prefix: 0951
Population: 1.41 million
Bank of China: 170 Jiefang Xi Jie

Literally meaning "Silver River", Yinchuan is one of China's more spartan capitals, with winter temperatures dipping as low as -20°C. But Yinchuan's remoteness is a blessing of sorts: it has some of the cleanest air of any city in China.

Yinchuan is located about 20km west of the Yellow River and is divided into an old city closer to the river, and a new city 10km further to the west. As with many Chinese cities that have become split this way, the old city is more pleasant and has more of a cohesive feel, while the new section is more reminiscent of a border town. Most of the old city is being demolished and modernized – and now of course has a KFC outlet and other chain stores.

Yinchuan's advantages from a for-eign investment perspective are low wages, a clean environment, tourist resources and a local government eager for investment. The main disadvantage is the tyranny of distance. A lot of work has been done on the infrastructure of the city and its environs. The airport expressway is top-class, and the airport terminal itself is as good as any in provincial China. But road and rail networks still leave something to be desired, though the government is working to improve them.

Remember that Yinchuan, and all of Ningxia, is an ancient home of Chinese Muslims. As such, certain places will frown upon alcohol and pork, among other things. It is important to respect the local culture.

Hotels

Ningxia International Hotel
★★★★★
365 Beijing Dong Lu, (0951) 672 8688
www.nx-hotel.com
Credit Cards:
Visa, Master Card, JCB, American Express, Domestic Cards
Apollo Hotel Yinchuan China
★★★★
123 Beijing Dong Lu, (0951) 786 8888
Standard room: RMB538
Credit Cards: Visa, Master Card, JCB, American Express
Shahu Hotel
★★★
58 Wenhua Xi Jie, Xingqing
(0951) 501 2128
www.nxshahu.com
Credit Cards:
Visa, Master Card, Domestic Cards

Qinghai

Population: 5.43 million
Area: 720,000 sq km
Capital: Xining
Airports: Xining

Qinghai, a sparsely populated province of about 5 million, is primarily known for its harsh terrain and extreme weather. Due to its high elevation (an average of more than 3,000 meters above sea level), along with Tibet it constitutes the region often referred to as the 'roof of the world'. More than half of Qinghai rises between 4,000 and 5,000 meter, and the province is home to the upper reaches of the Yangtze, Yellow and Lancang (Mekong) Rivers.

Qinghai's history, like its geography and culture, is closely linked to that of Tibet. Historically, the region was part of Tibet's Amdo province and it was not until 1928 that the region was brought under Chinese control. Almost half of Qinghai's population belongs to ethnic minorities, including Tibetans, Hui, Mongolians, Tu and Salars. In the 1960s and 1970s it became known as a place of exile, the location of vast camps to which criminals and people with unacceptable political backgrounds were shipped in the Cultural Revolution period. By the early 1980s, the system was largely dismantled.

Although one of the poorest regions in China's economically underdeveloped west, Qinghai is rich in energy resources and its numerous rivers are increasingly being tapped for hydroelectric power. The Qaidam Basin, which covers 250,000 sq km, is China's fourth-largest gas field and is expected to become China's most important energy reserve base, with oil reserves of 4.1 billion tons and proven gas reserves of 150 billion cubic meters. Qinghai is also a major producer of salt, chemicals and fertilizers.

Approximately half of Qinghai is grassland – fundamental to the province's animal husbandry and grain production – mostly found in the northeastern regions. Qinghai produces large numbers of sheep, yaks and horses as well as

0   km   130

Delingha
XINING
Gonghe   Ping'an
Tongren
Maqin

DESTINATIONS

secondary products including wool, mutton, beef, leather, and sausage casings. Its main agricultural products include spring wheat, highland barley, potatoes, beans and rapeseed.

Foreign investment in the province has been limited to a handful of mining and power projects and investment in Xining's service sector. The economy is likely to be boosted by the Qinghai-Tibet railway, which was completed in 2006.

The province has suffered considerable environmental degradation in recent decades, especially soil erosion and water pollution. Beijing is consequently pursuing a policy of development at minimal cost to the environment as well as implementing programs aimed at environmental regeneration.

Qinghai Economic Data			
	2005	2004	Change (%)
GDP (RMB bn)	54.3	46.6	16.5
GDP per capita (RMB)	10,045	8,606	16.7
Exports (US$ bn)	0.32	0.46	-30.43
Imports (US$ bn)	0.09	0.12	-25.00
Cars per 100 households	1.39	0.67	107.46
PCs per 100 households	21.68	16.46	31.71

Xining 西宁

Telephone prefix: 0971
Population: 2.1 million
Bank of China: 218 Dongguan Jie

Xining, at an altitude of 2,260 meters, is a bleak and uninteresting city, beset with problems of traffic and pollution. Trips outside town include Taer Si – located 25 km southeast of town – one of the most famous Tibetan monasteries.

Xining served for centuries as a major commercial center on the road to Tibet before coming under the Han Chinese sphere of influence.

Xining's economy largely serves the processing needs of northeast Qinghai's agricultural region, milling wheat, spinning wool and packing meat. A regional center for heavy industry and chemical production, the city also counts steel, machinery, textiles and chemicals among its major products.

One of Qinghai's best-known destinations is Qinghai Lake, China's

largest saltwater lake, located 150 km west of Xining.

Xining hosts an annual international cycling competition billed as the highest-altitude cycling competition in the world.

Xining Economic Data	
GDP 2005 (RMB bn)	20.63
Disposable income 2005 (RMB)	8,530

Hotels

Qinghai Hotel
★★★★
158 Huanghe Lu, (0971) 614 4888
www.qhhotel.com
Credit Cards:
Visa, Master Card, JCB, American Express, Domestic Cards
Jian Yin Hotel
★★★★
55 Xi Dajie, (0971) 826 1888
Standard room: RMB338
Xining Hotel
★★★★
348 Qiyi Lu, (0971) 845 8701
Standard room: RMB280

Restaurants

Muslim
Xiao Yuan Men 小圆门美食宫
188 Dongguan Dajie, (0971) 812 5529
Shalihai Meishi Cheng
沙力海美食城
491 Qiyi Lu, (0971) 821 5426
Cantonese/Hunan/seafood
Private Cuisine 老厨房私房菜
Xining Hotel, 348 Qiyi Lu
(0971) 845 4785
Tibetan
Suji Nima Tibetan Flavor
苏姬尼玛藏餐风情宫
1 Huanghe Lu, (0971) 610 2282

Hospitals

Qinghai Provincial People's Hospital 青海省人民医院
441 Gonghe Lu, (0971) 817 7911
Red Cross Hospital of Qinghai
青海红十字医院
55 Xi Dajie, (0971) 825 2601

Bookstores

Xinhua Bookstore 西宁市新华书店
71 Dongguan Dajie, (0971) 814 7780

Industrial parks

Xining Economic & Technological Development Zone
西宁经济技术开发区
(0971) 812 5306
www.xnkfq.com
Major Industries: Ecological protection, new high technologies, new materials and information technology

Shaanxi

Population: 37.20 million
Area: 205, 600 sq km
Capital: Xi'an
Airports: Xi'an, Xianyang, Yan'an, Hanzhong

Located in central China and encompassing the middle sections of the Yellow River, Shaanxi province is one of the cradles of Chinese civilization. Today its economy is still primarily agricultural, but has aspirations of diversifying. A key area of development is the software industry.

The province is perhaps best known for its provincial capital, Xi'an, which served as the capital city for some of China's oldest dynasties. The city's famous Terracotta Warriors are the chief draw for tourists to the region.

Shaanxi is one of China's most productive agricultural regions, with the Wei and Han River valleys and recently irrigated areas in the province's northwest experiencing the most intensive farming. Shaanxi is a major producer of cotton, rice, corn, millet, sorghum, wheat and sweet potatoes. Livestock, sheep in particular, is also an important part of the rural economy.

Energy is one of the driving factors behind Shaanxi's development. The region holds bountiful mineral resources, particularly coal and iron, and sits upon a portion of the vast Ordos Basin, which holds some of China's largest gas reserves. This is an important source of energy for China's bustling coastal cities, and pipelines between Shaanxi and Beijing and Shanghai have been built to help funnel resources to the more prosperous eastern areas.

Shaanxi Economic Data			
	2005	2004	Change (%)
GDP (RMB bn)	367.6	317.6	15.7
GDP per capita (RMB)	9,899	7,757	27.6
Exports (US$ bn)	3.08	2.40	28.33
Imports (US$ bn)	1.50	1.25	20.00
Cars per 100 households	0.44	0.35	25.71
PCs per 100 households	27.92	23.51	18.76

Xi'an 西安

Telephone prefix: 029
Population: 8.07 million
Bank of China: 38 Juhuayuan

Around 1,500 years ago, the historic city of Xi'an was one of the greatest and richest cities in the world. As the starting point for the Silk Road stretching across Asia to Europe, Xi'an was China's first international commercial center. At a time when Beijing was only a remote trading outpost and Shanghai barely even a fishing village, Xi'an was the largest city in the world, with a population of more than 400,000 (195 BC).

Jump forward a couple of millennia and Xi'an is again positioning itself as a commercial gateway – a strategic entry point to China's underdeveloped west and a key staging post on the "Neo-Eurasia Continental Bridge", effectively a revived version of the old Silk Road.

Located near the geographic center of modern-day China and renowned internationally as the home of the ancient Terracotta Warriors, Xi'an is rebuilding itself as a major engineering center, specializing in aerospace manufacturing, as well as automobiles, textiles and optics.

One of the oldest and most successful foreign investment projects is the Xi'an-Janssen pharmaceutical plant, a subsidiary of the US giant Johnson & Johnson. The US$190 million plant has become the largest pharmaceutical joint venture in China.

Another growing area of foreign interest is Xi'an's status as the center of China's aviation industry. The world's two aviation giants, Boeing and Airbus, both have deals with local manufacturers amid expectations that Xi'an will emerge as a major manufacturing center in the world's fastest-growing aviation market.

Xi'an is most famous around the world for the Terracotta Army. Designed as a permanent guard for the tomb of the first emperor of China, Qin Shihuang, the warriors were only discovered in 1974 by a team of peasants digging a well.

With its rich cultural and archaeological heritage Xi'an has long been one of China's top tourist destinations, a status that has in turn made it one of the best-connected second-tier cities in China. The city's new airport, which opened in October 2003, has flights to almost all of China's major cities as well as several international destinations in Korea, Japan and Southeast Asia.

Meanwhile Xi'an is also at the focus of a rapidly improving expanding highway and rail network with plans to spend more than $15 billion on expressway construction over the next 10 years, reinforcing the city's position as a road transport hub for western China. A subway system, originally slated to begin construction in 2002, has been delayed for years over concerns about disruptions to the city's many archeological sites. Ground has now been broken and Line 1 is scheduled to begin operation in 2009.

Xi'an Economic Data	
GDP 2005 (RMB bn)	127
Disposable income 2005 (RMB)	9,628

Hotels

ANA Grand Castle Hotel Xi'an
★★★★★
12 West Section Huancheng Nan Lu
(029) 8760 8888

Credit Cards: Visa, Master Card, JCB, American Express, Domestic Cards

Grand Mercure on Renmin Square
★★★★★
319 Dongxin Jie, (029) 8792 8888
www.mercure.com
Standard room:
RMB1,093.5 +15% Surcharge
Credit Cards: Visa, Master Card, JCB, American Express, Domestic Cards

Howard Johnson Ginwa Plaza Hotel Xi'an
★★★★★
18 West Section Huancheng Nan Lu
(029) 8842 1111
Standard room:
RMB1,377 +15% Surcharge
Credit Cards: Visa, Master Card, JCB, American Express

Hyatt Regency Xi'an
★★★★★
158 East Dajie, (029) 8769 1234
Standard room: RMB1,400
Credit Cards: Visa, Master Card, JCB, American Express

Jinshi International Hotel
★★★★★
398 East Section Nan'erhuan
(029) 8313 3888
www.jinshi-hotel.com
Standard room: RMB950
Credit Cards: Visa, Master Card, JCB, American Express

Paradise Resort
★★★★★
8 South Section Yanta Nan Lu
(029) 8766 3333
www.xianparadiseresort.com
Credit Cards: Visa, Master Card, JCB, American Express, Domestic Cards

Shangri-La Golden Flower Hotel Xi'an
★★★★★

8 Changle Xi Lu, (029) 8323 2981
Standard room: RMB1,431
Credit Cards: Visa, Master Card,
JCB, American Express
Sheraton Xi'an Hotel
★★★★★
262 Fenggao Dong Lu
(029) 8426 1888
Standard room: RMB1,539
Credit Cards: Visa, Master Card, JCB,
American Express, Domestic Cards
Sofitel on Renmin Square Xi'an
★★★★★
319 Dongxin Jie, (029) 8792 8888
Standard room: RMB1,620
Credit Cards:
Visa, Master Card, JCB, American
Express, Domestic Cards, Diners Club
Wan Nian Hotel
★★★★★
93 Changle Zhong Lu
(029) 8259 6666, *www.wnhotel.com*
Standard room: RMB889
Credit Cards: Visa, Master Card,
JCB, American Express
Aurum International Hotel Xi'an
★★★★

30 Nanxin Jie, (029) 8767 2888
Credit Cards: Visa, Master Card, JCB,
American Express, Domestic Cards
Bell Tower Hotel Xi'an
★★★★
110 Nan Dajie, (029) 8760 0000
Standard room:
RMB850 +15% Surcharge
Credit Cards: Visa, Master Card,
JCB, American Express
Diamond International Hotel
★★★★
177 Jiefang Lu, (029) 8576 8888
www.dihxa.com.cn
Credit Cards: Visa, Master Card, JCB,
American Express, Domestic Cards
Fortune Hotel Xi'an China
★★★★
58 Dongguanzheng Jie
(029) 8248 1666, *www.fulaihotel.com*
Standard room: RMB560
Credit Cards: Visa, Master Card
Fukai Hotel
★★★★
27 Nanxin Jie, (029) 8748 3760
Credit Cards: Visa, Master Card,
American Express, Domestic Cards

Gaosu Shenzhou Hotel
★★★★
9 Huancheng Dong Lu
(029) 8323 3888
www.gsszhotel.com
Standard room: RMB338
Credit Cards: Visa, Master Card,
JCB, American Express

Grand New World Hotel
★★★★
172 Lianhu Lu, (029) 8721 6868
Credit Cards:
Visa, Master Card, American Express

Hotel Royal Garden
★★★★
334 Dong Dajie, (029) 8723 5311
www.hotelroyalgardenxian.com
Standard room: RMB860
Credit Cards: Visa, Master Card,
JCB, American Express

Jianguo Hotel Xi'an
★★★★
2 Huzhu Lu, (029) 8323 8888
www.jghotelxa.com
Credit Cards:
Visa, Master Card, JCB, American
Express, Domestic Cards

Silk Lu Hotel
★★★★
53 Jiefang Lu, (029) 8768 9999
www.xasilkLuhotel.com
Standard room: RMB290
Credit Cards:
Visa, Master Card, American Express

The Good World Hotel Xi'an
★★★★
28 Lianhu Lu, (029) 8735 1188
www.xagwhotel.com
Credit Cards:
Visa, Master Card, JCB, American
Express, Domestic Cards

The Mercure on Renmin Square Xi'an
★★★★
319 Dongxin Jie, (029) 8792 8888
www.mercure.com/asia
Standard room:
RMB810 +15% Surcharge
Credit Cards:
Visa, Master Card, JCB, American
Express, Domestic Cards

Tianyu Gloria Plaza Hotel Xi'an
★★★★
15 Yanta Bei Lu, (029) 8786 8855
Standard room:
RMB830 +15% Surcharge
Credit Cards: Visa, Master Card,
JCB, American Express

Xi'an Garden Hotel
★★★★
40 Yanyin Lu, Dayanta
(029) 8760 1111
www.xagardenhotel.cn
Standard room: RMB890
Credit Cards:
Visa, Master Card, JCB, American
Express, Domestic Cards

Xi'an Hotel
★★★★
58 North Section Chang'an Lu
(029) 8766 6666
www.xahotel.com
Credit Cards:
Visa, Master Card, JCB, American
Express, Domestic Cards

Xi'an Le Garden Hotel
★★★★
8 Laodong Nan Lu, (029) 8426 3388
www.legardens.com
Standard room: RMB350
Credit Cards: Visa, Master Card,
JCB, American Express

Xi'an Purple Mountain Hotel
★★★★
328 Huancheng Xi Lu
(029) 8766 8888
Credit Cards: Visa, Domestic Cards

Dynasty Hotel
★★★★
55 North Section Huancheng Xi Lu
(029) 8862 6262
Standard room: RMB320
Credit Cards: Visa, Master Card,
JCB, American Express

City Hotel Xi'an
★★★
70 Nan Dajie, (029) 8721 9988
www.cityhotelxian.com
Standard room: RMB268
Credit Cards:
Visa, Master Card, JCB, American
Express, Domestic Cards

Gaoxin Business Hotel
★★★
4 Gaoxin'er Lu, (029) 8799 2222
Standard room: RMB436
Credit Cards: Visa, Master Card,
JCB, American Express

New Henderson Hotel
★★★
22 South Section Xi'erhuan Lu
(029) 8811 0088
www.newhendersonhotelxa.com
Credit Cards: Domestic Cards

Siemen Hotel Xi'an
★★★
72 West Section Huancheng Nan Lu
(029) 8469 6998
Standard room: RMB178

Xi'an Hongye Hotel
★★★
137 Hanguang Bei Lu
(029) 8810 8888
www.xahongye.com
Credit Cards: Domestic Cards

Xi'an Melody Hotel
★★★
86 Xi Dajie, (029) 8728 8888
Standard room: RMB498
Credit Cards: Visa, Master Card,

JCB, American Express
Yanlian Hotel
★★★
3 East Section Nan'erhuan Lu
(029) 8523 5000
www.yanlianhotel.com
Standard room: RMB420
Credit Cards: Domestic Cards

Restaurants

Jiaozi
Xian Dumpling Restaurant
西安饺子馆
229 Jiefang Lu, (029) 8742 7004
De Fa Chang Restaurant
大发昌饺子馆
Bell and Drum Tower Square, 3 Xi
Dajie, (029) 8721 4060

Japanese
Orppongi 六本木怀石料理
12 Nan Dajie, (029) 8726 0987

Shaanxi
Qinchao Waguan 秦朝瓦罐
6 Jinhua Bei Lu, (029) 8322 5388

Chinese
Xi'an Restaurant 西安饭庄
298 Dong Dajie, (029) 8768 0618

Bars & Clubs

The Old Gun Club
Dong Dajie
Chaplin's
110 Nan Dadao (Bell Tower Hotel)
Goal Bar 球迷酒吧
26 Fenggao Dong Lu
Rich Coco Bar
洛奇酒吧
11 Building 25, Baojixiang

Hospitals

Xi'an Gaoxin Hospital
西安高新医院
16 Tuanjie Nan Lu, Hi-Tech Develop-

ment Zone, (029) 8833 2020

Shaanxi Provincial People's Hospital 陕西省人民医院

256 Youyi Xi Lu, (029) 8525 1331

Bookstores

Xinhua Bookstore 西安市新华书店

214 Jiefang Lu, (029) 8741 4157

Industrial parks

Xi'an Economic & Technological Development Zone

西安经济技术开发区

(029) 8652 0267

www.xetdz.com.cn

Major Industries:

Electronics, biotechnology

Xi'an High-Tech Industrial Development Zone

西安高新技术产业开发区

(029) 8833 3833

www.xdz.com.cn

Major Industries:

Electronics, telecommunications, information technology

Yangling Agricultural High-Tech Industry Area

杨陵农业高新技术产业开发区

(029) 8701 9676, *www.ylagri.gov.cn*

Major Industries:

Agriculture, forestry, manufacturing, bioengineering, pharmaceutical production, agro-chemicals

Exhibiton centers

Shaanxi International Exhibition Center

14 Chang'an Bei Lu, (029) 8536 1570

www.sn-gzzx.com

Xi'an International Exhibition Center

1 Huizhan Lu

(029) 8533 2211, *www.xagzzx.com*

Xianyang 咸阳

Telephone prefix: 029
Population: 37.20 million

An important city in China's history, Xianyang served as the capital of the state of Qin during the Warring States period (roughly 500 BC until 221 BC) and remained so during the brief Qin Dynasty after that. Foreign investment in the city is small but growing.

Hotels

Imperial Hotel
★★★

60A Weiyang Xi Lu, Qindu

(029) 3331 3368

Credit Cards:

Visa, Master Card, JCB, American Express, Domestic Cards

Shandong

Population: 92.48 million
Area: 153,000 sq km
Capital: Ji'nan
Airports: Qingdao, Ji'nan, Yantai
Ports: Qingdao, Yantai, Weihai, Rizhao

S handong is located in China's northeast, with much of the province constituting a large peninsula that separates the Bohai and Yellow Seas. Located just south of Beijing and west of Japan and Korea, its location makes it very attractive for foreign investment. Like much of the northeastern region, Shandong is rich in natural mineral reserves and has one of the oldest mining histories in China. With a population of over 90 million, it is the second most populous province after Henan.

It is also the last stop for the Yellow River, which deposits the sediment that gives Shandong's soil its richness and supports the province's diverse agriculture. More than 60% of Shandong's area is in the river's flood plain, but droughts and upstream irrigation have hit Shandong's agriculture hard. The Yellow River now dries up on occasion before reaching the sea.

Shandong borders Jiangsu to the south, but its people are decidedly northerners and are known to be warm, friendly and hearty. The region has been inhabited for more than 4,000 years, which contributes to a strong sense of local culture. Shandong people are also known for their ability to imbibe massive amounts of China's national fire water – *baijiu*. Businesspeople attending Chinese banquets in Shandong should be cautious trying to outdrink officials or businessmen here. Shandong cuisine is one of the major schools of Chinese cooking. The style relies on frying and is both greasy and flavorsome.

The region has a rich history, having given birth to many prominent philosophers, administrators and military figures, most prominently the sage Confucius, whose ideas still have a profound effect on most of East Asia. Confucius conceived of a hierarchical structure for society in which children

obey parents, wives obey husbands, ordinary citizens obey officials, and officials obey the king. In return, the superior in each relationship has a responsibility to care for his inferior. In short, benevolent dictatorship as the ideal.

In the late 19th century, the foreign powers were dividing up a degenerate Chinese empire into spheres of influence, and the Germans established rights over Shandong and took out a formal lease on the port of Qingdao (Tsingtao). As a result, there are many examples of German architecture, most prominently railway stations. And of course, the Germans were responsible for the creation of Tsingtao Beer, arguably China's most famous brand.

Ji'nan 济南
Telephone prefix: 0531
Population: 6.42 million
Bank of China: 6 Xianggang Zhong Lu

Ji'nan is the capital of Shandong and with its night markets, tasty food and palpable history, is one of China's more pleasant provincial capitals. But huge swathes of the city have been leveled in recent years to make way for development. The older buildings and roads may have been charming, but they were also squalid and poorly built, so the reconstruction is a mixed blessing. Amongst the modern structures – faced with the standard white tiles and reflective blue glass – survive scattered architectural remnants of the city's brief German period a century ago.

The city's old center has been largely demolished and is now dominated by the massive expanse of Quancheng Square, which covers just under 17 hectares. The square provides a place to sit and people watch

Shandong Economic Data

	2005	2004	Change (%)
GDP (RMB bn)	1851.7	1502.1	23.3
GDP per capita (RMB)	20,096	16,925	18.7
Exports (US$ bn)	46.12	35.86	28.61
Imports (US$ bn)	30.61	24.82	23.33
Cars per 100 households	4.47	2.51	78.09
PCs per 100 households	45.64	37.71	21.03

during the hot summer. Locals tend to go there to cool off, meet up, practice ballroom dancing or fly kites.

Ji'nan is a short drive from the Yellow River. If the weather is agreeable and the river isn't too low, the trip can be a nice day's getaway from the city. Ji'nan doesn't have much in the way of nightlife and cannot compare with Qingdao's flourishing bar scene.

Jinan Economic Data	
GDP 2005 (RMB bn)	187.65
Disposable income 2005 (RMB)	13,578

Hotels

Crowne Plaza Ji'nan
★★★★★
3 Tianditan Jie, Lixia
(0531) 8602 9999
www.ichotelsgroup.com
Standard room: RMB750
Credit Cards: Visa, Master Card, JCB, American Express, Domestic Cards
International Hotel
★★★★★
421 Beiyuan Dajie, (0531) 8591 8888
www.cnlongdu.com
Standard room:
RMB888 +15% Surcharge
Credit Cards: Master Card, JCB
Shandong Hotel
★★★★★
2-1 Ma'anshan Lu, (0531) 8295 8888
www.sdhotel.com.cn
Standard room: RMB880
Credit Cards: Visa, Master Card, JCB, American Express
Sofitel Silver Plaza Ji'nan
★★★★★
66 Luoyuan Dajie, (0531) 8606 8888
Standard room: RMB1,245

Credit Cards: Visa, Master Card, JCB, American Express, Domestic Cards, Dinner Club
Gui Du Hotel
★★★★
1 Shengping Jie, (0531) 8690 0888
Standard room: RMB588
Credit Cards: Visa, Master Card, JCB, American Express
Gui You Hotel
★★★★
101 Yingxiongshan Lu
(0531) 8298 0088, *www.guiyou.com.cn*
Standard room: RMB580
Credit Cards:
Visa, Master Card, JCB
Huaneng Hotel
★★★★
17 Quancheng Lu, (0531) 8609 6888
www.hnhotel.com.cn
Standard room: RMB590
Credit Cards: Visa, Master Card, JCB, American Express, Domestic Cards
Huang Tai Hotel
★★★★
122 Jiangjun Lu, (0531) 8896 6988
www.huang-tai.com
Standard room: RMB480
Credit Cards: Visa, Master Card, JCB
Litian Hotel
★★★★
66 Jingyi Lu, (0531) 8268 8888
www.ltlthotel.com
Standard room: RMB680
Credit Cards: Visa, Master Card, JCB, American Express
Shandong Liangyou Fulin Hotel
★★★★
5 Luoyuan Dajie, (0531) 8695 6888
www.sdlyfl.com
Credit Cards: Visa, Master Card, JCB, American Express
Silver Plaza Quancheng Hotel

DESTINATIONS

★★★★
2 Nanmen Dajie
(0531) 8692 1911
Standard room:
RMB580 +10% Surcharge
Credit Cards: Visa, Master Card,
JCB, American Express
Yi Zheng Hotel
★★★★
108 Lishan Lu
(0531) 8503 5888
www.yizhenghotel.com
Standard room: RMB748
Credit Cards: Visa, Master Card,
JCB, American Express
Century Run Hua Hotel Ji'nan
★★★★
138 Wei'er Lu
(0531) 8290 1818
Standard room: RMB782
Credit Cards: Visa, Master Card,
JCB, American Express
Ji'nan Nanjiao Hotel
★★★★
2 Ma'anshan Lu
(0531) 8518 8888
www.jnnjhotel.com
Standard room: RMB580
Credit Cards:
Visa, Master Card, Domestic Cards
Ji'nan Fuhua Hotel
★★★
108 Qingqi Lu, Lixia
(0531) 8895 1818
Credit Cards: Visa, Master Card,
JCB, Domestic Cards

Restaurants

Chinese
Taohuayuan 桃花源美食城
16-2 Yanshan Xiao Qu, Heping Lu
(0531) 8893 0718
Ji'nan Restaurant 济南菜馆

2/F Huaneng Building,17 Quancheng
Lu, (0531) 8609 6888
Western
Eurasian Garden 欧亚花园西餐厅
6 Luoyuan Dajie, Jingqi Lu (News
Hotel), (0531) 8696 9999
**Mediterranean
地中海咖啡厅**
66 Leyuan Dajie (2/F Sofitel Silver
Plaza Ji'nan)
(0531) 8606 8888
Korean
Aliya Korea 柯丽亚韩国餐厅
6 Luoyuan Dajie,
Jingqi Lu (News Hotel)
(0531) 8696 9999
Barbeque
Western Restaurant 西餐厅
101 Yingxiongshan Lu (2/F Guiyou
Hotel), (0531) 8298 0088

Hospitals

Ji'nan Hospital 济南医院
74 Hougangzi Jie
(0531) 8695 4646
**Shandong College Second Hospital
山东大学第二医院**
247 Beiyuan Dajie
(0531) 8587 5201

Bookstores

Xinhua Bookstore 济南市新华书店
185 Quancheng Lu, (0531) 8619 3051

Industrial Parks

**Ji'nan High-Tech Industrial Development Zone
济南高新技术产业开发区**
(0531) 8887 1510
www.jctp.gov.cn
Major Industries:
Software, environmental technology,
export processing

Qingdao 青岛

Telephone prefix: 0532
Population: 8.19 million
Bank of China: 6 Xianggang Zhong Lu

Qingdao is one of the most pleasant coastal cities of northern China, popular with Chinese visitors and foreigners alike. It was ceded to Germany in 1898 on a 99-year lease, although they were forced to withdraw in 1914 at the start of the First World War.

Qingdao, which now has a population of 7 million, is most famous for being the home of Tsingtao Beer, a legacy of the German occupation, which launched production in 1903 and has become China's number one export brand. The city is also one of China's top commercial ports, a leading marine science center and headquarters for the northern command of the Chinese navy. Another top Chinese consumer brand, white goods manufacturer Haier, makes its

home in the city, as does Hisense, an up-and-coming electronics manufacturer.

Qingdao has become a favorite destination for foreign investment. Its advantages include good infrastructure, an accommodating and supportive local government and the city's prime position in the center of the Northeast Asian market, close to Korea and Japan. Qingdao's pleasant climate and beautiful beaches help to attract investment as well as tourists. The majority of the city's 50,000 foreign residents are South Korean or Japanese.

The standard and quality of life in Qingdao is considered to be as good as or better than in China's first-tier cities. The air is cleaner than Beijing or Shanghai and there is a very low crime rate. The colonial architecture – most visible in the old district in the west of town – gives Qingdao a cosmopolitan feel. Enterprises in Qingdao have an easier time retaining quality Chinese

staff, who tend to flee other cities in pursuit of higher wages in Shanghai or Shenzhen.

Qingdao's commercial and business district around Xianggang Lu in the east is a particularly clean and smart area of town, and this is where the Carrefour hypermart, top-name hotels, bars and restaurants are found. The city's backstreets provide a laid-back contrast to the "New China" aesthetic. Don't get too laid back here though: Qingdao traffic is chaotic, even by Chinese standards.

Qingdao is scheduled to host some water sports events for the 2008 Olympic Games. The city's business leaders are focusing on the games to elevate Qingdao's international profile and attract new foreign investment.

Qingdao has several beaches that are typically packed on holidays. The beaches are far from idyllic, but they are not bad considering Qingdao's relatively northern latitude and the overall state of China's environment.

Hotels

Best Western Qingdao Kilin Crown Hotel
★★★★★
197 Xiang Gang Dong Lu
(0532) 8889 1888
Credit Cards: Visa, Master Card, JCB, American Express, Domestic Cards
Crowne Plaza Qingdao
★★★★★
76 Xiang Gang Zhong Lu
(0532) 8571 8888
www.ichotelsgroup.com
Standard room: RMB698

Credit Cards:
Visa, Master Card, JCB, American Express, Domestic Cards
Grand Regency Hotel
★★★★★
110 Xiang Gang Zhong Lu
(0532) 8588 1818
www.regencyhotelqd.com
Standard room:
RMB1,145 +15% Surcharge
Credit Cards: Visa, Master Card, JCB, American Express
Hai Tian Hotel
★★★★★
48 Xiang Gang Xi Lu, (0532) 8387 1888
Credit Cards: Visa, Master Card, JCB, Domestic Cards, Diners Club
Huiquan Dynasty Hotel
★★★★★
9 Nanhai Lu, (0532) 8299 9888
www.hqdynastyhotel.com
Standard room: RMB660
Credit Cards:
Visa, Master Card, JCB, American Express, Domestic Cards
Qingdao Century Haifeng Hotel
★★★★★
459 Changjiang Zhong Lu
(0532) 8699 6666
Standard room: RMB568
Credit Cards: Visa, Master Card, JCB, American Express, Domestic Cards
Sea View Garden Hotel
★★★★★
2 Zhanghua Lu, Shinan
(0532) 8587 5777
www.seaviewgardenhotel.com
Credit Cards: Visa, Master Card, JCB, American Express, Domestic Cards
Shangri-La Hotel Qingdao
★★★★★
9 Xiang Gang Zhong Lu
(0532) 8388 3838

Credit Cards: Visa, Master Card, JCB, American Express

SPR Hotel

★★★★★

316 Xiang Gang Dong Lu

(0532) 8889 0394

www.spr.cc

Credit Cards: Visa, Master Card, JCB, American Express, Domestic Cards

Dong Fang Hotel

★★★★

4 Daxue Lu, (0532) 8286 5888

www.hotel-dongfang.com

Standard room: RMB788

Credit Cards:

Visa, Master Card, JCB, American Express, Domestic Cards

Haidu Hotel

★★★★

218 Changjiang Zhong Lu, Eco. & Tech. Dev. Zone, (0532) 8699 9888

www.qdhaiduhotel.com

Standard room: RMB718

Credit Cards: Visa, Master Card, JCB, American Express

Hotel Equatorial Qingdao

★★★★

28 Xiang Gang Zhong Lu

(0532) 8572 1688

Credit Cards: Visa, Master Card, JCB, American Express

Huanghai Hotel

★★★★

75 Yan'an Yi Lu, (0532) 8287 0215

www.huanghaihotel.com

Standard room: RMB680

Credit Cards: Visa, Master Card, JCB, American Express

Oceanwide Elite Hotel Qingdao

★★★★

29 Taiping Lu, (0532) 8299 6699

www.oweh.com

Credit Cards: Visa, Master Card, JCB, American Express, Domestic Cards

Qingdao Champs Elysees Business Hotel

★★★★

8 Shandong Lu, (0532) 8580 7768

www.sdelysees.com

Standard room: RMB598

Credit Cards: Visa, Master Card, JCB, American Express

Sophia International Hotel Qingdao

★★★★

217 Xiang Gang Dong Lu

(0532) 8897 1111

www.sophiahotel.com.cn

Credit Cards:

Visa, Master Card, JCB, American Express, Domestic Cards

Eastern Light International Hotel

★★★

39 Shandong Lu, (0532) 8581 4688

www.qddh-hotel.com

Credit Cards:

Visa, Master Card, JCB, American Express, Domestic Cards

Hailin Hotel

★★★

24 Haian Lu, Xiang Gang Dong Lu

(0532) 8801 6688

www.hailinhotel.com

Credit Cards: Visa, Domestic Cards

Huanhai Gloria Inn Qingdao

★★★

29 Donghai Xi Lu, (0532) 8387 8855

Standard room: RMB880

Credit Cards:

Visa, Master Card, JCB, American Express, Domestic Cards

Qingdao Golden Coast Hotel

★★★

Shilaoren National Resort

(0532) 8889 7888

www.golden-holiday.com

Credit Cards: Visa, Master Card, American Express, Domestic Cards

Qingdao Julinyuan Hotel

★★★

38 Biaoshan Lu, (0532) 8363 1888

www.jlyhotel.com

Standard room: RMB480

Red-Crowned Crane Hotel

★★★

Minhang Lu, Liuting International Airport, (0532) 8471 0777

www.rcchotel.com

Standard room: RMB418

Credit Cards: Visa, Master Card, JCB

Sunny World Hotel

★★★

1 Shantou Lu, (0532) 8596 6888

Credit Cards: Visa, Master Card, JCB, Domestic Cards

Restaurants

Chinese

Yuanhai Restaurant 粤海中餐厅

2 Zhanghua Lu, (0532) 8587 5777

Cantonese

Xiang Gong 香宫

9 Xiang Gang Zhong Lu, 1/F Shangri-La Hotel, (0532) 8388 3838

Cafe

SPR Coffee

25 Donghai Xi Lu

French

La Villa 维拉法国餐厅

5 Xiang Gang Zhong Lu

(0532) 8388 6833

Shandong

Qingdao Restaurant 青岛菜馆

2 Shandong Lu, (0532) 8386 0098

Barbeque

Open Air Barbeque of Oceanwide Elite Hotel

泛海名人酒店露天烧烤吧

29 Taiping Lu, (0532) 8288 6699

Bars & Clubs

BATS 蝙蝠吧
Shangri-La Hotel
New York 纽约吧
75 Yan'an Yi Lu
Honolulu 火奴鲁鲁吧
9 Hainan Lu

Hospitals

Qingdao Medical College Hospital
青岛大学医学院附属医院
16 Jiangsu Lu, (0532) 8291 1867

Bookstores

Xinhua Bookstore
青岛市新华书店
Banghai Zhong Lu, Nan Duan
(0532) 8587 5440

Consulates

Korea 韩国
8 Qinling Lu, (0532) 897 6001

Industrial Parks

**Qingdao Economic & Technological
Development Zone**

青岛经济技术开发区
(0532) 8698 8987
www.qda.gov.cn
Major Industries: Electronics and
household appliances, software
Qingdao Free Trade Zone
青岛保税区
(0532) 8676 6671
www.qdftz.com
Major Industries:
Export processing, logistics, warehousing
**Qingdao High-Tech Industrial
Development Zone**
青岛高新技术产业开发区
(0532) 8899 6893
www.hi-tech.chinaqingdao.net
Major Industries: Electronics and
household appliances, software

Exhibiton centers

**Qingdao International Convention
Center**
501 Jinyi Building, Yan'an San Lu
(0535) 578 5101
www.qdicec.com.cn

Yantai 烟台

Telephone prefix: 0535
Population: 6.48 million
Bank of China: 166 Jiefang Lu

Located on the Bohai Sea, Yantai is one of Shandong's principle ports. The city is surrounded by mountains and faces the sea, giving it a picturesque setting. Yantai has a relatively mild climate, and has numerous beaches.

Hotels

Golden Gulf Hotel
★★★★★
34 Haian Lu, (0535) 663 6999
www.yantaigoldengulfhotel.com
Standard room: RMB534
Credit Cards:
Visa, Master Card, JCB, American Express, Domestic Cards
Yantai Marina Hotel
★★★★★
128 Binhai Bei Lu, (0535) 212 9999
Standard room: RMB880
Credit Cards:
Visa, Master Card, JCB, American Express, Domestic Cards
Air Plaza Hotel Yantai
★★★★
78 Dahaiyang Lu, (0535) 658 3356
www.ytminhanghotel.com
Credit Cards:
Visa, Master Card, JCB, American Express, Domestic Cards
Yantai Pacific Hotel
★★★★
74 Shifu Jie, (0535) 658 8866
Standard room: RMB300
Credit Cards:
Visa, Master Card, JCB, American Express, Domestic Cards
Asia Hotel (Yantai)
★★★
116 Nan Dajie
(0535) 658 8888
www.asiahotel.cn
Standard room: RMB520
Credit Cards: Visa, Master Card, JCB, American Express
Bihai Hotel
★★★
236 Nan Dajie, (0535) 658 5888
www.bihaihotel.com
Credit Cards:
Visa, JCB, Domestic Cards

Weihai 威海

Telephone prefix: 0631
Population: 2.47 million

Weihai mainly serves as a commercial seaport, but the area is also well developed industry-wise, manufacturing hundreds of products such as plastics, silk, and medicine.

Hotels

Golden Bay Hotel Weihai
★★★★★
128 Beihuanhai Lu, Hi-Tech. Ind. Dev. Zone
(0631) 568 8777
www.whgoldenbayhotel.com
Standard room: RMB1,020
Credit Cards: Visa, Master Card, JCB, American Express

Weihai Gaosi Bay Hotel
★★★★★
2 Qingdao Bei Lu, (0631) 578 8888
Standard room: RMB520
Credit Cards: Visa, Master Card, JCB, American Express, Domestic Cards

Blue Sky Hotel
★★★★
1 Huanhai Lu, (0631) 523 1670
www.whbluesky.com
Credit Cards:
Visa, Master Card, Domestic Cards

Guangming Garden Hotel
★★★★
25 Wenhua Dong Lu, (0631) 528 6555
www.guangminghotel.com
Standard room: RMB560
Credit Cards: Visa, Master Card, JCB, American Express

Qiming Holiday Hotel
★★★★
28 Dongshan Lu, (0631) 366 6666

www.qmhotel.cn
Standard room: RMB620
Credit Cards: Visa, Master Card, JCB, American Express

Weihai Haijing Garden Hotel
★★★★
9 Lianlindao Lu, Huancui
(0631) 526 2999
Standard room: RMB760
Credit Cards: Visa, Master Card, JCB, American Express, Domestic Cards

Weihaiwei Hotel
★★★★
82 Haigang Lu, (0631) 528 5888
www.whwhotel.com.cn
Credit Cards: Visa, Master Card, JCB, American Express, Domestic Cards

Whiteswan Hotel
★★★★
12 Wenhua Dong Lu
(0631) 523 1891
www.whwhiteswanhotel.com.cn
Credit Cards: Visa, Master Card, JCB, American Express, Domestic Cards

Industrial Parks

Weihai Economic & Technological Development Zone
威海经济技术开发区
(0631) 598 0100, *www.eweihai.net.cn*
Major Industries: Autos, electronics, textiles, pharmaceuticals, chemicals, building materials

Weihai Torch High-Tech Industrial Development Zone
威海火炬高新技术产业开发区
(0631) 568 0118, *ww.whtdz.com.cn*
Major Industries: IT, bioengineering and pharmacy, new materials

Weihai Export Processing Zone
威海出口加工区
(0631) 598 1673, *www.whepz.com*
Major Industries: Food, electronics

Shanghai

Population: 17.78 million
Area: 6,340 sq km
Airports: Shanghai Pudong, Shanghai Hongqiao
Ports: Shanghai

Throughout most of China's 5,000-year history, Shanghai was a quiet fishing town dwarfed in size and importance by nearby Suzhou and Hangzhou. It was not until 1842, when the British arrived after their victory in the first Opium War, that things began to change and a major trading city began to emerge. Other nations followed the British into Shanghai. The French had their own concession, while other foreign nationalities

came together under the International Settlement. By 1900, Shanghai had a population of 1 million and had emerged as one of the world's top commercial centers.

In the early 20th century, celebrities and personalities from the West came to Shanghai to see what the hubbub was all about in the "Paris of the East". Charlie Chaplin, Albert Einstein, Noel Coward and others managed to visit the city before the party ended when the Japanese invaded China in the late 1930s.

After the city was secured by Communist forces in 1949, Shanghai spent decades being held up as a negative example for the rest of the country of the ills of foreign culture and capitalism, its economy effectively mothballed as local taxes were used to build up other parts of the country.

These days, the foreigners and multinationals are back in town and the engine of China's economic growth is gaining ground on its East Asian neighbors, including Hong Kong and Tokyo. This time, instead of being driven by opium, Shanghai's economy is being propelled by automobiles, steel, chemicals, semiconductors, electronics and manufactured goods. But just as in the past, it is Shanghai's position at the mouth of the Yangtze River, navigable deep into the Chinese hinterland, which affords the city its status as conduit between inland China and the world.

Although Shanghai's recent growth is impressive by any measure, the city is not content to be just a regional player. Shanghai aims to become a world-class economic and cultural center on the level of New York and London.

In the early 1990s when many multinationals were setting up in China for the first time, it was the general consensus that a Beijing office was preferable due the proximity it would have to the government. After about 1995, however, Shanghai started to attract significantly more foreign investment than the capital and now clearly leads as the top choice for international investment, absorbing US$6.9 billion in utilized investment in 2005, 6.6% of the national total.

An even greater indicator of Shanghai's prospects is the widespread optimism shown in the city's future as measured by a host of indicators. By the end of 2005, 124 regional headquarters of multinational companies and 170 foreign R&D centers were located in Shanghai. That year the city's contracted FDI totaled US$13.8 billion, an 18.3% rise over 2004.

Change in the city is the only constant. Swathes of the old Shanghai that were left almost untouched from the Communist victory in 1949 through to the early 1990s are being bulldozed to make way for new office, residential and retail complexes. High-rise cranes have dotted the horizon since the mid-1990s and the honk of taxi horns is the defining sound of the city.

All this construction is necessary to keep pace with one of the fastest growing urban economies in the world. In 2005, the city's GDP grew by 13.4%, barely down from 2004's record 13.5% growth.

By 2005, after years of rapid development, there was some concern of a bubble forming in the local real estate market. As some property prices soared to US$5,500 per square meter, home ownership was becoming a luxury many Shanghainese, even those with decent salaries, could not afford. The government introduced capital gains taxes and interest rates were raised mid-year, cooling the market from the boiling point to a simmer. Similar measures were applied in 2006, with more restrictions placed on home ownership to prevent quick turnarounds and speculation.

There is a constant need to improve the city's infrastructure. One project addressing these needs is the Hangzhou Bay Trans-Oceanic Bridge, a US$1.4 billion, 33-km bridge linking Shanghai to the port city of Ningbo to the south. Slated to open sometime in 2009, the bridge will almost halve the journey between the two cities and tie Shanghai in closer with another part of the thriving Yangtze Delta region.

Shanghai's light-speed evolution is also producing some of China's most futuristic-looking buildings, particularly in the Pudong New Area, most of which was rice paddies before 1990. The Oriental Pearl TV Tower, the Jinmao Tower and the Aurora Building, which features the world's largest LCD television screen, all contribute to the science-fiction feel of the Pudong skyline.

Getting richer
Meanwhile, with the city booming and their wallets expanding, the Shanghainese middle class is growing at a fast rate as the city's residents become bigger and bigger spenders. The average Shanghainese enjoyed RMB18,645 in disposable income in 2005, the highest in the nation. In recent years, retail sales have risen by an annual average of about 15%, with spending on luxury goods rising even faster.

The city's residents, both foreign and local, are some of the most cosmopolitan in the country, and have at their disposal more fashion outlets, nightclubs, bars, cafes and bookstores than probably any other Chinese city. Only in Shanghai can someone sit in Garden Books on Changle Lu and eat ice cream while reading a novel in English, then head off to Jean Georges for a five-star feast, before climbing to the terrace of Bar Rouge for drinks and a view of the city at its best.

Shanghai's history stills resonates profoundly throughout the city, and despite being economically penalized by the central government during for 1950s and 1960s for having been a center of Western decadence, Shanghai has never lost its unique character.

During the 1980s, the early years of Deng Xiaoping's era of reform,

Shanghai Economic Data			
	2005	2004	Change%
GDP (RMB bn)	915.4	807.3	13.4
GDP per capita (RMB)	51,474	55,307	-6.9
Exports (US$ bn)	90.72	73.51	23.41
Imports (US$ bn)	95.62	86.51	10.53
Cars per 100 households	3.80	3.60	5.56
PCs per 100 households	81.10	69.90	16.02

Shanghai still played second fiddle to Beijing and later the Pearl River Delta region, particularly Shenzhen. It was not until former Shanghai Mayors Jiang Zemin and Zhu Rongji were in power during the early 1990s that the Communist government urged Shanghai to resurrect itself as a preeminent Asian city. In 1990, Shanghai's return to prominence was given an invaluable boost by the establishment of the Pudong New Area, an area the size of Singapore sitting on the opposite bank of the Huangpu River from Shanghai's city center.

Before 1990, the area of Pudong that is now the financial district was filled with worker slums and derelict warehouses. Beyond was flat farmland. Today Lujiazui, the portion of Pudong opposite the Bund, is a symbol of the city's rapid rebound from the chokehold of central planning. It is also becoming the gateway between Shanghai and the world.

Yangshan, a massive deepwater port, opened its first phase in 2005. Located well off the southern coast off Pudong, it is linked to the city by the massive Donghai Bridge and

was built to better accommodate the larger ships being used in the international logistics industry.

Shanghai has the world's first commercial-use magnetically levitating (MagLev) train and plans to add another by 2010. While the current maglev travels between Pudong Airport and Longyang Lu (approximately in the middle of nowhere, hence its lack of passengers and revenues), the new one will link Shanghai with Hangzhou, cutting the travel time between the two cities from two hours to 27 minutes.

Shanghai's other airport, Hongqiao, is located much closer to the city center than Pudong. Since the opening of Pudong, Hongqiao has been used exclusively for domestic flights, so the international traveler would not be likely to use it. If it is necessary to book a round trip flight between Shanghai and another Chinese city, Hongqiao is usually preferable to Pudong because of its location.

Shanghai Economic Data	
GDP 2005 (RMB bn)	915.4
Disposable income 2005 (RMB)	18,645

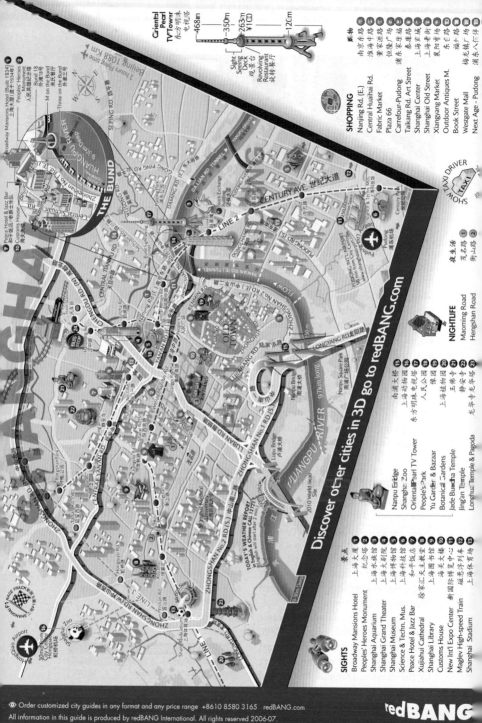

Hotels

Millenium Honqiao Hotel
★★★★★
2588 Yan An Xi Lu (021) 6208 5888
www.milleniumhongqiao.com
Standard room:
RMB1,320 +15% Surcharge
Credit Cards:
Visa, Master Card, JCB, American
Express, Domestic Cards

Hotel Equatorial Shanghai
★★★★
65 Yan'an Xi Lu, (021) 6248 1688
Standard room:
RMB1,865 +15% Surcharge
Credit Cards: Visa, Master Card,
JCB, Domestic Cards

Central Hotel Shanghai
★★★★★
555 Jiujiang Lu, (021) 5396 5000
www.centralhotelshanghai.com
Standard room: RMB1,450
Credit Cards:
Visa, Master Card, JCB, American
Express, Domestic Cards

Peace Hotel
★★★★★
20 Nanjing Dong Lu
(021) 6321 6888
Standard room: RMB1,680
Credit Cards: Visa, Master Card,
JCB, American Express

88 Xintiandi
★★★★★
380 Huangpi Nan Lu, (021) 5383 8833
www.88xintiandi.com
Credit Cards: Visa, Master Card,
JCB, American Express

Concord International Hotel
★★★★★
2068 Nanjing Xi Lu, (021) 6272 8860
Credit Cards: Visa, Master Card,
JCB, American Express

Crowne Plaza Fudan
★★★★★
199 Handan Lu, (021) 5552 9999
www.ichotelsgroup.com
Standard room:
RMB2,268 +15% Surcharge
Credit Cards:
Visa, Master Card, American Express

Crowne Plaza Pudong
★★★★★
1000 Yanggao Bei Lu, Pudong
(021) 5862 1000
www.ichotelsgroup.com
Standard room:
RMB988 +15% Surcharge
Credit Cards:
Visa, Master Card, JCB, American
Express, Domestic Cards

Four Seasons Hotel Shanghai
★★★★★
500 Weihai Lu, (021) 6256 8888
Standard room:
RMB3,300 +15% Surcharge
Credit Cards:
Visa, Master Card, JCB, American
Express, Diners Club

Grand Hyatt Shanghai
★★★★★
Jinmao Tower, 88 Shiji Dadao,
Pudong, (021) 5049 1234
Standard room:
RMB3,800+15% Surcharge
Credit Cards: Visa, Master Card,
JCB, American Express

Guangdong Hotel Shanghai
★★★★★
328 Yixian Lu, (021) 5117 1888
www.gdhhotels.com
Credit Cards:
Visa, Master Card, JCB, American
Express, Domestic Cards

Hilton Shanghai
★★★★★

250 Huashan Lu, (021) 6248 0000
Credit Cards: Visa, Master Card,
JCB, American Express
Home Hotel
★★★★★
288 Shaanxi Bei Lu, (021) 6288 1515
www.home-hotel.cn
Standard room: RMB1,580
Credit Cards: Visa, Master Card,
JCB, American Express
Howard Johnson Palm Beach Resort
★★★★★
1888 Hai'ou Lu, Fengxian Bay Resort
(021) 5712 1777
Standard room: RMB988
Credit Cards: Visa, Master Card,
JCB, American Express
Howard Johnson Plaza Hotel
★★★★★
595 Jiujiang Lu, (021) 3313 4888
Standard room:
RMB1,910 +15% Surcharge
Credit Cards:
Visa, Master Card, JCB, American
Express, Domestic Cards
Hua Ting Hotel & Towers Shanghai
★★★★★
1200 Caoxi Bei Lu, (021) 6439 1000
www.huating-hotel.com
Standard room:
RMB2,100 +15% Surcharge
Credit Cards:
Visa, Master Card, JCB, American
Express, Domestic Cards
InterContinental Pudong Shanghai
★★★★★
777 Zhangyang Lu, Pudong
(021) 5835 6666
Standard room: RMB2,666
Credit Cards: Visa, Master Card,
JCB, American Express
Jin Jiang Hotel Shanghai
★★★★★

59 Maoming Nan Lu
(021) 6258 2582
Credit Cards:
Visa, Master Card, JCB, American
Express, Domestic Cards
Jin Jiang Tower
★★★★★
161 Changle Lu, (021) 6415 1188
www.jinjiangtower.com
Standard room:
RMB2,328 +15% Surcharge
Credit Cards: Visa, Master Card,
JCB, American Express
JW Marriott Hotel Shanghai
★★★★★
399 Nanjing Xi Lu, (021) 5359 4969
Standard room: RMB3,200
Credit Cards: Visa, Master Card,
JCB, American Express
Lake Meilan Convention Center
★★★★★
888 Luofen Lu, (021) 5659 0888
www.luodian.com.cn
Standard room: RMB700
Credit Cards: Visa, Master Card,
JCB, American Express
Le Meridien She Shan Shanghai
★★★★★
1288 Linyinxin Lu, Sheshan
(021) 5779 9999
www.lemeridien.com
Standard room:
RMB2,300 +15% Surcharge
Credit Cards: Visa, Master Card,
JCB, American Express
New World Mayfair Hotel
★★★★★
1555 Dingxi Lu, (021) 6240 8888
Standard room: RMB988
Credit Cards: Visa, Master Card,
JCB, American Express
Okura Garden Hotel Shanghai
★★★★★

58 Maoming Nan Lu
(021) 6415 1111
www.gardenhotelshanghai.com
Credit Cards: Visa, Master Card,
JCB, American Express
Oriental Riverside
★★★★★
2727 Binjiang Dajie, Pudong
(021) 5037 0000
www.shicc.net
Standard room: RMB788
Credit Cards:
Visa, Master Card, JCB, American
Express, Domestic Cards
**Pudi Boutique Hotel Fuxing Parc
Shanghai**
★★★★★
99 Yandang Lu, (021) 5158 5888
www.accorhotels.com/asia
Standard room: RMB2,250
Credit Cards: Visa, Master Card,
JCB, American Express
Pudong Shangri-La Shanghai
★★★★★
33 Fucheng Lu, Pudong
(021) 6882 8888
www.shangri-la.com

Standard room: RMB2,850
Credit Cards: Visa, Master Card,
JCB, American Express
Purple Mountain Hotel
★★★★★
778 Dongfang Lu, Pudong
(021) 6886 8888
www.pmhotel.com.cn
Standard room: RMB791
Credit Cards:
Visa, Master Card, JCB, American
Express, Domestic Cards
**Radisson Hotel Shanghai New
World**
★★★★★
88 Nanjing Xi Lu, (021) 6359 9999
Credit Cards: Visa, Master Card,
JCB, American Express, Domestic
Cards, Diners Club
**Radisson Plaza Xing Guo Hotel
Shanghai**
★★★★★
78 Xingguo Lu, (021) 6212 9998
Standard room:
RMB1,830 (single), 1,990 (double)
Credit Cards:
Visa, Master Card, JCB, American

CHECK OUT

THE

NEWEST ROOMS

IN

SHANGHAI

Welcome to
Hotel Equatorial Shanghai

All of our 526 bedrooms have been completely
and fully refurbished. Combined with a very
central location, excellent choice of in house
dining and excellent gym and spa facilities it
makes for an even better stay in Shanghai.

65 Yanan Road West, Shanghai 200040, China
Tel: + 86 21 62481688   Fax: + 86 21 62481773
www.equatorial.com   info@sha.equatorial.com

Express
Regal International East Asia Hotel
★★★★★
516 Hengshan Lu, (021) 6415 5588
Standard room: RMB2,900 +15%
Surcharge
Credit Cards: Visa, Master Card,
JCB, American Express

Renaissance Shanghai Pudong Hotel
★★★★★
100 Changliu Lu, Lianyang New District, Pudong, (021) 3871 4888
Credit Cards:
Visa, Master Card, JCB, American
Express, Domestic Cards

Renaissance Yangtze Shanghai Hotel
★★★★★
2099 Yan'an Xi Lu, (021) 6275 0000
www.renaissancehotels.com
Standard room:
RMB2,650 +15% Surcharge
Credit Cards: Visa, Master Card,
JCB, American Express

Shanghai Grand Pacific Hotel
★★★★★
288 Shanxi Bei Lu, (021) 3218 4555
Standard room: RMB1,486
Credit Cards: Visa, Master Card,
JCB, American Express

**Shanghai Hong Qiao State Guest
Hotel**
★★★★★
1591 Hongqiao Lu, (021) 6219 8855
www.hqstateguesthotel.com
Standard room: RMB1,660
Credit Cards:
Visa, Master Card, JCB, American
Express, Domestic Cards

Shanghai JC Mandarin
★★★★★
1225 Nanjing Xi Lu, (021) 6279 1888
Standard room: RMB2,200
Credit Cards:

Visa, Master Card, JCB, American
Express, Domestic Cards

Shanghai Marriott Hotel Hongqiao
★★★★★
2270 Hongqiao Lu, (021) 6237 6000
Credit Cards:
Visa, Master Card, JCB, American
Express, Domestic Cards

**Sheraton Grand Shanghai Tai Ping
Yang Hotel**
★★★★★
5 Zunyi Nan Lu, (021) 6275 8888
Credit Cards:
Visa, Master Card, JCB, American
Express, Domestic Cards

**Sofitel Jin Jiang Oriental Pudong
Shanghai**
★★★★★
889 Yanggao Nan Lu, Pudong
(021) 5050 4888
Standard room: RMB2,405
Credit Cards:
Visa, Master Card, JCB, American
Express, Domestic Cards

Somerset Grand Shanghai
★★★★★
8 Ji'nan Lu, (021) 6385 6888
Credit Cards:
Visa, Master Card, JCB, American
Express, Domestic Cards

Somerset Xu Hui Shanghai
★★★★★
888 Shaanxi Nan Lu, (021) 6466 0888
Credit Cards:
Visa, Master Card, JCB, American
Express, Domestic Cards

St. Regis Hotel Shanghai
★★★★★
889 Dongfang Lu, Pudong
(021) 5050 4567
Standard room: RMB2,990
Credit Cards: Visa, Master Card,
JCB, American Express

Sun Island Resort & Clubs
★★★★★
2588 Shentai Lu, Zhujiajiao Town, Qingpu, (021) 6983 3888
www.sunislandclub.com
Credit Cards:
Visa, Master Card, JCB, American Express, Domestic Cards

The Ascott Pudong Shanghai
★★★★★
3 Pudong Dadao, Pudong
(021) 6886 0088
Credit Cards:
Visa, Master Card, JCB, American Express, Domestic Cards

The Portman Ritz-Carlton, Shanghai
★★★★★
1376 Nanjing Xi Lu, (021) 6279 8888
Credit Cards:
Visa, Master Card, JCB, American Express, Domestic Cards

The Regent Shanghai
★★★★★
1116 Yan'an Xi Lu, (021) 6115 9988
Standard room:
RMB2,500 +15% Surcharge

Credit Cards: Visa, Master Card, JCB, American Express

The Westin Shanghai Hotel & Residences
★★★★★
88 Henan Zhong Lu
(021) 6335 1888
Standard room: RMB2,990
Credit Cards: Visa, Master Card, JCB, American Express

Universal Ever-Rich Hotel Shanghai
★★★★★
3189 Bao'an Lu, (021) 5915 1188
www.ever-rich-hotel.com
Standard room: RMB667
Credit Cards:
Visa, Master Card, JCB, American Express, Domestic Cards

Hengshan Moller Villa Hotel
★★★★★
30 Shaanxi Nan Lu, (021) 6247 8881
www.mollervilla.com
Standard room: RMB850
Credit Cards: Visa, Master Card, JCB, American Express

Acme Riverside Service Apartment Shanghai

★★★★
1 Lane 588 Changyi Lu, Pudong
(021) 5133 7733
Standard room: RMB1,188
Credit Cards: Visa, Master Card,
JCB, American Express
City Hotel Shanghai
★★★★
5-7 Shanxi Nan Lu, (021) 6255 1133
Credit Cards:
Visa, Master Card, JCB, American
Express, Domestic Cards
**Courtyard by Marriott Shanghai-
Pudong**
★★★★
838 Dongfang Lu, Pudong
(021) 6886 7886
Standard room:
RMB2,200 (rack rate)
Credit Cards: Visa, Master Card,
JCB, American Express
Crowne Plaza Shanghai
★★★★
400 Panyu Lu, (021) 6145 8888
www.ichotelsgroup.com
Standard room: RMB2,000
Credit Cards: Visa, Master Card,
JCB, American Express
Diamond Court
★★★★
1168 Biyun Lu, Jinqiao, Pudong
(021) 5032 3232
www.diamondcourt.com
Standard room: RMB980
Credit Cards: Visa, Master Card,
JCB, American Express
**Four Points by Sheraton Shanghai,
Pudong**
★★★★
2111 Pudong Nan Lu
(021) 5039 9999
www.fourpoints.com/pudong
Standard room: RMB1,780

Credit Cards: Visa, Master Card,
JCB, American Express, Great Wall
Galaxy Hotel
★★★★
888 Zhongshan Xi Lu
(021) 6275 5888
www.galaxyhotel.com
Standard room: RMB1,400
Credit Cards:
Visa, Master Card, JCB, American
Express, Domestic Cards
Holiday Inn Downtown Shanghai
★★★★
285 Tianmu Xi Lu, (021) 6353 8008
Standard room:
RMB1,328 +15% Surcharge
Credit Cards: Visa, Master Card,
JCB, American Express
Holiday Inn Pudong Shanghai
★★★★
899 Dongfang Lu, Pudong
(021) 5830 6666
Standard room: RMB1,200
Credit Cards: Visa, Master Card,
JCB, American Express
Holiday Inn Vista Shanghai
★★★★
700 Changshou Lu, (021) 6276 8888
Standard room: RMB1,494
Credit Cards:
Visa, Master Card, JCB, American
Express, Domestic Cards
Honghe Hotel
★★★★
46 Guilin Lu, (021) 5421 8777
www.honghe-hotel.com
Standard room: RMB488
Credit Cards: Visa, Master Card,
JCB, American Express
**Hotel Zhongyou International
Shanghai**
★★★★
969 Dongfang Lu, Pudong

(021) 6875 8888
www.hotelzhongyou.net
Standard room:
RMB1,428 +15% Surcharge
Credit Cards: Visa, Master Card,
JCB, American Express
**Howard Johnson All Suites Hotel
Shanghai**
★★★★
1155 Yan'an Xi Lu, (021) 5238 2555
Standard room: RMB1,718
Credit Cards:
Visa, Master Card, JCB, American
Express, Domestic Cards
Jian Guo Hotel Shanghai
★★★★
439 Caoxi Bei Lu, (021) 6439 9299
www.jianguo.com
Standard room:
RMB1,300 +15% Surcharge
Credit Cards:
Visa, Master Card, JCB, American
Express, Domestic Cards
Jing An Hotel
★★★★
370 Huashan Lu, (021) 6248 1888
www.jinganhotel.net

Credit Cards:
Visa, Master Card, JCB, American
Express, Domestic Cards
Man Po Boutique Hotel
★★★★
660 Xinhua Lu, (021) 6280 1000
www.manpo.cn
Credit Cards: Visa, Master Card,
JCB, American Express, Domestic
Cards, Diners Club
Manhattan Business Hotel
★★★★
81-85 Dianchi Lu, (021) 6888 8123
www.manhattanhotel.com.cn
Credit Cards: Visa, Master Card,
JCB, American Express
**Metropark Service Apartment
(Shanghai)**
★★★★
103 Dongzhu'anbang Lu
(021) 6211 0088
Standard room: RMB640
Credit Cards: Visa, Master Card,
JCB, American Express
New Century Hotel
★★★★
1111 Liyang Lu, (021) 3608 4999

www.newcenturyhotelsh.com
Standard room: RMB468
Credit Cards:
Visa, Master Card, JCB, American Express, Domestic Cards

New Harbour Service Apartments
★★★★
88 Yongshou Lu, (021) 6355 1889
www.newharbour.com.cn
Credit Cards: Visa, Master Card, JCB, American Express

Novotel Atlantis Shanghai
★★★★
728 Pudong Dadao, Pudong
(021) 5036 6666
www.novotel.com/asia
Credit Cards:
Visa, Master Card, JCB, American Express, Domestic Cards

Phoenix-Mansion Service Apartment
★★★★
18 Huangyang Lu, Jinqiao, Pudong
(021) 5834 8888
www.phoenix-mansion.com
Standard room: RMB888
Credit Cards: Visa, Master Card, JCB, American Express

Pudong Conference Exhibition Hotel
★★★★
1810 Gaoke Xi Lu, Pudong
(021) 5089 8888
Credit Cards:
Visa, Master Card, JCB, American Express, Domestic Cards

Radisson SAS Lansheng Hotel Shanghai
★★★★
1000 Quyang Lu, (021) 5588 8000
Credit Cards: Visa, Master Card, JCB, American Express, Domestic Cards, Diners Club

Rainbow Hotel
★★★★
2000 Yan'an Xi Lu, (021) 6275 3388
www.e-rainbowhotel.com
Credit Cards:
Visa, Master Card, JCB, American Express, Domestic Cards

Ramada Plaza Pudong
★★★★
18 Xinjinqiao Lu, Pudong
(021) 5055 4666
www.ramada.com
Standard room: RMB1,240
Credit Cards: Visa, Master Card, JCB, American Express

Ramada Plaza Shanghai
★★★★
700 Jiujiang Lu, (021) 6350 0000
www.ramada.com
Standard room: RMB1,490
Credit Cards: Visa, Master Card, JCB, American Express

Ramada Pudong Airport Shanghai
★★★★
1100 Qihang Lu, Pudong Airport
(021) 3849 4949
www.ramada.com
Standard room:
RMB880 +15% Surcharge
Credit Cards:
Visa, Master Card, JCB, American Express, Domestic Cards

Ramada Shanghai Caohejing Hotel
★★★★
509 Caobao Lu, (021) 5464 9999
www.ramada.com
Standard room: RMB880
Credit Cards: Visa, Master Card, JCB, American Express

Regal Shanghai East Asia Hotel
★★★★
800 Lingling Lu, (021) 6426 6888
Standard room: RMB1,580

Credit Cards: Visa, Master Card, JCB, American Express
Rendezvous Merry Hotel Shanghai
★★★★
396 Yan'an Xi Lu, (021) 6249 5588
Credit Cards: Visa, Master Card, JCB, American Express, Diners Club
Royalton Hotel
★★★★
789 Wuyi Lu, (021) 5206 8000
Credit Cards:
Visa, Master Card, JCB, American Express, Domestic Cards
Ruitai Hongqiao Hotel
★★★★
555 Shuicheng Lu, (021) 6241 9600
www.ruitaihqhotel.com
Standard room: RMB680
Credit Cards: Visa, Master Card, JCB, American Express
Seagull Hotel
★★★★
60 Huangpu Lu, (021) 6325 1500
www.seagull-hotel.com
Standard room: RMB1,215
Credit Cards:
Visa, Master Card, JCB
Shaanxi Business Hotel Shanghai
★★★★
658 Yan'an Zhong Lu
(021) 5262 4866
Standard room: RMB498
Credit Cards: Visa, Master Card, JCB, American Express
Shanghai Eastern Airline Hotel
★★★★
2088 Zhongshan Bei Lu
(021) 5290 6688
Credit Cards:
Visa, Master Card, JCB, American Express, Domestic Cards
Shanghai Everbright Convention & Exhibition International Hotel

★★★★
66 Caobao Lu, (021) 6484 2500
www.secec.com
Credit Cards: Visa, Master Card, JCB, American Express, Domestic Cards, Diners Club
Shanghai Golden Jade Sunshine Hotel
★★★★
1888 Zhoujiazui Lu, (021) 6100 1888
www.hhmy-hotel.com
Credit Cards:
Visa, Master Card, JCB, American Express, Domestic Cards
Shanghai Worldfield Convention Hotel
★★★★
2106 Hongqiao Lu, (021) 6270 3388
Standard room:
RMB1,500 +15% Surcharge
Credit Cards: Visa, Master Card, JCB, American Express
Shanghai Yingyuan Hotel
★★★★
150 Qinghe Lu, (021) 5952 0952
www.shyyhotel.com
Standard room: RMB600
Credit Cards: Visa, Master Card, JCB, American Express
Sofitel Hyland Shanghai
★★★★
505 Nanjing Dong Lu
(021) 6351 5888
Standard room:
RMB2,490 +15% Surcharge
Credit Cards:
Visa, Master Card, JCB, American Express, Domestic Cards
Sun Shine International Plaza Service Apartment
★★★★
3721 Hongmei Lu, (021) 5422 0222
Standard room: RMB380

Credit Cards: Visa, Master Card, JCB, American Express

Supreme Tower

★★★★

600 Laoshan Dong Lu, Pudong

(021) 5831 1118

www.supremetower.com

Standard room: RMB1,330

Credit Cards: Visa, Master Card, JCB, American Express, Domestic Cards

The Bund Riverside Hotel

★★★★

398 Beijing Dong Lu, (021) 6352 2888

www.xxt-hotel.com

Credit Cards:

Visa, Master Card, JCB, American Express, Domestic Cards

The Panorama Shanghai

★★★★

53 Huangpu Lu, (021) 5393 0008

www.accorhotels-asia.com

Standard room: RMB764

Credit Cards: Visa, Master Card, JCB, American Express, Domestic Cards

Tongmao Hotel

★★★★

357 Songlin Lu, Pudong

(021) 5830 0000

Credit Cards: Visa, Master Card, JCB, American Express, Domestic Cards, Diners Club

Wanping Hotel Shanghai

★★★★

315 Wanping Lu, (021) 5467 9888

Credit Cards:

Visa, Master Card, JCB, American Express, Domestic Cards

Yihe Longbai Shanghai

★★★★

2451 Hongqiao Lu, (021) 6268 9111

Standard room: RMB1,527

Credit Cards: Visa, Master Card, American Express, Domestic Cards

Yue Hua Hotel

★★★★

88 Jianghai Lu, Nanqiao Town, Fengxian, (021) 5718 1888

www.yuehuahotel.com.cn

Standard room: RMB770

Credit Cards: Visa, Master Card, JCB, American Express

Peace Garden Apartment

★★★★

2222 Kongjiang Lu, (021) 5108 3737

www.peacegardenhotel.com
Credit Cards: Visa, Master Card, JCB, American Express

Restaurants

Continental/Fusion

Luna
Unit 1, House 15, North block Xintiandi, Lane 181, Taicang Lu with Madang Lu, (021) 6336 1717

Barbeque

Brasil Steak House 巴犀烧烤
1649 Nanjing Xi Lu, (021) 6255 9898

Beijing

Quanjude全聚德烤鸭店
4/F, 786 Huaihai Zhonglu
(021) 5404 5799
3/F, 778 Dongfang Lu (Purple Mountain Hotel), (021) 6886 8807
547 Tianmu Xi Lu, (021) 6353 8888

Cafe

Wagas 沃歌斯
B/F CITIC Square, 1168 Nanjing Xi Lu, (021) 5292 5228
B/F Hong Kong New World Plaza, 300 Huaihai Zhong Lu
(021) 6335 3739

Geow Yong Teo Hong 尧阳茶行
House 8, North Block, Xintiandi

Cantonese

Zen 香港采蝶轩
3/F Hong Kong Plaza, 283 Huaihai Zhong Lu, (021) 6390 6390
House 2, South Block, Xintiandi, 123 Xingye Lu, (021) 6385 6385

Bi Feng Tang 避风塘
175 Changle Lu, (021) 6467 0628
1/F Golden Magnolia Plaza, 1 Dapu Lu, (021) 5396 1328
1333 Nanjing Xi Lu, (021) 6279 0738

M on the Bund 米氏西餐厅
7/F, 20 Guangdong Lu
(021) 6350 9988

T8
House 8, North Block, Xintiandi, 181 Taicang Lu, (021) 6355 8999

Chinese

People 7 人间萤七
805 Julu Lu, (021) 5404 0707

Yinding Restaurant 银鼎大酒店
Building 5, 93 Binxi Jie
(0352) 209 8666

French

Flo 福楼
1/F-2/F Ciro's Plaza, 388 Nanjing Xi Lu, (021) 6334 5177

Jean Georges 法国餐厅
4/F, Three on the Bund, 3 Zhongshan Dong Yi Lu, (021) 6321 7733

La Seine 塞纳河
8 Ji'nan Lu, (021) 6384 3722

Hunan

Di Shui Dong 滴水洞
2/F, 56 Maoming Nan Lu
(021) 62532689
626 Xianxia Lu, (021) 3207 0213

Gu Yi 古意香味浓
87 Fumin Lu, (021) 6249 5628

Indian

Kitchen 印度小厨
572 Yongjia Lu, (021) 5465 1951

Indonesian

Bali Laguna 巴厘岛
189 Huashan Lu (inside Jing'an Park), (021) 6248 6970

International

New Heights 新视角餐厅酒廊
7/F, Three on the Bund, 3 Zhongshan Dong Yi Lu, (021) 6321 0909

American

Element Fresh 元素
112 Shanghai Centre, 1376 Nanjing Xi Lu, (021) 6279 8682

Moon River Diner 月亮河
Lane 3338 Hongmei Leisure Pedestrian Street, Gubei

DESTINATIONS

2F, BLDG 38, Zendai Thumb Plaza, 199 Fan Dian Lu

Italian

Da Marco 大马克

103 Dongzhu'anbang Lu

(021) 62104495

Japanese

Ooedo 大江户

30 Donghu Lu, (021) 5403 3332

Wuninosachi 海之幸

B/F Lippo Plaza, 222 Huaihai Zhong Lu, (021) 53822727

402 Shaanxi Nan Lu, (021) 6445 3406

2890 Yan'an Xi Lu, (021) 6262 5777

169 Xinle Lu, (021) 5403 0303

Nepalese

Nepali Kitchen 尼泊尔餐厅

178 Xinle Lu, (021) 5404 5077

Northeastern

Dongbei Ren 东北人

1 Shaanxi Nan Lu, (021) 5228 9898

Sichuan

China Moon 海上明月

3/F CITIC Square, 1168 Nanjing Xi Lu, (021) 3218 1379

Sichuan

Darling Harbor 达令港

19/F-20/F Paramount Hotel, 1728 Nanjing Xi Lu, (021) 6248 1818

6/F 755 Huaihai Zhong Lu

(021) 6445 3868

2/F Yuandong Plaza, 299 Xianxia Lu

(021) 6235 0368

Shanghainese

Shanghai Restaurant

徐家私菜精作坊

4/F Times Square 99 Huaihai Zhong Lu, (021) 6391 0152

Jade Garden 苏浙汇

388 Zhaojiabang Lu, (021) 6415 9918

Thai

Simply Thai 天泰餐厅

5C, Dongping Lu, (021) 6445 9551

North Block, Xintiandi

(021) 6326 2088

Vegetarian

Zao Zi Shu 枣子树

848 Huangjin Cheng Dao

(021) 6275 1798

258 Fengxian Lu, (021) 6215 7566

Vietnamese

Halong Bay 夏龙湾

2/F 158 Huaihai Zhong Lu

(021) 6386 5707

5/F Grand Gateway, 1 Hongqiao Lu

(021) 6447 9690

Latina

Barbeque/steakhouses

B1-B2 Yatai ShengHui Shopping Square, 2002 Shiji Da Dao, Pudong

(021) 50306673

Unit 2, House 18, North Block Xintiandi, Lane 181 Taicang Lu by Madang Lu, (021) 6320 3566

Café

Bonomi Café

30 Shaanxi Lu near Julu Lu

(021) 6247 5003

Fontainebleau Café

D43, 168 Hongbaoshi Lu by Yili Nan Lu, (021) 6295 9811

Cuban

El Cubano

3896 Hongmei Lu near Yanan Lu

(021) 6242 3349

Bars & Clubs

Blarney Stone

5A Dongping Lu

Upstairs at Park 97

Fuxing Park, Sinan Lu Men

Cotton Club 棉花吧

8 Fuxing Xi Lu

Face

Building 4, Ruijin Guest House, 118 Ruijin Er Lu

House of Blues and Jazz
158 Maoming Nan Lu
KABB
North Block, Xintiandi
Long Bar 长廊洒吧
2/F Shanghai Centre, 1376 Nanjing Xi Lu
Malone's 马龙美式酒吧
255 Tongren Lu
O'Malley's 欧玛莉
42 Taojiang Lu
Sasha's
9 Dongping Lu
CJW 星际/星球
South Block, Xintiandi
Big Bamboo
132 Nan Yang Lu

Hospitals

World Link 瑞新医疗
203 Shanghai Centre, 1376 Nanjing Xi Lu, (021) 6279 7688
www.worldlink-shanghai.com
World Link 瑞新医疗
3/F, 170 Danshui Lu
(021) 6385 9889
www.worldlink-shanghai.com

World Link 瑞新医疗
Mandarin City, 788 Hongxu Lu
(021) 6405 5788
www.worldlink-shanghai.com
Shanghai East International Medical Centre 上海东方国际医院
12/F 551 Pudong Nan Lu
(021) 5879 9999
www.seimc.com.cn
Shanghai United Family Hospital and Clinics 和睦家医院
1139 Xianxia Lu, (021) 5133 1900
www.shanghaiunited.com
International Medical Care Centre of Shanghai
上海第一人民医院国际医疗保健中心
585 Jiulong Lu, (021) 6324 3852 (24h)
Huashan Hospital: Foreigners' Clinic 华山医院国际诊所
1068 Changle Lu, (021) 6248 9999
CanAm International Medical Center Shanghai
新源国际医疗中心
966 Huaihai Zhong Lu
(021) 5403 9133
Ruijin Hospital: Foreigners' Clinic

瑞金医院外宾门诊
197 Ruijin Er Lu, (021) 6437 0045
Shanghai Humanity Hospital
上海博爱医院
1590 Huaihai Zhong Lu
(021) 6433 3999
Ruidong Hospital 瑞东医院
50, 1507 Lane Luoshan Lu
(021) 5833 9595

Bookstores

Garden Books 韬奋西文书局
325 Changle Lu,(021) 5404 8728
Shanghai Book Mall 上海书城
465 Fuzhou Lu, (021) 5353 4650
Chaterhouse 三联书店
B-E Time Square, Huaihai Zhong Lu
(021) 6391 8237
Foreign Language Book Store
外文书店
390 Fuzhou Lu
(021) 6322 3200

Local English Media

China Economic Review
www.chinaeconomicreview.com
that's Shanghai
www.thatsshanghai.com
City Weekend Shanghai
www.cityweekend.com.cn

Professional service providers

Shanghai Foreign Service
上海对外服务
15/F Jinling Building, 28 Jinling Xi
Lu, (021) 5456 4999
www.efesco.com
CIIC 中国国际技术智力合作
18/F Jianhui Building, 922 Hengshan
Lu, (021) 5459 4545
www.ciicsh.com
Shanghai Human Resources Service
上海人才服务中心

620 Zhongshan Xi Lu
(021) 6233 7211
www.shrc.com.cn

Commercial property agents

CB Richard Ellis
(021) 6289 1200
www.cbre.com.cn
Jones Lang LaSalle
(021) 6393 3333
www.joneslanglasalle.com.cn
Crispin Property Consultants
(021) 6372 2858
www.cpcproperty.com
Chesterton Petty
(021) 3877 1477
www.chesterton.com.cn
Colliers International
(021) 6237 0088
www.colliers.com

Consulates

Australia 澳大利亚
401, Shanghai Centre, 1376 Nanjing
Xi Lu, (021) 6279 8098
Austria 奥地利
3A Qi Hua Tower, 1375 Huaihai
Zhong Lu, (021) 6474 0268
Belgium 比利时
127 Wuyi Lu, (021) 6437 6579
India 印度
1008, Shanghai International Trade
Center, 2201 Yan'an Xi Lu
(021) 6275 8882
Brazil 巴西
10A-B, Qi Hua Tower, 1375 Huaihai
Zhong Lu, (021) 6437 0117
Canada 加拿大
604 West Tower, Shanghai Centre,
1376 Nanjing Xi Lu, (021) 6279 8400
Czech Republic 捷克共和国
12B, 1375 Huaihai Zhong Lu
(021) 6471 2420

Denmark 丹麦
701, Shanghai International Trade Centerm, (021) 6209 0500

Finland 芬兰
2501, CITIC Plaza, 1168 Nanjing Xi Lu, (021) 5292 9900

France 法国
21A, 23B, Qi Hua Tower, 1375 Huaihai Zhong Lu, (021) 6289 7414

Germany 德国
18/F New Century Plaza, 188 Wujiang Lu, (021) 6217 2884

Ireland 爱尔兰
700A Shanghai Centre, 1376 Nanjing Xi Lu, (021) 6279 8729

Israel 以色列
7/F New Town Mansion, 55 Loushanguan Lu, (021) 6209 8008

Italy 意大利
11A-11B, Qi Hua Tower, 1375 Huaihai Zhong Lu, (021) 6471 6980

Japan 日本
8 Wanshan Lu, (021) 5257 4766

Korea 韩国
60 Wanshan Lu, (021) 6295 5000

Malaysia 马来西亚
305, Equatorial Hotel, 65 Yan'an Xi Lu, (021) 6248 1688

Mexico 墨西哥
1375 Huaihai Zhong Lu
(021) 6437 9585

Netherlands 荷兰
4/F East Tower, Sun Plaza, 88 Xianxia Lu, (021) 6209 9076

New Zealand 新西兰
15/F Qi Hua Tower, 1375 Huaihai Zhong Lu, (021) 6471 1127

Norway 挪威
21, 3/F 12 Zhongshan Dong Yi Lu
(021) 6323 9988

Poland 波兰
618 Jianguo Xi Lu, (021) 6433 9288

Russia 俄罗斯
20 Huangpu Lu, (021) 6324 8383

Singapore 新加坡
89 Wanshan Lu, (021) 6278 5566

South Africa 南非
2706, 222 Yan'an Dong Lu
(021) 5359 4977

Sweden 瑞典
1530-1541, Shanghai Central Plaza, 381 Huaihai Zhong Lu
(021) 6391 6767

Switzerland 瑞士

22/Fs Building A, Far East Plaza, 319
Xianxia Lu, (021) 6270 0519
Thailand 泰国
3/F, 7 Zhongshan Dong Yi Lu
(021) 6323 4095
Turkey 土耳其
13B, 1375 Huaihai Dong Lu
(021) 6474 6838
UK 英国
301 Shanghai Centre, 1376 Nanjing
Xi Lu, (021) 6279 7650
Ukraine 乌克兰
Sun Plaza, 88 Xianxia Xi Lu
(021) 6295 3195
USA美国
1469 Huaihai Zhong Lu
(021) 6433 6880

Airline Offices

Air China 中国国际航空公司
1088 Yan'an Xi Lu
(021) 5239 7227
Air France 法国航空公司
1301, Novel Plaza, 128 Nanjing Xi Lu
4008 808 808
**Austrian Airlines
澳大利亚航空公司**
1103, 227 Huangpi Bei Lu
(021) 6375 9051
**China Eastern Airlines
中国东方航空公司**
200 Yan'an Xi Lu
(021) 6247 2255
**China Southern Airlines
中国南方航空公司**
238 Yan'an Xi Lu
(021) 6249 4918
Dragonair 港龙航空有限公司
2103, 138 Huaihai Zhong Lu
(021) 6375 9051
Finnair 芬兰航空公司
2406, 1168 Nanjing Xi Lu
(021) 5292 9400

KLM 荷兰皇家航空公司
301, 202 Hubin Lu, (021) 6884 6884
Lufthansa 德国汉莎航空公司
480 Pudian Lu, (021) 5830 4400
Shanghai Airlines 上海航空公司
212 Jiangning Lu, (021) 6255 0550
**Malaysia Airlines
马来西亚航空公司**
209 Shanghai Centre, 1376 Nanjing
Xi Lu, (021) 6279 8607
Singapore Airlines 新加坡航空公司
606-608 Kerry Center, 1515 Nanjing
Xi Lu, (021) 6289 1000
**Northwest Airlines
美国西北航空公司**
207 Shanghai Centre, 1376 Nanjing
Xi Lu, (021) 6884 6884
Swiss Airlines 瑞士航空公司
203B Shanghai Centre, 1376 Nanjing
Xi Lu, (021) 6279 7381

Industrial Parks

**Shanghai Jiading Industrial Zone
上海嘉定开发区**
(021) 6103 9558
www.shgszc.com
Major Industries:
Automobile components, optical
electronics, environmental protection equipment manufacturing
**Minhang Economic & Technologi-
cal 闵行经济技术开发区**
(021) 6430 0888
www.smudc.com
Major Industries: Machinery, heavy
industry, light industry
**Jinqiao Export Processing Zone
金桥出口加工区**
(021) 5899 1818
www.pdjq.com
Major Industries:
Information technology, electronics,
automobiles, biotechnology

Waigaoqiao Free Trade Zone
外高桥保税区
(021) 5869 8500
www.china-ftz.com
Major Industries: Export processing, logistics, warehousing
Zhangjiang High-Tech Park
张江高科技园区
(021) 5080 1818
www.zjpark.com
Major Industries:
Information technology, biotechnology, pharmaceuticals
Songjiang State-Level Export
松江出口加工区
(021) 5774 1102
www.zhaoshang-sh.com/kfqzs/ songjiangchukou
Major Industries:
Information technology, chemicals, biotechnology, light industry
Shanghai Baoshan Industrial Zone
上海宝山工业区
(021) 6687 9800
www.sbiz.gov.cn
Major Industries:
New materials, steel, metal

Shanghai Caohejing Export Processing Zone
漕河泾新兴技术开发区
(021) 6485 0000
www.caohejing.com
Major Industries:
Microelectronics, optical electronics, computers and software, new materials, bio-pharmaceuticals, meters and instruments, aerospace
Shanghai Chemical Industry Park
上海化学工业区
(021) 6712 0000
www.scip.com.cn
Major Industries: Petrochemical, precision chemical, new materials
Shanghai Comprehensive Industrial Development Zone
上海市工业综合开发区
(021) 5743 7066
www.fengpu.com
Major Industries: electronic information, biopharmaceutical
Shanghai Chongming Industrial Zone 上海崇明工业区
(021) 6103 9558
www.shgszc.com

Major Industries: Ship building, food processing, export processing

Shanghai Hongqiao Development Zone 上海虹桥开发区

(021) 6275 6888, *www.shudc.com*

Major Industries: Real estate, hotel building and management, restaurants and shopping malls, recreation facilities, transportation, service industries

Shanghai International Automobile City 上海国际汽车城

(021) 6950 2200, *www.shautocity.com*

Major Industries: Auto manufacturing, auto part production

Qingpu Industrial Zone 青浦工业区

(021) 5973 6914

industry.shqp.gov.cn

Major Industries:

Telecommunications, bio-pharmaceuticals, modern textile materials, and precision machinery processing

Jinshan Industrial Zone 金山工业区

(021) 5727 2000

www.jsgyq.com

Major Industries:

Fine chemicals, construction materials, and food processing

Kangqiao Industrial Zone 康桥工业区

(021) 5812 1488, *www.pudong.com.cn*

Major Industries: Electronics and electric appliances, automobile components, new construction materials

Zizhu Science-based Industrial Park 紫竹科学园区

(021) 6237 6300, *www.zizhupark.com*

Major Industries:

Information, new materials, bio-engineering, and modern agriculture

Spark Development Zone 星火开发区

(021) 6213 6254, *www.shspark.com*

Major Industries:

Textiles, pharmaceuticals, paper, construction materials

Lujiazui Finance & Trade Zone 上海陆家嘴金融贸易区

www.ljz.com.cn

Major Industries: modern services (finance, trade, and commerce)

Exhibition centers

Shanghai New International Expo Center

2345 Longyang Lu, Shanghai

(021) 2890 6666, *www.sniec.net*

Shanghai Mart

2299 Yan'an Xi Lu, Shanghai

(021) 6236 6888

www.shanghaimart.com.cn

Shanghai Everbright Convention & Exhibition Center

88 Caobao Lu, Shanghai

(021) 6451 6345, *www.secec.com*

INTEX Shanghai

88 Loushanguan Lu, Shanghai

(021) 6275 5800

www.intex-sh.com

Shanghai International Convention Center

2727 Bingjiang Dadao, Shanghai

(021) 5037 0000

www.shicc.net

Shanghai East Asia Exhibition Center

666 Tianyaoqiao Lu, Shanghai

(021) 6426 6666

www.ssc.sh.cn

Shanghai Agriculture Exhibition Center

2268 Hongqiao Lu

(021) 6237 6370, *www.shnzg.com*

Shanghai Exhibition Center

1000 Yan'an Zhong Lu, Shanghai

(021) 6249 0279

Shanxi

Population: 33.56 million
Area: 156,000 sq km
Capital: Taiyuan
Airport: Taiyuan
Ports: Taiyuan, Changzhi

Bordered by the Yellow River to the west and the Great Wall to the north, Shanxi province is situated in the northern central part of China. It borders the Taihang mountain range to the east and its name literally meaning 'west of the mountains'. Although its climate is relatively cool, Shanxi still sees a full range of seasons. Due to its proximity to the Gobi desert, the province is often susceptible to sandstorms.

Shanxi is situated largely on the 'Yellow Earth' loess plateau. The loess is the accumulation of eons of dust and sediment, and the region has seen continuous agricultural activity over thousands of years. There is some forest cover in Shanxi's southern reaches, but in general, the province is desperately short of trees.

Shanxi has a rich history, belonging to the region where Han Chinese civilization first appeared. But Shanxi continues to be counted among China's poorest provinces, facing a particular medley of critical challenges.

It is China's largest coal producer. Verifiable coal reserves amount to over 261 billion tons, one third of China's coal resources. Major coalfields lie around the cities of Taiyuan and Datong. Safety in the mines is mostly an afterthought, and fatal accidents are common.

A host of electric generation plants have sprung up among the coalfields, helping to ease strain on rail lines by converting the coal into electricity closer to the source. Shanxi provides Beijing with 25% of its power. In addition to exploitation of its iron ore, coal and other mineral deposits, metallurgy, chemicals, and machinery production are among Shanxi's main industries.

The environmental effects of Shanxi's industrial sector have been truly devastating, and the region is home to nearly half of the 30 most polluted cities in China. The semi-arid climate frequently leads to water shortages, and the water available is often heavily polluted. The primary problem is sulfur dioxide emissions from coal-fired plants, resulting in acid rain and air pollution. The impact of Shanxi's air problems extends as far as Japan.

Investment is badly needed to update the extraction of coal and other resources. Efforts are being made to attract high-tech industries to help diversify Shanxi's infrastructure and lessen its dependence on coal and heavy industry. Shanxi has some textile manufacturing and other light industry, but market-economy reforms have been slow to take effect.

Tourism has great potential due to the region's deep history. The top draw in recent years has been the town of Pingyao south of Taiyuan, which is included in UNESCO's list of world heritage sites.

Shanxi Economic Data			
	2005	2004	Change%
GDP (RMB bn)	418.0	357.1	17.1
GDP per capita (RMB)	12,495	9,105	37.2
Exports (US$ bn)	3.53	4.04	-12.62
Imports (US$ bn)	2.02	1.35	49.63
Cars per 100 households	3.13	1.23	154.47
PCs per 100 households	30.16	22.93	31.53

Taiyuan 太原
Telephone prefix: 0351
Population: 3.43 million
Bank of China: 288 Yinze Dajie

Taiyuan is situated at the geographic center of Shanxi along the north-south course of the Fen River. Founded about 2,500 years ago, Taiyuan witnessed and participated in the turbulent cycles of many Chinese dynasties. In the Ming (1368-1644) and Qing (1644-1911) dynasties particularly, Taiyuan was an important center of industry and trade. In the 1900 anti-foreigner uprisings referred to as the Boxer Rebellion, Taiyuan was the site of a massacre of foreigners and Christians.

Today, Taiyuan is one of China's most important industrial capitals. A vital transportation hub, Taiyuan lies within easy reach of Beijing by rail and highway, and provides a link to destinations further west and south. Lying relatively near the inland stretches of the Bohai Sea, Taiyuan offers easy access to large ports such as Qingdao and Tianjin.

Taiyuan differs little on the surface from other inland cities – the same massive redevelopment trend, shopping streets and office building developments.

Taiyuan's cultural interests include the Chongshan temple, originally built as a palace in the Sui Dynasty (581-618). In the 17th century it was refashioned into a temple, but was badly damaged by fire two hundred years later. Now only a fraction of its original size, it is still an impressive example of Ming-style architecture. The provincial museum is nearby, housed in the converted Confucian Temple and Chunyang Palace. Just 25 km outside of the city is the Jinci temple, worth seeing for the architectural contributions from various dynasties dating back nearly a thousand years.

Wutai Shan, one of China's four sacred Buddhist mountains, lies equidistant from Taiyuan and Datong. Here at least, Shanxi's captivating natural environment still remains relatively unspoiled. Picturesque monasteries and temples decorate the slopes.

Taiyuan Economic Data	
GDP 2005 (RMB bn)	89.55
Disposable income 2005 (RMB)	10,476

Hotels

World Trade Hotel
★★★★★
69 Fuxi Jie, (0351) 868 8888
www.sxwtc.com
Credit Cards:

Visa, Master Card, JCB, American Express, Domestic Cards
Grand Metropark Wanshi Hotel
★★★★★
126 Pingyang Lu, (0351) 765 8888
Standard room: RMB580
Credit Cards: Visa, Master Card, JCB, American Express
Imperial Garden Hotel
★★★★
186 Yingze Dajie, (0351) 481 2000
Credit Cards: Visa, Master Card, JCB, American Express, Domestic Cards, Diners Club
Sanjin International Hotel
★★★★
108 Yingze Dajie, (0351) 882 7777
Standard room: RMB618
Credit Cards: Visa, Master Card, JCB
Shanxi Grand Hotel
★★★★
5 Xinjian Nan Lu, (0351) 882 9999
www.sxgh.com
Standard room:
RMB680 +15% Surcharge
Credit Cards: Visa, Master Card, JCB, American Express
Shanxi Zhengxie Hotel
★★★★
35 Dongjihuying, (0351) 565 9988

Standard room: RMB498
Yingze Hotel
★★★★
189 Yingze Dajie, (0351) 882 8888
www.shanxiyingzehotel.com
Standard room: RMB1,180
Credit Cards: Visa, Master Card,
JCB, American Express
Yuyuan Hotel
★★★★
148 Kaihuasi Jie, (0351) 882 3333
www.yuyuanhotel.com
Credit Cards: Visa, Master Card, JCB,
American Express, Domestic Cards
Bingzhou Hotel
★★★
118 Yingze Dajie, (0351) 882 1188
www.bzfd.com
Credit Cards: Visa, Master Card, JCB,
American Express, Domestic Cards
Silver Dragon Hotel
★★★
15 Dongjihuying, (0351) 318 0888
www.sddragon.com
Credit Cards: Visa, JCB, American
Express, Domestic Cards
Xishan Hotel
★★★
78 Liuxiangbeikou, (0351) 413 2222
Standard room: RMB380, 418
Credit Cards: Domestic Cards

Restaurants

Shanxi
Jinyun Lou Restaurant
晋韵楼大酒店
188 Tiyu Xi Lu, (0351) 722 9666
Western
Rose Cafe 名人苑
5 Xinjiang Nan Lu (Shanxi Grand
Hotel), (0351) 882 9999
Local traditional
Mianshi Dian of Taiyuan

太原面食店
17 Jiefang Lu, (0351) 202 2230

Hospitals

Third People's Hospital of Taiyuan
太原第三人民医院
285 Shuangta Xi Jie, (0351) 759 5293
First Affiliated Hospital of Shanxi
Medical University
山西医科大学第一医院
13 Jiefang Nan Lu, (0351) 404 4111

Bookstores

Xinhua Bookstore 太原市新华书店
110 Jiefang Lu, (0351) 404 8859

Industrial Parks

Taiyuan Economic & Technological
Development Zone
太原经济技术开发区
(0351) 709 8055
Major Industries: Food processing,
medicine, electronics, machinery,
light industry, packaging
Taiyuan High-Tech Industrial
太原高新技术产业开发区
(0351) 703 3711, *www.tyctp.com.cn*
Major Industries: Electronics, photoelectronics, new materials
Taiyuan Economic & Technological
Development Zone
太原经济技术开发区
(0351) 709 269, www.tynewtown.com
Major Industries: Food processing,
medicine, electronics, machinery,
light industry, packaging
Taiyuan High-Tech Industrial
Development Zone
太原高新科技技术开发区
(0351) 703 3029
www.tyctp.com.cn
Major Industries: Electronics, photoelectronics, new materials

Datong 大同
Telephone prefix: 0352
Population: 3.12 million
Bank of China: 19 Donghuamen Jie

North Shanxi offers several significant attractions, visits to which would almost certainly mean staying at least a few nights in Datong. A major industrial city, Datong has a handful of four-star hotels. Yungang grottos, one of the three major Buddhist cliff-carving legacies in China, consist of tens of thousands of Buddhist images. Datong Steam Locomotive Plant was the last factory in the world to produce steam-powered locomotives, the last one of which rolled out in 1988. The factory today is a steam engine museum, treating visitors to an authentic 20-km steam engine ride and holding periodic Datong Steam Locomotive Festivals.

Hotels

Datong Hotel
★★★★
37 Yingbin Xi Lu, (0352) 586 8111
www.datonghotel.com
Credit Cards:
Visa, Master Card, JCB, American Express, Domestic Cards
Garden Hotel
★★★★
59 Da'nan Jie, (0352) 586 5888
www.huayuanhotel.com.cn
Standard room: RMB820
Credit Cards:
Visa, Master Card, JCB, American Express, Domestic Cards
Hong'an International Hotel
★★★★

28 Binxi Lu, (0352) 586 6666
Standard room:
RMB780 +15% Surcharge
Credit Cards:
Visa, Master Card, JCB, American Express, Domestic Cards
Jingyuan Guesthouse
★★★★
A3 Yongjun Nan Lu
(0352) 536 8000

Restaurants

International
Yungang International Hotel
云岗国际酒店
38 Daxi Jie
(0352) 586 9999
Chinese
Yungang Hotel 云冈宾馆
21 Yinbin Xi Jie, (0352) 586 3888
Kunlun Restaurant 昆仑饭店
89 Zhenhua Jie
(0352) 202 9658
Korean
Sorabol 萨拉伯尔
38 Daxi Jie, Yungang International Hotel, (0352) 586 2080
Cantonese
Tonghe Yuan Restaurant
同和园大饭店
11 Zhanqian Jie, 0352) 281 7222

Hospitals

Third People's Hospital of Datong
大同市第三人民医院
1 Yiwei Jie, Xinjian Nan Lu
(0352) 502 1001

Bookstores

Xinhua Bookstore
大同市新华书店
Yuhe Bei Lu, (0352)
602 9414

Sichuan

Population: 82.12 million
Area: 488,000 sq km
Capital: Chengdu
Airports: Chengdu, Mianyang, Panzhihua
Ports: Chengdu, Yibin, Luzhou, Nan-chong, Xichang

Home to about 82 million people, Sichuan province is one of the most populous provinces in China. For centuries it has been a key center for agriculture. Furthermore, with the Yangtze River flowing as one of its main waterways, it has had a long history of trade.

Economically, it gained a relatively privileged role in the 1950s with the decision of the Communist government to shift factories into remote inland regions to protect them from external attack. But when the reform process began in the early 1980s, Sichuan started to decline in importance, like most of the inland areas, while the coastal regions surged ahead. In the mid-1990s, the region of Chongqing city was hived off from Sichuan province to create a municipality reporting directly to Beijing, largely to support the construction of the Three Gorges Dam project on the Yangtze River.

Sichuan's economy is the biggest of the western provinces, but is still overwhelmingly agricultural in nature, and large areas of the province are poor. The plain that occupies the eastern portion of the province is fertile, and supports two rice crops per year. There are significant mineral deposits in the province, as well as rich oil and gas fields. The mountains which make up the western areas of the province also provide significant hydropower potential.

Sichuan is the most industrialized province in western China, and has benefited from Beijing's recent stress on investment in the west of the country. The province is a major producer of television sets, for instance. Sichuan has two state-level development zones for hi-tech industries – the Chengdu New and Hi-tech Industries Development Zone (CDDZ), and the

Mianyang New and Hi-tech Industries Development Zone (MYDZ), which have both played an important role in developing the provincial economy.

Of all the provinces in western China, Sichuan takes the lead in attracting foreign investment, most notably from IT companies such as Microsoft, Cisco, Intel, IBM and Motorola, who have all set up research and development centers in the province.

Tourism is becoming a major money earner for the province, with tourists coming from the coastal areas to experience the scenic beauty and deep wells of Chinese culture, stretching back more than 1,000 years. The history of the province, in fact, dates back to the 15th century BC. Beginning in the 9th century BC, the kingdoms of Shu (today's Chengdu) and Ba (today's Chongqing) emerged as cultural and administrative centers. Sichuan is also the principle natural habitat of the Giant Panda and the home of Mt Emei, one of China's most sacred mountains.

Sichuan Economic Data			
	2005	2004	Change%
GDP (RMB bn)	738.5	638.0	15.8
GDP per capita (RMB)	9,060	8,113	11.7
Exports (US$ bn)	4.70	3.98	18.09
Imports (US$ bn)	3.20	2.89	10.73
Cars per 100 households	2.37	2.14	10.75
PCs per 100 households	32.26	26.43	22.06

Chengdu 成都

Telephone prefix: 028
Population: 12.21 million
Bank of China: 35 Renmin Zhong Lu

Chengdu, the capital of Sichuan province, is famed for the spicy Sichuan food that has become popular around the globe. Many foreign businesses are attracted to Chengdu as a result of the low costs that can be as little as one third of those in cities like Shanghai. Other attractions include Chengdu's virtue as a gateway to all of western China, and the relaxed atmosphere for which all of Sichuan province is famous.

Chengdu is the biggest and richest city in western China, and as a result has a strong market potential for foreign retailers. A wander through the streets of downtown Chengdu certainly confirms that local residents like to shop. The city has three Parkson department stores, four branches of the French hypermarket chain Carrefour and several other chains well established or with plans to open soon. Carrefour meanwhile has moved its central and western China headquarters from Shanghai to Chengdu – a sign of the importance of western China in the company's growth strategy.

Another huge development, still awaiting approval from the central government, is the city's subway system. Ground has been broken on Line 1, which will run north-south and pass under Tianfu Sqaure in the city center. The plan calls for an eventual five lines.

Chengdu is also well known for its many extremely popular tea gardens, scattered about the city's many temples and parks. On a balmy summer's day there can be few better places to kick back and enjoy a bottomless cup of tea, playing cards and catching up on the news.

Chengdu's cavernous new steel and glass airport gives the immediate impression of a city that thinks well beyond its official status as a provincial capital. Already the major transport hub for southwestern China, Chengdu has its sights set on going global. Although more than 1,000 kilometers inland, road and rail links with the southern port of Beihai are being upgraded with central government funds. At the same time, work is underway to develop the inland container port at Chongqing, four hours' drive from Chengdu, further opening up China's vast interior to international trade. On the aviation scene meanwhile, Chengdu's airport was recently given the formal go-ahead to build a second runway; international carriers are starting to offer direct flights to European cities; and plans are under discussion for flights south to Australia. With daily flights already to Lhasa, Chengdu is also a gateway to Tibet.

Chengdu Economic Data	
GDP 2005 (RMB bn)	237.1
Disposable income 2005 (RMB)	11,359

Hotels

Chengdu Wangjiang Hotel
★★★★★
42 Xiashahepu, (028) 8479 0000
www.wangjianghotel.com
Standard room: RMB1,280
Credit Cards: Visa, Master Card, JCB, American Express

Crowne Plaza Chengdu
★★★★★
31 Zongfu Jie, (028) 8678 6666
www.ichotelsgroup.com
Standard room: RMB1,200
Credit Cards: Visa, Master Card, JCB, American Express

Jinjiang Hotel
★★★★★
80 Section 2 Renmin Nan Lu
(028) 8550 6666
www.jjhotel.com
Standard room: RMB669
Credit Cards:
Visa, Master Card, JCB, American Express, Domestic Cards

Kempinski Hotel Chengdu
★★★★★
42 Section 4 Remin Nan Lu
(028) 8526 9999
Standard room: RMB1,900
Credit Cards:
Visa, Master Card, JCB, American Express, Domestic Cards

Sheraton Chengdu Lido Hotel
★★★★★
15 Section 1 Renmin Zhong Lu
(028) 8676 8999
Standard room: RMB1,150
Credit Cards: Visa, Master Card, JCB, American Express

Sofitel Wanda Chengdu
★★★★★
15 Binjiang Zhong Lu
(028) 6666 9999
Standard room: RMB1,500
Credit Cards:
Visa, Master Card, JCB, American Express, Domestic Cards

Chengdu Tianfu Sunshine Hotel
★★★★
2 Taisheng Bei Lu, (028) 8692 2233
Standard room: RMB358
Credit Cards: Visa, Master Card, JCB, American Express

Islandia Water Hotel & Spa
★★★★
53-57 Taisheng Nan Lu
(028) 8298 8888
www.water-hotel.com
Standard room: RMB580
Credit Cards:
Visa, Master Card, JCB, American Express, Domestic Cards

Minshan Hotel
★★★★
55 Section 2 Renmin Nan Lu
(028) 8558 3333
www.minshan.com.cn
Standard room: RMB808-990
Credit Cards:
Visa, Master Card, JCB, American Express, Domestic Cards

Tai Yi Hotel
★★★★
209 Shuhan Lu, Yangxixian
(028) 8757 9999
www.tyhotel.cn
Standard room:
RMB780 +10% Surcharge
Credit Cards: Visa, Master Card, JCB, American Express

Tibet Hotel Chengdu
★★★★
10 Section 1 Renmin Bei Lu
(028) 8318 3388
www.tibet-hotel.com
Credit Cards: Visa, Master Card,

JCB, American Express, Domestic Cards

Xinhua International Hotel

★★★★

1-18 Guzhongsi Jie, (028) 8298 5588

www.xhgjjd.com

Credit Cards:
Visa, Master Card, JCB, American Express, Domestic Cards

Chaoyang Lake Hotel

★★★

Chaoyang Lake, Pujiang

(028) 8859 1108

www.cyhdjd.com

Credit Cards: Domestic Cards

Chengdu Pearl International Hotel

★★★

329 Section 2 Jiefang Lu

(028) 8642 9188

www.cdpih.com

Standard room: RMB458

Credit Cards: Visa, Master Card, JCB, American Express

Jing Hu Hotel

★★★

111 North Section 1 Erhuan Lu

(028) 8760 3168

www.jinghuhotel.com

Standard room: RMB360

Credit Cards:
Visa, Master Card, JCB, American Express, Domestic Cards

Lhasa Grand Hotel

★★★

88 Xiaojiahebei Jie, South Section 4 Yihuan Lu, (028) 8519 8998

www.lhasa-hotel.com

Credit Cards:
Visa, Master Card, JCB, American Express, Domestic Cards

Lu Tian Hua Hotel

★★★

220 Tongren Lu, (028) 8663 3338

www.lth-hotel.com

Standard room: RMB466

Credit Cards: Visa, Master Card, JCB, American Express

Sunjoy Inn

★★★

34 Section 4 Renmin Nan Lu

(028) 8552 0808

www.sunjoy-inn.com

Credit Cards:
Visa, Master Card, JCB, American Express, Domestic Cards

Restaurants

Hotpot

Tanyu Tou 谭鱼头

1/F 49 Renmin Nan Lu Si Duan

(028) 8522 2266

Italian

Red Brick Pizzeria 红砖意大利餐厅

77 Kehua Bei Lu, (028) 8521 4065

Fiesta Thai 非常泰

6 Linjiang Zhong Lu (Jiaotong Hotel)

(028) 8545 4530

American

Grandma's Kitchen 祖母的厨房

75 Kehua Bei Lu, (028) 8524 2835

Indian

Tandoor 坦道

34 Renmin Nan Lu (Xinzu Hotel)

(028) 8555 1958

Cafe

Rogers Coffee 罗杰斯咖啡

2 Lihua Jie, (028) 8672 1080

**Signature Cafe
签名咖啡**

1/F, 8 Daye Lu. (028) 8671 0705

Chinese

Chen Mapo Doufu 陈麻婆豆腐

197 Xiyulong Jie, (028) 8675 4512

Hospitals

People's Hospital of Sichuan

四川省人民医院
32 Yihuan Lu Xi Er Duan, Qingyang
Gong, (028) 8739 3999

Bookstores

Xinhua Bookstore 成都市新华书店
86 Renmin Nan Lu Yi Duan
(028) 8620 3938

Consulates

USA 美国
4 Lingshiguan Lu, (028) 8558 3992

Industrial Parks

Chengdu Economic & Technological Development Zone
成都经济技术开发区
(028) 8484 8844
www.cdetdz.com
Major Industries:
Foodstuff, new materials, timbering
Chengdu Export Processing Zone
成都出口加工区
(028) 8532 8899

www.scepz.gov.cn
Major Industries: IT, precision machinery, fine chemistry
Chengdu Hi-Tech Industrial Development Zone
成都高新技术产业开发区
(028) 8518 4155
www.china-cdht.com
Major Industries: IT, bio-pharmaceutical, precision machinery
Chengdu Cross-Straits Technological Industry Park
成都海峡两岸科技产业开发园
(028) 8263 0204
www.cdwenjiang.cn
Major Industries:
Biopharmaceutical, food & beverage, packaging, electronics

Exhibition centers

Chengdu International Exhibition & Convention Center
258 Shawan Lu, (028) 8764 9999
www.ecccn.com

DESTINATIONS

Mianyang 绵阳

Telephone prefix: 0816
Population: 2.47 million

With just over 2 million people, Mianyang is Sichuan's second-largest city, and relatively clean and prosperous. Only a few hours form Chengdu by car, Mianyang also has direct flights to Beijing, Shanghai, Guangzhou, Shenzhen, and Kunming. Today the city's economy revolves around the electronics industry, and is home to several research centers devoted to electronics, as well as large domestic corporations like Changhong Electronics Group. Because of its concentration on technological research, Mianyang is sometimes known as "Science City".

Hotels

Fuleshan International Hotel
★★★★
1 Section 1 Furong Lu
(0816) 228 4888

Mianzhou Hotel
★★★★
62 East Section Linyuan Lu
(0816) 635 0999
www.mianzhou-hotel.com
Standard room: RMB263
Credit Cards:
Visa, Master Card, JCB, American Express

Prince Hotel
★★★★
25 West Section Linyuan Lu
(0816) 635 8999
www.myprincehotel.com
Credit Cards:
Visa, Master Card, JCB, American Express, Domestic Cards

Industrial Parks

Mianyang New & Hi-Tech Industrial Development Zone
绵阳国家高新技术开发区
(0816) 253 1536
www.myship.gov.cn
Major Industries:
Electronic information, fine chemicals, new materials, bio-pharmaceuticals

Panzhihua 攀枝花
Telephone prefix: 0812
Population: 1.08 million
Bank of China: 14 Renmin Jie

Panzhihua, in southwest Sichuan, is a major iron and steel production center, and also one of the world's largest producers of titanium. One of China's latest hydroelectric dam projects is located close to Panzhihua. The dam is the tallest in Asia at 240 meters, and was built with the help of Italian engineers.

Panzhihua is an important stopping point on the Chengdu-Kunming train line for access to northern Yunnan. Due to its heavy reliance on industry, Panzhihua is one of the most polluted cities in China.

Hotels

Chuanhui Hotel
★★★★
Bingcao Gang, (0812) 355 1607
Standard Room: RMB368
Suite: RMB688

Restaurants

Seafood
Tiantian Yugang 天天渔港
2/F, 3/F Baoshan Hotel, Bingcao Gang, (0812)227 1111
Hotpot
Su Dajie Huoguo 苏大姐火锅
Jichang Lu entrance, Zhuhu Yuan
(0812) 333 8789
Chinese
Panzhihua Hotel 攀枝花宾馆
90, Section 1, Wangjiang Jie
(0812) 333 6631

Hospitals

**Panzhihua Central Hospital
攀枝花市中心医院**
60, Sancun, Dahe Bei Lu
(0812) 223 8001
**Panzhihua Zhongxi Jiehe Hospital
攀枝花市中西结合医院**
70 Taoyuan Hotel, Bingcao Gang
(0812) 333 6897

Bookstores

**Xinhua Bookstore
攀枝花市新华书店**
5/F Central Square, (0812) 333 5004

DESTINATIONS

Tianjin

Population: 10.43 million
Area: 11,300 sq km
Airports: Tianjin
Ports: Tianjin

Tianjin, whose name in Chinese means "emperor's quay" or "emperor's ferry", is nestled on the coast 120km east of Beijing. Largely seen as the port city for the landlocked capital, Tianjin is the principal shipping center for northern China, and hopes to be to its region what Shanghai is to the Yangtze River Delta. The third-largest city after Shanghai and Beijing, Tianjin is

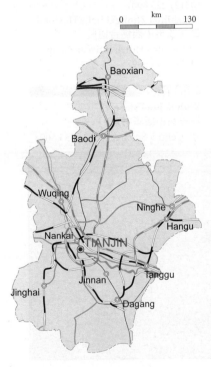

a municipality and reports directly to the central government.

The climate is characterized by hot, humid summers and dry, cold winters. The opening of the Grand Canal during the Sui dynasty (581-618) prompted the development of Tianjin into a trading center; when the Mongols established Beijing as their capital in the 13th century, Tianjin rose to prominence as a grain storage point. For the last 600 years it has served as a defensive position and trading port for Beijing, moving grain from the Yangtze River delta to the capital.

In 1856 Chinese soldiers in Tianjin boarded the Arrow, a Chinese-owned ship registered in Hong Kong and flying the British flag, on suspicion of piracy, smuggling and opium trading. In response the British and French sent gunboats to capture the forts around Tianjin and in 1858 the Treaty of Tianjin was signed, opening the city to foreign trade and legalizing the sale of opium. Britain built the first foreign concession in 1860, followed later by France, the United States, Germany and Japan.

During the Boxer Rebellion of 1900, the rebels seized control of much of Tianjin. Following their defeat by foreign troops, however, foreign concessions in the city were expanded and the city walls were torn down as punishment.

Early in the 20th century, heavy silting of the Hai River forced the city's port to move downstream to its present location at Tanggu. The largest port city in north China gradually grew into one of modern China's commercial centers and by 1931 the city's export volume was one quarter of the national total. The city was also the financial hub of north China, with 16 foreign banks and 10 Chinese banks by 1935. In 1937 Tianjin fell to Japan and remained under occupation until the Japanese surrender at the end of World War II.

During the occupation a major construction program was started to develop an artificial harbor including deep-water berthing facilities, but construction was not fully completed until 1952. Following the Communist takeover the city fell into a commercial slumber. China's closed door policy from the 1950s until the early 1980s rendered Tianjin's port virtually useless. The city developed heavy industries based on oil, natural gas, salt and minerals and was for three decades best known nationally for its production of Flying Pigeon bicycles.

The state of economic torpor was exacerbated by the devastating 1976 Tangshan earthquake, which killed well over 20,000 people in Tianjin and more than 250,000 in total.

When China's economy began to open to international business in the early 1980s, Tianjin was largely overlooked by investors rushing to the southern cities such as Guangzhou and Shenzhen. The large industrial state-owned enterprises (SOEs) that underpinned the city's economy became a burden as the country entered the market economy era.

Many SOEs now stand on the brink of bankruptcy. But in the past decade, Tianjin has taken some steps towards reclaiming its former com-

DESTINATIONS

mercial glory, and a major part of that rejuvenation has been the Tianjin Port, which went public in Hong Kong in May 2006, raising US$139 million. By October of the same year, the port had already seen 200 million tons of cargo pass through it, and was expected to hit 250 million tons by end-2006.

Tianjin's traditional industries include iron and steel, machine building, chemicals, textiles, construction materials, papermaking and food processing. Today the economy is oriented towards such industries as automobile manufacturing, shipbuilding, petrochemicals, metallurgy, telecommunications and the production of electronic goods such as TVs, cameras and computers.

Tianjin Municipality also sits on top of about 1 billion tons of petro-

leum and recent discoveries of oil deposits under the Bohai Sea have boosted the development of the region's petrochemical sector. Tianjin is one of the country's most important salt production areas. Deposits of manganese and boron in the area were the first to be found in China and geothermal energy in the area is scheduled to be developed.

Farmland takes up about 40% of Tianjin's total area. The agriculture sector is currently undergoing what the government calls "strategic restructuring". With rampant pollution and depletion of fishing areas, traditional fishing is being replaced by fish-breeding while poultry-raising and high-quality planting are being favored over the traditional crops of wheat, rice and maize.

Tianjin is home to a large number of development zones including one of the country's first, the Tianjin Economic and Technological Development Area (TEDA), which was established by the State Council in 1984. By 2004, TEDA had attracted more than 3,800 foreign companies

Tianjin Economic Data			
	2005	2004	Change%
GDP (RMB bn)	369.8	311.1	18.9
GDP per capita (RMB)	35,783	31,550	13.4
Exports (US$ bn)	27.38	20.86	31.26
Imports (US$ bn)	25.90	21.18	22.29
Cars per 100 households	3.00	2.33	28.76
PCs per 100 households	51.13	41.20	24.10

and had annual revenues of US$26.7 billion. Other development parks and zones include the Tianjin University Science Park, the Tianjin Export Processing Zone, the Tianjin High-Tech Park and the Tianjin Port Free Trade Zone, the biggest free trade zone in north China.

There is even a development zone specifically aimed at European small and medium enterprises with the uninventive name 'Europark'. The city provides comprehensive assistance to overseas investors through the Foreign Investment Service Center and a series of preferential policies have been adopted including approval for the establishment of foreign-funded banks, real estate projects and joint venture shopping centers.

Tianjin's long-term goal is to become the gateway to an integrated Beijing-Tianjin-Hubei region, similar to those around the Yangtze and Pear River deltas. Further integration within the region, like a new expressway and high speed rail link between Tianjin and Beijing are to be completed before the 2008 Olympics, facilitating travel between the two cities. Measures have also been stepped up to reduce spending on wasteful duplicate projects, like building identical facilities in both Beijing and Tianjin, in order to make the region more efficient. In this way, Tianjin hopes to be able to rival its neighbors to the south in the not too distant future.

Tianjin Economic Data	
GDP 2005 (RMB bn)	369.8
Disposable income 2005 (RMB)	12,639

Hotels

Hotel Nikko Tianjin
★★★★★
189 Nanjing Road, Heping District
(022) 8319 8888
www.nikkotianjin.com
Credit Cards: Visa, Master Card, JCB, American Express, Dinners Club

Golden Crown Hotel
★★★★★
18 Nanjing Lu, (022) 2303 8866
Standard room: RMB1,498
Credit Cards: Visa, Master Card, JCB, American Express

Renaissance Tianjin Hotel
★★★★★
105 Jianshe Lu, Heping
(022) 2302 6888
Credit Cards: Visa, Master Card, JCB, American Express, Domestic Cards

Renaissance Tianjin TEDA Hotel & Convention Centre
★★★★★
29 Second Dajie, Eco. & Tech. Dev. Zone, (022) 6621 8888
Standard room:
RMB1,600 +15% Surcharge
Credit Cards: Visa, Master Card, JCB, American Express, Domestic Cards

Sheraton Tianjin Hotel
★★★★★
Zijinshan Lu, (022) 2334 3388
Standard room:
RMB1,541 +15% Surcharge
Credit Cards: Visa, Master Card, JCB, American Express, Domestic Cards

Somerset Olympic Tower Tianjin
★★★★★
126 Chengdu Lu, Heping
(022) 2335 5888
Credit Cards: Visa, Master Card, JCB, American Express, Domestic Cards

TEDA International Hotel & Club

★★★★★
8 Second Dajie, Eco. & Tech. Dev. Zone, (022) 2532 6000
www.tedahotel.com
Credit Cards: Visa, American Express

China Tianjin Astor Hotel
★★★★
33 Tai'erzhuang Lu, Heping
(022) 2331 1688
Standard room:
RMB680 +15% Surcharge
Credit Cards: Visa, Master Card, JCB, American Express

Crystal Palace Hotel
★★★★
28 Youyi Lu, Hexi, (022) 2835 6888
Standard room: RMB568
Credit Cards: Visa, Master Card, JCB, American Express

Dickson Hotel
★★★★
18 Binshui Lu, Hexi, (022) 2836 4888
Credit Cards: Visa, Master Card, JCB, American Express

Geneva Hotel
★★★★
32 Youyi Lu, Hexi, (022) 2835 2222
Credit Cards: Visa, Master Card, JCB, American Express

Holiday Inn Binhai Tianjin
★★★★
Citizen Plaza, First Dajie, Eco. & Tech. Dev. Zone, (022) 6628 3388
www.holidayinn.com.cn
Standard room: RMB840
Credit Cards: Visa, Master Card, JCB, American Express, Domestic Cards

Holiday Inn Tianjin
★★★★
288 Zhongshan Lu, Hebei
(022) 2628 8888
Credit Cards: Visa, Master Card, JCB, American Express

Hyatt Regency Tianjin
★★★★
219 Jiefang Bei Lu, Heping
(022) 2330 1234
Standard room: RMB980
Credit Cards: Visa, Master Card, JCB, American Express, Domestic Cards

Jinwan Hotel
★★★★
358 Nanjing Lu, Nankai
(022) 2750 1188
Credit Cards:
Visa, Master Card, JCB, American Express, Domestic Cards

Meidu Hotel
★★★★
117 Weidi Lu, Hexi, (022) 2813 8588
Credit Cards:
Visa, Master Card, JCB, American Express, Domestic Cards

TEDA Central Hotel
★★★★
16 Third Dajie, Eco. & Tech. Dev. Zone, (022) 2520 6666
www.teda-hotel.com
Standard room: RMB988
Credit Cards:
Visa, Master Card, American Express

Tian Yu Hotel
★★★★
19 Diantai Lu, Heping
(022) 2360 3388, *www.ty-hotel.com*
Credit Cards:
Visa, Master Card, JCB, American Express, Domestic Cards

Tianjin Junyue Hotel
★★★★
16 Guizhou Lu, Heping
(022) 8558 8888
Standard room: RMB980
Credit Cards: Visa, Master Card, JCB, American Express

Tianjin Victory Hotel

A Shining Star In The Heart Of A Growing City

A striking landmark in the promising city -Tianjin, Hotel Nikko Tianjin is superbly located in the heart of the city's commercial center. Whether you are traveling for business or pleasure, we at Hotel Nikko recognize that every guest's needs are unique and we consistently deliver excellence at every corner around the world.

hotel nikko tianjin
天津日航酒店

NO.189 Nanjing Road, Heping District, Tianjin, 300051, China
Phone: +86-22 8319-8888
www.nikkotianjin.com

Opening in the spring of 2007

★★★★
11 Jintang Lu, Tanggu
(022) 2534 5833
www.victoryhotel.com
Credit Cards: Visa, Master Card,
JCB, American Express
Cairnhill International Hotel
★★★
2 Sanma Lu, Nankai, (022) 2735 1688
www.cairnhillhotel.com
Standard room: RMB258
Credit Cards: Visa, Master Card,
JCB, American Express
Hotel Ibis Tianjin
★★★
30 Third Dajie, Eco. & Tech. Dev.
Zone, (022) 5981 5100
www.ibishotel.com
Standard room: RMB198, 178
Credit Cards:
Visa, Master Card, JCB, American
Express, Domestic Cards
Ocean Hotel Tianjin
★★★
5 Ocean Square, Hebei

(022) 2420 5518
Standard room: RMB803
Credit Cards: Visa, Master Card,
JCB, American Express
Zhengda Hotel
★★★
6 Wanliucun Dajie, (022) 6059 2888
www.zhengdahotel.com
Credit Cards:
Visa, Master Card, JCB, American
Express, Domestic Cards

Restaurants

Japanese
Kahan 河畔餐厅
219 Jiefang Bei Lu, 2/F Hyatt
(022) 2330 1234
Western
Kiessling's Restaurant
起士林西餐厅
33 Zhejiang Lu, (022) 2332 1603
Friday's 星期五餐厅
7 Fukang Lu, (022) 2300 5555 ext.84
Shabere 夏倍乐
24 Xihucun Dajie, (022) 8741 0780

Chinese
Goubuli Restaurant 狗不理大酒店
322 Heping Lu, (022) 2303 1118
Chuyuntian Restaurant
楚云天酒楼
195 Baidi Lu, (022) 2738 6628
Japanese
Kahan 河畔餐厅
219 Jiefang Bei Lu, 2/F Hyatt
(022) 2330 1234
Korean
Sorabol 萨拉伯尔
873 Dagu Nan Lu, (022)2833 5588
Seafood
Lilac Garden 丁香花园
Xiamen Lu, Zhong Duan, People's
Park, (022) 2328 5555

Hospitals

Tianjin First Central Hospital
天津市第一中心医院
24 Fukang Lu, (022) 2362 6032
First Hospital of Tianjin
天津市第一医院
24 Guangming Lu
(022) 2446 3310
Tianjin Medical University Hospital
天津医科大学总医院
154 Anshan Dao, (022) 2351 4019

Bookstores

Xinhua Bookstore
天津市滨江道新华书店
165 Binjiang Dao, Heping District
(022) 2711 1290

Industrial Parks

**Tianjin Economic & Technological
Development Area**
天津技术开发区
(022) 2520 1111
www.teda.gov.cn
Major Industries: Electronics

Tianjin Export Processing Zone
天津出口加工区
(022) 6629 9621, *www.teda.gov.cn*
Major Industries: Export processing,
logistics, warehousing
**Tianjin Port Free Trade Zone /
Tianjin Airport Industrial Park**
天津港保税区/天津空港物流加
工区
(022) 2576 3844
www.teda.gov.cn
Major Industries: Export processing,
logistics, warehousing
Tianjin High-Tech Industrial Park
天津高科技园区
(022) 8371 5785
www.thip.gov.cn
Major Industries:
Electronics, information technology,
biotechnology, new materials

Exhibition centers

**Tianjin World Economy Trade &
Exhibition Center**
32 Youyi Lu, Hexi, Tianjin
(022) 2835 2222
www.tjtwtc.com

Tibet

Population: 2.77 million
Area: 1,220,000 sq km
Capital: Lhasa
Airports: Lhasa, Banda, Gonggar
Border Crossings: Nielamu, Pulan, Jilong, Riwu and Yadong

Tibet is a sprawling region located at the highest elevation of any place in the world. It borders the Karakoram Mountains to the west, the Kunlun Mountains to the north, and the Himalayas to the south, which include the world's highest peak, Mt Everest, straddling its border with Nepal. The region is sparsely populated, and its native inhabitants mainly engage in agriculture in the numerous river valleys. Nomadic groups also use the huge expanses of land for grazing.

The Tibetans have a unique culture with deep roots in Buddhism. They are optimistic and kind people. During its long history, Tibet has had periods of independent rule and periods when it has had different degrees of political connection with China and India. It was for centuries a theocracy – run by Buddhist monks, led by "incarnations" of the Dalai Lama, the most important figure in Tibet. Communist troops occupied Tibet in 1951.

In 1959, the young Dalai Lama escaped to India after an unsuccessful Tibetan revolt against Chinese control. The region saw widespread destruction of monasteries and temples during the 1960s and 1970s led by Maoist Red Guards, but some monasteries were allowed to re-open in the 1980s. Fitful negotiations have been held over the past decades between the exiled Tibetans and Beijing on terms for a return of the Dalai Lama, but they have always stalled over the degree of autonomy Tibet could be given. Meanwhile, tourism, immigration, the internet, fast food and property investments are changing Tibetan society, linking it ever more closely with the rest of China and the rest of the world.

Buddhism reached Tibet in the 7th century, and in a dispute in the 9th century, the Yellow Hats crushed the Red Hats and the Yellow Hats' leader adopted

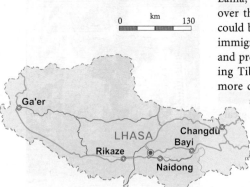

the title of Dalai Lama. Each Dalai Lama is considered the reincarnation of the last, and upon the death of a Dalai Lama, the monks search the land for a newborn child who shows signs of embodying his predecessor's spirit.

The present Dalai Lama, the 14th, was installed after the 13th Dalai Lama died in 1940. He received the Nobel Peace Prize in 1989. In 1999, the Dalai Lama announced that while he was not seeking independence from China, he wanted a form of self-rule that would satisfy Tibetans.

Tibet is the poorest of China's regions. Tourism is Tibet's top earning industry, accounting for about 10% of GDP. Around 1.8 million tourists visited the region in 2005, most of them from other parts of China. In July 2006, the number of tourists visiting Tibet was up 44% over July 2005.

Other economic activities include mining, wool and wool spinning, forestry, food processing and printing. With the development of animal husbandry, leather production is a key money earner. Much of Tibet in still without electricity, and power shortages are a major drag on development.

The region has big deposits of a wide range of minerals, most of them unexploited and often inaccessible. Agriculture is the main source of revenue for most Tibetans, and the main crops are highland barley and wheat.

In recent years China has placed more emphasis on Tibet's economic development. The completion of the Tibet-Qinghai railway, which became operational in mid-2006, will hopefully spur more activity. For Tibetans though, greater economic prosperity is a mixed blessing. Tibetan culture remained intact for hundreds of years primarily due to isolation. With growing influence from the

rest of China, there is a legitimate fear that some of Tibet's uniqueness may disappear. This would be a welcome side effect of development for Beijing, as the government feels a weaker distinct identity would also weaken any Tibetan independence movement.

Restrictions on travel to Tibet are stricter than for the rest of China, and travelers must obtain a special Tibet travel permit, available at any travel agency.

Tibet Economic Data			
	2005	2004	Change%
GDP (RMB bn)	25.1	22.0	14.1
GDP per capita (RMB)	9,114	7,779	17.2
Exports (US$ bn)	0.17	0.13	30.77
Imports (US$ bn)	0.04	0.07	-42.86
Cars per 100 households	3.00	2.00	50
PCs per 100 households	19.00	17.00	11.76

Lhasa 拉萨

Telephone prefix: 0891
Population: 270,000
Bank of China: 28 Linkuo Xi Lu

Lhasa, meaning the "sacred place of the Buddhas" in the Tibetan language, is an ancient city on the plateau with a history of over 1,300 years. It sits at an elevation of over 3,600 meters – one of the highest cities in the world.

Lhasa is divided into two sections – a modern Chinese area and a traditional Tibetan area. The most famous symbol of the city is Potala Palace, the former seat of the Dalai Lama, built in the 17th century. The Jokhang temple in the center of town dates back 1,300 years. It contains some of the greatest treasures of Tibetan culture, including a pure gold statue of Sakyamuni. The Barkhor is the name given to the pilgrim circuit that runs clockwise around the temple. A host of market and tea stalls has grown up to serve the streams of pilgrims and tourists. The Norbu Linka, once the summer residence of the Dalai Lama, is 3km west of the Potala Palace. The park here contains several small palaces and a zoo.

Tibetan boots, rugs, saddle blankets, jewelry, temple bells and prayer wheels are all sold in Lhasa, and you can watch carpets being woven at the Khawachen Carpet Factory on Jinzhu Xilu. Local beer halls put on shows of traditional Tibetan music and dancing, known as Longman, or 'royal music'.

Lhasa Economic Data	
GDP 2005 (RMB bn)	8.67
Disposable income 2005 (RMB)	9,500

Hotels

Century Hotel
★★★★
66 Beijing Zhong Lu
(0891) 682 7111
Standard room: RMB600
Credit Cards:
Visa, Master Card, JCB, American Express

Lhasa Hotel
★★★★
1 Minzu Lu
(0891) 683 2221
www.lhasahotel.com.cn
Credit Cards: Visa, Master Card, JCB, American Express

Restaurants

Tibetan

Celestial Snow Palace Restaurant
雪神宫
Close to Potala Palace
(0891) 682 5866

South Asian

Snowlands Restaurant 雪域餐厅
4 Zangyiyuan Lu (Snowlands Hotel)
(0891) 633 7323

Bars & Clubs

Potala Traditional Snack
布达拉风情酒吧
127 Beijing Zhong Lu
(0891) 633 6664

Hospitals

People's Hospital of Tibet
西藏自治区人民医院
Linkuo Bei Lu

(0891) 633 2462

Lhasa People's Hospital
拉萨市人民医院
Beijing Dong Lu
(0891) 632 3811

Bookstores

Xinhua Bookstore
西藏自治区新华书店
219 Beijing Xi Lu
(0891) 638 2362

Industrial Parks

Lhasa Economic & Technological Development Zone
拉萨经济技术开发区
(0891) 686 3035
www.invest-tibet.gov.cn
Major Industries:
Tibetan medicine, new materials, biopharmaceuticals

DESTINATIONS

Xinjiang

Population: 20.1 million
Area: 1,600, 000 sq km
Capital: Urumqi
Airports: Urumqi, Kashgar, Hetian, Kuche, Kelamayi, Aletai, Narat, Yili
Border Crossings: Shangkou, Baketu, Jimunai, Yierkeshitan, Hongqilapu, Tuergate, Wulasitai, Takeshiken, and Hongshanzui

Xinjiang (meaning New Frontier), a land of arid desert, deep depressions, ice-capped mountains and climatic extremes, was historically crossed by Silk Road caravans to and from Central Asia and beyond. As such, the region served as China's first and most important overland mercantile route.

Three times the size of France, this vast region extends over 1,600,000 square km in China's northwest – nearly one-sixth of China's total territory.

Formally known as Xinjiang Uyghur Autonomous Region, the region is divided into two basins by the Tianshan Mountains – the Jungar Basin, a grazing land to the north and the Tarim Basin (Taklamakan) a vast desert to the south. Xinjiang's terrain includes the great Altai, Tianshan and Kunlun mountains on its north, west and south, respectively.

China's second-largest border trade zone after Heilongjiang, Xinjiang borders Kazakhstan, Kirghizstan, Uzbekistan, Tajikistan, Afghanistan, Pakistan and India. Xinjiang has 16 designated border trade points with neighboring countries.

Xinjiang has been loosely controlled by China on and off since the Han Dynasty. It was conquered in the 8th century by the Tibetans; the region itself was established during the Qing dynasty in 1884. Relations between Xinjiang's mainly Muslim population and the Chinese authorities have been marked by sporadic cultural and religious conflicts. Massive Han Chinese immigration in recent decades has contributed to periodic outbreaks of discontent with Chinese rule.

Xinjiang's population is roughly 19 million, with Muslim, Tur-

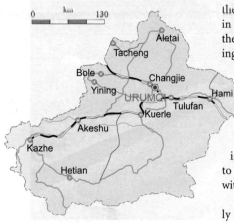

kic-speaking Uyghurs constituting nearly half the population. Uyghurs are closer to Central Asians in their language and ethnicity and do not look like traditional Han Chinese. Be aware that in many parts of the region it is forbidden to drink alcohol or eat pork.

The province is well known for its fruit, including grapes and melons. Wheat, barley, oats, sugar beets, hops and cotton are also grown and cattle, sheep, and horses are raised. Lop Nor, a largely dried-up salt lake in the Tarim basin, was the site of Chinese nuclear test explosions.

The vast oil fields in Karamay are among China's largest, and there are extensive deposits of coal, gold, silver, copper, lead, and zinc. The Chinese government sees Xinjiang as the country's largest oil and gas producer by 2010. Transport of these resources will be facilitated by the new west-east gas and oil pipeline. Other industries include textiles, cement production, and sugar refining. Karamay, Urumqi, and Korla are the major industrial centers.

Major export items include food and live animals, non-edible raw materials, machinery and transport equipment, textiles and other light industrial products. Major import goods included aluminum and steel products, chemical fertilizer, paper and paper products and medical equipment.

Kashgar, in the far west of Xinjiang, is connected to Urumqi by plane and rail (passing through Korla, Kuche and Aksu), while Urumqi itself is linked by air to major towns in China (and some international destinations mainly in Central Asia and Russia) and by rail to the rest of China via Lanzhou, Gansu province.

The Urumqi Foreign Economic Relations and Trade Fair is a major annual event promoting foreign trade and inward investment.

Xinjiang Economic Data			
	2005	2004	Change%
GDP (RMB bn)	260.4	220.9	17.9
GDP per capita (RMB)	13,108	11,199	17.0
Exports (US$ bn)	5.04	3.05	65.25
Imports (US$ bn)	2.90	2.59	11.97
Cars per 100 households	2.81	0.79	255.69
PCs per 100 households	23.86	17.84	33.74

Urumqi 乌鲁木齐

Telephone prefix: 0991
Population: 2.30 million
Bank of China: 2 Dongfeng Lu

Established as the capital of Xinjiang in 1884, Urumqi has a semi-arid continental climate and glories in the title of the world's furthest city from the sea.

Among international investors in Urumqi is France's Carrefour, which opened two stores in 2004. While the city has a fair selection of hotels, nightlife options are still limited. One reason would be the locals' tendency to frown on alcohol consumption.

Urumqi has over 10 billion tons of coal reserves and the Salt Lake is rich in minerals, including iron, copper, uranium and gold.

Apart from the stunning lake of Tian Chi 115km east of the city, Urumqi's most notable tourist sight is the Xinjiang Autonomous Region Museum which contains a remarkable collection of ancient non-Han Chinese mummies.

Urumqi Economic Data	
GDP 2005 (RMB bn)	57.1
Disposable income 2005 (RMB)	10816

Hotels

Hoi Tak Hotel Xinjiang
★★★★★
1 Dongfeng Lu, (0991) 232 2828
Standard room: RMB1,400
Credit Cards: Visa, Master Card, JCB, American Express
Hongfu Hotel Xinjiang
★★★★★
26 Huanghe Lu, (0991) 588 1588
www.hongfuhotel.com
Mirage Hotel
★★★★★
5 Xinhua Bei Lu, (0991) 293 7888
www.mirage-hotel.cn
Standard room: RMB1,200
Credit Cards: Visa, Master Card, JCB, American Express
Xinjiang Silver Star Hotel
★★★★★
134 Qitai Lu, (0991) 588 8888
www.silverstarhotel.com
Standard room: RMB1,200
Credit Cards: Visa, Master Card, JCB, American Express
Yin Du Hotel
★★★★★
39 Xibei Lu, (0991) 453 6688
www.yinduhotel.com
Standard room: RMB1,500
Credit Cards: Visa, Master Card, JCB, American Express
Royal International Hotel
★★★★★
2 Henan Xi Lu, (0991) 788 7888
www.ruihao.com.cn
Credit Cards: Visa, Master Card, JCB, American Express
Hong Xin Hotel
★★★★
61 Jiefang Bei Lu, (0991) 230 1688
www.hongxinhotel.com
Standard room: RMB300
Credit Cards:
Visa, Master Card, JCB, American Express, Domestic Cards
Hotel World Plaza
★★★★
2 Beijing Nan Lu, (0991) 383 6400
Standard room: RMB800
Credit Cards:
Visa, Master Card, JCB, American

Express, Domestic Cards

New Times Hotel

★★★★

7 Youhao Bei Lu, (0991) 429 2888

www.newtimes-hotel.com

Standard room: RMB780

Credit Cards: Visa, Master Card, JCB, American Express

Ramada Hotel Urumqi

★★★★

52 Changjiang Lu, (0991) 587 6688

www.ramada.com

Standard room: RMB588

Credit Cards: Visa, Master Card, JCB, American Express

Torch Hotel Xinjiang

★★★★

18 Diamond City, Beijing Nan Lu

(0991) 383 6699

www.torch-hotel.com.cn

Standard room: RMB299 (low season), 599 (high season)

Credit Cards: Visa, Master Card, JCB, American Express

Tu Ha Petroleum Hotel

★★★★

9 Jiangsu Dong Lu, (0991) 661 0066

www.hoteltuha.com

Credit Cards: Visa, Master Card, JCB, American Express

Xinjiang Grand Hotel

★★★★

168 Xinhua Bei Lu, (0991) 293 5888

www.hotelxj.cn

Standard room: RMB380

Credit Cards: Visa, Master Card, JCB, American Express

Daluqiao Hotel

★★★

1 Beijing Bei Lu, (0991) 788 8388

www.daluqiaohotel.com

Standard room: RMB400

Credit Cards: Domestic Cards

Restaurants

American

Western 绿洲西餐厅

168 Xinhua Bei Lu

(Xinjiang Grand Hotel)

(0991) 281 8788

Muslim

Kashgar 喀什葛里清餐厅

168 Xinhua Bei Lu

(Xinjiang Grand Hotel)

(0991) 281 8788

Silk Road 丝绸之路

2 Beijing Nan Lu

(0991) 383 6400

International

Panorama 天山阁

2 Beijing Nan Lu (Hotel World Plaza)

(0991) 383 6400

Hospitals

Urumqi Friendship Hospital 乌鲁木齐市友谊医院

22 Shengli Lu

(0991) 286 0270

People's Hospital of Xinjiang 新疆维吾尔自治区人民医院

91 Tianchi Lu

(0991) 856 2242

Bookstores

Xinhua Bookstore 乌鲁木齐市新华书店

346 Jiefang Nan Lu, (0991) 282 4939

Industrial Parks

Urumchi Economic & Technological Development Zone 乌鲁木齐经济技术开发区

(0991) 371 6656

www.uda.gov.cn

Major Industries:

Light industry, textiles, pharmaceutical, machinery, electronics

DESTINATIONS

Yunnan

Population: 44.5 million
Area: 394,000 sq km
Capital: Kunming
Airports: Kunming, Lijiang, Dali, Zhongdian, Diqin, Xishuangbanna, Mangshi, Simao, Zhaotong, Baoshan
Border Crossings: Ruili, Leiduo, Hekou

Located in China's southwest region just north of Myanmar and Laos, Yunnan is one of the most diverse regions in the country, with more ethnic minority groups than any other province in China. Seen as one of the main gateways between China and Southeast Asia, it will play an important role when the China-ASEAN free trade zone comes into effect in 2010.

Home to more than 30 of the country's 55 ethnic minority groups, Yunnan's cultural range is

unmatched. Minorities such as Tibetans, Bai, Dai, Naxi, Zhuang, Miao, Hani, Hui and Lisu live here and add to the distinctly Southeast Asian feel of the province. Almost half of the 43 million inhabitants are non-Han Chinese, and each group has its own distinct customs, festivals, dress and food.

Historically, Yunnan has played a minor role compared with other regions, often serving as a place to exile disgraced officials. The influence of the Chinese government in this distant province has varied widely over the centuries, and revolts against the Han by the local peoples have occurred regularly throughout history. In the 19th century, the region started to feel the influence of foreign powers, most notably the French, who claimed rights to the province along with several others in southern China. Yunnan also served as a link in the crucial supply route that fed resources to the Nationalists during World War II.

Today, raw material processing is the focus of Yunnan's heavy industry sector, which was until recently less developed than the light industry sector, but has grown fast since 1990. Light industrial activity is closely linked to the province's agriculture and natural resources, and cigarette manufacturing is the most important sector. Food processing, chemicals, metallurgy and power generation also feature prominently.

Yunnan contains a wealth of mineral resources but foreign investment, particularly by Canadian firms, has been primarily interested in gold. China's largest deposits of zinc are found here, particularly around the city of Gejiu, near the Vietnamese border. Most of China's deposits of lead, tin, and cadmium are also in Yunnan.

Yunnan has poured hundreds of millions of dollars into power infrastructure in the last few years, and the province is one of the most important energy sources in China's national power grid. New hydropower stations are being built on the upper and lower reaches of the Lan-

cang River and the province has built transmission facilities to send power eastwards to Guangdong province. A proposed dam project on the Nujiang River was suspended in 2004 due to an outcry from environmentalists who feared the virgin ecosystem would be damaged. However, in 2006, the Thai and Mynmar governments entered into an agreement to dam the river further downstream.

Yunnan is still a primarily agrarian region and boasts the highest agricultural output of all of China, with terrace farming making good use of precious land on the many hills and mountains in the province. Major food crops include rice, corn, potatoes and wheat. One third of the country's plant species are found in Yunnan.

Cash crops are important to the provincial economy, primarily tobacco – Yunnan is the country's largest producer (the small city of Yuxi is one of the biggest tobacco production bases in China). Yuxi Hongta

Tobacco is China's main tobacco group, producing the well-known Hongtashan brand cigarettes.

Another sector worth watching is tourism. Yunnan has the most developed tourism industry in western China, but many of the high-potential destinations still lack access and infrastructure. Main tourist draws include Kunming and the Stone Forest nearby, Xishuangbanna's rainforests and the wild border town of Ruili in the south and Lijiang, a World Heritage site, in the northwest. The extreme northwest is considered by many to be the source of the legend of Shangri-la, the fantastic land described in James Hilton's famous novel Lost Horizon. To emphasize this connection, the name of Zhongdian was changed to Shangri-la, or Xianggelila in Chinese.

Because of its remote location and position near Southeast Asia's Golden Triangle, Yunnan is experiencing two rapidly growing and

related social problems: HIV/AIDS and heroin usage. There are officially more than 16,000 HIV-positive residents in Yunnan, but the actual number is thought to be much higher. HIV infections here are chiefly linked to widespread prostitution and intravenous drug use, especially heroin. The drug comes from Southeast Asia and is generally smuggled to Dali, and is then distributed out to the rest of the country. As a result, Yunnan has some of the most progressive policies regarding drug treatment and AIDS prevention in the country, setting up addiction treatment centers and proactively distributing condoms.

Yunnan Economic Data			
	2005	2004	Change%
GDP (RMB bn)	347.3	308.2	12.7
GDP per capita (RMB)	7,835	6,733	16.4
Exports (US$ bn)	2.64	2.24	17.86
Imports (US$ bn)	2.10	1.51	39.07
Cars per 100 households	7.92	6.91	14.62
PCs per 100 households	29.44	25.73	14.42

Kunming 昆明

Telephone prefix: 0871
Population: 6.09 million
Bank of China: 515 Beijing Lu

Known as China's "spring city" for its year-round cool climate, Kunming is one of the most pleasant cities in China. The combination of high altitude and tropical latitude produces a climate with warm sun and cool breezes during the day and a slight chill at night.

Kunming's economy is essentially a microcosm of the provincial economy. Agriculture is a major contributor to many residents' incomes and tobacco-related ventures employ a large number of locals. Mining is also important – one of China's top five phosphate mines is located on the city's outskirts – and the area also holds significant iron ore and bauxite deposits. Growth in the tourism sector is a major driver in the local economy. Other key industries include food processing, machinery production, textiles, construction materials and chemicals.

Kunming is to be a key city in a proposed free trade zone between China and the Association of Southeast Asian Nations (ASEAN), scheduled to come into effect in 2010. Over the last 15 years, trade between China and Southeast Asia has increased an average of 20% each year. With the lowering of tariffs between China and ASEAN member states, the trend is expected to continue. In order to facilitate this growth, numerous highways and railroad links are being constructed with the primary goal of linking Singapore with Kunming, and in turn all of China.

In 1937 and 1938, Kunming absorbed 60,000 refugees fleeing the fighting between Japan and the Chinese armed forces. This was to have a profound impact on the city, which had a population of roughly 150,000 at the time. The city became a home of scholars fleeing from Japanese-

occupied north China and to this day, Kunming is the top academic center of southwestern China, with universities such as Yunnan University and Yunnan Normal University leading the region particularly in agricultural research.

The city is famous for its laid-back atmosphere, and boasts a number of coffeehouses including Salvador's and the French Café. It is a magnet for foreign students, and the young run in mixed circles, with most of the foreigners speaking good Chinese and counting locals among their best friends. It is common for young foreign students to stay in Kunming long after they finish their studies, sometimes for years at a time.

Kunming Economic Data	
GDP 2005 (RMB bn)	106.1
Disposable income 2005 (RMB)	9,618

Hotels

Bank Hotel Kunming
★★★★★
399 Qingnian Lu, (0871) 315 8888
www.bankhotel.com
Standard room: RMB1,318
Credit Cards: Visa, Master Card, JCB, American Express
Greenland Hotel
★★★★★
80 Tuodong Lu, (0871) 318 9999
Standard room: RMB1,012
Credit Cards: Visa, Master Card, JCB, American Express
Harbour Plaza Kunming
★★★★★
20 Honghua Bridge, (0871) 538 6688
Standard room: RMB1,050
Credit Cards: Visa, Master Card,

JCB, American Express
Horizon Hotel
★★★★★
432 Qingnian Lu, (0871) 318 6666
www.horizonhotel.net
Credit Cards:
Visa, Master Card, JCB, American Express, Domestic Cards
Kai Wah Plaza International Hotel
★★★★★
157 Beijing Lu, (0871) 356 2828
www.kaiwahplaza.com
Credit Cards: Visa, Master Card, JCB, American Express
Economic Trade Hotel
★★★★
298 Qingnian Lu, (0871) 319 0888
www.ynethotel.com
Credit Cards:
Visa, Master Card, Domestic Cards
Golden Dragon Hotel
★★★★
575 Beijing Lu, (0871) 313 3015
www.gdhotel.com.cn
Standard room: RMB820
Credit Cards:
Visa, Master Card, JCB, American Express, Domestic Cards
Kunming Hotel
★★★★
52 Dongfeng Dong Lu
(0871) 316 2063
www.kmhotel.com.cn
Standard room: RMB780
Credit Cards: Visa, Master Card, JCB, American Express, Domestic Cards, Diners Club
Kunming Jinjiang Hotel
★★★★
98 Beijing Lu, (0871) 313 8888
www.km-jinjiang.cn
Standard room: RMB480
Credit Cards: Visa, Master Card,

JCB, American Express

Mandarin Hotel Yunnan

★★★★

Building A Xinghe Bright, Guanshang Zhong Lu, (0871) 809 6666

Credit Cards:
Visa, Master Card, JCB, American Express, Domestic Cards

New Era Hotel

★★★★

99 Dongfeng Xi Lu, (0871) 362 4999

www.erahotel.com

Standard room: RMB840

Credit Cards: Visa, Master Card, JCB, American Express

New Nanjiang Hotel Kunming

★★★★

241 Dongfeng Xi Lu, (0871) 538 1999

www.nnjhotel.com

Standard room: RMB729

Credit Cards: Visa, Master Card, JCB

Sakura Hotel Kunming

★★★★

29 Dongfeng Dong Lu
(0871) 316 5888

www.sakurahotel.cn

Credit Cards: Visa, Master Card, JCB, American Express

Tai Long Hong Rui Hotel

★★★★

279 Chuncheng Lu, (0871) 355 9999

Credit Cards:
Visa, Master Card, JCB, American Express, Domestic Cards

Telecom International Hotel Kunming

★★★★

39 Huancheng Nan Lu
(0871) 330 5888

www.telhotel.com

Standard room: RMB764

Credit Cards: Visa, Master Card, JCB

Weilong Hotel

★★★★

42 Yanhe Lu, (0871) 361 6688

Credit Cards:
Visa, Master Card, JCB, American Express, Domestic Cards

Zhongyu Hotel Kunming

★★★★

87 Guanshang Zhong Lu
(0871) 715 5188

www.kmzyjd.com

Standard room: RMB688

Credit Cards: Visa, Master Card, JCB, American Express

Hydro Jintai Hotel

★★★

118 Huancheng Nan Lu
(0871) 333 3918

www.jintaihotel.com.cn

Standard room: RMB558

Credit Cards: Visa, Master Card, JCB, American Express

Yunnan Taoliyuan Hotel

★★★

170 Baohai Lu, Guanshang
(0871) 718 8806

www.taoliyuan-hotel.com.cn

Standard room: RMB388

Credit Cards: Domestic Cards

Restaurants

Al Medina Restaurant

2/F, Sightseeing Hotel (across from airport), (0871) 732 5655

Bangkok Café

曼谷咖啡厅

44 Wenhua Xiang, Wenlin Jie
(0871) 531 0669

Makye Ame 玛吉阿米

Jinhuapu Lu (Inside the Kunming office of Diqing Prefecture)
(0871) 833 6300

Pisa Pizza 比萨比萨

160 Wenlin Jie, (0871) 534 1359

DESTINATIONS

Pizza da Rocco 乐客比萨
202 Wenlin Jie, (0871) 538 6817
Red Star 红星公社
Jinhuapu Lu (next to Chunyuan Residential Area), (0871) 822 8345
Teresa's Pizza
40 Wenlin Jie #2
7 Shili Wuxing Huacaiyuan (Across from Kaiyuan Residential Area)
(86) 136 7879 0664
Watami 和民
47 Wenhua Xiang, Wenlin Jie
(0871) 691 2366
Wicker Basket 馨香烤屋
Kaiyuan Residential Area, Bldg 11, 1-4, (0871) 822 1382

Cafes

Anxiang Coffee Bar 岸香咖啡吧
98 Fu Chun Jie, (0871) 3605958
Blog Cafe 博客
46 Qingyun Jie, (0871) 5175609
City Garden Coffee Shop
城市花园咖啡店
138 Wujing Lu, (0871) 3115999

French Café 兰白红
70 Wenlin Jie, (0871) 5382391
Manabe 真锅咖啡馆
6 Sanshi Jie (Brilliant Plaza, South Bldg, Suite B), (0871) 3635868
Ming Tien Coffee 名典咖啡语茶
212 Baoshan Jie, (0871) 6400064
Prague Café 布拉格咖啡馆
40-5 Wenlin Jie, (0871) 0871 5332764
Salvador's Coffee House
萨尔瓦多名咖啡馆
76 Wenhua Xiang, Wenlin Jie
(0871) 0871 5363525
Kaiyuan Residential Area, Bldg 14
(0871) 0871 8225457
Tiziano Coffee 提香咖啡吧
25 Sanhe Ying, (0871) 3646920
Tranströmer Café 瑞云咖啡廊
101 Xiba Lu, (0871) 4114691
UBC Coffee 上岛咖啡
6 Sanshi Jie (Brilliant Plaza ground floor, room 116), (0871) 3649168
Yixiang Coffee 逸香咖啡语茶
171 Guofang Lu, (0871) 3628538
Yunjoy 云嘉

45 Wenhua Xiang, Wenlin Jie
(0871) 5516364

Bars & Clubs

Babi 芭比慢摇吧
Kundu, Xinwen Lu, (0871) 415 7888
Café de Camel
骆驼餐厅酒吧
62 Tuodong Lu, (0871) 319 5841
Cha Ma Bar 茶马吧
96 Dongfeng Dong Lu
(0871) 316 3000 x7/8
Chapter One
146 Wenlin Jie, (0871) 536 5635
New York Bar 纽约吧
20 Honghuaqiao
(Inside Harbour Plaza Hotel)
(0871) 538 6688 x3199
Silver Oak 银橡树
76 Wenhua Xiang, Wenlin Jie
(0871) 316 1379
Speakeasy Bar 说吧
445 Dongfeng Xi Lu
(0871) 532 7047
The Box 老夫子
69 Wenhua Xiang, Wenlin Jie
(0871) 536 2137
The Hump Bar 驼峰酒吧
Jinbi Plaza, (0871) 364 0359
Tsingtao Beer Bar 青岛啤酒吧
Kundu, 42 Wacang Zhuang
(0871) 361 9299

Hospitals

Yunnan Provincial People's Hospital 云南省第一人民医院
172 Jinbi Lu
(0871) 362 7731
First Affiliated Hospital of Kunming Medical College
昆明医学院第一附属医院
295 Xichang Lu
(0871) 5324888

Bookstores

Xinhua Bookstore
昆明市新华书店
56 Nanpin Jie
(0871) 364 3267

Consulates

Thailand 泰国
145, South Tower, Kunming Hotel, 52
Dongfeng Lu
(0871) 316 8916

Industrial Parks

Hekou Border Economic Cooperation
河口边境经济合作区
(0873) 342 4526
Major Industries:
Food processing, agribusiness
Kunming Economic & Technological Development Zone
昆明经济技术开发区
(0871) 727 5011
www.ketdz.gov.cn
Major Industries:
Mechanical manufacturing, biopharmaceuticals, tobacco
Kunming High-Tech Industrial Development Zone
昆明高新技术产业开发区
(0871) 831 2391
www.kmhnz.gov.cn
Major Industries:
Bioengineering, electronics information technology, photoelectronics, new materials

Exhibition centers

Kunming International Convention Exhibition Center
289 Chuncheng Lu, Kunming
(0871) 717 8999
www.kmicec.com

Lijiang 丽江
Telephone prefix: 0888
Population: 1.1 million

This famous city is perhaps best known for its proximity to Tiger Leaping Gorge, a very popular tourist attraction. The gorge is formed where the Yangtze River cuts between Jade Dragon Snow Mountain and Haba Mountain, with cliffs rising 2,000 meters. Legend has it that a tiger jumped across the gorge at its narrowest point (25 meters) to escape a hunter.

The city of Lijiang has over 1 million people, but the most visited area is the old town (more properly called Dayan town), which is an official UNESCO World Heritage Site and dates back some 800 years. The Naxi people are the area's traditional residents.

A massive earthquake in 1996 destroyed about one third of Lijiang, and rebuilding efforts since then have often brought condemnation from those who do not consider them authentic enough. Indeed, the government has pushed the tourist appeal of Lijiang, opening up an airport in 1995 and operating direct flights from Beijing, Shanghai and of course, Kunming.

Hotels

Guanfang Hotel Lijiang
★★★★★
Shangri-la Dajie
(0888) 518 8888
www.gfhotel-lijiang.com.cn
Credit Cards:
Visa, Master Card, JCB, American Express, Domestic Cards

Lijiang Treasure Harbour International Hotel
★★★★★
North Section Shangri-la Dajie
(0888) 311 6688
www.treasureharbour.cn
Credit Cards:
Visa, Master Card, JCB, American Express, Domestic Cards

Aviation Lijiang Guanguang Hotel
★★★★
Central Section Shangri-la Dajie, Dayan Town
(0888) 516 0188
www.lj-ggjd.com
Credit Cards:
Visa, Master Card, JCB, American Express, Domestic Cards

Jiannanchun Hotel
★★★★
8 Guangyi Jie, Dayan Town
(0888) 510 2222
www.jnchotel.com

Senlong Hotel
★★★★
Minzhu Lu, Guojing Nan Lu
(0888) 512 0666
www.senlonghotel.com
Standard room: RMB688
Credit Cards:
Visa, Master Card, JCB, American Express, Domestic Cards

Wang Fu Hotel Lijiang
★★★★
9 Yigu Lane, Nanmen Jie, Gucheng
(0888) 518 9666
www.ljhotel.cn
Standard room: RMB680
Credit Cards:
Visa, Master Card, JCB, American ExpressJ

Zhejiang

Population: 48.98 million
Area: 101,800sq km
Capital: Hangzhou
Airports: Hangzhou, Ningbo, Wenzhou, Zhoushan, Quzhou, Huangyang, Yiwu, Putuoshan
Ports: Ningbo, Wenzhou, Zhoushan, Zhapu

Located on China's east coast just south of Shanghai, Zhejiang is one of the most prosperous provinces in China. It is one of the country's major manufacturing centers, with cities like Hangzhou, Ningbo, and Wenzhou global leaders in the production of a wide range of consumer goods. Zhejiang has a moist, subtropical climate with cool winters and long, hot summers.

Zhejiang has a long history of economic prosperity. The Grand Canal, a historic north-south waterway, runs from Beijing to the north of Zhejiang, one of the most fertile and heavily populated regions in the whole of China. Tourism, particularly from the newly-moneyed Shanghai crowds that head south at weekends and during national holidays, is also becoming a major source of income for Zhejiang.

Zhejiang's factories are generally considered to be among the best in China and this is reflected in the high number of consumer goods manufactured there each year, a number that continues to grow at an astonishing rate. Silk is one of the most popular exports – Zhejiang today produces approximately one third of the nation's total silk output.

The region is also famous for its high-quality tea production. Even on the fringes of the capital, Hangzhou, there are tea fields growing famous Longjing (Dragon Well) tea, the best varieties of which can fetch astronomical prices – up to US$750 per kilogram. During the harvest, the population in tea-growing areas will swell to double or even triple as migrant workers swarm through the fields picking the valuable leaves.

Recently, increased competition

in Zhejiang's manufacturing sector has led to a more blasé attitude towards intellectual property rights, and in 2005 the province had more IPR infringements than anywhere else in China. Also, an emphasis on manufacturing has led to high energy consumption, and Zhejiang has been susceptible to power shortages, particularly in the summer months.

Growth industries in Zhejiang in recent years have included electronics and telecoms, largely thanks to the rapid growth of foreign investment in Zhejiang in these areas. Multinational companies of note that have already set up in Zhejiang include Motorola, Siemens and Toshiba. A large majority of foreign investment flowing into Zhejiang originates in Hong Kong with other major investors including the US, Taiwan, Japan and the UK.

One of the reasons that Zhejiang has been so successful is its avid encouragement of entrepreneurship, especially the support of small businesses. This development theory has been dubbed the "Zhejiang model."

As one of the wealthiest provinces, Zhejiang has become a magnet for luxury brands. High-end fashion labels like Armani have established stores in Hangzhou, as has the German auto maker Porsche.

Zhejiang Economic Data			
	2005	2004	Change%
GDP (RMB bn)	1343.8	1164.9	15.4
GDP per capita (RMB)	27,703	23,942	15.7
Exports (US$ bn)	76.80	58.16	32.05
Imports (US$ bn)	30.59	27.07	13.00
Cars per 100 households	8.71	3.52	147.44
PCs per 100 households	59.47	44.72	32.98

Hangzhou 杭州
Telephone prefix: 0571
Population: 7.50 million
Bank of China: 320 Yan'an Lu

Hangzhou has a history as a trade and administrative center that stretches back well over 1,000 years, and was one of the first cities in the world to register a population of more than a million. The city was notable enough to be referred to at length by Marco Polo – whether he visited China or not.

The city is situated beside the West Lake, one of the most beautiful natural features of China, and tourism has always been an important part of its economy. To that has now been added huge manufacturing capacity.

Hangzhou has become a magnet for foreign investment, with light manufacturing, electronics, and textiles leading the way. Mobile phone giants such as Motorola and Nokia have invested in the city, and the Xiaoshan Development Zone to the east of the city has major investments by companies including Coca-Cola, United Biscuits, and more than 40 Taiwanese enterprises.

Hangzhou has some of the most modern transportation facilities in China and is linked to Shanghai and other surrounding cities by numerous expressways. The city is additionally served by three airports and two rail stations making it an easy place to reach from nearly all parts of China.

In 2006 the government announced plans to introduce a maglev train line between Shanghai and Hangzhou, which would cut the travel time from two hours down to 45 minutes. But the train, if built, would not be operational for quite some time.

Hangzhou Economic Data	
GDP 2005 (RMB bn)	294.27
Disposable income 2005 (RMB)	16,601

Hotels

Hyatt Regency Hangzhou
★★★★★
28 Hubin Lu, (0571) 8779 1234
Credit Cards:
Visa, Master Card, JCB, American
Express, Diners Club
Fuchun Resort
★★★★★
Fuyang Section Hangfuyanjiang Lu
(0571) 6346 1111
www.fuchunresort.com
Credit Cards: Visa, Master Card,
JCB, American Express
Hangzhou Continental Hotel
★★★★★
2 Pinghai Lu, (0571) 8708 8088
www.hzch.com
Standard room:
RMB1,150 +15% Surcharge
Credit Cards: Visa, Master Card,
JCB, American Express
**Howard Johnson Oriental Hotel
Zhejiang**
★★★★★
288 Genshan Xi Lu, (0571) 8676 7888
Credit Cards: Visa, Master Card,
JCB, American Express
Jinma Palace Hangzhou
★★★★★
218 Tonghui Zhong Lu
(0571) 8288 7888
www.jinma-hotel.com
Standard room:
RMB798 +10% Surcharge
Credit Cards: Visa, Master Card,
JCB, American Express
**New Century Grand Hotel
Hangzhou**
★★★★★
818 Shixin Zhong Lu, Xiaoshan
(0571) 8288 8888
www.ncihotel.com

Credit Cards:
Visa, Master Card, JCB, American
Express, Domestic Cards
**New Century Resort Qiandao Lake
Hangzhou**
★★★★★
Qilin Island Qiandao Lake Town,
Chun'an, (0571) 6501 8888
www.ncihotel.com
Credit Cards:
Visa, Master Card, JCB, American
Express, Domestic Cards
Radisson Plaza Hotel Hangzhou
★★★★★
333 Tiyuchang Lu
(0571) 8515 8888
Standard room: RMB1,660
Credit Cards:
Visa, Master Card, JCB, American
Express, Domestic Cards
Shangri-La Hotel Hangzhou
★★★★★
78 Beishan Lu, (0571) 8797 7951
Standard room:
RMB1,650 +15% Surcharge
Credit Cards:
Visa, Master Card, JCB, American
Express, Domestic Cards
Sofitel Westlake Hangzhou
★★★★★
333 Xihu Dajie, (0571) 8707 5858
Standard room:
RMB1,500 +15% Surcharge
Credit Cards:
Visa, Master Card, JCB, American
Express, Domestic Cards
Sofitel Xanadu Resort Hangzhou
★★★★★
3318 Fengqing Dajie, Wenyan Town,
Xiaoshan, (0571) 8388 0888
Credit Cards: Visa, Master Card,
JCB, American Express, Diners Club
World Trade Center Grand Hotel

inviting

Located in the heart of the city by the West Lake, Hyatt Regency Hangzhou offers stylish accommodation, spectacular views, exciting dining experience and splendid meeting venues.

FEEL THE HYATT TOUCH®

28 Hu Bin Road, Hangzhou, Zhejiang 310006, People's Republic of China
TELEPHONE +86 571 8779 1234 FACSIMILE +86 571 8779 1818
hangzhou.regency.hyatt.com

Zhejiang
★★★★★
122 Shuguang Lu, (0571) 8799 0888
www.wtcgh.com
Credit Cards:
Visa, Master Card, JCB, American
Express, Domestic Cards

Zhejiang International Hotel
★★★★★
221 Tiyuchang Lu, (0571) 8577 0088
www.zjih.com
Standard room: RMB688
Credit Cards: Visa, Master Card,
JCB, American Express

Regal Plaza Hotel Hangzhou
★★★★★
370 Tiyuchang Lu, (0571) 5619 9999
www.regalplazahotel.com
Standard room: RMB1,388
Credit Cards:
Visa, Master Card, JCB, American
Express, Domestic Cards

Best Western Hangzhou
★★★★
511 Moganshan Lu
(0571) 8805 1000
Standard room: RMB680
Credit Cards:
Visa, Master Card, JCB, American
Express, Domestic Cards

Culture Plaza Hotel Zhejiang
★★★★
38 Wener Lu, (0571) 8882 5888
www.zjcphotel.com
Credit Cards: Visa, Master Card

Dragon Hotel
★★★★
120 Shuguang Lu, (0571) 8799 8833
www.dragon-hotel.com
Standard room:
RMB810 +15% Surcharge
Credit Cards:
Visa, Master Card, JCB, American

Express, Domestic Cards

Hai Wai Hai Hotel
★★★★
1 Kaifa Lu, Nanshan, Qiandaohu
Town, (0571) 6488 (0888)
www.haiwaihai.com
Standard room: RMB688
Credit Cards:
Visa, Master Card, JCB, American
Express, Domestic Cards

Hangzhou Capital-Star Hotel
★★★★
448 Wenhui Lu, (0571) 8838 6888
www.c-starhotel.com
Standard room: RMB980
Credit Cards: Visa, Master Card,
JCB, American Express

Hangzhou Friendship Hotel
★★★★
53 Pinghai Lu, (0571) 8707 7888
Standard room: RMB680
Credit Cards: Visa, Master Card,
JCB, American Express

**Hangzhou Fuyang Eden Holiday
Hotel**
★★★★
Xihushan Village, Shouxiang Town
(0571) 5678 8888
www.fuyang.com
Standard room: RMB680
Credit Cards: Domestic Cards

Hangzhou Hotel
★★★★
546 Yan'an Lu, (0571) 8516 6888
www.hangzhouhotel.com.cn
Standard room: RMB580
Credit Cards:
Visa, Master Card, American Express

**Hangzhou Huachen International
Hotel**
★★★★
25 Pinghai Lu, (0571) 8765 2222
www.hcgjhotel.com

Standard room: RMB450
Credit Cards:
Visa, Master Card, JCB, American Express, Domestic Cards
Hangzhou Sunny Hotel
★★★★
108 Jiefang Lu, (0571) 8721 8899
www.sunny-hotels.com
Credit Cards:
Visa, Master Card, JCB, American Express, Domestic Cards
Hangzhou Tianchengyuan Hotel
★★★★
166 Zhonghe Zhong Lu
(0571) 2802 1188
Standard room: RMB680
Credit Cards: Visa, Master Card, JCB, American Express
Hangzhou Tower Hotel
★★★★
1 Wulin Plaza, (0571) 8515 3911
Standard room: RMB780
Credit Cards: Visa, Master Card, JCB, American Express
Hangzhou Xinqiao Hotel
★★★★

226 Jiefang Lu, (0571) 8707 6688
www.hzxqhotel.com
Standard room: RMB880
Credit Cards: Visa, Master Card, JCB, American Express
Holiday Inn Hangzhou
★★★★
289 Jianguo Bei Lu
(0571) 8527 1188
Standard room: RMB722
Credit Cards: Visa, Master Card, American Express, Domestic Cards
International Hotel, Xiaoshan
★★★★
1 Wenhua Lu, Xiaoshan
(0571) 8265 6888
Standard room: RMB520
Credit Cards: Visa, Master Card, JCB, American Express
Jianfeng Hotel Hangzhou
★★★★
30 Qiutao Bei Lu, (0571) 8696 6688
Credit Cards: Domestic Cards
Milan Hotel
★★★★
346 Yan'an Lu, (0571) 8703 3111

Standard room: RMB378
Credit Cards:
Master Card, Domestic Cards
New Century Zhijiang Holiday
Resort
★★★★
4758 Jiangnan Dajie, Binjiang
(0571) 8669 6888
www.kaiyuangroup.com
Standard room: RMB580
Credit Cards: Visa, Master Card,
JCB, American Express
Ramada Plaza Hangzhou Haihua
★★★★
298 Qingchun Lu, (0571) 8721 5888
www.ramada.com
Standard room:
RMB919 +15% Surcharge
Credit Cards:
Visa, Master Card, JCB, American
Express, Domestic Cards
Redstar Culture Hotel Hangzhou
★★★★
280 Jianguo Nan Lu
(0571) 8770 3888
www.redstarhotel.com
Standard room: RMB328
Credit Cards:
Visa, Master Card, JCB, American
Express, Domestic Cards
Wanghu Hotel
★★★★
2 Huancheng Xi Lu, (0571) 8707 8888
www.lakeviewhotelhz.com
Credit Cards:
Visa, Master Card, JCB, American
Express, Domestic Cards
Wuyang International Hotel
★★★★
48 Qingchun Lu, (0571) 8721 8888
www.wuyanghotel.com
Standard room: RMB388
Credit Cards:

Visa, Master Card, JCB, American
Express, Domestic Cards
Zhejiang Grand Hotel
★★★★
595 Yan'an Lu, (0571) 8505 6666
www.zjghotel.com
Standard room: RMB680
Credit Cards:
Visa, Master Card, JCB, American
Express, Domestic Cards
Zhejiang Hotel
★★★★
447 Yan'an Lu, (0571) 8791 3333
www.zjfd.com
Credit Cards:
Visa, Master Card, JCB, American
Express, Domestic Cards
Zhejiang Xinyu City Hotel
★★★★
315 Wenhui Lu, (0571) 8539 4888
www.xycityhotel.com.cn
Standard room: RMB330
Credit Cards:
Visa, Master Card, JCB, American
Express, Domestic Cards
Hangzhou Huajiashan Resort
★★★★
25 Santaishan Lu, Xihu
(0571) 8797 6688
www.hzhjsz.com
Credit Cards:
Visa, Master Card, American Express
Zhejiang Railway Hotel
★★★★
8 Chengzhan Square, Shangcheng
(0571) 8783 0688
www.zjtdds.com
Standard room: RMB520
Credit Cards: Visa, Master Card

Restaurants

French
Les Ripailles莱利法式餐厅

152 Nanshan Lu, (0571) 8706 3228

Italian
Va Bene 华缤霓意大利餐厅
Xihutiandi, 147 Nanshan Lu
(0571) 8702 6333
Peppino 巴比诺
78 Beishan Lu (Shangri-La Hotel)
(0571) 8707 7951
Valentino 华伦天奴意大利餐厅
333 Tiyuchang Lu, (0571) 8515 8888

Western
Boton 伯顿西餐厅
2/F Great Wall Building, 346 Yan'an
Lu, (0571) 8708 5757
Caribbean Sea 加勒比海餐厅
58 Yan'an Nan Lu, (0571) 8780 9900
Oak Grill 橡树公园
289 Jianguo Bei Lu, (0571) 8527 1188
Laurel Lounge 桂雨厅
7 Shuguang Lu (Huang Long Hotel)
(0571) 8799 8833

Indian
Haveli 天度餐厅
77 Nanshan Lu, (0571) 8707 9677

Barbeque
Brasilia 巴西利亚南美音乐餐厅
2/F Hangzhou Opera House, 360
Tiyuchang Lu, (0571) 8515 0998

Paulaner BBQ
宝莱纳巴西烤肉
21/F Xinyu City Hotel, 315 Wenhui
Lu, (0571) 8539 4633

Cantonese
Zen 湖蝶
Xihutiandi, 147 Nanshan Lu
(0571) 8702 7711

Cafe
Tea & Wine Chapter
杭州茶酒年代
Xihutiandi, 147 Nanshan Lu
(0571) 8702 6993

Thai
Banana Leaf
蕉叶泰国餐厅
1/F-2/F, Overseas Hotel, 39 Hubin
Lu, (0571) 8707 2345

Japanese
Yimalikawa 伊万里川日本料理
2/F, 2 Pinghai Lu, (0571) 8708 8088

Chinese
Louwailou Restaurant 楼外楼
30 Gushan Lu, (0571) 8796 9682

Hospitals

**Hangzhou Hospital of Traditional
Chinese Medicine** 杭州中医院

453 Tiyuchang Lu, (0571) 8582 7888
Hangzhou Red-Cross Hospital
杭州红十字会医院
208 Huancheng Dong Lu
(0571) 5610 9999
First People's Hospital of Hangzhou
杭州第一人民医院
4 Xueshi Lu, (0571) 87065701

Bookstores

Xinhua Bookstore, Jiefang Branch
解放路新华书店
225 Jiefang Lu, (0571) 8792 4809

Industrial Parks

Hangzhou Economic & Technological Development Zone
杭州经济技术开发区
(0571) 8691 3653
www.heda.gov.cn
Major Industries:
Machinery, electronics, biopharmaceutical, textiles, chemical fibers, foodstuffs, high-tech chemicals
Hangzhou High-Tech Industrial

杭州高新技术产业开发区
(0571) 8821 7856
www.hhtz.com
Major Industries:
Electronics, new materials, medicine and biotechnology
Xiaoshan Economic & Technological Development Zone
萧山经济技术开发区
(0571) 8283 5906
www.xetz.gov.cn
Major Industries:
Electronics, IT, software development, biomedicine, new materials, photoelectronic systems

Exhibiton centers

Hangzhou Peace International Convention & Exhibition Center
158 Shaoxing Lu, (0571) 8581 7027
www.hzpiec.com
Hangzhou World Trade Center Zhejiang
122 Shuguang Lu, 0571) 8799 0888
www.wtcgh.com

Ningbo 宁波

Telephone prefix: 0574
Population: 6.32 million
Bank of China: 139 Yaoxing Jie

Ningbo has been an important trading port since the fifth century AD. It was a port of call for Arab traders in the 13th century, and in the mid-19th century was one of the first of China's cities to be forced open to Westerners and foreign trade. But it was quickly eclipsed by the rise of Shanghai just to the north, and many of its canny businessmen moved to the new foreign-dominated city.

To the east of Ningbo, on the coast at Beilungang, a deepwater container port was built to try to grab logistics business from Shanghai, and even from Keelung on Taiwan. But Shanghai is the key center and it has now opened its own deepwater terminal, Yangshan port.

Ningbo has a vibrant economy dominated by private companies. Textiles and garments, produced both for export and domestic sale, are a major component of its output. It is also a major center for electronics and industrial machinery production. Foreign companies with investments in the area include Esso, Xerox, Metro, LG, and Samsung.

For more than a century Ningbo, only 160km south of Shanghai, has suffered from the fact that the broad expanse of Hangzhou Bay separates the two cities. But the resourceful city has a plan to solve the problem – a bridge stretching 36 km over the open ocean.

In true Chinese style, it is a fantastic project of mammoth proportions – a six-lane highway stretching over the open ocean. Work on the bridge, which is budgeted to cost US$1.4 billion, has already begun and completion is expected in 2008, at which point driving time to Shanghai will apparently take just 90 minutes.

Hotels

CITIC Ningbo International Hotel
★★★★★
1 Jiangdong Bei Lu
(0574) 8775 7888
www.citichotel-nb.com
Credit Cards: Visa, Master Card, JCB, American Express
Grand Pacific Hotel
★★★★★
168 Nanhinjiang Lu
(0574) 6288 6288
Standard room: RMB1,242
Credit Cards:
Visa, Master Card, JCB, American Express, Domestic Cards
Hangzhou Bay Hotel
★★★★★
301 Shishan Lu, (0574) 6391 4888
www.hangzhoubayhotel.com
Credit Cards:
Visa, Master Card, JCB, American Express, Domestic Cards
Nanyuan Hotel Ningbo
★★★★★
2 Lingqiao Lu, (0574) 8709 5678
www.nanyuanhotel.com
Standard room: RMB1,030
Credit Cards:
Visa, Master Card, JCB, American Express, Domestic Cards
Xiangshan Harbour International Hotel

★★★★★
1111 Xiangshangang Lu
(0574) 6577 8888
www.xshih.com
Credit Cards:
Visa, Master Card, JCB, American
Express, Domestic Cards
Howard Johnson Plaza Hotel
Ningbo
★★★★★
230 Liuting Jie, (0574) 8729 1060
Standard room:
RMB1,388 +15% Surcharge
Credit Cards:
Visa, Master Card, JCB, American
Express, Domestic Cards
Cixi International Hotel
★★★★
625 Xincheng Dajie
(0574) 6392 8888
www.cxih.net
Credit Cards:
Visa, Master Card, JCB, American
Express, Domestic Cards
Good Sun International Business
Apartment
★★★★
966 Baizhang Dong Lu
(0574) 8706 3888
www.goodsun.cn
Credit Cards:
Visa, Master Card, JCB, American
Express, Domestic Cards
Jadedoor Hotel
★★★★
669 Songjiang Dong Lu
(0574) 8818 5999
www.jundu-hotel.com
Credit Cards:
Visa, Master Card, JCB, American
Express, Domestic Cards
New Century Hotel Ningbo
★★★★

812 Baizhang Dong Lu
(0574) 8706 8888
www.kaiyuangroup.com
Credit Cards: Visa, Master Card,
JCB, American Express
Ningbo World Hotel
★★★★
145 Zhongshan Dong Lu
(0574) 2788 0088
www.nbwhotel.com
Standard room: RMB818
Credit Cards: Visa, Master Card,
JCB, American Express
Pitman Hotel
★★★★
6 Tongtu Lu, Jiangdong
(0574) 8701 7888
www.pitmanhotel.com
Standard room: RMB215
Credit Cards: Visa, Master Card,
JCB, American Express
Xiangshan Gold Coast Hotel
★★★★
Songlanshan Resort, Xiangshan
(0574) 6570 6888
Credit Cards:
Visa, Master Card, JCB, American
Express, Domestic Cards
Xinzhou Hotel
★★★★
678 Zhongshan Dong Lu, Jiangdong
(0574) 8771 7678
www.xz-hotel.com
Standard room: RMB468
Credit Cards: Visa, Master Card,
JCB, American Express
New Golden Star Hotel
★★★★
555 Liuting Jie, (0574) 8708 7888
www.xjxhotel.com.cn
Standard room: RMB328 (executive
standard), 358 (business standard)
Credit Cards: Domestic Cards

CITIC NINGBO INTERNATIONAL HOTEL

The Citic Ningbo International Hotel is a five-star hotel in Ningbo,and get Quality Management System Certificate (ISO9001:2000) Environmental Management System Certification (ISO14001:2004) OHSAS Certification (OHSAS18001:1999).Our hotel situated in the heart of Ningbo city's financial and commercial center with spectacular river and city views. It is only 15km away from the Ningbo International Airport and 2km away from the railway station.

Our hotel consists of 286 various types of guest rooms. Each room is Internet ready for our computer age guests. Every executive room is specially equipped exclusive computer and fax machine. A number of restaurants provide Western and Chinese style cuisine. Wide ranges of recreational facilities are available in the hotel. A wide choice of conference and meeting rooms, including the Grand Ballroom provided with facilities of simultaneous interpretation.

中信宁波国际大酒店
CITIC NINGBO
★ ★ ★ ★ ★ INTERNATIONAL HOTEL

Address: 1 Jiangdong Bei-lu, Ningbo, Zhejiang, 315040 P.R.China
Tel: (86-574)87757888   Fax: (86-574)87334739
http://www.citichotel-nb.com   E-mail: nbcitic@mail.nbptt.zj.cn

Jinfeng Hotel
★★★
567 West Section Huancheng Bei Lu
(0574) 8721 3456
www.jfhotel.com
Standard room: RMB358
Credit Cards:
Visa, Master Card, JCB, American
Express, Domestic Cards

Yun Hai Hotel
★★★
2 Changchun Lu
(0574) 8709 8888
www.yunhaihotel.com
Credit Cards: Visa, Master Card, JCB,
American Express, Domestic Cards

Restaurants

Chinese
Shi Pu Restaurant 石浦大酒店
1118 Baizhang Dong Lu
(0574) 8783 8888

Seafood
Wuyi Restaurant 五一大酒店
51 Xianxue Jie, (0574) 8732 5151

Cafe
Ming Tien Coffee Language
名典咖啡语茶
112 Zhonghe Lu
(0574) 8686 7555
UBC 上岛咖啡
280 Liuting Jie, (0574) 8712 8968

Pizza
Italian Pizza House 意大利比萨屋
147 Jiefang Nan Lu, (0574) 8730 8768

Barbeque
Brazilian Barbeque 森吧阳光
46 Shuijing Jie
(0574) 8736 5555

Hunan
Sharndy Hunan Restaurant
湘地家乡餐馆
24-25 Qicao Jie, (0574) 8772 2007

Hospitals

Ningbo Hospital of Traditional Chinese Medicine 宁波中医院
64 Xiaowen Xiang, (0574) 8708 9090
Lihuili Hospital
宁波市李惠利医院
57 Xingning Lu, (0574) 8701 8701

Bookstores

Xinhua Bookstore
宁波市新华书店
71 Zhongshan Dong Lu
(0574) 8724 6576

Industrial Parks

Ningbo Economic & Technological Development Zone
宁波经济技术开发区
(0574) 8678 3420
www.netd.com.cn
Major Industries: Textiles, electronics, auto parts, petrochemicals
Ningbo Free Trade Zone
宁波保税区
(0574) 8688 5445
www.nftz.gov.cn
Major Industries: Information technology, machinery, bioengineering
Ningbo Daxie Island Development Zone 宁波大榭开发区
(0574) 8676 7047
www.citic-daxie.com
Major Industries:
Port transshipment, storage, petrochemicals, precision chemicals, building materials, medicine, machinery manufacturing, textiles

Exhibition centers

Ningbo International Convention & Exhibition Center
181 Huizhan Lu, (0574) 8705 2113
www.intex-nb.com

Shaoxing 绍兴

Telephone prefix: 0575
Population: 4.34 million
Bank of China: 201 Renmin Zhong Lu

Shaoxing is, or was, one of the most beautiful of the old east China canal towns. There are still streets and alleys that are reminiscent of the old China of Mandarin scholars, concubines and calligraphy, and many of the canals are still there too.

The town is famous for its rich rice wine with its distinctive fragrance. It is usually drunk hot, and if you drink too much you will feel truly awful the next morning.

Shaoxing's most famous son is the writer Lu Xun, who played a key role in dragging Chinese literature into the 20th century. He was the first major writer to use colloquial Chinese instead of the classical writing style, which made his books more accessible to common people. His best-known books are The Story of Ah-Q, and Diary of a Madman.

Hotels

Shaoxing International Hotel
★★★★★
100 Fushan Xi Lu, (0575) 516 6788
www.sxint.com
Standard room:
RMB888 +15% Surcharge
Credit Cards: Visa, Master Card, JCB, American Express
Xianheng Hotel
★★★★★
680 Jiefang Nan Lu, (0575) 806 8688
www.xianhengchina.com
Standard room:

RMB980 +15% Surcharge
Credit Cards: Visa, Master Card, JCB, American Express
Shaoxing Hotel
★★★★
9 Huanshan Lu, (0575) 515 5888
www.hotel-shaoxing.com
Credit Cards: Visa, Master Card, JCB, American Express, Domestic Cards
Shaoxing Yuedu Hotel
★★★★
1 Shengli Dong Lu, (0575) 514 8888
Standard room: RMB318
Credit Cards:
Visa, Master Card, Domestic Cards

Restaurants

Shanghai
Xianheng Restaurant 咸亨酒店
179 Luxun Zhong Lu ,(0575) 511 6666

Hositals

People's Hospital of Shaoxing
绍兴市人民医院
61 Dong Jie, (0575) 522 8888

Bookstores

Xinhua Bookstore 绍兴市新华书店
163 Shengli Dong Lu, (0575) 513 4696

DESTINATIONS

Wenzhou 温州

Telephone prefix: 0577
Population: 873,000
Bank of China: Xihu Jinyuan, Renmin Xi Lu

Wenzhou is a small coastal city in southeast Zhejiang noted for its intense love affair with capitalism. The city has virtually no state enterprises, and its private entrepreneurs are famous through China and the world for their clannish but effective business approach.

Wenzhou entrepreneurs are famous for arranging their own financing amongst their friends, and are not beholden to the state banks. There are some incredibly rich families in the city, and the Shanghai property market has been significantly affected in recent years by the infusion of Wenzhou investment funds.

In 2005, Wenzhou ranked fifth on the Forbes list of best cities for commerce in China.

Hotels

Dong Ou Hotel
★★★★
Dongjian Building, Wenzhou Dajie
(0577) 8676 7888
www.dongouhotel.com
Credit Cards:
Visa, Master Card, JCB, American Express, Domestic Cards
Olympic Hotel
★★★★
8 Minhang Lu, (0577) 8837 9999
www.chinaolympichotel.com
Credit Cards:
Visa, Master Card, JCB, American Express, Domestic Cards
Shunsheng Hotel
★★★★
36 Lucheng Lu, (0577) 8827 0000
www.shunshenghotel.com
Credit Cards:
Visa, Master Card, JCB, American Express, Domestic Cards
Victoria Grand Hotel Wenzhou
★★★★
320 Ma'anchi Dong Lu

(0577) 8827 8888
www.victoriagrandhotel.com
Credit Cards: Visa, Master Card, JCB,
American Express, Domestic Cards
Wenzhou Dynasty Hotel
★★★★
2 Minhang Lu, (0577) 8837 8888
Standard room:
RMB750 +10% Surcharge
Credit Cards: Visa, Master Card,
JCB, American Express
Wenzhou Guomao Grand Hotel
★★★★
1 Liming Xi Lu, (0577) 8831 1111
www.wzguomaohotel.com
Standard room: RMB398
Credit Cards: Visa, Master Card,
JCB, American Express
Wenzhou International Hotel
★★★★
1 Renmin Zhong Lu, (0577) 8825 1111
www.wzihotel.com
Standard room:
RMB780 +10% Surcharge
Credit Cards: Visa, Domestic Cards
Wenzhou Wanhao Grand Hotel
★★★★
East Wenzhou Railway Station
(0577) 8808 9888
www.wanhaohotel.com
Standard room: RMB678
Credit Cards: Visa, Master Card,
JCB, American Express
Rui Xing Hotel
★★★
135 Lucheng Lu, (0577) 8809 9999
www.wzruixing.com
Standard room: RMB328
Credit Cards: Domestic Cards

Restaurants

International
Victoria Grand Hotel

维多利亚大酒店
58 Ma'anchi Dong Lu
(0577) 8827 8888
Bordeaux Restaurant
波尔多西餐厅
Jingshan Shan Ding
(0577) 8853 9008
Yuntianlou Guoding Restaurant
云天楼国鼎酒店
Guoding Building, Xiaonan Lu
(0577) 8828 8888
Chinese
Yindu Restaurant
银都大酒店
Tangjiaqiao Bei Lu, (0577) 8651 1111
Guansong Lou 观松楼
2/F Fengsheng Building, Jiefang Bei
Lu, (0577) 8817 8888

Hospitals

First Affiliated Hospital of Wenzhou Medical College
温州医学院附属第一医院
2 Fuxue Xiang, (0577) 8806 9624
Wenzhou Second People's Hospital
温州市第二人民医院
32 Dajian Xiang, (0577) 8807 0114

Bookstores

Xinhua Bookstore
温州市新华书店
A 104, Hongde Building, Gongran
Lu, (0577) 822 5231

Industrial Parks

Wenzhou Economic & Technological Development Zone
温州经济技术开发区
(0577) 8891 7125
www.wetdz.gov.cn
Major Industries: Biotechnology,
genetic engineering, medicine, electronics, new materials, new energy

Hong Kong 香港
Telephone prefix: 00852
Population: 6.93 million

Hong Kong, whose name means fragrant harbor, is located next to Guangdong's Shenzhen on the eastern Pearl River Delta and the South China Sea. A Special Administrative Region (SAR), Hong Kong was returned to China from British rule in 1997. It is an important cultural, financial, and logistics center located conveniently at the crossroads of East and Southeast Asia.

Hong Kong occupies a relatively small area of 1,098 square km, and with a population of around 6.8 million, it has one of the world's highest population densities. The territory consists of Hong Kong Island, the Kowloon Peninsula, the New Territories, and 235 other islands. The climate is subtropical, tending to be temperate for nearly half the year. Typhoons often affect Hong Kong with, on average, six hitting its shores annually.

After the handover from Great Britain, Hong Kong's relationship with the mainland was in some ways tentative. For many Chinese, the return of Hong Kong was the end of the 150-year humiliating domination suffered by the Chinese at the hands of Western colonial powers. But there was also uncertainty about how the new government would impact on the economy and daily lives of Hong Kong citizens. Many Hong Kongers moved assets over-seas, and, exacerbated by the Asian financial crisis, the economy experienced a significant downturn. After a few years however, it became clear that in Hong Kong it was more or less business as usual, and the region has emerged in its current incarnation almost as confident and vibrant as ever.

With few natural resources and virtually no arable land, from the 1950s the local economy had been based on manufacturing. But today, as China's capabilities have grown, most capacity has been transferred to the mainland, with just 12% of Hong Kong's GDP now generated by industry. Hong Kong is one of the world's leading service based economies with services counting for 87.9% of GDP. It is also the world's freest market economy, being highly dependent on international trade and imports of food and raw materials due to its limited resources.

Hong Kong has a high standard of living with per capita GDP of US$25,622, comparable with the leading economies of Western Europe. While GDP growth was strong through the 1990s at an annual average of 5%, Hong Kong was hit particularly hard during the

Asian financial crisis in 1998, the global downturn in 2001-2002 and the SARS crisis of 2003. But the economy rebounded in the second half of 2003, with GDP reaching US$158 billion and growth of 3.2%, followed by growth at 7.9% and 7.3% in 2004 and 2005, respectively.

Closer ties

An important driver of growth for Hong Kong in the coming years will be the Closer Economic Partnership Arrangement (CEPA). This is a free-trade agreement between the Mainland and the Hong Kong SAR consistent with China's obligations as a member of the WTO (World Trade Organization). The agreement came into effect on January 2004 and immediately strengthened Hong Kong's position as the leading gateway to China. The CEPA promotes co-development of trade and services on an earlier schedule than the WTO requires by eliminating many tariffs, non-tariff barriers and other discriminatory measures on trade and facilitating cross-trade and investment.

Hong Kong's logistics and transport infrastructure includes one of the world's biggest container ports and the world's busiest air cargo center. The award-winning Hong Kong International Airport is one of the best connected in the world. Hong Kong is renowned for its efficiency, and for enterprises that excel in supply chain management, providing fast and reliable services. The government sees the strategic importance of the logistics capability between the mainland and Hong Kong and is planning to expand the transport network across the Pearl River Delta with projects such as the construction of the Shenzhen Western Corridor and the Hong Kong-Zhuhai-Macau Bridge.

Tourism is one of the fastest-growing sectors in Hong Kong. In 2005, Hong Kong welcomed 23.36

million visitors, 7.3% more than a year earlier. This included some 12.5 million tourists from the mainland. Although Disneyland Hong Kong was not the hit that Disney was expecting it to be, Hong Kong still saw tourism expenditure exceed HK$100 million for the year.

Hong Kong is a major international financial center in the Asia Pacific region. The Hong Kong stock market had a total market capitalization of US$1.46 trillion as of October 2006, ranked seventh in the world. That year saw a number of high-profile IPOs of mainland companies in Hong Kong, such as Bank of China and Industrial and Commercial Bank of China.

It is beneficial to set up a business in Hong Kong when dealing with mainland China, in order to access Hong Kong's strong competency base and services, as well as tax rates that are among the lowest and most straightforward in the world.

Importantly, no tax is paid by firms on foreign-sourced income of any kind. Registering a business is also a simple, straightforward procedure.

Visas for Hong Kong are not required for many travelers. British passport-holders can stay visa-free for up to 90 days; Americans for up to 60 days. Work permits and visas are increasingly more difficult for foreigners to get, requiring special skills or knowledge. With respect to PRC visas, there are many travel agencies and hotels where business or tourist visas can be acquired within a matter of hours.

Hong Kong Data			
	2005	2004	Change%
GDP (US$ bn)	177.7	165.8	7.3
GDP per capita (US$)	25,622	24,096	6.33
Exports of goods to mainland (HK$bn)	37.77	37.9	-0.4
Imports of goods from mainland (HK$bn)	1,049.34	918.28	14.27
Visitor arrivals from mainland (Million people)	12.54	12.25	2.37

Hotels

Grand Hyatt Hong Kong
香港凯悦酒店
★★★★★
1 Harbour Road, Wanchai, Hong
(0852) 2768 1234
Standard room: HK$2,814

Grand Stanford Hotel
海景嘉福酒店
★★★★★
70 Mody Road, Tsim Sha Tsui, Kowloon, (0852) 2721 5161
Standard room: HK$2,100

Hotel Intercontinental
香港洲际酒店
★★★★★
18 Salisbury Road, Tim Sha Tsui,
Kowloon, (0852) 2721 1211
Standard room: HK$2,290

Hotel Miramar 美丽华酒店
★★★★★
11A, 230 Nathan Road, Tim Sha
Tsui, Kowloon, (0852) 2368 1111
Standard room: HK$1,582

Hyatt Regency 凯悦酒店
★★★★★
67 Nathan Road, Tim Sha Tsui,
Kowloon, (0852) 2311 1234
Standard room: HK$1,469

Island Shangri-La Hong Kong
港岛香格里拉大酒店
★★★★★
Supreme Court Road, Pacific Place 2,
Central, Hong Kong Island
(0852) 2877 3838
Standard room: HK$2,306

Kowloon Shangri-la Hong Kong
九龙香格里拉大酒店
★★★★★
64 Mody Road, Tsim Sha Tsui, Kowloon, (0852) 2721 2111
Standard room: HK$2,475

New World Reaissance Hong Kong
新世界万丽酒店
★★★★★
22 Salisbury Road, Tsim Sha Tsui,
Kowloon, (0852) 2369 4111
Standard room: HK$2,260

redBANG

NEVER EVER LOS

Novotel Century Hong Kong Hotel
世纪香港酒店
★★★★★
238 Jaffe Road, Wanchai, Hong Kong Island, (0852) 2598 8888
Standard room: HK$1,230

Peninsula Hotel 半岛酒店
★★★★★
Salisbury Road, Tsim Sha Tsui, Kowloon, (0852) 2366 6251 / 29
Standard room: HK$3,051

Regal Airport Hong Kong Hotel
富豪香港酒店
★★★★★
9 Cheong Tat Road, Chek Lap Kok, Lantau, (0852) 2286 8888
Standard room: HK$1,808

Royal Plaza Hotel Hong Kong
帝京酒店
★★★★★
193 Prince Edward Road, Mong Kok, Kowloon, (0852) 2928 8822
Standard room: HK$1,102

Sheraton Hong Kong Hotel & Tower 香港喜来登酒店
★★★★★
20 Nathan Road, Tsim Sha Tsui, Kowloon, (0852) 2369 1111
Standard room: HK$2,769

The Metropole Hotel 京华国际酒店
★★★★★
75 Waterloo Road, Ho Man Tin, Kowloon, (0852) 2761 1711
Standard room: HK$1,142

Ritz-Carlton Hong Kong 丽嘉酒店
★★★★★
3 Connaught Road, Central, Hong Kong Island, (0852) 2877 6666
Standard room: HK$2,825

JW Marriott Hotel Hong Kong
香港万豪酒店
★★★★★
1 Pacific Place, 88 Queensway, Central, Hong Kong Island
(0852) 2810 8366
Standard room: HK$2,475

Mandarin Oriental Hotel
文华东方酒店
★★★★★
5 Connaught Road, Central, Hong Kong Island, (0852) 2522 0111
Standard room: HK$2,770

Nikko Hong Kong 香港日航酒店
★★★★★
72 Mody Road, Tsim Sha Tsui, Kowloon, Hong Kong Island
(0852) 2739 1111
Standard room: HK$1,500

Conrad Hong Kong 港丽酒店
★★★★★
Pacific Place, 88 Queensway, Central, Hong Kong Island, (0852) 2521 3838
Standard room: HK$2,994

Harbor Plaza 海逸酒店
★★★★★
20 Tak Fung Street, Hung Hom, Kowloon, (0852) 2621 3188
Standard room: HK$1,808

Gold Coast Hotel 黄金海岸酒店
★★★★★
1 Castle Peak Road, Castle Peak Bay, Kowloon, (0852) 2452 8888
Standard room: HK$1,100

The Emperor Happy Valley
英皇骏景酒店
★★★★★
1 Wang Tak Street, Happy Valley, Wanchai, Hong Kong Island
(0852) 2893 3693
Standard room: HK$1,300

Langham Hotel 朗庭酒店
★★★★★
8 Peking Road, Tsim Sha Tsui, Kowloon, (0852) 2375 1133
Standard room: HK$1,525

Renaissance Harbour View

万丽海景酒店
★★★★
1 Harbour Road, Wanchai, Hong Kong Island, (0852) 2802 8888
Standard room: HK$1,300
Royal Pacific & Towers
皇家太平洋酒店
★★★★
33 Canton Road, Tsim Sha Tsui (W), Kowloon, (0852) 2736 1188
Standard room: HK$1,695
Holiday Inn Golden Mile 假日酒店
★★★★
50 Nathan Road, Tsim Sha Tsui (W), Kowloon, (0852) 2369 3111
Standard room: HK$2,712
Harbor Plaza North Point 北角海逸
★★★★
665 King's Road, North Point, Hong Kong Island, (0852) 2187 8888
Standard room: HK$1,582
Excelsior Hong Kong 香港怡东酒店
★★★★
281 Gloucester Road, Causeway Bay, Hong Kong Island, (0852) 2894 8888
Standard room: HK$1,898

Bookstores

Jumbo Grade
1 Harbour View Street, Central
(0852) 2295 0008

Consulates

Argentina 阿根廷
12/F Jardine House, 1 Connaught Place, (0852) 2523 3208
Australia 澳大利亚
24/F Harbour Centre, 25 Harbour Road,(0852) 2827 8881
Austria 奥地利
2201 Chinachem Tower, 34-37 Connaught Road, (0852) 2522 8086
Belgium 比利时

9/F St John's Building, 33 Garden Road, (0852) 2524 3111
Brazil 巴西
Suite 2014 Sun Hung Kai Center, 24 Harbour Street, (0852) 2525 700
Canada 加拿大
11/F-14/F Tower 1, Exchange Square, 8 Connaught Place
(0852) 2810 4321
Czech Republic 捷克共和国
1204-05, Great Eagle Centre, 23 Harbour Road, (0852) 2802 2212
Denmark 丹麦
2402B, Great Eagle Centre, 23 Harbour Road, Wanchai
(0852) 2827 8101
Finland 芬兰
24/F Dah Sing Financial Center, 108 Gloucester Road, (0852) 2525 5385
France 法国
26/F Tower 2, Admiralty Centre, 18 Harcourt Road, (0852) 3196 6100
Greece 希腊
2503-2504 Two Pacific Place, 88 Queensway, (0852) 2774 1682
India 印度
16D, 26/F, United Centre, 95 Queenway, (0852) 2866 4027
Indonesia 印度尼西亚
2/F 127 Leighton Road, Causeway Bay, (0852) 2890 4421
Ireland 爱尔兰
6/F Chungnam Building, 1 Lockhart Road, (0852) 2527 4897
Israel 以色列
1701 Tower 2, Admiralty Centre,18 Harbour Road, (0852) 25296091
Italy 意大利
3206 Asia Pacific Finance Tower, 3 Garden Road, (0852) 2522 0033
Japan 日本
46/F One Exchange Square, 8 Connaught Place, (0852) 2522 1184

Korea 韩国
5/F Far East Finance Centre, 16 Harcourt Road, (0852) 2528 3666

Malaysia 马来西亚
24/F Malaysia Building, 50 Gloucester Road, (0852) 2821 0800

Netherlands荷兰
5702 Cheung Kong Center, 2 Queen's Road, (0852) 2522 5127

New Zealand 新西兰
6508 Central Plaza, 18 Harbour Road (0852) 2877 4488

Norway 挪威
24/F Dah Sing Financial Center, 108 Gloucester Road (Norway represented by Finland in Hong Kong) (0852) 2525 5385

Pakistan 巴基斯坦
3706 China Resources Building, 26 Harbour Road, (0852) 2827 0681

Poland 波兰
2009 Two Pacific Place, 88 Queensway, (0852) 2840 0814

Russia 俄罗斯
2932 Sun Hung Kai Center, 30 Harbour Road, (0852) 2877 7188

Singapore 新加坡
901 Tower 1, Admiralty Centre, 18 Harcourt Road, (0852) 2527 2212

South Africa 南非
2706 Great Eagle Centre, 23 Harbour Road, (0852) 2577 3279

Spain 西班牙
8/F Printing House, 18 Ice House Street, (0852) 2525 3041

Sri Lanka 斯里兰卡
22/F Dominion Centre, 43 Queens Road East, (0852) 2876 0828

Sweden 瑞典
804 Hong Kong Club Building, 3A Chater Road, (0852) 2521 1212

Switzerland 瑞士
16, 2/F Central Plaza, 18 Harbour Road, (0852) 2522 7147

Thailand 泰国
8/F Fairmont House, 8 Cotton Tree Drive, (0852) 2521 6481

Turkey 土耳其
301 Sino Plaza, 255-257 Gloucester Road, (0852) 2572 1331

USA 美国
26 Garden Road, (0852) 2523 9011

Macau 澳门

Telephone prefix: 00853
Population: 0.48 million

Macau, known principally as a gambling mecca, is located on the western edge of the Pearl River delta, just across from Hong Kong, and borders the city of Zhuhai in Guangdong province. It has a population of just 451,000 and a total area of just more than 27 sq km consisting of the Macau Peninsula, Taipa Island and Coloane Island (now one island due to land reclamation), all connected by bridges and causeways. Macau has long been tied to Hong Kong economically.

Formally established in the 16th century, Macau was the first permanent European settlement in the region. It was directly ruled by the Portuguese as a colony for centuries until both governments negotiated its return to China in 1999. Like Hong Kong, Macau will retain a 'high degree of autonomy' regarding internal affairs for 50 years, and the Chinese even invited some of the Portuguese administrators to stay on in the SAR government after the handover.

Macau has some historical sites of interest thanks to its mixed Portuguese heritage, but it is gambling that drives its economy. Gambling has been licensed since 1850 and from 1962 onwards was the monopoly of the Sociedade de Turismo e Diversoes de Macau (STDM). The monopoly was ended in 2002 when two new 20-year casino licenses were issued and two competitors of Las Vegas fame entered. The industry is experiencing explosive growth as greater numbers of principally mainland tourists visit to indulge in its attractions.

As a result of this growth, ambitious expansion plans have been initiated like the Cotai Strip – a multiuse development built on reclaimed land between Taipa and Coloane Islands which will have a series of Las Vegas-style casino hotels with participation from companies like Hilton, Four Seasons, Marriott, and Intercontinental. Phase one of the project is due to be completed in 2007, and the long term goal is to create a new self-sufficient city within the area.

Although the territory suffered in the 1998 Asian financial crisis, the global downturn in 2001, and SARS in 2003, its economy has grown at an astonishing rate since with growth of 11.9% in 2005 to US$11.5 billion. The recovery has been driven by an increase of mainland visitors to the territory as travel restrictions have been relaxed and the resulting increase in gambling profits, the taxing of which generates around 70% of government revenue.

Macau's transport infrastructure

MACAU

中國大陸
China
Mainland

孫文紀念公園
Sun Yat Sen Park

建孙
Built
1849年

500m (1640 feet)

LEGEND

- Hospital
- Museum
- Heritage Route 1
- Heritage Route 2
- Heritage Route 3
- Macau Race Track

內港
Inner
Harbour

白朗古將軍大馬路 Av. Marginal do Lam Mau

裙樓海邊大馬路 Av. Marginal do Patane

花地瑪堂區
Church of Our
Lady of Fatima

青洲
Ilha Verde

筷子基北灣
Baia Norte do Patane

R. da Ribeira do Patane

林則徐紀念館 M
Lin Zexu M.

Colina de Mong Ha

望廈

觀音堂
The Kun
Iam Temple

賽車跑道
Race Track Length
6200 m (20342 feet)

旅遊塔 M
Fire M.

Domus 主教堂
Chapel & Cemetery

東望洋新街 Av. Horta e Costa

二龍喉花園
Lou Lim Ieoc
Garden

松山隧道
Guia Tunnel
456 m (1500 feet)

St. Anthony's
Church

大三巴牌坊 M
Ruins of St Paul's M.

St. Michael's
Cemetery

東望洋山
Guia Hill

基督教墳場 M
& Cemetery
伊斯蘭墳場

START FINISH

大炮台 M
Monte
Fortress

聖老楞佐
St. Lazarus
Church

松山燈塔
Guia Fortress &
Lighthouse M.

St. Dominic's Church

崗頂劇院
Dom Pedro V
Theatre

St. Augustine's
Church

聖若瑟修院
St. Januario
Govt. Hospital

蓮花大馬路
Lotus Flower
in Full Bloom

澳門旅遊
Macau HK
Helicopter
Platform

Macau HK Ferry
Terminal

新馬路 Av. Almeida Ribeiro

亞馬喇前地

漁人碼頭
Fisherman's
Wharf

外港
Outer
Harbour

西望洋聖堂
Penha
Church

賈梅士花園
Cybernetic
Fountain

南灣湖
Nam Van
Lakes

澳門博物館
Handover Gifts
Museum of Macau

媽閣廟
A-Ma Temple

西灣湖
Sai Van
Lakes

觀音蓮花苑
Kun Iam
Ecumenical
Centre

友誼大橋
Friendship Bridge
2569 m (8429 feet)

西灣大橋
Sai Van Bridge
(7220 feet)

NIGHTLIFE

澳氹大橋
Taipa Bridge
1200 m (3937 feet)

澳門旅遊塔
Macau Tower
338 m (1109 feet)

To Taipa

南中國海
South China Sea

中式大船
Chinese Junk

redBANG®
NEVER EVER LOST®

for trade and tourism is an important constraint on its economy. Most tourists arrive by sea, since there is no direct land linkage from Hong Kong, although many mainland Zhuhai tourists travel by land to Macau. Air transport via Macau Airport is not successful due to high costs. Consequently, plans to create the Hong Kong-Zhuhai-Macau Bridge in the next years will provide an important alternative access to Macau to stimulate its economy. In terms of trade and logistics, Macau has been losing competitiveness for quite some time due to infrastructure insufficiencies. Despite its history as a successful port, it lacks the deep-water capacity and air cargo infrastructure necessary to meet modern trade needs.

Hotels

Hyatt Regency Hotel凯悦酒店
★★★★★
2 Estrada Almirante Marques
Esparteiro Taipa Island
(853) 831 234
Standard room: HK$805
New Century Hotel Macau
新世纪大酒店
★★★★★
889 Avenida Padre Tomas Pereira
(853) 831 111
Standard room: HK$800
The Landmark Hotel 置地广场酒店
★★★★★
555 Avenida da Amizade
(853) 781 781
Standard room: HK$1,190
Westin Resort 卫斯汀酒店
★★★★★
1918 Estrada de Hac Sa, Coloane
(853) 871 111

Standard room: HK$1,495
Ritz Macau
★★★★★
Rua do Comendador Kou Ho Neng
(853) 339 955
Standard room: HK$993
Lisboa Hotel 葡京酒店
★★★★★
2-4 Avenida de Lisboa
(853) 577 666
Standard room: HK$977
Mandarin Oriental 文华东方酒店
★★★★★
Avenida da Amizade, (853) 567 888
Standard room: HK$1,206
Pousada de Sao Tiago
圣地亚哥酒店
★★★★★
Avenida da Republica Fortaleza de Sao Tiago da Barra, (853) 378 111
Standard room: HK$1,863
Holiday Inn 假日酒店
★★★★★
82-86 Rua de Pequim
(853) 783 333
Standard room: HK$688
Hotel Grandeur 京澳酒店
★★★★★
199 Rua de Pequim, (853) 781 233
Standard room: HK$750
Beverly Plaza Hote 富豪酒店
★★★★
70 Avenida do Dr. Rodrigo Rodrigues, (853) 782 288
Standard room: HK$630
Pousada de Mong-ha 望厦宾馆
★★★★
Colina da Mong-Ha, (853) 515 222
Standard room: HK$700
Emperor Hotel 帝国酒店
★★★
Rua De Xangai, (853) 781 888
Standard room: HK$620

Reference

Maps	564
China fact file	566
PowerPoint fodder	567
Economic data	568
Chinese leader profiles	574
Trade events 2007	582
Airlines	676
Useful websites	685

REFERENCE

Administrative Regions

- Province
- Municipality
- Autonomous Region

Topography

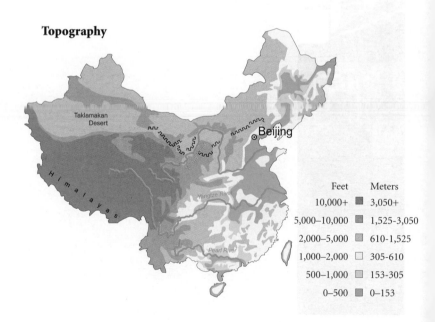

Feet		Meters
10,000+		3,050+
5,000–10,000		1,525-3,050
2,000–5,000		610-1,525
1,000–2,000		305-610
500–1,000		153-305
0–500		0–153

Gross Domestic Product (GDP)
By Province 2005 (RMB billions)

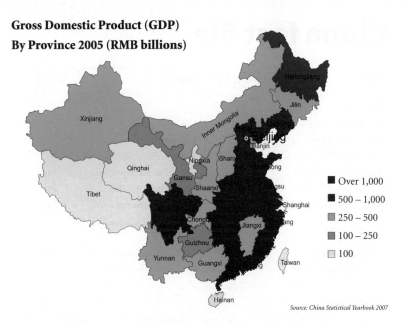

- Over 1,000
- 500 – 1,000
- 250 – 500
- 100 – 250
- 100

Source: China Statistical Yearbook 2007

Total Investment in Foreign-Funded
Enterprises By Province 2005 (US$ billions)

- Over 200
- 50 – 200
- 20 – 50
- 10 – 20
- 1 – 10
- Below 0.1

Source: China Statistical Yearbook 2007

China fact file

Area	9,560,900 sq km	Capital	Beijing

People

Population (millions)	1,307.56	Pop. per sq km	137
Pop. Under 15 (%)	20.3	Pop. over 65 (%)	7.7
Men per 100 women	106.19	Avg male life expectancy (yrs)	70.8
Crude birth rate (%)	13.2	Avg female life expectancy (yrs)	74.6
Urban pop: 2005 (%)	43	Urban pop: 1995 (%)	29.0
Adult Literacy (%)	93.02	Natural growth rate (%)	5.89

Economy

GDP (RMB billions)	18,308.48	GDP (US$ billions)	2,288.56
GDP per capita (RMB)	14,040	GDP per capita (US$)	1,755

Employment

Total workforce (millions)	758.25	Unemployment (% of workforce)	4.2
Emp. Primary sec. (% of workforce)	44.8	Emp. Secondary sec. (% of workforce)	23.8
Emp. Tertiary sec. (% of workforce)	31.4		

Health and education

Health spending as % of GDP	4.15	Doctors per 1,000 pop.	1.52
Hospital beds per 1,000 pop.	2.45	Education spending as % of GDP	2.16

Society

Number of households (millions)	539.10	Average number per household	3.13
Marriages per 1,000 pop.	12.6	Divorces per 1,000 pop.	2.21
Color TVs per 100 households	134.8	Computers per 100 households	41.5
Mobile phones per 100 pop.	30.26	Automobiles per 100 pop.	3.37
Avg annual income of urban households (RMB)			10,493
Avg annual living expenditure of urban households (RMB)			7,943

Exchange rate

RMB per US$ (Nov 2006) 7.87		RMB per EUR (Nov 2006) 10.08
RMB per GBP (Nov 2006) 14.87		RMB per HKD (Nov 2006) 1.01
RMB per JPY (Nov 2006) 0.07		RMB per AUD (Nov 2006) 6.03

PowerPoint fodder

Key facts(All figures for 2005 unless otherwise noted)

- East Asia has been the world's fastest-growing region for more than two decades
- China is the fastest-growing country in East Asia with an average annual GDP growth of approx. 9% since reforms began in 1979
- China's GDP: US$2.29 trillion, 4th in the world (US GDP 2005: US$12.48 trillion)
- GDP growth rates (%)

1998	1999	2000	2001	2002	2003	2004	2005
7.8	7.6	8.4	8.3	9.1	10.0	10.1	10.2

- GDP per capita. US$1,755 (US GDP per capita approx. US$40,100)
- Sources of GDP (%)

Industry	1980	2005
Primary	30	13
Secondary	47	
Tertiary	15	40

- China was the world's third-largest trading nation in 2005 (after the US and Germany)
- By June 2006, China's foreign exchange reserves stood at US$941 billion, 2nd in the world to Japan
- FDI in China: US$60.32 billion, 2nd in the world after the US
- Chinese exports in 1980: 50% primary goods and 50% manufactured goods; in 2005: 6% primary and 94% manufactured goods
- By the end of 2005, 44.8% of the labor force worked in primary industry; 23.8% in secondary; 31.4% in tertiary
- By the end of 2005, there were more than 4.3 million private enterprises in China, employing more than 58 million workers.
- By December 2005, there were 10.79 million private cars in China
- As of October 2005, there were 238 branches and representative offices of foreign banks in China
- In 2005, China's primary energy production amounted to 2.06 billion tons of coal equivalent (TCE) and total energy consumption reached 2.23 billion TCE, which made the country the second largest energy producer and consumer in the world. China imports about 12% of its energy needs
- Number of inbound tourists to mainland China: 120.29 million
- Number of outbound tourists: 31.02 million
- Number of air passengers: 138 million
- Shanghai port's cargo handling: 443 million tons, world's second-largest and China's largest; 18.084 million TEUs of containers
- Ningbo port's cargo-handling: 269 million tons; 5.21 million TEUs of containers
- Guangzhou port's cargo handling: 250 million tons; 4.68 million TEUs of containers
- China's total air cargo in: 3.07 million tons
- Amount of new railway that became operational: 1000 km
- China-US trade: US$211.51 billion
- China-EU trade: US$262.06 billion
- Almost 300,000 millionaires in mainland China (counted in US$)
- Number of returned students: 34,987

REFERENCE

Region	Gross Domestic Product (GDP) (RMB bn)			GDP Per Capita (RMB bn)		
	2005	2004	Y/Y Change (%)	2005	2004	Y/Y Change (%)
Anhui	537.5	475.9	12.9	8,675	7,768	11.7
Beijing	688.6	606.0	13.6	45,444	37,058	22.6
Chongqing	307.0	269.3	14.0	10982	9,608	14.3
Fujian	656.9	576.3	14.0	18,646	17,218	8.3
Gansu	193.4	168.8	14.6	7,477	5,970	25.2
Guangdong	2236.7	1886.5	18.6	24,435	19,707	24.0
Guangxi	407.6	343.4	18.7	8,788	7,196	22.1
Guizhou	197.9	167.8	17.9	5,052	4,215	19.9
Hainan	89.5	79.9	12.0	1,087	9,450	-88.5
Hebei	1009.6	847.8	19.1	14,782	12,918	14.4
Heilongjiang	551.2	475.1	16.0	14,434	13,897	3.9
Henan	1058.7	855.4	23.8	11,346	9,470	19.8
Hubei	652.0	563.3	15.7	11,431	10,500	8.9
Hunan	651.1	564.2	15.4	10,426	9,117	14.4
Inner Mongolia	389.6	304.1	28.1	16,331	11,305	44.5
Jiangsu	1830.6	1500.4	22.0	24,560	20,705	18.6
Jiangxi	405.7	345.7	17.4	9,440	8,189	15.3
Jilin	362.0	312.2	16.0	13,348	10,932	22.1
Liaoning	800.9	667.2	20.0	18,983	16,297	16.5
Ningxia	60.6	53.7	12.8	10,239	7,880	29.9
Qinghai	54.3	46.6	16.5	10,045	8,606	16.7
Shaanxi	367.6	317.6	15.7	9,899	7,757	27.6
Shandong	1851.7	1502.1	23.3	20,096	16,925	18.7
Shanghai	915.4	807.3	13.4	51,474	55,307	-6.9
Shanxi	418.0	357.1	17.1	12,495	9,105	37.2
Sichuan	738.5	638.0	15.8	9,060	8,113	11.7
Tianjin	369.8	311.1	18.9	35,783	31,550	13.4
Tibet	25.1	22.0	14.1	9,114	7,779	17.2
Xinjiang	260.4	220.9	17.9	13,108	11,199	17.0
Yunnan	347.3	308.2	12.7	7,835	6,733	16.4
Zhejiang	1343.8	1164.9	15.4	27,703	23,942	15.7
China	18308.5	15987.8	14.5	14,040	12,336	13.8

Source: China Statistical Yearbook, 2005 and 2004

Region	Imports (US$ bn)			Exports (US$ bn)		
	2005	2004	YOY Change (%)	2005	2004	YOY Change (%)
Anhui	3.93	3.28	19.82	5.18	3.94	31.47
Beijing	94.64	74.09	27.74	30.87	20.58	50.00
Chongqing	1.772	1.766	0.34	2.52	2.09	20.57
Fujian	19.57	18.15	7.82	34.84	29.40	18.50
Gansu	1.54	0.78	101.00	1.09	1.00	9.44
Guangdong	189.81	165.58	14.63	238.16	191.56	24.33
Guangxi	2.30	1.89	21.69	2.88	2.39	20.50
Guizhou	0.54	0.65	-16.92	0.86	0.87	-1.15
Hainan	1.52	2.31	-34.20	1.02	1.09	-6.42
Hebei	5.15	4.19	22.91	10.92	9.34	16.92
Heilongjiang	3.50	3.11	12.54	6.07	3.68	64.95
Henan	2.64	2.45	7.76	5.08	4.18	21.53
Hubei	4.63	3.39	36.58	4.43	3.38	31.07
Hunan	2.25	2.34	-3.85	3.75	3.10	20.97
Inner Mongolia	3.10	2.37	30.80	1.77	1.36	30.15
Jiangsu	104.96	83.36	25.91	122.97	87.50	40.54
Jiangxi	1.63	1.53	6.54	2.43	2.00	21.80
Jilin	4.06	5.08	-20.08	2.47	1.72	43.60
Liaoning	17.57	15.52	13.21	23.44	18.92	23.89
Ningxia	0.28	0.26	7.69	0.69	0.65	6.15
Qinghai	0.09	0.12	-25.00	0.32	0.46	-30.43
Shaanxi	1.50	1.25	20.00	3.08	2.40	28.33
Shandong	30.61	24.82	23.33	46.12	35.86	28.61
Shanghai	95.62	86.51	10.53	90.72	73.51	23.41
Shanxi	2.02	1.35	49.63	3.53	4.04	-12.62
Sichuan	3.20	2.89	10.73	4.70	3.98	18.09
Tianjin	25.90	21.18	22.29	27.38	20.86	31.26
Tibet	0.04	0.07	-42.86	0.17	0.13	30.77
Xinjiang	2.90	2.59	11.97	5.04	3.05	65.25
Yunnan	2.10	1.51	39.07	2.64	2.24	17.86
Zhejiang	30.59	27.07	13.00	76.80	58.16	32.05
China	659.95	561.42	17.55	761.95	593.37	28.41

Source: China Statistical Yearbook, 2005 and 2004

Region	Average Wages (RMB)			Number of Persons Employed in Private Enterprises (Millions)		
	2005	2004	YOY Change (%)	2005	2004	YOY Change (%)
Anhui	15,334	12,928	18.6	1.66	1.41	17.52
Beijing	34,191	29,674	15.2	2.95	2.73	7.88
Chongqing	16,630	14,357	15.8	1.06	1.00	5.50
Fujian	17,146	15,603	9.89	1.35	1.11	21.35
Gansu	14,939	13,623	9.66	0.48	0.42	14.52
Guangdong	23,959	22,116	8.33	5.26	4.35	20.94
Guangxi	15,461	13,579	13.86	0.84	0.66	26.52
Guizhou	14,344	12,431	15.39	0.51	0.37	36.76
Hainan	14,417	12,652	13.95	0.36	0.29	24.14
Hebei	14,707	12,925	13.79	2.42	2.24	7.90
Heilongjiang	14,458	12,557	15.14	0.952	0.84	13.33
Henan	14,282	12,114	17.9	1.39	1.20	15.50
Hubei	14,419	11,855	21.63	1.23	1.10	11.45
Hunan	15,659	13,928	12.43	2.00	1.74	15.17
Inner Mongolia	15,985	13,324	19.97	0.68	0.61	11.80
Jiangsu	20,957	18,202	15.14	7.97	5.62	41.85
Jiangxi	13,688	11,860	15.41	1.34	1.14	17.81
Jilin	14,409	12,431	15.91	0.88	0.99	-11.11
Liaoning	17,331	14,921	16.15	2.52	2.26	11.59
Ningxia	17,211	14,620	17.72	0.23	0.21	11.43
Qinghai	19,084	17,229	10.77	0.28	0.25	11.60
Shaanxi	14,976	13,024	14.99	1.55	1.52	1.64
Shandong	16,614	14,332	15.92	4.44	3.90	13.90
Shanghai	34,345	30,085	14.16	4.66	4.05	15.01
Shanxi	15,645	12,943	20.88	0.82	0.95	-13.37
Sichuan	15,826	14,063	12.54	2.38	1.88	26.60
Tianjin	25,271	21,754	16.17	0.89	0.77	15.19
Tibet	28,950	30,873	-6.22	0.05	0.04	22.50
Xinjiang	15,558	14,484	7.42	0.67	0.57	17.72
Yunnan	16,140	14,581	10.69	1.09	0.77	41.82
Zhejiang	25,896	23,506	10.17	5.35	5.17	3.46
China	18,364	16,024	14.6	58.24	50.17	16.09

Source: China Statistical Yearbook, 2005 and 2004

REFERENCE

Region	Total Investment in Foreign-Funded Enterprises (US$ bn)			Automobiles Owned Per 100 Urban Households		
	2005	2004	YOY Change (%)	2005	2004	YOY Change (%)
Anhui	15.48	12.94	19.63	0.76	0.53	43.39
Beijing	60.67	53.16	14.13	14.06	12.64	11.23
Chongqing	8.03	7.25	10.76	0.67	0.33	103.03
Fujian	75.33	68.88	9.36	1.70	1.42	19.72
Gansu	3.16	3.06	3.27	0.46	0.23	100
Guangdong	288.9	260.96	10.71	9.69	6.56	47.71
Guangxi	14.71	12.68	16.00	1.88	0.48	291.67
Guizhou	2.34	2.23	4.93	1.81	0.38	376.32
Hainan	9.2	8.63	6.60	3.52	2.25	56.44
Hebei	21.93	20.06	9.32	3.94	2.23	76.68
Heilongjiang	10.98	9.47	15.95	1.51	0.95	58.95
Henan	20.64	14.86	38.89	1.58	0.76	107.89
Hubei	25.78	22.69	13.62	0.92	0.31	196.77
Hunan	15.02	11.91	22.93	1.10	0.56	96.43
Inner Mongolia	12.64	10.81	16.93	3.64	3.47	4.89
Jiangsu	265.72	216.98	22.46	4.29	1.83	134.43
Jiangxi	18.49	16.33	13.23	0.73	0.36	102.78
Jilin	20.71	19.35	7.03	1.41	1.16	21.55
Liaoning	81.5	67.92	19.99	1.16	0.42	176.19
Ningxia	4.46	4.07	9.58	1.27	0.36	252.78
Qinghai	0.7	0.96	27.10	1.39	0.67	107.46
Shaanxi	13.7	12.46	9.95	0.44	0.35	25.71
Shangdong	78.62	69.41	13.27	4.47	2.51	78.09
Shanghai	200.67	172.19	16.54	3.80	3.60	5.56
Shanxi	7.71	6.91	11.58	3.13	1.23	154.47
Sichuan	16.6	13.98	18.74	2.37	2.14	10.75
Tianjin	56.77	47.04	20.68	3.00	2.33	28.76
Tibet	0.35	0.33	6.06	3.00	2.00	50
Xinjiang	1.85	1.45	27.59	2.81	0.79	255.69
Yunnan	8.42	7.89	6.72	7.92	6.91	14.62
Zhejiang	101.91	83.4	22.19	8.71	3.52	147.44
China	1174.89	999.3	17.57	3.04	2.18	39.45

Source: China Statistical Yearbook, 2005 and 2004

Region	Computers Owned Per 100 Urban Households			Registered FIEs		
	2005	2004	YOY Change (%)	2005	2004	YOY Change (%)
Anhui	25.97	19.31	34.49	2,165	2,114	2.41
Beijing	89.16	79.44	12.24	10,980	9,890	11.02
Chongqing	51.33	43.67	17.54	1,315	1,294	1.62
Fujian	54.89	46.56	17.89	17,854	17,236	3.59
Gansu	22.99	20.66	11.28	658	650	1.23
Guangdong	70.34	64.28	9.43	58,762	55,259	6.34
Guangxi	46.67	32.64	42.98	2,441	2,336	4.49
Guizhou	23.99	21.02	14.13	649	641	1.25
Hainan	36.21	18.96	90.98	2,456	2,329	5.45
Hebei	37.63	23.82	57.98	3,637	3,497	4.00
Heilongjiang	25.94	17.29	50.03	2,288	2,202	3.91
Henan	31.82	22.09	44.05	2,877	2,600	10.65
Hubei	42.42	32.40	30.03	4,284	4,173	2.66
Hunan	34.94	27.67	26.27	2,712	2,598	4.39
Inner Mongolia	23.17	19.02	21.82	914	847	7.91
Jiangsu	46.35	31.68	46.31	33,321	29,939	11.30
Jiangxi	32.03	19.98	60.31	3,980	3,415	16.54
Jilin	30.06	20.85	44.17	2,488	2,370	4.98
Liaoning	32.88	27.87	17.98	16,542	14,858	11.33
Ningxia	23.15	15.04	53.92	463	454	1.98
Qinghai	21.68	16.46	31.71	138	161	-14.29
Shaanxi	27.92	23.51	18.76	2,890	2,754	4.94
Shandong	45.64	37.71	21.03	20,153	19,251	4.69
Shanghai	81.10	69.90	16.02	28,978	26,657	8.71
Shanxi	30.16	22.93	31.53	776	705	10.07
Sichuan	32.26	26.43	22.06	4,075	3,789	7.55
Tianjin	51.13	41.20	24.10	10,933	9,938	10.01
Tibet	19.00	17.00	11.76	100	86	16.28
Xinjiang	23.86	17.84	33.74	345	331	4.23
Yunnan	29.44	25.73	14.42	1,817	1,761	3.18
Zhejiang	59.47	44.72	32.98	19,009	17,792	6.84
China	41.25	33.11	24.58	260,000	242,284	7.31

Source: China Statistical Yearbook, 2005 and 2004

Foreign Trade with Selected Regions (US$ bn)

Region	2005	2004	YOY change (%)
Hong Kong	136.70	112.67	21.33
Taiwan	91.23	78.30	16.51
Japan	184.39	167.84	9.86
South Korea	111.93	90.05	24.30
Singapore	33.15	26.68	24.25
Malaysia	30.70	26.26	16.91
Europe	262.05	211.39	23.97
Germany	63.25	54.11	16.89
United Kingdom	24.50	19.73	24.18
France	20.65	17.57	17.53
Italy	18.61	15.68	18.69
Netherlands	28.80	21.49	34.02
Ireland	4.61	3.33	38.44
Spain	10.52	7.22	45.71
Belgium	11.74	9.38	25.16
Russia	29.10	21.23	37.07
South Africa	7.27	5.91	23.01
Brazil	14.82	12.35	20.00
Argentina	5.12	4.11	24.57
Mexico	7.76	7.11	9.14
Canada	19.16	15.51	23.53
United States	211.51	169.60	24.71
Australia	27.26	20.39	33.69
New Zealand	2.68	2.49	7.63

Source: China Statistical Yearbook, 2005 and 2004

Chinese leader profiles

REFERENCE

Hu Jintao (born 1942)

In what was hailed as the first orderly transition of power in modern China, Hu Jintao became **General Secretary of the Communist Party** in November 2002, state **President** in March 2003, and in September 2004 replaced former President Jiang Zemin as **Chairman of the Central Military Commission**. This final post gave Hu direct control of the armed forces and completed the two-year handover process from Jiang Zemin's third generation of leaders (the first is represented by Mao Zedong, the second by Deng Xiaoping) to the so-called fourth generation. According to official records, Hu is a native of Anhui province, but Anhui is in fact his place of ancestral origin; his actual birthplace is in Jiangsu province. A moderate and cautious cadre with a photographic memory, Hu trained at Tsinghua University as a hydroelectric engineer and served for more than two decades in China's poor western provinces of Gansu, Guizhou and Tibet. He was picked by the late supreme leader Deng Xiaoping in 1992 to succeed Jiang Zemin as leader of China and served from 1993 to 2002 as President of the Party School. While serving as governor of Tibet, he put down a number of uprisings and was the first provincial leader to voice his support and congratulate the central government following the 1989 Tiananmen Square incident. Many observers regard Hu as more liberal than the members of Jiang Zemin's faction, and his pronouncements are watched for signs of his attitude towards political as well as economic reform.

Wen Jiabao (born 1942)

Premier Wen Jiabao is regarded as the most liberal of China's current leaders, although he is also viewed as a political survivor who is unlikely to rock the boat. A geologist by training, the mild-mannered **Premier of the State Council**, has cultivated an image as something of a man of the people as he steers the country's economic reforms. Like Hu, he has spent a considerable amount of time in China's impoverished west. Born in Tianjin, he was sent to Gansu province as a graduate at the height of the Cultural Revolution and remained there until the early 1980s. Wen was once a protégé of disgraced reformist Zhao Ziyang, the party chief who sided with the students in the 1989 Tiananmen protests and who died in 2005 while still under house arrest. Wen emerged from that period relatively unscathed politically and became a protégé of Zhao's successor, the fiery Zhu Rongji. As Premier, he controls China's economic policy and is one of the leading voices for more sustainable development and greater distribution of wealth. Wen is known as an able administrator and has continued with Zhu's tradition of market reforms combined with centralized control. He is seen as Hu Jintao's chief ally within the leadership.

Wu Bangguo (born 1941)

Wu Bangguo is **Chairman of the Politburo Standing Committee of the National People's Congress (NPC)**, China's rubber-stamp parliament, and a **Vice Premier of the State Council** under Wen Jiabao. He officially ranks second in the Politburo Standing Committee, although the influence of Wen Jiabao and Zeng Qinghong is probably greater. He replaced Li Peng as NPC Chairman and is a prominent member of the so-called "Shanghai Faction." A native of Anhui province, he began work as an electrical engineer in Shanghai in 1966, the first year of the Cultural Revolution, after graduating from Tsinghua University. He succeeded Jiang Zemin to become Shanghai's Communist Party chief in 1992. Wu is regarded as a diligent but unimaginative official who was often at odds with former premier Zhu Rongji when he worked under him as Vice Premier. In his career, he has taken on the reform of state industries and oversaw the controversial Three Gorges Dam project.

Jia Qinglin (born 1940)

Jia Qinglin is the **Chairman of the Chinese People's Political Consultative Conference (CPPCC)**, an advisory council. Jia, who is ranked fourth out of the nine members of the Politburo Standing Committee, was born in Hebei province and graduated from Hebei Engineering College as an electrical engineer. He owes his political survival and position almost entirely to Jiang Zemin, who protected him when a massive corruption and bribery scandal blew up in the mid-1990s in Fujian province, where Jia was Party chief and governor. Jia and Jiang have been close friends for more than three decades, with Jia reportedly acting as best man at Jiang's wedding. Following the corruption scandal, Jia Qinglin was promoted to Party chief of Beijing.

Zeng Qinghong (born 1939)

Zeng Qinghong is China's **Vice President** and seen as a member of the Shanghai Faction. As former President Jiang Zemin's right-hand man and chief advisor, he is regarded by many as the most powerful balancing force to the more liberal tendencies of Hu Jintao and Wen Jiabao. Although he officially ranks only fifth in the Party Politburo Standing Committee, he is seen as a potential challenger for the leadership should Hu make any serious mistakes. A native of Jiangxi province, Zeng is an engineer by training and spent a number of years in the army working as a technician. In the 1980s he worked in China's oil and energy sectors before being appointed to the Shanghai City Government. When Jiang Zemin was transferred to Beijing after the Tiananmen Square protests of 1989, the only advisor he chose to accompany him was Zeng. Through the 1990s, Zeng consolidated Jiang's control over the party, the government and the military. Unlike Hu and Wen, who are both from bourgeois families that suffered during the Cultural Revolution, Zeng comes from a privileged Party clan and was not sent to the countryside as they were. He is in charge of key areas including personnel and ideology.

Huang Ju (born 1938)

Huang Ju is **Executive Vice Premier of the State Council** and seen as a member of the Shanghai Faction. He trained as an electrical engineer at Tsinghua University and is a veteran mayor and Party chief of Shanghai. A native of Zhejiang province, he moved to Shanghai to work in a factory in the early 1960s and joined the Party at the beginning of the Cultural Revolution in the mid-1960s. He is a key protégé of Jiang Zemin. Huang was reportedly promoted to the Politburo Standing Committee on the specific recommendation of Jiang Zemin. He is ranked sixth out of the nine members of the Politburo Standing Committee. He was criticized in 1995 when his daughter married the son of a pro-Taiwan newspaperman in San Francisco.

Wu Guanzheng (born 1938)

Wu Guanzheng is the **Head of the Central Commission for Disciplinary Inspection**, China's highest anti-corruption body, and is ranked seventh in the Politburo Standing Committee. Wu is also Party chief of Shandong province, a post he has held since 1997. He is deemed a moderate with reformist tendencies who manages to maintain amicable relations with both the Hu Jintao and Shanghai Factions. Born in Jiangxi province, he graduated in thermal engineering from Tsinghua University and held the post of mayor in the large industrial town of Wuhan from 1983-1986 before becoming governor of Jiangxi. He is seen as a moderator among the top leaders.

Li Changchun (born 1944)

Li Changchun is known as the **Propaganda Chief of the Communist Party** and is **Party chief of Guangdong province**, a position he has held since 1998. He ranks eighth

in the Politburo Standing Committee. He was born in the northeastern province of Liaoning and graduated from Harbin Institute of Technology with a degree in electrical engineering. Li is a protégé of Jiang Zemin and seen as a

member of the Shanghai Faction with a strong record of reform and achievement. In 1983, aged 39, he became the youngest mayor and Party secretary of a major city, Shenyang, in Liaoning. He was credited with setting up one of China's first stock markets there in the mid-1980s and, as governor of Liaoning, with overseeing the country's first expressway, between Shenyang and Dalian. In the mid-1990s, before moving to Guangdong, Li was Party chief of the agricultural province of Henan. After serving a combined 14 years as a provincial governor and party chief, Li was promoted to the Politburo in 1997 – again the youngest ever member.

Luo Gan (born 1935)

Luo Gan is **Secretary of the Political and Legal Affairs Commission** and is ranked ninth in the Politburo Standing Committee. He is responsible for law enforcement and judiciary affairs, is known as a law and order specialist, and protégé of former Premier Li Peng. Luo was born in Shandong province and studied engineering at the Beijing Steel and Iron Institute. He moved to East Germany in 1954 and spent eight years there working in steel plants. He continued to work in the steel industry on his return to China and became Party chief of Henan province in the 1980s. Thanks largely to his connection with Li Peng, on whose behalf he gave instructions to the armed police during the Tiananmen student protests of 1989, Luo became a member of the Politburo in 1998 and served as security chief. He implemented a number of "strike hard" anti-crime campaigns. He won former President Jiang Zemin's support for his tough crackdown on the Falun Gong.

Wang Qishan (born 1948)

Wang Qishan was appointed **Mayor of Beijing** in February 2004, a post he had been acting in since former mayor Meng Xuenong was fired in April 2003 at the height of the SARS scare. Wang is also **Deputy Party Secretary for Beijing** and the **chairman of the organizing committee for the 2008 Beijing Olympics**. He was born in north China's Shanxi province and joined the Communist Party very late, in 1983. The most likely reason for this is that in 1969, at the height of the Cultural Revolution, Wang was sent to the countryside to work as a peasant farmer in neighboring Shaanxi province. He held a post at the provincial museum and eventually graduated from the history department of Northwest China University in 1976. He worked as an academic and later as a manager and political appointee at various financial institutions, including China Construction Bank, where he served as president. He is seen as a competent manager and an ally of the Shanghai Faction.

Han Zheng (born 1954)

Han Zheng was appointed **Mayor of Shanghai** in February 2003. This coveted position is seen as a launching pad for politicians who plan to move on to roles in central government and was once held by former President Jiang Zemin, former Premier Zhu Rongji and current Politburo Standing Committee member Huang Ju. Han did not graduate from university until 1994. Although he is reported in the media to be a former engineer, unlike the majority of China's senior leaders he holds a master's degree in economics and is referred to in Party files as a "senior economist". He was appointed vice mayor of Shanghai in 1998 and was reportedly instrumental in promoting the city's property boom. Han is seen as an associate of President Hu Jintao because of his previous membership in the Chinese Communist Youth League, a Hu Jintao power base.

Dai Xianglong (born 1944)

Dai Xianglong was appointed **Mayor of Tianjin** in January 2003. Dai, born in Jiangsu province, joined the Communist Party in May 1973 during the Cultural Revolution. Dai began his career working for the People's Bank of China. By 1985, Dai had become the vice governor of the Agriculture Bank of China. He subsequently served as Vice Chairman of China Communications Bank, and then President of China Pacific Insurance. In June 1995, Dai was appointed governor of the People's Bank of China, replacing former Chinese Premier Zhu Rongji. Working closely with Zhu, Dai helped bring the economy to a soft landing. During his time at the People's Bank, Dai also acted as the head of the central bank's powerful currency policy committee and became the focus of a great deal of media attention during the Asian financial crisis of 1997, when it was feared that China would succumb to pressures to devalue its currency.

Chen Geng (born 1946)

Chen Geng is **Chairman of the Board of Directors of PetroChina**, the nation's largest oil company, and **President of China National Petroleum Corporation (CNPC)**, PetroChina's state-owned parent company. Chen, born in Hebei province, graduated from Beijing Economics Institute (now known as the Capital University of Economics and Trade) with a major in Labor & Economics. In 1983, Chen became deputy director of Changqing Petroleum Exploration Bureau and later deputy director of the Labor Department under the Ministry of Petroleum Industry. Chen held a number of key posts in CNPC, including assistant general manager, deputy general manager and director of the board, before he was appointed president of the company in December 2002. In April 2004, Chen became chairman of PetroChina, replacing Ma Fucai, who resigned after a gas well explosion in Chongqing.

Chen Tonghai (born 1948)

Chen Tonghai, born in Shandong province in 1948, has been **Chairman of the Board of Directors of China Petroleum & Chemical Corporation (Sinopec Corp.)** since April 2003 and **President of Sinopec Group** since March 2003. Chen graduated from Northeast Petroleum Institute in 1976, majoring in oil production engineering. After working as deputy CPC secretary and secretary of Zhenhai General Petrochemical Works (a subsidiary of the former China Petrochemical Corporation), he was made executive vice mayor of Ningbo, Zhejiang province, and later executive deputy director of the Planning and Economic Commission of Zhejiang province and acting mayor of Ningbo before he was elected mayor of the city in February 1992. In January 1994, he became the vice minister of the State Planning Commission, where he served until he was appointed vice president of Sinopec Group in April 1998. Chen has taken a series of measures to restructure Sinopec since it was

listed in Hong Kong in 2000, such as downsizing the workforce through reassignments and reforming the salary system.

Fu Chengyu (born 1951)

Fu Chengyu is **Chairman and CEO of China National Offshore Oil Corporation (CNOOC) Limited, President of CNOOC,** CNOOC Limited's parent company, and **Chairman and CEO of China Oilfield Services Limited**, a listing oilfield service vehicle of CNOOC. Fu graduated from China's Northeast Petroleum Institute, majoring in geology, and later received a master's degree in petroleum engineering from the University of Southern California. After working in China's Daqing, Liaohe and Huabei oilfields, Fu joined CNOOC in 1982 and from 1983, he served as chairman of several joint management committees formed through joint ventures between CNOOC and international oil companies including BP Amoco, Chevron, Texaco, Phillips Petroleum, Shell and Agip. He was vice president of CNOOC Nanhai East Corporation from 1994 to 1995 and then became vice president of Phillips China Inc., responsible for the Xinjiang Development Project. Fu was appointed executive vice president and COO of CNOOC Limited in September 1999 and one year later he was made vice president of CNOOC and president of CNOOC Limited. Fu became the focus of media attention during CNOOC's failed bid for US Unocal in 2005, when he impressed lawmakers with his sophisticated lobbying and public relations skills, which are rarely seen in the Chinese business circle.

Liu Mingkang (born 1946)

Liu Mingkang was appointed **Chairman of the China Banking Regulatory Commission (CBRC)** in March 2003. Liu was born in Shanghai and received both his MBA degree and an honorary doctorate from the City University of London. After working as the department manager of the Bank of China (BOC) London branch for more than two years, Liu was appointed general manager of the trust and investment company affiliated to the BOC Jiangsu provincial branch in 1998. Then Liu moved to Fujian province, where he held a number of important positions in both banking institutions and government agencies, including vice president of BOC Fuzhou municipal branch, president of BOC Fujian provincial branch, deputy governor of Fujian province and head of the secretariat of Fujian provincial government. Liu was promoted to the positions of deputy governor of the State Development Bank of China and deputy governor of the People's Bank of China (PBOC) in 1998 and 1999, respectively. He served as chairman of China Everbright Group and chairman and president of BOC before presiding over CBRC.

Ma Kai (born 1946)

Ma Kai is **Director of National Development and Reform Commission (NDRC)** and a member of the 16th CPC Central Committee. Born in Shanghai, Ma graduated from the Department of Politics and Economy of the Chinese People's University and spent his early career in Beijing initially with the Planning Commission of Xicheng District and later became chief of the Pricing Bureau of Beijing Municipality and deputy chief of the National Price Bureau. In 1993, Ma was appointed vice-minister of the State Commission for Restructuring the Economy and two years later vice-minister of the State Development and Reform Commission. He additionally worked with the CPC Central Commission for Discipline Inspection during this period. Ma was elected deputy secretary-general of the State Council in 1998, heading the State Flood Control and Drought Relief Headquarters, the National Afforestation Committee and the 5th National Census Leading Group.

Shang Fulin (born 1951)

Shang Fulin has been the **Chairman of China Securities Regulatory Commission (CSRC)** and a member of Monetary Policy Committee of the People's Bank of China (PBOC) since December 2002. He was born in Ji'nan, Shandong province and graduated from Southwestern University of Finance and Economics with a PhD in finance. Shang started his banking career in 1973 when he joined PBOC, where he quickly moved through the ranks and served successively as deputy division chief, division chief, deputy director and director of the Planning and Budgeting Department (now Monetary Policy Department). He was appointed assistant governor of PBOC in 1994 and promoted to the position of deputy governor in 1996. Shang led teams to make monetary policies, design and construct the clearing and settlement system and solve the Y2K problems of the banking industry before he was appointed president of Agricultural Bank of China in February 2000 and worked there for more than two years.

Shi Zongyuan (born 1946)

Shi Zongyuan is **Director of the General Administration of Press and Publication (GAPP)** and a member of the 16th CPC Central Committee. Of Hui ethnicity, Shi was born in Hebei province and graduated from Northwestern Nationality College. He worked for Hezheng County government of Gansu province before he was appointed deputy head of Gansu CPC Autonomous Regional Committee in 1984 and later became head of the Regional Committee. In 1993, Shi began to serve as head of the publicity department of Gansu. In the late 1990s, Shi moved to Jilin province and held top positions in the Party school and publicity department of the CPC Jilin Provincial Committee before he was appointed head of GAPP in 2000.

Tian Congming (born 1943)

Tian Congming is **President of Xinhua News Agency** and a member of the 16th CPC Central Committee. Tian was born in Shaanxi province and graduated from Beijing Normal University. He started his career in the Inner Mongolia Autonomous Region, working for the regional branch of Xinhua News Agency for six years. In 1983, he began to hold party positions in the CPC Inner Mongolia Autonomous Regional Committee and in 1988 he became deputy secretary of the CPC Tibet Regional Committee. Wang moved to Beijing in 1990, serving as vice-minister of the Ministry of Radio, Film and Television, before he was appointed head of the state news agency in 2000.

Wang Taihua (born 1945)

Wang Taihua was appointed **Director of State Administration of Radio, Film & Television (SARFT)** and **Vice Minister of the CPC Propaganda Department** in December 2004. A native of Jiangxi province, Wang graduated from Jiangxi Teachers College with a major in Chinese language and literature and began his career as a middle school teacher. In 1985, Wang began to work for the Ganzhou municipal government and Jiangxi provincial government, serving as director of the Publicity Department of CPC Ganzhou Municipal Committee; deputy commissioner of the Ganzhou prefectural government and deputy secretary of CPC Jiangxi Provincial Committee. Wang became secretary of CPC Hefei City Committee of Anhui Province in 1992 and rose quickly to prominence, becoming deputy secretary of CPC Anhui Provincial Committee, vice-governor and acting governor of Anhui. Wang was elected governor of Anhui in February 1999 and became secretary of the CPC Anhui Provincial Committee in January 2000.

Wang Xiaochu (born 1958)

Wang Xiaochu has been **President of China Telecommunications Corporation (China Telecom)** since November 2004 and also serves as its General Manager. He is also currently the Chairman and CEO of China Telecom's listed arm, China Telecommunications Corporation Limited. Wang graduated from

Beijing Institute of Posts and Telecommunications and has over 24 years of management experience in the telecommunications industry. Wang served as director and deputy director of the Hangzhou Telecommunications Bureau in Zhejiang province, and director general of the Tianjin Posts and Telecommunications Administration before he joined the board of directors of China Mobile Hong Kong Ltd. in March 1999 and later became chairman and CEO of the company. Wang was responsible for the development of China Telecom's telephone network management systems and other information technology projects. He was honored with a National Award for Science and Technology and a Science and Technology Advancement Award by the former Ministry of Posts and Telecommunications.

Wu Dingfu (born 1946)

Wu Dingfu is **Chairman of the China Insurance Regulatory Commission (CIRC)** and an alternate member of the 16th CPC Central Committee. After graduating from Hubei University, majoring in Chinese language and literature, Wu spent his early career in Hubei province with various government agencies. Wu became a member of the National Audit Office in 1995 and headed the Commission for Discipline Inspection under the office. In November 1998, he began to serve as the first vice-chairman of CIRC, where he held the post until he was appointed chairman of the Commission four years later.

Zhou Xiaochuan (born 1948)

Zhou Xiaochuan was appointed **Governor of the People's Bank of China (BPOC)** in November 2002. A native of Jiangsu province, Zhou graduated from Beijing Chemical Engineering Institute and later received his PhD from Tsinghua University. Before heading China's leading banks, Zhou held various positions in government agencies, including deputy director of China Economic Restructuring Institute, assistant minister of the Ministry of Foreign Trade and Economic Cooperation and member of the State Economic Restructuring Commission. In 1991, Zhou was appointed vice-governor of the Bank of China (BOC) and in 1995 he began to serve as director of the State Administration of Foreign Exchanges. Zhou held the positions of vice-governor of PBOC, governor of the China Construction Bank (CCB) and chairman of China Securities Regulatory Commission (CSRC) before becoming chairman of the central bank in 2002.

Wang Hongju (born 1945)

Wang Hongju was appointed **Mayor of Chongqing** in January 2003. Born in Chongqing, Wang joined the Communist Party in February 1979 and was appointed deputy director, and later Secretary, of his local Party Committee. Wang quickly moved through the ranks serving a number of key posts in Sichuan province before being appointed deputy mayor of Chongqing at the first session of the first Chongqing People's Congress in June 1997.

Trade Events 2007

REFERENCE

The information listed below is subject to change. For a more up-to-date listing of upcoming expos and conferences in China please check the latest edition of *China Economic Review* magazine. Alternatively, please check online at: www.ChinaEconomicReview.com

Automobiles, Aviation & Transportation

9-11 March 2007
Auto Maintexpo China 2007
National Agricultural Exhibition Center, Beijing
www.autoexpo.com.cn
18-20 April 2007
China Commercial Vehicals 2007
Beijing Exhibition Center
www.businessmediachina.com/ccve.htm
13-15 March 2007
Personal Care Ingredients Asia 2007
Guangzhou Jinhan Exhibition Center
www.stepex.com/pcia
20-28 April 2007
Auto Shanghai 2007
Shanghai New Int'l Expo Center
www.auto-shanghai.com
25-27 April 2007
China Int'l Automotive Electronics Products & Technologies Show & Auto+IT Summit
Shanghai Everbright Convention & Exhibition Center
www.gracefair.com/aes_home.htm
19-22 September 2007
Aviation Expo China 2007
China Int'l Exhibition Center
www.beijingaviation.com
26-28 September 2007
ATOP 2007
Shanghai Int'l Exhibition Center
www.adsale.com.hk

Construction & Building Materials

28-30 March 2007
Domotex Asia/ China Floor 2007
Shanghai New Int'l Expo Center
www.domotexasiachinafloor.com
28-31 March 2007
Kitchen + Bath Business Expo China 2007
Shanghai Exhibition Center
www.kbbexpochina.com
2-4 April 2007
R+T Asia
Shanghai Everbright
Convention & Exhibition Center
www.vnuexhibitionsasia.com
4-7 April 2007
Expo Build China 2007
Shanghai New Int'l
Expo Center
www.cmpsinoexpo.com/expobuild
4-7 April 2007
Ceramics, Tile & Sanitary Ware China 2007
Shanghai New Int'l
Expo Center
www.ceramics-china.com.cn
6-9 July 2007
CBD(China Building & Decroating) 2007
Chinese Export Commodities Fairground, Guangzhou
www.merebo.com

Education

3-4 March 2007
CIEET Beijing 2007   China
World Trade Center, Beijing
www.cieet.com

6-7 March 2007
CIEET Chongqing 2007
Chongqing Int'l Convention & Exhibition Center
www.cieet.com

10-11 March 2007
CIEET Shanghai 2007
Shanghai East Asia Exhibition Center
www.cieet.com

13-14 March 2007
CIEET Nanjing 2007
Gr& Metro Park Hotel
www.cieet.com

17-18 March 2007
CIEET Guangzhou 2007
Dongfang Hotel
www.cieet.com

Electronics, Machines & Equipment

5-6 March 2007
IIC China 2007 Shenzhen
Shenzhen Convention & Exhibition Center
www.china.iicexpo.com

7-10 March 2007
CHIFA 2007
Guangzhou Int'l Convention & Exhibition Center
www.chifa-ptg.merebo.com

7-10 March 2007
PTG 2007
Guangzhou Int'l Convention & Exhibition Center
www.chifa-ptg.merebo.com

7-10 March 2007
METEX 2007 (Measurement & Testing Equipment)

Guangzhou Int'l Convention & Exhibition Center
www.chifa-ptg.merebo.com

8-9 March 2007
IIC China 2007 Beijing
China World Trade Center, Beijing
www.china.iicexpo.com

13-14 March 2007
IIC China 2007 Shanghai
Shanghai Mart
www.china.iicexpo.com

13-15 March 2007
FPD 2007 INTEX Shanghai
www.semi.org

20-23 March 2007
PCIM China 2007
Shanghai New Int'l Expo Center
www.mesago.de

20-23 March 2007
Semicon China 2007
Shanghai New Int'l Expo Center
www.semi.org

20-23 March 2007
Electronica & Productronica China 2007
Shanghai New Int'l Expo Center
www.global-electronics.net

29-31 March 2007
IEAE 2007 (Electronics)
Shanxi Int'l Exhibition Center
www.ieae.com.cn

24-27 April 2007
NEPCON Shanghai 2007
Shanghai Everbright Convention & Exhibition Center
www.nepconchina.com

24-27 April 2007
EMT China 2007
Shanghai Everbright Convention & Exhibition Center
www.nepconchina.com

25-27 April 2007
Intergrated Systems China 2007
Beijing Exhibition Center
www.is-china.com

5-7 June 2007
EP China Shanghai Int'l Exhibition Center
www.adsale.com.hk

Energy & Utilities

7-10 March 2007
AW China
Guangzhou Int'l Convention & Exhibition Center
www.waterchina.merebo.com
7-10 March 2007
Water China
Guangzhou Int'l Convention & Exhibition Center
www.waterchina.merebo.com
3-5 April 2007
CIO OE 2007 (Energy)
Beijing Exhibition Center
www.ciooe.com.cn
3-5 April 2007
CIPPE 2007
Beijing Exhibition Center
www.cippe.com.cn
3-5 April 2007
CIPE 2007
Beijing Exhibition Center
www.cipe.com.cn
3-5 April 2007
EXPEC 2007
Beijing Exhibition Center
www.expec.com.cn
23-25 April 2007
Int'l Exhibition on Nuclear Power Industry 2007
Shanghai
www.coastal.com.hk/nuclear

Finance

11-13 May 2007
Millionaire Fair

Shanghai Exhibition Center
www.millionairefair.com.cn
29-31 May 2007
Smart Cards + Smart Label, China & Users' Conference
China World Trade Center, Beijing
www.scfc.org.cn
29-31 May 2007
Int'l Payment Terminals EXPO & Conference 2007
China World Trade Center, Beijing
www.scfc.org.cn

Food & Beverage

7-10 March 2007
China Drinktec 2007
Guangzhou Int'l Convention & Exhibition Center
www.adsale.com.hk
15-17 March 2007
FI Asia-China 2007
Shanghai New Int'l Expo Center
www.fi-events.com
16-18 April 2007
Wine Culture China
China World Trade Center, Beijing
www.regall&.com
16-18 April 2007
Oil Tech China 2007
China World Trade Center, Beijing
www.regall&.com/eoliveoil
16-18 April 2007
Oil China
China World Trade Center, Beijing
www.regall&.com/eoliveoil
10-12 May 2007
Packtech & Foodtech
Shanghai New Int'l Expo Center
www.packtech-foodtech.com
11-13 May 2007
FDC China 2007
Chinese Export Commodities Fairground,

Guangzhou
www.fdcchina.com.cn

Furniture, Wood & Plastics

20-23 March 2007
Woodmac China 2007
Shanghai New Int'l Expo Center
www.woodmacchina.com

20-23 March 2007
Wood Build China 2007
INTEX Shanghai
www.woodbuildchina.net

20-23 March 2007
Furnitech China 2007
Shanghai New Int'l Expo Center
www.woodbuildchina.net

27-30 March 2007
InterZum Guangzhou 2007
Guangzhou Int'l Convention & Exhibition Center
www.interzum-guangzhou.com

21-24 April 2007
China Plas 2007
Guangzhou Int'l Convention & Exhibition Center
www.2456.com/chinaplas

Optics

8-10 March 2007
China (Shanghai Opitcs) Int'l Fair
Shanghai Everbright Convention & Exhibition Center
www.siof.cn

19-21 March 2007
Neon Show 2007
Chinese Export Commodities Fair Liuhua
Complex Center
www.trustexhibition.com

19-21 March 2007
Led China 2007
Chinese Export Commodities Fair Pazhou

Complex Center
www.ledchina-gz.com

20-23 March 2007
Laser China 2007
Shanghai New Int'l Expo Center
www.global-electronics.net

Pharmaceuticals & Health

2-5 April 2007
China Int'l Oral Healthcare & Products Expo & Technology Conference
Chinese Export Commodities Fair Liuhua
Complex Center
www.dentalsouthchina.com

2-5 April 2007
Dental South China
Chinese Export Commodities Fair Liuhua
Complex Center
www.dentalsouthchina.com

22-24 April 2007
China Med
China Int'l Exhibition Center,
Beijing
www.chinamed.net.cn

19-21 June 2007
P-MEC China 2007
Shanghai New Int'l Expo Center
www.cmpsinoexpo.com/cphi-china

19-21 June 2007
CPhI, ICSE & P-MEC China 2007
Shanghai New Int'l Expo Center
www.cmpsinoexpo.com/cphi-china

19-21 June 2007
Expo Bio (Biotechnology)
Chinese Export Commodities Fair Liuhua
Complex Center
www.biosouthchina.com

Pipeline

7-10 March 2007
PVP China

Guangzhou Int'l Convention & Exhibition Center
www.waterchina.merebo.com
28-30 March 2007
Flow Expo 2007
Guangzhou Gymnasium
www.flowexpo.com

Printing, Package & Paper

7-10 March 2007
Printing South China 2007
Guangzhou Int'l
Convention & Exhibition Center
www.adsale.com.hk
7-10 March 2007
Sino Print 07
Guangzhou Int'l
Convention & Exhibition Center
www.adsale.com.hk
7-10 March 2007
Sino Label 07
Guangzhou Int'l Convention & Exhibition Center
www.adsale.com.hk
19-21 March 2007
Sign China 2007
Chinese Export Commodities Fairground, Guangzhou
www.signchina-gz.com
19-21 March 2007
Printer China 2007
Guangzhou Jinhan Exhibition Center
www.signchina-gz.com
28-31 March 2007
Sino-Corrugated 2007
Shanghai New Int'l Expo Center
www.sino-corrugated.com

Textile, Clothing & Shoes

18-20 April 2007
China Shoes

Dongguan Int'l Conference & Exhibition Center
www.chinashoesexpo.com
18-20 April 2007
China Shoetec
Dongguan Int'l Conference & Exhibition Center
www.chinashoesexpo.com
1-4 June 2007
Shanghai Tex 2007
Shanghai New Int'l Expo Center
www.2456.com/shanghaitex2007
22-24 March 2007
InterTextile Beijing
Beijing Exhibition Center
www.interstoff.com
22-24 March 2007
Yarn Expo China World Trade Center, Beijing
www.messefrankfurt.com.hk
25-27 July 2007
Intertextile Pavilion Shenzhen
Shenzhen Convention & Exhibition Center
www.messefrankfurt.com.hk
29-31 August 2007
Intertextile Shanghai Home Textiles
Shanghai New Int'l Expo Center
www.messefrankfurt.com.hk

Tourism & Hospitality

22-25 March 2007
World Travel Fair 2007
Shanghai Exhibition Center
www.worldtravelfair.com.cn
4-7 April 2007
Hotelex Shanghai 2007
Shanghai New Int'l Expo Center
www.cmpsinoexpo.com/hotelex
21-21 June 2007
Beijing Int'l Tourism Expo 2007
Beijing Exhibition Center
www.cems.com.sg

Airlines

Air Asia
www.airasia.com

Xiamen to Thailand: 4 flights weekly

Air Asia Xiamen
1/F International Trade Building, 388 Hubing Nan Lu
Tel: (0592) 516 7777

Air Canada
www.aircanada.com

Beijing to Vancouver: 7 flights weekly
Shanghai to Vancouver: 7 flights weekly

Air Canada Beijing
C201 Lufthansa Center, 50 Liangmaqiao Lu
Tel: (010) 6468 2001
Air Canada Shanghai
390 Zhongxin Building, 1468 Nanjing Xi Lu
Tel: (021) 6279 2999

Air Europa
www.air-europa.com

Beijing to Madrid: 2 flights weekly
Shanghai to Madrid: 4 flights weekly

Air Europa Beijing
602 Cits Building, 1 Dongdan Bei Dajie
Tel: (010) 6522 1823
Air Europa Shanghai
2001 South Tower, Hong Kong Plaza, 283 Huaihai Zhong Lu
Tel: (021) 6288 1500

Air France
www.airfrance.com

Beijing to Paris: 14 flights weekly
Shanghai to Paris: 7 flights weekly
Guangzhou to Paris: 7 flights weekly
Hong Kong to Paris: 7 flights weekly
Air France Beijing
5/F Full Link Plaza, 18 Chaoyangmenwai Dajie
Tel: 4008 808 808
Air France Shanghai
Room1301, Novel Plaza, 128 Nanjing Xi Lu
Tel: 4008 808 808
Air France Guangzhou
13/F Gaosheng Building, 109 Tiyu Xi Lu
Tel: 4008 808 808
Air France Hong Kong
18/F Vicwood Plaza, 199 Des Voeux Road Central
Tel: (+852) 2501 9433

Air India
www.airindia.com

Shanghai to Delhi:
2 flights weekly
Hong Kong to Ahmedabad:
8 flights weekly

Air India Shanghai
1008 Kerry Center, 1515 Nanjing Xi Lu
Tel: (021) 5298 5698
Air India Hong Kong
29/F Vicwood Plaza, 199 Des Voeux Road Central
Tel: (+852) 2522 1176

Air Macau
www.airmacau.com.mo

Beijing to Macau: 14 flights weekly
Chengdu to Macau: 4 flights weekly
Guilin to Macau: 7 flights weekly
Haikou to Macau: 3 flights weekly
Kunming to Macau: 3 flights weekly

Nanjing to Macau: 4 flights weekly
Shanghai to Macau: 28 flights weekly
Shenzhen to Macau: 14 flights weekly
Xiamen to Macau: 7 flights weekly

Air Macau Beijing
8/F Scitech Tower, 22 Jianguomenwai Dajie
Tel: (010) 6515 8988
Air Macau Shanghai
104 Shanghai International Equatorial Hotel, 65 Yan'an Xi Lu
Tel: (021) 6248 1110

Alitalia
www.alitalia.com

Shanghai to Milan: 5 flights weekly

Alitalia Shanghai
3607 The Center, 989 Changle Lu
Tel: (021) 6103 1133

All Nippon Airways
www.anaskyweb.com

Beijing to Osaka: 7 flights weekly
Beijing to Tokyo: 14 flights weekly
Shanghai to Osaka: 14 flights weekly
Shanghai to Tokyo: 21 flights weekly
Guangzhou to Tokyo: 3 flights weekly
Hong Kong to Osaka: 7 flights weekly
Hong Kong to Tokyo: 14 flights weekly
Shenyang to Osaka: 2 flights weekly
Shenyang to Tokyo: 3 flights weekly
Dalian to Osaka: 4 flights weekly
Dalian to Tokyo: 7 flights weekly
Qingdao to Osaka: 3 flights weekly
Qingdao to Tokyo: 4 flights weekly
Xiamen to Osaka: 3 flights weekly
Xiamen to Tokyo: 3 flights weekly

All Nippon Airways Beijing
2/F Beijing Fortune Building, 5 Dongsanhuan Bei Lu
Tel: (010) 6590 9191
All Nippon Airways Shanghai
108A Shanghai Center, 1376 Nanjing Xi Lu

Tel: (021) 5696 2525
All Nippon Airways Guangzhou
3501 CITIC Plaza, 233 Tianhe Bei Lu
Tel: (020) 3877 2020

American Airlines
www.aa.com

Beijing to Los Angeles: 7 flights weekly
Beijing to New York: 7 flights weekly
Beijing to San Jose: 7 flights weekly
Beijing to Dallas: 7 flights weekly
Shanghai to Los Angeles: 7 flights weekly
Shanghai to New York: 7 flights weekly
Shanghai to San Jose: 7 flights weekly
Shanghai to Dallas: 7 flights weekly
Guangzhou to Los Angeles:
7 flights weekly
Guangzhou to New York:
7 flights weekly
Guangzhou to San Jose: 7 flights weekly
Guangzhou to Dallas: 14 flights weekly

American Airlines Beijing
37 Maizidian Jie
Tel: (010) 8527 6188
American Airlines Shanghai
702 Central Plaza, 227 Huangpi Bei Lu
Tel: (021) 6375 8686
American Airlines Guangzhou
1213 Garden Tower, 368 Huansi Dong Lu
Tel: (020) 8387 8389 ext.8018

Asiana Airlines
flyasiana.com

Beijing to Seoul: 13 flights weekly
Beijing to Pusan: 7 flights weekly
Shanghai to Seoul: 28 flights weekly
Shanghai to Daegu: 2 flights weekly
Shanghai to Jeju: 1 flight weekly
Yanji to Seoul: 2 flights weekly
Tianjin to Seoul: 3 flights weekly
Qingdao to Seoul: 7 flights weekly
Shenyang to Pusan: 2 flights weekly
Chengdu to Seoul: 3 flights weekly
Nanjing to Seoul: 4 flights weekly
Hangzhou to Seoul: 7 flights weekly
Xi'an to Seoul: 3 flights weekly

Yantai to Seoul: 16 flights weekly
Harbin to Seoul: 5 flights weekly
Guangzhou to Seoul: 7 flights weekly
Changchun to Seoul: 7 flights weekly

Asiana Airlines Beijing
102 Lufthansa Center, 50 Liangmaqiao Lu
Tel: (010) 6468 4000
Asiana Airlines Shanghai
2/F Rainbow Hotel, 2000 Yan'an Dong Lu
Tel: (021) 6219 4000
Asiana Airlines Guangzhou
905 South Tower, World Trade Center,
371-375 Huansi Dong Lu
Tel: (020) 8760 6677

Austrian Airlines
www.aua.com

Beijing to Vienna: 6 flights weekly
Shanghai to Vienna: 5 flights weekly

Austrian Airlines Beijing
C214 Kempinski Hotel, 50 Liangmaqiao Lu
Tel: (010) 6462 2161
Austrian Airlines Shanghai
2904 Raffles City, 268 Xizang Zhong Lu
Tel: (021) 6340 3411

British Airways
www.britishairways.com

Beijing to London: 6 flights weekly
Shanghai to London: 5 flights weekly

British Airways Beijing
210 Scitech Tower, 22 Jianguomenwai
Dajie
Tel: (010) 8511 5599
British Airways Shanghai
1038 Nanjing Xi Lu
Tel: 800 8108 012

Cathay Pacific Airways
www.cathaypacific.com

Beijing to Hong Kong: 14 flights weekly
Xiamen to Hong Kong: 3 flights weekly

Cathay Pacific Airways Beijing
1709 CITIC Building, 6 Xinyuan Nan Lu
Tel: (010) 8486 8532

Cebu Pacific
www.cebupacificair.com

Hong Kong to Manila: 14 flights weekly

Cebu Pacific Hong Kong
1805 Regent Center, 88 Queen's Road
Central
Tel: (+852) 2810 8500

China Eastern
Airlines www.ce-air.com

Beijing to Los Angeles: 7 flights weekly
Beijing to Nagoya: 5 flights weekly
Beijing to Osaka: 5 flights weekly
Beijing to Paris: 7 flights weekly
Beijing to Fukuoka: 4 flights weekly
Beijing to Delhi: 4 flights weekly
Beijing to Tokyo: 7 flights weekly
Shanghai to Bangkok: 7 flights weekly
Shanghai to Delhi: 5 flights weekly
Shanghai to Hong Kong: 70 flights weekly
Shanghai to London: 4 flights weekly
Shanghai to Los Angeles: 7 flights weekly
Shanghai to Melbourne: 3 flights weekly
Shanghai to Nagoya:
21 flights weekly
Shanghai to Osaka: 14 flights weekly
Shanghai to Paris: 12 flights weekly
Shanghai to Seoul: 28 flights weekly
Shanghai to Singapore: 21flights weekly
Shanghai to Sydney: 7 flights weekly
Shanghai to Tokyo: 22 flights weekly
Shanghai to Vancouver: 7 flights weekly
Shanghai to Moscow: 3 flights weekly

China Eastern Airlines Beijing
1/F, 12 Xinyuan Xili Zhong Jie
Tel: (010) 6468 1166
China Eastern Airlines Shanghai

200 Yan'an Xi Lu
Tel: (021) 95108

China Southern Airlines
www.cs-air.com

Beijing to Tokyo: 7 flights weekly
Beijing to Dubai: 3 flights weekly
Beijing to Amsterdam: 4 flights weekly
Beijing to Manila: 7 flights weekly
Beijing to Hanoi: 7 flights weekly
Beijing to Seoul: 7 flights weekly
Chengdu to Amsterdam: 2 flights weekly
Chongqing to Lhasa: 7 flights weekly
Guangzhou to Amsterdam:
7 flights weekly
Guangzhou to Bangkok: 7 flights weekly
Guangzhou to Hanoi: 7 flights weekly
Guangzhou to Hochiminh City:
7 flights weekly
Guangzhou to Los Angeles:
5 flights weekly
Guangzhou to Jakarta: 7 flights weekly
Guangzhou to Kuala Lumpur:
7 flights weekly
Guangzhou to Osaka: 14 flights weekly
Guangzhou to Paris: 5 flights weekly
Guangzhou to Sydney: 5 flight weekly
Guangzhou to Seoul: 17 flights weekly
Guangzhou to Tokyo: 14 flights weekly
Guangzhou to Singapore: 8 flights weekly
Guangzhou to Fukuoka: 5 flights weekly
Guangzhou to Manila: / flights weekly
Guangzhou to Lagos: 3 flights weekly
Guangzhou to Kathmandu: 2 flights weekly
Shanghai to Amsterdam: 7 flights weekly
Shanghai to Seoul: 7 flights weekly
Shenzhen to Nagoya: 7 flights weekly
Zhangjiajie to Xiamen: 7 flights weekly

China Southern Airlines Beijing
15 Xi Chang'an Jie
Tel: (010) 6465 3104
China Southern Airlines Shanghai
2011 Nanjing Xi Lu
Tel: (021) 6247 4496
China Southern Airlines Guangzhou
181 Dongfeng Xi Lu
Tel: (020) 8668 2000

Continental Airlines
www.continental.com

Beijing to New York: 7 flights weekly
Hong Kong to New York: 6 flights weekly
Hong Kong to Saipan: 2 flights weekly

Continental Airlines Beijing
500 Sunflower Tower, 37 Maizidian Jie
(010) 8527 6686
Continental Airlines Hong Kong
58/F The Center, 99 Queen's Road Central
(852) 3198 5777

Dragonair
www.dragonair.com

Beijing to Hong Kong: 56 flights weekly
Changsha to Hong Kong:
3 flights weekly
Chengdu to Hong Kong: 7 flights weekly
Chongqing to Hong Kong:
3 flights weekly
Dalian to Hong Kong: 3 flights weekly
Fuzhou to Hong Kong: 7 flights weekly
Guilin to Hong Kong: 4 flights weekly
Haikou to Hong Kong: 1 flights weekly
Hangzhou to Hong Kong:
21 flights weekly
Kunming to Hong Kong: 9 flights weekly
Nanjing to Hong Kong: 14 flights weekly
Ningbo to Hong Kong: 7 flights weekly
Qingdao to Hong Kong: / flights weekly
Sanya to Hong Kong: 4 flights weekly
Shanghai to Hong Kong:
105 flights weekly
Wuhan to Hong Kong: 2 flights weekly
Xiamen to Hong Kong: 14 flights weekly
Xi'an to Hong Kong: 2 flights weekly

Dragonair Beijing
1710 Office Tower 1, Henderson Center,
18 Jianguomennei Dajie
Tel: (010) 6518 2533
Dragonair Shanghai
2101-2104 Shanghai Square Office Tower,
138 Huaihai Zhong Lu
Tel: (021) 6375 6375
Dragonair Guangzhou

Garden Hotel, 368 Huanshi Dong Lu
Tel: (020) 8388 2498
Dragonair Hong Kong
4601-4605 COSCO Tower, 183 Queen's
Road Central
Tel: (+852) 3193 3888

El Al Israel Airlines
www.elal.co.il

Beijing to Tel Aviv: 2 flghts weekly
Hong Kong to Tel Aviv: 4 flights weekly

El Al Israel Airlines Beijing
2906 Jingguang Center, Hujialou
Tel: (010) 6597 4512
EL AL Israel Airlines Hong Kong
2205 Tower One, Lippo Center, 89
Queensway
Tel: (+852) 2521 1696

Emirates
www.emirates.com

Shanghai to Dubai: 7 flights weekly
Hong Kong to Dubai: 14 flights weekly

Emirates Shanghai
3302-3303 United Plaza, 1468 Nanjing Xi Lu
Tel: (021) 3222 9999
Emirates Hong Kong
11/F Henley Building, 5 Queen's Road
Central
Tel: (+852) 2801 8777

Finnair
www.finnair.com

Beijing to Helsinki: 6 flights weekly
Guangzhou to Helsinki: 3 flights weekly
Hong Kong to Helsinki: 3 flights weekly
Shanghai to Helsinki: 6 flights weekly

Finnair Beijing
204 Scitech Tower, 22 Jianguomenwai
Dajie

Tel: (010) 6512 7180
Finnair Shanghai
2406 CITIC Square, 1168 Nanjing Xi Lu
Tel: (021) 5292 9400
Finnair Guangzhou
3308-09A CITIC Plaza, 233 Tienhe Bei Lu
Tel: (020) 3877 3188
Finnair Hong Kong
2312 COSCO Tower, 183 Queen's Road
Central, Tel: (+852) 2117 1238

Garuda Indonesia
www.garuda-indonesia.com

Guangzhou to Jakarta: 7 flights weekly
Hong Kong to Jakarta: 7 flights weekly
Shanghai to Jakarta: 4 flights weekly

Garuda Indonesia Beijing
717-720 South Office Tower, Beijing
Kerry Center, 1 Guanghua Lu
Tel: (010) 6561 3399
Garuda Indonesia Guangzhou
1101 Asia International Hotel,
326 Huanshi Dong Lu
Tel: (020) 6120 6777
Garuda Indonesia Shanghai
10/F West Wing, East Ocean Center, 618
Yan'an Dong Lu, Tel: (021) 5385 5399
Garuda Indonesia Hong Kong
1501-1505 Dah Sing Financial Center,
108 Gloucester Road
Tel: (+852) 2522 9140/2840 0000

Iran Air
www.iranair.com

Beijing to Teheran: 2 flights weekly
Beijing to Tokyo: 1 flights weekly

Iran Air Beijing
701 CITIC Building, 19 Jianwai Dajie
Tel: (010) 6512 4945

Japan Airlines
www.jal.com

Beijing to Nagoya: 5 flights weekly
Beijing to Osaka: 7 flights weekly
Beijing to Tokyo: 14 flights weekly
Dalian to Osaka: 3 flights weekly
Dalian to Tokyo: 7 flights weekly
Guangzhou to Nagoya: 3 flights weekly
Guangzhou to Osaka: 7 flights weekly
Guangzhou to Tokyo: 7 flights weekly
Hangzhou to Osaka: 2 flights weekly
Hangzhou to Tokyo: 5 flights weekly
Hong Kong to Osaka: 14 flights weekly
Hong Kong to Tokyo: 21 flights weekly
Qingdao to Osaka: 4 flights weekly
Qingdao to Tokyo: 7 flights weekly
Shanghai to Fukuoka: 14 flights weekly
Shanghai to Nagoya: 14 flights weekly
Shanghai to Osaka: 28 flights weekly
Shanghai to Tokyo: 35 flights weekly
Xiamen to Tokyo: 3 flights weekly
Xi'an to Tokyo: 2 flights weekly

Japan Airlines Beijing
1/F Chang Fu Gong Office,
26 Jianguomenwai Dajie
Tel: 400 888 0808
Japan Airlines Shanghai
Plaza 66 Mall number 435, 1266 Nanjing
Xi Lu
Tel: 400 888 0808
Japan Airlines Guangzhou
A-203 China Hotel, Liuhua Lu
Tel: 400 888 0808
Japan Airlines Hong Kong
30/F Tower 6, The Gateway, Harbour
City, 9 Canton Road
Tel: 400 888 0808

KLM
www.klm.com

Beijing to Amsterdam: 14 flights weekly
Hong Kong to Amsterdam:
7 flights weekly
Shanghai to Amsterdam: 7 flights weekly
Chengdu to Amsterdam: 3 flights weekly

KLM Beijing
5/F West Wing, China World Trade
Center, 1 Jianguomenwai Dajie
Tel: 40081 40081

KLM Shanghai
301 Two Corporate Avenue,
202 Hubin Lu
Tel: 40081 40081
KLM Hong Kong
18/F Vicwood Plaza, 199 Des Voeux Road
Central
Tel: (+852) 2808 2111

Korean Airlines
www.koreanair.com

Beijing to Jeju: 2 flights weekly
Beijing to Daegu: 5 flights weekly
Beijing to Seoul: 8 flights weekly
Dalian to Seoul: 7 flights weekly
Jinan to Seoul: 2 flights weekly
Kunming to Seoul: 2 flights weekly
Qingdao to Busan: 3 flights weekly
Qingdao to Seoul: 14 flights weekly
Sanya to Seoul: 2 flights weekly
Shanghai to Busan: 14 flights weekly
Shanghai to Seoul: 21 flights weekly
Shenyang to Seoul: 18 flights weekly
Tianjin to Seoul: 11 flights weekly
Wuhan to Seoul: 2 flights weekly
Xiamen to Seoul: 3 flights weekly
Xi'an to Busan: 2 flights weekly
Yanji to Seoul: 3 flights weekly

Korean Airlines Beijing
1602 Hyundai Millennium Tower, 38
Xiaoyun Lu
Tel: 40065 88888
Korean Airlines Shanghai
3406 Maxdo Center, 8 Xingyi Lu
Tel: (021) 5208 2080

Lufthansa
www.lufthansa.com

Beijing to Frankfurt: 7 flights weekly
Beijing to Munich: 7 flights weekly
Guangzhou to Frankfurt:
7 flights weekly
Hong Kong to Frankfurt:
7 flights weekly
Hong Kong to Munich: 7 flights weekly

Shanghai to Frankfurt: 7 flights weekly
Shanghai to Munich: 7 flights weekly

Lufthansa Beijing
101, 50 Liangmaqiao Lu
Tel: (010) 6468 8838
Lufthansa Shanghai
3/F Building One, Corporate Avenue, 222 Huibin Lu
Tel: (021) 5352 4999
Lufthansa Guangzhou
1557-1559 China Hotel, Liuhua Lu
Tel: (020) 2832 6588
Lufthansa Hong Kong
10/F Guangdong Investment Tower, 148 Connaught Road Central
Tel: (+852) 2868 2313

Malaysia Airlines
www.malaysiaairlines.com

Beijing to Kuala Lumpur:
7 flights weekly
Chengdu to Kuala Lumpur:
0 flights weekly
Guangzhou to Kota Kinabalu:
3 flights weekly
Guangzhou to Kuala Lumpur:
7 flights weekly
Hong Kong to Kota Kinabalu:
7 flights weekly
Hong Kong to Kuala Lumpur:
14 flights weekly
Kunming to Kuala Lumpur:
3 flights weekly
Shanghai to Kota Kinabalu:
3 flights weekly
Shanghai to Kuala Lumpur:
7 flights weekly
Xiamen to Kuala Lumpur:
4 flights weekly
Xi'an to Kuala Lumpur: 0 flights weekly

Malaysia Airlines Beijing
1005 China World Tower 2, 1 Jianguomenwai Dajie
Tel: (010) 6505 2681
Malaysia Airlines Shanghai
209 East Wing, Shanghai Center, 1376 Nanjing Xi Lu

Tel: (021) 6279 8607
Malaysia Airlines Guangzhou
Shop M04-05 Garden Hotel, 368 Huanshi Dong Lu
Tel: (020) 8335 8868
Malaysia Airlines Hong Kong
23/F Central Tower, 28 Queen's Road Central
Tel: (+852) 2916 0088

Northwest Airlines
www.nwa.com

Beijing to Tokyo: 7 flights weekly
Guangzhou to Tokyo: 7 flights weekly
Hong Kong to Tokyo: 7 flights weekly
Shanghai to Tokyo: 7 flights weekly

Northwest Airlines Beijing
5/F West Wing, China World Trade Center, 1 Jianguomenwai Dajie
Tel: (010) 6505 3505
Northwest Airlines Shanghai
207 East Wing, Shanghai Center, 1376 Nanjing Xi Lu
Tel: (021) 6884 6884
Northwest Airlines Hong Kong
1908 COSCO Tower, 183 Queen's Road Central
Tel: (+852) 2810 4288

Pakistan International Airways
www.piac.com.pk

Beijing to Islamabad: 2 flights weekly
Hong Kong to Islamabad:
2 flights weekly
Urumchi to Islamabad:
0 flight weekly

Pakistan International Airways Beijing
617 China World Tower, 1 Jianguomenwai Dajie
Tel: (010) 6505 1681
Pakistan International Airways Hong Kong

1104A East Ocean Center, 98 Granville Road
Tel: (+852) 2366 4770

Philippine Airlines
www.philippineairlines.com

Hong Kong to Manila: 21 flights weekly
Shanghai to Manila: 7 flights weekly
Xiamen to Manila: 4 flights weekly

Philippine Airlines Shanghai
735A East Tower, Shanghai Center, 1376
Nanjing Xi Lu, Tel: (021) 6279 8765
Philippine Airlines Hong Kong
Shop G6 Ground Floor, East Ocean
Center, 98 Granville Road
Tel: (+852) 2301 9350

Qantas
www.qantas.com.au

Beijing to Sydney: 3 flights weekly
Beijing to Melbourne: 9 flights weekly
Shanghai to Sydney: 7 flights weekly
Shanghai to Melbourne:
1 flights weekly

Qantas Beijing
120 Lufthansa Center, 50 Liangmaqiao Lu
(010) 6467 3337
Qantas Shanghai
208 Shanghai Center, 1376 Nanjing Xi Lu
(021) 6279 8660

Royal Brunei Airways
www.bruneiair.com

Shanghai to Brunei: 4 flights weekly
Hong Kong to Brunei: 5 flights weekly

Royal Brunei Airways Beijing
S1098 Beijing Lufthansa Center, 50 Liangmaqiao Lu
(010) 6465 1625
Royal Brunei Airways Shanghai

303-306 Kerry Centre, 1515 Nanjing Xi Lu
(021) 5298 6688
Royal Brunei Airways Hong Kong
2505A, Caroline Center, 28 Yun Ping
Road, Causeway Bay, (+852) 3180 3232

Scandinavian Airlines
www.scandinavian.net

Beijing to Copenhagen:
7 flights weekly
Shanghai to Copenhagen:
6 flights weekly

SAS Beijing
1830 Sunflower Tower, 37 Maizidian Dajie
(010) 8527 6100
SAS Shanghai
3901 Nanzheng Plaza, 580 Nanjing Xi Lu
(021) 5228 5001, 800 810 3738

Silkair
www.silkair.com

Chongqing to Singapore: 3 flights weekly
Kunming to Singapore: 3 flights weekly
Xiamen to Singapore: 7 flights weekly
Fuzhou to Singapore: 0 flights weekly

Silkair Xiamen
G 11/F, International Plaza, 8 Lujiang
Road, (0592) 205 3257
Silkair Chongqing
3110-3111, Metropolitan Tower, 68
Zourong Lu, (023) 6373 1881

Singapore Airlines
www.singaporeair.com

Shanghai to Singapore: 28 flights weekly
Beijing to Singapore:
21 flights weekly
Hong Kong to Singapore:
35 flights weekly
Shenzhen to Singapore:

6 flights weekly
Nanjing to Singapore:
7 flights weekly

Singapore Airlines Shanghai
606-608 Kerry Center, 1515 Nanjing Xi
Lu, (021) 6289 1000
Singapore Airlines Beijing
8/F China World Tower 2, 1 Jianguomenwai Dajie, (010) 6505 2233
Singapore Airlines Guangzhou
2807-2808 Dongshan Plaza, 69 Xianlie
Zhong Lu, (020) 8755 6300

SriLankan Airlines
www.srilankan.aero

Beijing to Colombo: 3 flights weekly
Hongkong to Colombo: 4 flights weekly

Srilankan Beijing
S119 Lufthansa Center, 50 Liangmaqiao
Lu, (010) 6461 7208
Srilankan Hong Kong
2703 Tower 1, Lippo Center, 89 Queens-
way, Admiralty, (+852) 2521 0708

Thai Airways International
www.thaiair.com

Beijing to Bangkok: 7 flights weekly
Guangzhou to Bangkok: 7 flights weekly
Kunming to Bangkok:
6 flights weekly
Shanghai to Bangkok:
7 flights weekly
Xiamen to Bangkok:
3 flights weekly
Chengdu to Bangkok:
3 flights weekly
Hong Kong to Seoul:
7 flights weekly
Hong Kong to Bangkok:
28 flights weekly

Thai Airways Beijing
303-304 Office Tower W3, Oriental Plaza,

1 East Chang'an Dajie
(010) 8515 0088
Thai Airways Guangzhou
G3 West Wing, The Garden Hotel, 368
Huanshi Dong Lu
(020) 8365 2603
Thai Airways Shanghai
105 Kerry Centre, 1515 Nanjing Xi Lu
(021) 5298 5555
Thai Airways Hong Kong
A 24/F, United Center
95 Queensway
(+852) 2876 6888

Ukraine Aerosvit Airlines
www.aerosvit.ua

Beijing to Kiev: 2 flights weekly

Ukraine Aerosvit Airlines Beijing
978 Poly Plaza Hotel, Dongzhimen Nan
Dajie, (010) 6501 0937

United Airlines
www.united.com

Beijing to San Francisco:
7 flights weekly
Beijing to Chicago:
7 flights weekly
Shanghai to San Francisco:
7 flights weekly
Shanghai to Chicago:
7 flights weekly
Hong Kong to Francisco: 7 flights weekly
Hong Kong to Chicago: 10 flights weekly

United Airlines Beijing
W101, 50 Liangmaqiao Lu
(010) 6463 1111
United Airlines Shanghai
33/F Central Plaza, 381 Huaihai Zhong
Lu, (021) 3311 4567
United Airlines Hong Kong
2901 Gloucester Tower, The Landmark,
11 Pedder Street Central
(852) 2810 4888

REFERENCE

Useful websites

Business and Investment

China Economic Review
The top source of China business info for over 15 years
www.chinaeconomicreview.com

China Logistics News
www.chinaeconomicreview.com/logistics

China Property News
www.chinaeconomicreview.com/property

China Hotel News
www.chinaeconomicreview.com/hotels

China MBA News
www.chinaeconomicreview.com/mba

China IT News
www.chinaeconomicreview.com/it

ChinaBiz
www.cbiz.cn

SinoProjects
Database of daily updated listings, postings and information
www.sinoprojects.com/English/Online/index.htm

Hong Kong Trade Development Council
www.tcdtrade.com

ChinaMarket
Sourcing in China
www.chinamarket.com.cn/index_e.html

Alibaba
Sourcing in China
www.alibaba.com

News and Media

China Economic Review
The top source of China business info for over 15 years
www.chinaeconomicreview.com

Xinhua Finance
www.xinhuafinance.com

South China Morning Post
www.scmp.com

China Daily
www.chinadaily.com.cn

People's Daily
www.english.peopledaily.com.cn

Shanghai Daily
www.shanghaidaily.com

China View
www.chinaview.cn

China Org
www.china.org.cn/english

CRI English
www.crienglish.com

CCTV
www.cctv.com.cn/english

Beijing Review
www.bjreview.com.cn

SinoLinx
www.sinolinx.com

Newsvine
www.newsvine.com

News Blogs

China Press
www.shanghaidaily.com/press

China Digital Times
www.chinadigitaltimes.net
China Herald
www.chinaherald.net

Blogs

A Glimpse of the World
New York Times Shanghai correspondent Howard French
www.howardwfrench.com
China Blog List
www.chinabloglist.org
China Stock Blog
www.china.seekingalpha.com
Danwei
www.danwei.org
Imagethief
www.news.imagethief.com/blogs/china/default.aspx
China Law Blog
www.chinalawblog.com
Shanghaiist
www.shanghaiist.com
Shanghai Streets
www.shanghaistreets.net
Shanghai Jazz Scene
www.shanghaijazzscene.com/blog
China Challenges
chinachallenges.blogs.com/my_weblog
Peking Duck
www.pekingduck.org/
All Roads Lead to China
www.allroadsleadtochina.com
China Word of Mouth Blog
www.samflemming.com
Virtual China
www.virtual-china.org

Entertainment, Networking, and Listings

LinkedIn
Professional networking site
www.linkedin.com
YPHH Networking
Networking events in China's major cities
www.yphh.com
Xianzai.com
City sites with events and classifieds
www.xianzai.com
Culture X China
Learn about China's culture and meet new friends
www.culturexchina.com
Asia Xpat
Find a job, apartment, maid, teacher, etc.
www.asiaxpat.com
Move and Stay
Relocate anywhere in the world
www.moveandstay.com
Spa China
A magazine dedicated to China's spa and wellness industry
www.spachina.com

Beijing

That's Beijing
www.thatsbj.com
The Beijing Page
www.beijingpage.com

Shanghai

that's Shanghai

www.thatssh.com
City Weekend
www.cityweekend.com.cn
Smart Shanghai
www.smartshanghai.com

Guangzhou

That's Guangzhou
www.thatsgz.com

Kunming

Go Kunming
www.gokunming.com

Reference

Currency Conversion
www.xe.com
Document China
Photos of China
www.documentchina.com

Travel

Ctrip Travel
www.english.ctrip.com
China Travel
www.linktrip.com
Chinese Railway Timetables in English
www.chinatt.org

History, Culture, Language

Tales of Old China
www.talesofoldchina.com
China Culture

www.chinaculture.org
Chinese History
www.orpheus.ucsd.edu/
chinesehistory
Chinese Characters and Culture
www.zhongwen.com
Online Chinese Tools
www.mandarintools.com

Development and Social Issues

China Development Gateway
www.chinagateway.com.cn
China Development Brief
www.chinadevelopmentbrief.com

Government Bodies

Government Organizational Chart
www.cbw.com/govern
General Government Information
http://www.chinatoday.com/gov/
a.htm
Ministry of Commerce
www.fdi.gov.cn
Ministry of Foreign Affairs
www.fmprc.gov.cn/eng
National Bureau of Statistics
www.stats.gov.cn/english

Reference

Wikipedia
http://en.wikipedia.org/wiki/People's_
Republic_of_China
CIA Factbook
http://www.cia.gov/cia/publications/
factbook/geos/ch.html

A

accounting firms	209
administrative regions	30
agriculture	104
air travel	49
airlines	587
Anhui	238
Anqing	243
Anshan	447
antique markets	57
ATMs	40
automobiles	109
aviation	115

B

banking	119
banknotes	40
banks, foreign	40
Baoding	372
Baotou	406
Beihai	348
Beijing	245
Beijing map	248
Bo'ao	366
business schools	216

C

cement	124
Changchun	431
Changsha	397
Changzhou	422
Chaozhou	339
Chengdu	504
China fact file	566
China map	31; 564
China's dynasties	24
Chinese instruction	89
Chinese language guide	74
Chinese leader profiles	574

Chongqing	276
cigar lounges	65
climate	34
company setup	194
consumer trends	128
credit cards	40
currency, foreign	40

D

daily necessities	93
Dalian	441
Daqing	380
Datong	501
dining etiquette	58
Dongguan	333
drinking and smoking	62
driving	47

E

economic data	567
electricity	47
electronics	133
energy	137
environment	141
executive search firms	200

F

finding a place to live	83
finding an office	202
finding staff	198
Foshan	334
Fujian	283
Fuzhou	285

G

Gansu	294
Guangdong	300
Guangxi	340

Guangzhou	303
Guilin	345
Guiyang	352
Guizhou	349
gyms	88

H

Haikou	356
Hainan	354
Hangzhou	537
Harbin	376
health	65
Hebei	367
Hefei	239
Heilongjiang	373
Henan	381
hired help	92
history	12
Hohhot	404
Hong Kong	552
Hong Kong map	556
hotels	50
Hubei	389
Hunan	396

I

industry overviews	100
Inner Mongolia	402
insurance	146
internet access	45

J

Jiangsu	407
Jiangxi	424
Jiayuguan	299
Jilin	429
Jilin City	434
Ji'nan	462
Jingdezhen	428

K

Kaifeng	388
Kunming	529
Kunshan	420

L

Lanzhou	296
law firms	212
learning Chinese	89
Lhasa	520
Liaoning	436
Lijiang	534
logistics	
overview	150
firms	229
Luoyang	386

M

Macau	560
Macau map	561
massage	68
MBA/EMBA programs	216
money matters	40

N

Nanchang	426
Nanjing	408
Nanning	342
Nantong	418
Ningbo	545
Ningxia	448

P

Panzhihua	509
phones	43
preview of 2007	25
professional service providers	234

public holidays	37

Q

Qingdao	465
Qinghai	451
Qiqihar	379
Quanzhou	290

R

real estate	156
registering a company	197
relocation services	185
residence registration	82
residential property agents	85
retail	160

S

safety	71
Sanya	360
schools, international	97
securities	164
semiconductors	171
serviced offices	204
Shaanxi	454
Shandong	461
Shanghai	472
Shanghai map	476
Shantou	334
Shanxi	497
Shaoxing	549
Shenyang	438
Shenzhen	315
Shenzhen map	316
Shijiazhuang	369
shopping	54
Sichuan	502
silk shops	56
SIM cards	44
spas	69

sports clubs	88
steel	175
supermarkets	94
Suzhou	412

T

tailors	54
Taiyuan	498
Tangshan	371
taxation	209
taxis	47
tea	54
telecommunications	179
telephones	43
textiles	184
Tianjin	510
Tibet	518
time	37
tipping	62
tourism	188
trade events 2007	582
translation firms	234
transportation	47
travelers' cheques	42

U

Urumqi	524
useful websites	596

V

visas	38

W

web design firms	234
Weihai	471
Wenzhou	550
Wi-Fi	46
Wuhan	390

INDEX

INDEX

Wuhu	242
Wuxi	416

X

Xiamen	288
Xi'an	455
Xiangtan	401
Xianyang	460
Xining	452
Xinjiang	522

Y

Yangzhou	421
Yantai	470
Yichang	397
Yinchuan	450
Yunnan	526

Z

Zhejiang	535
Zhengzhou	382
Zhongshan	332
Zhuhai	324

Advertisers' index

APBC	203
Asia Pacific Access	87
Center Hotel Shanghai	479
Citic Ningbo International	547
Dave's Tailor	55
Equatorial Hotel Qingdao	467
Frasers Hospitality	35
Gloria Plaza Hotel	2
Hotel Equatorial Shanghai	481
Hotel Nikko Tianjin	515
Hotel reservation service	51
Hyatt hangzhou	539
Panalpina	3
Regue	207
Schenker	153
Shanghai Eastern Logistics	155
Staff Service	199
The executive center	205